MODERN LIBRARY

To my real
Valentine — my
husband, Ted Nowlin

Hilda G. Nowlin

February 14, 1951

AN ANTHOLOGY OF
FAMOUS
ENGLISH AND AMERICAN
POETRY

AN ANTHOLOGY
OF
FAMOUS
ENGLISH AND
AMERICAN
POETRY

>>>

Edited, with Introductions, by
WILLIAM ROSE BENÉT
AND CONRAD AIKEN

>>>

THE MODERN LIBRARY
NEW YORK

THE MODERN LIBRARY

IS PUBLISHED BY

RANDOM HOUSE, INC.

BENNETT A. CERF · DONALD S. KLOPFER · ROBERT K. HAAS

Manufactured in the United States of America

Printed by Parkway Printing Company   *Bound by H. Wolff*

CONTENTS

English

CONTENTS

CONTENTS

CONTENTS

American

English Poetry

Introduction

THIS anthology, like any other, involves personal predilection, though it endeavors to be catholic in taste. My only criterion has been what I consider excellent. Some of my choices will certainly display an idiosyncrasy not shared by readers of different temperament. One is also limited as to scope by a book's planned size. Which only means that there is really more good English verse accumulated from the past than an ordinary volume will hold—what Saintsbury has called "the grace and the glory of the written word that conquers Time." That is what I have striven to present here. Perhaps on a good deal of it we may agree.

However well-read in English poetry one conceives oneself to be, the average memory endlessly loses and recaptures things fine and fantastic. New delights lie in wait, old experiences are continually refreshed. As an instance of this, I had, till lately, thought myself quite familiar with the famous old ballad of Sir Andrew Barton— and, to be sure, I had by heart the famous sixty-fourth and sixty-fifth verses; but on rereading it, the other day, I realized how far I had forgotten the masterly description of the marksmanship of William Horsley, to say nothing of the strange mixture of cruelty and chivalry which caused the Lord Howard to strike off the dead Sir Andrew's head, and throw him overboard, at the same time seeing that he bore with him, strapped around his middle, a good three hundred crowns, "Wheresoever thou lands it will bury thee!" Old English poetry is full of such queer and delightful turns. It is full, also, of such less-well-known magnificences as this verse from Kit Smart's "A Song to David."

> Strong is the lion—like a coal
> His eyeball—like a bastion's mole
> His chest against the foes:
> Strong the gier-eagle on his sail;
> Strong against tide the enormous whale
> Emerges as he goes.

Hence it is a golden wonder, constantly renewed. Coming again upon the lyrical felicity of one who was a popular London physician toward the end of the reign of great Elizabeth, one marvels at such lines as:

> Kind are her answers,
> But her performance keeps no day;
> Breaks time, as dancers
> From their own music when they stray.

Much could be said of the song in English poetry, such as Thomas Campion wrote so well in his "Four Books of Airs"—a kind of poem of great rarity in this different age. Now what a nation feeds upon, for the most part, is the stupid stereotype of what are called "popular songs," sung on the stage, and blatting about "sweet memoree." We have nothing in English verse today to approach the exquisite rhyme of Campion—though, strangely enough, he argued ably *against* rhyme, excelling in unrhymed iambic and trochaic measure. Nor have we a Herrick:

> Her eyes the glow-worm lend thee,
> The shooting stars attend thee—

It is as though the Machine Age had stilled or corrupted the voice for singing and the ear for music, in verse. The new cerebral mode, "straining harsh discords and unpleasing sharps," has not only no grace notes but little sense of the true lyric. Incidentally, its love-poetry, also is almost a matter of the higher mathematics. It may claim to have adopted the imagery of science, as John Donne did first in his own time; but it has little or nothing of the brave lustiness of Donne, just as it seems to have eschewed both warmth and wit. But ours are, perhaps, more serious concerns, such as result in increasingly destructive wars, and create from our most amazing scientific discoveries merely so many clever gadgets.

However, perhaps the above is too severe. Certainly we live in an entirely different age from that even of the last great singers before the first Great War. I think, nevertheless, that far too many excuses have been made for modern poetry on the score of our epoch being too dynamic, disastrous, and bewildering. Must poets be coddled? To the Elizabethans, the increase of geographical discovery, and the growth of human knowledge, in their own time, must have seemed just as confusing; and they created stirring dramatic verse and great song. Today we have more books, but have we more profound thought? Certainly modern English poetry has no such profuse lingual beauty, no such rich zest for life.

Yet my quarrel with some modern poets is not because they are endeavoring to interpret a complicated period of the world's history, but that their efforts are, for the most part, so limited in scope and understanding. As one young modern poet has said, "There is a kind of intellectual hysteria about most modern poetry." One would think that some of its practitioners existed in an historical vacuum.

The modern reader, certainly, does not feel so closely in touch with the poets of our day as did the peruser, say, of that early anthology of English song, *The Phoenix Nest*, whence time has culled some of the rarest delights of Lodge and Breton. Much later on, in the Victorian era, the great poets of England were household friends. Today, for a poet to attain any sort of popularity seems to be a black mark against him in the minds of modern critics; and a great deal of highly esoteric posturing is hailed as poetry's top and flower. But there I shall halt my strictures. There is also much in modern English verse to admire, much that is fresh, vigorous, beautiful, of the spirit.

It may be that in an age of unfaith, a time of constant turmoil, a period of transition from a still-lingering feudalism in society, of war against a maniacal ideology and a recrudescence of foul cruelty, an age of tyrannical power and spiritual callousness, it is marvelous that we should have any poetry at all. But even this era of devastation seems to give signs of a better one succeeding, of the coming to birth of a renewed strength of the spirit. As for England, that at one point in the War rose phoenix-like from her ashes of early appeasement and then bitter defeat, when has she not been associated with great poetry, poetry that is the strength of the soul? The most noble and liberal English minds have continually been full of it. Her statesmen have respected her poets—where our Congress, still largely of the unlettered and rough-and-ready breed, could do little lately but jeer when a distinguished American poet became an Assistant Secretary of State—incidentally quite forgetting the example of John Hay.

English poets have long been an influence in their country's affairs. Among them, in this respect, Milton is, of course, outstanding. Earlier, Raleigh and Sidney served their country nobly as adventurer and warrior. Earlier still, Chaucer was employed upon diplomatic missions abroad, and was Comptroller of the Customs in the port of London; Spenser held government office. Matt Prior was England's Ambassador to France, and took a leading part, in the eighteenth century, in framing the Treaty of Utrecht, which was, indeed, called "Matt's Peace," he being, parenthetically, one of the best and most characteristic of eighteenth-century love poets! The list could be greatly extended. As for poetry's standing among modern Englishmen of action, one of the best recent anthologies has been compiled by a viceroy of India, Field Marshal Sir Archibald Percival Wavell, who, it seems, possesses a prodigious memory for English verse, as did Viscount Allenby, the High Commissioner for Egypt. When we examine the genuine bond we have with the English, we find one of the strongest strands of it to be that many of us were brought up in the high tradition of English poetry. It has long permeated and enriched our mutual relations.

Tradition notwithstanding, in no national poetry do you find a greater variety of expression than in the English. Not only have the British Isles possessed the most comprehensive and many-faceted of writers in Shakespeare, but the great luminaries of their poetry have been as different in style as Pope from Burns, Tennyson from Browning, Masefield from de la Mare. Let it be at once admitted that the Scotch and the Irish have contributed greatly to what we inclusively term English poetry. You will note particularly the presence of William Butler Yeats in this volume. Indeed, after Hardy's death, he remained for a while the greatest poetic figure in Britain. These differing racial strains in the Island Race, and the saliently independent character of English, Scotch, and Irish have given British poetry color and tang. If, as some surmise, a form of socialism is likely to come to England, it is nevertheless sure to have a character all its own, allowing free play to English independence, though strictly consorting with that sense of justice that inhabits the hearts of the highest type of Englishman. In saying this, I do not speak of governments. In the dawn of the day of world freedom, governments may more truly convey the world-conscious desires of the common people everywhere. In that day too, perhaps, the people themselves will take a more immediate interest in those international affairs that involve their future and their fate. In such participation today the average Briton could point the way to many of us Americans who pride ourselves upon our democracy.

But in the last analysis, it is the poets who chiefly point the way, as they have always done. It is the poets who sense the weather of the world, and feel in which direction the wind of human history is blowing. Of late, driven in upon themselves, many of them have been chary of prophesying. But after such a world convulsion as the present, we may reasonably expect them to re-establish themselves in the domain of art and of life. If we owe some of our highest standards of living to the revelations, exhortations, admonitions in English verse, we may be sure that they will continually be secured and enlarged by new rhythmic voices. And perhaps we may be allowed to hope that thus the walls of a new spiritual city will rise to music, as did those fabled of old time.

WILLIAM ROSE BENÉT

Cape Ann, Mass.

GEOFFREY CHAUCER

The Nun's Priest's Tale

*Here biginneth the Nonne Preestes Tale of the Cok and Hen, Chauntecleer
and Pertelote*

A POVRE widwe, somdel stape in age,
   Was whylom dwelling in a narwe cotage,
Bisyde a grove, stonding in a dale.
This widwe, of which I telle yow my tale,
Sin thilke day that she was last a wyf,
In pacience ladde a ful simple lyf,
For litel was hir catel and hir rente;
By housbondrye, of such as God hir sente,
She fond hir-self, and eek hir doghtren two.
Three large sowes hadde she, and namo,
Three kyn, and eek a sheep that highte Malle,
Ful sooty was hir bour, and eek hir halle,
In which she eet ful many a sclendre meel.
Of poynaunt sauce hir neded never a deel.
No deyntee morsel passed thurgh hir throte;
Hir dyete was accordant to hir cote.
Repleccioun ne made hir never syk;
Attempree dyete was al hir phisyk,
And exercyse, and hertes suffisaunce.
The goute lette hir no-thing for to daunce,
N'apoplexye shente nat hir heed;
No wyn ne drank she, neither whyt ne reed;
Hir bord was served most with whyt and blak,
Milk and broun breed, in which she fond no lak,
Seynd bacoun, and somtyme an ey or tweye,
For she was as it were a maner deye.
   A yerd she hadde, enclosed al aboute
With stikkes, and a drye dich with-oute,
In which she hadde a cok, hight Chauntecleer,
In al the land of crowing nas his peer.
His vois was merier than the mery orgon

9

On messe-dayes that in the chirche gon;
Wel sikerer was his crowing in his logge,
Than is a clokke, or an abbey orlogge.
By nature knew he ech ascencioun
Of equinoxial in thilke toun;
For whan degrees fiftene were ascended,
Thanne crew he, that it mighte nat ben amended.
His comb was redder than the fyn coral,
And batailed, as it were a castel-wal.
His bile was blak, and as the jeet it shoon;
Lyk asur were his legges, and his toon;
His nayles whytter than the lilie flour,
And lyk the burned gold was his colour.
This gentil cok hadde in his governaunce
Sevene hennes, for to doon al his plesaunce,
Whiche were his sustres and his paramours,
And wonder lyk to him, as of colours.
Of whiche the faireste hewed on hir throte
Was cleped faire damoysele Pertelote.
Curteys she was, discreet, and debonaire,
And compaignable, and bar hir-self so faire,
Sin thilke day that she was seven night old,
That trewely she hath the herte in hold
Of Chauntecleer loken in every lith;
He loved hir so, that wel was him therwith.
But such a joye was it to here hem singe,
Whan that the brighte sonne gan to springe,
In swete accord, "my lief is faren in londe."
For thilke tyme, as I have understonde,
Bestes and briddes coude speke and singe.
    And so bifel, that in a daweninge,
As Chauntecleer among his wyves alle
Sat on his perche, that was in the halle,
And next him sat this faire Pertelote,
This Chauntecleer gan gronen in his throte,
As man that in his dreem is drecched sore.
And whan that Pertelote thus herde him rore,
She was agast, and seyde, "O herte dere,
What eyleth yow, to grone in this manere?
Ye been a verray sleper, fy for shame!"
And he answerde and seyde thus, "Madame,
I pray yow, that ye take it nat a-grief:

By god, me mette I was in swich meschief
Right now, that yet myn herte is sore afright.
Now god," quod he, "my swevene recche aright,
And keep my body out of foul prisoun!
Me mette, how that I romed up and doun
Withinne our yerde, wher-as I saugh a beste,
Was lyk an hound, and wolde han maad areste
Upon my body, and wolde han had me deed.
His colour was bitwixe yelwe and reed;
And tipped was his tail, and bothe his eres,
With blak, unlyk the remenant of his heres;
His snowte smal, with glowinge eyen tweye.
Yet of his look for fere almost I deye;
This caused me my groning, doutelees."
    "Avoy," quod she, "fy on yow, hertelees!
Allas!" quod she, "for, by that god above,
Now han ye lost myn herte and al my love;
I can nat love a coward, by my feith.
For certes, what so any womman seith,
We alle desyren, if it mighte be,
To han housbondes hardy, wyse, and free,
And secree, and no nigard, ne no fool,
Ne him that is agast of every tool,
Ne noon avauntour, by that god above!
How dorste ye seyn for shame unto your love,
That any thing mighte make yow aferd?
Have ye no mannes herte, and han a berd?
Allas! and conne ye been agast of swevenis?
No-thing, god wot, but vanitee, in sweven is.
Swevenes engendren of replecciouns,
And ofte of fume, and of complecciouns,
Whan humours been to habundant in a wight.
Certes this dreem, which ye han met tonight,
Cometh of the grete superfluitee
Of youre rede *colera*, pardee,
Which causeth folk to dreden in here dremes
Of arwes, and of fyr with rede lemes,
Of grete bestes, that they wol hem byte,
Of contek, and of whelpes grete and lyte;
Right as the humour of malencolye
Causeth ful many a man, in sleep, to crye,
For fere of blake beres, or boles blake,

Or elles, blake develes wole hem take.
Of othere humours coude I telle also,
That werken many a man in sleep ful wo;
But I wol passe as lightly as I can.

  Lo Catoun, which that was so wys a man,
Seyde he nat thus, ne do no fors of dremes?
Now, sire," quod she, "whan we flee fro the bemes,
For Goddes love, as tak som laxatyf;
Up peril of my soule, and of my lyf,
I counseille yow the beste, I wol nat lye,
That bothe of colere and of malencolye
Ye purge yow; and for ye shul nat tarie,
Though in this toun is noon apotecarie,
I shal my-self to herbes techen yow,
That shul ben for your hele, and for your prow;
And in our yerd tho herbes shal I finde,
The whiche han of hir propertee, by kinde,
To purgen yow binethe, and eek above.
Forget not this, for goddes owene love!
Ye been ful colerik of compleccioun.
Ware the sonne in his ascencioun
Ne fynde yow nat repleet of humours hote;
And if it do, I dar wel leye a grote,
That ye shul have a fevere terciane,
Or an agu, that may be youre bane.
A day or two ye shul have digestyves
Of wormes, er ye take your laxatyves,
Of lauriol, centaure, and fumetere,
Or elles of ellebor, that groweth there,
Of catapuce, or of gaytres' beryis,
Of erbe yve, growing in our yerd, that mery is;
Pekke hem up right as they growe, and ete hem in.
Be mery, housbond, for your fader kin!
Dredeth no dreem; I can say yow namore."

  "Madame," quod he, "*graunt mercy* of your lore.
But nathelees, as touching daun Catoun,
That hath of wisdom such a greet renoun,
Though that he bad no dremes for to drede,
By god, men may in olde bokes rede
Of many a man, more of auctoritee
Than ever Catoun was, so mote I thee,
That al the revers seyn of his sentence,

And han wel founden by experience,
That dremes ben significaciouns,
As wel of joye as tribulaciouns
That folk enduren in this lyf present.
Ther nedeth make of this noon argument;
The verray preve sheweth it in dede.

  Oon of the gretteste auctours that men rede
Seith thus, that whylom two felawes wente
On pilgrimage, in a ful good entente;
And happed so, they come into a toun,
Wher-as ther was swich congregacioun
Of peple, and eek so streit of herbergage
That they ne founde as muche as o cotage
In which they bothe mighte y-logged be.
Wherefor thay mosten, of necessitee,
As for that night, departen compaignye;
And ech of hem goth to his hostelrye,
And took his logging as it wolde falle.
That oon of hem was logged in a stalle,
Fer in a yerd, with oxen of the plough;
That other man was logged wel y-nough,
As was his aventure, or his fortune,
That us governeth alle as in commune.

  And so bifel, that, longe er it were day,
This man mette in his bed, ther-as he lay,
How that his felawe gan up-on him calle,
And seyde, 'allas! for in an oxes stalle
This night I shal be mordred ther I lye.
Now help me, dere brother, er I dye;
In alle haste com to me,' he sayde.
This man out of his sleep for fere abrayde;
But whan that he was wakned of his sleep,
He turned him, and took of this no keep;
Him thoughte his dreem nas but a vanitee.
Thus twyës in his sleping dremed he.
And atte thridde tyme yet his felawe
Cam, as him thoughte, and seide, 'I am now slawe;
Bihold my blody woundes, depe and wyde!
Arys up erly in the morwe-tyde,
And at the west gate of the toun,' quod he,
'A carte ful of dong ther shaltow see,
In which my body is hid ful prively;

Do thilke carte aresten boldely.
My gold caused my mordre, sooth to sayn;'
And tolde him every poynt how he was slayn,
With a ful pitous face, pale of hewe.
And truste wel, his dreem he fond ful trewe;
For on the morwe, as sone as it was day,
To his felawes in he took the way;
And whan that he cam to this oxes stale,
After his felawe he bigan to calle.

The hostiler answered him anon,
And seyde, 'sire, your felawe is agon,
As sone as day he wente out of the toun.'
This man gan fallen in suspecioun,
Remembering on his dremes that he mette,
And forth he goth, no lenger wolde he lette,
Unto the west gate of the toun, and fond
A dong-carte, as it were to donge lond,
That was arrayed in the same wyse
As ye han herd the dede man devyse;
And with an hardy herte he gan to crye
Vengeaunce and justice of this felonye:—
'My felawe mordred is this same night,
And in this carte he lyth gapinge upright.
I crye out on the ministres,' quod he,
'That sholden kepe and reulen this citee;
Harrow! allas! her lyth my felawe slayn!'
What sholde I more un-to this tale sayn?
The peple out-sterte, and caste the cart to grounde,
And in the middel of the dong they founde
The dede man, that mordred was al newe.

O blisful god, that art so just and trewe!
Lo, how that thou biwreyest mordre alway!
Mordre wol out, that see we day by day.
Mordre is so wlatsom and abhominable
To god, that is so just and resonable,
That he ne wol nat suffre it heled be;
Though it abyde a yeer, or two, or three,
Mordre wol out, this my conclusioun.
And right anoon, ministres of that toun
Han hent the carter, and so sore him pyned,
And eek the hostiler so sore engyned,
That thay biknewe hir wikkednesse anoon,

And were an-hanged by the nekke-boon.
  Here may men seen that dremes been to drede.
And certes, in the same book I rede,
Right in the nexte chapitre after this,
(I gabbe nat, so have I joye or blis,)
Two men that wolde han passed over see,
For certeyn cause, in-to a fer contree,
If that the wind ne hadde been contrarie,
That made hem in a citee for to tarie,
That stood ful mery upon an haven-syde.
But on a day, agayn the even-tyde,
The wind gan chaunge, and blew right as hem leste.
Jolif and glad they wente un-to hir reste,
And casten hem ful erly for to saille;
But to that oo man fil a greet mervaille.
That oon of hem, in sleping as he lay,
Him mette a wonder dreem, agayn the day;
Him thoughte a man stood by his beddes syde,
And him comaunded, that he sholde abyde,
And seyde him thus, 'if thou to-morwe wende,
Thou shalt be dreynt; my tale is at an ende.'
He wook, and tolde his felawe what he mette,
And preyde him his viage for to lette;
As for that day, he preyde him to abyde.
His felawe, that lay by his beddes syde,
Gan for to laughe, and scorned him ful faste.
'No dreem,' quod he, 'may so myn herte agaste,
That I wol lette for to do my thinges.
I sette not a straw by thy dreminges,
For swevenes been but vanitees and japes.
Men dreme al-day of owles or of apes,
And eke of many a mase ther withal;
Men dreme of thing that never was ne shal.
But sith I see that thou wolt heer abyde,
And thus for-sleuthen wilfully thy tyde,
God wot it reweth me; and have good day.'
And thus he took his leve, and wente his way.
But er that he hadde halfe his cours y-seyled,
Noot I nat why, ne what mischaunce it eyled,
But casuelly the shippes botme rente,
And ship and man under the water wente
In sighte of othere shippes it byside,

That with hem seyled at the same tyde.
And therfor, faire Pertelote so dere,
By swiche ensamples olde maistow lere,
That no man sholde been to recchelees
Of dremes, for I sey thee, doutelees,
That many a dreem ful sore is for to drede.

   Lo, in the lyf of seint Kenelm, I rede,
That was Kenulphus sone, the noble king
Of Mercenrike, how Kenelm mette a thing;
A lyte er he was mordred, on a day,
His mordre in his avisioun he say.
His norice him expouned every del
His sweven, and bad him for to kepe him wel
For traisoun; but he nas but seven yeer old,
And therfore litel tale hath he told
Of any dreem, so holy was his herte.
By god, I hadde lever than my sherte
That ye had rad his legende, as have I.
Dame Pertelote, I sey yow trewely,
Macrobeus, that writ th'avisioun
In Affrike of the worthy Cipioun,
Affermeth dremes, and seith that they been
Warning of thinges that men after seen.

   And forther-more, I pray yow loketh wel
In th'olde testament, of Daniel,
If he held dremes any vanitee.
Reed eek of Joseph, and ther shul ye see
Wher dremes ben somtyme (I sey nat alle)
Warning of thinges that shul after falle.
Loke of Egipt the king, daun Pharao,
His bakere and his boteler also,
Wher they ne felte noon effect in dremes.
Who-so wol seken actes of sondry remes,
May rede of dremes many a wonder thing.

   Lo Cresus, which that was of Lyde king,
Mette he nat that he sat upon a tree,
Which signified he sholde anhanged be?
Lo heer Andromacha, Ectores wyf,
That day that Ector sholde lese his lyf,
She dremed on the same night biforn,
How that the lyf of Ector sholde be lorn,
If thilke day he wente in-to bataille;

She warned him, but it mighte nat availle;
He wente for to fighte nathelees,
But he was slayn anoon of Achilles.
But thilke tale is al to long to telle,
And eek it is ny day, I may nat dwelle.
Shortly I seye, as for conclusioun,
That I shal han of this avisioun
Adversitee; and I seye forther-more,
That I ne telle of laxatyves no store,
For they ben venimous, I woot it wel;
I hem defye, I love hem never a del.
    Now let us speke of mirthe, and stinte al this;
Madame Pertelote, so have I blis,
Of o thing god hath sent me large grace;
For whan I see the beautee of your face,
Ye ben so scarlet-reed about your yën,
It maketh al my drede for to dyen;
For, also siker as *In principio*,
Mulier est hominis confusio;
Madame, the sentence of this Latin is—
Womman is mannes joye and al his blis.
For whan I fele a-night your softe syde,
Al-be-it that I may nat on you ryde,
For that our perche is maad so narwe, alas!
I am so ful of joye and of solas
That I defye bothe sweven and dreem."
And with that word he fley doun fro the beem,
For it was day, and eek his hennes alle;
And with a chuk he gan hem for to calle,
For he had founde a corn, lay in the yerd.
Royal he was, he was namore aferd;
He fethered Pertelote twenty tyme,
And trad as ofte, er that it was pryme.
He loketh as it were a grim leoun;
And on his toos he rometh up and doun,
Him deyned not to sette his foot to grounde.
He chukketh, whan he hath a corn y-founde,
And to him rennen thanne his wyves alle.
Thus royal, as a prince is in his halle,
Leve I this Chauntecleer in his pasture;
And after wol I telle his aventure.
    Whan that the month in which the world bigan,

That highte March, whan god first maked man,
Was complet, and [y]-passed were also,
Sin March bigan, thritty dayes and two,
Bifel that Chauntecleer, in al his pryde,
His seven wyves walking by his syde,
Caste up his eyen to the brighte sonne,
That in the signe of Taurus hadde y-ronne
Twenty degrees and oon, and somwhat more;
And knew by kynde, and by noon other lore,
That it was pryme, and crew with blisful stevene.
"The sonne," he sayde, "is clomben up on hevene
Fourty degrees and oon, and more, y-wis.
Madame Pertelote, my worldes blis,
Herkneth thise blisful briddes how they singe,
And see the fresshe floures how they springe;
Ful is myn herte of revel and solas."
But sodeinly him fil a sorweful cas;
For ever the latter ende of joye is wo.
God woot that worldly joye is sone ago;
And if a rethor coude faire endyte,
He in a cronique saufly mighte it wryte,
As for a sovereyn notabilitee.
Now every wys man, lat him herkne me;
This storie is al-so trewe, I undertake,
As is the book of Launcelot de Lake,
That wommen holde in ful gret reverence.
Now wol I torne agayn to my sentence.
   A col-fox, ful of sly iniquitee,
That in the grove hadde woned yeres three,
By heigh imaginacioun forn-cast,
The same night thurgh-out the hegges brast
Into the yerd, ther Chauntecleer the faire
Was wont, and eek his wyves, to repaire;
And in a bed of wortes stille he lay,
Til it was passed undern of the day,
Wayting his tyme on Chauntecleer to falle,
As gladly doon thise homicydes alle,
That in awayt liggen to mordre men.
O false mordrer, lurking in thy den!
O newe Scariot, newe Genilon!
False dissimilour, O Greek Sinon,
That broghtest Troye al outrely to sorwe!

O Chauntecleer, acursed be that morwe,
That thou into that yerd flough fro the bemes!
Thou were ful wel y-warned by thy dremes,
That thilke day was perilous to thee.
But what that god forwoot mot nedes be,
After the opinioun of certeyn clerkis.
Witnesse on him, that any perfit clerk is,
That in scole is gret altercacioun
In this matere, and greet disputisoun,
And hath ben of an hundred thousand men.
But I ne can not bulte it to the bren,
As can the holy doctour Augustyn,
Or Boëce, or the bishop Bradwardyn,
Whether that goddes worthy forwiting
Streyneth me nedely for to doon a thing,
(Nedely clepe I simple necessitee);
Or elles, if free choys be graunted me
To do that same thing, or do it noght,
Though god forwoot it, er that it was wroght;
Or if his witing streyneth nevere a del
But by necessitee condicionel.
I wol not han to do of swich matere;
My tale is of a cok, as ye may here,
That took his counseil of his wyf, with sorwe,
To walken in the yerd upon that morwe
That he had met the dreem, that I yow tolde.
Wommennes counseils been ful ofte colde;
Wommannes counseil broghte us first to wo,
And made Adam fro paradys to go,
Ther-as he was ful mery, and wel at ese.—
But for I noot, to whom it mighte displese,
If I counseil of wommen wolde blame,
Passe over, for I seyde it in my game.
Rede auctours, wher they trete of swich matere,
And what thay seyn of wommen ye may here.
Thise been the cokkes wordes, and nat myne;
I can noon harm of no womman divyne.—
    Faire in the sond, to bathe hir merily,
Lyth Pertelote, and alle hir sustres by,
Agayn the sonne; and Chauntecleer so free
Song merier than the mermayde in the see;
For Phisiologus seith sikerly,

How that they singen wel and merily.
And so bifel that, as he caste his yë,
Among the wortes, on a boterflye,
He was war of this fox that lay ful lowe.
No-thing ne liste him thanne for to crowe,
But cryde anon, "cok, cok," and up he sterte,
As man that was affrayed in his hertc.
For naturelly a beest desyreth flee
Fro his contrarie, if he may it see,
Though he never erst had seyn it with his yë.
　This Chauntecleer, whan he gan him espye,
He wolde han fled, but that the fox anon
Seyde, "Gentil sire, allas! wher wol ye gon?
Be ye affrayed of me that am your freend?
Now certes, I were worse than a feend,
If I to yow wolde harm or vileinye.
I am nat come your counseil for t'espye;
But trewely, the cause of my cominge
Was only for to herkne how that ye singe.
For trewly ye have as mery a stevene
As eny aungel hath, that is in hevene;
Therwith ye han in musik more felinge
Than hadde Boëce, or any that can singe.
My lord your fader (god his soule blesse!)
And eek your moder, of hir gentilesse,
Han in myn hous y-been, to my gret ese;
And certes, sire, ful fayn wolde I yow plese.
But for men speke of singing, I wol saye,
So mote I brouke wel myn eyen tweye,
Save yow, I herde never man so singe,
As dide your fader in the morweninge;
Certes, it was of herte, al that he song.
And for to make his voys the more strong,
He wolde so peyne him, that with bothe his yën
He moste winke, so loude he wolde cryen,
And stonden on his tiptoon ther-with-al,
And strecche forth his nekke long and smal.
And eek he was of swich discrecioun,
That ther nas no man in no regioun
That him in song or wisdom mighte passe.
I have wel rad in daun Burnel the Asse,
Among his vers, how that ther was a cok,

For that a preestes son yaf him a knok
Upon his leg, whyl he was yong and nyce,
He made him for to lese his benefyce.
But certeyn, there nis no comparisoun
Bitwix the wisdom and discrecioun
Of youre fader, and of his subtiltee.
Now singeth, sire, for seinte Charitee,
Let see, conne ye your fader countrefete?"
This Chauntecleer his winges gan to bete,
As man that coude his tresoun nat esype,
So was he ravisshed with his flaterye.

   Allas! ye lordes, many a fals flatour
Is in your courtes, and many a losengeour,
That plesen yow wel more, by my feith,
Than he that soothfastnesse unto yow seith.
Redeth Ecclesiaste of flaterye;
Beth war, ye lordes, of hir trecherye.

   This Chauntecleer stood hye up-on his toos,
Strecching his nekke, and heeld his eyen cloos,
And gan to crowe loude for the nones;
And daun Russel the fox sterte up at ones,
And by the gargat hente Chauntecleer,
And on his bak toward the wode him beer,
For yet ne was ther no man that him sewed.
O destinee, that mayst nat been eschewed!
Allas, that Chauntecleer fleigh fro the bemes!
Allas, his wyf ne roghte nat of dremes!
And on a Friday fil al this meschaunce.
O Venus, that art goddesse of plesaunce,
Sin that thy servant was this Chauntecleer,
And in thy service dide al his poweer,
More for delyt, than world to multiplye,
Why woldestow suffre him on thy day to dye?
O Gaufred, dere mayster soverayn,
That, whan thy worthy king Richard was slayn
With shot, compleynedest his deth so sore,
Why ne hadde I now thy sentence and thy lore,
The Friday for to chyde, as diden ye?
(For on a Friday soothly slayn was he.)
Than wolde I shewe yow how that I coude pleyne
For Chauntecleres drede, and for his peyne.

   Certes, swich cry ne lamentacioun

Was never of ladies maad, whan Ilioun
Was wonne, and Pirrus with his streite swerd,
When he hadde hent king Priam by the berd,
And slayn him (as saith us *Eneydos*),
As maden alle the hennes in the clos,
Whan they had seyn of Chauntecleer the sighte.
But sovereynly dame Pertelote shrighte,
Ful louder than dide Hasdrubales wyf,
Whan that hir housbond hadde lost his lyf,
And that the Romayns hadde brend Cartage;
She was so ful of torment and rage,
That wilfully into the fyr she sterte,
And brende hir-selven with a stedfast herte.
O woful hennes, right so cryden ye,
As, whan that Nero brende the citee
Of Rome, cryden senatoures wyves,
For that hir housbondes losten alle hir lyves;
Withouten gilt this Nero hath hem slayn.
Now wol I torne to my tale agayn:—
    This sely widwe, and eek hir doghtres two,
Herden thise hennes crye and maken wo,
And out at dores sterten they anoon,
And syen the fox toward the grove goon,
And bar upon his bak the cok away;
And cryden, "Out! harrow! and weylaway!
Ha, ha, the fox!" and after him they ran,
And eek with staves many another man;
Ran Colle our dogge, and Talbot, and Gerland,
And Malkin, with a distaf in hir hand;
Ran cow and calf, and eek the verray hogges
So were they fered for berking of the dogges
And shouting of the men and wimmen eke,
They ronne so, hem thoughte hir herte breke.
They yelleden as feendes doon in helle;
The dokes cryden as men wolde hem quelle;
The gees for fere flowen over the trees;
Out of the hyve cam the swarm of bees;
So hidous was the noyse, a! *benedicte*!
Certes, he Jakke Straw, and his meynee,
Ne made never shoutes half so shrille,
Whan that they wolden any Fleming kille,
As thilke day was maad upon the fox.

Of bras thay broghten bemes, and of box,
Of horn, of boon, in whiche they blewe and pouped,
And therwithal thay shryked and they houped;
It semed as that heven sholde falle.
Now, gode men, I pray yow herkneth alle!
   Lo, how fortune turneth sodeinly
The hope and pryde eek of hir enemy!
This cok, that lay upon the foxes bak,
In al his drede, un-to the fox he spak,
And seyde, "sire, if that I were as ye,
Yet sholde I seyn (as wis god helpe me),
Turneth agayn, ye proude cherles alle!
A verray pestilence up-on yow falle!
Now am I come un-to this wodes syde,
Maugree your heed, the cok shal heer abyde;
I wol him ete in feith, and that anon."—
The fox answerde, "in feith, it shal be don,"—
And as he spak that word, al sodeinly
This cok brak from his mouth deliverly,
And heighe up-on a tree he fleigh anon.
And whan the fox saugh that he was y-gon,
"Allas!" quod he, "O Chauntecleer, allas!
I have to yow," quod he, "y-doon trespas,
In-as-muche as I maked yow aferd,
Whan I yow hente, and broghte out of the yerd;
But, sire, I dide it in no wikke entente;
Com doun, and I shal telle yow what I mente.
I shal seye sooth to yow, god help me so."
"Nay than," quod he, "I shrewe us bothe two,
And first I shrewe my-self, bothe blood and bones,
If thou bigyle me ofter than ones.
Thou shalt na-more, thurgh thy flaterye,
Do me to singe and winke with myn yë.
For he that winketh, whan he sholde see,
Al wilfully, god lat him never thee!"
"Nay," quod the fox, "but god yeve him meschaunce,
That is so undiscreet of governaunce,
That jangleth whan he sholde holde his pees."
   Lo, swich it is for to be recchelees,
And necligent, and truste on flaterye.
But ye that holden this tale a folye,
As of a fox, or of a cok and hen,

Taketh the moralitee, good men.
For seint Paul seith, that al that writen is,
To our doctryne it is y-write, y-wis.
Taketh the fruyt, and lat the chaf be stille.
  Now, gode god, if that it be thy wille,
As seith my lord, so make us alle good men;
And bringe us to his heighe blisse. Amen.

Here is ended the Nonne Preestes Tale

JOHN SKELTON

To Mistress Margaret Hussey

MERRY Margaret,
        As midsummer flower,
Gentle as falcon
Or hawk of the tower,
With solace and gladness,
Much mirth and no madness,
All good and no badness;
So joyously,
So maidenly,
So womanly,
Her demeaning;
In every thing
Far, far passing
That I can indite,
Or suffice to write
Of merry Margaret,
As midsummer flower,
Gentle as falcon
Or hawk of the tower.
As patient and as still,
And as full of good will,
As the fair Isyphill,
Coliander,
Sweet pomander,
Good Cassander;

Steadfast of thought,
Well made, well wrought.
Far may be sought
Erst than ye can find
So courteous, so kind,
As merry Margaret,
This midsummer flower,
Gentle as falcon
Or hawk of the tower.

SIR THOMAS WYATT

Forget Not Yet

FORGET not yet the tried intent
Of such a truth as I have meant;
My great travail so gladly spent
      Forget not yet!

Forget not yet when first began
The weary life ye know, since whan
The suit, the service none tell can;
      Forget not yet!

Forget not yet the great assays,
The cruel wrong, the scornful ways,
The painful patience in denays,
      Forget not yet!

Forget not! oh! forget not this,
How long ago hath been, and is
The mind that never meant amiss—
      Forget not yet!

Forget not then thine own approved,
The which so long hath thee so loved,

denays] denials

Whose steadfast faith yet never moved—
Forget not this!

HENRY HOWARD, EARL OF SURREY

Brittle Beauty

BRITTLE beauty that nature made so frail,
  Whereof the gift is small, and short the season,
Flow'ring today tomorrow apt to fail,
Fickle treasure, abhorrèd of reason,
Dangerous to deal with, vain, of none avail,
Costly in keeping, passed not worth two peason,
Slippery in sliding as an eelès tail,
Hard to attain, once gotten not geason,
Jewel of jeopardy that peril doth assail,
False and untrue, enticèd oft to treason,
Enemy to youth (that most may I bewail!),
Ah, bitter sweet! infecting as the poison,
Thou farest as fruit that with the frost is taken:
Today ready ripe, tomorrow all too shaken.

CHIDIOCK TICHBORNE

Written on the Eve of Execution

MY prime of youth is but a frost of cares,
  My feast of joy is but a dish of pain,
My crop of corn is but a field of tares,
  And all my good is but vain hope of gain;
My life is fled, and yet I saw no sun;
And now I live, and now my life is done.

My tale was heard, and yet it was not told;
  My fruit is fallen, and yet my leaves are **green**;
My youth is spent, and yet I am not old;
  I saw the world, and yet I was not seen;
My thread is cut, and yet it is not spun;
And now I live, and now my life is done.

I sought my death and found it in the womb,
  I lookt for life and saw it was a shade,
I trod the earth and knew it was my tomb,
  And now I die, and now I was but made;
My glass is full, and now my glass is run,
And now I live, and now my life is done.

SIR WALTER RALEIGH

The Passionate Man's Pilgrimage

Supposed to be written by one at the point of death

GIVE me my scallop shell of quiet,
  My staff of faith to walk upon,
My scrip of joy, immortal diet,
My bottle of salvation:
My gown of glory, hope's true gage,
And thus I'll make my pilgrimage.

Blood must be my body's balmer,
No other balm will there be given
Whilst my soul like a white palmer
Travels to the land of heaven,
Over the silver mountains,
Where spring the nectar fountains;
And there I'll kiss
The bowl of bliss,
And drink my eternal fill
On every milken hill.

My soul will be a-dry before,
But after it, will ne'er thirst more.

And by the happy blissful way
More peaceful pilgrims I shall see,
That have shook off their gowns of clay,
And go apparelled fresh like me.
I'll bring them first
To slake their thirst,
And then to taste those nectar suckets
At the clear wells
Where sweetness dwells,
Drawn up by saints in crystal buckets.

And when our bottles and all we
Are filled with immortality;
Then the holy paths we'll travel
Strewed with rubies thick as gravel,
Ceilings of diamonds, sapphire floors,
High walls of coral and pearl bowers.

From thence to heaven's bribeless hall
Where no corrupted voices brawl,
No conscience molten into gold,
Nor forg'd accusers bought and sold,
No cause deferred, nor vain-spent journey,
For there Christ is the King's Attorney:
Who pleads for all without degrees,
And he hath angels, but no fees.

When the grand twelve million jury
Of our sins with sinful fury,
Gainst our souls black verdicts give,
Christ pleads his death, and then we live.
Be thou my speaker, taintless pleader,
Unblotted lawyer, true proceeder,
Thou movest salvation even for alms,
Not with a bribéd lawyer's palms.

And this is my eternal plea,
To him that made heaven, earth and sea,
Seeing my flesh must die so soon,

And want a head to dine next noon,
Just at the stroke when my veins start and spread
Set on my soul an everlasting head.
Then am I ready like a palmer fit,
To tread those blest paths which before I writ.

EDMUND SPENSER

Prothalamion

CALM was the day, and through the trembling air
  Sweet breathing Zephyrus did softly play,
A gentle spirit, that lightly did delay
Hot Titan's beams, which then did glister fair;
When I whose sullen care,
Through discontent of my long fruitless stay
In prince's court, and expectation vain
Of idle hopes, which still do fly away
Like empty shadows, did afflict my brain,
Walked forth to ease my pain
Along the shore of silver streaming Thames,
Whose rutty bank, the which his river hems,
Was painted all with variable flowers,
And all the meads adorned with dainty gems,
Fit to deck maidens' bowers,
And crown their paramours,
Against the bridal day, which is not long:
  Sweet Thames, run softly, till I end my song.

There, in a meadow, by the river's side,
A flock of nymphs I chanced to espy,
All lovely daughters of the flood thereby,
With goodly greenish locks all loose untied,
As each had been a bride;
And each one had a little wicker basket,
Made of fine twigs entrailed curiously,
In which they gathered flowers to fill their flasket,

And with fine fingers cropped full featously
The tender stalks on high.
Of every sort, which in that meadow grew,
They gathered some; the violet pallid blue,
The little daisy, that at evening closes,
The virgin lily, and the primrose true,
With store of vermeil roses,
To deck their bridegrooms' posies,
Against the bridal day, which was not long:
   Sweet Thames, run softly, till I end my song.

With that, I saw two swans of goodly hue
Come softly swimming down along the Lee;
Two fairer birds I yet did never see.
The snow, which doth the top of Pindus strew,
Did never whiter shew,
Nor Jove himself, when he a swan would be
For love of Leda, whiter did appear:
Yet Leda was they say as white as he,
Yet not so white as these, nor nothing near.
So purely white they were,
That even the gentle stream, the which them bare,
Seemed foul to them, and bade his billows spare
To wet their silken feathers, lest they might
Soil their fair plumes with water not so fair,
And mar their beauties bright,
That shone as heaven's light,
Against their bridal day, which was not long:
   Sweet Thames, run softly, till I end my song.

Eftsoons the nymphs, which now had flowers their fill,
Ran all in haste, to see that silver brood,
As they came floating on the crystal flood.
Whom when they saw, they stood amazed still,
Their wondering eyes to fill.
Them seemed they never saw a sight so fair,
Of fowls so lovely, that they sure did deem
Them heavenly born, or to be that same pair
Which through the sky draw Venus' silver team;
For sure they did not seem
To be begot of any earthly seed,
But rather angels or of angels' breed:

Yet were they bred of Somers-heat they say,
In sweetest season, when each flower and weed
The earth did fresh array,
So fresh they seemed as day,
Even as their bridal day, which was not long:
  Sweet Thames, run softly, till I end my song.

Then forth they all out of their baskets drew
Great store of flowers, the honour of the field,
That to the sense did fragrant odours yield,
All which upon those goodly birds they threw,
And all the waves did strew,
That like old Peneus' waters they did seem,
When down along by pleasant Tempe's shore,
Scattered with flowers, through Thessaly they stream,
That they appear through lilies' plenteous store,
Like a bride's chamber floor.
Two of those nymphs, meanwhile, two garlands bound,
Of freshest flowers which in that mead they found,
The which presenting all in trim array,
Their snowy foreheads therewithal they crowned,
Whilst one did sing this lay,
Prepared against that day,
Against their bridal day, which was not long:
  Sweet Thames, run softly, till I end my song.

"Ye gentle birds, the world's fair ornament,
And heaven's glory, whom this happy hour
Doth lead unto your lovers' blissful bower,
Joy may you have and gentle heart's content
Of your love's couplement:
And let fair Venus, that is queen of love,
With her heart-quelling sun upon you smile,
Whose smile, they say, hath virtue to remove
All love's dislike, and friendship's faulty guile
For ever to assoil.
Let endless peace your steadfast hearts accord,
And blessed plenty wait upon your board,
And let your bed with pleasures chaste abound,
That fruitful issue may to you afford,
Which may your foes confound,
And make your joys redound,

    Somers-heat] summer's heat = Somerset

Upon your bridal day, which is not long:
   Sweet Thames, run softly, till I end my song."

So ended she; and all the rest around
To her redoubled that her undersong,
Which said, their bridal day should not be long.
And gentle echo from the neighbour ground
Their accents did resound.
So forth those joyous birds did pass along,
Adown the Lee, that to them murmured low,
As he would speak, but that he lacked a tongue,
Yet did by signs his glad affection show,
Making his stream run slow.
And all the fowl which in his flood did dwell
'Gan flock about these twain, that did excel
The rest so far as Cynthia doth shend
The lesser stars. So they, enranged well,
Did on those two attend,
And their best service lend,
Against their wedding day, which was not long:
   Sweet Thames, run softly, till I end my song.

At length they all to merry London came,
To merry London, my most kindly nurse,
That to me gave his life's first native source;
Though from another place I take my name,
An house of ancient fame.
There when they came, whereas those bricky towers,
The which on Thames' broad aged back do ride,
Where now the studious lawyers have their bowers
There whilom wont the Templar Knights to bide,
Till they decayed through pride:
Next whereunto there stands a stately place,
Where oft I gained gifts and goodly grace
Of that great lord, which therein wont to dwell,
Whose want too well now feels my friendless case.
But ah! here fits not well
Old woes but joys to tell
Against the bridal day, which is not long:
   Sweet Thames, run softly, till I end my song.

Yet therein now doth lodge a noble peer,
Great England's glory and the world's wide wonder,

shend] shame

Whose dreadful name late through all Spain did thunder,
And Hercules' two pillars standing near
Did make to quake and fear.
Fair branch of honour, flower of chivalry,
That fillest England with thy triumph's fame,
Joy have thou of thy noble victory,
And endless happiness of thine own name
That promiseth the same:
That through thy prowess and victorious arms,
Thy country may be freed from foreign harms;
And great Elisa's glorious name may ring
Through all the world, filled with thy wide alarms,
Which some brave Muse may sing
To ages following,
Upon the bridal day, which is not long:
   Sweet Thames, run softly, till I end my song.

From those high towers this noble lord issuing,
Like radiant Hesper when his golden hair
In th' Ocean billows he hath bathed fair,
Descended to the river's open viewing,
With a great train ensuing.
Above the rest were goodly to be seen
Two gentle knights of lovely face and feature
Beseeming well the bower of any queen,
With gifts of wit and ornaments of nature,
Fit for so goodly stature;
That like the twins of Jove they seemed in sight,
Which deck the baldric of the heavens bright.
They two forth pacing to the river's side,
Received those two fair birds, their love's delight,
Which at th' appointed tide
Each one did make his bride,
Against their bridal day, which is not long:
   Sweet Thames, run softly, till I end my song.

Amoretti

XXXIV

LIKE as a ship, that through the ocean wide,
  By conduct of some star doth make her way,
Whenas a storm hath dimmed her trusty guide,
Out of her course doth wander far astray;

So I, whose star, that wont with her bright ray
Me to direct, with clouds is overcast,
Do wander now, in darkness and dismay,
Through hidden perils round about me placed;
Yet hope I well that, when this storm is past,
My Helicè, the lodestar of my life,
Will shine again, and look on me at last,
With lovely light to clear my cloudy grief:
   Till then I wander care-full, comfortless,
   In secret sorrow, and sad pensiveness.

LXXV

One day I wrote her name upon the strand,
But came the waves and washèd it away:
Again I wrote it with a second hand,
But came the tide and made my pains his prey.
"Vain man," said she, "that dost in vain essay
A mortal thing so to immortalize;
For I myself shall like to this decay,
And eke my name be wipèd out likewise."
"Not so," quoth I; "let baser things devise
To die in dust, but you shall live by fame;
My verse your virtues rare shall eternize,
And in the heavens write your glorious name:
   Where, whenas Death shall all the world subdue,
   Our love shall live, and later life renew."

SIR PHILIP SIDNEY

"Astrophel to Stella"

I

LOVING in truth, and fain in verse my love to show,
  That she, dear she, might take some pleasure of my pain,
Pleasure might cause her read, reading might make her know,
  Knowledge might pity win, and pity grace obtain,

I sought fit words to paint the blackest face of woe;
  Studying inventions fine, her wits to entertain,
Oft turning others' leaves to see if thence would flow
  Some fresh and fruitful showers upon my sun-burned brain.
But words came halting forth, wanting Invention's stay;
  Invention, Nature's child, fled step-dame Study's blows,
And others' feet still seemed but strangers in my way.
    Thus, great with child to speak, and helpless in my throes,
      Biting my truant pen, beating myself for spite,
      "Fool," said my Muse to me, "look in thy heart and write."

XXXI

With how sad steps, O Moon, thou climb'st the skies!
  How silently, and with how wan a face!
  What! may it be that even in heavenly place
That busy archer his sharp arrows tries?
Sure, if that long-with-love-acquainted eyes
  Can judge of love, thou feel'st a lover's case;
  I read it in thy looks; thy languished grace
To me, that feel the like, thy state descries.
Then, even of fellowship, O Moon, tell me,
  Is constant love deemed there but want of wit?
Are beauties there as proud as here they be?
  Do they above love to be loved, and yet
    Those lovers scorn whom that love doth possess?
    Do they call virtue there ungratefulness?

XXXIX

  Come, sleep, O sleep, the certain knot of peace,
    The baiting place of wit, the balm of woe,
  The poor man's wealth, the prisoner's release,
    Th' indifferent judge between the high and low;
  With shield of proof shield me from out the prease
    Of those fierce darts despair at me doth throw;
  O make me in those civil wars to cease;
    I will good tribute pay, if thou do so.
  Take thou of me smooth pillows, sweetest bed,
    A chamber deaf to noise and blind to light,
  A rosy garland and a weary head;
    And if these things, as being thine by right,

prease] crowd

Move not thy heavy grace, thou shalt in me,
Livelier than elsewhere, Stella's image see.

XLI

Having this day my horse, my hand, my lance
  Guided so well that I obtained the prize,
  Both by the judgment of the English eyes
And of some sent from that sweet enemy, France;
Horsemen my skill in horsemanship advance,
  Town-folks my strength; a daintier judge applies
  His praise to sleight which from good use doth rise;
Some lucky wits impute it but to chance;
Others, because of both sides I do take
  My blood from them who did excel in this,
Think Nature me a man of arms did make.
  How far they shot awry! The true cause is,
    Stella looked on, and from her heavenly face
    Sent forth the beams which made so fair my race.

FULKE GREVILLE, LORD BROOKE

Epitaph on Sir Philip Sidney

SILENCE augmenteth grief, writing increaseth rage,
  Staled are my thoughts, which loved and lost the wonder of our
    age:
Yet quickened now with fire, though dead with frost ere now,
Enraged I write I know not what; dead, quick, I know not how.

Hard-hearted minds relent and rigour's tears abound,
And envy strangely rues his end, in whom no fault she found.
Knowledge her light hath lost; valour hath slain her knight.
Sidney is dead; dead is my friend; dead is the world's delight.

Place, pensive, wails his fall whose presence was her pride;
Time crieth out, "My ebb is come; his life was my spring tide."

Fame mourns in that she lost the ground of her reports;
Each living wight laments his lack, and all in sundry sorts.

He was (woe worth that word!) to each well-thinking mind
A spotless friend, a matchless man, whose virtue ever shined,
Declaring in his thoughts, his life, and that he writ,
Highest conceits, longest foresights, and deepest works of wit.

He, only like himself, was second unto none,
Whose death (though life) we rue, and wrong, and all in vain do
    moan.
Their loss, not him, wail they, that fill the world with cries,
Death slew not him, but he made death his ladder to the skies.

Now sink of sorrow I, who live, the more the wrong!
Who wishing death, whom death denies, whose thread is all too
    long;
Who tied to wretched life, who looks for no relief,
Must spend my ever dying days in never ending grief.

Heart's ease and only I, like parallels, run on,
Whose equal length keep equal breadth, and never meet in one;
Yet for not wronging him, my thoughts, my sorrow's cell,
Shall not run out, though leak they will, for liking him so well.

Farewell to you, my hopes, my wonted waking dreams,
Farewell, sometimes enjoyed joy; eclipsed are thy beams.
Farewell, self-pleasing thoughts, which quietness brings forth;
And farewell, friendship's sacred league, uniting minds of worth.

And farewell, merry heart, the gift of guiltless minds,
And all sports which for life's restore variety assigns;
Let all that sweet is void; in me no mirth may dwell.
Philip, the cause of all this woe, my life's content, farewell!

Now rhyme, the son of rage, which art no kin to skill,
And endless grief, which deads my life, yet knows not how to kill,
Go, seek that hapless tomb, which if ye hap to find,
Salute the stones, that keep the limbs, that held so good a mind.

GEORGE PEELE

A Farewell to Arms

TO QUEEN ELIZABETH

HIS golden locks Time hath to silver turn'd;
  O Time too swift, O swiftness never ceasing!
His youth 'gainst Time and Age hath ever spurn'd,
  But spurn'd in vain; youth waneth by increasing:
Beauty, strength, youth, are flowers but fading seen;
Duty, faith, love, are roots, and ever green.

His helmet now shall make a hive for bees,
  And, lovers' sonnets turn'd to holy psalms,
A man-at-arms must now serve on his knees,
  And feed on prayers, which are Age his alms:
But though from court to cottage he depart,
His saint is sure of his unspotted heart.

And when he saddest sits in homely cell,
  He'll teach his swains this carol for a song—
"Blest be the hearts that wish my sovereign well,
  Curst be the souls that think her any wrong."
Goddess, allow this aged man his right,
To be your beadsman now that was your knight.

ROBERT GREENE

The Description of Sir Geoffrey Chaucer

HIS stature was not very tall,
  Lean he was, his legs were small,
Hosed within a stock of red,

A buttoned bonnet on his head,
From under which did hang, I ween,
Silver hairs both bright and sheen.
His beard was white, trimmed round,
His countenance blithe and merry found.
A sleeveless jacket large and wide,
With many plights and skirts side,
Of water camlet did he wear;
A whittle by his belt he bare,
His shoes were corned, broad before,
His inkhorn at his side he wore,
And in his hand he bore a book.
Thus did this ancient poet look.

ROBERT SOUTHWELL

The Burning Babe

AS I in hoary winter's night stood shivering in the snow,
    Surprised I was with sudden heat which made my heart to
      glow;
And lifting up a fearful eye to view what fire was near,
A pretty Babe all burning bright did in the air appear;
Who, scorched with excessive heat, such floods of tears did shed,
As though his floods should quench his flames which with his tears
      were fed.
"Alas!" quoth he, "but newly born in fiery heats I fry,
Yet none approach to warm their hearts or feel my fire but I.
My faultless breast the furnace is, the fuel wounding thorns;
Love is the fire, and sighs the smoke, the ashes shame and scorns;
The fuel justice layeth on, and mercy blows the coals;
The metal in this furnace wrought are men's defiled souls:
For which, as now on fire I am to work them to their good,
So will I melt into a bath to wash them in my blood."
With this he vanished out of sight and swiftly shrunk away,
And straight I called unto mind that it was Christmas day.

MARK ALEXANDER BOYD

Sonet

FRA bank to bank, fra wood to wood I rin,
  Ourhailit with my feeble fantasie;
Like til a leaf that fallis from a tree,
Or til a reed ourblawin with the win.

Twa gods guides me: the ane of tham is blin,
  Yea and a bairn brocht up in vanitie;
The next a wife ingenrit of the sea,
And lichter nor a dauphin with her fin.

Unhappy is the man for evermair
  That tills the sand and sawis in the air;
  But twice unhappier is he, I lairn,
That feidis in his hairt a mad desire,
And follows on a woman throw the fire,
  Led by a blind and teachit by a bairn.

MICHAEL DRAYTON

To the Cambro-Britons and Their Harp, His Ballad of Agincourt

FAIR stood the wind for France,
  When we our sails advance,
Nor now to prove our chance,
  Longer will tarry;
But putting to the main
At Kaux, the mouth of Seine,

With all his martial train,
  Landed King Harry.

And taking many a fort,
Furnished in warlike sort,
Marcheth towards Agincourt,
  In happy hour;
Skirmishing day by day
With those that stopped his way,
Where the French gen'ral lay
  With all his power.

Which in his height of pride,
King Henry to deride,
His ransom to provide
  To the King sending;
Which he neglects the while
As from a nation vile,
Yet with an angry smile
  Their fall portending.

And turning to his men,
Quoth our brave Henry then:
Though they to one be ten,
  Be not amazéd.
Yet have we well begun,
Battles so bravely won
Have ever to the sun
  By fame been raiséd.

And for myself, quoth he,
This my full rest shall be,
England ne'er mourn for me,
  Nor more esteem me;
Victor I will remain,
Or on this earth lie slain,
Never shall she sustain
  Loss to redeem me.

Poitiers and Crécy tell,
When most their pride did swell,
Under our swords they fell;

No less our skill is
Than when our grandsire great,
Claiming the regal seat
By many a warlike feat,
    Lopped the French lilies.

The Duke of York so dread
The eager vaward led;
With the main Henry sped
    Amongst his henchmen.
Excester had the rear,
A braver man not there,
O Lord, how hot they were
    On the false Frenchmen!

They now to fight are gone,
Armor on armor shone,
Drum now to drum did groan,
    To hear was wonder,
That with the cries they make
The very earth did shake,
Trumpet to trumpet spake,
    Thunder to thunder.

Well it thine age became,
O noble Erpingham,
Which didst the signal aim
    To our hid forces;
When from a meadow by,
Like a storm suddenly,
The English archery
    Stuck the French horses.

With Spanish yew so strong,
Arrows a cloth-yard long,
That like to serpents stung,
    Piercing the weather;
None from his fellow starts,
But playing manly parts,
And like true English hearts,
    Stuck close together.

When down their bows they threw,
And forth their bilboes drew,
And on the French they flew,
  Not one was tardy;
Arms were from shoulders sent,
Scalps to the teeth were rent,
Down the French peasants went;
  Our men were hardy.

This while our noble King,
His broad sword brandishing,
Down the French host did ding,
  As to o'erwhelm it;
And many a deep wound lent,
His arms with blood besprent,
And many a cruel dent
  Bruiséd his helmet.

Gloster, that Duke so good,
Next of the royal blood,
For famous England stood
  With his brave brother;
Clarence, in steel so bright,
Though but a maiden knight,
Yet in that furious fight,
  Scarce such another.

Warwick in blood did wade,
Oxford the foe invade,
And cruel slaughter made,
  Still as they ran up;
Suffolk his axe did ply,
Beaumont and Willoughby
Bare them right doughtily,
  Ferrers and Fanhope.

Upon Saint Crispin's day
Fought was this noble fray,
Which fame did not delay
  To England to carry;

Oh, when shall English men
With such acts fill a pen,
Or England breed again
    Such a King Harry?

———— •◆• ————

CHRISTOPHER MARLOWE

———— •◆• ————

Hero and Leander

FIRST SESTIAD

ON Hellespont, guilty of true love's blood,
    In view, and opposite, two cities stood,
Sea borderers, disjoined by Neptune's might;
The one Abydos, the other Sestos hight.
At Sestos, Hero dwelt; Hero the fair,
Whom young Apollo courted for her hair,
And offered as a dower his burning throne,
Where she should sit for men to gaze upon.
The outside of her garments were of lawn,
The lining purple silk, with gilt stars drawn;
Her wide sleeves green, and bordered with a grove,
Where Venus in her naked glory strove
To please the careless and disdainful eyes
Of proud Adonis, that before her lies;
Her kirtle blue, whereon was many a stain,
Made with the blood of wretched lovers slain.
Upon her head she ware a myrtle wreath,
From whence her veil reached to the ground beneath.
Her veil was artificial flowers and leaves,
Whose workmanship both man and beast deceives.
Many would praise the sweet smell as she passed,
When 'twas the odour which her breath forth cast;
And there for honey bees have sought in vain,
And, beat from thence, have lighted there again.
About her neck hung chains of pebble-stone.
Which, lightened by her neck, like diamonds shone.

She ware no gloves, for neither sun nor wind
Would burn or parch her hands, but to her mind
Or warm or cool them, for they took delight
To play upon those hands, they were so white.
Buskins of shells all silvered used she,
And branched with blushing coral to the knee,
Where sparrows perched, of hollow pearl and gold,
Such as the world would wonder to behold:
Those with sweet water oft her handmaid fills,
Which, as she went, would chirrup through the bills.
Some say, for her the fairest Cupid pined,
And, looking in her face, was strooken blind.
But this is true, so like was one the other,
As he imagined Hero was his mother;
And oftentimes into her bosom flew,
About her naked neck his bare arms threw,
And laid his childish head upon her breast,
And with still panting rocked, there took his rest.
So lovely fair was Hero, Venus' nun,
As Nature wept, thinking she was undone,
Because she took more from her than she left,
And of such wondrous beauty her bereft;
Therefore, in sign her treasure suffered wrack,
Since Hero's time hath half the world been black.
Amorous Leander, beautiful and young,
(Whose tragedy divine Musaeus sung)
Dwelt at Abydos; since him dwelt there none
For whom succeeding times make greater moan.
His dangling tresses that were never shorn,
Had they been cut and unto Colchos borne,
Would have allured the venturous youth of Greece
To hazard more than for the Golden Fleece.
Fair Cynthia wished his arms might be her sphere;
Grief makes her pale, because she moves not there.
His body was as straight as Circe's wand;
Jove might have sipped out nectar from his hand.
Even as delicious meat is to the taste,
So was his neck in touching, and surpassed
The white of Pelop's shoulder. I could tell ye,
How smooth his breast was, and how white his belly,
And whose immortal fingers did imprint
That heavenly path, with many a curious dint,

That runs along his back; but my rude pen
Can hardly blazen forth the loves of men,
Much less of powerful gods: let it suffice,
That my slack muse sings of Leander's eyes,
Those orient cheeks and lips, exceeding his
That leapt into the water for a kiss
Of his own shadow, and despising many,
Died ere he could enjoy the love of any.
Had wild Hippolytus Leander seen,
Enamoured of his beauty had he been;
His presence made the rudest peasant melt,
That in the vast uplandish country dwelt;
The barbarous Thracian soldier, moved with nought,
Was moved with him, and for his favour sought.
Some swore he was a maid in man's attire,
For in his looks were all that men desire,
A pleasant smiling cheek, a speaking eye,
A brow for love to banquet royally;
And such as knew he was a man would say,
Leander, thou art made for amorous play:
Why art thou not in love, and loved of all?
Though thou be fair, yet be not thine own thrall.

The men of wealthy Sestos, every year,
(For his sake whom their goddess held so dear,
Rose-cheeked Adonis) kept a solemn feast.
Thither resorted many a wand'ring guest,
To meet their loves; such as had none at all,
Came lovers home from this great festival.
For every street, like to a firmament,
Glistered with breathing stars, who where they went,
Frighted the melancholy earth, which deemed
Eternal heaven to burn, for so it seemed,
As if another Phaeton had got
The guidance of the sun's rich chariot.
But far above the loveliest Hero shined,
And stole away th' enchanted gazer's mind;
For like sea-nymphs' inveigling harmony,
So was her beauty to the standers by.
Nor that night-wand'ring pale and watery star
(When yawning dragons draw her thirling car
From Latmos' mount up to the gloomy sky,
Where, crowned with blazing light and majesty,

She proudly sits) more over-rules the flood,
Than she the hearts of those that near her stood.
Even as when gaudy nymphs pursue the chase,
Wretched Ixion's shaggy-footed race,
Incensed with savage heat, gallop amain
From steep pine-bearing mountains to the plain:
So ran the people forth to gaze upon her,
And all that viewed her were enamoured on her.
And as in fury of a dreadful fight,
Their fellows being slain or put to flight,
Poor soldiers stand with fear of death dead strooken,
So at her presence all, surprised and tooken,
Await the sentence of her scornful eyes:
He whom she favours lives, the other dies.
There might you see one sigh, another rage,
And some (their violent passions to assuage)
Compile sharp satires; but alas too late,
For faithful love will never turn to hate.
And many, seeing great princes were denied,
Pined as they went, and thinking on her died.
On this feast day, O cursèd day and hour,
Went Hero thorough Sestos, from her tower
To Venus' temple, where unhappily,
As after chanced, they did each other spy.
So fair a church as this had Venus none;
The walls were of discoloured jasper stone,
Wherein was Proteus carvèd, and o'er head,
A lively vine of green sea-agate spread;
Where by one hand, light headed Bacchus hung,
And with the other, wine from grapes outwrung.
Of crystal shining fair the pavement was;
The town of Sestos called it Venus' glass.
There might you see the gods in sundry shapes,
Committing heady riots, incest, rapes:
For know, that underneath this radiant floor
Was Danaë's statue in a brazen tower,
Jove slyly stealing from his sister's bed,
To dally with Idalian Ganymed,
And for his love Europa bellowing loud,
And tumbling with the Rainbow in a cloud:
Blood-quaffing Mars heaving the iron net,
Which limping Vulcan and his Cyclops set;

Love kindling fire, to burn such towns as Troy,
Sylvanus weeping for the lovely boy
That now is turned into a cypress tree,
Under whose shade the woòd-gods love to be.
And in the midst a silver altar stood;
There Hero sacrificing turtles' blood,
Vailed to the ground, veiling her eye-lids close,
And modestly they opened as she rose:
Thence flew Love's arrow with the golden head,
And thus Leander was enamouréd.
Stone still he stood, and evermore he gazed,
Till with the fire that from his count'nance blazed,
Relenting Hero's gentle heart was strook,
Such force and virtue hath an amorous look.
  It lies not in our power to love, or hate,
For will in us is over-ruled by fate.
When two are stript long ere the course begin,
We wish that one should lose, the other win;
And one especially do we affect
Of two gold ingots like in each respect.
The reason no man knows, let it suffice,
What we behold is censured by our eyes.
Where both deliberate, the love is slight,
Who ever loved, that loved not at first sight?

WILLIAM SHAKESPEARE

XVIII

SHALL I compare thee to a summer's day?
  Thou art more lovely and more temperate:
Rough winds do shake the darling buds of May,
And summer's lease hath all too short a date:
Sometime too hot the eye of heaven shines,
And often is his cold complexion dimm'd;
And every fair from fair sometime declines,
By chance, or nature's changing course, untrimm'd:
But thy eternal summer shall not fade,

Nor lose possession of that fair thou ow'st;
Nor shall Death brag thou wander'st in his shade,
When in eternal lines to time thou grow'st:
 So long as men can breathe, or eyes can see,
 So long lives this, and this gives life to thee.

XXIX

When, in disgrace with fortune and men's eyes,
I all alone beweep my outcast state,
And trouble deaf heaven with my bootless cries,
And look upon myself, and curse my fate,
Wishing me like to one more rich in hope,
Featur'd like him, like him with friends possess'd,
Desiring this man's art, and that man's scope,
With what I most enjoy contented least;
Yet in these thoughts myself almost despising,
Haply I think on thee,—and then my state,
Like to the lark at break of day arising
From sullen earth, sings hymns at heaven's gate;
 For thy sweet love remember'd such wealth brings
 That then I scorn to change my state with kings.

XXX

When to the sessions of sweet silent thought
I summon up remembrance of things past,
I sigh the lack of many a thing I sought,
And with old woes new wail my dear times' waste:
Then can I drown an eye, unus'd to flow,
For precious friends hid in death's dateless night,
And weep afresh love's long since cancell'd woe,
And moan the expense of many a vanish'd sight:
Then can I grieve at grievances forgone,
And heavily from woe to woe tell o'er
The sad account of fore-bemoaned moan,
Which I new pay as if not paid before.
 But if the while I think on thee, dear friend,
 All losses are restor'd and sorrows end.

LV

Not marble, not the gilded monuments
Of princes, shall outlive this powerful rime;

But you shall shine more bright in these contents
Than unswept stone, besmear'd with sluttish time.
When wasteful war shall statues overturn,
And broils root out the work of masonry,
Nor mars his sword nor war's quick fire shall burn
The living record of your memory.
'Gainst death and all-oblivious enmity
Shall you pace forth; your praise shall still find room,
Even in the eyes of all posterity
That wear this world out to the ending doom.
    So, till the judgment that yourself arise,
      You live in this, and dwell in lovers' eyes.

LX

Like as the waves make towards the pebbled shore,
So do our minutes hasten to their end;
Each changing place with that which goes before,
In sequent toil all forwards do contend.
Nativity, once in the main of light,
Crawls to maturity, wherewith being crown'd,
Crooked eclipses 'gainst his glory fight,
And Time that gave doth now his gift confound.
Time doth transfix the flourish set on youth
And delves the parallels in beauty's brow,
Feeds on the rarities of nature's truth,
And nothing stands but for his scythe to mow:
    And yet to times in hope my verse shall stand,
      Praising thy worth, despite his cruel hand.

LXVI

Tired with all these, for restful death I cry,
As, to behold desert a beggar born,
And needy nothing trimmed in jollity,
And purest faith unhappily forsworn,
And gilded honor shamefully misplaced,
And maiden virtue rudely strumpeted,
And right perfection wrongfully disgraced,
And strength by limping sway disablèd,
And art made tongue-tied by authority,
And folly doctor-like controlling skill,
And simple truth miscalled simplicity,

And captive good attending captain ill:
  Tired with all these, from these would I be gone,
  Save that, to die, I leave my love alone.

LXXIII

That time of year thou may'st in me behold
When yellow leaves, or none, or few, do hang
Upon those boughs which shake against the cold,
Bare ruin'd choirs, where late the sweet birds sang.
In me thou see'st the twilight of such day
As after sunset fadeth in the west;
Which by and by black night doth take away,
Death's second self, that seals up all in rest.
In me thou see'st the glowing of such fire,
That on the ashes of his youth doth lie,
As the death-bed whereon it must expire
Consum'd with that which it was nourish'd by.
  This thou perceiv'st, which makes thy love more strong,
  To love that well which thou must leave ere long.

LXXXVII

Farewell! thou art too dear for my possessing,
And like enough thou know'st thy estimate:
The charter of thy worth gives thee releasing;
My bonds in thee are all determinate.
For how do I hold thee but by thy granting?
And for that riches where is my deserving?
The cause of this fair gift in me is wanting,
And so my patent back again is swerving.
Thyself thou gav'st, thy own worth then not knowing,
Or me, to whom thou gav'st it, else mistaking;
So thy great gift, upon misprision growing,
Comes home again, on better judgment making.
  Thus have I had thee, as a dream doth flatter,
  In sleep a king, but, waking, no such matter.

XCIV

They that have power to hurt and will do none,
That do not do the thing they most do show,
Who, moving others, are themselves as stone,
Unmovèd, cold, and to temptation slow;

They rightly do inherit heaven's graces,
And husband nature's riches from expense:
They are the lords and owners of their faces,
Others but stewards of their excellence.
The summer's flower is to the summer sweet,
Though to itself it only live and die,
But if that flower with base infection meet,
The basest weed outbraves his dignity:
For sweetest things turn sourest by their deeds:
Lilies that fester smell far worse than weeds.

CVI

When in the chronicle of wasted time
I see descriptions of the fairest wights,
And beauty making beautiful old rime,
In praise of ladies dead and lovely knights,
Then, in the blazon of sweet beauty's best,
Of hand, of foot, of lip, of eye, of brow,
I see their antique pen would have express'd
Even such a beauty as you master now.
So all their praises are but prophecies
Of this our time, all you prefiguring;
And, for they look'd but with divining eyes,
They had not skill enough your worth to sing:
For we, which now behold these present days,
Have eyes to wonder, but lack tongues to praise.

CXVI

Let me not to the marriage of true minds
Admit impediments. Love is not love
Which alters when it alteration finds,
Or bends with the remover to remove:
O, no! it is an ever-fixed mark,
That looks on tempests and is never shaken;
It is the star to every wandering bark,
Whose worth's unknown, although his height be taken.
Love's not Time's fool, though rosy lips and cheeks
Within his bending sickle's compass come;
Love alters not with his brief hours and weeks,
But bears it out even to the edge of doom.
If this be error, and upon me prov'd,
I never writ, nor no man ever lov'd.

Songs

(FROM THE TWO GENTLEMEN OF VERONA)

WHO is Silvia? what is she?
  That all our swains commend her?
Holy, fair, and wise is she;
The heaven such grace did lend her,
  That she might admirèd be.

Is she kind as she is fair?
For beauty lives with kindness:
  Love doth to her eyes repair,
To help him of his blindness;
  And, being help'd, inhabits there.

Then to Silvia let us sing,
That Silvia is excelling;
  She excels each mortal thing
Upon the dull earth dwelling:
  To her let us garlands bring.

(FROM LOVE'S LABOUR'S LOST)

WHEN daisies pied and violets blue,
  And lady-smocks all silver-white,
And cuckoo-buds of yellow hue
  Do paint the meadows with delight,
The cuckoo then, on every tree,
Mocks married men; for thus sings he,
    Cuckoo!
  Cuckoo, cuckoo!
  O word of fear,
Unpleasing to a married ear!

When shepherds pipe on oaten straws,
  And merry larks are ploughmen's clocks,
When turtles tread, and rooks, and daws,
  And maidens bleach their summer smocks,
The cuckoo then, on every tree,
Mocks married men, for thus sings he—
    Cuckoo!

Cuckoo, cuckoo!
O word of fear,
Unpleasing to a married ear!

(FROM LOVE'S LABOUR'S LOST)

WHEN icicles hang by the wall,
    And Dick the shepherd blows his nail,
And Tom bears logs into the hall,
    And milk come frozen home in pail,
When blood is nipp'd, and ways be foul,
Then nightly sings the staring owl,
        To-whit!
To-who!—a merry note,
While greasy Joan doth keel the pot.

When all aloud the wind doth blow,
    And coughing drowns the parson's saw,
And birds sit brooding in the snow,
    And Marian's nose looks red and raw,
When roasted crabs hiss in the bowl,
Then nightly sings the staring owl,
        To-whit!
To-who!—a merry note,
While greasy Joan doth keel the pot.

Fairy Songs

(FROM A MIDSUMMER NIGHT'S DREAM)

I

OVER hill, over dale,
    Thorough bush, thorough brier,
Over park, over pale,
    Thorough flood, thorough fire,
I do wander everywhere
Swifter than the moon's sphere;
And I serve the Fairy Queen,
To dew her orbs upon the green.

The cowslips tall her pensioners be;
In their gold coats spots you see;
Those be rubies, fairy favours,
In those freckles live their savours:
I must go seek some dewdrops here,
And hang a pearl in every cowslip's ear.

II

You spotted snakes with double tongue,
Thorny hedge-hogs, be not seen;
Newts and blind-worms, do no wrong;
Come not near our fairy queen:

Philomel, with melody,
Sing in our sweet lullaby
Lulla, lulla, lullaby, lulla, lulla, lullaby
Never harm,
Nor spell, nor charm,
Come our lovely lady nigh;
So, good night, with lullaby.

Weaving spiders come not here:
Hence, you long-legg'd spinners, hence!
Beetles black, approach not near;
Worm nor snail, do no offence.

Philomel, with melody,
Sing in our sweet lullaby
Lulla, lulla, lullaby, lulla, lulla, lullaby
Never harm,
Nor spell, nor charm,
Come our lovely lady nigh;
So, good night, with lullaby.

III

Now the hungry lion roars,
And the wolf behowls the moon;
Whilst the heavy ploughman snores,
All with weary task fordone.

Now the wasted brands do glow,
  Whilst the screech-owl, screeching loud,
Puts the wretch that lies in woe
  In remembrance of a shroud.

Now it is the time of night
  That the graves, all gaping wide,
Every one lets forth his spright,
  In the church-way paths to glide:

And we fairies, that do run
  By the triple Hecate's team,
From the presence of the sun,
  Following darkness like a dream,

Now are frolic; not a mouse
Shall disturb this hallow'd house.
I am sent with broom before,
To sweep the dust behind the door.

Casket Song

(FROM THE MERCHANT OF VENICE)

TELL me where is fancy bred,
  Or in the heart, or in the head?
How begot, how nourishèd?
    Reply, reply.

It is engendered in the eyes,
With gazing fed; and fancy dies
In the cradle where it lies.

Let us all ring fancy's knell;
I'll begin it—Ding dong bell.
    Ding dong bell.

Balthasar's Song

(FROM MUCH ADO ABOUT NOTHING)

SIGH no more, ladies, sigh no more,
  Men were deceivers ever;
One foot in sea, and one on shore,
  To one thing constant never:
      Then sigh not so,
      But let them go,
  And be you blithe and bonny,
Converting all your sounds of woe
  Into Hey nonny, nonny.

Sing no more ditties, sing no mo
  Of dumps so dull and heavy;
The fraud of men was ever so,
  Since summer first was leavy.
      Then sigh not so,
      But let them go,
  And be you blithe and bonny,
Converting all your sounds of woe
  Into Hey nonny, nonny.

Amien's Songs

(FROM AS YOU LIKE IT)

I

UNDER the greenwood tree,
  Who loves to lie with me,
And tune his merry note
Unto the sweet bird's throat,
Come hither, come hither, come hither—
    Here shall he see
    No enemy
But winter and rough weather.

Who doth ambition shun,
And loves to live i' the sun,
Seeking the food he eats,
And pleased with what he gets,
Come hither, come hither, come hither—
Here shall he see
No enemy
But winter and rough weather.

II

Blow, blow, thou winter wind,
Thou art not so unkind
As man's ingratitude;
Thy tooth is not so keen,
Because thou art not seen,
Although thy breath be rude.
Heigh-ho, sing heigh-ho, unto the green holly:
Most friendship is feigning, most loving mere folly.
Then heigh-ho, the holly!
This life is most jolly.

Freeze, freeze, thou bitter sky,
That dost not bite so nigh
As benefits forgot:
Though thou the waters warp,
Thy sting is not so sharp
As friend remember'd not.
Heigh-ho, sing heigh-ho, unto the green holly:
Most friendship is feigning, most loving mere folly.
Then heigh-ho, the holly!
This life is most jolly.

Feste's Songs

(FROM TWELFTH NIGHT)

I

O MISTRESS mine, where are you roaming?
O! stay and hear; your true love's coming,
That can sing both high and low.

Trip no further, pretty sweeting;
Journeys end in lovers meeting,
   Every wise man's son doth know.

What is love? 'Tis not hereafter;
Present mirth hath present laughter;
   What's to come is still unsure.
In delay there lies no plenty;
Then come kiss me, sweet and twenty;
   Youth's a stuff will not endure.

II

Come away, come away, death,
   And in sad cypress let me be laid;
Fly away, fly away, breath;
   I am slain by a fair cruel maid.
My shroud of white, stuck all with yew,
   O! prepare it.
My part of death, no one so true
   Did share it.

Not a flower, not a flower sweet,
   On my black coffin let there be strown;
Not a friend, not a friend greet
   My poor corse, where my bones shall be thrown.
A thousand thousand sighs to save,
   Lay me, O! where
Sad true lover never find my grave,
   To weep there.

III

When that I was and a little tiny boy,
   With hey, ho, the wind and the rain,
A foolish thing was but a toy,
   For the rain it raineth every day.

But when I came to man's estate,
   With hey, ho, the wind and the rain,
'Gainst knaves and thieves men shut their gate,
   For the rain it raineth every day.

But when I came, alas, to wive,
   With hey, ho, the wind and the rain,
By swaggering could I never thrive,
   For the rain it raineth every day.

But when I came unto my beds,
   With hey, ho, the wind and the rain,
With toss-pots still had drunken heads,
   For the rain it raineth every day.

A great while ago the world begun,
   With hey, ho, the wind and the rain,
But that's all one, our play is done,
   And we'll strive to please you every day.

Ophelia's Songs

(FROM HAMLET)

I

HOW should I your true love know
   From another one?
By his cockle hat and staff,
   And his sandal shoon.

He is dead and gone, lady,
   He is dead and gone;
At his head a grass-green turf,
   At his heels a stone.

White his shroud as the mountain snow,
   Larded with sweet flowers,
Which bewept to the grave did go
   With true-love showers.

II

And will he not come again?
And will he not come again?
   No, no, he is dead:
   Go to thy death-bed:
He never will come again.

His beard was as white as snow,
All flaxen was his poll:
  He is gone, he is gone,
   And we cast away moan;
God ha' mercy on his soul!

Song for Mariana

(FROM MEASURE FOR MEASURE)

TAKE, O take those lips away
  That so sweetly were forsworn;
And those eyes, the break of day,
  Lights that do mislead the morn.
But my kisses bring again,
          Bring again;
Seals of love, but seal'd in vain,
          Seal'd in vain.

Song to Imogen

(FROM CYMBELINE)

HARK! hark! the lark at heaven's gate sings,
  And Phoebus gins arise,
His steeds to water at those springs
  On chaliced flowers that lies;
And winking Mary-buds begin
  To ope their golden eyes;
With everything that pretty bin,
  My lady sweet, arise!
  Arise, arise!

Fidele's Dirge

(FROM CYMBELINE)

FEAR no more the heat o' the sun,
  Nor the furious winter's rages;
Thou thy worldly task hast done,

Home art gone, and ta'en thy wages,
Golden lads and girls all must,
As chimney-sweepers, come to dust.

Fear no more the frown o' the great,
   Thou art past the tyrant's stroke:
Care no more to clothe and eat;
   To thee the reed is as the oak:
The sceptre, learning, physic, must
All follow this, and come to dust.

Fear no more the lightning-flash,
   Nor the all-dreaded thunder-stone;
Fear not slander, censure rash;
   Thou hast finish'd joy and moan:
All lovers young, all lovers must
Consign to thee, and come to dust.

Ariel's Songs

(FROM THE TEMPEST)

I

COME unto these yellow sands,
   And then take hands:
Curtsied when you have, and kist
   The wild waves whist,
Foot it featly here and there;
And, sweet sprites, the burthen bear.
         Hark, hark!
            Bow-wow.
         The watch-dogs bark:
            Bow-wow.
      Hark, hark! I hear
The strain of strutting chanticleer
Cry Cock-a-diddle-dow!

II

Full fathom five thy father lies:
   Of his bones are coral made;

Those are pearls that were his eyes:
    Nothing of him that doth fade
But doth suffer a sea-change
Into something rich and strange.
Sea-nymphs hourly ring his knell:
    Ding-dong.
Hark! now I hear them—
    Ding dong bell.

III.

Where the bee sucks, there suck I;
In a cowslip's bell I lie;
There I couch when owls do cry.
On the bat's back I do fly
After summer merrily:
Merrily, merrily, shall I live now,
Under the blossom that hangs on the bough.

THOMAS NASHE

RICH men, trust not in wealth
    Gold cannot buy you health:
Physic himself must fade;
All things to end are made;
The plague full swift goes by.
I am sick, I must die—
    Lord have mercy on us!

Beauty is but a flower
Which wrinkles will devour;
Brightness falls from the air;
Queens have died young, and fair;
Dust hath closed Helen's eye.
I am sick, I must die—
    Lord have mercy on us!

Strength stoops unto the grave,
Worms feed on Hector brave;

Swords may not fight with fate;
Earth still holds ope her gate;
Come, come, the bells do cry.
I am sick, I must die—
　　Lord have mercy on us!

———•———

THOMAS CAMPION

———•———

Laura

ROSE-CHEEK'D *Laura*, come;
　　Sing thou smoothly with thy beauty's
Silent music, either other
　　　Sweetly gracing.

Lovely forms do flow
From concent divinely framèd:
Heaven is music, and thy beauty's
　　　Birth is heavenly.

These dull notes we sing
Discords need for helps to grace them;
Only beauty purely loving
　　　Knows no discord;

But still moves delight,
Like clear springs renew'd by flowing,
Ever perfect, ever in them-
　　　selves eternal.

SONGS FROM LUTE BOOKS

Kind are her answers,
But her performance keeps no day;
　　Breaks time, as dancers
From their own music when they stray.
　　All her free favours
And smooth words wing my hopes in vain.
O! did ever voice so sweet but only feign?

Can true love yield such delay,
 Converting joy to pain?

 Lost is our freedom
When we submit to women so.
 Why do we need them
When in their best they work our woe?
 There is no wisdom
Can alter ends by Fate prefixed.
O! why is the good of man with evil mixed?
 Never were days yet called two,
  But one night went betwixt.

Now winter nights enlarge
 The number of their hours,
And clouds their storms discharge
 Upon the airy towers.
Let now the chimmeys blaze
 And cups o'erflow with wine;
Let well-tuned words amaze
 With harmony divine.
Now yellow waxen lights
 Shall wait on honey love,
While youthful revels, masques, and courtly sights
 Sleep's leaden spells remove.
This time doth well dispense
 With lovers' long discourse;
Much speech hath some defence,
 Though beauty no remorse.
All do not all things well;
 Some measures comely tread,
Some knotted riddles tell,
 Some poems smoothly read.
The summer hath his joys,
 And winter his delights;
Though love and all his pleasures are but toys,
 They shorten tedious nights.

Thrice toss these oaken ashes in the air;
Thrice sit thou mute in this enchanted chair;

Then thrice three times tie up this true love's knot,
And murmur soft: "She will, or she will not."

Go burn these poisonous weeds in yon blue fire,
These screech-owl's feathers and this prickling briar,
This cypress gathered at a dead man's grave,
That all thy fears and cares an end may have.

Then come, you fairies, dance with me a round;
Melt her hard heart with your melodious sound.
In vain are all the charms I can devise;
She hath an art to break them with her eyes.

BEN JONSON

Hymn to Diana

QUEEN and Huntress, chaste and fair,
    Now the sun is laid to sleep,
Seated in thy silver chair
    State in wonted manner keep;
        Hesperus entreats thy light,
        Goddess excellently bright.

Earth, let not thy envious shade
    Dare itself to interpose;
Cynthia's shining orb was made
    Heaven to clear when day did close;
        Bless us then with wished sight,
        Goddess excellently bright.

Lay thy bow of pearl apart
    And thy crystal-shining quiver;
Give unto the flying hart
    Space to breathe, how short soever;
        Thou that mak'st a day of night,
        Goddess excellently bright.

To Celia

DRINK to me only with thine eyes,
   And I will pledge with mine;
Or leave a kiss but in the cup
   And I'll not look for wine.
The thirst that from the soul doth rise
   Doth ask a drink divine;
But might I of Jove's nectar sup,
   I would not change for thine.

I sent thee late a rosy wreath,
   Not so much honoring thee
As giving it a hope that there
   It could not withered be;
But thou thereon didst only breathe
   And sent'st it back to me;
Since when it grows, and smells, I swear
   Not of itself but thee!

The Triumph

SEE the Chariot at hand here of Love,
   Wherein my Lady rideth!
Each that draws is a swan or a dove,
   And well the car Love guideth.
As she goes, all hearts do duty
         Unto her beauty;
And enamour'd do wish, so they might
         But enjoy such a sight,
That they still were to run by her side,
Through swords, through seas, whither she would ride.

Do but look on her eyes, they do light
   All that Love's world compriseth!
Do but look on her hair, it is bright
   As Love's star when it riseth!
Do but mark, her forehead's smoother
         Than words that soothe her;
And from her arch'd brows such a grace
         Sheds itself through the face,

As alone there triumphs to the life
All the gain, all the good, of the elements' strife.

Have you seen but a bright lily grow
   Before rude hands have touch'd it?
Have you mark'd but the fall of the snow
   Before the soil hath smutch'd it?
Have you felt the wool of beaver,
            Or swan's down ever?
Or have smelt o' the bud o' the brier,
            Or the nard in the fire?
Or have tasted the bag of the bee?
O so white, O so soft, O so sweet is she!

First Three Verses of an Ode

TO THE IMMORTAL MEMORY AND FRIENDSHIP OF THAT NOBLE
PAIR, SIR LUCIUS CARY AND SIR H. MORISON

IT is not growing like a tree
   In bulk, doth make man better be;
Or standing long an oak, three hundred year,
To fall a log at last, dry, bald, and sere:
            A lily of a day
            Is fairer far in May,
   Although it fall and die that night;
   It was the plant and flower of light.
In small proportions we just beauties see;
And in short measures, life may perfect be.

   Call, noble *Lucius,* then for wine,
   And let thy looks with gladness shine:
Accept this garland, plant it on thy head,
And think—nay, know—thy *Morison's* not dead.
            He leap'd the present age,
            Possest with holy rage
   To see that bright eternal Day
   Of which we Priests and Poets say
Such truths as we expect for happy men;
And there he lives with memory—and *Ben*

Jonson: who sung this of him, ere he went
                Himself to rest,
Or taste a part of that full joy he meant
                To have exprest
        In this bright Asterism
        Where it were friendship's schism—
Were not his *Lucius* long with us to tarry—
                To separate these twy
                Lights, the Dioscuri,
And keep the one half from his *Harry*.
But fate doth so alternate the design,
Whilst that in Heav'n, this light on earth must shine.

JOHN DONNE

The Good-Morrow

I WONDER by my troth, what thou, and I
    Did, till we lov'd? were we not wean'd till then?
But suck'd on countrey pleasures, childishly?
Or snorted we in the seaven sleepers den?
T'was so; But this, all pleasures fancies bee.
If ever any beauty I did see,
Which I desir'd, and got, t'was but a dreame of thee.

And now good morrow to our waking soules,
Which watch not one another out of feare;
For love, all love of other sights controules,
And makes one little roome, an every where.
Let sea-discoverers to new worlds have gone,
Let Maps to other, worlds on worlds have showne,
Let us possesse one world, each hath one, and is one.

My face is thine eye, thine in mine appeares,
And true plaine hearts doe in the faces rest,

Where can we finde two better hemispheares
Without sharpe North, without declining West?
What ever dyes, was not mixt equally;
If our two loves be one, or, thou and I
Love so alike, that none doe slacken, none can die.

Song

GOE, and catche a falling starre,
    Get with child a mandrake roote,
Teil me, where all past yeares are,
    Or who cleft the Divels foot,
Teach me to heare Mermaides singing,
    Or to keep off envies stinging,
            And finde
            What winde
Serves to advance an honest minde.

If thou beest borne to strange sights,
    Things invisible to see,
Ride ten thousand daies and nights,
    Till age snow white haires on thee,
Thou, when thou retorn'st, wilt tell mee
All strange wonders that befell thee,
            And sweare
            No where
Lives a woman true, and faire.

If thou findst one, let mee know,
    Such a Pilgrimage were sweet;
Yet doe not, I would not goe,
    Though at next doore wee might meet,
Though shee were true, when you met her,
And last, till you write your letter,
            Yet shee
            Will bee
False, ere I come, to two, or three.

The Undertaking

I HAVE done one braver thing
  Than all the *Worthies* did,
And yet a braver thence doth spring,
  Which is, to keepe that hid.

It were but madnes now t'impart
  The skill of specular stone,
When he which can have learn'd the art
  To cut it, can finde none.

So, if I now should utter this,
  Others (because no more
Such stuffe to worke upon, there is,)
  Would love but as before.

But he who lovelinesse within
  Hath found, all outward loathes,
For he who colour loves, and skinne,
  Loves but their oldest clothes.

If, as I have, you also doe
  Vertue'attir'd in woman see,
And dare love that, and say so too,
  And forget the Hee and Shee;

And if this love, though placed so,
  From prophane men you hide,
Which will no faith on this bestow,
  Or, if they doe, deride:

Then you have done a braver thing
  Than all the *Worthies* did;
And a braver thence will spring,
  Which is, to keepe that hid.

The Sunne Rising

BUSIE old foole, unruly Sunne,
  Why dost thou thus,
Through windowes, and through curtaines call on us?
Must to thy motions lovers seasons run?
    Sawcy pedantique wretch, goe chide
    Late schoole boyes, and sowre prentices,
  Goe tell Court-huntsmen, that the King will ride,
  Call countrey ants to harvest offices;
Love, all alike, no season knowes, nor clyme,
Nor houres, dayes, moneths, which are the rags of time.

    Thy beames, so reverend, and strong
    Why shouldst thou thinke?
I could eclipse and cloud them with a winke,
But that I would not lose her sight so long:
    If her eyes have not blinded thine,
    Looke, and tomorrow late, tell mee,
  Whether both the 'India's of spice and Myne
  Be where thou leftst them, or lie here with mee.
Aske for those Kings whom thou saw'st yesterday,
And thou shalt heare, All here in one bed lay.
    She'is all States, and all Princes, I,
    Nothing else is.
Princes doe but play us; compar'd to this,
All honor's mimique; All wealth alchimie.
    Thou sunne art halfe as happy'as wee,
    In that the world's contracted thus;
  Thine age askes ease, and since thy duties bee
  To warme the world, that's done in warming us.
Shine here to us, and thou art every where;
This bed thy center is, these walls, thy spheare.

The Anniversary

ALL kings, and all their favourites,
  All glory of honours, beauties, wits,
The sun itself, which makes time, as they pass,
Is elder by a year now than it was

When thou and I first one another saw.
All other things to their destruction draw,
    Only our love hath no decay;
This no tomorrow hath, nor yesterday;
Running it never runs from us away,
But truly keeps his first, last, everlasting day.

    Two graves must hide thine and my corse;
    If one might, death were no divorce.
Alas! as well as other princes, we
—Who prince enough in one another be—
Must leave at last in death these eyes and ears,
Oft fed with true oaths, and with sweet salt tears;
    But souls where nothing dwells but love
    —All other thoughts being inmates—then shall prove
This or a love increasèd there above,
When bodies to their graves, souls from their graves remove.

    And then we shall be throughly blest;
    But now no more than all the rest.
Here upon earth we're kings, and none but we
Can be such kings, nor of such subjects be.
Who is so safe as we? where none can do
Treason to us, except one of us two.
    True and false fears let us refrain,
Let us love nobly, and live, and add again
Years unto years unto years, till we attain
To write threescore; this is the second of our reign.

The Extasie

WHERE, like a pillow on a bed,
    A Pregnant banke swel'd up, to rest
The violets reclining head,
    Sat we two, one anothers best.
Our hands were firmely cimented
    With a fast balme, which thence did spring,
Our eye-beames twisted, and did thred
    Our eyes, upon one double string;
So to'entergraft our hands, as yet
    Was all the meanes to make us one,

And pictures in our eyes to get
   Was all our propagation.
As 'twixt two equall Armies, Fate
   Suspends uncertaine victorie,
Our soules, (which to advance their state,
   Were gone out,) hung 'twixt her, and mee.
And whil'st our soules negotiate there,
   Wee like sepulchrall statues lay;
All day, the same our postures were,
   And wee said nothing, all the day.
If any, so by love refin'd,
   That he soules language understood,
And by good love were growen all minde,
   Within convenient distance stood,
He (though he knew not which soul spake,
   Because both meant, both spake the same)
Might thence a new concoction take,
   And part farre purer than he came.
This Extasie doth unperplex
   'We said) and tell us what we love,
Wee see by this, it was not sexe,
   Wee see, we saw not what did move:
But as all severall soules containe
   Mixture of things, they know not what,
Love, these mixt soules, doth mixe againe,
   And makes both one, each this and that.
A single violet transplant,
   The strength, the colour, and the size,
(All which before was poore, and scant,)
   Redoubles still, and multiplies.
When love, with one another so
   Interinanimates two soules,
That abler soule, which thence doth flow,
   Defects of lonelinesse controules.
Wee then, who are this new soule, know,
   Of what we are compos'd, and made,
For, th'Atomies of which we grow,
   Are soules, whom no change can invade.
But O alas, so long, so farre
   Our bodies why doe wee forbeare?
They are ours, though they are not wee, Wee are
   The intelligences, they the spheares.

We owe them thankes, because they thus,
   Did us, to us, at first convay,
Yeelded their forces, sense, to us,
   Nor are drosse to us, but allay.
On man heavens influence workes not so,
   But that it first imprints the ayre,
Soe soule into the soule may flow,
   Though it to body first repaire.
As our blood labours to beget
   Spirits, as like soules as it can,
Because such fingers need to knit
   That subtile knot, which makes us man:
So must pure lovers soules descend
   T'affections, and to facultics,
Which sense may reach and apprehend,
   Else a great Prince in prison lies.
To'our bodies turne wee then, that so
   Weake men on love reveal'd may looke;
Loves mysteries in soules doe grow,
   But yet the body is his booke.
And if some lover, such as wee,
   Have heard this dialogue of one,
Let him still marke us, he shall see
   Small change, when we'are to bodies gone.

The Relique

WHEN my grave is broke up againe
   Some second ghest to entertaine,
(For graves have learn'd that woman-head
To be to more than one a Bed)
   And he that digs it, spies
A bracelet of bright haire about the bone,
   Will he not let'us alone,
And thinke that there a loving couple lies,
Who thought that this device might be some way
To make their soules, at the last busie day,
Meet at this grave, and make a little stay?

   If this fall in a time, or land,
   Where mis-devotion doth command,

Then, he that digges us up, will bring
Us, to the Bishop, and the King,
To make us Reliques; then
Thou shalt be a Mary Magdalen, and I
A something else thereby;
All women shall adore us, and some men;
And since at such time, miracles are sought,
I would have that age by this paper taught
What miracles wee harmlesse lovers wrought.

First, we lov'd well and faithfully,
Yet knew not what wee lov'd, nor why,
Difference of sex no more wee knew,
Than our Guardian Angells doe;
Comming and going, wee
Perchance might kisse, but not between those meales;
Our hands ne'r toucht the seales,
Which nature, injur'd by late law, sets free:
These miracles wee did; but now alas,
All measure, and all language, I should passe,
Should I tell what a miracle shee was.

X

Death be not proud, though some have called thee
Mighty and dreadfull, for, thou art not soe,
For, those, whom thou think'st, thou dost overthrow,
Die not, poore death, nor yet canst thou kill mee.
From rest and sleepe, which but thy pictures bee,
Much pleasure, then from thee, much more must flow,
And soonest our best men with thee doe goe,
Rest of their bones, and soules deliverie.
Thou art slave to Fate, Chance, kings, and desperate men,
And dost with poyson, warre, and sicknesse dwell,
And poppie, or charmes can make us sleepe as well,
And better than thy stroake; why swell'st thou then?
One short sleepe past, wee wake eternally,
And death shall be no more; death, thou shalt die.

XIV

Batter my heart, three person'd God; for, you
As yet but knocke, breathe, shine, and seeke to mend,

That I may rise, and stand, o'erthrow mee,'and bend
Your force, to breake, blowe, burn and make me new.
I, like an usurpt towne, to'another due,
Labour to'admit you, but Oh, to no end,
Reason your viceroy in mee, mee should defend,
But is captiv'd, and proves weake or untrue.
Yet dearely'I love you,'and would be loved faine,
But am bethroth'd unto your enemie:
Divorce mee,'untie, or breake that knot againe,
Take mee to you, imprison mee, for I
Except you'enthrall mee, never shall be free,
Nor ever chast, except you ravish mee.

A Hymne to God the Father

I

WILT thou forgive that sinne where I begunne,
　　Which is my sin, though it were done before?
Wilt thou forgive those sinnes, through which I runne,
　　And do run still: though still I do deplore?
　　　　When thou hast done, thou hast not done,
　　　　　　For, I have more.

II

Wilt thou forgive that sinne by which I'have wonne
　　Others to sinne? and, made my sinne their doore?
Wilt thou forgive that sinne which I did shunne
　　A yeare, or two: but wallowed in, a score?
　　　　When thou hast done, thou hast not done,
　　　　　　For, I have more.

III

I have a sinne of feare, that when I have spunne
　　My last thred, I shall perish on the shore;
Sweare by thy selfe, that at my death thy sonne
　　Shall shine as he shines now, and heretofore;
　　　　And, having done that, Thou haste done,
　　　　　　I feare no more.

JOHN WEBSTER

FROM THE DUCHESS OF MALFI

Ferdinand. Is she dead?
Bosola.　　　She is what you would have her.
　　　　　　Fix your eye here.
Ferdinand. Constantly.
Bosola.　　　Do you not weep?
　　　　　　Other sins only speak; murder shrieks out.
　　　　　　The element of water moistens the earth,
　　　　　　But blood flies upward and bedews the heavens.
Ferdinand. Cover her face: mine eyes dazzle: she died young.

FROM THE WHITE DEVIL

Funeral Dirge for Marcello

　　　　　　　　　　　　(His Mother sings it)
Call for the Robin-red-breast, and the Wren,
Since o'er shady groves they hover,
And with leaves and flowers do cover
The friendless bodies of unburied men.
Call unto his funeral dole
The Ant, the Field-mouse, and the Mole,
To raise him hillocks that shall keep him warm,
And (when gay tombs are robb'd) sustain no harm;
But keep the wolf far thence, that's foe to men,
For with his nails he'll dig them up again.

GEORGE WITHER

Shall I, Wasting in Despair

SHALL I, wasting in despair,
Die because a woman's fair?
Or make pale my cheeks with care
'Cause another's rosy are?
Be she fairer than the day,
Or the flowery meads in May,
If she be not so to me
What care I how fair she be?

Should my heart be grieved or pined
'Cause I see a woman kind?
Or a well-disposèd nature
Joinèd with a lovely feature?
Be she meeker, kinder than
Turtle-dove, or pelican,
If she be not so to me,
What care I how kind she be?

Shall a woman's virtues move
Me to perish for her love?
Or her well-deserving, known,
Make me quite forget my own?
Be she with that goodness blest
Which may gain her name of best,
If she be not such to me
What care I how good she be?

'Cause her fortune seems too high,
Shall I play the fool, and die?
Those that bear a noble mind,
Where they want of riches find,
Think what with them they would do
That without them dare to woo;

And unless that mind I see,
What care I though great she be?

Great, or good, or kind, or fair,
I will ne'er the more despair:
If she love me, this believe
I will die ere she shall grieve:
If she slight me when I woo,
I can scorn and let her go;
   For if she be not for me,
    What care I for whom she be?

ROBERT HERRICK

A SWEET disorder in the dress
  Kindles in clothes a wantonness:
A lawn about the shoulders thrown
Into a fine distraction;
An erring lace, which here and there
Enthrals the crimson stomacher;
A cuff neglectful, and thereby
Ribbons to flow confusedly;
A winning wave, deserving note,
In the tempestuous petticoat;
A careless shoe-string, in whose tie
I see a wild civility;
Do more bewitch me than when art
Is too precise in every part.

To the Virgins: to Make Much of Time

GATHER ye rosebuds while ye may,
  Old time is still a-flying;
And the same flower that smiles today,
  Tomorrow will be dying.

The glorious lamp of heaven, the sun,
  The higher he's a-getting,
The sooner will his race be run,
  And nearer he's to setting.

That age is best which is the first,
  When youth and blood are warmer;
But being spent, the worse and worst
  Times still succeed the former.

Then be not coy, but use your time,
  And while ye may, go marry;
For having lost but once your prime,
  You may for ever tarry.

Night Piece to Julia

HER eyes the glow-worm lend thee,
  The shooting stars attend thee:
    And the elves also,
    Whose little eyes glow,
Like the sparks of fire, befriend thee.

No Will-o'-the-Wisp mislight thee,
Nor snake or slow-worm bite thee;
    But on, on thy way,
    Not making a stay,
Since ghost there's none to affright thee.

Let not the dark thee cumber;
What though the moon does slumber?
    The stars of the night
    Will lend thee their light,
Like tapers clear, without number.

Then, Julia, let me woo thee,
Thus, thus to come unto me;
    And when I shall meet
    Thy silv'ry feet,
My soul I'll poure into thee.

Upon Julia's Clothes

WHENAS in silks my Julia goes,
    Then, then, methinks, how sweetly flows
That liquefaction of her clothes.

Next, when I cast mine eyes, and see
That brave vibration each way free,
Oh, how that glittering taketh me!

His Winding Sheet

COME thou, who art the wine and wit
    Of all I've writ:
The grace, the glory, and the best
    Piece of the rest.
Thou art of what I did intend
    The all and end;
And what was made, was made to meet
    Thee, thee, my sheet.
Come then and be to my chaste side
    Both bed and bride:
We two, as reliques left, will have
    One rest, one grave:
And hugging close, we will not fear
    Lust entering here:
Where all desires are dead and cold
    As is the mould;
And all affections are forgot,
    Or trouble not.
Here, here, the slaves and prisoners be
    From shackles free:
And weeping widows long oppress'd
    Do here find rest.
The wrongèd client ends his laws
    Here, and his cause.
Here those long suits of Chancery lie
    Quiet, or die:
And all Star-Chamber bills do cease
    Or hold their peace.

Here needs no Court for our Request
    Where all are best,
All wise, all equal, and all just
    Alike i' th' dust.
Nor need we here to fear the frown
    Of court or crown:
Where fortune bears no sway o'er things,
    There all are kings.
In this securer place we'll keep
    As lull'd asleep;
Or for a little time we'll lie
    As robes laid by;
To be another day re-worn,
    Turn'd, but not torn:
Or like old testaments engross'd,
    Lock'd up, not lost.
And for a while lie here conceal'd,
    To be reveal'd
Next at the great Platonick year,
    And then meet here.

---◆---

GEORGE HERBERT

The Quip

THE merry World did on a day
    With his train-bands and mates agree
To meet together, where I lay,
    And all in sport to jeer at me.

First, Beauty crept into a rose,
    Which when I plucked not, "Sir," said she,
"Tell me, I pray, whose hands are those?"—
    But Thou shalt answer, Lord, for me.

Platonick year] the perfect or cyclic year, when the sun, moon, and five
planets end their revolutions together and start anew. See *Timæus*.

Then Money came, and clinking still,
　　"What tune is this, poor man?" said he:
"I heard in Music you had skill."
　　But Thou shalt answer, Lord, for me.

Then came brave Glory puffing by
　　In silks that whistled—who but he?
He scarce allowed me half an eye—
　　But Thou shalt answer, Lord, for me.

Then came quick Wit and Conversation,
　　And he would needs a comfort be,
And, to be short, make an oration—
　　But Thou shalt answer, Lord, for me

Yet when the hour of Thy design
　　To answer these fine things shall come,
Speak not at large, say, I am Thine,
　　And then they have their answer home.

The Pulley

WHEN God at first made Man,
　　Having a glass of blessings standing by—
Let us (said He) pour on him all we can;
Let the world's riches, which dispersèd lie,
　　Contract into a span.

So strength first made a way,
Then beauty flow'd, then wisdom, honour, pleasure:
When almost all was out, God made a stay,
Perceiving that, alone of all His treasure,
　　Rest in the bottom lay.

For if I should (said He)
Bestow this jewel also on My creature,
He would adore My gifts instead of Me,
And rest in Nature, not the God of Nature:
　　So both should losers be.

Yet let him keep the rest,
But keep them with repining restlessness;

Let him be rich and weary, that at least,
If goodness lead him not, yet weariness
        May toss him to My breast.

JAMES SHIRLEY

A Dirge

THE glories of our blood and state,
    Are shadows, not substantial things,
There is no armour against fate,
    Death lays his icy hand on Kings,
        Sceptre and Crown
        Must tumble down,
And in the dust be equal made
With the poor crookèd scythe and spade.

Some men with swords may reap the field,
    And plant fresh laurels where they kill,
But their strong nerves at last must yield,
    They tame but one another still;
        Early or late,
        They stoop to fate,
And must give up their murmuring breath,
When they, pale Captives, creep to death.

The garlands wither on your brow,
    Then boast no more your mighty deeds,
Upon Death's purple Altar now,
    See, where the Victor-victim bleeds.
        Your heads must come
        To the cold Tomb;
Only the actions of the just
Smell sweet, and blossom in their dust.

JOHN MILTON

On the Morning of Christ's Nativity

THIS is the Month, and this the happy morn
　　Wherein the Son of Heav'ns eternal King,
Of wedded Maid, and Virgin Mother born,
Our great redemption from above did bring;
For so the holy sages once did sing,
　　That he our deadly forfeit should release,
And with his Father work us a perpetual peace.

That glorious Form, that Light unsufferable,
And that far-beaming blaze of Majesty,
Wherwith he wont at Heav'ns high Councel-Table,
To sit the midst of Trinal Unity,
He laid aside; and here with us to be,
　　Forsook the Courts of everlasting Day,
And chose with us a darksom House of mortal Clay.

Say Heav'nly Muse, shall not thy sacred vein
Afford a present to the Infant God?
Hast thou no verse, no hymn, or solemn strein,
To welcom him to this his new abode,
Now while the Heav'n by the Suns team untrod,
　　Hath took no print of the approching light,
And all the spangled host keep watch in squadrons bright?

See how from far upon the Eastern rode
The Star-led Wisards haste with odours sweet,
O run, prevent them with thy humble ode,
And lay it lowly at his blessed feet;
Have thou the honour first, thy Lord to greet,
　　And joyn thy voice unto the Angel Quire,
From out his secret Altar toucht with hallow'd fire.

The Hymn

IT was the Winter wilde,
  While the Heav'n-borne-childe,
   All meanly wrapt in the rude manger lies;
Nature in aw to him
Had dofft her gawdy trim,
   With her great Master so to sympathize:
It was no season then for her
To wanton with the Sun her lusty Paramour.

Only with speeches fair
She woo's the gentle Air
   To hide her guilty front with innocent Snow,
And on her naked shame,
Pollute with sinfull blame,
   The Saintly Vail of Maiden white to throw,
Confounded, that her Maker's eyes
Should look so neer upon her foul deformities.

But he her fears to cease,
Sent down the meek-eyd Peace,
   She crown'd with Olive green, came softly sliding
Down through the turning sphear
His ready Harbinger,
   With Turtle wing the amorous clouds dividing,
And waving wide her mirtle wand,
She strikes a universall Peace through Sea and Land.

No War, or Battails sound
Was heard the World around,
   The idle spear and shield were high up hung;
The hooked Chariot stood
Unstain'd with hostile blood,
   The Trumpet spake not to the armed throng,
And Kings sate still with awfull eye,
As if they surely knew their sovran Lord was by.

But peacefull was the night
Wherin the Prince of light
   His raign of peace upon the earth began:

The Windes with wonder whist,
Smoothly the waters kist,
   Whispering new joyes to the milde Ocean,
Who now hath quite forgot to rave,
While Birds of Calm sit brooding on the charmed wave.

The Stars with deep amaze
Stand fixt in stedfast gaze,
   Bending one way their pretious influence,
And will not take their flight,
For all the morning light,
   Or *Lucifer* that often warn'd them thence;
But in their glimmering Orbs did glow,
Untill their Lord himself bespake, and bid them go.

And though the shady gloom
Had given day her room,
   The Sun himself with-held his wonted speed,
And hid his head for shame,
As his inferiour flame,
   The new enlightn'd world no more should need;
He saw a greater Sun appear
Than his bright Throne, or burning Axletree could bear.

The Shepherds on the Lawn,
Or ere the point of dawn,
   Sate simply chatting in a rustick row;
Full little thought they than,
That the mighty *Pan*
   Was kindly come to live with them below;
Perhaps their loves, or els their sheep,
Was all that did their silly thoughts so busie keep.

When such musick sweet
Their hearts and ears did greet,
   As never was by mortall finger strook,
Divinely-warbled voice
Answering the stringed noise,
   As all their souls in blisfull rapture took:
The Air such pleasure loth to lose,
With thousand echo's still prolongs each heav'nly close.

Nature that heard such sound
Beneath the hollow round
  Of *Cynthia's* seat, the Airy region thrilling,
Now was almost won
To think her part was don,
  And that her raign had here its last fulfilling;
She knew such harmony alone
Could hold all Heav'n and Earth in happier union.

At last surrounds their sight
A Globe of circular light,
  That with long beams the shame-fac't night array'd,
The helmed Cherubim
And sworded Seraphim,
  Are seen in glittering ranks with wings displaid,
Harping in loud and solemn quire,
With unexpressive notes to Heav'ns new-born Heir.

Such Musick (as 'tis said)
Before was never made,
  But when of old the sons of morning sung,
While the Creator Great
His constellations set,
  And the well-balanc't world on hinges hung,
And cast the dark foundations deep,
And bid the weltring waves their oozy channel keep.

Ring out ye Crystall sphears,
Once bless our human ears,
  (If ye have power to touch our senses so)
And let your silver chime
Move in melodious time;
  And let the Base of Heav'ns deep Organ blow,
And with your ninefold harmony
Make up full consort to th' Angelike symphony.

For if such holy Song
Enwrap our fancy long,
  Time will run back, and fetch the age of gold,
And speckl'd vanity
Will sicken soon and die,
  And leprous sin will melt from earthly mould,

And Hell it self will pass away,
And leave her dolorous mansions to the peering day.

Yea Truth, and Justice then
Will down return to men,
　　Th' enameld *Arras* of the Rain-bow wearing,
And Mercy set between,[1]
Thron'd in Celestiall sheen,
　　With radiant feet the tissued clouds down stearing,
And Heav'n as at som festivall,
Will open wide the Gates of her high Palace Hall.

But wisest Fate sayes no,
This must not yet be so,
　　The Babe lies yet in smiling Infancy,
That on the bitter cross
Must redeem our loss;
　　So both himself and us to glorifie:
Yet first to those ychain'd in sleep,
The wakefull trump of doom must thunder through the deep,

With such a horrid clang
As on mount *Sinai* rang
　　While the red fire, and smouldring clouds out brake:
The aged Earth agast
With terrour of that blast,
　　Shall from the surface to the center shake;
When at the worlds last session,
The dreadfull Judge in middle Air shall spread his throne.

And then at last our bliss
Full and perfect is,
　　But now begins; for from this happy day
Th' old Dragon under ground
In straiter limits bound,
　　Not half so far casts his usurped sway,
And wrath to see his Kingdom fail,
Swindges the scaly Horrour of his foulded tail.

The Oracles are dumm,
No voice or hideous humm

[1] Orb'd in a Rain-bow; and like glories wearing Mercy will sit between.

Runs through the arched roof in words deceiving.
Apollo from his shrine
Can no more divine,
  With hollow shreik the steep of *Delphos* leaving.
No nightly trance, or breathed spell,
Inspire's the pale-ey'd Priest from the prophetic cell.

The lonely mountains o're,
And the resounding shore,
  A voice of weeping heard, and loud lament;
From haunted spring, and dale
Edg'd with poplar pale,
  The parting Genius is with sighing sent,
With flowre-inwov'n tresses torn
The Nimphs in twilight shade of tangled thickets mourn.

In consecrated Earth,
And on the holy Hearth,
  The *Lars*, and *Lemures* moan with midnight plaint,
In Urns, and Altars round,
A drear, and dying sound
  Affrights the *Flamins* at their service quaint;
And the chill Marble seems to sweat,
While each peculiar power forgoes his wonted seat.

Peor, and *Baalim,*
Forsake their Temples dim,
  With that twice-batter'd god of *Palestine,*
And mooned *Ashtaroth,*
Heav'ns Queen and Mother both,
  Now sits not girt with Tapers holy shine,
The Libyc *Hammon* shrinks his horn,
In vain the *Tyrian* Maids their wounded *Thamuz* mourn.

And sullen *Moloch* fled,
Hath left in shadows dred,
  His burning Idol all of blackest hue,
In vain with Cymbals ring,
They call the grisly king,
  In dismall dance about the furnace blue;
The brutish gods of *Nile* as fast,
Isis and *Orus*, and the Dog *Anubis* hast.

Nor is *Osiris* seen
In *Memphian* Grove, or Green,
   Trampling the unshowr'd Grasse with lowings loud:
Nor can he be at rest
Within his sacred chest,
   Naught but profoundest Hell can be his shroud,
In vain with Timbrel'd Anthems dark
The sable-stoled Sorcerers bear his worshipt Ark.

He feels from *Juda's* Land
The dredded Infants hand,
   The rayes of *Bethlehem* blind his dusky eyn;
Nor all the gods beside,
Longer dare abide,
   Not *Typhon* huge ending in snaky twine:
Our Babe to shew his Godhead true,
Can in his swadling bands controul the damned crew.

So when the Sun in bed,
Curtain'd with cloudy red,
   Pillows his chin upon an Orient wave,
The flocking shadows pale,
Troop to th' infernall jail,
   Each fettr'd Ghost slips to his severall grave,
And the yellow-skirted *Fayes*,
Fly after the Night-steeds, leaving their Moon-lov'd maze.

But see the Virgin blest,
Hath laid her Babe to rest.
   Time is our tedious Song should here have ending,
Heav'ns youngest teemed Star,
Hath fixt her polisht Car,
   Her sleeping Lord with Handmaid Lamp attending:
And all about the Courtly Stable,
Bright-harnest Angels sit in order serviceable.

L'Allegro

HENCE loathed Melancholy
   Of Cerberus, and blackest midnight born,
In Stygian Cave forlorn
   'Mongst horrid shapes, and shreiks, and sights unholy,

Find out som uncouth cell,
  Where brooding darkness spreads his jealous wings,
And the night-Raven sings;
  There under Ebon shades, and low-brow'd Rocks,
As ragged as thy Locks,
  In dark Cimmerian desert ever dwell.
But com thou Goddes fair and free,
In Heav'n ycleap'd Euphrosyne,
And by men, heart-easing Mirth,
Whom lovely Venus at a birth
With two sister Graces more
To Ivy-crowned Bacchus bore;
Or whether (as som Sager sing)
The frolick Wind that breathes the Spring,
Zephir with Aurora playing,
As he met her once a Maying,
There on Beds of Violets blew,
And fresh-blown Roses washt in dew,
Fill'd her with thee a daughter fair,
So bucksom, blith, and debonair.
Haste thee nymph, and bring with thee
Jest and youthful Jollity,
Quips and Cranks, and wanton Wiles,
Nods, and Becks, and Wreathed Smiles,
Such as hang on Hebe's cheek,
And love to live in dimple sleek;
Sport that wrinkled Care derides,
And Laughter holding both his sides.
Com, and trip it as ye go
On the light fantastick toe,
And in thy right hand lead with thee,
The Mountain Nymph, sweet Liberty;
And if I give thee honour due,
Mirth, admit me of thy crue
To live with her, and live with thee,
In unreproved pleasures free;
To hear the Lark begin his flight,
And singing startle the dull night,
From his watch-towre in the skies,
Till the dappled dawn doth rise;
Then to com in spight of sorrow,
And at my window bid good morrow,

Through the Sweet-Briar, or the Vine,
Or the twisted Eglantine.
While the Cock with lively din,
Scatters the rear of darkness thin,
And to the stack, or the Barn dore,
Stoutly struts his Dames before,
Oft list'ning how the Hounds and horn
Chearly rouse the slumbring morn,
From the side of som Hoar Hill,
Through the high wood echoing shrill.
Som time walking not unseen
By Hedge-row Elms, on Hillocks green,
Right against the Eastern gate,
Wher the great Sun begins his state,
Rob'd in flames, and Amber light,
The clouds in thousand Liveries dight.
While the Plowman neer at hand,
Whistles o'er the Furrow'd Land,
And the Milkmaid singeth blithe,
And the Mower whets his sithe,
And every Shepherd tells his tale
Under the Hawthorn in the dale.
Strait mine eye hath caught new pleasures
Whilst the Lantskip round it measures,
Russet Lawns, and Fallows Gray,
Where the nibling flocks do stray,
Mountains on whose barren brest
The labouring clouds do often rest:
Meadows trim with Daisies pide,
Shallow Brooks, and Rivers wide.
Towers, and Battlements it sees
Boosom'd high in tufted Trees,
Where perhaps som beauty lies,
The Cynosure of neighbouring eyes.
Hard by, a Cottage chimney smokes,
From betwixt two aged Okes,
Where Corydon and Thyrsis met,
Are at their savory dinner set
Of Hearbs, and other Country Messes,
Which the neat-handed Phillis dresses;
And then in haste her Bowre she leaves,
With Thestylis to bind the Sheaves;

Or if the earlier season lead
To the tann'd Haycock in the Mead,
Som times with secure delight
The up-land Hamlets will invite,
When the merry Bells ring round,
And the jocond rebecks sound
To many a youth, and many a maid,
Dancing in the Chequer'd shade;
And young and old com forth to play
On a Sunshine Holyday,
Till the live-long day-light fail,
Then to the Spicy Nut-brown Ale,
With stories of many a feat,
How Faery Mab the junkets eat,
She was pincht, and pull'd she sed,
And he by Friars Lanthorn led;
Tells how the drudging Goblin swet,
To earn his Cream-bowle duly set,
When in one night, ere glimps of morn,
His shadowy Flale hath thresh'd the Corn
That ten day-labourers could not end,
Then lies him down the Lubbar Fend.
And stretch'd out all the Chimney's length,
Basks at the fire his hairy strength;
And Crop-full out of dores he flings,
Ere the first Cock his Mattin rings.
Thus don the Tales, to bed they creep,
By whispering Windes soon lull'd asleep.
Towred Cities please us then,
And the busie hum of men,
Where throngs of Knights and Barons bold,
In weeds of Peace high triumphs hold,
With store of Ladies, whose bright eies
Rain influence, and judge the prise
Of Wit, or Arms, while both contend
To win her Grace, whom all commend.
There let Hymen oft appear
In Saffron robe, with Taper clear,
And pomp, and feast, and revelry,
With mask, and antique Pageantry,
Such sights as youthful Poets dream
On Summer eeves by haunted stream.

Then to the well-trod stage anon,
If Jonsons learned Sock be on,
Or sweetest Shakespear fancies childe,
Warble his native Wood-notes wilde.
And ever against eating Cares,
Lap me in soft Lydian Aires,
Married to immortal verse
Such as the meeting soul may pierce
In notes, with many a winding bout
Of linked sweetness long drawn out,
With wanton heed, and giddy cunning,
The melting voice through mazes running;
Untwisting all the chains that ty
The hidden soul of harmony.
That Orpheus self may heave his head
From golden slumber on a bed
Of heapt Elysian flowres, and hear
Such streins as would have won the ear
Of Pluto, to have quite set free
His half regain'd Eurydice.
These delights, if thou canst give,
Mirth with thee, I mean to live.

Lycidas

A LAMENT FOR A FRIEND DROWNED IN HIS PASSAGE FROM CHESTER ON
THE IRISH SEAS, 1637

YET once more, O ye Laurels, and once more
  Ye Myrtles brown, with Ivy never sere,
I come to pluck your Berries harsh and crude,
And with forced fingers rude,
Shatter your leaves before the mellowing year.
Bitter constraint, and sad occasion dear,
Compels me to disturb your season due:
For Lycidas is dead, dead ere his prime,
Young Lycidas, and hath not left his peer:
Who would not sing for Lycidas? he knew
Himself to sing, and build the lofty rhyme.
He must not float upon his watery bier
Unwept, and welter to the parching wind,

Without the meed of some melodious tear.
  Begin, then, Sisters of the sacred well,
That from beneath the seat of Jove doth spring;
Begin, and somewhat loudly sweep the string.
Hence with denial vain, and coy excuse,
So may some gentle Muse
With lucky words favor my destined Urn,
And as he passes turn,
And bid fair peace be to my sable shroud.
For we were nursed upon the self-same hill,
Fed the same flock, by fountain, shade, and rill;
Together both, ere the high Lawns appeared
Under the opening eye-lids of the Morn,
We drove a-field, and both together heard
What time the Grey-fly winds her sultry horn,
Battening our flocks with the fresh dews of night,
Oft till the Star that rose, at Evening, bright
Toward Heaven's descent had sloped his westering wheel,
Meanwhile the Rural ditties were not mute,
Tempered to the Oaten Flute;
Rough Satyrs danced, and Fauns with cloven heel,
From the glad sound would not be absent long,
And old Damætas loved to hear our song.
  But O the heavy change, now thou art gone,
Thee, Shepherd, thee the Woods, and desert Caves,
With wild Thyme and the gadding Vine o'ergrown,
And all their echoes mourn.
The Willows, and the Hazel Copses green,
  Shall now no more be seen,
Fanning their joyous Leaves to thy soft lays.
As killing as the Canker to the Rose,
Or Taint-worm to the weanling Herds that graze,
Or Frost to Flowers, that their gay wardrobe wear,
When first the White-thorn blows;
Such, Lycidas, thy loss to Shepherd's ear.
  Where were ye, Nymphs, when the remorseless deep
Closed o'er the head of your loved Lycidas?
For neither were ye playing on the steep,
Where your old Bards, the famous Druids, lie,
Nor on the shaggy top of Mona high,
Nor yet where Deva spreads her wizard stream:
Ay me, I fondly dream!

Had ye been there—for what could that have done?
What could the Muse herself that Orpheus bore,
The Muse herself, for her enchanting son
Whom Universal nature did lament,
When, by the rout that made the hideous roar,
His gory visage down the stream was sent,
Down the swift Hebrus to the Lesbian shore?
   Alas! What boots it with uncessant care
To tend the homely slighted Shepherd's trade,
And strictly meditate the thankless Muse,
Were it not better done, as others use,
To sport with Amaryllis in the shade,
Or with the tangles of Neæra's hair?
Fame is the spur that the clear spirit doth raise
(That last infirmity of Noble mind)
To scorn delights, and live laborious days;
But the fair Guerdon when we hope to find,
And think to burst out into sudden blaze,
Comes the blind Fury with the abhorrèd shears,
And slits the thin-spun life. "But not the praise,"
Phœbus replied, and touched my trembling ears;
"Fame is no plant that grows on mortal soil,
Nor in the glistering foil
Set off to the world, nor in broad rumor lies,
But lives and spreads aloft by those pure eyes,
And perfect witness of all-judging Jove;
As he pronounces lastly on each deed,
Of so much fame in Heaven expect thy meed."
   O fountain Arethuse, and thou honored flood,
Smooth-sliding Mincius, crowned with vocal reeds,
That strain I heard was of a higher mood:
But now my Oat proceeds,
And listens to the Herald of the Sea
That came in Neptune's plea.
He asked the Waves, and asked the Felon winds,
What hard mishap hath doomed this gentle swain?
And questioned every gust of rugged wings
That blows from off each beakèd Promontory.
They knew not of his story,
And sage Hippotades their answer brings,
That not a blast was from his dungeon strayed,
The Air was calm, and on the level brine,

Sleek Panope with all her sisters played.
It was that fatal and perfidious Bark
Built in the eclipse, and rigged with curses dark,
That sunk so low that sacred head of thine.
   Next Camus, reverend Sire, went footing slow,
His Mantle hairy, and his Bonnet sedge,
Inwrought with figures dim, and on the edge
Like to that sanguine flower inscribed with woe.
"Ah, who hath reft," (quoth he) "my dearest pledge?"
Last come, and last did go,
The Pilot of the Galilean Lake.
Two massy Keys he bore of metals twain,
(The Golden opes, the Iron shuts amain).
He shook his Mitred locks, and stern bespake,
"How well could I have spared for thee, young swain,
Enow of such as, for their bellies' sake,
Creep and intrude, and climb into the fold!
Of other care they little reckoning make,
Than how to scramble at the shearers' feast,
And shove away the worthy bidden guest.
Blind mouths! that scarce themselves know how to hold
A Sheep-hook, or have learned aught else the least
That to the faithful Herdman's art belongs!
What recks it them? What need they? They are sped;
And when they list, their lean and flashy songs
Grate on their scrannel Pipes of wretched straw,
The hungry Sheep look up, and are not fed,
But swoln with wind, and the rank mist they draw,
Rot inwardly, and foul contagion spread:
Besides what the grim Wolf with privy paw
Daily devours apace, and nothing said.
But that two-handed engine at the door,
Stands ready to smite once, and smite no more."
   Return Alpheus, the dread voice is past,
That shrunk thy streams; return Sicilian Muse,
And call the Vales, and bid them hither cast
Their Bells, and Flowerets of a thousand hues.
Ye valleys low, where the mild whispers use,
Of shades and wanton winds, and gushing brooks,
On whose fresh lap the swart Star sparely looks,
Throw hither all your quaint enamelled eyes,
That on the green turf suck the honied showers,

And purple all the ground with vernal flowers.
Bring the rathe Primrose that forsaken dies,
The tufted Crow-toe, and pale Jessamine,
The white Pink, and the Pansy freaked with jet,
The glowing Violet,
The Musk-rose, and the well-attired Woodbine,
With Cowslips wan that hang the pensive head,
And every flower that sad embroidery wears:
Bid Amaranthus all his beauty shed,
And Daffadillies fill their cups with tears,
To strew the Laureate Hearse where Lycid lies.
For so to interpose a little ease,
Let our frail thoughts dally with false surmise.
Ay me! Whilst thee the shores, and sounding Seas
Wash far away, where e'er thy bones are hurled,
Whether beyond the stormy Hebrides,
Where thou perhaps under the whelming tide
Visit'st the bottom of the monstrous world;
Or whether thou, to our moist vows denied,
Sleep'st by the fable of Bellerus old,
Where the great vision of the guarded Mount
Looks toward Namancos and Bayona's hold;
Look homeward, Angel, now, and melt with ruth:
And, O ye Dolphins, waft the hapless youth.
  Weep no more, woful Shepherds, weep no more,
For Lycidas your sorrow is not dead,
Sunk though he be beneath the watery floor.
So sinks the day-star in the Ocean bed,
And yet anon repairs his drooping head,
And tricks his beams, and with new-spangled Ore,
Flames in the forehead of the morning sky:
So Lycidas sunk low, but mounted high,
Through the dear might of Him that walked the waves
Where, other groves and other streams along,
With Nectar pure his oozy Locks he laves,
And hears the unexpressive nuptial Song,
In the blest Kingdoms meek of joy and love.
There entertain him all the Saints above,
In solemn troops, and sweet Societies,
That sing, and singing in their glory move,
And wipe the tears for ever from his eyes.
Now, Lycidas, the Shepherds weep no more;

Henceforth thou art the Genius of the shore,
In thy large recompense, and shalt be good
To all that wander in that perilous flood.
   Thus sang the uncouth Swain to the Oaks and rills,
While the still morn went out with Sandals grey,
He touched the tender stops of various Quills,
With eager thought warbling his Doric lay:
And now the Sun had stretched out all the hills,
And now was dropt into the Western bay;
At last he rose, and twitched his Mantle blue:
Tomorrow to fresh Woods, and Pastures new.

Sonnet XVI

WHEN I consider how my light is spent,
    Ere half my days, in this dark world and wide,
  And that one Talent which is death to hide,
    Lodg'd with me useless, though my Soul more bent
To serve therewith my Maker, and present
  My true account, lest he returning chide,
  Doth God exact day-labour, light deny'd,
  I fondly ask; But patience to prevent
That murmur, soon replies, God doth not need
  Either man's work or his own gifts, who best
  Bear his milde yoak, they serve him best, his State
Is Kingly. Thousands at his bidding speed
  And post o'er Land and Ocean without rest:
  They also serve who only stand and waite.

FROM PARADISE LOST

HIM the Almighty Power
  Hurld headlong flaming from th' ethereal skie
With hideous ruine and combustion down
To bottomless perdition, there to dwell
In adamantine chains and penal fire,
Who durst defie th' Omnipotent to arms.
Nine times the space that measures day and night
To mortal men, he with his horrid crew
Lay vanquisht, rowling in the fiery gulfe,
Confounded though immortal. But his doom

Reserv'd him to more wrath; for now the thought
Both of lost happiness and lasting pain
Torments him; round he throws his baleful eyes
That witness'd huge affliction and dismay,
Mixt with obdurate pride and stedfast hate.
At once as far as Angels kenn he views
The dismal situation waste and wilde,
A dungeon horrible, on all sides round
As one great furnace flam'd; yet from those flames
No light, but rather darkness visible
Serv'd only to discover sights of woe,
Regions of sorrow, doleful shades, where peace
And rest can never dwell, hope never comes
That comes to all; but torture without end
Still urges, and a fiery deluge, fed
With ever-burning sulphur unconsum'd.
Such place Eternal Justice had prepar'd
For those rebellious, here their prison ordain'd.
In utter darkness, and their portion set
As far remov'd from God and light of Heav'n
As from the center thrice to th' utmost pole.
O how unlike the place from whence they fell!
There the companions of his fall, o'rewhelm'd
With Floods and Whirlwinds of tempestuous fire,
He soon discerns, and weltring by his side
One next himself in power, and next in crime,
Long after known in *Palestine,* and nam'd
Bëëlzebub. To whom th' Arch-Enemy,
And thence in Heav'n call'd Satan, with bold words
Breaking the horrid silence thus began.

If thou beest he; But O how fall'n! how chang'd
From him, who in the happy Realms of Light
Cloth'd with transcendent brightness didst outshine
Myriads though bright: If he whom mutual league,
United thoughts and counsels, equal hope,
And hazard in the Glorious Enterprize,
Joynd with me once, now misery hath joynd
In equal ruin: into what Pit thou seest
From what highth fal'n, so much the stronger provd
He with his Thunder: and till then who knew
The force of those dire Arms? yet not for those
Nor what the Potent Victor in his rage

Can else inflict do I repent or change,
Though chang'd in outward lustre; that fixt mind
And high disdain, from sence of injur'd merit,
That with the mightiest rais'd me to contend,
And to the fierce contention brought along
Innumerable force of Spirits arm'd
That durst dislike his reign, and me preferring,
His utmost power with adverse power oppos'd
In dubious Battel on the Plains of Heav'n,
And shook his throne. What though the field be lost?
All is not lost; the unconquerable Will,
And study of revenge, immortal hate,
And courage never to submit or yield:
And what is else not to be overcome?

He scarce had ceas't when the superiour Fiend
Was moving toward the shore; his ponderous shield,
Ethereal temper, massy, large and round,
Behind him cast; the broad circumference
Hung on his shoulders like the moon, whose orb
Through optic glass the Tuscan artist [1] views
At ev'ning from the top of Fesole,
Or in Valdarno, to descry new lands,
Rivers or mountains in her spotty globe.
His spear, to equal which the tallest pine
Hewn on Norwegian hills, to be the mast
Of some great ammiral, were but a wand,[2]
He walkt with, to support uneasie steps
Over the burning marle, not like those steps
On Heavens azure; and the torrid clime
Smote on him sore besides, vaulted with fire.
Nathless he so endur'd, till on the beach
Of that inflaméd sea, he stood and call'd
His legions, Angel forms, who lay intrans't
Thick as autumnal leaves that strow the brooks
In Vallombrosa,[3] where th' Etrurian shades
High overarch't imbowr; or scatterd sedge
Afloat, when with fierce winds Orion arm'd

[1] Galileo, whom Milton had met at Florence, improved the telescope. Fiesole is on a hill overlooking Florence which lies in the valley of the Arno.
[2] Admiral, the flagship of a fleet.
[3] A "shady valley" eighteen miles from Florence. Milton is said to have passed several days at a monastery there.

Hath vext the Red-Sea [4] coast, whose waves orethrew
Busiris [5] and his Memphian [6] chivalrie,
While with perfidious hatred they pursu'd
The sojourners of Goshen, who beheld
From the safe shore their floating carkases
And broken chariot wheels; so thick bestrown
Abject and lost lay these, covering the flood,
Under amazement of their hideous change.
He call'd so loud, that all the hollow Deep
Of Hell resounded. Princes, Potentates,
Warriers, the flowr of Heav'n, once yours, now lost,
If such astonishment as this can sieze
Eternal spirits; or have ye chos'n this place
After the toyl of battel to repose
Your wearied vertue, for the ease you find
To slumber here, as in the vales of Heav'n?
Or in this abject posture have ye sworn
To adore the Conquerour who now beholds
Cherube and Seraph rowling in the flood
With scatter'd arms and ensigns, till anon
His swift pursuers from Heav'n gates discern
Th' advantage, and descending tread us down
Thus drooping, or with linked thunderbolts
Transfix us to the bottom of this gulfe?
Awake, arise, or be for ever fall'n.

FROM SAMSON AGONISTES

O WHEREFORE was my birth from Heaven foretold
    Twice by an Angel, who at last in sight
Of both my Parents all in flames ascended
From off the Altar, where an Off'ring burn'd,
As in a fiery column charioting
His Godlike presence, and from some great act
Or benefit reveal'd to *Abraham's* race?
Why was my breeding order'd and prescrib'd
As of a person separate to God,

[4] The Hebrew name means "Sea of Sedge."
[5] Though Busiris was an earlier ruler than the Pharaoh who was drowned in the Red Sea, Milton identifies him with that oppressor of the Israelites.
[6] Egyptian

Design'd for great exploits; if I must dye
Betray'd, Captiv'd, and both my Eyes put out,
Made of my Enemies the scorn and gaze;
To grind in Brazen Fetters under task
With this Heav'n-gifted strength? O glorious strength
Put to the labour of a Beast, debas't
Lower then bondslave! Promise was that I
Should *Israel* from *Philistian* yoke deliver;
Ask for this great Deliverer now, and find him
Eyeless in *Gaza* at the Mill with slaves,
Himself in bonds under *Philistian* yoke;
Yet stay, let me not rashly call in doubt
Divine Prediction; what if all foretold
Had been fulfilld but through mine own default,
Whom have I to complain of but my self?
Who this high gift of strength committed to me,
In what part lodg'd, how easily bereft me,
Under the Seal of silence could not keep,
But weakly to a woman must reveal it
O'recome with importunity and tears.
O impotence of mind, in body strong!
But what is strength without a double share
Of wisdom, vast, unwieldy, burdensom,
Proudly secure, yet liable to fall
By weakest suttleties, not made to rule,
But to subserve where wisdom bears command.
God, when he gave me strength, to shew withal
How slight the gift was, hung it in my Hair.
But peace, I must not quarrel with the will
Of highest dispensation, which herein
Happ'ly had ends above my reach to know:
Suffices that to me strength is my bane,
And proves the sourse of all my miseries;
So many, and so huge, that each apart
Would ask a life to wail, but chief of all,
O loss of sight, of thee I most complain!
Blind among enemies, O worse than chains,
Dungeon, or beggery, or decrepit age!
Light the prime work of God to me is extinct,
And all her various objects of delight
Annull'd, which might in part my grief have eas'd,
Inferiour to the vilest now become

Of man or worm; the vilest here excel me,
They creep, yet see, I dark in light expos'd
To daily fraud, contempt, abuse and wrong,
Within doors, or without, still as a fool,
In power of others, never in my own;
Scarce half I seem to live, dead more than half.
O dark, dark, dark, amid the blaze of noon,
Irrecoverably dark, total Eclipse
Without all hope of day!

SIR JOHN SUCKLING

Why So Pale and Wan?

WHY so pale and wan, fond lover?
        Prithee, why so pale?
Will, when looking well can't move her,
        Looking ill prevail?
        Prithee, why so pale?

Why so dull and mute, young sinner?
        Prithee, why so mute?
Will, when speaking well can't win her,
        Saying nothing do 't?
        Prithee, why so mute?

Quit, quit for shame! This will not move;
        This cannot take her;
If of herself she will not love,
        Nothing can make her:
        The devil take her!

Out Upon It

OUT upon it, I have lov'd
        Three whole days together;
And am like to love three more,
        If it prove fair weather.

Time shall moult away his wings
  Ere he shall discover
In the whole wide world again
  Such a constant lover.

But the spite on 't is, no praise
  Is due at all to me:
Love with me had made no stays,
  Had it any been but she.

Had it any been but she,
  And that very Face,
There had been at least ere this
  A dozen dozen in her place.

RICHARD CRASHAW

Wishes to His Supposed Mistress

WHOE'ER she be—
    That not impossible She
That shall command my heart and me:

Where'er she lie,
Lock'd up from mortal eye
In shady leaves of destiny:

Till that ripe birth
Of studied Fate stand forth,
And teach her fair steps to our earth:

Till that divine
Idea take a shrine
Of crystal flesh, through which to shine:

Meet you her, my Wishes,
Bespeak her to my blisses,
And be ye call'd my absent kisses.

I wish her Beauty,
That owes not all its duty
To gaudy tire, or glist'ring shoe-tie:

Something more than
Taffata or tissue can,
Or rampant feather, or rich fan.

A Face, that's best
By its own beauty drest,
And can alone commend the rest.

A Face, made up
Out of no other shop
Than what Nature's white hand sets ope.

A Cheek, where youth
And blood, with pen of truth,
Write what the reader sweetly ru'th.

A Cheek, where grows
More than a morning rose,
Which to no box his being owes.

Lips, where all day
A lover's kiss may play,
Yet carry nothing thence away.

Looks, that oppress
Their richest tires, but dress
And clothe their simplest nakedness.

Eyes, that displace
The neighbour diamond, and outface
That sunshine by their own sweet grace.

Tresses, that wear
Jewels but to declare
How much themselves more precious are:

Whose native ray
Can tame the wanton day
Of gems that in their bright shades play.

Each ruby there,
Or pearl that dare appear,
Be its own blush, be its own tear.

A well-tamed Heart,
For whose more noble smart
Love may be long choosing a dart.

Eyes, that bestow
Full quivers on love's bow,
Yet pay less arrows than they owe.

Smiles, that can warm
The blood, yet teach a charm,
That chastity shall take no harm.

Blushes, that bin
The burnish of no sin,
Nor flames of aught too hot within.

Joys, that confess
Virtue their mistress,
And have no other head to dress.

Fears, fond and slight
As the coy bride's, when night
First does the longing lover right.

Days, that need borrow
No part of their good-morrow
From a fore-spent night of sorrow.

Days, that in spite
Of darkness, by the light
Of a clear mind, are day all night.

Nights, sweet as they,
Made short by lovers' play,
Yet long by th' absence of the day.

Life, that dares send
A challenge to his end,
And when it comes, say, "Welcome, friend!"

Sydneian showers
Of sweet discourse, whose powers
Can crown old Winter's head with flowers.

Soft silken hours,
Open suns, shady bowers;
'Bove all, nothing within that lowers.

Whate'er delight
Can make Day's forehead bright,
Or give down to the wings of Night.

I wish her store
Of worth may leave her poor
Of wishes; and I wish—no more.

Now, if Time knows
That Her, whose radiant brows
Weave them a garland of my vows;

Her, whose just bays
My future hopes can raise,
A trophy to her present praise;

Her, that dares be
What these lines wish to see;
I seek no further, it is She.

'Tis She, and here,
Lo! I unclothe and clear
My Wishes' cloudy character.

May she enjoy it
Whose merit dare apply it,
But modesty dares still deny it!

Such worth as this is
Shall fix my flying Wishes,
And determine them to kisses.

Let her full glory,
My fancies, fly before ye;
Be ye my fictions—but her story.

RICHARD LOVELACE

Going to the Warres

(TO LUCASTA)

TELL me not (sweet) I am unkinde,
  That from the Nunnerie
Of thy chaste breast, and quiet minde,
  To Warre and Armes I flie.

True; a new Mistresse now I chase,
  The first Foe in the Field;
And with a stronger Faith imbrace
  A Sword, a Horse, a Shield.

Yet this Inconstancy is such,
  As you too shall adore;
I could not love thee (Deare) so much,
  Lov'd I not Honour more.

To Althea from Prison

WHEN Love with unconfinèd wings
  Hovers within my gates,
And my divine Althea brings
  To whisper at the grates;
When I lie tangled in her hair
  And fetter'd to her eye,
The birds that wanton in the air
  Know no such liberty.

When flowing cups run swiftly round
  With no allaying Thames,
Our careless heads with roses bound,
  Our hearts with loyal flames;

When thirsty grief in wine we steep,
　　When healths and draughts go free—
Fishes that tipple in the deep
　　Know no such liberty.

When, like committed linnets, I
　　With shriller throat shall sing
The sweetness, mercy, majesty,
　　And glories of my King;
When I shall voice aloud how good
　　He is, how great should be,
Enlargèd winds, that curl the flood,
　　Know no such liberty.

Stone walls do not a prison make,
　　Nor iron bars a cage;
Minds innocent and quiet take
　　That for an hermitage;
If I have freedom in my love
　　And in my soul am free,
Angels alone, that soar above,
　　Enjoy such liberty.

ABRAHAM COWLEY

Beauty

BEAUTY, thou wild fantastic ape,
　　Who dost in ev'ry country change thy shape!
Here black, there brown, here tawny, and there white;
Thou flatt'rer which compli'st with every sight!
　　Thou Babel which confound'st the eye
With unintelligible variety!
　　Who hast no certain What, nor Where,
But vari'st still, and dost thy self declare
Inconstant, as thy she-possessors are.

　　Beauty, love's scene and masquerade,
So gay by well-plac'd lights, and distance made!
False coin, with which th' impostor cheats us still;

The stamp and colour good, but metal ill!
  Which light, or base we find, when we
Weigh by enjoyment, and examine thee!
  For though thy being be but show,
'Tis chiefly night which men to thee allow:
And choose t' enjoy thee, when thou least art thou.

  Beauty, thou active, passive ill!
Which diest thy self as fast at thou dost kill!
Thou tulip, who thy stock in paint dost waste,
Neither for physic good, nor smell, nor taste.
  Beauty, whose flames but meteors are,
Short-liv'd and low, though thou wouldst seem a star,
  Who dar'st not thine own home descry,
Pretending to dwell richly in the eye,
When thou, alas, dost in the fancy lie.

ANDREW MARVELL

To His Coy Mistress

HAD we but world enough, and time,
    This coyness, Lady, were no crime.
We would sit down, and think which way
To walk and pass our long love's day.
Thou by the Indian Ganges' side
Shouldst rubies find: I by the tide
Of Humber would complain. I would
Love you ten years before the Flood;
And you should, if you please, refuse
Till the conversion of the Jews.
My vegetable love should grow
Vaster than empires, and more slow:
An hundred years should go to praise
Thine eyes and on thy forehead gaze;
Two hundred to adore each breast,
But thirty thousand to the rest;
An age at least to every part,
And the last age should show your heart.

For, Lady, you deserve this state;
Nor would I love at lower rate.

But at my back I always hear
Time's wingèd charriot hurrying near;
And yonder all before us lie
Desarts of vast eternity.
Thy beauty shall no more be found,
Nor, in thy marble vault, shall sound
My echoing song: then worms shall try
That long preserv'd virginity,
And your quaint honour turn to dust,
And into ashes all my lust.
The grave's a fine and private place,
But none I think do there embrace.

Now therefore, while the youthful hew
Sits on thy skin like morning dew,
And while thy willing soul transpires
At every pore with instant fires,
Now let us sport us while we may,
And now, like amorous birds of prey,
Rather at once our time devour
Than languish in his slow-chapt power.
Let us roll all our strength and all
Our sweetness up into one ball,
And tear our pleasures with rough strife
Thorough the iron gates of life.
Thus, though we cannot make our sun
Stand still, yet we will make him run.

The Definition of Love

MY love is of a birth as rare
As 'tis for object strange and high;
It was begotten by despair
Upon impossibility.

Magnanimous despair alone
Could show me so divine a thing,
Where feeble hope could ne'r have flown
But vainly flapt its tinsel wing.

And yet I quickly might arrive
Where my extended soul is fixt,
But fate does iron wedges drive,
And alwaies crouds it self betwixt.

For fate with jealous eye does see
Two perfect loves, nor lets them close;
Their union would her ruine be,
And her tyrannick pow'r depose.

And therefore her decrees of steel
Us as the distant poles have plac'd,
(Though loves whole world on us doth wheel)
Not by themselves to be embrac'd.

Unless the giddy heaven fall,
And earth some new convulsion tear;
And, us to joyn, the world should all
Be cramp'd into a planisphere.[1]

As lines, so loves, oblique may well
Themselves in every angle greet;
But ours so truly paralel,
Though infinite, can never meet.

Therefore the love which us doth bind,
But fate so enviously debarrs,
Is the conjunction of the mind,
And opposition of the stars.

HENRY VAUGHAN

Peace

MY soul, there is a country
    Far beyond the stars,
Where stands a wingèd sentry
    All skilful in the wars:

---

[1] Projection of a sphere on a plane.

There, above noise and danger,
   Sweet Peace sits crown'd with smiles,
And One born in a manger
   Commands the beauteous files.
He is thy gracious Friend,
   And—O my soul, awake!—
Did in pure love descend
   To die here for thy sake.
If thou canst get but thither,
   There grows the flower of Peace,
The Rose that cannot wither,
   Thy fortress, and thy ease.
Leave then thy foolish ranges;
   For none can thee secure
But One who never changes—
   Thy God, thy life, thy cure.

JOHN DRYDEN

Zimri

SOME of their Chiefs were Princes of the Land:
In the first rank of these did *Zimri* [1] stand:
A man so various, that he seem'd to be
Not one, but all Mankind's Epitome.
Stiff in opinions, always in the wrong;
Was Every thing by starts, and Nothing long:
But, in the course of one revolving Moon,
Was Chymist, Fidler, States-man, and Buffoon;
Then all for Women, Painting, Rhiming, Drinking;
Besides ten thousand Freaks that dy'd in thinking.
Blest Madman, who coud every hour employ,
With something New to wish, or to enjoy!
Railing and praising were his usual Theams;
And both (to shew his judgment) in Extreams:

[1] The Duke of Buckingham, a mercurial statesman and the literary enemy of Dryden.

So over Violent, or over Civil,
That every Man, with him, was God or Devil.
In squandring Wealth was his peculiar Art:
Nothing went unrewarded, but Desert.
Begger'd by fools, whom still he found too late:
He had his Jest, and they had his Estate.
He laugh'd himself from Court; then sought Relief
By forming Parties, but could ne'r be Chief:
For, spight of him, the weight of Business fell
On *Absalom* and wise *Achitophel*:
Thus wicked but in Will, of Means bereft,
He left not Faction, but of that was left.

Shadwell

ALL humane things are subject to decay,
And, when Fate summons, Monarchs must obey:
This *Fleckno* found, who, like *Augustus,* young
Was call'd to Empire and had govern'd long:
In Prose and Verse was own'd, without dispute
Through all the realms of Non-sense, absolute.
This aged Prince now flourishing in Peace,
And blest with issue of a large increase,
Worn out with business, did at length debate
To settle the Succession of the State;
And pond'ring which of all his Sons was fit
To Reign, and wage immortal War with Wit,
Cry'd, 'tis resolv'd; for Nature pleads that He
Should onely rule, who most resembles me:
Sh——alone my perfect image bears,
Mature in dullness from his tender years;
Sh——alone of all my Sons is he
Who stands confirm'd in full stupidity.
The rest to some faint meaning make pretence,
But *Sh*——never deviates into sense.
Some beams of Wit on other souls may fall,
Strike through and make a lucid intervall;
But *Sh*——Genuine Night admits no Ray,
His rising Fogs prevail upon the Day;
Besides, his goodly Fabrick fills the Eye,
And seems design'd for thoughtless Majesty;

Thoughtless as Monarch-Oaks that shade the Plain,
And spread in solemn State, supinely Reign;
Heywood and *Shirly* were but Types of Thee,
Thou last great Prophet of Tautology.
Ev'n I a Dunce of more renown than they,
Was sent before but to prepair thy way;
I coursly Cloath'd in Drugget Russet, came
To teach the Nations in thy greater name.

Alexander's Feast

Or, the Power of Music

AN ODE IN HONOUR OF ST. CECILIA'S DAY:

1697

'TWAS at the royal feast, for Persia won,
     By Philip's warlike son:
   Aloft in awful state
   The god-like heroe sate
     On his imperial throne;
His valiant peers were plac'd around;
Their brows with roses and with myrtles bound.
   (So should desert in arms be crown'd:)
The lovely Thais by his side,
Sate like a blooming Eastern bride
In flow'r of youth and beauty's pride.
     Happy, happy, happy pair!
        None but the brave,
        None but the brave,
   None but the brave deserve the fair.

CHORUS

Happy, happy, happy pair!
   None but the brave,
   None but the brave,
None but the brave deserves the fair.

   Timotheus[1] plac'd on high
      Amid the tuneful quire,

[1] Alexander's favorite musician.

With flying fingers touch'd the lyre:
  The trembling notes ascend the sky,
    And heav'nly joys inspire.
The song began from Jove;
Who left his blissful seats above,
(Such is the pow'r of mighty love.)
A dragon's fiery form bely'd the god:
Sublime on radiant spires he rode,
When he to fair Olympia press'd:
And while he sought her snowy breast:
Then, round her slender waist he curl'd,
And stamp'd an image of himself, a sov'raign of the world.
The list'ning crowd admire the lofty sound,
A present deity, they shout around:
A present deity, the vaulted roofs rebound.

        With ravish'd ears
        The monarch hears,
        Assumes the god,
        Affects to nod,
    And seems to shake the spheres.

                    CHORUS

        With ravish'd ears
        The monarch hears,
        Assumes the god,
        Affects to nod,
    And seems to shake the spheres.

The praise of Bacchus then the sweet musician sung,
  Of Bacchus ever fair, and ever young:
    The jolly god in triumph comes;
    Sound the trumpets; beat the drums;
      Flush'd with a purple grace
      He shows his honest face:
Now give the hautboys breath; he comes, He comes.
    Bacchus ever fair and young
        Drinking joys did first ordain;
    Bacchus blessings are a treasure;
    Drinking is the soldiers pleasure;

Rich the treasure;
Sweet the pleasure;
Sweet is pleasure after pain.

CHORUS

Bacchus blessings are a treasure,
Drinking is the soldiers pleasure;
Rich the treasure,
Sweet the pleasure,
Sweet is pleasure after pain.

ooth'd with the sound the king grew vain;
Fought all his battails o'er again;
And thrice he routed all his foes, and thrice he slew the slain.
The master saw the madness rise,
His glowing cheeks, his ardent eyes;
And while he heav'n and earth defy'd,
Chang'd his hand, and check'd his pride.
He chose a mournful muse,
Soft pity to infuse;
He sung Darius great and good,
By too severe a fate,
Fallen, fallen, fallen, fallen,
Fallen from his high estate,
And weltring in his blood:

Deserted at his utmost need
By those his former bounty fed;
On the bare earth expos'd he lies,
With not a friend to close his eyes.
With down-cast looks the joyless victor sate,
Revolving in his alter'd soul
The various turns of chance below;
And, now and then, a sigh he stole,
And tears began to flow.

CHORUS

Revolving in his alter'd soul
The various turns of chance below;
And, now and then, a sigh he stole,
And tears began to flow.

The mighty master smil'd to see
That love was in the next degree;
'Twas but a kindred-sound to move,
For pity melts the mind to love.
  Softly sweet, in Lydian measures,
  Soon he sooth'd his soul to pleasures.
War, he sung, is toil and trouble;
Honour but an empty bubble.
  Never ending, still beginning,
Fighting still, and still destroying,
  If the world be worth thy winning,
  Think, O think, it worth enjoying.
  Lovely Thais sits beside thee,
  Take the good the gods provide thee.
The many rend the skies, with loud applause;
So love was crown'd, but musique won the cause.
  The prince, unable to conceal his pain,
      Gaz'd on the fair
      Who caus'd his care,
  And sigh'd and look'd, sigh'd and look'd,
  Sigh'd and look'd, and sigh'd again:
At length, with love and wine at once oppress'd,
The vanquish'd victor sunk upon her breast.

CHORUS

The prince, unable to conceal his pain,
    Gaz'd on the fair
    Who caus'd his care,
  And sigh'd and look'd, sigh'd and look'd,
  Sigh'd and look'd, and sigh'd again;
At length, with love and wine at once oppress'd,
The vanquish'd victor sunk upon her breast.

Now strike the golden lyre again;
A lowder yet, and yet a lowder strain.
Break his bands of sleep asunder,
And rouze him, like a rattling peal of thunder.
  Hark, hark, the horrid sound
    Has rais'd up his head;
    As awak'd from the dead,
  And amaz'd he stares around.
  Revenge, revenge, Timotheus cries,

See the Furies arise!
See the snakes that they rear,
How they hiss in their hair,
And the sparkles that flash from their eyes!
Behold a ghastly band,
Each a torch in his hand!
Those are Grecian ghosts, that in battail were slain,
          And unbury'd remain
          Inglorious on the plain:
          Give the vengeance due
          To the valiant crew.
Behold how they toss their torches on high,
          How they point to the Persian abodes,
And glitt'ring temples of their hostile gods.
The princes applaud with a furious joy;
And the king seized a flambeau with zeal to destroy;
          Thais led the way,
          To light him to his prey,
And, like another Hellen, fir'd another Troy.

CHORUS

And the king seiz'd a flambeau with zeal to destroy;
          Thais led the way,
          To light him to his prey,
And, like another Hellen, fir'd another Troy.

          Thus long ago,
      'Ere heaving bellows learn'd to blow,
          While organs yet were mute,
          Timotheus, to his breathing flute
          And sounding lyre,
Cou'd swell the soul to rage, or kindle soft desire.
      At last divine Cecelia came,
      Inventress of the vocal frame;
The sweet enthusiast, from her sacred store,
      Enlarg'd the former narrow bounds,
      And added length to solemn sounds,
With Nature's mother-wit, and arts unknown before.
      Let old Timotheus yield the prize,
          Or both divide the crown:
      He rais'd a mortal to the skies;
          She drew an angel down.

GRAND CHORUS

At last divine Cecilia came,
Inventress of the vocal frame;
The sweet enthusiast, from her sacred store,
Enlarg'd the former narrow bounds,
And added length to solemn sounds,
With Nature's mother-wit, and arts unknown before.
Let old Timotheus yield the prize,
Or both divide the crown:
He rais'd a mortal to the skies;
She drew an angel down.

MATTHEW PRIOR

Song

THE merchant, to secure his treasure,
Conveys it in a borrowed name:
Euphelia serves to grace my measure,
But Chloe is my real flame.

My softest verse, my darling lyre,
Upon Euphelia's toilet lay—
When Chloe noted her desire
That I should sing, that I should play.

My lyre I tune, my voice I raise,
But with my numbers mix my sighs;
And whilst I sing Euphelia's praise,
I fix my soul on Chloe's eyes.

Fair Chloe blushed: Euphelia frowned:
I sung, and gazed; I played, and trembled:
And Venus to the Loves around
Remarked how ill we all dissembled.

ALEXANDER POPE

FROM ESSAY ON MAN

KNOW then thy-self, presume not God to scan,
 The proper study of Mankind is Man.
Plac'd on this isthmus of a middle state,
A Being darkly wise, and rudely great:
With too much knowledge for the Sceptic side,
With too much weakness for the Stoic's pride,
He hangs between; in doubt to act, or rest;
In doubt to deem himself a God, or Beast;
In doubt his Mind or Body to prefer;
Born but to die, and reas'ning but to err;
Alike in ignorance, his reason such,
Whether he thinks too little, or too much:
Chaos of Thought and Passion, all confus'd;
Still by himself abus'd, or disabus'd;
Created half to rise, and half to fall;
Great lord of all things, yet a prey to all;
Sole judge of truth, in endless error hurl'd:
The glory, jest, and riddle of the world!

Self-love, the spring of motion, acts the soul;
Reason's comparing balance rules the whole.
Man, but for that, no action could attend,
And, but for this, were active to no end:
Fix'd like a plant on his peculiar spot,
To draw nutrition, propagate, and rot;
Or, meteor-like, flame lawless through the void,
Destroying others, by himself destroy'd.
Most strength the moving principle requires;
Active its task, it prompts, impels, inspires.
Sedate and quiet the comparing lies,
Form'd but to check, delib'rate, and advise.
Self-love still stronger, as its objects nigh;
Reason's at distance, and in prospect lie:
That sees immediate good by present sense;
Reason, the future and the consequence.

Thicker than arguments, temptations throng,
At best more watchful this, but that more strong.
The action of the stronger to suspend
Reason still use, to reason still attend.
Attention, habit and experience gains;
Each strengthens reason, and self-love restrains.

Vice is a monster of so frightful mien,
As, to be hated, needs but to be seen;
Yet seen too oft, familiar with her face,
We first endure, then pity, then embrace.
But where th' extreme of vice, was ne'er agreed:
Ask where's the north? at York, 'tis on the Tweed;
In Scotland, at the Orcades; and there,
At Greenland, Zembla, or the Lord knows where.
No creature owns it in the first degree,
But thinks his neighbour farther gone than he;
Ev'n those who dwell beneath its very zone,
Or never feel the rage, or never own;
What happier natures shrink at with affright,
The hard inhabitant contends is right.

Honour and shame from no condition rise;
Act well your part, there all the honour lies.
Fortune in men has some small diff'rence made,
One flaunts in rags, one flutters in brocade;
The cobbler apron'd, and the parson gown'd,
The friar hooded, and the monarch crown'd.
"What differ more," you cry, "than crown and cowl?"
I'll tell you, friend! a wise man and a fool.
You'll find, if once the monarch acts the monk,
Or, cobbler-like, the parson will be drunk,
Worth makes the man, and want of it, the fellow;
The rest is all but leather or prunella.
Stuck o'er with titles and hung round with strings,
That thou mayst be by kings, or whores of kings,
Boast the pure blood of an illustrious race,
In quiet flow from Lucrece to Lucrece:
But by your father's worth if yours you rate,
Count me those only who were good and great.
Go! if your ancient, but ignoble blood
Has crept through scoundrels ever since the flood,

Go! and pretend your family is young;
Nor own, your fathers have been fools so long.
What can ennoble sots, or slaves, or cowards?
Alas! not all the blood of all the Howards.
  Look next on greatness; say where greatness lies?
"Where, but among the heroes and the wise?"
Heroes are much the same, the point's agreed,
From Macedonia's madman to the Swede;
The whole strange purpose of their lives to find,
Or make, an enemy of all mankind!
Not one looks backward, onward still he goes,
Yet ne'er looks forward farther than his nose.
No less alike the politic and wise;
All sly slow things, with circumspective eyes:
Men in their loose unguarded hours they take,
Not that themselves are wise, but others weak.
But grant that those can conquer, these can cheat;
'Tis phrase absurd to call a villain great:
Who wickedly is wise, or madly brave,
Is but the more a fool, the more a knave.
Who noble ends by noble means obtains,
Or failing, smiles in exile or in chains,
Like good Aurelius let him reign, or bleed
Like Socrates, that man is great indeed.
  What's fame? a fancied life in others' breath,
A thing beyond us, ev'n before our death.
Just what you hear, you have, and what's unknown
The same (my Lord) if Tully's, or your own.
All that we feel of it begins and ends
In the small circle of our foes or friends;
To all beside as much an empty shade
An Eugene living, as a Cæsar dead;
Alike or when, or where, they shone, or shine,
Or on the Rubicon, or on the Rhine.
A wit's a feather, and a chief a rod;
An honest man's the noblest work of God.

FROM AN ESSAY ON CRITICISM

BUT most by numbers judge a poet's song;
  And smooth or rough, with them, is right or wrong:
In the bright Muse though thousand charms conspire,

Her voice is all these tuneful fools admire;
Who haunt Parnassus but to please their ear,
Not mend their minds; as some to church repair,
Not for the doctrine, but the music there.
These equal syllables alone require,
Though oft the ear the open vowels tire;
While expletives their feeble aid do join;
And ten low words oft creep in one dull line:
While they ring round the same unvaried chimes,
With sure returns of still expected rhymes;
Where'er you find "the cooling western breeze,"
In the next line, it "whispers through the trees":
If crystal streams "with pleasing murmurs creep,"
The reader's threaten'd (not in vain) with "sleep":
Then, at the last and only couplet fraught
With some unmeaning thing they call a thought,
A needless Alexandrine ends the song,
That, like a wounded snake, drags its slow length along.
Leave such to tune their own dull rhymes, and know
What's roundly smooth, or languishingly slow;
And praise the easy vigour of a line,
Where Denham's strength, and Waller's sweetness join.
True ease in writing comes from art, not chance,
As those move easiest who have learn'd to dance.
'Tis not enough no harshness gives offense,
The sound must seem an echo to the sense:
Soft is the strain when Zephyr gently blows,
And the smooth stream in smoother numbers flows;
But when loud surges lash the sounding shore,
The hoarse, rough verse should like the torrent roar:
When Ajax strives some rock's vast weight to throw,
The line too labours, and the words move slow;
Not so, when swift Camilla[1] scours the plain,
Flies o'er th' unbending corn, and skims along the main.
Hear how Timotheus' varied lays surprise,
And bid alternate passions fall and rise!
While, at each change, the son of Libyan Jove
Now burns with glory, and then melts with love;
Now his fierce eyes with sparkling fury glow,
Now sighs steal out, and tears begin to flow:
Persians and Greeks like turns of nature found,

[1] See Ben Jonson's *Every Man out of his Humour*. [Pope.]

And the world's victor stood subdu'd by sound!
The pow'r of music all our hearts allow,
And what Timotheus was, is Dryden now.

THOMAS GRAY

Elegy Written in a Country Churchyard

THE curfew tolls the knell of parting day,
    The lowing herd wind slowly o'er the lea,
The ploughman homeward plods his weary way,
    And leaves the world to darkness and to me.

Now fades the glimm'ring landscape on the sight,
    And all the air a solemn stillness holds,
Save where the beetle wheels his droning flight,
    And drowsy tinklings lull the distant folds;

Save that from yonder ivy-mantled tow'r
    The moping owl does to the moon complain
Of such, as wand'ring near her secret bow'r,
    Molest her ancient solitary reign.

Beneath those rugged elms, that yew-tree's shade,
    Where heaves the turf in many a mold'ring heap,
Each in his narrow cell forever laid,
    The rude forefathers of the hamlet sleep.

The breezy call of incense-breathing Morn,
    The swallow twitt'ring from the straw-built shed,
The cock's shrill clarion, or the echoing horn,
    No more shall rouse them from their lowly bed.

For them no more the blazing hearth shall burn,
    Or busy housewife ply her evening care:
No children run to lisp their sire's return,
    Or climb his knees the envied kiss to share.

Oft did the harvest to their sickle yield,
　Their furrow oft the stubborn glebe has broke;
How jocund did they drive their team afield!
　How bow'd the woods beneath their sturdy stroke!

Let not Ambition mock their useful toil,
　Their homely joys, and destiny obscure;
Nor Grandeur hear with a disdainful smile,
　The short and simple annals of the poor.

The boast of heraldry, the pomp of pow'r,
　And all that beauty, all that wealth e'er gave,
Awaits alike th' inevitable hour.
　The paths of glory lead but to the grave.

Nor you, ye proud, impute to these the fault,
　If Mem'ry o'er their tomb no trophies raise,
Where through the long-drawn aisle and fretted vault
　The pealing anthem swells the note of praise.

Can storied urn or animated bust
　Back to its mansion call the fleeting breath?
Can Honour's voice provoke the silent dust,
　Or Flatt'ry soothe the dull cold ear of Death?

Perhaps in this neglected spot is laid
　Some heart once pregnant with celestial fire;
Hands that the rod of empire might have sway'd,
　Or wak'd to ecstasy the living lyre.

But Knowledge to their eyes her ample page
　Rich with the spoils of time did ne'er unroll;
Chill Penury repress'd their noble rage,
　And froze the genial current of the soul.

Full many a gem of purest ray serene,
　The dark unfathom'd caves of ocean bear:
Full many a flow'r is born to blush unseen,
　And waste its sweetness on the desert air.

Some village-Hampden,[1] that with dauntless breast
 The little tyrant of his fields withstood;
Some mute inglorious Milton here may rest,
 Some Cromwell guiltless of his country's blood.

Th' applause of list'ning senates to command,
 The threats of pain and ruin to despise,
To scatter plenty o'er a smiling land,
 And read their hist'ry in a nation's eyes,

Their lot forbade: nor circumscrib'd alone
 Their growing virtues, but their crimes confin'd;
Forbade to wade through slaughter to a throne,
 And shut the gates of mercy on mankind,

The struggling pangs of conscious truth to hide,
 To quench the blushes of ingenuous shame,
Or heap the shrine of Luxury and Pride
 With incense kindled at the Muse's flame.

Far from the madding crowd's ignoble strife,
 Their sober wishes never learn'd to stray;
Along the cool sequester'd vale of life
 They kept the noiseless tenour of their way.

Yet ev'n these bones from insult to protect
 Some frail memorial still erected nigh,
With uncouth rhymes and shapeless sculpture deck'd,
 Implores the passing tribute of a sigh.

Their names, their years, spelt by th' unletter'd Muse,
 The place of fame and elegy supply:
And many a holy text around she strews,
 That teach the rustic moralist to die.

For who to dumb forgetfulness a prey,
 This pleasing anxious being e'er resign'd,
Left the warm precincts of the cheerful day,
 Nor cast one longing ling'ring look behind?

[1] John Hampden, who opposed Charles I's attempt to collect ship-money.

On some fond breast the parting soul relies,
  Some pious drops the closing eye requires;
Ev'n from the tomb the voice of Nature cries,
  Ev'n in our ashes live their wonted fires.

For thee, who mindful of th' unhonour'd dead
  Dost in these lines their artless tale relate;
If chance, by lonely contemplation led,
  Some kindred spirit shall inquire thy fate,

Haply some hoary-headed swain may say,
  "Oft have we seen him at the peep of dawn
Brushing with hasty steps the dews away
  To meet the sun upon the upland lawn.

"There, at the foot of yonder nodding beech
  That wreathes its old fantastic roots so high,
His listless length at noontide would he stretch,
  And pore upon the brook that babbles by.

"Hard by yon wood, now smiling as in scorn,
  Mutt'ring his wayward fancies he would rove,
Now drooping, woeful wan, like one forlorn,
  Or craz'd with care, or cross'd in hopeless love.

"One morn I miss'd him on the 'custom'd hill,
  Along the heath and near his fav'rite tree;
Another came; nor yet beside the rill,
  Nor up the lawn, nor at the wood was he;

"The next with dirges due in sad array
  Slow through the church-way path we saw him borne.
Approach and read (for thou canst read) the lay,
  Grav'd on the stone beneath yon aged thorn."

THE EPITAPH

Here rests his head upon the lap of Earth
  A youth to Fortune and to Fame unknown:
Fair Science frown'd not on his humble birth,
  And Melancholy mark'd him for her own.

Large was his bounty, and his soul sincere,
    Heav'n did a recompense as largely send:
He gave to Mis'ry all he had, a tear:
    He gain'd from Heav'n ('twas all he wish'd) a friend.

No farther seek his merits to disclose,
    Or draw his frailties from their dread abode,
(There they alike in trembling hope repose)
    The bosom of his Father and his God.

WILLIAM COLLINS

Ode to Evening

IF aught of oaten stop, or pastoral song,
    May hope, chaste Eve, to soothe thy modest ear,
        Like thy own solemn springs,
        Thy springs, and dying gales,

O nymph reserv'd, while now the bright-hair'd sun
Sits in yon western tent, whose cloudy skirts,
        With brede[1] ethereal wove,
        O'er hang his wavy bed:

Now air is hush'd, save where the weak-ey'd bat,
With short shrill shriek flits by on leathern wing,
        Or where the beetle winds
        His small but sullen horn,

As oft he rises 'midst the twilight path,
Against the Pilgrim borne in heedless hum:
        Now teach me, maid compos'd,
        To breathe some soften'd strain,

Whose numbers, stealing thro' my darkning vale,
May not unseemly with its stillness suit,
        As, musing slow, I hail
        Thy genial lov'd return!

[1] embroidery (braid).

For when thy folding-star arising shews
His play circlet, at his warning lamp
 The fragrant Hours, and elves
 Who slept in flowers the day,

And many a nymph who wreaths her brows with sedge,
And sheds the fresh'ning dew, and lovelier still,
 The pensive Pleasures sweet
 Prepare thy shadowy car.

Then lead, calm vot'ress, where some sheety lake
Cheers the lone heath, or some time-hallow'd pile,
 Or upland fallows grey
 Reflect its last cool gleam.

But when chill blust'ring winds, or driving rain,
Forbid my willing feet, be mine the hut
 That from the mountain's side,
 Views wilds, and swelling floods,

And hamlets brown, and dim-discover'd spires,
And hears their simple bell, and marks o'er all
 Thy dewy fingers draw
 The gradual dusky veil.

While Spring shall pour his show'rs, as oft he wont,
And bathe thy breathing tresses, meekest Eve!
 While Summer loves to sport,
 Beneath thy ling'ring light;

While sallow Autumn fills thy lap with leaves,
Or Winter yelling thro' the troublous air,
 Affrights thy shrinking train,
 And rudely rends thy robes;

So long, sure-found beneath the sylvan shed,
Shall Fancy, Friendship, Science, rose-lip'd Health
 Thy gentlest influence own,
 And hymn thy fav'rite name!

CHRISTOPHER SMART

FROM A SONG TO DAVID

FOR adoration, David's psalms
　　Lift up the heart to deeds of alms;
　　　And he, who kneels and chants,
Prevails his passions to control,
Finds meat and med'cine to the soul,
　　　Which for translation pants.

For adoration, beyond match,
The scholar bullfinch aims to catch
　　　The soft flute's iv'ry touch;
And, careless on the hazel spray,
The daring redbreast keeps at bay
　　　The damsel's greedy clutch.

For adoration, in the skies,
The Lord's philosopher espies
　　　The dog, the ram, and rose;
The planet's ring, Orion's sword;
Nor is his greatness less ador'd
　　　In the vile worm that glows.

For adoration, on the strings
The western breezes work their wings,[1]
　　　The captive ear to soothe.—
Hark! 'tis a voice—how still, and small—
That makes the cataracts to fall,
　　　Or bids the sea be smooth.

For adoration, incense comes
From bezoar,[2] and Arabian gums;

[1] Æolian harp. [Smart.]
[2] Bezoar is literally a counter-poison or antidote; then the name was given to various substances formerly held as antidotes, as a concretion found in the stomach or intestines of some animal; then to alleged stones or concretions of various kinds, usually in ignorance of its original meaning, as here. [*N.E.D.*]

And on the civet's[3] fur.
But as for pray'r, or ere it faints,
Far better is the breath of saints
    Than galbanum and myrrh.

For adoration, from the down
Of dam'sins[4] to th' anana's[5] crown,
    God sends to tempt the taste;
And while the luscious zest invites,
The sense, that in the scene delights,
    Commands desire be chaste.

For adoration, all the paths
Of grace are open, all the baths
    Of purity refresh;
And all the rays of glory beam
To deck the man of God's esteem,
    Who triumphs o'er the flesh.

For adoration, in the dome
Of Christ the sparrows find an home;
    And on his olives perch:
The swallow also dwells with thee,
O man of God's humility,
    Within his Saviour Church.

Sweet is the dew that falls betimes,
And drops upon the leafy limes;
    Sweet Hermon's fragrant air:[6]
Sweet is the lily's silver bell,
And sweet the wakeful tapers smell
    That watch for early pray'r.

Sweet the young nurse with love intense,
Which smiles o'er sleeping innocence;
    Sweet when the lost arrive:
Sweet the musician's ardour beats,

[3] An animal ranking in size and appearance between the fox and the weasel, which yields a secretion, called by the same name, used in perfumery. [*N.E.D.*]
[4] Damsons.
[5] The pineapple.
[6] A mountain in Judea. See Psalms, CXXXIII, 3: "As the dew of Hermon, and as the dew that descended upon the mountains of Zion."

While his vague mind's in quest of sweets,
The choicest flow'rs to hive.

Sweeter in all the strains of love
The language of thy turtle dove
  Pair'd to thy swelling chord;
Sweeter with ev'ry grace endu'd
The glory of thy gratitude,
  Respir'd unto the Lord.

Strong is the horse upon his speed;
Strong in pursuit the rapid glede,[7]
  Which makes at once his game:
Strong the tall ostrich on the ground;
Strong through the turbulent profound
  Shoots xiphias[8] to his aim.

Strong is the lion—like a coal
His eyeball—like a bastion's mole
  His chest against the foes:
Strong, the gier-eagle on his sail,
Strong against tide, th' enormous whale
  Emerges as he goes.

But stronger still, in earth and air,
And in the sea, the man of pray'r,
  And far beneath the tide;
And in the seat to faith assign'd,
Where ask is have, where seek is find
  Where knock is open wide.

Beauteous the fleet before the gale;
Beauteous the multitudes in mail,
  Rank'd arms and crested heads:
Beauteous the garden's umbrage mild,
Walk, water, meditated wild,
  And all the bloomy beds.

[7] The kite.
[8] The sword-fish. [Smart.]

Beauteous the moon full on the lawn;
And beauteous, when the veil's withdrawn,
　　The virgin to her spouse:
Beauteous the temple deck'd and fill'd,
When to the heav'n of heav'ns they build
　　Their heart-directed vows.

Beauteous, yea beauteous more than these,
The shepherd king upon his knees,
　　For his momentous trust;
With wish of infinite conceit,
For man, beast, mute, the small and great,
　　And prostrate dust to dust.

Precious the bounteous widow's mite;
And precious, for extreme delight,
　　The largess from the churl:[9]
Precious the ruby's blushing blaze,
And alba's blest imperial rays,
　　And pure cerulean pearl.

Precious the penitential tear;
And precious is the sigh sincere,
　　Acceptable to God:
And precious are the winning flow'rs,
In gladsome Israel's feast of bow'rs,
　　Bound on the hallow'd sod.

More precious that diviner part
Of David, ev'n the Lord's own heart,
　　Great, beautiful, and new:
In all things where it was intent,
In all extremes, in each event,
　　Proof—answ'ring true to true.

Glorious the sun in mid career;
Glorious th' assembled fires appear;
　　Glorious the comet's train;
Glorious the trumpet and alarm;
Glorious th' almighty stretch'd-out arm;
　　Glorious th' enraptur'd main:

[9] [I] Samuel XXV, 18. [Smart.]

Glorious the northern lights a-stream;
Glorious the song, when God's the theme:
   Glorious the thunder's roar;
Glorious hosannah from the den;
Glorious the catholic amen;
   Glorious the martyr's gore:

Glorious—more glorious, is the crown
Of Him that brought salvation down
   By meekness, call'd thy Son;
Thou that stupendous truth believ'd,
And now the matchless deed's achiev'd,
   Determin'd, dar'd, and done.

OLIVER GOLDSMITH

FROM THE DESERTED VILLAGE

SWEET smiling village, loveliest of the lawn,
  Thy sports are fled, and all thy charms withdrawn;
Amidst thy bowers the tyrant's hand is seen,
And desolation saddens all thy green:
One only master[1] grasps the whole domain,
And half a tillage stints thy smiling plain:
No more thy glassy brook reflects the day,
But chok'd with sedges, works its weedy way.
Along thy glades, a solitary guest,
The hollow-sounding bittern guards its nest;
Amidst thy desert walks the lapwing flies,
And tires their echoes with unvaried cries.
Sunk are thy bowers in shapeless ruin all,
And the long grass o'ertops the mould'ring wall;
And trembling, shrinking from the spoiler's hand,
Far, far away, thy children leave the land.

  Ill fares the land, to hast'ning ills a prey,
Where wealth accumulates, and men decay:

---

[1] By the repeated Enclose Acts landlords could enclose common land in order to improve their holdings. Naturally there were many harsh expulsions.

Princes and lords may flourish, or may fade;
A breath can make them, as a breath has made;
But a bold peasantry, their country's pride,
When once destroy'd, can never be supplied.

Beside yon straggling fence that skirts the way,
With blossom'd furze unprofitably gay,
There, in his noisy mansion, skill'd to rule,
The village master taught his little school;
A man severe he was, and stern to view;
I knew him well, and every truant knew;
Well had the boding tremblers learn'd to trace
The day's disasters in his morning face;
Full well they laugh'd, with counterfeited glee,
At all his jokes, for many a joke had he;
Full well the busy whisper, circling round,
Convey'd the dismal tidings when he frown'd;
Yet he was kind; or if severe in aught,
The love he bore to learning was in fault;
The village all declar'd how much he knew;
'Twas certain he could write, and cypher too;
Lands he could measure, terms and tides presage,
And e'en the story ran that he could gauge.
In arguing too, the parson own'd his skill,
For e'en though vanquish'd, he could argue still;
While words of learned length and thund'ring sound
Amazed the gazing rustics rang'd around,
And still they gaz'd, and still the wonder grew,
That one small head could carry all he knew.

But past is all his fame. The very spot
Where many a time he triumph'd, is forgot.
Near yonder thorn, that lifts its head on high,
Where once the sign-post caught the passing eye,
Low lies that house where nut-brown draughts inspir'd,
Where grey-beard mirth and smiling toil retir'd,
Where village statesmen talk'd with looks profound,
And news much older than their ale went round.
Imagination fondly stoops to trace
The parlour splendours of that festive place;
The white-wash'd wall, the nicely sanded floor,
The varnish'd clock that click'd behind the door;

The chest contriv'd a double debt to pay,
A bed by night, a chest of drawers by day;
The pictures plac'd for ornament and use,
The twelve good rules,[2] the royal game of goose;[3]
The hearth, except when winter chill'd the day,
With aspen boughs, and flow'rs, and fennel gay;
While broken tea-cups, wisely kept for show,
Rang'd o'er the chimney, glisten'd in a row.

WILLIAM COWPER

FROM THE TASK

GOD made the country, and man made the town.
What wonder then that health and virtue, gifts
That can alone make sweet the bitter draught
That life holds out to all, should most abound
And least be threaten'd in the fields and groves?
Possess ye, therefore, ye, who, borne about
In chariots and sedans, know no fatigue
But that of idleness, and taste no scenes
But such as art contrives, possess ye still
Your element; there only can ye shine,
There only minds like your's can do no harm.
Our groves were planted to console at noon
The pensive wand'rer in their shades. At eve
The moon-beam, sliding softly in between
The sleeping leaves, is all the light they wish,
Birds warbling all the music. We can spare
The splendour of your lamps; they but eclipse
Our softer satellite. Your songs confound
Our more harmonious notes: the thrush departs
Scar'd, and th' offended nightingale is mute.
There is a public mischief in your mirth;

---

[2] King Charles I's "Twelve Good Rules," the wall-motto of many a house, were supposedly found in his study after his death.
[3] A game played with dice.

It plagues your country. Folly such as your's,
Grac'd with a sword, and worthier of a fan,
Has made, what enemies could ne'er have done,
Our arch of empire, stedfast but for you,
A mutilated structure, soon to fall.

On the Loss of the Royal George [1]

WRITTEN WHEN THE NEWS ARRIVED TO THE MARCH IN *Scipio*

TOLL for the brave!
    The brave that are no more!
All sunk beneath the wave,
    Fast by their native shore!

Eight hundred of the brave,
    Whose courage well was tried,
Had made the vessel heel,
    And laid her on her side.

A land-breeze shook the shrouds,
    And she was overset;
Down went the Royal George,
    With all her crew complete.

Toll for the brave!
    Brave Kempenfelt is gone;
His last sea-fight is fought;
    His work of glory done.

It was not in the battle;
    No tempest gave the shock;
She sprang no fatal leak;
    She ran upon no rock.

His sword was in the sheath;
    His fingers held the pen,
When Kempenfelt went down
    With twice four hundred men.

[1] While being refitted, the *Royal George* sank August 29, 1782.

Weigh the vessel up,
    Once dreaded by our foes!
And mingle with our cup
    The tears that England owes.

Her timbers yet are sound,
    And she may float again
Full charg'd with England's thunder,
    And plough the distant main.

But Kempenfelt is gone,
    His victories are o'er;
And he and his eight hundred
    Shall plough the wave no more.

ANONYMOUS

Edward

"WHY dois your brand sae drap wi bluid,
            Edward, Edward,
Why dois your brand sae drap wi bluid,
    And why sae sad gang yee O?"
"O I hae killed my hauke [1] sae guid,
            Mither, mither,
O I hae killed my hauke sae guid,
    And I had nae mair bot hee O."

"Your haukis bluid was nevir sae reid,
            Edward, Edward,
Your haukis bluid was nevir sae reid,
    My deir son I tell thee O."
"O I hae killed my reid-roan steid,
            Mither, mither,
O I hae killed my reid-roan steid,
    That erst was sae fair and frie O."

hawk

"Your steid was auld, and ye hae gat mair,
Edward, Edward,
Your steid was auld, and ye hae gat mair,
  Sum other dule ye drie [2] O.
"O I hae killed my fadir deir,
Mither, mither,
O I hae killed my fadir deir,
  Alas, and wae is mee O!"

"And whatten penance wul ye drie for that,
Edward, Edward?
And whatten penance will ye drie for that?
  My deir son, now tell me O."
"Ile set my feit in yonder boat,
Mither, mither,
Ile set my feit in yonder boat,
  And Ile fare ovir the sea O."

"And what wul ye doe wi your towirs and your ha,[3]
Edward, Edward?
And what wul ye doe wi your towirs and your ha,
  That were sae fair to see O?"
"Ile let thame stand tul they doun fa,
Mither, mither,
Ile let thame stand tul they doun fa,
  For here nevir mair maun I bee O."

"And what wul ye leive to your bairns and your wife,
Edward, Edward?
And what wul ye leive to your bairns and your wife,
  Whan ye gang ovir the sea O?"
"The warldis room, late them beg thrae life,
Mither, mither,
The warldis room, late them beg thrae life,
  For thame nevir mair wul I see O."

"And what wul ye leive to your ain mither deir,
Edward, Edward?
And what wul ye leive to your ain mither deir?
  My deir son, now tell me O."

[2] grief you suffer
[3] hall

"The curse of hell frae me sall ye beir,
    Mither, mither,
The curse of hell frae me sall ye beir,
  Sic counseils ye gave to me O."

The Twa Corbies

AS I was walking all alane,
  I heard twa corbies making a mane;
The tane unto the t'other say,
  "Where sall we gang and dine today?"

"In behint yon auld fail dyke,
I wot their lies a new slain knight;
And naebody kens that he lies there
But his hawk, his hound, and lady fair.

"His hound is to the hunting gane,
His hawk to fetch the wild-fowl hame,
His lady's ta'en another mate,
So we may mak our dinner sweet.

"Ye'll sit on his white hause-bane,
And I'll pike out his bonny blue een;
Wi ae lock o his gowden hair,
We'll theek our nest when it grows bare.

"Mony a one for him makes mane,
But nane sall ken where he is gane;
Oer his white banes, when they are bare,
The wind sall blaw for evermair."

Thomas the Rhymer

TRUE Thomas lay on Huntlie bank;
  A ferlie he spied wi' his e'e;
And there he saw a ladye bright
  Come riding down by the Eildon Tree.

Her skirt was o' the grass-green silk,
  Her mantle o' the velvet fyne;

At ilka tett o' her horse's mane,
  Hung fifty siller bells and nine.

True Thomas he pu'd aff his cap,
  And louted low down on his knee:
"Hail to thee, Mary, Queen of Heaven!
  For thy peer on earth could never be."

"O no, O no, Thomas," she said,
  "That name does not belang to me;
I'm but the Queen o' fair Elfland,
  That am hither come to visit thee.

"Harp and carp, Thomas," she said;
  "Harp and carp along wi' me;
And if ye dare to kiss my lips,
  Sure of your bodie I will be."

"Betide me weal, betide me woe,
  That weird shall never daunten me."
Syne he has kiss'd her rosy lips,
  All underneath the Eildon Tree.

"Now ye maun go wi' me," she said,
  "True Thomas, ye maun go wi' me;
And ye maun serve me seven years,
  Thro' weal or woe as may chance to be."

She's mounted on her milk-white steed,
  She's ta'en true Thomas up behind;
And aye, whene'er her bridle rang,
  The steed gaed swifter than the wind.

O they rade on, and farther on,
  The steed gaed swifter than the wind;
Until they reach'd a desert wide,
  And living land was left behind.

"Light down, light down now, true Thomas,
  And lean your head upon my knee;
Abide ye there a little space,
  And I will show you ferlies three.

"O see ye not yon narrow road,
   So thick beset wi' thorns and briers?
That is the Path of Righteousness,
   Though after it but few inquires.

"And see ye not yon braid, braid road,
   That lies across the lily leven?
That is the Path of Wickedness,
   Though some call it the Road to Heaven.

"And see ye not yon bonny road
   That winds about the fernie brae?
That is the Road to fair Elfland,
   Where thou and I this night maun gae.

"But, Thomas, ye sall haud your tongue,
   Whatever ye may hear or see;
For speak ye word in Elflyn-land,
   Ye'll ne'er win back to your ain countrie."

O they rade on, and farther on,
   And they waded rivers abune the knee;
And they saw neither sun nor moon,
   But they heard the roaring of the sea.

It was mirk, mirk night, there was nae starlight,
   They waded thro' red blude to the knee;
For a' the blude that's shed on the earth
   Rins through the springs o' that countrie.

Syne they came to a garden green,
   And she pu'd an apple frae a tree:
"Take this for thy wages, true Thomas;
   It will give thee the tongue that can never lee."

"My tongue is my ain," true Thomas he said;
   "A gudely gift ye wad gie to me!
I neither dought to buy or sell
   At fair or tryst where I might be.

"I dought neither speak to prince or peer,
   Nor ask of grace from fair ladye!"—

"Now haud thy peace, Thomas," she said,
    "For as I say, so must it be."

He has gotten a coat of the even cloth,
    And a pair o' shoon of the velvet green;
And till seven years were gane and past,
    True Thomas on earth was never seen.

Sir Patrick Spens

1. *The Sailing*

THE king sits in Dunfermline town
    Drinking the blude-red wine;
"O whare will I get a skeely skipper
    To sail this new ship o' mine?"

O up and spak an eldern knight,
    Sat at the king's right knee;
"Sir Patrick Spens is the best sailor
    That ever sail'd the sea."

Our king has written a braid letter,
    And seal'd it with his hand,
And sent it to Sir Patrick Spens,
    Was walking on the strand.

"To Noroway, to Noroway,
    To Noroway o'er the faem;
The king's daughter o' Noroway,
    'Tis thou must bring her hame."

The first word that Sir Patrick read
    So loud, loud laugh'd he;
The neist word that Sir Patrick read
    The tear blinded his e'e.

"O wha is this has done this deed
    And tauld the king o' me,
To send us out, at this time o' year,
    To sail upon the sea?

"Be it wind, be it weet, be it hail, be it sleet,
　　Our ship must sail the faem;
The king's daughter o' Noroway,
　　'Tis we must fetch her hame."

They hoysed their sails on Monenday morn
　　Wi' a' the speed they may;
They hae landed in Noroway
　　Upon a Wodensday.

II. *The Return*

"Mak ready, mak ready, my merry men a':
　　Our gude ship sails the morn."
"Now ever alack, my master dear,
　　I fear a deadly storm.

"I saw the new moon late yestreen
　　Wi' the auld moon in her arm;
And if we gang to sea, master,
　　I fear we'll come to harm."

They hadna sail'd a league, a league,
　　A league but barely three,
When the lift grew dark, and the wind blew loud,
　　And gurly grew the sea.

The ankers brak, and the topmast lap,
　　It was sic a deadly storm:
And the waves cam owre the broken ship
　　Till a' her sides were torn.

"Go fetch a web o' the silken claith,
　　Another o' the twine,
And wap them into our ship's side,
　　And let nae the sea come in."

They fetch'd a web o' the silken claith,
　　Another o' the twine,

lift] sky.
lap] sprang.

And they wapp'd them round that gude ship's side,
  But still the sea came in.

O laith, laith were our gude Scots lords
  To wet their cork-heel'd shoon;
But lang or a' the play was play'd
  They wat their hats aboon.

And mony was the feather bed
  That flatter'd on the faem;
And mony was the gude lord's son
  That never mair cam hame.

O lang, lang may the ladies sit,
  Wi' their fans into their hand,
Before they see Sir Patrick Spens
  Come sailing to the strand!

And lang, lang may the maidens sit
  Wi' their gowd kames in their hair,
A-waiting for their ain dear loves!
  For them they'll see nae mair.

Half-owre, half-owre to Aberdour,
  'Tis fifty fathoms deep;
And there lies gude Sir Patrick Spens,
  Wi' the Scots lords at his feet!

Fair Annie

"IT'S narrow, narrow, make your bed,
  And learn to lie your lane;
For I'm ga'n oer the sea, Fair Annie,
  A braw bride to bring hame.
Wi her I will get gowd and gear;
  Wi you I neer got nane.

"But wha will bake my bridal bread,
  Or brew my bridal ale?

---

flatter'd] tossed afloat.
kames] combs.

And wha will welcome my brisk bride,
    That I bring oer the dale?"

"It's I will bake your bridal bread,
    And brew your bridal ale,
And I will welcome your brisk bride,
    That you bring oer the dale."

"But she that welcomes my brisk bride
    Maun gang like maiden fair;
She maun lace on her robe sae jimp,
    And braid her yellow hair."

"But how can I gang maiden-like,
    When maiden I am nane?
Have I not born seven sons to thee,
    And am with child again?"

She's taen her young son in her arms,
    Another in her hand,
And she's up to the highest tower,
    To see him come to land.

"Come up, come up, my eldest son,
    And look oer yon sea-strand,
And see your father's new-come bride,
    Before she come to land."

"Come down, come down, my mother dear,
    Come frae the castle wa!
I fear, if langer ye stand there,
    Ye'll let yoursell down fa."

And she gaed down, and farther down,
    Her love's ship for to see,
And the topmast and the mainmast
    Shone like the silver free.

And she's gane down, and farther down,
    The bride's ship to behold,
And the topmast and the mainmast
    They shone just like the gold.

She's taen her seven sons in her hand,
    I wot she didna fail;
She met Lord Thomas and his bride,
    As they came oer the dale.

"You're welcome to your house, Lord Thomas,
    You're welcome to your land;
You're welcome with your fair ladye,
    That you lead by the hand.

"You're welcome to your ha's, ladye,
    You're welcome to your bowers;
You're welcome to your hame, ladye,
    For a' that's here is yours."

"I thank thee, Annie; I thank thee, Annie,
    Sae dearly as I thank thee;
You're the likest to my sister Annie,
    That ever I did see.

"There came a knight out oer the sea,
    And steald my sister away;
The shame scoup in his company,
    And land whereer he gae!"

She hang ae napkin at the door,
    Another in the ha,
And a' to wipe the trickling tears,
    Sae fast as they did fa.

And aye she served the lang tables,
    With white bread and with wine,
And aye she drank the wan water,
    To had her colour fine.

And aye she served the lang tables,
    With white bread and with brown;
And ay she turned her round about,
    Sae fast the tears fall down.

And he's taen down the silk napkin,
    Hung on a silver pin,

And aye he wipes the tear trickling
    A'down her cheik and chin.

And aye he turn'd him round about,
    And smil'd amang his men;
Says, Like ye best the old ladye,
    Or her that's new come hame?

When bells were rung and mass was sung,
    And a' men bound to bed,
Lord Thomas and his new-come bride
    To their chamber they were gaed.

Annie made her bed a little forbye,
    To hear what they might say;
"And ever alas!" Fair Annie cried,
    "That I should see this day!

"Gin my seven sons were seven young rats,
    Running on the castle wa,
And I were a grey cat mysell,
    I soon would worry them a'.

"Gin my seven sons were seven young hares,
    Running oer yon lilly lee,
And I were a grew hound mysell,
    Soon worried they a' should be."

And wae and sad Fair Annie sat,
    And drearie was her sang,
And ever, as she sobbd and grat,
    "Wae to the man that did the wrang!"

"My gown is on," said the new-come bride,
    "My shoes are on my feet,
And I will to Fair Annie's chamber,
    And see what gars her greet.

"What ails ye, what ails ye, Fair Annie,
    That ye make sic a moan?
Has your wine barrels cast the girds,
    Or is your white bread gone?

"O wha was't was your father, Annie,
    Or wha was't was your mother?
And had ye ony sister, Annie,
    Or had ye ony brother?"

"The Earl of Wemyss was my father,
    The Countess of Wemyss my mother;
And a' the folk about the house
    To me were sister and brother."

"If the Earl of Wemyss was your father,
    I wot sae was he mine;
And it shall not be for lack o gowd
    That ye your love sall tine.

"For I have seven ships o mine ain,
    A' loaded to the brim,
And I will gie them a' to thee,
    Wi four to thine eldest son:
But thanks to a' the powers in heaven
    That I gae maiden hame!"

Clerk Saunders

CLERK SAUNDERS and may Margaret
    Walk'd owre yon garden green;
And deep and heavy was the love
    That fell thir twa between.

"A bed, a bed," Clerk Saunders said,
    "A bed for you and me!"
"Fye na, fye na," said may Margaret,
    "Till anes we married be!"

"Then I'll take the sword frae my scabbard
    And slowly lift the pin;
And you may swear, and save your aith,
    Ye ne'er let Clerk Saunders in.

"Take you a napkin in your hand,
    And tie up baith your bonnie e'en,

And you may swear, and save your aith,
  Ye saw me na since late yestreen."

It was about the midnight hour,
  When they asleep were laid,
When in and came her seven brothers,
  Wi' torches burning red:

When in and came her seven brothers,
  Wi' torches burning bright:
They said, "We hae but one sister,
  And behold her lying with a knight!"

Then out and spake the first o' them,
  "I bear the sword shall gar him die."
And out and spake the second o' them,
  "His father has nae mair but he."

And out and spake the third o' them,
  "I wot that they are lovers dear."
And out and spake the fourth o' them,
  "They hae been in love this mony a year."

Then out and spake the fifth o' them,
  "It were great sin true love to twain."
And out and spake the sixth o' them,
  "It were shame to slay a sleeping man."

Then up and gat the seventh o' them,
  And never a word spake he;
But he has striped his bright brown brand
  Out through Clerk Saunders' fair bodye.

Clerk Saunders he started, and Margaret she turn'd
  Into his arms as asleep she lay;
And sad and silent was the night
  That was atween thir twae.

And they lay still and sleepit sound
  Until the day began to daw';
And kindly she to him did say,
  "It is time, true love, you were awa'."

But he lay still, and sleepit sound,
 Albeit the sun began to sheen;
She look'd atween her and the wa',
 And dull and drowsie were his e'en.

Then in and came her father dear;
 Said, "Let a' your mourning be;
I'll carry the dead corse to the clay,
 And I'll come back and comfort thee."

"Comfort weel your seven sons,
 For comforted I will never be:
I ween 'twas neither knave nor loon
 Was in the bower last night wi' me."

The clinking bell gaed through the town
 To carry the dead corse to the clay;
And Clerk Saunders stood at may Margaret's window,
 I wot, an hour before the day.

"Are ye sleeping, Marg'ret?" he says,
 "Or are ye waking presentlie?
Give me my faith and troth again,
 I wot, true love, I gied to thee."

"Your faith and troth ye sall never get,
 Nor our true love sall never twin,
Until ye come within my bower,
 And kiss me cheik and chin."

"My mouth it is full cold, Marg'ret;
 It has the smell, now, of the ground;
And if I kiss thy comely mouth,
 Thy days of life will not be lang.

"O cocks are crowing a merry midnight;
 I wot the wild fowls are boding day;
Give me my faith and troth again,
 And let me fare me on my way."

"Thy faith and troth thou sallna get,
 And our true love sall never twin,

twin] break in two

Until ye tell what comes o' women,
 I wot, who die in strong traivelling?"

"Their beds are made in the heavens high,
 Down at the foot of our good Lord's knee,
Weel set about wi' gillyflowers;
 I wot, sweet company for to see.

"O cocks are crowing a merry midnight;
 I wot the wild fowls are boding day;
The psalms of heaven will soon be sung,
 And I, ere now, will be miss'd away."

Then she has taken a crystal wand,
 And she has stroken her troth thereon;
She has given it him out at the shot-window,
 Wi' mony a sad sigh and heavy groan.

"I thank ye, Marg'ret; I thank ye, Marg'ret;
 And ay I thank ye heartilie;
Gin ever the dead come for the quick,
 Be sure, Marg'ret, I'll come for thee."

It's hosen and shoon, and gown alone,
 She climb'd the wall, and follow'd him,
Until she came to the green forest,
 And there she lost the sight o' him.

"Is there ony room at your head, Saunders?
 Is there ony room at your feet?
Or ony room at your side, Saunders,
 Where fain, fain, I wad sleep?"

"There's nae room at my head, Marg'ret,
 There's nae room at my feet;
My bed it is fu' lowly now,
 Amang the hungry worms I sleep.

"Cauld mould is my covering now,
 But and my winding-sheet;
The dew it falls nae sooner down
 Than my resting-place is weet.

"But plait a wand o' bonny birk,
　And lay it on my breast;
And shed a tear upon my grave,
　And wish my saul gude rest."

Then up and crew the red, red cock,
　And up and crew the gray:
' 'Tis time, 'tis time, my dear Marg'ret,
　That you were going away.

'And fair Marg'ret, and rare Marg'ret,
　And Marga'ret o' veritie,
Gin e'er ye love another man,
　Ne'er love him as ye did me."

The Unquiet Grave

"THE wind doth blow today, my love,
　And a few small drops of rain;
I never had but one true-love,
　In cold grave she was lain.

"I'll do as much for my true-love
　As any young man may;
I'll sit and mourn all at her grave
　For a twelvemonth and a day."

The twelvemonth and a day being up,
　The dead began to speak:
"Oh who sits weeping on my grave,
　And will not let me sleep?"

" 'Tis I, my love, sits on your grave,
　And I will not let you sleep;
For I crave one kiss of your clay-cold lips,
　And that is all I seek."

You crave one kiss of my clay-cold lips;
　But my breath smells earthy strong;
If you have one kiss of my clay-cold lips,
　Your time will not be long.

" 'Tis down in yonder garden green,
    Love, where we used to walk,
The finest flower that ere was seen
    Is withered to a stalk.

"The stalk is withered dry, my love,
    So will our hearts decay;
So make yourself content, my love,
    Till God calls you away."

The Wife of Usher's Well

THERE lived a wife at Usher's Well,
    And a wealthy wife was she;
She had three stout and stalwart sons,
    And sent them o'er the sea.

They had not been a week from her,
    A week but barely one,
When word came to the mother herself,
    That her three sons were gone.

They had not been a week from her,
    A week but barely three,
When word came to the mother herself,
    That her sons she'd never see.

"I wish the wind may never cease,
    Nor fishes in the flood,
Till my three sons come home to me,
    In earthly flesh and blood!"

It fell about the Martinmas,
    When nights are long and dark,
The mother's three sons they all came home,
    And their hats were of birch bark.

It neither grew in marsh or trench
    Nor yet in any ditch;
But at the gates of Paradise
    That birch grew fair and rich.

"Blow up the fire, my maidens!
  Bring water from the well!
For all my house shall feast this night,
  Since my three sons are well."

And she has made to them a bed,
  She's made it large and wide;
And she's taken her mantle her about,
  Sat down at the bed-side.

Up then crew the red, red cock,
  And up and crew the gray;
The eldest to the youngest said,
  " 'Tis time we were away."

The cock he had not crowed but once,
  And clapped his wings at dawn,
When the youngest to the eldest said,
  "Brother, we must be gone.

"The cock doth crow, the light doth grow,
  The channeling worm doth chide;
If we be missed out of our place,
  A sore pain we must abide."

"Lie still, lie still, but a little wee while,
  Lie still but if we may,
If our mother should miss us when she wakes,
  She will go mad ere day."

"Fare ye well, my mother dear!
  Farewell to barn and byre!
And fare ye well, the bonny lass,
  That kindles my mother's fire."

The Maid Freed from the Gallows

"O GOOD Lord Judge, and sweet Lord Judge,
      Peace for a little while!
Methinks I see my own father,
  Come riding by the stile.

"O father, O father, a little of your gold,
    And likewise of your fee!
To keep my body from yonder grave,
    And my neck from the gallows-tree."

"None of my gold now shall you have,
    Nor likewise of my fee;
For I am come to see you hangd,
    And hangéd you shall be."

"O good Lord Judge, and sweet Lord Judge,
    Peace for a little while!
Methinks I see my own mother,
    Come riding by the stile.

"O mother, O mother, a little of your gold,
    And likewise of your fee,
To keep my body from yonder grave,
    And my neck from the gallows-tree!"

"None of my gold now shall you have,
    Nor likewise of my fee;
For I am come to see you hangd,
    And hangéd you shall be."

"O good Lord Judge, and sweet Lord Judge,
    Peace for a little while!
Methinks I see my own brother,
    Come riding by the stile.

"O brother, O brother, a little of your gold,
    And likewise of your fee,
To keep my body from yonder grave,
    And my neck from the gallows-tree!"

"None of my gold now shall you have,
    Nor likewise of my fee;
For I am come to see you hangd
    And hangéd you shall be."

"O good Lord Judge, and sweet Lord Judge,
    Peace for a little while!

Methinks I see my own sister
   Come riding by the stile.

"O sister, O sister, a little of your gold,
   And likewise of your fee,
To keep my body from yonder grave,
   And my neck from the gallows-tree!"

"None of my gold now shall you have,
   Nor likewise of my fee;
For I am come to see you hangd
   And hangéd you shall be."

"O good Lord Judge, and sweet Lord Judge,
   Peace for a little while!
Methinks I see my own true-love,
   Come riding by the stile.

"O true-love, O true-love, a little of your gold,
   And likewise of your fee,
To save my body from yonder grave,
   And my neck from the gallows-tree."

"Some of my gold now you shall have,
   And likewise of my fee,
For I am come to see you saved,
   And savéd you shall be."

The Bonnie Earl of Murray

YE Highlands and ye Lawlands.
   Oh! where hae ye been?
They hae slain the Earl of Murray,
   And hae laid him on the green.

Now wae be to thee, Huntly,
   And wherefore did you sae?
I bade you bring him wi' you,
   But forbade you him to slay.

He was a braw gallant,
   And he rid at the ring;

And the bonnie Earl of Murray,
   Oh! he might hae been a king.

He was a braw gallant,
   And he play'd at the ba';
And the bonnie Earl of Murray
   Was the flower amang them a'.

He was a braw gallant,
   And he play'd at the glove;
And the bonnie Earl of Murray,
   Oh! he was the Queen's luve.

Oh! lang will his lady
   Look owre the castle Down,
Ere she see the Earl of Murray
   Come sounding thro' the town.

Helen of Kirconnell

I WISH I were where Helen lies,
   Night and day on me she cries;
O that I were where Helen lies,
   On fair Kirconnell lea!

Curst be the heart that thought the thought,
And curst the hand that fired the shot,
When in my arms burd Helen dropt,
   And died to succour me!

O think na ye my heart was sair,
When my Love dropp'd and spak nae mair!
There did she swoon wi' meikle care,
   On fair Kirconnell lea.

As I went down the water side,
None but my foe to be my guide,
None but my foe to be my guide,
   On fair Kirconnell lea;

I lighted down my sword to draw,
I hackèd him in pieces sma',

I hackèd him in pieces sma',
  For her sake that died for me.

O Helen fair, beyond compare!
I'll mak a garland o' thy hair,
Shall bind my heart for evermair,
  Until the day I die!

O that I were where Helen lies!
Night and day on me she cries;
Out of my bed she bids me rise,
  Says, "Haste, and come to me!"

O Helen fair! O Helen chaste!
If I were with thee, I'd be blest,
Where thou lies low and taks thy rest,
  On fair Kirconnell lea.

I wish my grave were growing green,
A winding-sheet drawn owre me e'en,
And I in Helen's arms lying,
  On fair Kirconnell lea.

I wish I were where Helen lies!
Night and day on me she cries;
And I am weary of the skies,
  For her sake that died for me.

Binnorie

THERE were twa sisters sat in a bour;
  Binnorie, O Binnorie!
There cam a knight to be their wooer,
  By the bonnie milldams o' Binnorie.

He courted the eldest with glove and ring,
But he lo'ed the youngest abune a thing.

The eldest she was vexèd sair,
And sair envìed her sister fair.

Upon a morning fair and clear,
She cried upon her sister dear:

"O sister, sister, tak my hand,
And let's go down to the river-strand."

She's ta'en her by the lily hand,
And led her down to the river-strand.

The youngest stood upon a stane,
The eldest cam and push'd her in.

"O sister, sister, reach your hand!
And ye sall be heir o' half my land:

"O sister, reach me but your glove!
And sweet William sall be your love."

Sometimes she sank, sometimes she swam,
Until she cam to the miller's dam.

Out then cam the miller's son,
And saw the fair maid soummin' in.

"O father, father, draw your dam!
There's either a mermaid or a milk-white swan."

The miller hasted and drew his dam,
And there he found a drown'd womàn.

You couldna see her middle sma',
Her gowden girdle was sae braw.

You couldna see her lily feet,
Her gowden fringes were sae deep.

All amang her yellow hair
A string o' pearls was twisted rare.

You couldna see her fingers sma',
Wi' diamond rings they were cover'd a'.

And by there came a harper fine,
That harpit to the king at dine.

And when he look'd that lady on,
He sigh'd and made a heavy moan.

He's made a harp of her breast-bane,
Whose sound wad melt a heart of stane.

He's ta'en three locks o' her yellow hair,
And wi' them strung his harp sae rare.

He went into her father's hall,
And there was the court assembled all.

He laid his harp upon a stane,
And straight it began to play by lane.

"O yonder sits my father, the King,
And yonder sits my mother, the Queen;

"And yonder stands my brother Hugh,
And by him my William, sweet and true."

But the last tune that the harp play'd then—
  Binnorie, O Binnorie!
Was, "Woe to my sister, false Helèn!"
  By the bonnie milldams o' Binnorie.

A Lyke-Wake Dirge

THIS ae nighte, this ae nighte,
  —Every nighte and alle,
Fire and sleet and candle-lighte,
  And Christe receive thy saule.

When thou from hence away art past,
  —Every nighte and alle,
To Whinny-muir thou com'st at last;
  And Christe receive thy saule.

If ever thou gavest hosen and shoon,
  —*Every nighte and alle,*
Sit thee down and put them on;
  And Christe receive thy saule.

If hosen and shoon thou ne'er gav'st nane
  —*Every nighte and alle,*
The whinnes sall prick thee to the bare bane;
  And Christe receive thy saule.

From Whinny-muir when thou may'st pass,
  —*Every nighte and alle,*
To Brig o' Dread thou com'st at last;
  And Christe receive thy saule.

From Brig o' Dread when thou may'st pass,
  —*Every nighte and alle,*
To Purgatory fire thou com'st at last;
  And Christe receive thy saule.

If ever thou gavest meat or drink,
  —*Every nighte and alle,*
The fire sall never make thee shrink;
  And Christe receive thy saule.

If meat or drink thou ne'er gav'st nane,
  —*Every nighte and alle,*
The fire will burn thee to the bare bane;
  And Christe receive thy saule.

This ae nighte, this ae nighte,
  —*Every nighte and alle,*
Fire and sleet and candle-lighte,
  And Christe receive thy saule.

"Western Wind, when wilt thou blow"

WESTERN wind, when wilt thou blow,
  That the small rain down can rain?
Christ, that my love were in my arms
And I in my bed again!

Lily, Germander, and Sops-in-Wine

AND can the physician make sick men well?
  And can the magician a fortune divine?
Without lily, germander, and sops-in-wine,
        With sweet-briar
        And bon-fire
        And strawberry wire
        And columbine.

Within and out, in and out, round as a ball,
With hither and thither, as straight as a line,
With lily, germander, and sops-in-wine,
        With sweet-briar
        And bon-fire
        And strawberry wire
        And columbine.

When Saturn did live, there lived no poor,
The king and the beggar with roots did dine,
With lily, germander, and sops-in-wine,
        With sweet-briar
        And bon-fire
        And strawberry wire
        And columbine.

Phyllida's Love Call

Phyl. CORYDON, arise, my Corydon!
          Titan shineth clear.
  Cor. Who is it that calleth Corydon?
          Who is it that I hear?
Phyl. Phyllida, thy true Love, calleth thee,
          Arise then, arise then,
            Arise and keep thy flock with me!
  Cor. Phyllida, my true Love, is it she?
          I come then, I come then,
            I come and keep my flock with thee.

Phyl. Here are cherries ripe, my Corydon;
    Eat them for my sake.
Cor. Here's my oaten pipe, my lovely one,
    Sport for thee to make.
Phyl. Here are threads, my true Love, fine as silk,
    To knit thee, to knit thee
    A pair of stockings white as milk.
Cor. Here are reeds, my true Love, fine and neat,
    To make thee, to make thee
    A bonnet to withstand the heat.

Phyl. I will gather flowers, my Corydon,
    To set in thy cap.
Cor. I will gather pears, my lovely one,
    To put in thy lap.
Phyl. I will buy my true Love garters gay
    For Sundays, for Sundays,
    To wear about his legs so tall.
Cor. I will buy my true Love yellow say
    For Sundays, for Sundays,
    To wear about her middle small.

Phyl. When my Corydon sits on a hill
    Making melody—
Cor. When my lovely one goes to her wheel
    Singing cheerily—
Phyl. Sure methinks my true Love doth excel
    For sweetness, for sweetness,
    Sir Pan, that old Arcadian knight.
Cor. And methinks my true Love bears the bell
    For clearness, for clearness,
    Beyond the nymphs that be so bright.
Phyl. Had my Corydon, my Corydon,
    Been, alack! her swain—
Cor. Had my lovely one, my lovely one,
    Been in Ida plain—
Phyl. Cynthia Endymion had refused,
    Preferring, preferring,
    My Corydon to play withal.
Cor. The queen of love had been excused,
    Bequeathing, bequeathing,
    My Phyllida the golden ball.

Phyl. Yonder comes my mother, Corydon,
   Whither shall I fly?
Cor. Under yonder beech, my lovely one,
   While she passeth by.
Phyl. Say to her thy true Love was not here;
   Remember, remember,
    Tomorrow is another day.
Cor. Doubt me not, my true Love, do not fear;
   Farewell then, farewell then,
   Heaven keep our loves alway.

A Song of Ale

 Back and side go bare, go bare,
  Both hand and foot go cold,
 But belly, God send thee good ale enough
  Whether it be new or old!

BUT if that I may have truly
 Good ale my belly full,
I shall look like one, by sweet Saint John,
 Were shorn against the wool.
Though I go bare, take you no care,
 I am nothing a-cold,
I stuff my skin so full within
 Of jolly good ale and old.

I cannot eat but little meat,
 My stomach is not good;
But sure I think that I could drink
 With him that weareth an hood.
Drink is my life; although my wife
 Some time do chide and scold,
Yet spare I not to ply the pot
 Of jolly good ale and old.

I love no roast but a brown toast,
 Or a crab in the fire;
A little bread shall do me stead;
 Much bread I never desire.
Nor frost, nor snow, nor wind I trow,
 Can hurt me if it would,

I am so wrapped within and lapped
   With jolly good ale and old.

I care right nough, I take no thought
   For clothes to keep me warm;
Have I good drink, I surely think
   Nothing can do me harm:
For truly than I fear no man,
   Be he never so bold,
When I am armed and throughly warmed
   With jolly good ale and old.

But now and than I curse and ban,
   They make their ale so small;
God give them care and evil to fare!
   They stry the malt and all.
Such peevish pew, I tell you true,
   Not for a crown of gold,
There cometh one sip within my lip,
   Whether it be new or old.

Good ale and strong maketh me among
   Full jocund and full light,
That oft I sleep and take no keep
   From morning until night.
Then start I up and flee to the cup;
   The right way on I hold;
My thirst to staunch, I fill my paunch
   With jolly good ale and old.

And Kit my wife, that as her life
   Loveth well good ale to seek,
Full oft drinketh she, that ye may see
   The tears run down her cheek.
Then doth she troll to me the bowl,
   As a good malt-worm should,
And say "Sweet-heart, I have take my part
   Of jolly good ale and old."

They that do drink till they nod and wink,
   Even as good fellows should do,
They shall not miss to have the bliss,
   That good ale hath brought them to.

And all poor souls that scour black bowls,
   And them hath lustily trolled,
God save the lives of them and their wives,
   Whether they be young or old!

Tom o' Bedlam's Song

FROM the hagg and hungrie goblin
   That into raggs would rend ye
And the spirit that stands by the naked man
   In the Book of Moones defend yee!
That of your five sounde sences
   You never be forsaken
Nor wander from your selves with Tom
   Abroad to begg your bacon.

   While I doe sing "Any foode any feeding
     Feedinge, drinke or clothing"
   Come dame or maid, be not afraid,
     Poor Tom will iniure nothing.

Of thirty bare yeares have I
   Twice twenty bin enragèd
And of forty bin three tymes fifteene
   In durance soundlie cagèd
On the lordlie loftes of Bedlam
   With stubble softe and dainty,
Braue braceletts strong, sweet whips ding-dong,
   With wholsome hunger plenty.
    And nowe I sing &c.

With a thought I tooke for Maudlin
   And a cruse of cockle pottage
With a thing thus tall, skie blesse you all,
   I befell into this dotage.
I slept not since the Conquest,
   Till then I never wakèd
Till the rogysh boy of loue where I lay
   Mee found and strip't mee naked.
    And nowe I sing &c.

When I short have shorne my sowre face
And swigg'd my horny barrel
In an oaken inne I pound my skin
As a suite of guilt apparell.
The moon's my constant Mistrisse
And the lowlie owle my morrowe
The flaming Drake and the Nightcrowe make
Mee musicke to my sorrowe.
    While I doe sing &c.

The palsie plagues my pulses
When I prigg your pigs or pullen,
Your culvers take, or matchles make
Your Chanticleare or sullen.
When I want prouant with Humfrie
I sup, and when benighted
I repose in Powles with waking soules
Yet neuere am affrighted.
    But I doe sing &c.

I knowe more then Apollo,
For oft when hee ly's sleeping
I see the starres att bloudie warres
In the wounded welkin weeping,
The moone embrace her shepheard
And the quene of Love her warryor,
While the first doth horne the star of morne
And the next the heavenly Farrier.
    While I doe sing &c.

The Gipsie snap and Pedro
Are none of Tom's comradoes.
The punk I skorne and the cut purse sworn
And the roaring boyes bravadoe
The meeke the white the gentle,
Me handle touch and spare not
But those that crosse Tom Rynosseros
Doe what the panther dare not.
    Although I sing &c.

With an host of furious fancies
Whereof I am commander,

With a burning speare, and a horse of aire,
To the wildernesse I wander.
By a knight of ghostes and shadowes
I summon'd am to tourney
Ten leagues beyond the wide world's end.
Mee thinke it is noe journey.
    Yet will I sing &c.

THOMAS CHATTERTON

Mynstrelles Songe [1]

O! SYNGE untoe mie roundelaie,
    O! droppe the brynie teare wythe mee,
Daunce ne moe atte hallie daie,
Lycke a reynynge ryver bee;
        Mie love ys dedde,
        Gon to hys death-bedde,
        Al under the wyllowe tree.

Blacke hys cryne [2] as the wyntere nyghte,
Whyte hys rode [3] as the sommer snowe,
Rodde hys face as the mornynge lyghte;
Cale [4] he lyes ynne the grave belowe;
        Mie love ys dedde,
        Gon to hys deathe-bedde,
        Al under the wyllowe tree.

Swote [5] hys tyngue as the throstles note,
Quycke ynn daunce as thoughte canne bee,
Defte hys taboure, codgelle stote; [6]

[1] Published in *Ælla, a Tragycal Enterlude.*
[2] Hair.
[3] Skin.
[4] Cold.
[5] Sweet.
[6] Cudgel stout.

O! hee lyes bie the wyllowe tree:
    Mie love ys dedde,
    Gonne to hys deathe-bedde,
    Alle underre the wyllowe tree.

Harke! the ravenne flappes hys wynge,
In the briered delle belowe;
Harke! the dethe-owle loude dothe synge,
To the nyghte-mares as heie goe;
    Mie love ys dedde,
    Gonne to hys deathe-bedde,
    Al under the wyllowe tree.

See! the whyte moone sheenes onne hie;
Whyterre ys mie true loves shroude;
Whyterre yanne the mornynge skie,
Whyterre yanne the evenynge cloude;
    Mie love ys dedde,
    Gon to hys deathe-bedde,
    Al under the wyllowe tree.

Heere, uponne mie true loves grave,
Schalle the baren fleurs be layde,
Nee one hallie Seyncte to save
Al the celness [7] of a mayde.
    Mie love ys dedde,
    Gonne to hys deathe-bedde,
    Alle under the wyllowe tree.

Wythe mie hondes I'lle dente the brieres
Rounde his hallie corse to gre,[8]
Ouphante fairie,[9] lyghte youre fyres,
Heere mie boddie stylle schalle bee.
    Mie love ys dedde,
    Gon to hys deathe-bedde,
    Al under the wyllowe tree.

Comme, wythe acorne-coppe and thorne,
Drayne mie hartys blodde awaie;
Lyfe and all yttes goode I scorne,

[7] Coolness.
[8] Grow.
[9] Elfin fairy.

Daunce bie nete, or feaste by daie.
   Mie love ys dedde,
   Gon to hys deathe-bedde,
   Al under the wyllowe tree.

Waterre wytches, crownede wythe reytes,[10]
Bere mee to yer leathalle [11] tyde.
I die; I comme; mie true love waytes.
Thos the damselle spake, and dyed.

GEORGE CRABBE

The Vicar

FROM INEBRIETY

THE vicar at the table's front presides,
   Whose presence a monastic life derides;
The reverend wig, in sideway order placed,
The reverend band, by rubric stains disgraced,
The leering eye, in wayward circles roll'd,
Mark him the pastor of a jovial fold,
Whose various texts excite a loud applause,
Favouring the bottle, and the good old cause.
See! the dull smile which fearfully appears,
When gross indecency her front uprears;
The joy conceal'd, the fiercer burns within,
As masks afford the keenest gust to sin;
Imagination helps the reverend sire,
And spreads the sails of sub-divine desire;
But when the gay immoral joke goes round,
When shame and all her blushing train are drown'd,
Rather than hear his God blasphemed, he takes
The last loved glass, and then the board forsakes.
Not that religion prompts the sober thought,
But slavish custom has the practice taught;

[10] Sea weeds.
[11] Deadly.

Besides, this zealous son of warm devotion
Has a true Levite bias for promotion.
Vicars must with discretion go astray,
Whilst bishops may be damn'd the nearest way.

WILLIAM BLAKE

To the Muses

WHETHER on Ida's shady brow,
    Or in the chambers of the East,
The chambers of the sun, that now
From ancient melody have ceas'd;

Whether in Heaven ye wander fair,
Or the green corners of the earth,
Or the blue regions of the air
Where the melodious winds have birth;

Whether on crystal rocks ye rove,
Beneath the bosom of the sea
Wand'ring in many a coral grove,
Fair Nine, forsaking Poetry!

How have you left the ancient love
That bards of old enjoy'd in you!
The languid strings do scarcely move!
The sound is forc'd, the notes are few!

Songs of Innocence

Introduction

PIPING down the alleys wild,
    Piping songs of pleasant glee,
On a cloud I saw a child,
And he laughing said to me:

"Pipe a song about a Lamb!"
So I piped with merry cheer.
"Piper, pipe that song again;"
So I piped: he wept to hear.

"Drop thy pipe, thy happy pipe;
Sing thy songs of happy cheer:"
So I sang the same again,
While he wept with joy to hear.

"Piper, sit thee down and write
In a book, that all may read."
So he vanish'd from my sight,
And I pluck'd a hollow reed,

And I made a rural pen,
And I stain'd the water clear,
And I wrote my happy songs
Every child may joy to hear.

The Lamb

LITTLE Lamb, who made thee?
    Dost thou know who made thee?
Gave thee life, and bid thee feed,
By the stream and o'er the mead;
Gave thee clothing of delight,
Softest clothing, woolly, bright;
Gave thee such a tender voice,
Making all the vales rejoice?
    Little Lamb, who made thee?
    Dost thou know who made thee?

    Little Lamb, I'll tell thee,
    Little Lamb, I'll tell thee:
He is calléd by thy name,
For He calls Himself a Lamb.
He is meek, and He is mild;
He became a little child.
I a child, and thou a lamb,
We are calléd by His name.

Little Lamb, God bless thee!
Little Lamb, God bless thee!

The Little Black Boy

MY mother bore me in the southern wild,
And I am black, but O! my soul is white;
White as an angel is the English child,
But I am black, as if bereav'd of light.

My mother taught me underneath a tree,
And, sitting down before the heat of day,
She took me on her lap and kisséd me,
And, pointing to the east, began to say:

"Look on the rising sun,—there God does live,
And gives His light, and gives His heat away;
And flowers and trees and beasts and men receive
Comfort in morning, joy in the noonday.

"And we are put on earth a little space,
That we may learn to bear the beams of love;
And these black bodies and this sunburnt face
Is but a cloud, and like a shady grove."

A Cradle Song

SWEET dreams, form a shade
O'er my lovely infant's head;
Sweet dreams of pleasant streams
By happy, silent, moony beams.

Sweet sleep, with soft down
Weave thy brows an infant crown.
Sweet sleep, Angel mild,
Hover o'er my happy child.

Sweet smiles, in the night
Hover over my delight;
Sweet smiles, mother's smiles,
All the livelong night beguiles.

Sweet moans, dovelike sighs,
Chase not slumber from thy eyes.
Sweet moans, sweeter smiles,
All the dovelike moans beguiles.

Sleep, sleep, happy child,
All creation slept and smil'd;
Sleep, sleep, happy sleep,
While o'er thee thy mother weep.

Sweet babe, in thy face
Holy image I can trace.
Sweet babe, once like thee,
Thy Maker lay and wept for me,

Wept for me, for thee, for all,
When He was an infant small.
Thou His image ever see,
Heavenly face that smiles on thee,

Smiles on thee, on me, on all;
Who became an infant small.
Infant smiles are His own smiles;
Heaven and earth to peace beguiles.

Holy Thursday

'TWAS on a Holy Thursday, their innocent faces clean,
 The children walking two and two, in red and blue and
green,
Grey-headed beadles walk'd before, with wands as white as snow,
Till into the high dome of Paul's they like Thames' waters flow.

O what a multitude they seem'd, these flowers of London town!
Seated in companies they sit with radiance all their own.
The hum of multitudes was there, but multitudes of lambs,
Thousands of little boys and girls raising their innocent hands.

Now like a mighty wind they raise to Heaven the voice of song,
Or like harmonious thunderings the seats of Heaven among.
Beneath them sit the agéd men, wise guardians of the poor;
Then cherish pity, lest you drive an angel from your door.

Songs of Experience

The Tyger

TYGER! Tyger! burning bright
In the forests of the night,
What immortal hand or eye
Could frame thy fearful symmetry?

In what distant deeps or skies
Burnt the fire of thine eyes?
On what wings dare he aspire?
What the hand dare seize the fire?

And what shoulder, and what art,
Could twist the sinews of thy heart?
And when thy heart began to beat,
What dread hand? and what dread feet?

What the hammer? what the chain?
In what furnace was thy brain?
What the anvil? what dread grasp
Dare its deadly terrors clasp?

When the stars threw down their spears
And water'd heaven with their tears,
Did he smile his work to see?
Did he who made the Lamb make thee?

Tyger! Tyger! burning bright
In the forests of the night,
What immortal hand or eye
Dare frame thy fearful symmetry?

A Poison Tree

I WAS angry with my friend:
I told my wrath, my wrath did end.
I was angry with my foe:
I told it not, my wrath did grow.

And I water'd it in fears,
Night and morning with my tears;
And I sunnéd it with smiles,
And with soft deceitful wiles.

And it grew both day and night,
Till it bore an apple bright;
And my foe beheld it shine,
And he knew that it was mine,

And into my garden stole
When the night had veil'd the pole:
In the morning glad I see
My foe outstretch'd beneath the tree.

"Never Seek to Tell Thy Love"

NEVER seek to tell thy love,
    Love that never told can be;
For the gentle wind does move
Silently, invisibly.

I told my love, I told my love,
I told her all my heart,
Trembling, cold, in ghastly fears,
Ah! she doth depart.

Soon as she was gone from me,
A traveller came by,
Silently, invisibly:
He took her with a sigh.

Auguries of Innocence[1]

TO see a World in a grain of sand,
　And a Heaven in a wild flower,
Hold Infinity in the palm of your hand,
And Eternity in an hour.
A robin redbreast in a cage
Puts all Heaven in a rage.
A dove-house fill'd with doves and pigeons
Shudders Hell thro' all its regions.
A dog starv'd at his master's gate
Predicts the ruin of the State.
A horse misus'd upon the road
Calls to Heaven for human blood.
Each outcry of the hunted hare
A fibre from the brain does tear.
A skylark wounded in the wing,
A cherubim does cease to sing.
The game-cock clipt and arm'd for fight
Does the rising sun affright.
Every wolf's and lion's howl
Raises from Hell a Human soul.
The wild deer, wandering here and there,
Keeps the Human soul from care.
The lamb misus'd breeds public strife,
And yet forgives the butcher's knife.
The bat that flits at close of eve
Has left the brain that won't believe.
The owl that calls upon the night
Speaks the unbeliever's fright.
He who shall hurt the little wren
Shall never be belov'd by men.
He who the ox to wrath has mov'd
Shall never be by woman lov'd.
The wanton boy that kills the fly

[1] From poems in Pickering MS., written *circa* 1801-1803; also published by Rossetti, 1863. "The title 'Auguries of Innocence' probably, as Mr. Yeats conjectures, refers only to the opening quatrain, although the MS. itself has no space or line separating it from the couplets which follow. These proverbs are here placed in the sequence in which they appear in the MS., where they were doubtless transcribed from scattered jottings elsewhere." [John Sampson, editor of Oxford edition, wherein his own rearrangement is appended to the reading here used.]

Shall feel the spider's enmity.
He who torments the chafer's sprite
Weaves a bower in endless night.
The caterpillar on the leaf
Repeats to thee thy mother's grief.
Kill not the moth nor butterfly,
For the Last Judgment draweth nigh.
He who shall train the horse to war
Shall never pass the polar bar.
The beggar's dog and widow's cat,
Feed them, and thou wilt grow fat.
The gnat that sings his summer's song
Poison gets from Slander's tongue.
The poison of the snake and newt
Is the sweat of Envy's foot.
The poison of the honey-bee
Is the artist's jealousy.
The prince's robes and beggar's rags
Are toadstools on the miser's bags.
A truth that's told with bad intent
Beats all the lies you can invent.
It is right it should be so;
Man was made for joy and woe;
And when this we rightly know,
Thro' the world we safely go.
Joy and woe are woven fine,
A clothing for the soul divine;
Under every grief and pine
Runs a joy with silken twine.
The babe is more than swaddling-bands;
Throughout all these human lands
Tools were made, and born were hands,
Every farmer understands.
Every tear from every eye
Becomes a babe in Eternity;
This is caught by Females bright,
And return'd to its own delight.
The bleat, the bark, bellow, and roar
Are waves that beat on Heaven's shore.
The babe that weeps the rod beneath
Writes revenge in realms of death.
The beggar's rags, fluttering in air,

Does to rags the heavens tear.
The soldier, arm'd with sword and gun,
Palsied strikes the summer's sun.
The poor man's farthing is worth more
Than all the gold on Afric's shore.
One mite wrung from the labourer's hands
Shall buy and sell the miser's lands
Or, if protected from on high,
Does that whole nation sell and buy.
He who mocks the infant's faith
Shall be mock'd in Age and Death.
He who shall teach the child to doubt
The rotting grave shall ne'er get out.
He who respects the infant's faith
Triumphs over Hell and Death.
The child's toys and the old man's reasons
Are the fruits of the two seasons.
The questioner, who sits so sly,
Shall never know how to reply.
He who replies to words of Doubt
Doth put the light of knowledge out.
The strongest poison ever known
Came from Caesar's laurel crown.
Nought can deform the human race
Like to the armour's iron brace.
When gold and gems adorn the plough
To peaceful arts shall Envy bow.
A riddle, or the cricket's cry,
Is to Doubt a fit reply.
The emmet's inch and eagle's mile
Make lame Philosophy to smile.
He who doubts from what he sees
Will ne'er believe, do what you please.
If the Sun and Moon should doubt,
They'd immediately go out.
To be in a passion you good may do,
But no good if a passion is in you.
The whore and gambler, by the state
Licensed, build that nation's fate.
The harlot's cry from street to street
Shall weave Old England's winding-sheet.
The winner's shout, the loser's curse,

Dance before dead England's hearse.
Every night and every morn
Some to misery are born.
Every morn and every night
Some are born to sweet delight.
Some are born to sweet delight,
Some are born to endless night.
We are led to believe a lie
When we see not thro' the eye,
Which was born in a night, to perish in a night,
When the Soul slept in beams of light.
God appears, and God is Light,
To those poor souls who dwell in Night;
But does a Human Form display
To those who dwell in realms of Day.

Preface to Milton

AND did those feet in ancient time
Walk upon England's mountains green?
And was the holy Lamb of God
On England's pleasant pastures seen?

And did the countenance divine
Shine forth upon our clouded hills?
And was Jerusalem builded here
Among these dark Satanic mills?

Bring me my bow of burning gold!
Bring me my arrows of desire!
Bring me my spear! O clouds, unfold!
Bring me my chariot of fire!

I will not cease from mental fight,
Nor shall my sword sleep in my hand,
Till we have built Jerusalem
In England's green and pleasant land.

Eternity

HE who binds to himself a joy
 Does the wingèd life destroy;
But he who kisses the joy as it flies
Lives in eternity's sun-rise.

Night

THE sun descending in the west,
 The evening star does shine;
The birds are silent in their nest.
 And I must seek for mine.
  The moon, like a flower
  In heaven's high bower,
  With silent delight
  Sits and smiles on the night.

Farewell, green fields and happy grove,
 Where flocks have took delight:
Where lambs have nibbled, silent move
 The feet of angels bright;
  Unseen they pour blessing
  And joy without ceasing
  On each bud and blossom,
  On each sleeping bosom.

They look in every thoughtless nest
 Where birds are cover'd warm;
They visit caves of every beast,
 To keep them all from harm:
  If they see any weeping
  That should have been sleeping,
  They pour sleep on their head,
  And sit down by their bed.

When wolves and tigers howl for prey,
 They pitying stand and weep,
Seeking to drive their thirst away
 And keep them from the sheep.

But, if they rush dreadful,
The angels, most heedful,
Receive each mild spirit,
New worlds to inherit.

And there the lion's ruddy eyes
  Shall flow with tears of gold:
And pitying the tender cries,
  And walking round the fold:
    Saying, "Wrath by His meekness,
    And, by His health, sickness,
    Are driven away
    From our immortal day.

"And now beside thee, bleating lamb,
  I can lie down and sleep,
Or think on Him who bore thy name,
  Graze after thee, and weep.
    For, wash'd in life's river,
    My bright mane for ever
    Shall shine like the gold
    As I guard o'er the fold."

ROBERT BURNS

Mary Morison [1]

O MARY, at thy window be,
  It is the wish'd, the trysted hour!
Those smiles and glances let me see,
  That make the miser's treasure poor:
How blythely wad I bide the stoure,[2]
  A weary slave frae sun to sun,
Could I the rich reward secure,
  The lovely Mary Morison.

[1] Written in 1780 or 1781, and sent to Thomson in a letter of 20 March 1793; published in *Works*, 1800.
[2] suffer hardship, or struggle

Yestreen, when to the trembling string
  The dance gaed thro' the lighted ha',
To thee my fancy took its wing,
  I sat, but neither heard nor saw:
Tho' this was fair, and that was braw,[3]
  And yon the toast of a' the town,
I sigh'd, and said amang them a',
  "Ye are na Mary Morison."

O Mary, canst thou wreck his peace,
  Wha for thy sake wad gladly die?
Or canst thou break that heart of his,
  Whase only faut is loving thee?
If love for love thou wilt na gie,[4]
  At least be pity to me shown!
A thought ungentle canna be
  The thought o' Mary Morison.

[3] handsome, fine
[4] not give

To a Mouse[1]

ON TURNING HER UP IN HER NEST WITH THE PLOUGH, NOVEMBER, 1785

WEE, sleekit,[2] cow'rin', tim'rous beastie,
  O what a panic's in thy breastie!
Thou need na start awa sae hasty,
    Wi' bickering brattle! [3]
I wad be laith to rin an' chase thee
    Wi' murd'ring pattle! [4]

I'm truly sorry man's dominion
Has broken Nature's social union,
An' justifies that ill opinion
    Which makes thee startle
At me, thy poor earth-born companion,
    An' fellow-mortal!

[1] Published in 1786.
[2] sleek
[3] with hasty scamper
 plow-staff

I doubt na, whiles, but thou may thieve;
What then? poor beastie, thou maun live!
A daimen-icker in a thrave[5]
   'S a sma' request:
I'll get a blessin' wi' the lave,
   And never miss 't!

Thy wee bit housie, too, in ruin!
Its silly wa's the win's are strewin'!
An' naething, now, to big[6] a new ane
   O' foggage green! [7]
An' bleak December's winds ensuin',
   Baith snell [8] an' keen!

Thou saw the fields laid bare and waste,
An' weary winter comin' fast,
An' cozie here, beneath the blast,
   Thou thought to dwell,
Till crash! the cruel coulter past
   Out-thro' thy cell.

That wee bit heap o' leaves an' stibble
Has cost thee mony a weary nibble!
Now thou's turn'd out, for a' thy trouble,
   But house or hald,[9]
To thole[10] the winter's sleety dribble,
   An' cranreuch[11] cauld!

But, Mousie, thou art no thy lane,[12]
In proving foresight may be vain:
The best laid schemes o' mice an' men
   Gang aft a-gley,[13]
An' lea'e us nought but grief an' pain
   For promis'd joy.

[5] An occasional ear in twenty-four sheaves.
[6] build
[7] coarse grass
[8] bitter
[9] without house or possession
[10] endure
[11] hoar-frost
[12] not alone
[13] astray

Still thou art blest compar'd wi' me!
The present only toucheth thee:
But oh! I backward cast my e'e
        On prospects drear!
An' forward tho' I canna see,
        I guess an' fear!

Address to the Unco Guid, or the Rigidly Righteous[1]

> *My son, these maxims make a rule,*
> *And lump them aye thegither:*
> *The rigid righteous is a fool,*
> *The rigid wise anither:*
> *The cleanest corn that e'er was dight,[2]*
> *May hae some pyles o' caff in;*
> *So ne'er a fellow-creature slight*
> *For random fits o' daffin.*
>   SOLOMON (Eccles. vii. 16).

O YE wha are sae guid yoursel,
        Sae pious and sae holy,
Ye've nought to do but mark and tell
        Your neibour's fauts and folly!
Whase life is like a weel-gaun[3] mill,
        Supplied wi' store o' water:
The heapéd happer's[4] ebbing still,
        And still the clap plays clatter:

Hear me, ye venerable core,[5]
        As counsel for poor mortals,
That frequent pass douce[6] Wisdom's door,
        For glaikit[7] Folly's portals;
I, for their thoughtless careless sakes,
        Would here propone[8] defences,—
Their donsie[9] tricks, their black mistakes,
        Their failings and mischances.

[1] Written in 1786; published in *Poems, Chiefly in the Scottish Dialect,* 1787.
[2] winnowed
[3] well-going
[4] hopper's
[5] corps, company
[6] grave
[7] giddy
[8] propose
[9] restive

Ye see your state wi' their's compar'd,
   And shudder at the niffer;[10]
But cast a moment's fair regard—
   What makes the mighty differ?
Discount what scant occasion gave,
   That purity ye pride in,
And (what's aft mair than a' the lave[11])
   Your better art o' hidin'.

Think, when your castigated pulse
   Gies now and then a wallop,
What ragins must his veins convulse,
   That still eternal gallop!
Wi' wind and tide fair i' your tail,
   Right on ye scud your sea-way;
But in the teeth o' baith to sail,
   It makes an unco[12] leeway.

See Social life and Glee sit down,
   All joyous and unthinking,
Till, quite transmogrified,[13] they're grown
   Debauchery and Drinking:
O would they stay to calculate
   Th' eternal consequences;
Or your more dreaded hell to state,
   Damnation of expenses!

Ye high, exalted, virtuous Dames,
   Tied up in godly laces,
Before ye gie poor Frailty names,
   Suppose a change o' cases;
A dear lov'd lad, convenience snug,
   A treacherous inclination—
But, let me whisper i' your lug,[14]
   Ye're aiblins[15] nae temptation.

Then gently scan your brother man,
   Still gentler sister woman;

[10] exchange
[1] rest
[12] uncommon
[13] transformed
[14] ear
[15] perhaps

Tho' they may gang a kennin wrang,
  To step aside is human.
One point must still be greatly dark,
  The moving why they do it;
And just as lamely can ye mark
  How far perhaps they rue it.

Who made the heart, 'tis He alone
  Decidedly can try us;
He knows each chord, its various tone,
  Each spring, its various bias.
Then at the balance let's be mute,
  We never can adjust it;
What's done we partly may compute,
  But know not what's resisted.

Ae Fond Kiss

AE fond kiss, and then we sever;
  Ae fareweel, alas, for ever!
Deep in heart-wrung tears I'll pledge thee,
Warring sighs and groans I'll wage thee!

Who shall say that Fortune grieves him
While the star of hope she leaves him?
Me, nae cheerfu' twinkle lights me,
Dark despair around benights me.

I'll ne'er blame my partial fancy;
Naething could resist my Nancy;
But to see her was to love her,
Love but her, and love for ever.

Had we never loved sae kindly,
Had we never loved sae blindly,
Never met—or never parted,
We had ne'er been broken-hearted.

Fare thee weel, thou first and fairest!
Fare thee weel, thou best and dearest!
Thine be ilka joy and treasure,
Peace, enjoyment, love, and pleasure!

Ae fond kiss, and then we sever!
Ae fareweel, alas, for ever!
Deep in heart-wrung tears I'll pledge thee,
Warring sighs and groans I'll wage thee!

Highland Mary[1]

YE banks and braes, and streams around
   The castle o' Montgomery,
Green be your woods and fair your flowers,
   Your waters never drumlie!
There Summer first unfald her robes,
   And there the langest tarry;
For there I took the last fareweel,
   O' my sweet Highland Mary.

How sweetly bloomed the gay, green birk,
   How rich the hawthorn's blossom,
As underneath their fragrant shade
   I clasped her to my bosom!
The golden hours on angel wings
   Flew o'er me and my dearie;
For dear to me as light and life
   Was my sweet Highland Mary.

Wi' monie a vow and locked embrace
   Our parting was fu' tender;
And, pledging aft to meet again,
   We tore oursels asunder.
But O, fell Death's untimely frost,
   That nipt my flower sae early!
Now green's the sod, and cauld's the clay,
   That wraps my Highland Mary!

O pale, pale now, those rosy lips,
   I aft hae kissed sae fondly;
And closed for ay, the sparkling glance
   That dwalt on me sae kindly;

[1] Written in 1792. Put in select collection of original Scotch Airs II, in 1799. The song concerns Mary Campbell.

And moldering now in silent dust
 That heart that lo'ed me dearly!
But still within my bosom's core
 Shall live my Highland Mary.

My Love Is Like a Red Red Rose

MY love is like a red red rose
  That's newly sprung in June:
My love is like the melodie
 That's sweetly play'd in tune.

So fair art thou, my bonnie lass,
 So deep in love am I:
And I will love thee still, my dear,
 Till a' the seas gang dry.

Till a' the seas gang dry, my dear,
 And the rocks melt wi' the sun:
And I will love thee still, my dear,
 While the sands o' life shall run.

And fare thee weel, my only love,
 And fare thee weel awhile!
And I will come again, my love,
 Tho' it were ten thousand mile.

For A' That and A' That

IS there, for honest poverty,
 That hangs his head, and a' that?
The coward-slave, we pass him by,
 We dare be poor for a' that!
  For a' that, and a' that,
   Our toils obscure, and a' that;
  The rank is but the guinea stamp;
   The man's the gowd[1] for a' that.

¹ gold

What tho' on hamely fare we dine,
  Wear hodden-gray,[2] and a' that;
Gie fools their silks, and knaves their wine,
  A man's a man for a' that.
    For a' that, and a' that,
      Their tinsel show, and a' that;
    The honest man, tho' e'er sae poor,
      Is King o' men for a' that.

Ye see yon birkie,[3] ca'd a lord,
  Wha struts, and stares, and a' that;
Tho' hundreds worship at his word,
  He's but a coof [4] for a' that:
    For a' that, and a' that,
      His riband, star, and a' that,
    The man of independent mind,
      He looks and laughs at a' that.

A prince can mak a belted knight,
  A marquis, duke, and a' that;
But an honest man's aboon[5] his might,
  Guid faith he mauna fa'[6] that!
    For a' that, and a' that,
      Their dignities, and a' that,
    The pith o' sense, and pride o' worth,
      Are higher rank than a' that.

Then let us pray that come it may
  As come it will for a' that,
That sense and worth o'er a' the earth,
  Shall bear the gree and a' that;
    For a' that, and a' that,
      It's comin' yet for a' that,
    That man to man, the world o'er,
      Shall brithers be for a' that.

[2] coarse gray woolen
[3] conceited fellow
[4] fool, ninny
[5] above
[6] claim

WILLIAM WORDSWORTH

Lucy

II

SHE dwelt among the untrodden ways
  Beside the springs of Dove,
A Maid whom there were none to praise
  And very few to love:

A violet by a mossy stone
  Half hidden from the eye!
Fair as a star, when only one
  Is shining in the sky.

She lived unknown, and few could know
  When Lucy ceased to be;
But she is in her grave, and oh,
  The difference to me!

V

A slumber did my spirit seal;
  I had no human fears:
She seem'd a thing that could not feel
  The touch of earthly years.

No motion has she now, no force;
  She neither hears nor sees;
Roll'd round in earth's diurnal course,
  With rocks, and stones, and trees.

Composed upon Westminster Bridge

EARTH has not anything to show more fair:
  Dull would he be of soul who could pass by
  A sight so touching in its majesty:
This City now doth like a garment wear
The beauty of the morning; silent, bare,
  Ships, towers, domes, theatres, and temples lie
  Open unto the fields, and to the sky;
All bright and glittering in the smokeless air.
Never did sun more beautifully steep
  In his first splendour valley, rock, or hill;
Ne'er saw I, never felt, a calm so deep!
  The river glideth at his own sweet will:
Dear God! the very houses seem asleep;
  And all that mighty heart is lying still!

London, 1802

MILTON! thou shouldst be living at this hour:
  England hath need of thee: she is a fen
Of stagnant waters: altar, sword, and pen,
Fireside, the heroic wealth of hall and bower,
Have forfeited their ancient English dower
Of inward happiness. We are selfish men;
Oh! raise us up, return to us again;
And give us manners, virtue, freedom, power.
Thy soul was like a Star, and dwelt apart;
Thou hadst a voice whose sound was like the sea:
Pure as the naked heavens, majestic, free,
So didst thou travel on life's common way,
In cheerful godliness; and yet thy heart
The lowliest duties on herself did lay.

The Solitary Reaper

BEHOLD her, single in the field,
  Yon solitary Highland Lass!
Reaping and singing by herself;
Stop here, or gently pass!

Alone she cuts and binds the grain,
And sings a melancholy strain;
O listen! for the Vale profound
Is overflowing with the sound.

No Nightingale did ever chaunt
More welcome notes to weary bands
Of travelers in some shady haunt,
Among Arabian sands:
A voice so thrilling ne'er was heard
In spring-time from the Cuckoo-bird,
Breaking the silence of the seas
Among the farthest Hebrides.

Will no one tell me what she sings?—
Perhaps the plaintive numbers flow
For old, unhappy, far-off things,
And battles long ago:
Or is it some more humble lay,
Familiar matter of today?
Some natural sorrow, loss, or pain,
That has been, and may be again?

Whate'er the theme, the Maiden sang
As if her song could have no ending;
I saw her singing at her work,
And o'er the sickle bending;—
I listened, motionless and still;
And, as I mounted up the hill,
The music in my heart I bore,
Long after it was heard no more.

Written between 1803 and 1805; published in 1807. In her entry of 13 September 1803 in *Recollections of a Tour Made in Scotland,* Dorothy Wordsworth describes the reapers and goes on to say, "It is not uncommon in the more lonely parts of the Highlands to see a single person so employed. The following poem was suggested to William by a beautiful sentence in Thomas Wilkinson's 'Tour in Scotland.'" Wordsworth himself pointed out the entry in Wilkinson: "Passed a female who was reaping alone: she sung in Erse, as she bended over her sickle; the sweetest human voice I ever heard: her strains were tenderly melancholy, and felt delicious, long after they were heard no more."

Daffodils

I WANDER'D lonely as a cloud
  That floats on high o'er vales and hills,
When all at once I saw a crowd,
A host of golden daffodils,
Beside the lake, beneath the trees
Fluttering and dancing in the breeze.

Continuous as the stars that shine
And twinkle on the milky way,
They stretched in never-ending line
Along the margin of a bay:
Ten thousand saw I at a glance
Tossing their heads in sprightly dance.

The waves beside them danced, but they
Out-did the sparkling waves in glee:
A poet could not but be gay
In such a jocund company!
I gazed—and gazed—but little thought
What wealth the show to me had brought.

For oft, when on my couch I lie
In vacant or in pensive mood,
They flash upon that inward eye
Which is the bliss of solitude;
And then my heart with pleasure fills,
And dances with the daffodils.

Ode

INTIMATIONS OF IMMORTALITY FROM RECOLLECTIONS OF EARLY
CHILDHOOD

The Child is father of the Man;
And I could wish my days to be
Bound each to each by natural piety.

I

THERE was a time when meadow, grove, and stream,
The earth, and every common sight,
To me did seem
Apparelled in celestial light,
The glory and the freshness of a dream.
It is not now as it hath been of yore;—
Turn wheresoe'er I may,
By night or day,
The things which I have seen I now can see no more.

II

The Rainbow comes and goes,
And lovely is the Rose,
The Moon doth with delight
Look round her when the heavens are bare,
Waters on a starry night
Are beautiful and fair;
The sunshine is a glorious birth;
But yet I know, where'er I go,
That there hath past away a glory from the earth.

III

Now, while the birds thus sing a joyous song,
And while the young lambs bound
As to the tabor's sound,
To me alone there came a thought of grief:
A timely utterance gave that thought relief,
And I again am strong:
The cataracts blow their trumpets from the steep;
Nor more shall grief of mine the season wrong;

I hear the Echoes through the mountains throng,
The Winds come to me from the fields of sleep,
  And all the earth is gay;
   Land and sea
  Give themselves up to jollity,
   And with the heart of May
  Doth every Beast keep holiday;—
   Thou Child of Joy,
Shout round me, let me hear thy shouts, thou happy Shepherd-boy!

IV

Ye blessèd Creatures, I have heard the call
 Ye to each other make; I see
The heavens laugh with you in your jubilee;
 My heart is at your festival,
  My head hath its coronal,
The fulness of your bliss, I feel—I feel it all.
   Oh evil day! if I were sullen
   While Earth herself is adorning,
    This sweet May-morning,
   And the Children are culling
    On every side,
   In a thousand valleys far and wide,
   Fresh flowers; while the sun shines warm,
And the Babe leaps up on his Mother's arm:—
   I hear, I hear, with joy I hear!
   —But there's a Tree, of many, one,
A single Field which I have looked upon,
Both of them speak of something that is gone:
   The Pansy at my feet
   Doth the same tale repeat:
Whither is fled the visionary gleam?
Where is it now, the glory and the dream?

V

Our birth is but a sleep and a forgetting:
The Soul that rises with us, our life's Star,
  Hath had elsewhere its setting,
   And cometh from afar:
  Not in entire forgetfulness,
  And not in utter nakedness,

But trailing clouds of glory do we come
    From God, who is our home:
Heaven lies about us in our infancy!
Shades of the prison-house begin to close
    Upon the growing Boy,
But He beholds the light, and whence it flows,
    He sees it in his joy;
The Youth, who daily farther from the east
    Must travel, still is Nature's Priest,
    And by the vision splendid
    Is on his way attended;
At length the Man perceives it die away,
And fade into the light of common day.

VI

Earth fills her lap with pleasures of her own;
Yearnings she hath in her own natural kind,
And, even with something of a Mother's mind,
    And no unworthy aim,
    The homely Nurse doth all she can
To make her Foster-child, her Inmate Man,
    Forget the glories he hath known,
And that imperial palace whence he came.

VII

Behold the Child among his new-born blisses,
A six years' Darling of a pigmy size!
See, where 'mid work of his own hand he lies,
Fretted by sallies of his mother's kisses,
With light upon him from his father's eyes!
See, at his feet, some little plan or chart,
Some fragment from his dream of human life,
Shaped by himself with newly-learned art;
    A wedding or a festival,
    A mourning or a funeral;
    And this hath now his heart,
    And unto this he frames his song:
    Then will he fit his tongue
To dialogues of business, love, or strife;
    But it will not be long
    Ere this be thrown aside,
    And with new joy and pride

The little Actor cons another part;
Filling from time to time his "humorous stage" [1]
With all the Persons, down to palsied Age,
That Life brings with her in her equipage;
    As if his whole vocation
    Were endless imitation.

VIII

Thou, whose exterior semblance doth belie
    Thy Soul's immensity;
Thou best Philosopher, who yet dost keep
Thy heritage, thou Eye among the blind,
That, deaf and silent, read'st the eternal deep,
Haunted for ever by the eternal mind,—
    Mighty Prophet! Seer blest!
    On whom those truths do rest,
Which we are toiling all our lives to find,
In darkness lost, the darkness of the grave;
Thou, over whom thy Immortality
Broods like the Day, a Master o'er a Slave,
A Presence which is not to be put by;
Thou little Child yet glorious in the might
Of heaven-born freedom on thy being's height,
Why with such earnest pains dost thou provoke
The years to bring the inevitable yoke,
Thus blindly with thy blessedness at strife?
Full soon thy Soul shall have her earthly freight,
And custom lie upon thee with a weight,
Heavy as frost, and deep almost as life!

IX

    O joy! that in our embers
    Is something that doth live,
    That nature yet remembers
    What was so fugitive!
The thought of our past years in me doth breed
Perpetual benediction: not indeed
For that which is most worthy to be blest;
Delight and liberty, the simple creed

---

[1] See *As You Like It,* II, vii, 139-166, the speech of Jacques, beginning "All the world's a stage."

Of Childhood, whether busy or at rest,
With new-fledged hope still fluttering in his breast:—
    Not for these I raise
    The song of thanks and praise;
    But for those obstinate questionings
    Of sense and outward things,
    Fallings from us, vanishings;
    Blank misgivings of a Creature
Moving about in worlds not realised,
High instincts before which our mortal Nature
Did tremble like a guilty Thing surprised:
    But for those first affections,
    Those shadowy recollections,
    Which, be they what they may,
Are yet the fountain-light of all our day,
Are yet a master-light of all our seeing;
    Uphold us, cherish, and have power to make
Our noisy years seem moments in the being
Of the eternal Silence: truths that wake,
    To perish never:
Which neither listlessness, nor mad endeavour,
    Nor Man nor Boy,
Nor all that is at enmity with joy,
Can utterly abolish or destroy!
    Hence in a season of calm weather
    Though inland far we be,
Our Souls have sight of that immortal sea
    Which brought us hither,
    Can in a moment travel thither,
And see the Children sport upon the shore,
And hear the mighty waters rolling evermore.

x

Then sing, ye Birds, sing, sing, a joyous song!
    And let the young Lambs bound
    As to the tabor's sound!
We in thought will join your throng,
    Ye that pipe and ye that play,
    Ye that through your hearts today
    Feel the gladness of the May!
What though the radiance which was once so bright

Be now for ever taken from my sight,
    Though nothing can bring back the hour
Of splendour in the grass, of glory in the flower;
        We will grieve not, rather find
        Strength in what remains behind;
        In the primal sympathy
        Which having been must ever be;
        In the soothing thoughts that spring
        Out of human suffering;
        In the faith that looks through death,
In years that bring the philosophic mind.

XI

And O, ye Fountains, Meadows, Hills, and Groves,
Forebode not any severing of our loves!
Yet in my heart of hearts I feel your might;
I only have relinquished one delight
To live beneath your more habitual sway.
I love the Brooks which down their channels fret,
Even more than when I tripped lightly as they;
The innocent brightness of a new-born Day
        Is lovely yet;
The Clouds that gather round the setting sun
Do take a sober colouring from an eye
That hath kept watch o'er man's mortality;
Another race hath been, and other palms are won.
Thanks to the human heart by which we live,
Thanks to its tenderness, its joys, and fears,
To me the meanest flower that blows can give
Thoughts that do often lie too deep for tears.

   Written in the period between 1803 (1802?) and 1806; published in 1807. It is
exceedingly important to realize that the poem is, in effect, an "answer" to Coleridge's
Ode on Dejection. A comparison of the two pieces, with respect to ideas, form, and
verbal echoes, is illuminating. Wordsworth's own note is as follows:
   "This was composed during my residence at Town-end, Grasmere. Two years at
least passed between the writing of the four first stanzas and the remaining part. To
the attentive and competent reader the whole sufficiently explains itself; but there may
be no harm in adverting here to particular feelings or *experiences* of my own mind
on which the structure of the poem partly rests. Nothing was more difficult for me
in childhood than to admit the notion of death as a state applicable to my own being.
I have said elsewhere—
            A simple child,
        That lightly draws its breath,
        And feels its life in every limb,
        What should it know of death!—

She Was a Phantom of Delight

SHE was a Phantom of delight
When first she gleamed upon my sight;
A lovely Apparition, sent
To be a moment's ornament;
Her eyes as stars of Twilight fair;
Like Twilight's, too, her dusky hair;
But all things else about her drawn
From May-time and the cheerful Dawn;
A dancing Shape, an Image gay,
To haunt, to startle, and way-lay.

I saw her upon nearer view,
A Spirit, yet a Woman too!
Her household motions light and free,
And steps of virgin-liberty;

But it was not so much from feelings of animal vivacity that *my* difficulty came as from a sense of the indomitableness of the Spirit within me. I used to brood over the stories of Enoch and Elijah, and almost to persuade myself that, whatever might become of others, I should be translated, in something of the same way, to heaven. With a feeling congenial to this, I was often unable to think of external things as having external existence, and I communed with all that I saw as something not apart from, but inherent in, my own immaterial nature. Many times while going to school have I grasped at a wall or tree to recall myself from this abyss of idealism to the reality. At that time I was afraid of such processes. In later periods of life I have deplored, as we have all reason to do, a subjugation of an opposite character, and have rejoiced over the remembrances, as is expressed in the lines—

> Obstinate questionings
> Of sense and outward things,
> Fallings from us, vanishings, etc.

To that dream-like vividness and splendour which invest objects of sight in childhood, every one, I believe, if he would look back, could bear testimony, and I need not dwell upon it here: but having in the poem regarded it as presumptive evidence of a prior state of existence, I think it right to protest against a conclusion, which has given pain to some good and pious persons, that I meant to inculcate such a belief. It is far too shadowy a notion to be recommended to faith, as more than an element in our instincts of immortality. But let us bear in mind that, though the idea is not advanced in revelation, there is nothing there to contradict it, and the fall of Man presents an analogy in its favor. Accordingly, a pre-existent state has entered into the popular creeds of many nations; and, among all persons acquainted with classic literature, is known as an ingredient in Platonic philosophy. Archimedes said that he could move the world if he had a point whereon to rest his machine. Who has not felt the same aspirations as regards the world of his own mind? Having to wield some of its elements when I was impelled to write this poem on the 'Immortality of the Soul,' I took hold of the notion of pre-existence as having sufficient foundation in humanity for authorising me to make for my purpose the best use of it I could as a poet."

A countenance in which did meet
Sweet records, promises as sweet;
A Creature not too bright or good
For human nature's daily food;
For transient sorrows, simple wiles,
Praise, blame, love, kisses, tears, and smiles.

And now I see with eye serene
The very pulse of the machine;
A Being breathing thoughtful breath,
A Traveller between life and death;
The reason firm, the temperate will,
Endurance, foresight, strength, and skill;
A perfect Woman, nobly planned,
To warn, to comfort, and command;
And yet a Spirit still, and bright
With something of angelic light.

The World Is Too Much with Us

THE world is too much with us: late and soon,
   Getting and spending, we lay waste our powers:
Little we see in Nature that is ours;
We have given our hearts away, a sordid boon!
This Sea that bares her bosom to the moon;
The winds that will be howling at all hours,
And are up-gathered now like sleeping flowers;
For this, for everything, we are out of tune;
It moves us not.—Great God! I'd rather be
A Pagan suckled in a creed outworn;
So might I, standing on this pleasant lea,
Have glimpses that would make me less forlorn;
Have sight of Proteus rising from the sea;
Or hear old Triton blow his wreathèd horn.

SIR WALTER SCOTT

Coronach

FROM "THE CROSS OF FIRE"

HE is gone on the mountain,
    He is lost to the forest,
Like a summer-dried fountain,
    When our need was the sorest.
The font, reappearing,
    From the rain-drops shall borrow,
But to us comes no cheering,
    To Duncan no morrow!

The hand of the reaper
    Takes the ears that are hoary,
But the voice of the weeper
    Wails manhood in glory.
The autumn winds rushing
    Waft the leaves that are searest,
But our flower was in flushing,
    When blighting was nearest.

Fleet foot on the correi,
    Sage counsel in cumber,
Red hand in the foray,
    How sound is thy slumber!
Like the dew on the mountain,
    Like the foam on the river,
Like the bubble on the fountain,
    Thou art gone, and for ever!

MacGregor's Gathering

THE moon's on the lake, and the mist's on the brae,
And the Clan has a name that is nameless by day;
   Then gather, gather, gather, Grigalach!
   Gather, gather, gather, etc.

Our signal for fight, that from monarchs we drew,
Must be heard but by night in our vengeful haloo!
   Then haloo, Grigalach! haloo, Grigalach!
   Haloo, haloo, haloo, Grigalach, etc.

Glen Orchy's proud mountains, Coalchuirn and her towers,
Glenstrae and Glenlyon no longer are ours;
   We're landless, landless, landless, Grigalach!
   Landless, landless, landless, etc.

But doom'd and devoted by vassal and lord,
MacGregor has still both his heart and his sword!
   Then courage, courage, courage, Grigalach!
   Courage, courage, courage, etc.

If they rob us of name, and pursue us with beagles,
Give their roofs to the flame, and their flesh to the eagles!
   Then vengeance, vengeance, vengeance, Grigalach!
   Vengeance, vengeance, vengeance, etc.

While there's leaves in the forest, and foam on the river,
MacGregor, despite them, shall flourish for ever!
   Come then, Grigalach, come then, Grigalach!
   Come then, come then, come then, etc.

Through the depths of Loch Katrine the steed shall career,
O'er the peak of Ben-Lomond the galley shall steer,
And the rocks of Craig-Royston like icicles melt,
Ere our wrongs be forgot, or our vengeance unfelt!
   Then gather, gather, gather, Grigalach!
   Gather, gather, gather, etc.

Sound, Sound the Clarion

SOUND, sound the clarion, fill the fife!
　To all the sensual world proclaim,
One crowded hour of glorious life
　Is worth an age without a name.

SAMUEL TAYLOR COLERIDGE

The Rime of the Ancient Mariner

PART I

*An ancient Mariner
meeteth three Gal-
lants bidden to a
wedding-feast, and
detaineth one.*

IT is an ancient Mariner,
　And he stoppeth one of three.
"By thy long grey beard and glittering eye,
Now wherefore stopp'st thou me?

The Bridegroom's doors are opened wide,
And I am next of kin;
The guests are met, the feast is set:
May'st hear the merry din."

He holds him with his skinny hand,
"There was a ship," quoth he.
"Hold off! unhand me, grey-beard loon!"
Eftsoons his hand dropt he.

*The Wedding-Guest
is spell-bound by the
eye of the old sea-
faring man, and con-
strained to hear his
tale.*

He holds him with his glittering eye—
The Wedding-Guest stood still,
And listens like a three years' child:
The Mariner hath his will.

The Wedding-Guest sat on a stone:
He cannot choose but hear;
And thus spake on that ancient man,
The bright-eyed Mariner.

"The ship was cheered, the harbour cleared,
Merrily did we drop
Below the kirk, below the hill,
Below the lighthouse top.

The Sun came up upon the left,
Out of the sea came he!
And he shone bright, and on the right
Went down into the sea.

Higher and higher every day,
Till over the mast at noon—"
The Wedding-Guest here beat his breast,
For he heard the loud bassoon.

The bride hath paced into the hall,
Red as a rose is she;
Nodding their heads before her goes
The merry minstrelsy.

The Wedding-Guest he beat his breast,
Yet he cannot choose but hear;
And thus spake on that ancient man,
The bright-eyed Mariner.

"And now the STORM-BLAST came, and he
Was tyrannous and strong:
He struck with his o'ertaking wings,
And chased us south along.

With sloping masts and dipping prow,
As who pursued with yell and blow
Still treads the shadow of his foe,
And forward bends his head,
The ship drove fast, loud roared the blast,
And southward aye we fled.

And now there came both mist and snow,
And it grew wondrous cold:
And ice, mast-high, came floating by,
As green as emerald.

The land of ice, and
of fearful sounds
where no living
thing was to be seen.

And through the drifts the snowy clifts
Did send a dismal sheen:
Nor shapes of men nor beasts we ken—
The ice was all between.

The ice was here, the ice was there,
The ice was all around:
It cracked and growled, and roared and howled,
Like noises in a swound!

Till a great sea-bird,
called the Albatross,
came through the
snow-fog, and was
received with great
joy and hospitality.

At length did cross an Albatross,
Thorough the fog it came;
As if it had been a Christian soul,
We hailed it in God's name.

It ate the food it ne'er had eat,
And round and round it flew.
The ice did split with a thunder-fit;
The helmsman steered us through!

And lo! the Albatross
proveth a bird of
good omen, and fol-
loweth the ship as it
returned northward
through fog and float-
ing ice.

And a good south wind sprung up behind;
The Albatross did follow,
And every day, for food or play,
Came to the mariners' hollo!

In mist or cloud, on mast or shroud,
It perched for vespers nine;
Whiles all the night, through fog-smoke white,
Glimmered the white Moon-shine."

The ancient Mariner
inhospitably killeth
the pious bird of good
omen.

"God save thee, ancient Mariner!
From the fiends, that plague thee thus!—
Why look'st thou so?"—With my cross-bow
I shot the ALBATROSS.

PART II

The Sun now rose upon the right:
Out of the sea came he,
Still hid in mist, and on the left
Went down into the sea.

And the good south wind still blew behind,
But no sweet bird did follow,
Nor any day for food or play
Came to the mariners' hollo!

And I had done a hellish thing,
And it would work 'em woe:
For all averred, I had killed the bird
That made the breeze to blow.
Ah wretch! said they, the bird to slay,
That made the breeze to blow!

Nor dim nor red, like God's own head,
The glorious Sun uprist:
Then all averred, I had killed the bird
That brought the fog and mist.
'Twas right, said they, such birds to slay,
That bring the fog and mist.

The fair breeze blew, the white foam flew,
The furrow followed free;
We were the first that ever burst
Into that silent sea.

Down dropt the breeze, the sails dropt down,
'Twas sad as sad could be;
And we did speak only to break
The silence of the sea!

All in a hot and copper sky,
The bloody Sun, at noon,
Right up above the mast did stand,
No bigger than the Moon.

Day after day, day after day,
We stuck, nor breath nor motion;
As idle as a painted ship
Upon a painted ocean.

Water, water, every where,
And all the boards did shrink;
Water, water, every where,
Nor any drop to drink.

The very deep did rot: O Christ!
That ever this should be!
Yea, slimy things did crawl with legs
Upon the slimy sea.

About, about, in reel and rout
The death-fires danced at night;
The water, like a witch's oils,
Burnt green, and blue and white.

A Spirit had followed them; one of the invisible inhabitants of this planet, neither departed souls nor angels; concerning whom the learned Jew, Josephus, and the Platonic Constantinopolitan, Michael Psellus, may be consulted. They are very numerous, and there is no climate or element without one or more.

And some in dreams assuréd were
Of the Spirit that plagued us so;
Nine fathoms deep he had followed us
From the land of mist and snow.

And every tongue, through utter drought,
Was withered at the root;
We could not speak, no more than if
We had been choked with soot.

The shipmates, in their sore distress, would fain throw the whole guilt on the ancient Mariner: in sign whereof they hang the dead sea-bird round his neck.

Ah! well a-day! what evil looks
Had I from old and young!
Instead of the cross, the Albatross
About my neck was hung.

PART III

There passed a weary time. Each throat
Was parched, and glazed each eye.
A weary time! a weary time!
How glazed each weary eye,
When looking westward, I beheld
A something in the sky.

The ancient Mariner beholdeth a sign in the element afar off.

At first it seemed a little speck,
And then it seemed a mist;
It moved and moved, and took at last
A certain shape, I wist.[1]

A speck, a mist, a shape, I wist!
And still it neared and neared:

[1] believed, knew

As if it dodged a water-sprite,
It plunged and tacked and veered.

At its nearer ap-
proach, it seemeth
him to be a ship; and
at a dear ransom he
freeth his speech
from the bonds of
thirst.

With throats unslaked, with black lips baked,
We could nor laugh nor wail;
Through utter drought all dumb we stood!
I bit my arm, I sucked the blood,
And cried, A sail! a sail!

With throats unslaked, with black lips baked,
Agape they heard me call:

A flash of joy;

Gramercy! they for joy did grin,
And all at once their breath drew in,
As they were drinking all.

And horror follows.
For can it be a ship
that comes onward
without wind or
tide?

See! see! (I cried) she tacks no more!
Hither to work us weal;
Without a breeze, without a tide,
She steadies with upright keel!

The western wave was all a-flame.
The day was well nigh done!
Almost upon the western wave
Rested the broad bright Sun;
When that strange shape drove suddenly
Betwixt us and the Sun.

It seemeth him but
the skeleton of a
ship.

And straight the Sun was flecked with bars,
(Heaven's Mother send us grace!)
As if through a dungeon-grate he peered
With broad and burning face.

And its ribs are
seen as bars on the
face of the setting
Sun.

Alas! (thought I, and my heart beat loud)
How fast she nears and nears!
Are those *her* sails that glance in the Sun,
Like restless gossameres?

The Spectre-Woman
and her Death-mate,
and no other on
board the skeleton
ship.

Are those *her* ribs through which the Sun
Did peer, as through a grate?
And is that Woman all her crew?
Is that a DEATH? and are there two?
Is DEATH that woman's mate?

Her lips were red, *her* looks were free,
Her locks were yellow as gold:
Her skin was as white as leprosy,
The Night-mare LIFE-IN-DEATH was she,
Who thicks man's blood with cold.

The naked hulk alongside came,
And the twain were casting dice;
"The game is done! I've won! I've won!"
Quoth she, and whistles thrice.

The Sun's rim dips; the stars rush out:
At one stride comes the dark;
With far-heard whisper, o'er the sea,
Off shot the spectre-bark.

We listened and looked sideways up!
Fear at my heart, as at a cup,
My life-blood seemed to sip!
The stars were dim, and thick the night,
The steersman's face by his lamp gleamed white;
From the sails the dew did drip—
Till clomb above the eastern bar
The hornéd Moon, with one bright star
Within the nether tip.

One after one, by the star-dogged Moon,
Too quick for groan or sigh,
Each turned his face with a ghastly pang,
And cursed me with his eye.

Four times fifty living men,
(And I heard nor sigh nor groan)
With heavy thump, a lifeless lump,
They dropped down one by one.

The souls did from their bodies fly,—
They fled to bliss or woe!
And every soul, it passed me by,
Like the whizz of my cross-bow!

PART IV

The Wedding-Guest
feareth that a Spirit
is talking to him;

"I fear thee, ancient Mariner!
I fear thy skinny hand!
And thou art long, and lank, and brown,
As is the ribbed sea-sand.[2]

I fear thee and thy glittering eye,
And thy skinny hand, so brown."—

But the ancient
Mariner assureth him
of his bodily life, and
proceedeth to relate
his horrible penance.

Fear not, fear not, thou Wedding-Guest!
This body dropt not down.

Alone, alone, all, all alone,
Alone on a wide wide sea!
And never a saint took pity on
My soul in agony.

He despiseth the
creatures of the calm,

The many men, so beautiful!
And they all dead did lie:
And a thousand thousand slimy things
Lived on; and so did I.

And envieth that
they should live, and
so many lie dead.

I looked upon the rotting sea,
And drew my eyes away;
I looked upon the rotting deck,
And there the dead men lay.

I looked to heaven, and tried to pray;
But or ever a prayer had gusht,
A wicked whisper came, and made
My heart as dry as dust.

I closed my lids, and kept them close,
And the balls like pulses beat;
For the sky and the sea, and the sea and the sky
Lay like a load on my weary eye,
And the dead were at my feet.

[2] For the last two lines of this stanza, I am indebted to Mr. WORDSWORTH. It was on a delightful walk from Nether Stowey to Dulverton, with him and his sister, in the Autumn of 1797, that this Poem was planned, and in part composed. [Coleridge.]

*But the curse liveth
for him in the eye of
the dead men.*

The cold sweat melted from their limbs,
Nor rot nor reek did they:
The look with which they looked on me
Had never passed away.

An orphan's curse would drag to hell
A spirit from on high;
But oh! more horrible than that
Is the curse in a dead man's eye!
Seven days, seven nights, I saw that curse,
And yet I could not die.

*In his loneliness and
fixedness he yearneth
towards the journey-
ing Moon, and the
stars that still sojourn,
yet still move onward,
and every where the
blue sky belongs to
them, and is their ap-
pointed rest, and their
native country and
their own natural
homes, which they
enter unannounced,
as lords that are cer-
tainly expected and
yet there is a silent
joy at their arrival.*

The moving Moon went up the sky,
And no where did abide:
Softly she was going up,
And a star or two beside—

Her beams bemocked the sultry main,
Like April hoar-frost spread;
But where the ship's huge shadow lay,
The charmèd water burnt alway
A still and awful red.

*By the light of the
Moon he beholdeth
God's creatures of the
great calm.*

Beyond the shadow of the ship,
I watched the water-snakes:
They moved in tracks of shining white,
And when they reared, the elfish light
Fell off in hoary flakes.

Within the shadow of the ship
I watched their rich attire:
Blue, glossy green, and velvet black,
They coiled and swam; and every track
Was a flash of golden fire.

*Their beauty and
their happiness.*

*He blesseth them in
his heart.*

O happy living things! no tongue
Their beauty might declare:
A spring of love gushed from my heart,
And I blessed them unaware:
Sure my kind saint took pity on me,
And I blessed them unaware.

The spell begins to break.

The self-same moment I could pray;
And from my neck so free
The Albatross fell off, and sank
Like lead into the sea.

PART V

Oh sleep! it is a gentle thing,
Beloved from pole to pole!
To Mary Queen the praise be given!
She sent the gentle sleep from Heaven,
That slid into my soul.

By grace of the holy Mother, the ancient Mariner is refreshed with rain.

The silly buckets on the deck,
That had so long remained,
I dreamt that they were filled with dew;
And when I awoke, it rained.

My lips were wet, my throat was cold,
My garments all were dank;
Sure I had drunken in my dreams,
And still my body drank.

I moved, and could not feel my limbs:
I was so light—almost
I thought that I had died in sleep,
And was a blessèd ghost.

He heareth sounds and seeth strange sights and commotions in the sky and the element.

And soon I heard a roaring wind:
It did not come anear;
But with its sound it shook the sails,
That were so thin and sere.

The upper air burst into life!
And a hundred fire-flags sheen,[3]
To and fro they were hurried about!
And to and fro, and in and out,
The wan stars danced between.

And the coming wind did roar more loud,
And the sails did sigh like sedge;

[3] bright

And the rain poured down from one black cloud;
The Moon was at its edge.

The thick black cloud was cleft, and still
The Moon was at its side:
Like waters shot from some high crag,
The lightning fell with never a jag,
A river steep and wide.

The bodies of the
ship's crew are in-
spired [*inspirited,*
S. L.] *and the ship*
moves on;

The loud wind never reached the ship,
Yet now the ship moved on!
Beneath the lightning and the Moon
The dead men gave a groan.

They groaned, they stirred, they all uprose,
Nor spake, nor moved their eyes;
It had been strange, even in a dream,
To have seen those dead men rise.

The helmsman steered, the ship moved on;
Yet never a breeze up-blew;
The mariners all 'gan work the ropes,
Where they were wont to do;
They raised their limbs like lifeless tools—
We were a ghastly crew.

The body of my brother's son
Stood by me, knee to knee:
The body and I pulled at one rope,
But he said nought to me.[4]

But not by the souls
of the men, nor by
dæmons of earth or
middle air, but by a
blessed troop of
angelic spirits, sent
down by the in-
vocation of the
guardian saint.

"I fear thee, ancient Mariner!"
Be calm, thou Wedding-Guest!
'Twas not those souls that fled in pain,
Which to their corses came again,
But a troop of spirits blest:

For when it dawned—they dropped their arms,
And clustered round the mast;

[4] After this line there originally followed these two lines:
    "And I quak'd to think of my own voice
      How frightful it would be!"

Sweet sounds rose slowly through their mouths,
And from their bodies passed.

Around, around, flew each sweet sound,
Then darted to the Sun;
Slowly the sounds came back again,
Now mixed, now one by one.

Sometimes a-dropping from the sky
I heard the sky-lark sing;
Sometimes all little birds that are,
How they seemed to fill the sea and air
With their sweet jargoning!

And now 'twas like all instruments,
Now like a lonely flute;
And now it is an angel's song,
That makes the heavens be mute.

It ceased; yet still the sails made on
A pleasant noise till noon,
A noise like of a hidden brook
In the leafy month of June,
That to the sleeping woods all night
Singeth a quiet tune.

Till noon we quietly sailed on,
Yet never a breeze did breathe:
Slowly and smoothly went the ship,
Moved onward from beneath.

The lonesome Spirit from the south-pole carries on the ship as far as the Line, in obedience to the angelic troop, but still requireth vengeance.

Under the keel nine fathom deep,
From the land of mist and snow,
The spirit slid: and it was he
That made the ship to go.
The sails at noon left off their tune,
And the ship stood still also.

The Sun, right up above the mast,
Had fixed her to the ocean:
But in a minute she 'gan stir,
With a short uneasy motion—

Backwards and forwards half her length
With a short uneasy motion.

Then like a pawing horse let go,
She made a sudden bound:
It flung the blood into my head,
And I fell down in a swound.

How long in that same fit I lay,
I have not to declare;
But ere my living life returned,
I heard and in my soul discerned
Two voices in the air.

"Is it he?" quoth one, "Is this the man?
By him who died on cross,
With his cruel bow he laid full low
The armless Albatross.

The spirit who bideth by himself
In the land of mist and snow,
He loved the bird that loved the man
Who shot him with his bow."

The other was a softer voice,
As soft as honey-dew:
Quoth he, "The man hath penance done,
And penance more will do."

PART VI

FIRST VOICE

"But tell me, tell me! speak again,
Thy soft response renewing—
What makes that ship drive on so fast?
What is the ocean doing?"

SECOND VOICE

"Still as a slave before his lord,
The ocean hath no blast;
His great bright eye most silently
Up to the Moon is cast—

If he may know which way to go;
For she guides him smooth or grim.
See, brother, see! how graciously
She looketh down on him."

FIRST VOICE

The Mariner hath been cast into a trance; for the angelic power causeth the vessel to drive northward faster than human life could endure.

"But why drives on that ship so fast,
Without or wave or wind?"

SECOND VOICE

"The air is cut away before,
And closes from behind.

Fly, brother, fly! more high, more high!
Or we shall be belated:
For slow and slow that ship will go,
When the Mariner's trance is abated."

The supernatural motion is retarded; the Mariner awakes, and his penance begins anew.

I woke, and we were sailing on
As in a gentle weather:
'Twas night, calm night, the moon was high;
The dead men stood together.

All stood together on the deck,
For a charnel-dungeon fitter:
All fixed on me their stony eyes,
That in the Moon did glitter.

The pang, the curse, with which they died,
Had never passed away:
I could not draw my eyes from theirs,
Nor turn them up to pray.

The curse is finally expiated.

And now this spell was snapt: once more
I viewed the ocean green,
And looked far forth, yet little saw
Of what had else been seen—

Like one, that on a lonesome road
Doth walk in fear and dread,
And having once turned round walks on,

And turns no more his head;
Because he knows, a frightful fiend
Doth close behind him tread.

But soon there breathed a wind on me,
Nor sound nor motion made:
Its path was not upon the sea,
In ripple or in shade.

It raised my hair, it fanned my cheek
Like a meadow-gale of spring—
It mingled strangely with my fears,
Yet it felt like a welcoming.

Swiftly, swiftly flew the ship,
Yet she sailed softly too:
Sweetly, sweetly blew the breeze—
On me alone it blew.

*And the ancient
Mariner beholdeth his
native country.*

Oh! dream of joy! is this indeed
The light-house top I see?
Is this the hill? is this the kirk?
Is this mine own countree?

We drifted o'er the harbour-bar,
And I with sobs did pray—
O let me be awake, my God!
Or let me sleep alway.

The harbour-bay was clear as glass,
So smoothly it was strewn!
And on the bay the moonlight lay,
And the shadow of the Moon.

The rock shone bright, the kirk no less,
That stands above the rock:
The moonlight steeped in silentness
The steady weathercock.

*The angelic spirits
leave the dead bodies,*

And the bay was white with silent light,
Till rising from the same,
Full many shapes, that shadows were,
In crimson colours came.

A little distance from the prow
Those crimson shadows were:
I turned my eyes upon the deck—
Oh, Christ! what saw I there!

Each corse lay flat, lifeless and flat,
And, by the holy rood!
A man all light, a seraph-man,
On every corse there stood.

This seraph-band, each waved his hand:
It was a heavenly sight!
They stood as signals to the land,
Each one a lovely light;

This seraph-band, each waved his hand,
No voice did they impart—
No voice; but oh! the silence sank
Like music on my heart.

But soon I heard the dash of oars,
I heard the Pilot's cheer;
My head was turned perforce away
And I saw a boat appear.

The Pilot and the Pilot's boy,
I heard them coming fast:
Dear Lord in Heaven! it was a joy
The dead men could not blast.

I saw a third—I heard his voice:
It is the Hermit good!
He singeth loud his godly hymns
That he makes in the wood.
He'll shrieve my soul, he'll wash away
The Albatross's blood.

PART VII

This Hermit good lives in that wood
Which slopes down to the sea.
How loudly his sweet voice he rears!
He loves to talk with marineres
That come from a far countree.

He kneels at morn, and noon, and eve—
He hath a cushion plump:
It is the moss that wholly hides
The rotted old oak-stump.

The skiff-boat neared: I heard them talk,
"Why, this is strange, I trow!
Where are those lights so many and fair,
That signal made but now?"

Approacheth the ship with wonder.

"Strange, by my faith!" the Hermit said—
"And they answered not our cheer!
The planks looked warped! and see those sails,
How thin they are and sere!
I never saw aught like to them,
Unless perchance it were

Brown skeletons of leaves that lag
My forest-brook along;
When the ivy-tod[5] is heavy with snow,
And the owlet whoops to the wolf below,
That eats the she-wolf's young."

"Dear Lord! it hath a fiendish look—
(The Pilot made reply)
I am a-feared"—"Push on, push on!"
Said the Hermit cheerily.

The boat came closer to the ship,
But I nor spake nor stirred;
The boat came close beneath the ship,
And straight a sound was heard.

The ship suddenly sinketh.

Under the water it rumbled on,
Still louder and more dread:
It reached the ship, it split the bay;
The ship went down like lead.

The ancient Mariner is saved in the Pilot's boat.

Stunned by that loud and dreadful sound,
Which sky and ocean smote,
Like one that hath been seven days drowned

[5] ivy-bush

My body lay afloat;
But swift as dreams, myself I found
Within the Pilot's boat.

Upon the whirl, where sank the ship,
The boat spun round and round;
And all was still, save that the hill
Was telling of the sound.

I moved my lips—the Pilot shrieked
And fell down in a fit;
The holy Hermit raised his eyes,
And prayed where he did sit.

I took the oars: the Pilot's boy,
Who now doth crazy go,
Laughed loud and long, and all the while
His eyes went to and fro.
"Ha! ha!" quoth he, "full plain I see,
The Devil knows how to row."

And now, all in my own countree,
I stood on the firm land!
The Hermit stepped forth from the boat,
And scarcely he could stand.

The ancient Mariner earnestly entreateth the Hermit to shrieve him; and the penance of life falls on him.

"O shrieve me, shrieve me, holy man!"
The Hermit crossed his brow.
"Say quick," quoth he, "I bid thee say—
What manner of man art thou?"

Forthwith this frame of mine was wrenched
With a woful agony,
Which forced me to begin my tale;
And then it left me free.

And ever and anon through out his future life an agony constraineth him to travel from land to land;

Since then, at an uncertain hour,
That agony returns:
And till my ghastly tale is told,
This heart within me burns.

I pass, like night, from land to land;
I have strange power of speech;

That moment that his face I see,
I know the man that must hear me:
To him my tale I teach.

What loud uproar bursts from that door!
The wedding-guests are there:
But in the garden-bower the bride
And bride-maids singing are:
And hark the little vesper bell,
Which biddeth me to prayer!

O Wedding-Guest! this soul hath been
Alone on a wide wide sea:
So lonely 'twas, that God himself
Scarce seeméd there to be.

O sweeter than the marriage-feast,
'Tis sweeter far to me,
To walk together to the kirk
With a goodly company!—

To walk together to the kirk,
And all together pray,
While each to his great Father bends,
Old men, and babes, and loving friends
And youths and maidens gay!

And to teach, by his own example, love and reverence to all things that God made and loveth.

Farewell, farewell! but this I tell
To thee, thou Wedding-Guest!
He prayeth well, who loveth well
Both man and bird and beast.

He prayeth best, who loveth best
All things both great and small;
For the dear God who loveth us,
He made and loveth all.

The Mariner, whose eye is bright,
Whose beard with age is hoar,
Is gone: and now the Wedding-Guest
Turned from the bridegroom's door.

He went like one that hath been stunned,
And is of sense forlorn:
A sadder and a wiser man,
He rose the morrow morn.

Kubla Khan

IN Xanadu did Kubla Khan
A stately pleasure-dome decree:
Where Alph, the sacred river, ran
Through caverns measureless to man
  Down to a sunless sea.
So twice five miles of fertile ground
With walls and towers were girdled round:
And there were gardens bright with sinuous rills,
Where blossomed many an incense-bearing tree;
And here were forests ancient as the hills,
Enfolding sunny spots of greenery.

But oh! that deep romantic chasm which slanted
Down the green hill athwart a cedarn cover!
A savage place! as holy and enchanted
As e'er beneath a waning moon was haunted
By woman wailing for her demon-lover!
And from this chasm, with ceaseless turmoil seething,
As if this earth in fast thick pants were breathing,
A mighty fountain momently was forced:
Amid whose swift half-intermitted burst
Huge fragments vaulted like rebounding hail,
Or chaffy grain beneath the thresher's flail:
And 'mid these dancing rocks at once and ever
It flung up momently the sacred river.
Five miles meandering with a mazy motion
Through wood and dale the sacred river ran,
Then reached the caverns measureless to man,
And sank in tumult to a lifeless ocean:
And 'mid this tumult Kubla heard from far
Ancestral voices prophesying war!

The shadow of the dome of pleasure
  Floated midway on the waves;

Where was heard the mingled measure
From the fountain and the caves.
It was a miracle of rare device,
A sunny pleasure-dome with caves of ice!

A damsel with a dulcimer
In a vision once I saw:
It was an Abyssinian maid,
And on her dulcimer she played,
Singing of Mount Abora.
Could I revive within me
Her symphony and song,
To such a deep delight 'twould win me,
That with music loud and long,
I would build that dome in air,
That sunny dome! those caves of ice!
And all who heard should see them there,
And all should cry, Beware! Beware!
His flashing eyes, his floating hair!
Weave a circle round him thrice,
And close your eyes with holy dread,
For he on honey-dew hath fed,
And drunk the milk of Paradise.

———•—•—•———

JOSEPH BLANCO WHITE

———•—•—•———

Mysterious Night

MYSTERIOUS Night, when our first parent knew
Thee from report divine, and heard thy name,
Did he not tremble for this lovely frame,
This glorious canopy of light and blue?
Yet neath a curtain of translucent dew,
Bathed in the rays of the great setting flame,
Hesperus with the host of heaven came,
And lo, creation widen'd in man's view.
Who could have thought such darkness lay conceal'd
Within thy beams, O Sun! Or who could find,

Whilst fly and leaf and insect stood reveal'd,
That to such countless orbs thou mad'st us blind!
Why do we then shun Death with anxious strife?
If Light can thus deceive, wherefore not Life?

WALTER SAVAGE LANDOR

Rose Aylmer[1]

AH, what avails the sceptred race,
   Ah, what the form divine!
What every virtue, every grace!
   Rose Aylmer, all were thine.
Rose Aylmer, whom these wakeful eyes
   May weep, but never see,
A night of memories and of sighs
   I consecrate to thee.

On Seeing a Hair of Lucretia Borgia

BORGIA, thou once wert almost too august
   And high for adoration; now thou'rt dust;
All that remains of thee these plaits unfold,
Calm hair, meandering in pellucid gold.

Past ruin'd Ilion Helen lives

PAST ruin'd Ilion Helen lives,
   Alcestis rises from the shades;
Verse calls them forth; 'tis verse that gives
   Immortal youth to mortal maids.

[1] This and the following poem were published in *Simonidea,* 1806. It was inspired
by news of the death in India of Rose, the daughter of Henry, Baron Aylmer, who
had been Landor's devoted friend during the poet's early years in Wales, 1795-1798.

Soon shall Oblivion's deepening veil
Hide all the peopled hills you see,
The gay, the proud, while lovers hail
These many summers you and me.

Dirce

STAND close around, ye Stygian set,
With Dirce in one boat convey'd!
Or Charon, seeing, may forget
That he is old and she a shade.

Death Stands above Me

DEATH stands above me, whispering low
I know not what into my ear:
Of his strange language all I know
Is, there is not a word of fear.

On His Seventy-fifth Birthday

I STROVE with none; for none was worth my strife,
Nature I loved, and next to Nature, Art;
I warmed both hands before the fire of life,
It sinks, and I am ready to depart.

THOMAS MOORE

The Harp That Once through Tara's Halls

THE harp that once through Tara's[1] halls
The soul of music shed,
Now hangs as mute on Tara's walls,
As if that soul were fled.—

[1] Tara, near Dublin, was a residence of the early Irish kings.

So sleeps the pride of former days,
  So glory's thrill is o'er,
And hearts, that once beat high for praise,
  Now feel that pulse no more.

No more to chiefs and ladies bright
  The harp of Tara swells;
The chord alone, that breaks at night,
  Its tale of ruin tells.
Thus Freedom now so seldom wakes,
  The only throb she gives,
Is when some heart indignant breaks,
  To show that still she lives.

Believe Me, If All Those Endearing Young Charms

BELIEVE me, if all those endearing young charms,
  Which I gaze on so fondly today,
Were to change by tomorrow, and fleet in my arms,
  Like fairy-gifts fading away,
Thou wouldst still be adored, as this moment thou art,
  Let thy loveliness fade as it will,
And around the dear ruin each wish of my heart
  Would entwine itself verdantly still.

It is not while beauty and youth are thine own,
  And thy cheeks unprofaned by a tear,
That the fervour and faith of a soul can be known,
  To which time will but make thee more dear;
No, the heart that has truly loved never forgets,
  But as truly loves on to the close,
As the sun-flower turns on her god, when he sets,
  The same look which she turned when he rose.

Oft, in the Stilly Night

OFT, in the stilly night,
  Ere Slumber's chain has bound me,
Fond Memory brings the light
  Of other days around me;

The smiles, the tears,
Of boyhood's years,
The words of love then spoken;
The eyes that shone,
Now dimm'd and gone,
The cheerful hearts now broken!
Thus, in the stilly night,
Ere Slumber's chain has bound me,
Sad Memory brings the light
Of other days around me.

When I remember all
The friends, so link'd together,
I've seen around me fall,
Like leaves in wintry weather;
I feel like one
Who treads alone
Some banquet-hall deserted,
Whose lights are fled,
Whose garlands dead,
And all but he departed!
Thus, in the stilly night,
Ere Slumber's chain has bound me,
Sad Memory brings the light
Of other days around me.

GEORGE GORDON NOEL, LORD BYRON

Childe Harold's Pilgrimage

CANTO III

XXI

THERE was a sound of revelry by night,
And Belgium's capital had gather'd then
Her Beauty and her Chivalry, and bright
The lamps shone o'er fair women and brave men;

A thousand hearts beat happily; and when
Music arose with its voluptuous swell,
Soft eyes look'd love to eyes which spake again,
And all went merry as a marriage bell;
But hush! hark! a deep sound strikes like a rising knell!

XXII

Did ye not hear it?—No; 't was but the wind,
Or the car rattling o'er the stony street;
On with the dance! let joy be unconfined;
No sleep till morn, when Youth and Pleasure meet
To chase the glowing Hours with flying feet—
But hark!—that heavy sound breaks in once more,
As if the clouds its echo would repeat;
And nearer, clearer, deadlier than before!
Arm! Arm! it is—it is—the cannon's opening roar!

XXIII

Within a window'd niche of that high hall
Sate Brunswick's fated chieftain;[1] he did hear
That sound the first amidst the festival,
And caught its tone with Death's prophetic ear;
And when they smiled because he deem'd it near,
His heart more truly knew that peal too well
Which stretch'd his father on a bloody bier,
And roused the vengeance blood alone could quell;
He rush'd into the field, and, foremost fighting, fell.

XXIV

Ah! then and there was hurrying to and fro,
And gathering tears, and tremblings of distress,
And cheeks all pale, which but an hour ago
Blush'd at the praise of their own loveliness;
And there were sudden partings, such as press
The life from out young hearts, and choking sighs
Which ne'er might be repeated; who could guess
If ever more should meet those mutual eyes,
Since upon night so sweet such awful morn could rise!

[1] Frederick William, Duke of Brunswick, who fell in the first part of the battle. His father had been killed in 1806.

XXV

And there was mounting in hot haste: the steed,
The mustering squadron, and the clattering car,
Went pouring forward with impetuous speed,
And swiftly forming in the ranks of war;
And the deep thunder peal on peal afar;
And near, the beat of the alarming drum
Roused up the soldier ere the morning star;
While thronged the citizens with terror dumb,
Or whispering, with white lips—"The foe! they come! they come!"

XXVI

And wild and high the "Cameron's gathering" rose!
The war-note of Lochiel, which Albyn's hills
Have heard, and heard, too, have her Saxon foes:—
How in the noon of night that pibroch thrills,
Savage and shrill! But with the breath which fills
Their mountain-pipe, so fill the mountaineers
With the fierce native daring which instils
The stirring memory of a thousand years,
And Evan's, Donald's fame rings in each clansman's ears!

XXVII

And Ardennes waves above them her green leaves,
Dewy with nature's tear-drops, as they pass,
Grieving, if aught inanimate e'er grieves,
Over the unreturning brave,—alas!
Ere evening to be trodden like the grass
Which now beneath them, but above shall grow
In its next verdure, when this fiery mass
Of living valour, rolling on the foe
And burning with high hope, shall moulder cold and low.

XXVIII

Last noon beheld them full of lusty life,
Last eve in Beauty's circle proudly gay,
The midnight brought the signal-sound of strife,
The morn the marshalling in arms,—the day
Battle's magnificently-stern array!

The thunder-clouds close o'er it, which when rent
The earth is covered thick with other clay,
Which her own clay shall cover, heaped and pent,
Rider and horse,—friend, foe,—in one red burial blent!

CANTO IV

XXVII

The moon is up, and yet it is not night;
Sunset divides the sky with her; a sea
Of glory streams along the Alpine height
Of blue Friuli's mountains; Heaven is free
From clouds, but of all colours seems to be,—
Melted to one vast Iris of the West,—
Where the Day joins the past Eternity,
While, on the other hand, meek Dian's crest
Floats through the azure air—an island of the blest!

XXVIII

A single star is at her side, and reigns
With her o'er half the lovely heaven; but still
Yon sunny sea heaves brightly, and remains
Roll'd o'er the peak of the far Rhætian hill,
As Day and Night contending were, until
Nature reclaim'd her order:—gently flows
The deep-dyed Brenta, where their hues instil
The odorous purple of a new-born rose,
Which streams upon her stream, and glass'd within it glows,

XXIX

Fill'd with the face of heaven, which, from afar,
Comes down upon the waters; all its hues,
From the rich sunset to the rising star,
Their magical variety diffuse:
And now they change; a paler shadow strews
Its mantle o'er the mountains; parting day
Dies like the dolphin, whom each pang imbues
With a new colour as it gasps away,
The last still loveliest,—till—'t is gone—and all is gray.

She Walks in Beauty

I

SHE walks in beauty, like the night
   Of cloudless climes and starry skies
And all that's best of dark and bright
   Meet in her aspect and her eyes:
Thus mellow'd to that tender light
   Which heaven to gaudy day denies.

II

One shade the more, one ray the less,
   Had half impair'd the nameless grace
Which waves in every raven tress,
   Or softly lightens o'er her face;
Where thoughts serenely sweet express
   How pure, how dear their dwelling-place.

III

And on that cheek, and o'er that brow,
   So soft, so calm, yet eloquent,
The smiles that win, the tints that glow,
   But tell of days in goodness spent,
A mind at peace with all below,
   A heart whose love is innocent!

When We Two Parted

WHEN we two parted
   In silence and tears,
Half broken-hearted,
To sever for years,
Pale grew thy cheek and cold,
Colder thy kiss;
Truly that hour foretold
Sorrow to this!

The dew of the morning
Sunk chill on my brow;
It felt like the warning
Of what I feel now.
Thy vows are all broken,
And light is thy fame:
I hear thy name spoken
And share in its shame.

They name thee before me,
A knell to mine ear;
A shudder comes o'er me—
Why wert thou so dear?
They know not I knew thee
Who knew thee too well:
Long, long shall I rue thee
Too deeply to tell.

In secret we met:
In silence I grieve
That thy heart could forget,
Thy spirit deceive.
If I should meet thee
After long years,
How should I greet thee?—
With silence and tears.

FROM DON JUAN

I

THE isles of Greece, the isles of Greece!
   Where burning Sappho loved and sung,
Where grew the arts of war and peace,
   Where Delos[1] rose, and Phœbus sprung!
Eternal summer gilds them yet,
But all, except their sun, is set.

---

[1] The island of Delos had supposedly risen from the sea to become the birthplace of Apollo.

2

This Scian and the Teian muse,[2]
　The hero's harp, the lover's lute,
Have found the fame your shores refuse;
　Their place of birth alone is mute
To sounds which echo further west
Than your sires' "Islands of the Blest."

3

The mountains look on Marathon—
　And Marathon looks on the sea;
And musing there an hour alone,
　I dream'd that Greece might still be free;
For standing on the Persians' grave,
I could not deem myself a slave.

4

A king[3] sate on the rocky brow
　Which looks o'er sea-born Salamis;
And ships, by thousands, lay below,
　And men in nations;—all were his!
He counted them at break of day—
And when the sun set where were they?

5

And where are they? and where art thou,
　My country? On thy voiceless shore
The heroic lay is tuneless now—
　The heroic bosom beats no more!
And must thy lyre, so long divine,
Degenerate into hands like mine?

6

'T is something, in the dearth of fame,
　Though link'd among a fetter'd race,
To feel at least a patriot's shame,
　Even as I sing, suffuse my face;

[2] The island of Scio claimed to be the birthplace of Homer; Teos, in Asia Minor, that of Anacreon.
[3] Xerxes, King of Persia, whose fleet was defeated at Salamis by the Greeks.

For what is left the poet here?
For Greeks a blush—for Greece a tear.

7

Must *we* but weep o'er days more blest?
    Must *we* but blush?—Our fathers bled.
Earth! render back from out thy breast
    A remnant of our Spartan dead!
Of the three hundred grant but three,
To make a new Thermopylæ!

8

What, silent still? and silent all?
    Ah! no;—the voices of the dead
Sound like a distant torrent's fall,
    And answer, "Let one living head,
But one arise,—we come, we come!"
'T is but the living who are dumb.

9

In vain—in vain: strike other chords;
    Fill high the cup with Samian wine!
Leave battles to the Turkish hordes,
    And shed the blood of Scio's vine!
Hark! rising to the ignoble call—
How answers each bold Bacchanal!

10

You have the Pyrrhic dance as yet;
    Where is the Pyrrhic phalanx gone?
Of two such lessons, why forget
    The nobler and the manlier one?
You have the letters Cadmus gave[4]
Think ye he meant them for a slave?

11

Fill high the bowl with Samian wine!
    We will not think of themes like these!

[4] Cadmus was said to have introduced the alphabet from Phoenicia into Greece.

It made Anacreon's song divine:
 He served—but served Polycrates—
A tyrant; but our masters then .
Were still, at least, our countrymen.

12

The tyrant of the Chersonese
 Was freedom's best and bravest friend;
That tyrant was Miltiades!
 Oh! that the present hour would lend
Another despot of the kind!
Such chains as his were sure to bind.

13

Fill high the bowl with Samian wine!
 On Suli's rock, and Parga's shore,[5]
Exists the remnant of a line
 Such as the Doric mothers bore;
And there, perhaps, some seed is sown,
The Heracleidan blood might own.

14

Trust not for freedom to the Franks—
 They have a king who buys and sells;
In native swords, and native ranks,
 The only hope of courage dwells:
But Turkish force, and Latin fraud,
Would break your shield, however broad.

15

Fill high the bowl with Samian wine!
 Our virgins dance beneath the shade—
I see their glorious black eyes shine;
 But gazing on each glowing maid,
My own the burning tear-drop laves,
To think such breasts must suckle slaves.

16

Place me on Sunium's marbled steep,
 Where nothing, save the waves and I,

[5] Both places in Albania.

May hear our mutual murmurs sweep;
There, swan-like, let me sing and die:
A land of slaves shall ne'er be mine—
Dash down yon cup of Samian wine!

So, We'll Go No More a Roving

I

SO, we'll go no more a roving
  So late into the night,
Though the heart be still as loving,
  And the moon be still as bright.

II

For the sword outwears its sheath,
  And the soul wears out the breast,
And the heart must pause to breathe,
  And love itself have rest.

III

Though the night was made for loving,
  And the day returns too soon,
Yet we'll go no more a roving
  By the light of the moon.

On This Day I Complete My Thirty-sixth Year

MISSOLONGHI,[1] JAN. 22, 1824

'TIS time this heart should be unmoved,
  Since others it hath ceased to move:
Yet, though I cannot be beloved,
    Still let me love!

My days are in the yellow leaf;
  The flowers and fruits of love are gone;
The worm, the canker, and the grief
    Are mine alone!

[1] Byron had gone there to assist the war for Greek independence. He contracted a fever and died on 19 April of the same year.

The fire that on my bosom preys
   Is lone as some volcanic isle;
No torch is kindled at its blaze—
    A funeral pile.

The hope, the fear, the jealous care,
   The exalted portion of the pain
And power of love, I cannot share,
    But wear the chain.

But 't is not *thus*—and 't is not *here*—
   Such thoughts should shake my soul, nor *now,*
Where glory decks the hero's bier,
    Or binds his brow.

The sword, the banner, and the field,
   Glory and Greece, around me see!
The Spartan, borne upon his shield,
    Was not more free.

Awake! (not Greece—she *is* awake!)
   Awake, my spirit! Think through *whom*
Thy life-blood tracks its parent lake,
    And then strike home!

Tread those reviving passions down,
   Unworthy manhood!—unto thee
Indifferent should the smile or frown
    Of beauty be.

If thou regrett'st thy youth, *why live?*
   The land of honourable death
Is here:—up to the field, and give
    Away thy breath!

Seek out—less often sought than found—
   A soldier's grave, for thee the best;
Then look around, and choose thy ground,
    And take thy rest.

PERCY BYSSHE SHELLEY

Hymn to Intellectual Beauty[1]

I

THE awful shadow of some unseen Power
  Floats though unseen among us,—visiting
This various world with as inconstant wing
As summer winds that creep from flower to flower,—
Like moonbeams that behind some piny mountain shower,
    It visits with inconstant glance
    Each human heart and countenance;
Like hues and harmonies of evening,—
    Like clouds in starlight widely spread,—
    Like memory of music fled,—
    Like aught that for its grace may be
Dear, and yet dearer for its mystery.

II

Spirit of BEAUTY, that dost consecrate
  With thine own hues all thou dost shine upon
Of human thought or form,—where art thou gone?
Why dost thou pass away and leave our state,
This dim vast vale of tears, vacant and desolate?
    Ask why the sunlight not for ever
    Weaves rainbows o'er yon mountain-river,
Why aught should fail and fade that once is shown,
    Why fear and dream and death and birth

---

[1] Written in 1816; published in Leigh Hunt's *Examiner*, 19 January 1817. According to Mrs. Shelley, it was conceived during Shelley's voyage on Lake Geneva with Lord Byron. Material beauty as observed on earth shows but "broken lights" of that ideal or "intellectual" beauty, which is perfect, immaterial, and eternal, and in itself the peak of human contemplation. This Platonic concept is so frequent and important in English poetry that the first "vocation of the scholar" is to read of it at first hand in Plato's own work, chiefly in *The Symposium*, 211–212 (appropriately, in Shelley's translation, if possible). This "intellectual beauty" is, of course, prefigured in Shelley's own *Alastor*.

Cast on the daylight of this earth
Such gloom,—why man has such a scope
For love and hate, despondency and hope?

III

No voice from some sublimer world hath ever
   To sage or poet these responses given—
   Therefore the names of Demon, Ghost, and Heaven,
Remain the records of their vain endeavour,
Frail spells—whose uttered charm might not avail to sever,
   From all we hear and all we see,
   Doubt, chance, and mutability.
Thy light alone—like mist o'er mountains driven,
   Or music by the night-wind sent
   Through strings of some still instrument,
   Or moonlight on a midnight stream,
Gives grace and truth to life's unquiet dream.

IV

Love, Hope, and Self-esteem, like clouds depart
   And come, for some uncertain moments lent.
   Man were immortal, and omnipotent,
Didst thou, unknown and awful as thou art,
Keep with thy glorious train firm state within his heart.
   Thou messenger of sympathies,
   That wax and wane in lovers' eyes—
Thou—that to human thought art nourishment,
   Like darkness to a dying flame!
   Depart not as thy shadow came,
   Depart not—lest the grave should be,
Like life and fear, a dark reality.

V

While yet a boy I sought for ghosts, and sped
   Through many a listening chamber, cave and ruin,
   And starlight wood, with fearful steps pursuing
Hopes of high talk with the departed dead.
I called on poisonous names with which our youth is fed;
   I was not heard—I saw them not—
   When musing deeply on the lot

Of life, at that sweet time when winds are wooing
    All vital things that wake to bring
    News of birds and blossoming,—
    Sudden, thy shadow fell on me;
I shrieked, and clasped my hands in ecstasy!

VI

I vowed that I would dedicate my powers
    To thee and thine—have I not kept the vow? [2]
    With beating heart and streaming eyes, even now
I call the phantoms of a thousand hours
Each from his voiceless grave: they have in visioned bowers
    Of studious zeal or love's delight
    Outwatched with me the envious night—
They know that never joy illumed my brow
    Unlinked with hope that thou wouldst free
    This world from its dark slavery,
    That thou—O awful LOVELINESS,
Wouldst give whate'er these words cannot express.

VII

The day becomes more solemn and serene
    When noon is past—there is a harmony
    In autumn, and a lustre in its sky,
Which through the summer is not heard or seen,
As if it could not be, as if it had not been!
    Thus let thy power, which like the truth
    Of nature on my passive youth
Descended, to my onward life supply
    Its calm—to one who worships thee,
    And every form containing thee,
    Whom, SPIRIT fair, thy spells did bind
To fear himself, and love all human kind.

[2] *Cf.* Wordsworth's "dedication" of spirit in *The Prelude.*

Ode to the West Wind[1]

I

O WILD West Wind, thou breath of Autumn's being,
   Thou, from whose unseen presence the leaves dead
Are driven, like ghosts from an enchanter fleeing,

Yellow, and black, and pale, and hectic red,
Pestilence-stricken multitudes: O thou,
Who chariotest to their dark wintry bed

The wingéd seeds, where they lie cold and low,
Each like a corpse within its grave, until
Thine azure sister of the Spring shall blow

Her clarion o'er the dreaming earth, and fill
(Driving sweet buds like flocks to feed in air)
With living hues and odours plain and hill:

Wild Spirit, which art moving everywhere;
Destroyer and preserver; hear, oh, hear!

II

Thou on whose stream, mid the steep sky's commotion,
Loose clouds like earth's decaying leaves are shed,
Shook from the tangled boughs of Heaven and Ocean,

Angels of rain and lightning: there are spread
On the blue surface of thine aëry surge,
Like the bright hair uplifted from the head

[1] Written in 1819; published with *Prometheus Unbound*, 1820. "This poem was conceived and chiefly written in a wood that skirts the Arno, near Florence, and on a day when that tempestuous wind, whose temperature is at once mild and animating, was collecting the vapours which pour down the autumnal rains. They began, as I foresaw, at sunset with a violent tempest of hail and rain, attended by that magnificent thunder and lightning peculiar to the Cisalpine regions. The phenomenon alluded to at the conclusion of the third stanza is well known to naturalists. The vegetation at the bottom of the sea, of rivers, and of lakes, sympathizes with that of the land in the change of seasons, and is consequently influenced by the winds which announce it." [Shelley.]

Observe that Shelley gives the *terza rima* of Dante (properly, continuous verse with rhyme a-b-a, b-c-b, c-d-c, etc.) stanzaic form by concluding each division with a couplet. The whole poem is a technical masterpiece.

Of some fierce Maenad, even from the dim verge
Of the horizon to the zenith's height,
The locks of the approaching storm. Thou dirge

Of the dying year, to which this closing night
Will be the dome of a vast sepulchre,
Vaulted with all thy congregated might

Of vapours, from whose solid atmosphere
Black rain, and fire, and hail, will burst: O hear!

III

Thou who didst waken from his summer dreams
    The blue Mediterranean, where he lay,
Lull'd by the coil of his crystàlline streams,

    Beside a pumice isle in Baiæ's bay,
And saw in sleep old palaces and towers
    Quivering within the wave's intenser day,

All overgrown with azure moss, and flowers
    So sweet, the sense faints picturing them! Thou
For whose path the Atlantic's level powers

    Cleave themselves into chasms, while far below
The sea-blooms and the oozy woods which wear
    The sapless foliage of the ocean, know

Thy voice, and suddenly grow gray with fear,
And tremble and despoil themselves: O hear!

IV

If I were a dead leaf thou mightest bear;
    If I were a swift cloud to fly with thee;
A wave to pant beneath thy power, and share

    The impulse of thy strength, only less free
Than thou, O uncontrollable! if even
    I were as in my boyhood, and could be

The comrade of thy wanderings over heaven,
  As then, when to outstrip thy skiey speed
Scarce seem'd a vision—I would ne'er have striven

As thus with thee in prayer in my sore need.
Oh, lift me as a wave, a leaf, a cloud!
I fall upon the thorns of life! I bleed!

A heavy weight of hours has chained and bowed
One too like thee: tameless, and swift, and proud.

v

Make me thy lyre, even as the forest is;
What if my leaves are falling like its own!
The tumult of thy mighty harmonies

Will take from both a deep, autumnal tone,
Sweet though in sadness. Be thou, spirit fierce,
My spirit! Be thou me, impetuous one!

Drive my dead thoughts over the universe
Like withered leaves to quicken a new birth!
And, by the incantation of this verse,

Scatter, as from an unextinguished hearth
Ashes and sparks, my words among mankind!
Be through my lips to unawakened earth

The trumpet of a prophecy! O Wind,
If Winter comes, can Spring be far behind?

The Indian Serenade

I

I ARISE from dreams of thee
  In the first sweet sleep of night,
When the winds are breathing low,
And the stars are shining bright;
I arise from dreams of thee,
  And a spirit in my feet

Hath led me—who knows how?
To thy chamber window, sweet!

II

The wandering airs they faint
On the dark, the silent stream;
The champak odours fail
Like sweet thoughts in a dream;
The nightingale's complaint,
It dies upon her heart,
As I must die on thine,
Oh, belovèd as thou art!

III

Oh, lift me from the grass!
I die! I faint! I fail!
Let thy love in kisses rain
On my lips and eyelids pale,
My cheek is cold and white, alas!
My heart beats loud and fast,
Oh! press it to thine own again,
Where it will break at last.

To a Skylark

HAIL to thee, blithe spirit!
   Bird thou never wert—
That from heaven or near it
   Pourest thy full heart
In profuse strains of unpremeditated art.

Higher still and higher
   From the earth thou springest,
Like a cloud of fire;
   The blue deep thou wingest,
And singing still dost soar, and soaring ever singest.

In the golden light'ning
   Of the sunken sun,

O'er which clouds are bright'ning,
Thou dost float and run,
Like an unbodied joy whose race is just begun.

The pale purple even
Melts around thy flight;
Like a star of heaven,
In the broad daylight
Thou art unseen, but yet I hear thy shrill delight—

Keen as are the arrows
Of that silver sphere
Whose intense lamp narrows
In the white dawn clear,
Until we hardly see, we feel that it is there.

All the earth and air
With thy voice is loud,
As, when night is bare,
From one lonely cloud
The moon rains out her beams, and heaven is overflow'd.

What thou art we know not;
What is most like thee?
From rainbow clouds there flow not
Drops so bright to see,
As from thy presence showers a rain of melody:—

Like a poet hidden
In the light of thought,
Singing hymns unbidden,
Till the world is wrought
To sympathy with hopes and fears it heeded not:

Like a high-born maiden
In a palace tower,
Soothing her love-laden
Soul in secret hour
With music sweet as love, which overflows her bower:

Like a glow-worm golden
In a dell of dew,

Scattering unbeholden
  Its aëreal hue
Among the flowers and grass, which screen it from the view!

  Like a rose embowered
   In its own green leaves,
  By warm winds deflowered,
   Till the scent it gives
Makes faint with too much sweet those heavy-wingéd thieves:

  Sound of vernal showers
   On the twinkling grass,
  Rain-awakened flowers,
   All that ever was
Joyous, and clear, and fresh, thy music doth surpass:

  Teach us, Sprite or Bird,
   What sweet thoughts are thine:
  I have never heard
   Praise of love or wine
That panted forth a flood of rapture so divine.

  Chorus Hymeneal,
   Or triumphal chant,
  Matched with thine would be all
   But an empty vaunt,
A thing wherein we feel there is some hidden want.

  What objects are the fountains
   Of thy happy strain?
  What fields, or waves, or mountains?
   What shapes of sky or plain?
What love of thine own kind? what ignorance of pain?

  With thy clear keen joyance
   Languor cannot be:
  Shadow of annoyance
   Never came near thee:
Thou lovest—but ne'er knew love's sad satiety.

  Waking or asleep,
   Thou of death must deem

Things more true and deep
Than we mortals dream,
Or how could thy notes flow in such a crystal stream?

We look before and after,
And pine for what is not:
Our sincerest laughter
With some pain is fraught;
Our sweetest songs are those that tell of saddest thought.

Yet, if we could scorn
Hate and pride and fear,
If we were things born
Not to shed a tear,
I know not how thy joy we ever should come near.

Better than all measures
Of delightful sound,
Better than all treasures
That in books are found,
Thy skill to poet were, thou scorner of the ground!

Teach me half the gladness
That thy brain must know;
Such harmonious madness
From my lips would flow,
The world should listen then, as I am listening now.

To Night

I

SWIFTLY walk o'er the western wave,
        Spirit of Night!
Out of the misty eastern cave,
Where, all the long and lone daylight,
Thou wovest dreams of joy and fear,
Which make the terrible and dear,—
        Swift be thy flight!

II

Wrap thy form in a mantle gray,
  Star-inwrought!
Blind with thine hair the eyes of Day;
Kiss her until she be wearied out,
Then wander o'er city, and sea, and land,
Touching all with thine opiate wand—
  Come, long-sought!

III

When I arose and saw the dawn,
  I sighed for thee;
When light rode high, and the dew was gone,
And noon lay heavy on flower and tree,
And the weary Day turned to his rest,
Lingering like an unloved guest,
  I sighed for thee.

IV

Thy brother Death came, and cried,
  Wouldst thou me?
Thy sweet child Sleep, the filmy-eyed,
Murmured like a noontide bee,
Shall I nestle near thy side?
Wouldst thou me?—And I replied,
  No, not thee!

V

Death will come when thou art dead,
  Soon, too soon—
Sleep will come when thou art fled;
Of neither would I ask the boon
I ask of thee, belovéd Night—
Swift be thine approaching flight,
  Come soon, soon!

When the Lamp Is Shatter'd

WHEN the lamp is shatter'd,
    The light in the dust lies dead;
  When the cloud is scatter'd,
The rainbow's glory is shed:
  When the lute is broken,
Sweet tones are remember'd not
  When the lips have spoken,
Loved accents are soon forgot.

  As music and splendour
Survive not the lamp and the lute,
  The heart's echoes render
No song when the spirit is mute—
  No song but sad dirges,
Like the wind through a ruin'd cell,
  Or the mournful surges
That ring the dead seaman's knell.

  When hearts have once mingled,
Love first leaves the well-built nest;
  The weak one is singled
To endure what it once possest.
  O Love, who bewailest
The frailty of all things here,
  Why choose you the frailest
For your cradle, your home, and your bier?

  Its passions will rock thee,
As the storms rock the ravens on high:
  Bright reason will mock thee,
Like the sun from a wintry sky.
  From thy nest every rafter
Will rot, and thine eagle home
  Leave thee naked to laughter,
When leaves fall and cold winds come.

Song

TO THE MEN OF ENGLAND

I

MEN of England, wherefore plough
For the lords who lay ye low?
Wherefore weave with toil and care
The rich robes your tyrants wear?

II

Wherefore feed, and clothe, and save,
From the cradle to the grave,
Those ungrateful drones who would
Drain your sweat—nay, drink your blood?

III

Wherefore, Bees of England, forge
Many a weapon, chain, and scourge,
That these stingless drones may spoil
The forced produce of your toil?

IV

Have ye leisure, comfort, calm,
Shelter, food, love's gentle balm?
Or what is it ye buy so dear
With your pain and with your fear?

V

The seed ye sow, another reaps;
The wealth ye find, another keeps;
The robes ye weave, another wears;
The arms ye forge, another bears.

VI

Sow seed,—but let no tyrant reap;
Find wealth,—let no impostor heap;

Weave robes,—let not the idle wear;
Forge arms,—in your defence to bear.

VII

Shrink to your cellars, holes, and cells;
In halls ye deck another dwells.
Why shake the chains ye wrought? Ye see
The steel ye tempered glance on ye.

VIII

With plough and spade, and hoe and loom,
Trace your grave, and build your tomb,
And weave your winding-sheet, till fair
England be your sepulchre.

Choruses from Prometheus Unbound

ON a poet's lips I slept
Dreaming like a love-adept
In the sound his breathing kept;
Nor seeks nor finds he mortal blisses,
But feeds on the aëreal kisses
Of shapes that haunt thought's wildernesses.
He will watch from dawn to gloom
The lake-reflected sun illume
The yellow bees in the ivy-bloom,
Nor heed nor see, what things they be;
But from these create he can
Forms more real than living man,
Nurslings of immortality!

—Act I.

Life of Life! thy lips enkindle
With their love the breath between them;
And thy smiles before they dwindle
Make the cold air fire; then screen them
In those looks, where whoso gazes
Faints, entangled in their mazes.

Child of Light! thy limbs are burning
Through the vest which seems to hide them;

As the radiant lines of morning
   Through the clouds ere they divide them;
And this atmosphere divinest
Shrouds thee wheresoe'er thou shinest.

Fair are others; none beholds thee,
   But thy voice sounds low and tender
Like the fairest, for it folds thee
   From the sight, that liquid splendour,
And all feel, yet see thee never,
As I feel now, lost for ever!

Lamp of Earth! where'er thou movest
   Its dim shapes are clad with brightness,
And the souls of whom thou lovest
   Walk upon the winds with lightness,
Till they fail, as I am failing,
Dizzy, lost, yet unbewailing!

—ACT II, SCENE V.

Fragments

The Waning Moon

AND like a dying lady, lean and pale,
   Who totters forth, wrapped in a gauzy veil,
Out of her chamber, led by the insane
And feeble wanderings of her fading brain,
The moon arose up in the murky East,
A white and shapeless mass.

To the Moon

I

ART thou pale for weariness
   Of climbing heaven, and gazing on the earth,
   Wandering companionless
Among the stars that have a different birth,—
And ever-changing, like a joyless eye
That finds no object worth its constancy?

JOHN KEATS

On First Looking into Chapman's Homer

MUCH have I travell'd in the realms of gold,
    And many goodly states and kingdoms seen;
  Round many western islands have I been
Which bards in fealty to Apollo hold.
Oft of one wide expanse had I been told
    That deep-brow'd Homer ruled as his demesne;
    Yet did I never breathe its pure serene
Till I heard Chapman speak out loud and bold:
Then felt I like some watcher of the skies
    When a new planet swims into his ken;
Or like stout Cortez when with eagle eyes
    He star'd at the Pacific—and all his men
Look'd at each other with a wild surmise—
    Silent, upon a peak in Darien.

La Belle Dame Sans Merci

O WHAT can ail thee, knight-at-arms,
    Alone and palely loitering?
The sedge has wither'd from the lake,
    And no birds sing.

O what can ail thee, knight-at-arms,
    So haggard and so woe-begone?
The squirrel's granary is full,
    And the harvest's done.

I see a lily on thy brow
    With anguish moist and fever dew;
And on thy cheeks a fading rose
    Fast withereth too.

I met a lady in the meads,
    Full beautiful—a faëry's child,

Her hair was long, her foot was light,
    And her eyes were wild.

I made a garland for her head,
    And bracelets too, and fragrant zone;
She look'd at me as she did love,
    And made sweet moan.

I set her on my pacing steed,
    And nothing else saw all day long,
For sidelong would she bend, and sing
    A faëry's song.

She found me roots of relish sweet,
    And honey wild, and manna dew,
And sure in language strange she said,
    I love thee true!

She took me to her elfin grot,
    And there she wept and sigh'd full sore,
And there I shut her wild, wild eyes
    With kisses four.

And there she lullèd me asleep,
    And there I dream'd, ah! woe betide!
The latest dream I ever dream'd
    On the cold hill side.

I saw pale kings and princes too,
    Pale warriors, death-pale were they all;
They cried—La Belle Dame sans Merci
    Hath thee in thrall!

I saw their starved lips in the gloam,
    With horrid warning gapéd wide,
And I awoke and found me here,
    On the cold hill's side.

And this is why I sojourn here,
    Alone and palely loitering,
Though the sedge is wither'd from the lake,
    And no birds sing.

Ode on Melancholy

NO, no, go not to Lethe, neither twist
    Wolf's-bane, tight-rooted, for its poisonous wine;
Nor suffer thy pale forehead to be kiss'd
  By nightshade, ruby grape of Proserpine;
Make not your rosary of yew-berries,
    Nor let the beetle, nor the death-moth be
      Your mournful Psyche, nor the downy owl
A partner in your sorrow's mysteries;
    For shade to shade will come too drowsily,
      And drown the wakeful anguish of the soul.

But when the melancholy fit shall fall
  Sudden from heaven like a weeping cloud,
That fosters the droop-headed flowers all,
  And hides the green hill in an April shroud;
Then glut thy sorrow on a morning rose,
    Or on the rainbow of the salt sand-wave,
      Or on the wealth of globed peonies;
Or if thy mistress some rich anger shows,
    Emprison her soft hand, and let her rave,
      And feed deep, deep upon her peerless eyes.

She dwells with Beauty—Beauty that must die;
  And Joy, whose hand is ever at his lips
Bidding adieu; and aching Pleasure nigh,
  Turning to Poison while the bee-mouth sips:
Ay, in the very temple of delight
Veil'd Melancholy has her sovran shrine,
    Though seen of none save him whose strenuous tongue
Can burst Joy's grape against his palate fine;
His soul shall taste the sadness of her might,
    And be among her cloudy trophies hung.

Ode to a Nightingale

I

MY heart aches, and a drowsy numbness pains
   My sense, as though of hemlock I had drunk,
Or emptied some dull opiate to the drains
   One minute past, and Lethe-wards had sunk:
'Tis not through envy of thy happy lot,
   But being too happy in thine happiness,—
      That thou, light-winged Dryad of the trees,
         In some melodious plot
      Of beechen green, and shadows numberless,
         Singest of summer in full-throated ease.

II

O, for a draught of vintage! that hath been
   Cool'd a long age in the deep-delved earth,
Tasting of Flora and the country green,
   Dance, and Provençal song, and sunburnt mirth!
O for a beaker full of the warm South,
   Full of the true, the blushful Hippocrene,
      With beaded bubbles winking at the brim,
         And purple-stained mouth;
      That I might drink, and leave the world unseen,
         And with thee fade away into the forest dim:

III

Fade far away, dissolve, and quite forget
   What thou among the leaves hast never known,
The weariness, the fever, and the fret
   Here, where men sit and hear each other groan;
Where palsy shakes a few, sad, last gray hairs,
   Where youth grows pale, and spectre-thin, and dies;
      Where but to think is to be full of sorrow
         And leaden-eyed despairs,
      Where Beauty cannot keep her lustrous eyes,
         Or new Love pine at them beyond tomorrow.

IV

Away! away! for I will fly to thee,
　Not charioted by Bacchus and his pards,
But on the viewless wings of Poesy,
　Though the dull brain perplexes and retards:
Already with thee! tender is the night,
　And haply the Queen-moon is on her throne,
　　Cluster'd around by all her starry Fays;
　　　But here there is no light,
　Save what from heaven is with the breezes blown
　　Through verdurous glooms and winding mossy ways.

V

I cannot see what flowers are at my feet,
　Nor what soft incense hangs upon the boughs,
But, in embalmed darkness, guess each sweet
　Wherewith the seasonable month endows
The grass, the thicket, and the fruit-tree wild;
　White hawthorn, and the pastoral eglantine;
　　Fast fading violets cover'd up in leaves;
　　　And mid-May's eldest child,
　The coming musk-rose, full of dewy wine,
　　The murmurous haunt of flies on summer eves.

VI

Darkling I listen; and, for many a time
　I have been half in love with easeful Death,
Call'd him soft names in many a mused rhyme,
　To take into the air my quiet breath;
Now more than ever seems it rich to die,
　To cease upon the midnight with no pain,
　　While thou art pouring forth thy soul abroad
　　　In such an ecstasy!
　Still wouldst thou sing, and I have ears in vain—
　　To thy high requiem become a sod.

VII

Thou wast not born for death, immortal Bird!
　No hungry generations tread thee down;
The voice I hear this passing night was heard
　In ancient days by emperor and clown:

Perhaps the self-same song that found a path
  Through the sad heart of Ruth, when, sick for home,
    She stood in tears amid the alien corn;
      The same that oft-times hath
  Charm'd magic casements, opening on the foam
    Of perilous seas, in faery lands forlorn.

VIII

Forlorn! the very word is like a bell
  To toll me back from thee to my sole self!
Adieu! the fancy cannot cheat so well
  As she is fam'd to do, deceiving elf.
Adieu! adieu! thy plaintive anthem fades
  Past the near meadows, over the still stream,
    Up the hill-side; and now 'tis buried deep
      In the next valley-glades:
  Was it a vision, or a waking dream?
    Fled is that music:—Do I wake or sleep?

Ode on a Grecian Urn

I

THOU still unravish'd bride of quietness,
    Thou foster-child of silence and slow time,
Sylvan historian, who canst thus express
  A flowery tale more sweetly than our rhyme:
What leaf-fring'd legend haunts about thy shape
  Of deities or mortals, or of both,
    In Tempe or the dales of Arcady?
What men or gods are these? What maidens loth?
  What mad pursuit? What struggle to escape?
    What pipes and timbrels? What wild ecstasy?

II

Heard melodies are sweet, but those unheard
  Are sweeter; therefore, ye soft pipes, play on;
Not to the sensual ear, but, more endeared,
  Pipe to the spirit ditties of no tone:

Fair youth, beneath the trees, thou canst not leave
 Thy song, nor ever can those trees be bare;
 Bold lover, never, never canst thou kiss
Though winning near the goal—yet, do not grieve;
 She cannot fade, though thou hast not thy bliss,
  For ever wilt thou love, and she be fair!

III

Ah, happy, happy boughs! that cannot shed
 Your leaves, nor ever bid the Spring adieu;
And, happy melodist, unwearied,
 For ever piping songs for ever new;
More happy love! more happy, happy love!
  For ever warm and still to be enjoy'd,
  For ever panting, and for ever young,
All breathing human passion far above,
  That leaves a heart high-sorrowful and cloy'd,
  A burning forehead, and a parching tongue.

IV

Who are these coming to the sacrifice?
 To what green altar, O mysterious priest,
Lead'st thou that heifer lowing at the skies,
 And all her silken flanks with garlands drest?
What little town by river or sea shore,
 Or mountain-built with peaceful citadel,
 Is emptied of its folk, this pious morn?
And, little town, thy streets for evermore
 Will silent be; and not a soul to tell
 Why thou art desolate, can e'er return.

V

O Attic shape! Fair attitude! with brede
 Of marble men and maidens overwrought,
With forest branches and the trodden weed;
 Thou, silent form, dost tease us out of thought
As doth eternity: Cold Pastoral!
 When old age shall this generation waste,
  Thou shalt remain, in midst of other woe
Than ours, a friend to man, to whom thou say'st,
 "Beauty is truth, truth beauty,"—that is all
  Ye know on earth, and all ye need to know.

To Autumn

I

SEASON of mists and mellow fruitfulness,
  Close bosom-friend of the maturing sun;
Conspiring with him how to load and bless
With fruit the vines that round the thatch-eves run;
To bend with apples the moss'd cottage-trees,
And fill all fruit with ripeness to the core;
To swell the gourd, and plump the hazel shells
With a sweet kernel; to set budding more,
And still more, later flowers for the bees,
Until they think warm days will never cease,
For Summer has o'er-brimm'd their clammy cells.

Who hath not seen thee oft amid thy store?
Sometimes whoever seeks abroad may find
Thee sitting careless on a granary floor,
Thy hair soft-lifted by the winnowing wind;
Or on a half-reap'd furrow sound asleep,
Drows'd with the fume of poppies, while thy hook
Spares the next swath and all its twinèd flowers:
And sometimes like a gleaner thou dost keep
Steady thy laden head across a brook;
Or by a cider-press, with patient look,
Thou watchest the last cozings hours by hours.

Where are the songs of Spring? Ay, where are they?
Think not of them, thou hast thy music too—
While barrèd clouds bloom the soft-dying day,
And touch the stubble-plains with rosy hue;
Then in a wailful choir the small gnats mourn
Among the river sallows, borne aloft
Or sinking as the light wind lives or dies;
And full-grown lambs loud bleat from hilly bourn;
Hedge-crickets sing; and now with treble soft
The red-breast whistles from a garden-croft;
And gathering swallows twitter in the skies.

Last Sonnet

BRIGHT Star, would I were steadfast as thou art—
Not in lone splendour hung aloft the night,
And watching, with eternal lids apart,
Like Nature's patient sleepless Eremite,
The moving waters at their priest-like task
Of pure ablution round earth's human shores,
Or gazing on the new soft-fallen mask
Of snow upon the mountains and the moors—
No—yet still steadfast, still unchangeable,
Pillow'd upon my fair love's ripening breast,
To feel for ever its soft fall and swell,
Awake for ever in a sweet unrest,
Still, still to hear her tender-taken breath,
And so live ever—or else swoon to death.

----◆----

JOHN CLARE

----◆----

ONE gloomy eve I roam'd about
Neath Oxey's hazel bowers,
While timid hares were darting out,
To crop the dewy flowers;
And soothing was the scene to me,
Right pleasèd was my soul,
My breast was calm as summer's sea
When waves forget to roll.

But short was Even's placid smile,
My startled soul to charm,
When Nelly lightly skipt the stile,
With milk-pail on her arm:
One careless look on me she flung,
As bright as parting day;
And like a hawk from covert sprung,
It pounced my peace away.

THE nodding oxeye bends before the wind,
 The woodbine quakes lest boys their flowers should find,
And prickly dogrose spite of its array
Can't dare the blossom-seeking hand away,
While thistles wear their heavy knobs of bloom
Proud as a warhorse wears its haughty plume,
And by the roadside danger's self defy;
On commons where pined sheep and oxen lie
In ruddy pomp and ever thronging mood
It stands and spreads like danger in a wood,
And in the village street where meanest weeds
Can't stand untouch'd to fill their husks with seeds,
The haughty thistle o'er all danger towers,
In every place the very wasp of flowers.

GEORGE DARLEY

The Fallen Star

A STAR is gone! a star is gone!
 There is a blank in Heaven;
One of the cherub choir has done
 His airy course this even.

He sat upon the orb of fire
 That hung for ages there,
And lent his music to the choir
 That haunts the nightly air.

But when his thousands years are pass'd,
 With a cherubic sigh
He vanish'd with his car at last,
 For even cherubs die!

Hear how his angel-brothers mourn—
 The minstrels of the spheres—
Each chiming sadly in his turn
 And dropping splendid tears.

The planetary sisters all
  Join in the fatal song,
And weep this hapless brother's fall,
  Who sang with them so long.

But deepest of the choral band
  The Lunar Spirit sings,
And with a bass-according hand
  Sweeps all her sullen strings.

From the deep chambers of the dome
  Where sleepless Uriel lies,
His rude harmonic thunders come
  Mingled with mighty sighs.

The thousand car-borne cherubim,
  The wandering eleven,
All join to chant the dirge of him
  Who fell just now from Heaven.

THOMAS LOVELL BEDDOES

Song

HOW many times do I love thee, dear?
  Tell me how many thoughts there be
    In the atmosphere
    Of a new-fall'n year,
Whose white and sable hours appear
  The latest flake of Eternity:—
So many times do I love thee, dear.

How many times do I love again?
  Tell me how many beads there are
    In a silver chain
    Of evening rain,
Unravelled from the tumbling main,
  And threading the eye of a yellow star:—
So many times do I love again.

A Crocodile

FRAGMENT OF "THE LOST MAN"

HARD by the lilied Nile I saw
A duskish river-dragon stretched along,
The brown habergeon of his limbs enamelled
With sanguine almandines and rainy pearl:
And on his back there lay a young one sleeping,
No bigger than a mouse; with eyes like beads,
And a small fragment of its speckled egg
Remaining on its harmless, pulpy snout;
A thing to laugh at, as it gaped to catch
The baulking, merry flies. In the iron jaws
Of the great devil-beast, like a pale soul
Fluttering in rocky hell, lightsomely flew
A snowy troculus, with roseate beak
Tearing the hairy leeches from his throat.

Dream-Pedlary

I

IF there were dreams to sell,
What would you buy?
Some cost a passing bell;
Some a light sigh,
That shakes from Life's fresh crown
Only a roseleaf down.
If there were dreams to sell,
Merry and sad to tell,
And the crier rang his bell,
What would you buy?

II

A cottage lone and still,
With bowers nigh,
Shadowy, my woes to still,
Until I die.

Such pearl from Life's fresh crown
Fain would I shake me down.
Were dreams to have at will,
This would best heal my ill,
　This would I buy.

III

. But there were dreams to sell,
　Ill didst thou buy;
Life is a dream, they tell,
　Waking, to die.
Dreaming a dream to prize,
Is wishing ghosts to rise;
　And, if I had the spell
　To call the buried, well,
　　Which one would I?

IV

If there were ghosts to raise,
　What shall I call,
Out of hell's murky haze,
　Heaven's blue hall?
Raise my loved longlost boy
To lead me to his joy.
　There are no ghosts to raise;
　Out of death lead no ways;
　　Vain is the call.

V

Know'st thou no ghosts to sue?
　No love thou hast.
Else lie, as I will do
　And breathe thy last.
So out of Life's fresh crown
Fall like a rose-leaf down.
　Thus are the ghosts to woo;
　Thus are all dreams made true,
　　Ever to last!

JAMES CLARENCE MANGAN

Dark Rosaleen

O MY Dark Rosaleen,
  Do not sigh, do not weep!
The priests are on the ocean green,
  They march along the deep,
There's wine from the royal Pope,
  Upon the ocean green;
And Spanish ale shall give you hope,
  My Dark Rosaleen!
  My own Rosaleen!
Shall glad your heart, shall give you hope,
Shall give you health, and help, and hope,
  My Dark Rosaleen!

Over hills, and through dales,
  Have I roamed for your sake;
All yesterday I sailed with sails
  On river and on lake.
The Erne, at its highest flood,
  I dashed across unseen,
For there was lightning in my blood,
  My Dark Rosaleen!
  My own Rosaleen!
Oh! there was lightning in my blood,
Red lightning lightened through my blood,
  My Dark Rosaleen!

All day long in unrest,
  To and fro do I move,
The very soul within my breast
  Is wasted for you, love!
The heart in my bosom faints
  To think of you, my Queen,
My life of life, my saint of saints,
  My Dark Rosaleen!
  My own Rosaleen!

To hear your sweet and sad complaints,
My life, my love, my saint of saints,
  My Dark Rosaleen!

Woe and pain, pain and woe,
  Are my lot, night and noon,
To see your bright face clouded so,
  Like to the mournful moon.
But yet will I rear your throne
  Again in golden sheen;
'Tis you shall reign, shall reign alone,
  My Dark Rosaleen!
  My own Rosaleen!
'Tis you shall have the golden throne,
'Tis you shall reign, shall reign alone,
  My Dark Rosaleen!

Over dews, over sands,
  Will I fly, for your weal:
Your holy delicate white hands
  Shall girdle me with steel.
At home, in your emerald bowers,
  From morning's dawn till e'en,
You'll pray for me, my flower of flowers,
  My Dark Rosaleen!
  My fond Rosaleen!
You'll think of me through daylight hours,
My virgin flower, my flower of flowers,
  My Dark Rosaleen!

I could scale the blue air,
  I could plough the high hills,
O, I could kneel all night in prayer,
  To heal your many ills!
And one beamy smile from you
  Would float like light between
My toils and me, my own, my true,
  My Dark Rosaleen!
  My fond Rosaleen!
Would give me life and soul anew,
A second life, a soul anew,
  My Dark Rosaleen!

O, the Erne shall run red,
  With redundance of blood,
The earth shall rock beneath our tread,
  And flames wrap hill and wood,
And gun-peal and slogan-cry
  Wake many a glen serene,
Ere you shall fade, ere you shall die,
  My Dark Rosaleen!
  My own Rosaleen!
The Judgment Hour must first be nigh,
Ere you can fade, ere you can die,
  My Dark Rosaleen!

ELIZABETH BARRETT BROWNING

Sonnets from the Portuguese[1]

I

I THOUGHT once how Theocritus had sung
Of the sweet years, the dear and wished-for years,
Who each one in a gracious hand appears
To bear a gift for mortals, old or young:
And, as I mused it in his antique tongue,
I saw, in gradual vision through my tears,
The sweet, sad years, the melancholy years,
Those of my own life, who by turns had flung
A shadow across me. Straightway I was 'ware,
So weeping, how a mystic Shape did move
Behind me, and drew me backward by the hair;
And a voice said in mastery, while I strove,—
"Guess now who holds thee?"—"Death," I said. But, there,
The silver answer rang—"Not Death, but Love."

[1] These sonnets celebrate the love of Robert Browning and Elizabeth Barrett, who finally gave them one morning in 1847 to her husband, telling him to tear them up if he did not like them. Though they were meant to be private, Browning held that their high quality—"the finest sonnets written in any language since Shakespeare"—demanded publication. They appeared in 1850. The title, recalling Camoëns, the Portuguese poet, was selected by Browning, because of his liking for his wife's earlier love poem, *Catarina to Camoëns.*

III

Unlike are we, unlike, O princely Heart!
Unlike our uses and our destinies.
Our ministering two angels look surprise
On one another, as they strike athwart
Their wings in passing. Thou, bethink thee, art
A guest for queens to social pageantries,
With gages[2] from a hundred brighter eyes
Than tears even can make mine, to play thy part
Of chief musician. What hast *thou* to do
With looking from the lattice-lights at me,
A poor, tired, wandering singer, singing through
The dark, and leaning up a cypress-tree?
The chrism is on thine head,—on mine, the dew,—
And Death must dig the level where these agree.

XIV

If thou must love me, let it be for naught
Except for love's sake only. Do not say,
"I love her for her smile—her look—her way
Of speaking gently,—for a trick of thought
That falls in well with mine, and certes brought
A sense of pleasant ease on such a day"—
For these things in themselves, Belovèd, may
Be changed, or change for thee—and love, so wrought,
May be unwrought so. Neither love me for
Thine own dear pity's wiping my cheeks dry:
A creature might forget to weep, who bore
Thy comfort long, and lose thy love thereby!
But love me for love's sake, that evermore
Thou mayst love on, through love's eternity.

XXII

When our two souls stand up erect and strong,
Face to face, silent, drawing nigh and nigher,
Until the lengthening wings break into fire
At either curvèd point,—what bitter wrong
Can the earth do to us, that we should not long
Be here contented? Think. In mounting higher,

---

[2] pledges

The angels would press on us and aspire
To drop some golden orb of perfect song
Into our deep, dear silence. Let us stay
Rather on earth, Belovéd,—where the unfit
Contrarious moods of men recoil away
And isolate pure spirits, and permit
A place to stand and love in for a day,
With darkness and the death-hour rounding it.

XLIII

How do I love thee? Let me count the ways.
I love thee to the depth and breadth and height
My soul can reach, when feeling out of sight
For the ends of Being and ideal Grace.
I love thee to the level of everyday's
Most quiet need, by sun and candle-light.
I love thee freely, as men strive for Right;
I love thee purely, as they turn from Praise.
I love thee with the passion put to use
In my old griefs, and with my childhood's faith.
I love thee with a love I seemed to lose
With my lost saints,—I love thee with the breath,
Smiles, tears, of all my life!—and, if God choose,
I shall but love thee better after death.

Grief

I TELL you, hopeless grief is passionless;
That only men incredulous of despair,
  Half-taught in anguish, through the midnight air
Beat upward to God's throne in loud access
Of shrieking and reproach. Full desertness
  In souls as countries lieth silent-bare
  Under the blanching, vertical eye-glare
Of the absolute Heavens. Deep-hearted man, express
Grief for thy Dead in silence like to death—
  Most like a monumental statue set
In everlasting watch and moveless woe
Till itself crumble to the dust beneath.
  Touch it; the marble eyelids are not wet:
If it could weep, it could arise and go.

ALFRED LORD TENNYSON

The Lady of Shalott

PART I

ON either side the river lie
　Long fields of barley and of rye,
That clothe the wold and meet the sky;
And thro' the field the road runs by
　　To many-towered Camelot;
And up and down the people go,
Gazing where the lilies blow
Round an island there below,
　　The island of Shalott.

Willows whiten, aspens quiver,
Little breezes dusk and shiver
Thro' the wave that runs for ever
By the island in the river
　　Flowing down to Camelot.
Four gray walls, and four gray towers,
Overlook a space of flowers,
And the silent isle imbowers
　　The Lady of Shalott.

By the margin, willow-veil'd,
Slide the heavy barges trail'd
By slow horses; and unhail'd
The shallop flitteth silken-sail'd
　　Skimming down to Camelot:
But who hath seen her wave her hand?
Or at the casement seen her stand?
Or is she known in all the land,
　　The Lady of Shalott?

Only reapers, reaping early
In among the bearded barley,

Hear a song that echoes cheerly
From the river winding clearly,
    Down to tower'd Camelot:
And by the moon the reaper weary,
Piling sheaves in uplands airy,
Listening, whispers " 'Tis the fairy
    Lady of Shalott."

PART II

There she weaves by night and day
A magic web with colours gay.
She has heard a whisper say,
A curse is on her if she stay
    To look down to Camelot.
She knows not what the curse may be,
And so she weaveth steadily,
And little other care hath she,
    The Lady of Shalott.

And moving thro' a mirror clear
That hangs before her all the year,
Shadows of the world appear.
There she sees the highway near
    Winding down to Camelot:
There the river eddy whirls,
And there the surly village-churls,
And the red cloaks of market girls,
    Pass onward from Shalott.

Sometimes a troop of damsels glad,
An abbot on an ambling pad,
Sometimes a curly shepherd-lad,
Or long-hair'd page in crimson clad,
    Goes by to tower'd Camelot;
And sometimes thro' the mirror blue
The knights come riding two and two:
She hath no loyal knight and true,
    The Lady of Shalott.

But in her web she still delights
To weave the mirror's magic sights,
For often thro' the silent nights

A funeral, with plumes and lights
    And music, went to Camelot:
Or when the moon was overhead,
Came two young lovers lately wed;
"I am half sick of shadows," said
    The Lady of Shalott.

PART III

A bow-shot from her bower-eaves,
He rode between the barley-sheaves,
The sun came dazzling thro' the leaves,
And flamed upon the brazen greaves
    Of bold Sir Lancelot.
A red-cross knight for ever kneel'd
To a lady in his shield,
That sparkled on the yellow field,
    Beside remote Shalott.

The gemmy bridle glitter'd free,
Like to some branch of stars we see
Hung in the golden Galaxy.
The bridle bells rang merrily
    As he rode down to Camelot:
And from his blazon'd baldric slung
A mighty silver bugle hung,
And as he rode his armour rung,
    Beside remote Shalott.

All in the blue unclouded weather
Thick-jewell'd shone the saddle-leather,
The helmet and the helmet-feather
Burn'd like one burning flame together,
    As he rode down to Camelot.
As often thro' the purple night,
Below the starry clusters bright,
Some bearded meteor, trailing light,
    Moves over still Shalott.

His broad clear brow in sunlight glow'd;
On burnish'd hooves his war-horse trode;
From underneath his helmet flow'd
His coal-black curls as on he rode,
    As he rode down to Camelot.

From the bank and from the river
He flash'd into the crystal mirror,
"Tirra lirra," by the river
    Sang Sir Lancelot.

She left the web, she left the loom,
She made three paces thro' the room,
She saw the water-lily bloom,
She saw the helmet and the plume,
    She look'd down to Camelot.
Out flew the web and floated wide;
The mirror crack'd from side to side;
"The curse is come upon me," cried
    The Lady of Shalott.

PART IV

In the stormy east-wind straining,
The pale yellow woods were waning,
The broad stream in his banks complaining,
Heavily the low sky raining
    Over tower'd Camelot;
Down she came and found a boat
Beneath a willow left afloat,
And round about the prow she wrote
    The Lady of Shalott.

And down the river's dim expanse
Like some bold seër in a trance,
Seeing all his own mischance—
With a glassy countenance
    Did she look to Camelot.
And at the closing of the day
She loosed the chain, and down she lay;
The broad stream bore her far away,
    The Lady of Shalott.

Lying, robed in snowy white
That loosely flew to left and right—
The leaves upon her falling light—
Thro' the noises of the night
    She floated down to Camelot:

And as the boat-head wound along
The willowy hills and fields among,
They heard her singing her last song,
 The Lady of Shalott.

Heard a carol, mournful, holy,
Chanted loudly, chanted lowly,
Till her blood was frozen slowly,
And her eyes were darken'd wholly,
 Turn'd to tower'd Camelot.
For ere she reach'd upon the tide
The first house by the water-side,
Singing in her song she died,
 The Lady of Shalott.

Under tower and balcony,
By garden-wall and gallery,
A gleaming shape she floated by,
Dead-pale between the houses high,
 Silent into Camelot.
Out upon the wharfs they came,
Knight and burgher, lord and dame,
And round the prow they read her name,
 The Lady of Shalott.

Who is this? and what is here?
And in the lighted palace near
Died the sound of royal cheer;
And they cross'd themselves for fear,
 All the knights at Camelot:
But Lancelot mused a little space;
He said, "She has a lovely face;
God in his mercy lend her grace,
 The Lady of Shalott."

Songs from The Princess

AS thro' the land at eve we went,
 And pluck'd the ripen'd ears,
We fell out, my wife and I,
O we fell out I know not why,
 And kiss'd again with tears.

And blessings on the falling out
  That all the more endears,
When we fall out with those we love
  And kiss again with tears!
For when we came where lies the child
  We lost in other years,
There above the little grave,
O there above the little grave,
  We kiss'd again with tears.

    The splendour falls on castle walls
      And snowy summits old in story:
    The long light shakes across the lakes,
      And the wild cataract leaps in glory.
Blow, bugle, blow, set the wild echoes flying,
Blow, bugle; answer, echoes, dying, dying, dying.

    O hark, O hear! how thin and clear,
      And thinner, clearer, farther going!
    O sweet and far from cliff and scar
      The horns of Elfland faintly blowing!
Blow, let us hear the purple glens replying:
Blow, bugle; answer, echoes, dying, dying, dying.

    O love, they die in yon rich sky,
      They faint on hill or field or river:
    Our echoes roll from soul to soul,
      And grow for ever and for ever.
Blow, bugle, blow, set the wild echoes flying,
And answer, echoes, answer, dying, dying, dying.

  Tears, idle tears, I know not what they mean,
Tears from the depth of some divine despair
Rise in the heart, and gather to the eyes,
In looking on the happy Autumn-fields,
And thinking of the days that are no more.

  Fresh as the first beam glittering on a sail,
That brings our friends up from the underworld,
Sad as the last which reddens over one
That sinks with all we love below the verge;
So sad, so fresh, the days that are no more.

Ah, sad and strange as in dark summer dawns
The earliest pipe of half-awaken'd birds
To dying ears, when unto dying eyes
The casement slowly grows a glimmering square;
So sad, so strange, the days that are no more.

Dear as remember'd kisses after death,
And sweet as those by hopeless fancy feign'd
On lips that are for others; deep as love,
Deep as first love, and wild with all regret;
O Death in Life, the days that are no more.

Ask me no more: the moon may draw the sea;
    The cloud may stoop from heaven and take the shape
    With fold to fold, of mountain or of cape;
But O too fond, when have I answer'd thee?
        Ask me no more.

Ask me no more: what answer should I give?
    I love not hollow cheek or faded eye:
    Yet, O my friend, I will not have thee die!
Ask me no more, lest I should bid thee live;
        Ask me no more.

Ask me no more: thy fate and mine are seal'd:
    I strove against the stream and all in vain:
    Let the great river take me to the main:
No more, dear love, for at a touch I yield;
        Ask me no more.

"Now sleeps the crimson petal, now the white;[1]
Nor waves the cypress in the palace walk;
Nor winks the gold fin in the porphyry font:
The fire-fly wakens: waken thou with me.

Now droops the milkwhite peacock like a ghost,
And like a ghost she glimmers on to me.

---

[1] This and the following song were read aloud by the Princess, who watched during the night by the wounded Prince. Her love for him breaks down her vows of isolation.

Now lies the Earth all Danaë to the stars,
And all thy heart lies open unto me.

Now slides the silent meteor on, and leaves
A shining furrow, as thy thoughts in me.

Now folds the lily all her sweetness up,
And slips into the bosom of the lake:
So fold thyself, my dearest, thou, and slip
Into my bosom and be lost in me."

"Come down, O maid, from yonder mountain height:
What pleasure lives in height (the shepherd sang)
In height and cold, the splendour of the hills?
But cease to move so near the Heavens, and cease
To glide a sunbeam by the blasted Pine,
To sit a star upon the sparkling spire;
And come, for Love is of the valley, come,
For Love is of the valley, come thou down
And find him; by the happy threshold, he,
Or hand in hand with Plenty in the maize,
Or red with spirted purple of the vats,
Or foxlike in the vine; nor cares to walk
With Death and Morning on the silver horns,
Nor wilt thou snare him in the white ravine,
Nor find him dropt upon the firths of ice,
That huddling slant in furrow-cloven falls
To roll the torrent out of dusky doors:
But follow; let the torrent dance thee down
To find him in the valley; let the wild
Lean-headed Eagles yelp alone, and leave
The monstrous ledges there to slope, and spill
Their thousand wreaths of dangling watersmoke,
That like a broken purpose waste in air:
So waste not thou; but come; for all the vales
Await thee; azure pillars of the hearth
Arise to thee; the children call, and I
Thy shepherd pipe, and sweet is every sound,
Sweeter thy voice, but every sound is sweet;
Myriads of rivulets hurrying thro' the lawn,
The moan of doves in immemorial elms,
And murmuring of innumerable bees.

In Memoriam A. H. H.

XV

TONIGHT the winds begin to rise
  And roar from yonder dropping day:
The last red leaf is whirl'd away,
The rooks are blown about the skies;

The forest crack'd, the waters curl'd,
  The cattle huddled on the lea;
  And wildly dash'd on tower and tree
The sunbeam strikes along the world:

And but for fancies, which aver
  That all thy motions gently pass
  Athwart a plane of molten glass,
I scarce could brook the strain and stir

That makes the barren branches loud;
  And but for fear it is not so,
  The wild unrest that lives in woe
Would dote and pore on yonder cloud

That rises upward always higher,
  And onward drags a labouring breast,
  And topples round the dreary west,
A looming bastion fringed with fire.

L

Be near me when my light is low,
  When the blood creeps, and the nerves prick
  And tingle; and the heart is sick,
And all the wheels of Being slow.

Be near me when the sensuous frame
  Is rack'd with pangs that conquer trust;
  And Time, a maniac scattering dust,
And Life, a Fury slinging flame.

Be near me when my faith is dry,
  And men the flies of latter spring,
  That lay their eggs, and sting and sing
And weave their petty cells and die.

Be near me when I fade away,
  To point the term of human strife,
  And on the low dark verge of life
The twilight of eternal day.

LIV

Oh yet we trust that somehow good
  Will be the final goal of ill,
  To pangs of nature, sins of will,
Defects of doubt, and taints of blood;

That nothing walks with aimless feet;
  That not one life shall be destroy'd,
  Or cast as rubbish to the void,
When God hath made the pile complete;

That not a worm is cloven in vain;
  That not a moth with vain desire
  Is shrivell'd in a fruitless fire,
Or but subserves another's gain.

Behold, we know not anything;
  I can but trust that good shall fall
  At last—far off—at last, to all,
And every winter change to spring.

So runs my dream: but what am I?
  An infant crying in the night:
  An infant crying for the light:
And with no language but a cry.

LV

The wish, that of the living whole
  No life may fail beyond the grave,
  Derives it not from what we have
The likest God within the soul?

Are God and Nature then at strife,
   That Nature lends such evil dreams?
   So careful of the type she seems,
So careless of the single life;

That I, considering everywhere
   Her secret meaning in her deeds,
   And finding that of fifty seeds
She often brings but one to bear,

I falter where I firmly trod,
   And falling with my weight of cares
   Upon the great world's altar-stairs
That slope thro' darkness up to God,

I stretch lame hands of faith, and grope,
   And gather dust and chaff, and call
   To what I feel is Lord of all,
And faintly trust the larger hope.

LVI

"So careful of the type?" but no.
   From scarped cliff and quarried stone
   She cries, "A thousand types are gone:
I care for nothing, all shall go.

"Thou makest thine appeal to me:
   I bring to life, I bring to death:
   The spirit does not mean the breath:
I know no more." And he, shall he,

Man, her last work, who seem'd so fair,
   Such splendid purpose in his eyes,
   Who roll'd the psalm to wintry skies,
Who built him fanes of fruitless prayer,

Who trusted God was love indeed
   And love Creation's final law—
   Tho' Nature, red in tooth and claw
With ravine, shriek'd against his creed—

Who loved, who suffer'd countless ills,
  Who battled for the True, the Just,
  Be blown about the desert dust,
Or seal'd within the iron hills?

No more? A monster then, a dream,
  A discord. Dragons of the prime,
  That tare each other in their slime,
Were mellow music match'd with him.

O life as futile, then, as frail!
  O for thy voice to soothe and bless!
  What hope of answer, or redress?
Behind the veil, behind the veil.

XCV

By night we linger'd on the lawn,
  For underfoot the herb was dry;
  And genial warmth; and o'er the sky
The silvery haze of summer drawn;

And calm that let the tapers burn
  Unwavering: not a cricket chirr'd:
  The brook alone far-off was heard,
And on the board the fluttering urn:

And bats went round in fragrant skies,
  And wheel'd or lit the filmy shapes
  That haunt the dusk, with ermine capes
And woolly breasts and beaded eyes;

While now we sang old songs that peal'd
  From knoll to knoll, where, couch'd at ease,
  The white kine glimmer'd, and the trees
Laid their dark arms about the field.

But when those others, one by one,
  Withdrew themselves from me and night,
  And in the house light after light
Went out, and I was all alone,

A hunger seized my heart; I read
   Of that glad year which once had been,
   In those fall'n leaves which kept their green,
The noble letters of the dead:

And strangely on the silence broke
   The silent-speaking words, and strange
   Was love's dumb cry defying change
To test his worth; and strangely spoke

The faith, the vigour, bold to dwell
   On doubts that drive the coward back,
   And keen thro' wordy snares to track
Suggestion to her inmost cell.

So word by word, and line by line,
   The dead man touch'd me from the past,
   And all at once it seem'd at last
The living soul was flash'd on mine,

And mine in this was wound, and whirl'd
   About empyreal heights of thought,
   And came on that which is, and caught
The deep pulsations of the world,

Æonian music measuring out
   The steps of Time—the shocks of Chance—
   The blows of Death. At length my trance
Was cancell'd, stricken thro' with doubt.

Vague words! but ah, how hard to frame
   In matter-moulded forms of speech,
   Or ev'n for intellect to reach
Thro' memory that which I became:

Till now the doubtful dusk reveal'd
   The knolls once more where, couch'd at ease,
   The white kine glimmer'd, and the trees
Laid their dark arms about the field:

And suck'd from out the distant gloom
   A breeze began to tremble o'er

The large leaves of the sycamore,
And fluctuate all the still perfume,

And gathering freshlier overhead,
   Rock'd the full-foliaged elms, and swung
   The heavy-folded rose, and flung
The lilies to and fro, and said

"The dawn, the dawn," and died away;
   And East and West, without a breath,
   Mixt their dim lights, like life and death,
To broaden into boundless day.

ROBERT BROWNING

Home-Thoughts from Abroad

OH, to be in England
   Now that April's there,
And whoever wakes in England
Sees, some morning, unaware,
That the lowest boughs and the brush-wood sheaf
Round the elm-tree bole are in tiny leaf,
While the chaffinch sings on the orchard bough
In England—now!

And after April, when May follows,
And the whitethroat builds, and all the swallows—
Hark! where my blossomed pear-tree in the hedge
Leans to the field and scatters on the clover
Blossoms and dewdrops—at the bent-spray's edge—
That's the wise thrush; he sings each song twice over,
Lest you should think he never could recapture
The first fine careless rapture!
And though the fields look rough with hoary dew,
All will be gay when noontide wakes anew
The buttercups, the little children's dower,
—Far brighter than this gaudy melon-flower!

A Toccata of Galuppi's[1]

I

OH Galuppi, Baldassaro, this is very sad to find!
I can hardly misconceive you; it would prove me deaf and
blind;
But although I take your meaning, 'tis with such a heavy mind!

II

Here you come with your old music, and here's all the good it brings.
What, they lived once thus at Venice where the merchants were the
kings,
Where St. Mark's is, where the Doges used to wed the sea with
rings?

III

Ay, because the sea's the street there; and 'tis arched by . . . what
you call
. . . Shylock's bridge[2] with houses on it, where they kept the carni-
val:
I was never out of England—it's as if I saw it all.

IV

Did young people take their pleasure when the sea was warm in
May?
Balls and masks begun at midnight, burning ever to mid-day,
When they made up fresh adventures for the morrow, do you say?

V

Was a lady such a lady, cheeks so round and lips so red,—
On her neck the small face buoyant, like a bell-flower on its bed,
O'er the breast's superb abundance where a man might base his
head?

[1] Baldassare Galuppi (1706–1785) was an Italian composer, chiefly of opera. During
the latter part of his life he was organist at St. Mark's, Venice. The toccata, as the
name implies (Italian *toccare*, to touch), is a "touch-piece," built up of a rapid succession of notes, scale passages, *etc.*, played *staccato*. It is light, free, and rather more
showy than profound. In the poem it typifies the life of Venice.

[2] The Rialto.

VI

Well, and it was graceful of them—they'd break talk off and afford
—She, to bite her mask's black velvet—he, to finger on his sword,
While you sat and played Toccatas, stately at the clavichord?

VII

What? Those lesser thirds[3] so plaintive, sixths diminished, sigh on
sigh,
Told them something? Those suspensions, those solutions—"Must
we die?"
Those commiserating sevenths—"Life might last! we can but try!"

VIII

"Were you happy?"—"Yes."—"And are you still as happy?"—"Yes.
And you?"
—"Then, more kisses!"—"Did I stop them, when a million seemed
so few?"
Hark, the dominant's persistence, till it must be answered to!

IX

So, an octave struck the answer. Oh, they praised you, I dare say!
"Brave Galuppi! that was music! good alike at grave and gay!
I can always leave off talking when I hear a master play!"

X

Then they left you for their pleasure: till in due time, one by one,
Some with lives that came to nothing, some with deeds as well un-
done,
Death stepped tacitly and took them where they never see the sun.

XI

But when I sit down to reason, think to take my stand nor swerve,
While I triumph o'er a secret wrung from nature's close reserve,
In you come with your cold music till I creep thro' every nerve.

[3] This and the following technical terms in music are described, at least in their
effect, by the phrases that follow them.

XII

Yes, you, like a ghostly cricket, creaking where a house was burned:
"Dust and ashes, dead and done with, Venice spent what Venice
    earned.
The soul, doubtless, is immortal—where a soul can be discerned.

XIII

"Yours for instance: you know physics, something of geology,
Mathematics are your pastime; souls shall rise in their degree;
Butterflies may dread extinction,—you'll not die, it cannot be!

XIV

"As for Venice and her people, merely born to bloom and drop,
Here on earth they bore their fruitage, mirth and folly were the crop:
What of soul was left, I wonder, when the kissing had to stop?

XV

"Dust and ashes!" So you creak it, and I want the heart to scold.
Dear dead women, with such hair, too—what's become of all the
    gold
Used to hang and brush their bosoms? I feel chilly and grown old.

A Grammarian's Funeral

Shortly after the revival of learning in Europe

LET us begin and carry up this corpse,
    Singing together.
Leave we the common crofts, the vulgar thorpes
    Each in its tether
Sleeping safe on the bosom of the plain,
    Cared-for till cock-crow:
Look out if yonder be not day again
    Rimming the rock-row!
That's the appropriate country; there, man's thought,
    Rarer, intenser,
Self-gathered for an outbreak, as it ought,
    Chafes in the censer.

Leave we the unlettered plain its herd and crop;
  Seek we sepulture
On a tall mountain, citied to the top,
  Crowded with culture!
All the peaks soar, but one the rest excels;
  Clouds overcome it;
No! yonder sparkle is the citadel's
  Circling its summit.
Thither our path lies; wind we up the heights:
  Wait ye the warning?
Our low life was the level's and the nights;
  He's for the morning.
Step to a tune, square chests, erect each head,
  'Ware the beholders!
This is our master, famous calm and dead,
  Borne on our shoulders.

Sleep, crop and herd! sleep, darkling thorpe and croft,
  Safe from the weather!
He, whom we convoy to his grave aloft,
  Singing together,
He was a man born with thy face and throat,
  Lyric Apollo!
Long he lived nameless: how should spring take note
  Winter would follow?
Till lo, the little touch, and youth was gone!
  Cramped and diminished,
Moaned he, "New measures, other feet anon!
  My dance is finished"?
No, that's the world's way: (keep the mountain-side,
  Make for the city!)
He knew the signal, and stepped on with pride
  Over men's pity;
Left play for work, and grappled with the world
  Bent on escaping:
"What's in the scroll," quoth he, "thou keepest furled?
  Show me their shaping,
Theirs who most studied man, the bard and sage,—
  Give!"—So, he gowned him,
Straight got by heart that book to its last page:
  Learned, we found him.

Yea, but we found him bald too, eyes like lead,
  Accents uncertain:
"Time to taste life," another would have said,
  "Up with the curtain!"
This man said rather, "Actual life comes next?
  Patience a moment!
Grant I have mastered learning's crabbed text,
  Still there's the comment.
Let me know all! Prate not of most or least,
  Painful or easy!
Even to the crumbs I'd fain eat up the feast,
  Ay, nor feel queasy."
Oh, such a life as he resolved to live,
  When he had learned it,
When he had gathered all books had to give!
  Sooner, he spurned it.
Image the whole, then execute the parts—
  Fancy the fabric
Quite, ere you build, ere steel strike fire from quartz,
  Ere mortar dab brick!
(Here's the town-gate reach'd: there's the market-place
  Gaping before us.)
Yea, this in him was the peculiar grace
  (Hearten our chorus!)
That before living he'd learn how to live—
  No end to learning:
Earn the means first—God surely will contrive
  Use for our earning.
Others mistrust and say, "But time escapes:
  Live now or never!"
He said, "What's time? Leave Now for dogs and apes!
  Man has Forever."

Back to his book then: deeper drooped his head:
  Calculus racked him:
Leaden before, his eyes grew dross of lead:
  Tussis attacked him.
"Now, master, take a little rest!"—not he!
  (Caution redoubled,
Step two abreast, the way winds narrowly!)
  Not a whit troubled

Back to his studies, fresher than at first,
  Fierce as a dragon
He (soul-hydroptic with a sacred thirst)
  Sucked at the flagon.
Oh, if we draw a circle premature,
  Heedless of far gain,
Greedy for quick returns of profit, sure
  Bad is our bargain!
Was it not great? did not he throw on God,
  (He loves the burthen)—
God's task to make the heavenly period
  Perfect the earthen?
Did not he magnify the mind, show clear
  Just what it all meant?
He would not discount life, as fools do here,
  Paid by instalment!
He ventured neck or nothing—heaven's success
  Found, or earth's failure:
"Wilt thou trust death or not?" He answered "Yes:
  Hence with life's pale lure!"
That low man seeks a little thing to do,
  Sees it and does it:
This high man, with a great thing to pursue,
  Dies ere he knows it.
That low man goes on adding one to one,
  His hundred's soon hit:
This high man, aiming at a million,
  Misses an unit.
That, has the world here—should he need the next,
  Let the world mind him!
This, throws himself on God, and unperplexed
  Seeking shall find him
So, with the throttling hands of death at strife,
  Ground he at grammar;
Still, through the rattle, parts of speech were rife:
  While he could stammer
He settled *Hoti's* business—let it be!—
  Properly based *Oun*—
Gave us the doctrine of the enclitic *De,*
  Dead from the waist down.
Well, here's the platform, here's the proper place:
  Hail to your purlieus,

All ye highfliers of the feathered race,
　　Swallows and curlews!
Here's the top-peak; the multitude below
　　Live, for they can, there:
This man decided not to Live but Know—
　　Bury this man there?
Here—here's his place, where meteors shoot, clouds form,
　　Lightnings are loosened,
Stars come and go! Let joy break with the storm.
　　Peace let the dew send!
Lofty designs must close in like effects:
　　Loftily lying,
Leave him—still loftier than the world suspects,
　　Living and dying.

"Childe Roland to the Dark Tower Came"

I

MY first thought was, he lied in every word,
　　That hoary cripple, with malicious eye
Askance to watch the working of his lie
On mine, and mouth scarce able to afford
Suppression of the glee, that pursed and scored
　　Its edge, at one more victim gained thereby.

II

What else should he be set for, with his staff?
　　What, save to waylay with his lies, ensnare
　　All travellers who might find him posted there,
And ask the road? I guessed what skull-like laugh
Would break, what crutch 'gin write my epitaph
　　For pastime in the dusty thoroughfare,

III

If at his counsel I should turn aside
　　Into that ominous tract which, all agree,
　　Hides the Dark Tower. Yet acquiescingly
I did turn as he pointed: neither pride
Nor hope rekindling at the end descried,
　　So much as gladness that some end might be.

IV

For, what with my whole world-wide wandering,
  What with my search drawn out thro' years, my hope
  Dwindled into a ghost not fit to cope
With that obstreperous joy success would bring,—
I hardly tried now to rebuke the spring
  My heart made, finding failure in its scope.

V

As when a sick man very near to death
  Seems dead indeed, and feels begin and end
  The tears and takes the farewell of each friend,
And hears one bid the other go, draw breath
Freelier outside, ("since all is o'er," he saith,
  "And the blow fallen no grieving can amend;")

VI

While some discuss if near the other graves
  Be room enough for this, and when a day
  Suits best for carrying the corpse away,
With care about the banners, scarves and staves:
And still the man hears all, and only craves
  He may not shame such tender love and stay.

VII

Thus, I had so long suffered in this quest,
  Heard failure prophesied so oft, been writ
  So many times among "The Band"—to wit,
  The knights who to the Dark Tower's search addressed
Their steps—that just to fail as they, seemed best,
  And all the doubt was now—should I be fit?

VIII

. So, quiet as despair, I turned from him,
  That hateful cripple, out of his highway
  Into the path he pointed. All the day
Had been a dreary one at best, and dim
Was settling to its close, yet shot one grim
  Red leer to see the plain catch its estray.

IX

For mark! no sooner was I fairly found
  Pledged to the plain, after a pace or two,
  Than, pausing to throw backward a last view
O'er the safe road, 'twas gone; grey plain all round:
Nothing but plain to the horizon's bound.
  I might go on; nought else remained to do.

X

So, on I went. I think I never saw
  Such starved ignoble nature; nothing throve:
  For flowers—as well expect a cedar grove!
But cockle, spurge, according to their law
Might propagate their kind, with none to awe,
  You'd think; a burr had been a treasure-trove.

XI

No! penury, inertness and grimace,
  In some strange sort, were the land's portion. "See
  Or shut your eyes," said Nature peevishly,
"It nothing skills: I cannot help my case:
'Tis the Last Judgment's fire must cure this place,
  Calcine its clods and set my prisoners free."

XII

If there pushed any ragged thistle-stalk
  Above its mates, the head was chopped; the bents
  Were jealous else. What made those holes and rents
In the dock's harsh swarth leaves, bruised as to baulk
All hope of greenness? 'tis a brute must walk
  Pashing their life out, with a brute's intents.

XIII

As for the grass, it grew as scant as hair
  In leprosy; thin dry blades pricked the mud
  Which underneath looked kneaded up with blood.
One stiff blind horse, his every bone a-stare,
Stood stupified, however he came there:
  Thrust out past service from the devil's stud!

XIV

Alive? he might be dead for aught I know,
  With that red gaunt and colloped neck a-strain,
  And shut eyes underneath the rusty mane;
Seldom went such grotesqueness with such woe;
I never saw a brute I hated so;
  He must be wicked to deserve such pain.

XV

I shut my eyes and turned them on my heart.
  As a man calls for wine before he fights,
  I asked one draught of earlier, happier sights,
Ere fitly I could hope to play my part.
Think first, fight afterwards—the soldier's art:
  One taste of the old time sets all to rights.

XVI

Not it! I fancied Cuthbert's reddening face
  Beneath its garniture of curly gold,
  Dear fellow, till I almost felt him fold
An arm in mine to fix me to the place,
That way he used. Alas, one night's disgrace!
  Out went my heart's new fire and left it cold.

XVII

Giles then, the soul of honour—there he stands
  Frank as ten years ago when knighted first.
  What honest men should dare (he said) he durst.
Good—but the scene shifts—faugh! what hangman's hands
Pin to his breast a parchment? His own bands
  Read it. Poor traitor, spit upon and curst!

XVIII

Better this present than a past like that;
  Back therefore to my darkening path again!
  No sound, no sight as far as eye could strain.
Will the night send a howlet or a bat?
I asked: when something on the dismal flat
  Came to arrest my thoughts and change their train.

XIX

A sudden little river crossed my path
  As unexpected as a serpent comes.
  No sluggish tide congenial to the glooms;
This, as it frothed by, might have been a bath
For the fiend's glowing hoof—to see the wrath
  Of its black eddy bespate with flakes and spumes.

XX

So petty yet so spiteful! all along,
  Low scrubby alders kneeled down over it;
  Drenched willows flung them headlong in a fit
Of mute despair, a suicidal throng:
The river which had done them all the wrong,
  Whate'er that was, rolled by, deterred no whit.

XXI

Which, while I forded,—good saints, how I feared
  To set my foot upon a dead man's cheek,
  Each step, or feel the spear I thrust to seek
For hollows, tangled in his hair or beard!
—It may have been a water-rat I speared,
  But, ugh! it sounded like a baby's shriek.

XXII

Glad was I when I reached the other bank.
  Now for a better country. Vain presage!
  Who were the strugglers, what war did they wage,
Whose savage trample thus could pad the dank
Soil to a plash? Toads in a poisoned tank,
  Or wild cats in a red-hot iron cage—

XXIII

The fight must so have seemed in that fell cirque.
  What penned them there, with all the plain to choose?
  No foot-print leading to that horrid mews,
None out of it. Mad brewage set to work
Their brains, no doubt, like galley-slaves the Turk
  Pits for his pastime, Christians against Jews.

XXIV

And more than that—a furlong on—why, there!
  What bad use was that engine for, that wheel,
  Or brake, not wheel—that harrow fit to reel
Men's bodies out like silk? with all the air
Of Tophet's tool, on earth left unaware,
  Or brought to sharpen its rusty teeth of steel.

XXV

Then came a bit of stubbed ground, once a wood,
  Next a marsh, it would seem, and now mere earth
  Desperate and done with; (so a fool finds mirth,
Makes a thing and then mars it, till his mood
Changes and off he goes!) within a rood—
  Bog, clay and rubble, sand and stark black dearth.

XXVI

Now blotches rankling, coloured gay and grim,
  Now patches where some leanness of the soil's
  Broke into moss or substances like boils;
Then came some palsied oak, a cleft in him
Like a distorted mouth that splits its rim
  Gaping at death, and dies while it recoils.

XXVII

And just as far as ever from the end!
  Nought in the distance but the evening, nought
  To point my footstep further! At the thought,
A great black bird, Apollyon's bosom-friend,
Sailed past, nor beat his wide wing dragon-penned
  That brushed my cap—perchance the guide I sought.

XXVIII

For, looking up, aware I somehow grew,
  'Spite of the dusk, the plain had given place
  All round to mountains—with such name to grace
Mere ugly heights and heaps now stolen in view.
How thus they had surprised me,—solve it, you!
  How to get from them was no clearer case.

XXIX

Yet half I seemed to recognise some trick
  Of mischief happened to me, God knows when—
  In a bad dream perhaps. Here ended, then,
Progress this way. When, in the very nick
Of giving up, one time more, came a click
  As when a trap shuts—you're inside the den!

XXX

Burningly it came on me all at once,
  This was the place! those two hills on the right,
  Crouched like two bulls locked horn in horn in fight;
While to the left, a tall scalped mountain . . . Dunce,
Dotard, a-dozing at the very nonce,
  After a life spent training for the sight!

XXXI

What in the midst lay but the Tower itself?
  The round squat turret, blind as the fool's heart,
  Built of brown stone, without a counterpart
In the whole world. The tempest's mocking elf
Points to the shipman thus the unseen shelf
  He strikes on, only when the timbers start.

XXXII

Not see? because of night perhaps?—Why, day
  Came back again for that! before it left,
  The dying sunset kindled through a cleft:
The hills, like giants at a hunting, lay,
Chin upon hand, to see the game at bay,—
  "Now stab and end the creature—to the heft!"

XXXIII

Not hear? when noise was everywhere! it tolled
  Increasing like a bell. Names in my ears,
  Of all the lost adventurers my peers,—
How such a one was strong, and such was bold,
And such was fortunate, yet each of old
  Lost, lost! one moment knelled the woe of years.

XXXIV

There they stood, ranged along the hillsides, met
  To view the last of me, a living frame
  For one more picture! in a sheet of flame
I saw them and I knew them all. And yet
Dauntless the slug-horn to my lips I set,
  And blew. *"Childe Roland to the Dark Tower came."*

Song from Paracelsus

HEAP cassia, sandal-buds and stripes
    Of labdanum, and aloe-balls,
Smear'd with dull nard an Indian wipes
    From out her hair: such balsam falls
    Down sea-side mountain pedestals,
From tree-tops where tired winds are fain,
Spent with the vast and howling main,
  To treasure half their island-gain.

And strew faint sweetness from some old
    Egyptian's fine worm-eaten shroud
Which breaks to dust when once unroll'd;
    Or shredded perfume, like a cloud
    From closet long to quiet vow'd,
With moth'd and dropping arras hung,
Mouldering her lute and books among,
  As when a queen, long dead, was young.

Song

NAY, but you, who do not love her,
    Is she not pure gold, my mistress?
Holds earth aught—speak truth—above her?
    Aught like this tress, see, and this tress,
And this last fairest tress of all,
So fair, see, ere I let it fall!

Because, you spend your lives in praising;
  To praise, you search the wide world over;

So, why not witness, calmly gazing,
  If earth holds aught—speak truth—above her?
Above this tress, and this I touch
But cannot praise, I love so much!

Never the Time and the Place

NEVER the time and the place
      And the loved one all together!
  This path—how soft to pace!
    This May—what magic weather!
  Where is the loved one's face?
In a dream that loved one's face meets mine,
  But the house is narrow, the place is bleak
Where, outside, rain and wind combine
  With a furtive ear, if I strive to speak,
  With a hostile eye at my flushing cheek,
With a malice that marks each word, each sign!
O enemy sly and serpentine,
  Uncoil thee from the waking man!
    Do I hold the Past
    Thus firm and fast
  Yet doubt if the Future hold I can?
  This path so soft to pace shall lead
  Through the magic of May to herself indeed!
  Or narrow if needs the house must be,
Outside are the storms and strangers: we—
Oh, close, safe, warm sleep I and she,
    —I and she!

Prospice

FEAR death?—to feel the fog in my throat,
      The mist in my face,
When the snows begin, and the blasts denote
      I am nearing the place,
The power of the night, the press of the storm,
      The post of the foe;
Where he stands, the Arch Fear in a visible form,
      Yet the strong man must go:

For the journey is done and the summit attained,
　　And the barriers fall,
Though a battle's to fight ere the guerdon be gained,
　　The reward of it all.
I was ever a fighter, so—one fight more,
　　The best and the last!
I would hate that death bandaged my eyes, and forbore,
　　And bade me creep past.
No! let me taste the whole of it, fare like my peers
　　The heroes of old,
Bear the brunt, in a minute pay glad life's arrears
　　Of pain, darkness and cold.
For sudden the worst turns the best to the brave,
　　The black minute's at end,
And the elements' rage, the fiend-voices that rave,
　　Shall dwindle, shall blend,
Shall change, shall become first a peace out of pain,
　　Then a light, then thy breast,
O thou soul of my soul! I shall clasp thee again,
　　And with God be the rest!

EDWARD FITZGERALD

FROM THE RUBÁIYÁT OF OMAR KHAYYÁM

A　Book of Verses underneath the Bough,
　　A Jug of Wine, a Loaf of Bread—and Thou
　Beside me singing in the Wilderness—
Oh, Wilderness were Paradise enow!

Some for the Glories of this World; and some
Sigh for the Prophet's Paradise to come;
　Ah, take the Cash, and let the Credit go,
Nor heed the rumble of a distant Drum!

Look to the blowing Rose about us—"Lo,
Laughing," she says, "into the world I blow,

At once the silken tassel of my Purse
Tear, and its Treasure on the Garden throw."

And those who husbanded the Golden grain,
And those who flung it to the winds like Rain,
   Alike to no such aureate Earth are turned
As, buried once, Men want dug up again.

The Worldly Hope men set their Hearts upon
Turns Ashes—or it prospers; and anon,
   Like Snow upon the Desert's dusty Face,
Lighting a little hour or two—was gone.

Think, in this battered caravanserai
Whose Portals are alternate Night and Day,
   How Sultán after Sultán with his Pomp
Abode his destined Hour, and went his way.

They say the Lion and the Lizard keep
The Courts where Jamshyd gloried and drank deep:
   And Bahrám, that great Hunter—the Wild Ass
Stamps o'er his Head, but cannot break his Sleep.

I sometimes think that never blows so red
The Rose as where some buried Cæsar bled;
   That every Hyacinth the Garden wears
Dropped in her Lap from some once lovely Head.

And this reviving Herb whose tender Green
Fledges the River-Lip on which we lean—
   Ah, lean upon it lightly! for who knows
From what once lovely Lip it springs unseen!

Ah, my Beloved, fill the Cup that clears
Today of past Regret and future Fears:
   Tomorrow!—Why, Tomorrow I may be
Myself with Yesterday's sev'n thousand Years.

For some we loved, the loveliest and the best
That from his Vintage rolling Time hath pressed,
   Have drunk their Cup a Round or two before,
And one by one crept silently to rest.

And we that now make merry in the Room
They left, and Summer dresses in new bloom,
   Ourselves must we beneath the Couch of Earth
Descend—ourselves to make a Couch—for whom?

Ah, make the most of what we yet may spend,
Before we too into the Dust descend;
   Dust into Dust, and under Dust, to lie,
Sans Wine, sans Song, sans Singer, and—sans End!

Yet Ah, that Spring should vanish with the Rose!
That Youth's sweet-scented manuscript should close!
   The Nightingale that in the branches sang,
Ah whence, and whither flown again, who knows!

Would but the Desert of the Fountain yield
One glimpse—if dimly, yet indeed, revealed,
   To which the fainting Traveller might spring,
As springs the trampled herbage of the field!

Would but some winged Angel ere too late
Arrest the yet unfolded Roll of Fate,
   And make the stern Recorder otherwise
Enregister, or quite obliterate!

Ah Love! could you and I with Him conspire
To grasp this sorry Scheme of Things entire,
   Would not we shatter it to bits—and then
Remould it nearer to the Heart's desire!

Yon rising Moon that looks for us again—
How oft hereafter will she wax and wane;
   How oft hereafter rising look for us
Through this same Garden—and for *one* in vain!

And when like her, oh Sákí, you shall pass
Among the Guests Star-scattered on the Grass,
   And in your joyous errand reach the spot
Where I made One—turn down an empty Glass!

WILLIAM BELL SCOTT

The Witch's Ballad

O I hae come from far away,
From a warm land far away,
A southern land across the sea,
With sailor-lads about the mast,
Merry and canny, and kind to me.

And I hae been to yon town
To try my luck in yon town;
Nort, and Mysie, Elspie too.
Right braw we were to pass the gate,
Wi' gowden clasps on girdles blue.

Mysie smiled wi' miminy mouth,
Innocent mouth, miminy mouth;
Elspie wore a scarlet gown,
Nort's grey eyes were unco' gleg.
My Castile comb was like a crown.

We walk'd abreast all up the street,
Into the market up the street;
Our hair with marigolds was wound,
Our bodices with love-knots laced,
Our merchandise with tansy bound.

Nort had chickens, I had cocks,
Gamesome cocks, loud-crowing cocks;
Mysie ducks, and Elspie drakes,—
For a wee groat or a pound;
We lost nae time wi' gives and takes.

—Lost nae time, for weil we knew,
In our sleeves full well we knew,
When the gloaming came that night,

Duck nor drake, nor hen nor cock
Would be found by candle-light.

And when our chaffering all was done,
  All was paid for, sold and done,
We drew a glove on ilka hand,
We sweetly curtsied, each to each,
And deftly danced a saraband.

The market-lassies look'd and laugh'd,
  Left their gear, and look'd and laugh'd;
They made as they would join the game,
But soon their mithers, wild and wud,
With whack and screech they stopp'd the same.

Sae loud the tongues o' randies grew,
  The flytin' and the skirlin' grew,
At all the windows in the place,
Wi' spoons or knives, wi' needle or awl,
Was thrust out every hand and face.

And down each stair they throng'd anon,
  Gentle, semple, throng'd anon:
Souter and tailor, frowsy Nan,
The ancient widow young again,
Simpering behind her fan.

Without a choice, against their will,
  Doited, dazed, against their will,
The market lassie and her mither,
The farmer and his husbandman,
Hand in hand dance a' thegither.

Slow at first, but faster soon,
  Still increasing, wild and fast,
Hoods and mantles, hats and hose,

wud = mad.
randies = viragoes.
flyin' = scolding.
skirlin' = shrieking.
souter = cobbler.
doited = mazed.

Blindly doff'd and cast away,
Left them naked, heads and toes.

They would have torn us limb from limb,
    Dainty limb from dainty limb;
But never one of them could win
Across the line that I had drawn
With bleeding thumb a-widdershin.

But there was Jeff the provost's son,
    Jeff the provost's only son;
There was Father Auld himsel',
The Lombard frae the hostelry,
And the lawyer Peter Fell.

All goodly men we singled out,
    Waled them well, and singled out,
And drew them by the left hand in;
Mysie the priest, and Elspie won
The Lombard, Nort the lawyer carle,
I mysel' the provost's son.

Then, with cantrip kisses seven,
    Three times round with kisses seven,
Warp'd and woven there spun we
Arms and legs and flaming hair,
Like a whirlwind on the sea.

Like a wind that sucks the sea,
    Over and in and on the sea,
Good sooth it was a mad delight;
And every man of all the four
Shut his eyes and laugh'd outright.

Laugh'd as long as they had breath,
    Laugh'd while they had sense or breath;
And close about us coil'd a mist
Of gnats and midges, wasps and flies,
Like the whirlwind shaft it rist.

a-widdershin = the wrong way of the sun: or E. to W. through N.
waled = chose.
cantrip = magic.

Drawn up I was right off my feet,
  Into the mist and off my feet;
And, dancing on each chimmey-top,
I saw a thousand darling imps
Keeping time with skip and hop.

And on the provost's brave ridge-tile,
  On the provost's grand ridge-tile,
The Blackamoor first to master me
I saw, I saw that winsome smile.
The mouth that did my heart beguile,
And spoke the great Word over me,
In the land beyond the sea.

I call'd his name, I call'd aloud,
  Alas! I call'd on him aloud;
And then he fill'd his hand with stour,
And threw it towards me in the air;
My mouse flew out, I lost my pow'r!

My lusty strength, my power were gone;
  Power was gone, and all was gone.
He will not let me love him more!
Of bell and whip and horse's tail
He cares not if I find a store.

But I am proud if he is fierce!
  I am as proud as he is fierce;
I'll turn about and backward go,
If I meet again that Blackamoor,
And he'll help us then, for he shall know
I seek another paramour.

And we'll gang once more to yon town,
  Wi' better luck to yon town;
We'll walk in silk and cramoisie,
And I shall wed the provost's son
My lady of the town I'll be!

stour = dust.
cramoisie = crimson.

For I was born a crown'd king's child,
 Born and nursed a king's child,
King o' a land ayont the sea,
Where the Blackamoor kiss'd me first,
And taught me art and glamourie.

Each one in her wame shall hide
 Her hairy mouse, her wary mouse,
Fed on madwort and agramie,—
Wear amber beads between her breasts,
And blind-worm's skin about her knee.

The Lombard shall be Elspie's man,
 Elspie's gowden husband-man;
Nort shall take the lawyer's hand;
The priest shall swear another vow:
We'll dance again the saraband!

———•—•—•———

EMILY BRONTË

———•—•—•———

The Prisoner

A FRAGMENT

IN the dungeon-crypts idly did I stray,
 Reckless of the lives wasting there away;
"Draw the ponderous bars! open, Warder stern!"
He dared not say me nay—the hinges harshly turn.

"Our guests are darkly lodged," I whisper'd, gazing through
The vault, whose grated eye showed heaven more grey than blue;
(This was when glad Spring laughed in awaking pride);
"Ay, darkly lodged enough!" returned my sullen guide.

Then, God forgive my youth; forgive my careless tongue;
I scoffed, as the chill chains on the damp flagstones rung:

ayont = beyond.
glamourie = wizardy.

"Confined in triple walls, art thou so much to fear,
That we must bind thee down and clench thy fetters here?"

The captive raised her face; it was as soft and mild
As sculptured marble saint, or slumbering unwean'd child;
It was so soft and mild, it was so sweet and fair,
Pain could not trace a line, nor grief a shadow there!

The captive raised her hand and pressed it to her brow:
"I have been struck," she said, "and I am suffering now;
Yet these are little worth, your bolts and irons strong;
And, were they forged in steel, they could not hold me long."

Hoarse laughed the jailor grim: "Shall I be won to hear;
Dost think, fond, dreaming wretch, that *I* shall grant thy prayer?
Or, better still, wilt melt my master's heart with groans?
Ah! sooner might the sun thaw down these granite stones.

"My master's voice is low, his aspect bland and kind,
But hard as hardest flint the soul that lurks behind;
And I am rough and rude, yet not more rough to see
Than is the hidden ghost that has its home in me."

About her lips there played a smile of almost scorn:
"My friend," she gently said, "you have not heard me mourn;
When you my kindred's lives, *my* lost life, can restore,
Then may I weep and sue,—but never, friend, before!

"Still, let my tyrants know, I am not doomed to wear
Year after year in gloom, and desolate despair;
A messenger of Hope comes every night to me,
And offers for short life, eternal liberty.

"He comes with western winds, with evening's wandering airs,
With that clear dusk of heaven that brings the thickest stars.
Winds take a pensive tone, and stars a tender fire,
And visions rise, and change, that kill me with desire.

"Desire for nothing known in my maturer years,
When joy grew mad with awe, at counting future tears.
When, if my spirit's sky was full of flashes warm,
I knew not whence they came, from sun or thunder-storm.

"But, first, a hush of peace—a soundless calm descends;
The struggle of distress, and fierce impatience ends;
Mute music soothes my breast—unuttered harmony,
That I could never dream, till Earth was lost to me.

"Then dawns the Invisible; the Unseen its truth reveals;
My outward sense is gone, my inward essence feels:
Its wings are almost free—its home, its harbour found,
Measuring the gulf, it stoops—and dares the final bound.

"Oh! dreadful is the check—intense the agony—
When the ear begins to hear, and the eye begins to see;
When the pulse begins to throb, the brain to think again;
The soul to feel the flesh, and the flesh to feel the chain.

"Yet I would lose no sting, would wish no torture less;
The more that anguish racks, the earlier it will bless;
And robed in fires of hell, or bright with heavenly shine,
If it but herald death, the vision is divine!"

She ceased to speak, and we, unanswering, turned to go—
We had no further power to work the captive woe:
Her cheek, her gleaming eye, declared that man had given
A sentence, unapproved, and overruled by Heaven.

Then like a tender child whose hand did just enfold
Safe in its eager grasp a bird it wept to hold,
When pierced with one wild glance from the troubled hazel eye,
It gushes into tears and lets its treasure fly,

Thus ruth and selfish love, together striving, tore
The heart all newly taught to pity and adore;
If I should break the chain, I felt my bird would go;
Yet I must break the chain, or seal the prisoner's woe.

ARTHUR HUGH CLOUGH

Say not the struggle nought availeth

SAY not the struggle nought availeth,
　　The labour and the wounds are vain,
The enemy faints not, nor faileth,
　　And as things have been things remain.

If hopes were dupes, fears may be liars;
　　It may be, in yon smoke concealed,
Your comrades chase e'en now the fliers,
　　And, but for you, possess the field.

For while the tired waves, vainly breaking,
　　Seem here no painful inch to gain,
Far back, through creeks and inlets making,
　　Comes silent, flooding in, the main,

And not by eastern windows only,
　　When daylight comes, comes in the light,
In front, the sun climbs slow, how slowly,
　　But westward, look, the land is bright!

MATTHEW ARNOLD

Shakespeare

OTHERS abide our question. Thou art free.
　　We ask and ask—Thou smilest and art still,
Out-topping knowledge. For the loftiest hill,
Who to the stars uncrowns his majesty,

Planting his steadfast footsteps in the sea,
Making the heaven of heavens his dwelling-place,
Spares but the cloudy border of his base
To the foil'd searching of mortality;

And thou, who didst the stars and sunbeams know,
Self-school'd, self-scann'd, self-honour'd, self-secure,
Didst tread on earth unguess'd at.—Better so!

All pains the immortal spirit must endure,
All weakness which impairs, all griefs which bow,
Find their sole speech in that victorious brow.

The Scholar-Gipsy

GO, for they call you, shepherd, from the hill;
　　Go, shepherd, and untie the wattled cotes!
　No longer leave thy wistful flock unfed,
Nor let thy bawling fellows rack their throats,
　Nor the cropp'd herbage shoot another head.
　　But when the fields are still,
　And the tired men and dogs all gone to rest,
　And only the white sheep are sometimes seen
　Cross and recross the strips of moon-blanch'd green,
Come, shepherd, and again begin the quest!
Here, where the reaper was at work of late—
　In this high field's dark corner, where he leaves
　His coat, his basket, and his earthen cruse,
　And in the sun all morning binds the sheaves,
　　Then here, at noon, comes back his stores to use—
　　Here will I sit and wait,
　While to my ear from uplands far away
　The bleating of the folded flocks is borne,
　With distant cries of reapers in the corn—
All the live murmur of a summer's day.

Screen'd is this nook o'er the high, half-reap'd field,
　And here till sun-down, shepherd! will I be.
　Through the thick corn the scarlet poppies peep,
And round green roots and yellowing stalks I see
　Pale pink convolvulus in tendrils creep;
　　And air-swept lindens yield

Their scent, and rustle down their perfum'd showers
  Of bloom on the bent grass where I am laid,
    And bower me from the August sun with shade;
And the eye travels down to Oxford's towers.

And near me on the grass lies Glanvil's book—
  Come, let me read the oft-read tale again:
    The story of that Oxford scholar poor,
  Of pregnant parts and quick inventive brain,
    Who, tired of knocking at Preferment's door,
      One summer morn forsook
His friends, and went to learn the Gipsy lore,
  And roam'd the world with that wild brotherhood,
  And came, as most men deem'd, to little good,
But came to Oxford and his friends no more.

But once, years after, in the country lanes,
  Two scholars, whom at college erst he knew,
    Met him, and of his way of life inquired.
  Whereat he answer'd that the Gipsy crew,
    His mates, had arts to rule as they desired
      The workings of men's brains;
And they can bind them to what thoughts they will:
  "And I," he said, "the secret of their art,
  When fuly learn'd, will to the world impart:
But it needs Heaven-sent moments for this skill!"

This said, he left them, and return'd no more,
  But rumours hung about the country-side,
    That the lost Scholar long was seen to stray,
  Seen by rare glimpses, pensive and tongue-tied,
    In hat of antique shape, and cloak of grey,
      The same the Gipsies wore.
Shepherds had met him on the Hurst in spring;
  At some lone alehouse in the Berkshire moors,
  On the warm ingle-bench, the smock-frock'd boors
Had found him seated at their entering,

But, 'mid their drink and clatter, he would fly:
  And I myself seem half to know thy looks,
    And put the shepherds, Wanderer, on thy trace;

And boys who in lone wheatfields scare the rooks
I ask if thou hast pass'd their quiet place;
　　Or in my boat I lie
Moor'd to the cool bank in the summer heats,
'Mid wide grass meadows which the sunshine fills,
And watch the warm green-muffled Cumnor hills,
And wonder if thou haunt'st their shy retreats.

For most, I know, thou lov'st retired ground!
Thee at the ferry Oxford riders blithe,
　　Returning home on summer-nights, have met
Crossing the stripling Thames at Bab-lock-hithe,
Trailing in the cool stream thy fingers wet,
　　As the punt's rope chops round;
And leaning backward in a pensive dream,
And fostering in thy lap a heap of flowers
Pluck'd in shy fields and distant Wychwood bowers,
And thine eyes resting on the moonlit stream.

And then they land, and thou art seen no more!—
Maidens, who from the distant hamlets come
To dance around the Fyfield elm in May,
Oft through the darkening fields have seen thee roam,
Or cross a stile into the public way;
　　Oft thou hast given them store
Of flowers—the frail-leaf'd, white anemony,
Dark bluebells drench'd with dews of summer eves,
And purple orchises with spotted leaves—
But none hath words she can report of thee!

And, above Godstow Bridge, when hay-time's here
In June, and many a scythe in sunshine flames,
Men who through those wide fields of breezy grass,
Where black-wing'd swallows haunt the glittering Thames
To bathe in the abandon'd lasher pass,
　　Have often pass'd thee near
Sitting upon the river bank o'ergrown;
Mark'd thine outlandish garb, thy figure spare,
Thy dark vague eyes, and soft abstracted air—
But, when they came from bathing, thou wast gone!

At some lone homestead in the Cumnor hills,
  Where at her open door the housewife darns,
    Thou hast been seen, or hanging on a gate
  To watch the threshers in the mossy barns.
      Children, who early range these slopes and late
        For cresses from the rills,
  Have known thee eying, all an April-day,
    The springing pastures and the feeding kine;
    And mark'd thee, when the stars come out and shine,
  Through the long dewy grass move slow away.

In autumn, on the skirts of Bagley Wood—
  Where most the gipsies by the turf-edged way
    Pitch their smoked tents, and every bush you see
  With scarlet patches tagg'd and shreds of grey,
      Above the forest-ground called Thessaly—
        The blackbird, picking food,
  Sees thee, nor stops his meal, nor fears at all;
    So often has he known thee past him stray,
    Rapt, twirling in thy hand a wither'd spray,
  And waiting for the spark from heaven to fall.

And once, in winter, on the causeway chill
  Where home through flooded fields foot-travellers go,
    Have I not pass'd thee on the wooden bridge,
  Wrapt in thy cloak and battling with the snow,
      Thy face tow'rd Hinksey and its wintry ridge?
        And thou hast climb'd the hill,
  And gain'd the white brow of the Cumnor range;
    Turn'd once to watch, while thick the snow-flakes fall,
    The line of festal light in Christ-Church hall—
  Then sought thy straw in some sequester'd grange.

But what—I dream! Two hundred years are flown
  Since first thy story ran through Oxford halls,
    And the grave Glanvil did the tale inscribe
  That thou wert wander'd from the studious walls
      To learn strange arts, and join a gipsy-tribe;
        And thou from earth art gone
  Long since, and in some quiet churchyard laid—
    Some country-nook, where o'er thy unknown grave

Tall grasses and white flowering nettles wave,
Under a dark, red-fruited yew-tree's shade.

—No, no, thou hast not felt the lapse of hours!
    For what wears out the life of mortal men?
        'Tis that from change to change their being rolls;
    'Tis that repeated shocks, again, again,
        Exhaust the energy of strongest souls
            And numb the elastic powers.
    Till having used our nerves with bliss and teen,
        And tired upon a thousand schemes our wit,
        To the just-pausing Genius we remit
    Our worn-out life, and are—what we have been.

Thou hast not lived, why should'st thou perish, so?
    Thou hadst *one* aim, *one* business, *one* desire;
        Else wert thou long since number'd with the dead!
    Else hadst thou spent, like other men, thy fire!
        The generations of thy peers are fled,
            And we ourselves shall go;
    But thou possessest an immortal lot,
        And we imagine thee exempt from age
        And living as thou liv'st on Glanvil's page,
    Because thou hadst—what we, alas! have not.

For early didst thou leave the world, with powers
    Fresh, undiverted to the world without,
        Firm to their mark, not spent on other things;
    Free from the sick fatigue, the languid doubt,
        Which much to have tried, in much been baffled, brings.
            O life unlike to ours!
    Who fluctuate idly without term or scope,
        Of whom each strives, nor knows for what he strives,
        And each half lives a hundred different lives;
    Who wait like thee, but not, like thee, in hope.

Thou waitest for the spark from heaven! and we,
    Light half-believers of our casual creeds,
        Who never deeply felt, nor clearly will'd,
    Whose insight never has born fruit in deeds,
        Whose vague resolves never have been fulfill'd;
            For whom each year we see

Breeds new beginnings, disappointments new;
  Who hesitate and falter life away,
  And lose tomorrow the ground won today—
Ah! do not we, wanderer! await it too?

Yes, we await it!—but it still delays,
  And then we suffer! and amongst us one,
  Who most has suffer'd, takes dejectedly
His seat upon the intellectual throne;
  And all his store of sad experience he
    Lays bare of wretched days;
  Tells us his misery's birth and growth and signs,
  And how the dying spark of hope was fed,
  And how the breast was soothed, and how the head,
And all his hourly varied anodynes.

This for our wisest! and we others pine,
  And wish the long unhappy dream would end,
  And waive all claim to bliss, and try to bear;
With close-lipp'd patience for our only friend,
  Sad patience, too near neighbour to despair—
    But none has hope like thine!
  Thou through the fields and through the woods dost stray,
  Roaming the country-side, a truant boy,
  Nursing thy project in unclouded joy,
And every doubt long blown by time away.

O born in days when wits were fresh and clear,
  And life ran gaily as the sparkling Thames;
  Before this strange disease of modern life,
With its sick hurry, its divided aims,
  Its heads o'ertax'd, its palsied hearts, was rife—
    Fly hence, our contact fear!
  Still fly, plunge deeper in the bowering wood!
  Averse, as Dido did with gesture stern
  From her false friend's approach in Hades turn,
Wave us away, and keep thy solitude!

Still nursing the unconquerable hope,
  Still clutching the inviolable shade,
  With a free, onward impulse brushing through,
By night, the silver'd branches of the glade—

Far on the forest-skirts, where none pursue,
  On some mild pastoral slope
Emerge, and resting on the moonlit pales
Freshen thy flowers as in former years
With dew, or listen with enchanted ears,
From the dark dingles, to the nightingales!

But fly our paths, our feverish contact fly!
  For strong the infection of our mental strife,
    Which, though it gives no bliss, yet spoils for rest;
And we should win thee from thy own fair life,
  Like us distracted, and like us unblest.
    Soon, soon thy cheer would die,
Thy hopes grow timorous, and unfix'd thy powers,
  And thy clear aims be cross and shifting made;
  And then thy glad perennial youth would fade,
Fade, and grow old at last, and die like ours.

Then fly our greetings, fly our speech and smiles!
  —As some grave Tyrian trader, from the sea,
    Descried at sunrise an emerging prow
Lifting the cool-hair'd creepers stealthily,
  The fringes of a southward-facing brow
    Among the Ægean isles;
And saw the merry Grecian coaster come,
  Freighted with amber grapes, and Chian wine,
  Green, bursting figs, and tunnies steep'd in brine—
And knew the intruders on his ancient home,

The young light-hearted masters of the waves—
  And snatch'd his rudder, and shook out more sail,
    And day and night held on indignantly
O'er the blue Midland waters with the gale,
  Betwixt the Syrtes and soft Sicily,
    To where the Atlantic raves
Outside the western straits, and unbent sails
  There where down cloudy cliffs, through sheets of foam,
  Shy traffickers, the dark Iberians come;
And on the beach undid his corded bales.

COVENTRY PATMORE

The Toys

MY little Son, who look'd from thoughtful eyes
And moved and spoke in quiet grown-up wise,
Having my law the seventh time disobey'd,
I struck him, and dismiss'd
With hard words and unkiss'd,
—His Mother, who was patient, being dead.
Then, fearing lest his grief should hinder sleep,
I visited his bed,
But found him slumbering deep,
With darken'd eyelids, and their lashes yet
From his late sobbing wet.
And I, with moan,
Kissing away his tears, left others of my own;
For, on a table drawn beside his head,
He had put, within his reach,
A box of counters and a red-vein'd stone,
A piece of glass abraded by the beach,
And six or seven shells,
A bottle with bluebells,
And two French copper coins, ranged there with careful art,
To comfort his sad heart.
So when that night I pray'd
To God, I wept, and said:
"Ah, when at last we lie with trancèd breath,
And Thou rememberest of what toys
We made our joys,
How weakly understood
Thy great commanded good,
Then, fatherly not less
Than I whom Thou has moulded from the clay,
Thou'lt leave Thy wrath, and say,
'I will be sorry for their childishness.'"

A Farewell

WITH all my will, but much against my heart,
 We two now part.
My Very Dear,
Our solace is, the sad road lies so clear.
It needs no art,
With faint, averted feet
And many a tear,
In our opposed paths to persevere.
Go thou to East, I West.
We will not say
There's any hope, it is so far away.
But, O, my Best,
When the one darling of our widowhead,
The nursling Grief,
Is dead,
And no dews blur our eyes
To see the peach-bloom come in evening skies,
Perchance we may,
Where now this night is day,
And even through faith of still averted feet,
Making full circle of our banishment,
Amazed meet;
The bitter journey to the bourne so sweet
Seasoning the termless feast of our content
With tears of recognition never dry.

Magna est Veritas

HERE, in this little Bay,
 Full of tumultuous life and great repose,
Where, twice a day,
The purposeless, glad ocean comes and goes,
Under high cliffs, and far from the huge town,
I sit me down.
For want of me the world's course will not fail:
When all its work is done, the lie shall rot;
The truth is great, and shall prevail,
When none cares whether it prevail or not.

DANTE GABRIEL ROSSETTI

The Blessed Damozel

THE blessed damozel leaned out
　　From the gold bar of Heaven;
Her eyes were deeper than the depth
　　Of waters stilled at even;
She had three lilies in her hand,
　　And the stars in her hair were seven.

Her robe, ungirt from clasp to hem,
　　No wrought flowers did adorn,
But a white rose of Mary's gift,
　　For service meetly worn;
Her hair that lay along her back
　　Was yellow like ripe corn.

Herseemed she scarce had been a day
　　One of God's choristers;
The wonder was not yet quite gone
　　From that still look of hers;
Albeit, to them she left, her day
　　Had counted as ten years.

(To one, it is ten years of years.
　　. . . Yet now, and in this place,
Surely she leaned o'er me—her hair
　　Fell all about my face. . . .
Nothing: the autumn-fall of leaves.
　　The whole year sets apace.)

It was the rampart of God's house
　　That she was standing on;
By God built over the sheer depth
　　The which is Space begun;
So high, that looking downward thence
　　She scarce could see the sun.

It lies in Heaven, across the flood
   Of ether, as a bridge.
Beneath, the tides of day and night
   With flame and darkness ridge
The void, as low as where this earth
   Spins like a fretful midge.

Around her, lovers, newly met
   'Mid deathless love's acclaims,
Spoke evermore among themselves
   Their heart-remembered names;
And the souls mounting up to God
   Went by her like thin flames.

And still she bowed herself and stooped
   Out of the circling charm;
Until her bosom must have made
   The bar she leaned on warm,
And the lilies lay as if asleep
   Along her bended arm.

From the fixed place of Heaven she saw
   Time like a pulse shake fierce
Through all the worlds. Her gaze still strove
   Within the gulf to pierce
Its path; and now she spoke as when
   The stars sang in their spheres.

The sun was gone now; the curled moon
   Was like a little feather
Fluttering far down the gulf; and now
   She spoke through the still weather.
Her voice was like the voice the stars
   Had when they sang together.

(Ah sweet! Even now, in that bird's song,
   Strove not her accents there,
Fain to be hearkened? When those bells
   Possessed the mid-day air,
Strove not her steps to reach my side
   Down all the echoing stair?)

"I wish that he were come to me,
  For he will come," she said.
"Have I not prayed in Heaven?—on earth,
  Lord, Lord, has he not pray'd?
Are not two prayers a perfect strength?
  And shall I feel afraid?

"When round his head the aureole clings,
  And he is clothed in white,
I'll take his hand and go with him
  To the deep wells of light;
As unto a stream we will step down,
  And bathe there in God's sight.

"We two will stand beside that shrine,
  Occult, withheld, untrod,
Whose lamps are stirred continually
  With prayer sent up to God;
And see our old prayers, granted, melt
  Each like a little cloud.

"We two will lie i' the shadow of
  That living mystic tree
Within whose secret growth the Dove
  Is sometimes felt to be,
While every leaf that His plumes touch
  Saith His Name audibly.

"And I myself will teach to him,
  I myself, lying so,
The songs I sing here; which his voice
  Shall pause in, hushed and slow,
And find some knowledge at each pause,
  Or some new thing to know."

(Alas! We two, we two, thou say'st!
  Yea, one wast thou with me
That once of old. But shall God lift
  To endless unity
The soul whose likeness with thy soul
  Was but its love for thee?)

"We two," she said, "will seek the groves
　　Where the lady Mary is,
With her five handmaidens, whose names
　　Are five sweet symphonies,
Cecily, Gertrude, Magdalen,
　　Margaret and Rosalys.

"Circlewise sit they, with bound locks
　　And foreheads garlanded;
Into the fine cloth white like flame
　　Weaving the golden thread,
To fashion the birth-robes for them
　　Who are just born, being dead.

"He shall fear, haply, and be dumb:
　　Then will I lay my cheek
To his, and tell about our love,
　　Not once abashed or weak:
And the dear Mother will approve
　　My pride, and let me speak.

"Herself shall bring us, hand in hand,
　　To Him round whom all souls
Kneel, the clear-ranged unnumbered heads
　　Bowed with their aureoles:
And angels meeting us shall sing
　　To their citherns and citoles.

"There will I ask of Christ the Lord
　　Thus much for him and me:—
Only to live as once on earth
　　With Love,—only to be,
As then awhile, for ever now
　　Together, I and he."

She gazed and listened and then said,
　　Less sad of speech than mild,—
"All this is when he comes." She ceased.
　　The light thrilled towards her, fill'd
With angels in strong level flight.
　　Her eyes prayed, and she smil'd.

(I saw her smile.) But soon their path
  Was vague in distant spheres:
And then she cast her arms along
  The golden barriers,
And laid her face between her hands,
  And wept. (I heard her tears.)

The Woodspurge

THE wind flapped loose, the wind was still,
  Shaken out dead from tree and hill:
I had walked on at the wind's will,—
I sat now, for the wind was still.

Between my knees my forehead was, —
My lips, drawn in, said not Alas!
My hair was over in the grass,
My naked ears heard the day pass.

My eyes, wide open, had the run
Of some ten weeds to fix upon;
Among those few, out of the sun,
The woodspurge flowered, three cups in one.

From perfect grief there need not be
Wisdom or even memory:
One thing then learnt remains to me,—
The woodspurge has a cup of three.

GEORGE MEREDITH

Modern Love

XLIII

MARK where the pressing wind shoots javelin-like,
Its skeleton shadow on the broad-backed wave!
Here is a fitting spot to dig Love's grave;
Here where the ponderous breakers plunge and strike,
And dart their hissing tongues high up the sand:
In hearing of the ocean, and in sight
Of those ribbed wind-streaks running into white.
If I the death of Love had deeply planned,
I never could have made it half so sure,
As by the unblest kisses which upbraid
The full-waked sense; or failing that, degrade!
'Tis morning: but no morning can restore
What we have forfeited. I see no sin:
The wrong is mixed. In tragic life, God wot,
No villain need be! Passions spin the plot:
We are betrayed by what is false within.

XLVII

We saw the swallows gathering in the sky,
And in the osier-isle we heard them noise.
We had not to look back on summer joys,
Or forward to a summer of bright dye:
But in the largeness of the evening earth
Our spirits grew as we went side by side.
The hour became her husband and my bride.
Love, that had robbed us so, thus blessed our dearth!
The pilgrims of the year waxed very loud
In multitudinous chatterings, as the flood
Full brown came from the West, and like pale blood
Expanded to the upper crimson cloud.

Love, that had robbed us of immortal things,
This little moment mercifully gave,
Where I have seen across the twilight wave
The swan sail with her young beneath her wings.

L

Thus piteously Love closed what he begat:
The union of this ever-diverse pair!
These two were rapid falcons in a snare,
Condemned to do the flitting of the bat.
Lovers beneath the singing sky of May,
They wandered once; clear as the dew on flowers:
But they fed not on the advancing hours:
Their hearts held cravings for the buried day.
Then each applied to each that fatal knife,
Deep questioning, which probes to endless dole.
Ah, what a dusty answer gets the soul
When hot for certainties in this our life!—
In tragic hints here see what evermore
Moves dark as yonder midnight ocean's force,
Thundering like ramping hosts of warrior horse,
To throw that faint thin line upon the shore!

Lucifer in Starlight

ON a starr'd night Prince Lucifer uprose.
  Tired of his dark dominion swung the fiend
Above the rolling ball in cloud part screen'd,
Where sinners hugg'd their spectre of repose.
Poor prey to his hot fit of pride were those.
  And now upon his western wing he lean'd,
  Now his huge bulk o'er Afric's sands careen'd,
Now the black planet shadow'd Arctic snows.
Soaring through wider zones that prick'd his scars
  With memory of the old revolt from Awe,
He reach'd a middle height, and at the stars,
Which are the brain of heaven, he look'd, and sank.
Around the ancient track march'd, rank on rank,
  The army of unalterable law.

CHRISTINA ROSSETTI

Goblin Market

MORNING and evening
Maids heard the goblins cry:
"Come buy our orchard fruits,
Come buy, come buy:
Apples and quinces,
Lemons and oranges,
Plump unpecked cherries,
Melons and raspberries,
Bloom-down-cheeked peaches,
Swart-headed mulberries,
Wild free-born cranberries,
Crab apples, dewberries,
Pine-apples, blackberries,
Apricots, strawberries;—
All ripe together
In summer weather,—
Morns that pass by,
Fair eves that fly;
Come buy, come buy:
Our grapes fresh from the vine,
Pomegranates full and fine,
Dates and sharp bullaces,
Rare pears and greengages,
Damsons and bilberries,
Taste them and try:
Currants and gooseberries,
Bright-fire-like barberries,
Figs to fill your mouth,
Citrons from the South,
Sweet to tongue and sound to eye;
Come buy, come buy."

Evening by evening
Among the brookside rushes,
Laura bowed her head to hear,
Lizzie veiled her blushes:
Crouching close together
In the cooling weather,
With clasping arms and cautioning lips,
With tingling cheeks and finger tips.
"Lie close," Laura said,
Pricking up her golden head:
"We must not look at goblin men,
We must not buy their fruits:
Who knows upon what soil they fed
Their hungry thirsty roots?"
"Come buy," call the goblins
Hobbling down the glen.
"Oh," cried Lizzie, "Laura, Laura,
You should not peep at goblin men."
Lizzie covered up her eyes,
Covered close lest they should look;
Laura reared her glossy head,
And whispered like the restless brook:
"Look, Lizzie, look, Lizzie,
Down the glen tramp little men.
One hauls a basket,
One bears a plate,
One lugs a golden dish
Of many pounds weight.
How fair the vine must grow
Whose grapes are so luscious;
How warm the wind must blow
Through those fruit bushes."
"No," said Lizzie: "No, no, no;
Their offers should not charm us,
Their evil gifts would harm us."
She thrust a dimpled finger
In each ear, shut eyes and ran:
Curious Laura chose to linger
Wondering at each merchant man.
One had a cat's face,
One whisked a tail,

One tramped at a rat's pace,
One crawled like a snail,
One like a wombat prowled obtuse and furry,
One like a ratel tumbled hurry skurry.
She heard a voice like voice of doves
Cooing all together:
They sounded kind and full of loves
In the pleasant weather.

Laura stretched her gleaming neck
Like a rush-imbedded swan,
Like a lily from the beck,
Like a moonlit poplar branch,
Like a vessel at the launch
When its last restraint is gone.

Backwards up the mossy glen
Turned and trooped the goblin men,
With their shrill repeated cry,
"Come buy, come buy."
When they reached where Laura was
They stood stock still upon the moss,
Leering at each other,
Brother with queer brother;
Signalling each other,
Brother with sly brother.
One set his basket down,
One reared his plate;
One began to weave a crown
Of tendrils, leaves, and rough nuts brown
(Men sell not such in any town);
One heaved the golden weight
Of dish and fruit to offer her:
"Come buy, come buy," was still their cry.
Laura stared but did not stir,
Longed but had no money:
The whisk-tailed merchant bade her taste
In tones as smooth as honey,
The cat-faced purr'd,
The rat-paced spoke a word
Of welcome, and the snail-paced even was heard;
One parrot-voiced and jolly

Cried "Pretty Goblin" still for "Pretty Polly";—
One whistled like a bird.

But sweet-tooth Laura spoke in haste:
"Good folk, I have no coin;
To take were to purloin:
I have no copper in my purse,
I have no silver either,
And all my gold is on the furze
That shakes in windy weather
Above the rusty heather."
"You have much gold upon your head,"
They answered all together:
"Buy from us with a golden curl."
She clipped a precious golden lock,
She dropped a tear more rare than pearl,
Then sucked their fruit globes fair or red:
Sweeter than honey from the rock,
Stronger than man-rejoicing wine,
Clearer than water flowed that juice;
She never tasted such before,
How should it cloy with length of use?
She sucked and sucked and sucked the more
Fruits which that unknown orchard bore;
She sucked until her lips were sore;
Then flung the emptied rinds away
But gathered up one kernel stone,
And knew not was it night or day
As she turned home alone.

Lizzie met her at the gate
Full of wise upbraidings:
"Dear, you should not stay so late,
Twilight is not good for maidens;
Should not loiter in the glen
In the haunts of goblin men.
Do you not remember Jeanie,
How she met them in the moonlight,
Took their gifts both choice and many,
Ate their fruits and wore their flowers
Plucked from bowers
Where summer ripens at all hours?

But ever in the moonlight
She pined and pined away;
Sought them by night and day,
Found them no more but dwindled and grew grey;
Then fell with the first snow,
While to this day no grass will grow
Where she lies low:
I planted daisies there a year ago
That never blow.
You should not loiter so."
"Nay, hush," said Laura:
"Nay, hush, my sister:
I ate and ate my fill,
Yet my mouth waters still;
Tomorrow night I will
Buy more:" and kissed her:
"Have done with sorrow;
I'll bring you plums tomorrow
Fresh on their mother twigs,
Cherries worth getting;
You cannot think what figs
My teeth have met in,
What melons icy-cold
Piled on a dish of gold
Too huge for me to hold,
What peaches with a velvet nap,
Pellucid grapes without one seed:
Odorous indeed must be the mead
Whereon they grow, and pure the wave they drink
With lilies at the brink,
And sugar-sweet their sap."

Golden head by golden head,
Like two pigeons in one nest
Folded in each other's wings,
They lay down in their curtained bed:
Like two blossoms on one stem,
Like two flakes of new-fall'n snow,
Like two wands of ivory
Tipped with gold for awful kings.
Moon and stars gazed in at them,
Wind sang to them lullaby,

Lumbering owls forbore to fly,
Not a bat flapped to and fro
Round their nest:
Cheek to cheek and breast to breast
Locked together in one nest.

Early in the morning
When the first cock crowed his warning,
Neat like bees, as sweet and busy,
Laura rose with Lizzie:
Fetched in honey, milked the cows,
Aired and set to rights the house,
Kneaded cakes of whitest wheat,
Cakes for dainty mouths to eat,
Next churned butter, whipped up cream,
Fed their poultry, sat and sewed;
Talked as modest maidens should:
Lizzie with an open heart,
Laura in an absent dream,
One content, one sick in part;
One warbling for the mere bright day's delight,
One longing for the night.

At length slow evening came:
They went with pitchers to the reedy brook;
Lizzie most placid in her look,
Laura most like a leaping flame.
They drew the gurgling water from its deep;
Lizzie plucked purple and rich golden flags,
Then turning homewards said: "The sunset flushes
Those furthest loftiest crags;
Come, Laura, not another maiden lags,
No wilful squirrel wags,
The beasts and birds are fast asleep."
But Laura loitered still among the rushes
And said the bank was steep.

And said the hour was early still,
The dew not fall'n, the wind not chill:
Listening ever, but not catching
The customary cry,
"Come buy, come buy,"

With its iterated jingle
Of sugar-baited words:
Not for all her watching
Once discerning even one goblin
Racing, whisking, tumbling, hobbling;
Let alone the herds
That used to tramp along the glen,
In groups or single,
Of brisk fruit-merchant men.

Till Lizzie urged, "O Laura, come;
I hear the fruit-call but I dare not look:
You should not loiter longer at this brook:
Come with me home.
The stars rise, the moon bends her arc,
Each glowworm winks her spark,
Let us get home before the night grows dark:
For clouds may gather
Though this is summer weather,
Put out the lights and drench us through;
Then if we lost our way what should we do?"

Laura turned cold as stone
To find her sister heard that cry alone,
That goblin cry,
"Come buy our fruits, come buy."
Must she then buy no more such dainty fruit?
Must she no more such succous pasture find,
Gone deaf and blind?
Her tree of life drooped from the root:
She said not one word in her heart's sore ache;
But peering thro' the dimness, nought discerning,
Trudged home, her pitcher dripping all the way;
So crept to bed, and lay
Silent till Lizzie slept;
Then sat up in a passionate yearning,
And gnashed her teeth for baulked desire, and wept
As if her heart would break.

Day after day, night after night,
Laura kept watch in vain
In sullen silence of exceeding pain.

She never caught again the goblin cry:
"Come buy, come buy;"—
She never spied the goblin men
Hawking their fruits along the glen:
But when the noon waxed bright
Her hair grew thin and grey;
She dwindled, as the fair full moon doth turn
To swift decay and burn
Her fire away.

One day remembering her kernel-stone
She set it by a wall that faced the south;
Dewed it with tears, hoped for a root,
Watched for a waxing shoot,
But there came none;
It never saw the sun,
It never felt the trickling moisture run:
While with sunk eyes and faded mouth
She dreamed of melons, as a traveller sees
False waves in desert drouth
With shade of leaf-crowned trees,
And burns the thirstier in the sandful breeze.

She no more swept the house,
Tended the fowls or cows,
Fetched honey, kneaded cakes of wheat,
Brought water from the brook:
But sat down listless in the chimney-nook
And would not eat.

Tender Lizzie could not bear
To watch her sister's cankerous care
Yet not to share.
She night and morning
Caught the goblins' cry:
"Come buy our orchard fruits,
Come buy, come buy:"—
Beside the brook, along the glen,
She heard the tramp of goblin men,
The voice and stir
Poor Laura could not hear;
Longed to buy fruit to comfort her,

But feared to pay too dear.
She thought of Jeanie in her grave,
Who should have been a bride;
But who for joys brides hope to have
Fell sick and died
In her gay prime,
In earliest Winter time,
With the first glazing rime,
With the first snow-fall of crisp Winter time.

Till Laura dwindling
Seemed knocking at Death's door:
Then Lizzie weighed no more
Better and worse;
But put a silver penny in her purse,
Kissed Laura, crossed the heath with clumps of furze
At twilight, halted by the brook:
And for the first time in her life
Began to listen and look.

Laughed every goblin
When they spied her peeping:
Came towards her hobbling,
Flying, running, leaping,
Puffing and blowing,
Chuckling, clapping, crowing,
Clucking and gobbling,
Mopping and mowing,
Full of airs and graces,
Pulling wry faces,
Demure grimaces,
Cat-like and rat-like,
Ratel- and wombat-like,
Snail-paced in a hurry,
Parrot-voiced and whistler,
Helter skelter, hurry skurry,
Chattering like magpies,
Fluttering like pigeons,
Gliding like fishes,—
Hugged her and kissed her:
Squeezed and caressed her:
Stretched up their dishes,

Panniers, and plates:
"Look at our apples
Russet and dun,
Bob at our cherries,
Bite at our peaches,
Citrons and dates,
Grapes for the asking,
Pears red with basking
Out in the sun,
Plums on their twigs;
Pluck them and suck them,
Pomegranates, figs."—

"Good folk," said Lizzie,
Mindful of Jeanie:
"Give me much and many:"—
Held out her apron,
Tossed them her penny.
"Nay, take a seat with us,
Honour and eat with us,"
They answered grinning:
"Our feast is but beginning.
Night yet is early,
Warm and dew-pearly,
Wakeful and starry:
Such fruits as these
No man can carry;
Half their bloom would fly,
Half their dew would dry,
Half their flavour would pass by.
Sit down and feast with us,
Be welcome guest with us,
Cheer you and rest with us."—
"Thank you," said Lizzie: "But one waits
At home alone for me:
So without further parleying,
If you will not sell me any
Of your fruits though much and many,
Give me back my silver penny
I tossed you for a fee."—
They began to scratch their pates,
No longer wagging, purring,

But visibly demurring,
Grunting and snarling.
One called her proud,
Cross-grained, uncivil;
Their tones waxed loud,
Their looks were evil.
Lashing their tails
They trod and hustled her,
Elbowed and jostled her,
Clawed with their nails,
Barking, mewing, hissing, mocking,
Tore her gown and soiled her stocking,
Twitched her hair out by the roots,
Stamped upon her tender feet,
Held her hands and squeezed their fruits
Against her mouth to make her eat.

White and golden Lizzie stood,
Like a lily in a flood,—
Like a rock of blue-veined stone
Lashed by tides obstreperously,—
Like a beacon left alone
In a hoary roaring sea,
Sending up a golden fire,—
Like a fruit-crowned orange-tree
White with blossoms honey-sweet
Sore beset by wasp and bee,—
Like a royal virgin town
Topped with gilded dome and spire
Close beleaguered by a fleet
Mad to tug her standard down.

One may lead a horse to water,
Twenty cannot make him drink.
Though the goblins cuffed and caught her,
Coaxed and fought her,
Bullied and besought her,
Scratched her, pinched her black as ink,
Kicked and knocked her,
Mauled and mocked her,
Lizzie uttered not a word;
Would not open lip from lip

Lest they should cram a mouthful in:
But laughed in heart to feel the drip
Of juice that syrupped all her face,
And lodged in dimples of her chin,
And streaked her neck which quaked like curd.
At last the evil people
Worn out by her resistance
Flung back her penny, kicked their fruit
Along whichever road they took, .
Not leaving root or stone or shoot;
Some writhed into the ground,
Some dived into the brook
With ring and ripple,
Some scudded on the gale without a sound,
Some vanished in the distance.

In a smart, ache, tingle,
Lizzie went her way;
Knew not was it night or day;
Sprang up the bank, tore thro' the furze,
Threaded copse and dingle,
And heard her penny jingle
Bouncing in her purse,—
Its bounce was music to her ear.
She ran and ran
As if she feared some goblin man
Dogged her with gibe or curse
Or something worse:
But not one goblin skurried after,
Nor was she pricked by fear;
The kind heart made her windy-paced
That urged her home quite out of breath with haste
And inward laughter.

She cried "Laura," up the garden,
"Did you miss me?
Come and kiss me.
Never mind my bruises,
Hug me, kiss me, suck my juices
Squeezed from globin fruits for you,
Goblin pulp and goblin dew.
Eat me, drink me, love me;

Laura, make much of me:
For your sake I have braved the glen
And had to do with goblin merchant men."

Laura started from her chair,
Flung her arms up in the air,
Clutched her hair:
"Lizzie, Lizzie, have you tasted
For my sake the fruit forbidden?
Must your light like mine be hidden,
Your young life like mine be wasted,
Undone in mine undoing
And ruined in my ruin,
Thirsty, cankered, goblin-ridden?"—
She clung about her sister,
Kissed and kissed and kissed her:
Tears once again
Refreshed her shrunken eyes,
Dropping like rain
After long sultry drouth;
Shaking with aguish fear, and pain,
She kissed and kissed her with a hungry mouth.

Her lips began to scorch,
That juice was wormwood to her tongue,
She loathed the feast:
Writhing as one possessed she leaped and sung,
Rent all her robe, and wrung
Her hands in lamentable haste,
And beat her breast.
Her locks streamed like the torch
Borne by a racer at full speed,
Or like the mane of horses in their flight,
Or like an eagle when she stems the light
Straight toward the sun,
Or like a caged thing freed,
Or like a flying flag when armies run.

Swift fire spread through her veins, knocked at her heart,
Met the fire smouldering there
And overbore its lesser flame;
She gorged on bitterness without a name:

Ah! fool, to choose such part
Of soul-consuming care!
Sense failed in the mortal strife:
Like the watch-tower of a town
Which an earthquake shatters down,
Like a lightning-stricken mast,
Like a wind-uprooted tree
Spun about,
Like a foam-topped waterspout
Cast down headlong in the sea,
She fell at last;
Pleasure past and anguish past,
Is it death or is it life?

   Life out of death.
That night long Lizzie watched by her,
Counted her pulse's flagging stir,
Felt for her breath,
Held water to her lips, and cooled her face
With tears and fanning leaves:
But when the first birds chirped about their eaves,
And early reapers plodded to the place
Of golden sheaves,
And dew-wet grass
Bowed in the morning winds so brisk to pass,
And new buds with new day
Opened of cup-like lilies on the stream,
Laura awoke as from a dream,
Laughed in the innocent old way,
Hugged Lizzie but not twice or thrice;
Her gleaming locks showed not one thread of grey,
Her breath was sweet as May
And light danced in her eyes.

   Days, weeks, months, years
Afterwards, when both were wives
With children of their own;
Their mother-hearts beset with fears,
Their lives bound up in tender lives;
Laura would call the little ones
And tell them of her early prime,
Those pleasant days long gone

Of not-returning time:
Would talk about the haunted glen,
The wicked, quaint fruit-merchant men,
Their fruits like honey to the throat
But poison in the blood;
(Men sell not such in any town:)
Would tell them how her sister stood
In deadly peril to do her good,
And win the fiery antidote:
Then joining hands to little hands
Would bid them cling together,
"For there is no friend like a sister
In calm or stormy weather;
To cheer one on the tedious way,
To fetch one if one goes astray,
To lift one if one totters down,
To strengthen whilst one stands."

Remember

REMEMBER me when I am gone away,
Gone far away into the silent land;
When you can no more hold me by the hand,
Nor I half turn to go, yet turning stay.
Remember me when no more, day by day,
You tell me of our future that you planned;
Only remember me; you understand
It will be late to counsel then or pray.
Yet if you should forget me for a while
And afterwards remember, do not grieve;
For if the darkness and corruption leave
A vestige of the thoughts that once I had,
Better by far you should forget and smile
Than that you should remember and be sad.

WILLIAM MORRIS

The Gilliflower of Gold

A GOLDEN gilliflower today
  I wore upon my helm alway,
And won the prize of this tourney.
    Hah! hah! la belle jaune giroflée.

However well Sir Giles might sit,
His sun was weak to wither it;
Lord Miles's blood was dew on it:
    Hah! hah! la belle jaune giroflée.

Although my spear in splinters flew,
From John's steel-coat, my eye was true;
I wheel'd about, and cried for you,
    Hah! hah! la belle jaune giroflée.

Yea, do not doubt my heart was good,
Though my sword flew like rotten wood,
To shout, although I scarcely stood,
    Hah! hah! la belle jaune giroflée.

My hand was steady too, to take
My axe from round my neck, and break
John's steel-coat up for my love's sake.
    Hah! hah! la belle jaune giroflée.

When I stood in my tent again,
Arming afresh, I felt a pain
Take hold of me, I was so fain—
    Hah! hah! la belle jaune giroflée.

To hear *"Honneur aux fils des preux!"*
Right in my ears again, and shew
The gilliflower blossomed new.
    Hah! hah! la belle jaune giroflée.

The Sieur Guillaume against me came,
His tabard bore three points of flame
From a red heart: with little blame—
 Hah! hah! la belle jaune giroflée.

Our tough spears crackled up like straw;
He was the first to turn and draw
His sword, that had nor speck nor flaw,—
 Hah! hah! la belle jaune giroflée.

But I felt weaker than a maid,
And my brain, dizzied and afraid,
Within my helm a fierce tune play'd,—
 Hah! hah! la belle jaune giroflée.

Until I thought of your dear head,
Bow'd to the gilliflower bed,
The yellow flowers stain'd with red;—
 Hah! hah! la belle jaune giroflée.

Crash! how the swords met, *"giroflée!"*
The fierce tune in my helm would play,
"La belle! la belle! jaune giroflée!"
 Hah! hah! la belle jaune giroflée.

Once more the great swords met again,
"La belle! la belle!" but who fell then?
Le Sieur Guillaume, who struck down ten;—
 Hah! hah! la belle jaune giroflée.

And as with mazed and unarm'd face
Toward my own crown and the Queen's place,
They led me at a gentle pace—
 Hah! hah! la belle jaune giroflée.

I almost saw your quiet head
Bow'd o'er the gilliflower bed,
The yellow flowers stain'd with red.
 Hah! hah! la belle jaune giroflée.

The Voice of Toil

I HEARD men saying, Leave hope and praying,
All days shall be as all have been;
Today and tomorrow bring fear and sorrow,
The never-ending toil between.

When Earth was younger mid toil and hunger,
In hope we strove, and our hands were strong;
Then great men led us, with words they fed us,
And bade us right the earthly wrong.

Go read in story their deeds and glory,
Their names amidst the nameless dead;
Turn then from lying to us slow-dying
In that good world to which they led;

Where faster and faster our iron master,
The thing we made, forever drives,
Bids us grind treasure and fashion pleasure
For other hopes and other lives.

Where home is a hovel and dull we grovel,
Forgetting that the world is fair;
Where no babe we cherish, lest its very soul perish;
Where mirth is crime, and love a snare.

Who now shall lead us, what God shall heed us
As we lie in the hell our hands have won?
For us are no rulers but fools and befoolers,
The great are fallen, the wise men gone.

I heard men saying, Leave tears and praying,
The sharp knife heedeth not the sheep;
Are we not stronger than the rich and the wronger,
When day breaks over dreams and sleep?

Come, shoulder to shoulder, ere the world grows older!
Help lies in naught but thee and me;
Hope is before us, the long years that bore us
Bore leaders more than men may be.

Let dead hearts tarry and trade and marry,
And trembling nurse their dreams of mirth,
While we the living our lives are giving
To bring the bright new world to birth.

Come, shoulder to shoulder ere Earth grows older!
The Cause spreads over land and sea;
Now the world shaketh, and fear awaketh,
And joy at last for thee and me.

JAMES THOMSON

FROM THE CITY OF DREADFUL NIGHT

I

THE City is of Night; perchance of Death,
    But certainly of Night; for never there
Can come the lucid morning's fragrant breath
    After the dewy dawning's cold grey air;
The moon and stars may shine with scorn or pity;
The sun has never visited that city,
    For it dissolveth in the daylight fair.

Dissolveth like a dream of night away;
    Though present in distempered gloom of thought
And deadly weariness of heart all day.
    But when a dream night after night is brought
    Throughout a week, and such weeks few or many
Recur each year for several years, can any
    Discern that dream from real life in aught?

For life is but a dream whose shapes return,
    Some frequently, some seldom, some by night
And some by day, some night and day: we learn,
    The while all change and many vanish quite,
In their recurrence with recurrent changes

A certain seeming order; where this ranges
  We count things real; such is memory's might.

A river girds the city west and south,
  The main north channel of a broad lagoon,
Regurging with the salt tides from the mouth;
  Waste marshes shine and glister to the moon
For leagues, then moorland black, then stony ridges;
Great piers and causeways, many noble bridges,
  Connect the town and islet suburbs strewn.

Upon an easy slope it lies at large,
  And scarcely overlaps the long curved crest
Which swells out two leagues from the river marge.
  A trackless wilderness rolls north and west,
Savannahs, savage woods, enormous mountains,
Bleak uplands, black ravines with torrent fountains;
  And eastward rolls the shipless sea's unrest.

The city is not ruinous, although
  Great ruins of an unremembered past,
With others of a few short years ago,
  More sad, are found within its precincts vast.
The street-lamps always burn; but scarce a casement
In house or palace front from room to basement
  Doth glow or gleam athwart the mirk air cast.

The street-lamps burn amidst the baleful glooms,
  Amidst the soundless solitudes immense
Of rangèd mansions dark and still as tombs.
  The silence which benumbs or strains the sense
Fulfils with awe the soul's despair unweeping:
Myriads of habitants are ever sleeping,
  Or dead, or fled from nameless pestilence!

Yet as in some necropolis you find
  Perchance one mourner to a thousand dead,
So there; worn faces that look deaf and blind
  Like tragic masks of stone. With weary tread,
Each wrapped in his own doom, they wander, wander,
Or sit foredone and desolately ponder
  Through sleepless hours with heavy drooping head.

Mature men chiefly, few in age or youth,
  A woman rarely, now and then a child:
A child! If here the heart turns sick with ruth
  To see a little one from birth defiled,
Or lame or blind, as preordained to languish
Through youthless life, think how it bleeds with anguish
  To meet one erring in that homeless wild.

They often murmur to themselves, they speak
  To one another seldom, for their woe
Broods maddening inwardly and scorns to wreak
  Itself abroad; and if at whiles it grow
To frenzy which must rave, none heeds the clamour,
Unless there waits some victim of like glamour,
  To rave in turn, who lends attentive show.

The City is of Night, but not of Sleep;
  There sweet sleep is not for the weary brain;
The pitiless hours like years and ages creep,
  A night seems termless hell. This dreadful strain
Of thought and consciousness which never ceases,
Or which some moments' stupor but increases,
  This, worse than woe, makes wretches there insane.

They leave all hope behind who enter there:
  One certitude while sane they cannot leave,
One anodyne for torture and despair;
  The certitude of Death, which no reprieve
Can put off long; and which, divinely tender,
But waits the outstretched hand to promptly render
  That draught whose slumber nothing can bereave.

IV

He stood alone within the spacious square,
  Declaiming from the central grassy mound,
With head uncovered and with streaming hair,
  As if large multitudes were gathered round:
A stalwart shape, the gestures full of might,
The glances burning with unnatural light:—

As I came through the desert thus it was,
As I came through the desert: All was black,

In heaven no single star, on earth no track;
A brooding hush without a stir or note,
The air so thick it clotted in my throat;
And thus for hours; then some enormous things
Swooped past with savage cries and clanking wings:
    But I strode on austere;
    No hope could have no fear.

As I came through the desert thus it was,
As I came through the desert: Eyes of fire
Glared at me throbbing with a starved desire;
The hoarse and heavy and carnivorous breath
Was hot upon me from deep jaws of death;
Sharp claws, swift talons, fleshless fingers cold
Plucked at me from the bushes, tried to hold:
    But I strode on austere;
    No hope could have no fear.

As I came through the desert thus it was,
As I came through the desert: Lo you, there,
That hillock burning with a brazen glare;
Those myriad dusky flames with points a-glow
Which writhed and hissed and darted to and fro;
A Sabbath of the Serpents, heaped pell-mell
For Devil's roll-call and some *fête* of hell:
    Yet I strode on austere;
    No hope could have no fear.

As I came through the desert thus it was,
As I came through the desert: Meteors ran
And crossed their javelins on the black sky-span;
The zenith opened to a gulf of flame,
The dreadful thunderbolts jarred earth's fixed frame;
The ground all heaved in waves of fire that surged
And weltered round me sole there unsubmerged:
    Yet I strode on austere;
    No hope could have no fear.

As I came through the desert thus it was,
As I came through the desert: Air once more,
And I was close upon a wild sea-shore;
Enormous cliffs arose on either hand,

The deep tide thundered up a league-broad strand;
White foambelts seethed there, wan spray swept and flew;
The sky broke, moon and stars and clouds and blue:
    And I strode on austere;
    No hope could have no fear.

As I came through the desert thus it was,
As I came through the desert: On the left
The sun arose and crowned a broad crag-cleft;
There stopped and burned out black, except a rim,
A bleeding, eyeless socket, red and dim;
Whereon the moon fell suddenly south-west,
And stood above the right-hand cliffs at rest:
    Still I strode on austere;
    No hope could have no fear.

As I came through the desert thus it was,
As I came through the desert: From the right
A shape came slowly with a ruddy light;
A woman with a red lamp in her hand,
Bareheaded and barefooted on that strand;
O desolation moving with such grace!
O anguish with such beauty in thy face!
    I fell as on my bier,
    Hope travailed with such fear.

As I came through the desert thus it was,
As I came through the desert: I was twain,
Two selves distinct that cannot join again;
One stood apart and knew but could not stir,
And watched the other stark in swoon and her;
And she came on, and never turned aside,
Between such sun and moon and roaring tide:
    And as she came more near
    My soul grew mad with fear.

As I came through the desert thus it was,
As I came through the desert: Hell is mild
And piteous matched with that accursèd wild;
A large black sign was on her breast that bowed,
A broad black band ran down her snow-white shroud;
That lamp she held was her own burning heart,

Whose blood-drops trickled step by step apart:
  The mystery was clear;
  Mad rage had swallowed fear.

As I came through the desert thus it was,
As I came through the desert: By the sea
She knelt and bent above that senseless me;
Those lamp-drops fell upon my white brow there,
She tried to cleanse them with her tears and hair;
She murmured words of pity, love, and woe,
She heeded not the level rushing flow:
  And mad with rage and fear,
  I stood stonebound so near.

As I came through the desert thus it was,
As I came through the desert: When the tide
Swept up to her there kneeling by my side,
She clasped that corpse-like me, and they were borne
Away, and this vile me was left forlorn;
I know the whole sea cannot quench that heart,
Or cleanse that brow, or wash those two apart:
  They love; their doom is drear,
  Yet they nor hope nor fear;
  But I, what do I here?

ALGERNON CHARLES SWINBURNE

Chorus from Atalanta in Calydon

WHEN the hounds of spring are on winter's traces,
  The mother of months in meadow or plain
Fills the shadows and windy places
  With lisp of leaves and ripple of rain;
And the brown bright nightingale amorous
Is half assuaged for Itylus,
For the Thracian ships and the foreign faces.
  The tongueless vigil, and all the pain.

Come with bows bent and with emptying of quivers,
　　Maiden most perfect, lady of light,
With a noise of winds and many rivers,
　　With a clamour of waters, and with might:
Bind on thy sandals, O thou most fleet,
Over the splendour and speed of thy feet;
For the faint east quickens, the wan west shivers,
　　Round the feet of the day and the feet of the night.

Where shall we find her, how shall we sing to her,
　　Fold our hands round her knees, and cling?
O that man's heart were as fire and could spring to her,
　　Fire, or the strength of the streams that spring!
For the stars and the winds are unto her
As raiment, as songs of the harp-player;
For the risen stars and the fallen cling to her,
　　And the southwest-wind and the west-wind sing.

For winter's rains and ruins are over,
　　And all the season of snows and sins;
The days dividing lover and lover,
　　The light that loses, the night that wins;
And time remember'd is grief forgotten,
And frosts are slain and flowers begotten,
And in green underwood and cover
　　Blossom by blossom the spring begins.

The full streams feed on flower of rushes,
　　Ripe grasses trammel a travelling foot,
The faint fresh flame of the young year flushes
　　From leaf to flower and flower to fruit;
And fruit and leaf are as gold and fire,
And the oat is heard above the lyre,
And the hoofèd heel of a satyr crushes
　　The chestnut-husk at the chestnut-root.

And Pan by noon and Bacchus by night,
　　Fleeter of foot than the fleet-foot kid,
Follows with dancing and fills with delight
　　The Maenad and the Bassarid;
And soft as lips that laugh and hide
The laughing leaves of the trees divide,

And screen from seeing and leave in sight
  The god pursuing, the maiden hid.

The ivy falls with the Bacchanal's hair
  Over her eyebrows hiding her eyes;
The wild vine slipping down leaves bare
  Her bright breast shortening into sighs;
The wild vine slips with the weight of its leaves,
But the berried ivy catches and cleaves
To the limbs that glitter, the feet that scare
  The wolf that follows, the fawn that flies.

The Garden of Proserpine

HERE, where the world is quiet;
  Here, where all trouble seems
Dead winds' and spent waves' riot
  In doubtful dreams of dreams;
I watch the green field growing
For reaping folk and sowing,
For harvest-time and mowing,
  A sleepy world of streams.

I am tired of tears and laughter,
  And men that laugh and weep;
Of what may come hereafter
  For men that sow to reap:
I am weary of days and hours,
Blown buds of barren flowers,
Desires and dreams and powers
  And everything but sleep.

Here life has death for neighbour,
  And far from eye or ear
Wan waves and wet winds labour,
  Weak ships and spirits steer;
They drive adrift, and whither
They wot not who make thither;
But no such winds blow hither,
  And no such things grow here.

No growth of moor or coppice,
  No heather-flower or vine,
But bloomless buds of poppies,
  Green grapes of Proserpine,
Pale beds of blowing rushes
Where no leaf blooms or blushes
Save this whereout she crushes
  For dead men deadly wine.

Pale, without name or number,
  In fruitless fields of corn,
They blow themselves and slumber
  All night till light is born;
And like a soul belated,
In hell and heaven unmated,
By cloud and mist abated
  Comes out of darkness morn.

Though one were strong as seven,
  He too with death shall dwell,
Nor wake with wings in heaven,
  Nor weep for pains in hell;
Though one were fair as roses,
His beauty clouds and closes;
And well though love reposes,
  In the end it is not well.

Pale, beyond porch and portal,
  Crowned with calm leaves, she stands
Who gathers all things mortal
  With cold immortal hands;
Her languid lips are sweeter
Than love's who fears to greet her
To men that mix and meet her
  From many times and lands.

She waits for each and other,
  She waits for all men born;
Forgets the earth her mother,
  The life of fruits and corn;
And spring and seed and swallow
Take wing for her and follow

Where summer song rings hollow
  And flowers are put to scorn.

There go the loves that wither,
  The old loves with wearier wings;
And all dead years draw thither,
  And all disastrous things;
Dead dreams of days forsaken,
Blind buds that snows have shaken,
Wild leaves that winds have taken,
  Red strays of ruined springs.

We are not sure of sorrow,
  And joy was never sure;
Today will die tomorrow;
  Time stoops to no man's lure;
And love, grown faint and fretful,
With lips but half regretful
Sighs, and with eyes forgetful
  Weeps that no loves endure.

From too much love of living,
  From hope and fear set free,
We thank with brief thanksgiving
  Whatever gods may be
That no life lives for ever;
That dead men rise up never;
That even the weariest river
  Winds somewhere safe to sea.

Then star nor sun shall waken,
  Nor any change of light:
Nor sound of waters shaken,
  Nor any sound or sight:
Nor wintry leaves nor vernal,
Nor days nor things diurnal:
Only the sleep eternal
  In an eternal night.

Super Flumina Babylonis

BY the waters of Babylon we sat down and wept,
    Remembering thee,
That for ages of agony hast endured, and slept,
    And wouldst not see.

By the waters of Babylon we stood up and sang,
    Considering thee,
That a blast of deliverance in the darkness rang,
    To set thee free.

And with trumpets and thunderings and with morning song
    Came up the light;
And thy spirit uplifted thee to forget thy wrong
    As day doth night.

And thy sons were dejected not any more, as then
    When thou wast shamed;
When thy lovers went heavily without heart, as men
    Whose life was maimed.

In the desolate distances, with a great desire,
    For thy love's sake,
With our hearts going back to thee, they were filled with fire,
    Were nigh to break.

It was said to us: "Verily ye are great of heart,
    But ye shall bend;
Ye are bondmen and bondwomen, to be scourged and smart,
    To toil and tend."

And with harrows men harrowed us, and subdued with spears,
    And crushed with shame;
And the summer and winter was, and the length of years,
    And no change came.

By the rivers of Italy, by the sacred streams,
    By town, by tower,
There was feasting with revelling, there was sleep with dreams,
    Until thine hour.

And they slept and they rioted on their rose-hung beds,
    With mouths on flame,
And with love-locks vine-chapleted, and with rose-crowned heads
    And robes of shame.

And they knew not their forefathers, nor the hills and streams
    And words of power,
Nor the gods that were good to them, but with songs and dreams
    Filled up their hour.

By the rivers of Italy, by the dry streams' beds,
    When thy time came,
There was casting of crowns from them, from their young men's
      heads,
    The crowns of shame.

By the horn of Eridanus, by the Tiber mouth,
    As thy day rose,
They arose up and girded them to the north and south,
    By seas, by snows.

As a water in January the frost confines,
    Thy kings bound thee;
As a water in April is, in the new-blown vines,
    Thy sons made free.

And thy lovers that looked for thee, and that mourned from far,
    For thy sake dead,
We rejoiced in the light of thee, in the signal star
    Above thine head.

In thy grief had we followed thee, in thy passion loved,
    Loved in thy loss;
In thy shame we stood fast to thee, with thy pangs were moved,
    Clung to thy cross.

By the hillside of Calvary we beheld thy blood,
    Thy bloodred tears,
As a mother's in bitterness, an unebbing flood,
    Years upon years.

And the north was Gethsemane, without leaf or bloom,
    A garden sealed;
And the south was Aceldama, for a sanguine fume
    Hid all the field.

By the stone of the sepulchre we returned to weep,
    From far, from prison;
And the guards by it keeping it we beheld asleep,
    But thou wast risen.

And an angel's similitude by the unsealed grave,
    And by the stone:
And the voice was angelical, to whose words God gave
    Strength like his own.

"Lo, the graveclothes of Italy that are folded up
    In the grave's gloom!
And the guards as men wrought upon with charmed cup,
    By the open tomb.

"And her body most beautiful, and her shining head,
    These are not here;
For your mother, for Italy, is not surely dead:
    Have ye no fear.

"As of old time she spake to you, and you hardly heard,
    Hardly took heed,
So now also she saith to you, yet another word,
    Who is risen indeed.

"By my saying she saith to you, in your ears she saith,
    Who hear these things,
Put no trust in men's royalties, nor in great men's breath,
    Nor words of kings.

"For the life of them vanishes and is no more seen,
    Nor no more known;
Nor shall any remember him if a crown hath been,
    Or where a throne.

"Unto each man his handiwork, unto each his crown,
    The just Fate gives;

Whoso takes the world's life on him and his own lays down,
    He, dying so, lives.

"Whoso bears the whole heaviness of the wronged world's weight
    And puts it by,
It is well with him suffering, though he face man's fate;
    How should he die?

"Seeing death has no part in him any more, no power
    Upon his head;
He has bought his eternity with a little hour,
    And is not dead.

"For an hour, if ye look for him, he is no more found,
    For one hour's space;
Then ye lift up your eyes to him and behold him crowned,
    A deathless face.

"On the mountains of memory, by the world's well-springs,
    In all men's eyes,
Where the light of the life of him is on all past things,
    Death only dies.

"Not the light that was quenched for us, nor the deeds that were,
    Nor the ancient days,
Nor the sorrows not sorrowful, nor the face most fair
    Of perfect praise."

So the angel of Italy's resurrection said,
    So yet he saith;
So the son of her suffering, that from breasts nigh dead
    Drew life, not death.

That the pavement of Golgotha should be white as snow,
    Not red, but white;
That the waters of Babylon should no longer flow,
    And men see light.

THOMAS HARDY

The Darkling Thrush

I LEANT upon a coppice gate
    When Frost was spectre-gray,
And Winter's dregs made desolate
    The weakening eye of day.
The tangled bine-stems scored the sky
    Like strings of broken lyres,
And all mankind that haunted nigh
    Had sought their household fires.

The land's sharp features seemed to be
    The Century's corpse outleant,[1]
His crypt the cloudy canopy,
    The wind his death-lament.
The ancient pulse of germ and birth
    Was shrunken hard and dry,
And every spirit upon earth
    Seemed fervorless as I.

At once a voice arose among
    The bleak twigs overhead
In a full-hearted evensong
    Of joy illimited;
An aged thrush, frail, gaunt, and small,
    In blast-beruffled plume,
Had chosen thus to fling his soul
    Upon the growing gloom.

So little cause for carolings
    Of such ecstatic sound
Was written on terrestrial things
    Afar or nigh around,
That I could think there trembled through
    His happy good-night air

[1] The poem was written in December, 1900.

Some blessed Hope, whereof he knew
And I was unaware.

Afterwards

WHEN the present has latched its postern behind my tremu-
lous stay,
And the May month flaps its glad green leaves like wings,
Delicate-filmed as new-spun silk, will the people say,
"He was a man who used to notice such things?"

If it be in the dusk when, like an eyelid's soundless blink,
The dewfall-hawk comes crossing the shades to alight
Upon the wind-warped upland thorn, will a gazer think,
"To him this must have been a familiar sight"?

If I pass during some nocturnal blackness, mothy and warm,
When the hedgehog travels furtively over the lawn,
Will they say, "He strove that such innocent creatures should come
to no harm,
"But he could do little for them; and now he is gone"?

If, when hearing that I have been stilled at last, they stand at the
door,
Watching the full-starred heavens that winter sees,
Will this thought rise on those who will meet my face no more,
"He was one who had an eye for such mysteries"?

And will any say when my bell of quittance is heard in the gloom,
And a crossing breeze cuts a pause in its outrollings,
Till they rise again, as they were a new bell's boom,
"He hears it not now, but used to notice such things"?

Let Me Enjoy

(MINOR KEY)

LET me enjoy the earth no less
Because the all-enacting Might
That fashioned forth its loveliness
Had other aims than my delight.

About my path there flits a Fair,
Who throws me not a word or sign;
I'll charm me with her ignoring air,
And laud the lips not meant for mine.

From manuscripts of moving song
Inspired by scenes and dreams unknown,
I'll pour out raptures that belong
To others, as they were my own.

And some day hence, towards Paradise
And all its blest—if such should be—
I will lift glad, afar-off eyes,
Though it contain no place for me.

The Blinded Bird

SO zestfully canst thou sing?
     And all this indignity,
With God's consent, on thee!
Blinded ere yet a-wing
By the red-hot needle thou,
I stand and wonder how
So zestfully thou canst sing!

Resenting not such wrong,
Thy grievous pain forgot,
Eternal dark thy lot,
Groping thy whole life long,
After that stab of fire;
Enjailed in pitiless wire;
Resenting not such wrong!

Who hath charity? This bird.
Who suffereth long and is kind,
Is not provoked, though blind
And alive ensepulchred?
Who hopeth, endureth all things?
Who thinketh no evil, but sings?
Who is divine? This bird.

ROBERT BRIDGES

My Delight and Thy Delight

MY delight and thy delight
Walking, like two angels white,
In the gardens of the night:

My desire and thy desire
Twining to a tongue of fire,
Leaping live, and laughing higher;

Through the everlasting strife
In the mystery of life.

Love, from whom the world begun,
Hath the secret of the sun.

Love can tell, and love alone,
Whence the million stars were strewn,
Why each atom knows its own,
How, in spite of woe and death,
Gay is life, and sweet is breath:

This he taught us, this we knew,
Happy in his science true,
Hand in hand as we stood
'Neath the shadows of the wood,
Heart to heart as we lay
In the dawning of the day.

I Will Not Let Thee Go

I WILL not let thee go.
Ends all our month-long love in this?
Can it be summed up so,
Quit in a single kiss?
I will not let thee go.

I will not let thee go.
If thy words' breath could scare thy deeds,
  As the soft south can blow
  And toss the feathered seeds,
  Then might I let thee go.

I will not let thee go.
Had not the great sun seen, I might;
  Or were he reckoned slow
  To bring the false to light,
  Then might I let thee go.

I will not let thee go.
The stars that crowd the summer skies
  Have watched us so below
  With all their million eyes,
  I dare not let thee go.

I will not let thee go.
Have we not chid the changeful moon,
  Now rising late, and now
  Because she set too soon,
  And shall I let thee go?

I will not let thee go.
Have not the young flowers been content,
  Plucked ere their buds could blow,
  To seal our sacrament?
  I cannot let thee go.

I will not let thee go.
I hold thee by too many bands:
  Thou sayest farewell, and lo!
  I have thee by the hands,
  And will not let thee go.

London Snow

WHEN men were all asleep the snow came flying,
    In large white flakes falling on the city brown,
Stealthily and perpetually settling and loosely lying,
    Hushing the latest traffic of the drowsy town;

Deadening, muffling, stifling its murmurs failing;
Lazily and incessantly floating down and down:
    Silently sifting and veiling road, roof and railing;
Hiding difference, making unevenness even,
Into angles and crevices softly drifting and sailing.
    All night it fell, and when full inches seven
It lay in the depth of its uncompacted lightness,
The clouds blew off from a high and frosty heaven;
    And all woke earlier for the unaccustomed brightness
Of the winter dawning, the strange unheavenly glare:
The eye marvelled—marvelled at the dazzling whiteness;
    The ear hearkened to the stillness of the solemn air;
No sound of wheel rumbling nor of foot falling,
And the busy morning cries came thin and spare.
    Then boys I heard, as they went to school, calling,
They gathered up the crystal manna to freeze
Their tongues with tasting, their hands with snowballing;
    Or rioted in a drift, plunging up to the knees;
Or peering up from under the white-mossed wonder,
"O look at the trees!" they cried, "O look at the trees!"
    With lessened load a few carts creak and blunder,
Following along the white deserted way,
A country company long dispersed asunder:
    When now already the sun, in pale display
Standing by Paul's high dome, spread forth below
His sparkling beams, and awoke the stir of the day.
    For now doors open, and war is waged with the snow;
And trains of somber men, past tale of number,
Tread long brown paths, as toward their toil they go:
    But even for them awhile no cares encumber
Their minds diverted; the daily word is unspoken,
The daily thoughts of labor and sorrow slumber
At the sight of the beauty that greets them, for the charm they have
      broken.

GERARD MANLEY HOPKINS

God's Grandeur

THE world is charged with the grandeur of God.
  It will flame out, like shining from shook foil;
It gathers to a greatness, like the ooze of oil
Crushed. Why do men then now not reck his rod?
Generations have trod, have trod, have trod;
  And all is seared with trade; bleared, smeared with toil;
  And wears man's smudge and shares man's smell: the soil
Is bare now, nor can foot feel, being shod.

And for all this, nature is never spent;
  There lives the dearest freshness deep down things;
And though the last lights off the black West went
  Oh, morning, at the brown brink eastward, springs—
Because the Holy Ghost over the bent
  World broods with warm breast and with ah! bright wings.

Pied Beauty

GLORY be to God for dappled things—
  For skies of couple-colour as a brinded cow;
    For rose-moles all in stipple upon trout that swim;
Fresh-firecoal chestnut-falls; finches' wings;
  Landscape plotted and pieced—fold, fallow, and plough;
    And áll trádes, their gear and tackle and trim.

All things counter, original, spare, strange;
  Whatever is fickle, freckled (who knows how?)
    With swift, slow; sweet, sour; adazzle, dim;
He fathers-forth whose beauty is past change:
                    Praise him.

The Windhover

TO CHRIST OUR LORD

I CAUGHT this morning morning's minion kingdom of day-
  light's dauphin, dappledawn-drawn
Falcon, in his riding
Of the rolling level underneath him steady air, and striding
High there, how he rung upon the rein of a wimpling wing
In his ecstasy! then off, off forth on swing,
  As a skate's heel sweeps smooth on a bow-bend: the hurl **and**
    gliding
Rebuffed the big wing. My heart in hiding
Stirred for a bird,—the achieve of, the mastery of the thing!
Brute beauty and valour and act, oh, air, pride, plume, here
  Buckle! AND the fire that breaks from thee then, a billion
Times told lovelier, more dangerous, O my chevalier!
  No wonder of it: shéer plód makes plough down sillion
Shine, and blue-bleak embers, ah my dear,
  Fall, gall themselves, and gash gold-vermilion.

Spring and Fall

TO A YOUNG CHILD

MÁRGARÉT, are you gríeving
  Over Goldengrove unleaving?
Leáves, líke the things of man, you
With your fresh thoughts care for, can you?
Áh! ás the heart grows older
It will come to such sights colder
By and by, nor spare a sigh
Though worlds of wanwood leafmeal lie;
And yet you wíll weep and know why.
Now no matter, child, the name:
Sórrow's spríngs áre the same.
Nor mouth had, no nor mind, expressed
What heart heard of, ghost guessed:
It ís the blight man was born for,
It is Margaret you mourn for.

Carrion Comfort

NOT, I'll not, carrion comfort, Despair, not feast on thee;
   Not untwist—slack they may be—these last strands of man
In me ór, most weary, cry *I can no more*. I can;
Can something, hope, wish day come, not choose not to be.
But ah, but O thou terrible, why wouldst thou rude on me
Thy wring-world right foot rock? lay a lionlimb against me? scan
With darksome devouring eyes my bruiséd bones? and fan,
O in turns of tempest, me heaped there; me frantic to avoid thee
   and flee?
  Why? That my chaff might fly; my grain lie, sheer and clear.
Nay in all that toil, that coil, since (seems) I kissed the rod,
Hand rather, my heart lo! lapped strength, stole joy, would laugh,
   chéer.
Cheer whom though? the hero whose heaven-handling flung me,
   fóot tród
Me? or me that fought him? O which one? is it each one? That
   night, that year
Of now done darkness I wretch lay wrestling with (my God!) my
   God.

WILLIAM ERNEST HENLEY

Invictus

OUT of the night that covers me,
   Black as the Pit from pole to pole,
I thank whatever gods may be
   For my unconquerable soul.

In the fell clutch of circumstance
   I have not winced nor cried aloud.
Under the bludgeonings of chance
   My head is bloody, but unbowed.

Beyond this place of wrath and tears
  Looms but the Horror of the shade,
And yet the menace of the years
  Finds, and shall find, me unafraid.

It matters not how strait the gate,
  How charged with punishments the scroll,
I am the master of my fate:
  I am the captain of my soul.

Ballade Made in Hot Weather

TO C. M.

FOUNTAINS that frisk and sprinkle
  The moss they overspill;
Pools that the breezes crinkle;
The wheel beside the mill,
With its wet, weedy frill;
Wind-shadows in the wheat;
A water-cart in the street;
The fringe of foam that girds
An islet's ferneries;
A green sky's minor thirds—
To live, I think of these!

Of ice and glass the tinkle,
Pellucid, silver-shrill;
Peaches without a wrinkle;
Cherries and snow at will,
From china bowls that fill
The senses with a sweet
Incuriousness of heat;
A melon's dripping sherds;
Cream-clotted strawberries;
Dust dairies set with curds—
To live, I think of these!

Vale-lily and periwinkle;
Wet stone-crop on the sill;
The look of leaves a-twinkle

With windlets clear and still;
The feel of a forest rill
That wimples fresh and fleet
About one's naked feet;
The muzzles of drinking herds;
Lush flags and bulrushes;
The chirp of rain-bound birds—
To live, I think of these!

Envoy

Dark aisles, new packs of cards,
Mermaidens' tails, cool swards,
Dawn dews and starlit seas,
White marbles, whiter words—
To live, I think of these!

To A. D.

THE nightingale has a lyre of gold,
    The lark's is a clarion call,
And the blackbird plays but a boxwood flute,
    But I love him best of all.

For his song is all of the joy of life,
    And we in the mad, spring weather,
We two have listened till he sang
    Our hearts and lips together.

ALICE MEYNELL

In Early Spring

O SPRING, I know thee! Seek for sweet surprise
    In the young children's eyes.
But I have learnt the years, and know the yet
    Leaf-folded violet.

Mine ear, awake to silence, can foretell
  The cuckoo's fitful bell.
I wander in a grey time that encloses
  June and the wild hedge-roses.
A year's procession of the flowers doth pass
  My feet, along the grass.
And all you sweet birds silent yet, I know
  The notes that stir you so,
Your songs yet half devised in the dim dear
  Beginnings of the year.
In these young days you meditate your part;
  I have it all by heart.
I know the secrets of the seeds of flowers
  Hidden and warm with showers,
And how, in kindling Spring, the cuckoo shall
  Alter his interval.
But not a flower or song I ponder is
  My own, but memory's.
I shall be silent in those days desired
  Before a world inspired.
O dear brown birds, compose your old song-phrases,
  Earth, thy familiar daisies.

The poet mused upon the dusky height,
  Between two stars towards night,
His purpose in his heart. I watched, a space,
  The meaning of his face:
There was the secret, fled from earth and skies,
  Hid in his gray young eyes.
My heart and all the Summer wait his choice,
  And wonder for his voice.
Who shall foretell his songs, and who aspire
  But to divine his lyre?
Sweet Earth, we know thy dimmest mysteries,
  But he is lord of his.

Renouncement

I MUST not think of thee; and, tired yet strong,
  I shun the thought that lurks in all delight—
The thought of thee—and in the blue Heaven's height,
And in the dearest passage of a song.

Oh, just beyond the fairest thoughts that throng
This breast, the thought of thee waits, hidden yet bright;
But it must never, never come in sight;
I must stop short of thee the whole day long.
But when sleep comes to close each difficult day,
When night gives pause to the long watch I keep,
And all my bonds I needs must loose apart,
Must doff my will as raiment laid away,—
With the first dream that comes with the first sleep
I run, I run, I am gathered to thy heart.

Chimes

BRIEF, on a flying night,
    From the shaken tower,
A flock of bells take flight.
    And go with the hour.

Like birds from the cote to the gales,
    Abrupt—O hark!
A fleet of bells set sails,
    And go to the dark.

Sudden the cold airs swing.
    Alone, aloud,
A verse of bells takes wing
    And flies with the cloud.

One wept whose only child was dead

ONE wept whose only child was dead,
    New-born, ten years ago.
"Weep not; he is in bliss," they said.
    She answered, "Even so,

"Ten years ago was born in pain
    A child, not now forlorn.
But oh, ten years ago, in vain,
    A mother, a mother was born."

ROBERT LOUIS STEVENSON

The Vagabond

(TO AN AIR OF SCHUBERT)

GIVE to me the life I love,
　Let the lave go by me,
Give the jolly heaven above
　And the byway nigh me.
Bed in the bush with stars to see,
　Bread I dip in the river—
There's the life for a man like me,
　There's the life for ever.

Let the blow fall soon or late,
　Let what will be o'er me;
Give the face of earth around
　And the road before me.
Wealth I seek not, hope nor love,
　Nor a friend to know me;
All I seek the heaven above
　And the road below me.

Or let autumn fall on me
　Where afield I linger,
Silencing the bird on tree,
　Biting the blue finger:
White as meal the frosty field—
　Warm the fireside haven—
Not to autumn will I yield,
　Not to winter even!

Let the blow fall soon or late,
　Let what will be o'er me;
Give the face of earth around,
　And the road before me.

Wealth I ask not, hope nor love,
  Nor a friend to know me.
All I ask the heaven above,
  And the road below me.

Requiem

UNDER the wide and starry sky
    Dig the grave and let me lie.
Glad did I live and gladly die,
  And I laid me down with a will.

This be the verse you grave for me:
  Here he lies where he longed to be;
Home is the sailor, home from sea,
  And the hunter home from the hill.

OSCAR WILDE

The Ballad of Reading Gaol

I

HE did not wear his scarlet coat,
  For blood and wine are red,
And blood and wine were on his hands
  When they found him with the dead,
The poor dead woman whom he loved,
  And murdered in her bed.

He walked amongst the Trial Men
  In a suit of shabby grey;
A cricket cap was on his head,
  And his step seemed light and gay;
But I never saw a man who looked
  So wistfully at the day.

I never saw a man who looked
  With such a wistful eye
Upon that little tent of blue
  Which prisoners call the sky,
And at every drifting cloud that went
  With sails of silver by.

I walked, with other souls in pain,
  Within another ring,
And was wondering if the man had done
  A great or little thing,
When a voice behind me whispered low,
  "That fellow's got to swing."

Dear Christ! the very prison walls
  Suddenly seemed to reel,
And the sky above my head became
  Like a casque of scorching steel;
And, though I was a soul in pain,
  My pain I could not feel.

I only knew what hunted thought
  Quickened his step, and why
He looked upon the garish day
  With such a wistful eye;
The man had killed the thing he loved,
  And so he had to die.

Yet each man kills the thing he loves,
  By each let this be heard,
Some do it with a bitter look,
  Some with a flattering word,
The coward does it with a kiss,
  The brave man with a sword!

Some kill their love when they are young,
  And some when they are old;
Some strangle with the hands of Lust,
  Some with the hands of Gold:
The kindest use a knife, because
  The dead so soon grow cold.

Some love too little, some too long,
    Some sell, and others buy;
Some do the deed with many tears,
    And some without a sigh:
For each man kills the thing he loves,
    Yet each man does not die.

He does not die a death of shame
    On a day of dark disgrace,
Nor have a noose about his neck,
    Nor a cloth upon his face,
Nor drop feet foremost through the floor
    Into an empty space.

He does not sit with silent men
    Who watch him night and day;
Who watch him when he tries to weep,
    And when he tries to pray;
Who watch him lest himself should rob
    The prison of its prey.

He does not wake at dawn to see
    Dread figures throng his room,
The shivering Chaplain robed in white,
    The Sheriff stern with gloom,
And the Governor all in shiny black,
    With the yellow face of Doom.

He does not rise in piteous haste
    To put on convict-clothes,
While some coarse-mouthed Doctor gloats, and notes
    Each new and nerve-twitched pose,
Fingering a watch whose little ticks
    Are horrible hammer blows.

He does not know that sickening thirst
    That sands one's throat, before
The hangman with his gardener's gloves
    Slips through the padded door,
And binds one with three leathern thongs,
    That the throat may thirst no more.

He does not bend his head to hear
  The Burial Office read,
Nor, while the terror of his soul
  Tells him he is not dead,
Cross his own coffin, as he moves
  Into the hideous shed.

He does not stare upon the air
  Through a little roof of glass:
He does not pray with lips of clay
  For his agony to pass:
Nor feel upon his shuddering cheek
  That kiss of Caiaphas.

II

Six weeks our guardsman walked the yard,
  In the suit of shabby grey:
His cricket cap was on his head,
  And his step seemed light and gay,
But I never saw a man who looked
  So wistfully at the day.

I never saw a man who looked
  With such a wistful eye
Upon that little tent of blue
  Which prisoners call the sky,
And at every wandering cloud that trailed
  Its ravelled fleeces by.

He did not wring his hands, as do
  Those witless men who dare
To try to rear the changeling Hope
  In the cave of black Despair:
He only looked upon the sun,
  And drank the morning air.

He did not wring his hands nor weep,
  Nor did he peek or pine,
But he drank the air as though it held
  Some healthful anodyne;
With open mouth he drank the sun
  As though it had been wine!

And I and all the souls in pain,
   Who tramped the other ring,
Forgot if we ourselves had done
   A great or little thing,
And watched with gaze of dull amaze
   The man who had to swing.

And strange it was to see him pass
   With a step so light and gay,
And strange it was to see him look
   So wistfully at the day,
And strange it was to think that he
   Had such a debt to pay.

For oak and elm have pleasant leaves
   That in the spring-time shoot:
But grim to see is the gallows-tree,
   With its adder-bitten root,
And, green or dry, a man must die
   Before it bears its fruit!

The loftiest place is that seat of grace
   For which all worldlings try:
But who would stand in hempen band
   Upon a scaffold high,
And through a murderer's collar take
   His last look at the sky?

It is sweet to dance to violins
   When Love and Life are fair:
To dance to flutes, to dance to lutes
   Is delicate and rare:
But it is not sweet with nimble feet
   To dance upon the air!

So with curious eyes and sick surmise
   We watched him day by day,
And wondered if each one of us
   Would end the self-same way,
For none can tell to what red Hell
   His sightless soul may stray.

At last the dead man walked no more
   Amongst the Trial Men,
And I knew that he was standing up
   In the black dock's dreadful pen,
And that never would I see his face
   In God's sweet world again.

Like two doomed ships that pass in storm,
   We had crossed each other's way:
But we made no sign, we said no word,
   We had no word to say;
For we did not meet in the holy night,
   But in the shameful day.

A prison wall was round us both,
   Two outcast men we were:
The world had thrust us from its heart,
   And God from out his care:
And the iron gin that waits for Sin
   Had caught us in its snare.

III

In Debtor's Yard the stones are hard,
   And the dripping wall is high,
So it was there he took the air
   Beneath the leaden sky,
And by each side a Warder walked,
   For fear the man might die.

Or else he sat with those who watched
   His anguish night and day;
Who watched him when he rose to weep,
   And when he crouched to pray;
Who watched him lest himself should rob
   Their scaffold of its prey.

The Governor was strong upon
   The Regulations Act:
The Doctor said that Death was but
   A scientific fact:
And twice a day the Chaplain called,
   And left a little tract.

And twice a day he smoked his pipe,
  And drank his quart of beer:
His soul was resolute, and held
  No hiding-place for fear;
He often said that he was glad
  The hangman's hands were near.

But why he said so strange a thing
  No Warder dared to ask:
For he to whom a watcher's doom
  Is given as his task,
Must set a lock upon his lips,
  And make his face a mask.

Or else he might be moved, and try
  To comfort or console:
And what should Human Pity do
  Pent up in Murderers' Hole?
What word of grace in such a place
  Could help a brother's soul?

With slouch and swing around the ring
  We trod the Fools' Parade!
We did not care: we knew we were
  The Devil's Own Brigade:
And shaven head and feet of lead
  Make a merry masquerade.

We tore the tarry rope to shreds
  With blunt and bleeding nails;
We rubbed the doors, and scrubbed the floors,
  And cleaned the shining rails:
And, rank by rank, we soaped the plank,
  And clattered with the pails.

We sewed the sacks, we broke the stones,
  We turned the dusty drill:
We banged the tins, and bawled the hymns,
  And sweated on the mill:
But in the heart of every man
  Terror was lying still.

So still it lay that every day
  Crawled like a weed-clogged wave:
And we forgot the bitter lot
  That waits for fool and knave,
Till once, as we tramped in from work,
  We passed an open grave.

With yawning mouth the yellow hole
  Gaped for a living thing;
The very mud cried out for blood
  To the thirsty asphalt ring:
And we knew that ere one dawn grew fair,
  Some prisoner had to swing.

Right in we went, with soul intent
  On Death and Dread and Doom:
The hangman, with his little bag,
  Went shuffling through the gloom:
And each man trembled as he crept
  Into his numbered tomb.

That night the empty corridors
  Were full of forms of Fear,
And up and down the iron town
  Stole feet we could not hear,
And through the bars that hide the stars
  White faces seemed to peer.

He lay as one who lies and dreams
  In a pleasant meadow-land,
The watchers watched him as he slept,
  And could not understand
How one could sleep so sweet a sleep
  With a hangman close at hand.

But there is no sleep when men must weep
  Who never yet have wept:
So we—the fool, the fraud, the knave—
  That endless vigil kept,
And through each brain on hands of pain
  Another's terror crept.

Alas! it is a fearful thing
   To feel another's guilt!
For, right within, the sword of Sin
   Pierced to its poisoned hilt,
And as molten lead were the tears we shed
   For the blood we had not spilt.

The Warders with their shoes of felt
   Crept by each padlocked door,
And peeped and saw, with eyes of awe,
   Grey figures on the floor,
And wondered why men knelt to pray
   Who never prayed before.

All through the night we knelt and prayed,
   Mad mourners of a corse!
The troubled plumes of midnight were
   The plumes upon a hearse:
And bitter wine upon a sponge
   Was the savour of Remorse.

The grey cock crew, the red cock crew,
   But never came the day;
And crooked shapes of terror crouched
   In the corners where we lay:
And each evil sprite that walks by night
   Before us seemed to play.

They glided past, they glided fast,
   Like travellers through a mist:
They mocked the moon in a rigadoon
   Of delicate turn and twist,
And with formal pace and loathsome grace
   The phantoms kept their tryst.

With mop and mow, we saw them go,
   Slim shadows hand and hand:
About, about, in ghostly rout
   They trod a saraband:
And the damned grotesques made arabesques,
   Like the wind upon the sand!

With pirouettes of marionettes
   They tripped on pointed tread:
But with flutes of Fear they filled the ear,
   As their grisly masque they led,
And loud they sang, and long they sang,
   For they sang to wake the dead.

"Oho!" they cried, *"The world is wide,*
   But fettered limbs go lame!
And once, or twice, to throw the dice
   Is a gentlemanly game,
But he does not win who plays with Sin
   In the Secret House of Shame."

No things of air these antics were,
   That frolicked with such glee:
To men whose lives were held in gyves,
   And whose feet might not go free,
Ah! wounds of Christ! they were living things,
   Most terrible to see.

Around, around, they waltzed and wound;
   Some wheeled in smirking pairs;
With the mincing step of a demirep
   Some sidled up the stairs:
And with subtle sneer, and fawning leer,
   Each helped us at our prayers.

The morning wind began to moan,
   But still the night went on;
Through its giant loom the web of gloom
   Crept till each thread was spun:
And, as we prayed, we grew afraid
   Of the Justice of the Sun.

The moaning wind went wandering round
   The weeping prison-wall:
Till like a wheel of turning steel
   We felt the minutes crawl:
O moaning wind! what had we done
   To have such a seneschal?

At last I saw the shadowed bars,
  Like a lattice wrought in lead,
Move right across the whitewashed wall
  That faced my three-planked bed,
And I knew that somewhere in the world
  God's dreadful dawn was red.

At six o'clock we cleaned our cells,
  At seven all was still,
But the sough and swing of a mighty wing
  The prison seemed to fill,
For the Lord of Death with icy breath,
  Had entered in to kill.

He did not pass in purple pomp,
  Nor ride a moon-white steed.
Three yards of cord and a sliding board
  Are all the gallows' need:
So with rope of shame the Herald came
  To do the secret deed.

We were as men who through a fen
  Of filthy darkness grope:
We did not dare to breathe a prayer,
  Or to give our anguish scope:
Something was dead in each of us,
  And what was dead was Hope.

For Man's grim Justice goes its way,
  And will not swerve aside:
It slays the weak, it slays the strong,
  It has a deadly stride:
With iron heel it slays the strong,
  The monstrous parricide!

We waited for the stroke of eight:
  Each tongue was thick with thirst:
For the stroke of eight is the stroke of Fate
  That makes a man accursed,
And Fate will use a running noose
  For the best man and the worst.

We had no other thing to do,
    Save to wait for the sign to come:
So, like things of stone in a valley lone,
    Quiet we sat and dumb:
But each man's heart beat thick and quick,
    Like a madman on a drum!

With sudden shock, the prison-clock
    Smote on the shivering air,
And from all the jail rose up a wail
    Of impotent despair,
Like the sound that frightened marshes hear
    From some leper in his lair.

And as one sees most dreadful things
    In the crystal of a dream,
We saw the greasy hempen rope
    Hooked to the blackened beam,
And heard the prayer the hangman's snare
    Strangled into a scream.

And all the woe that moved him so
    That he gave that bitter cry,
And the wild regrets, and the bloody sweats,
    None knew so well as I:
For he who lives more lives than one
    More deaths than one must die.

IV

There is no chapel on the day
    On which they hang a man:
The Chaplain's heart is far too sick,
    Or his face is far too wan,
Or there is that written in his eyes
    Which none should look upon.

So they kept us close till nigh on noon,
    And then they rang the bell,
And the Warders with their jingling keys
    Opened each listening cell,
And down the iron stair we tramped,
    Each from his separate Hell.

Out into God's sweet air we went,
    But not in wonted way,
For this man's face was white with fear,
    And that man's face was grey,
And I never saw sad men who looked
    So wistfully at the day.

I never saw sad men who looked
    With such a wistful eye
Upon that little tent of blue
    We prisoners call the sky,
And at every careless cloud that passed
    In happy freedom by.

But there were those amongst us all
    Who walked with downcast head,
And knew that, had each got his due,
    They should have died instead:
He had but killed a thing that lived,
    Whilst they had killed the dead.

For he who sins a second time
    Wakes a dead soul to pain,
And draws it from its spotted shroud,
    And makes it bleed again,
And makes it bleed great gouts of blood,
    And makes it bleed in vain!

Like ape or clown, in monstrous garb
    With crooked arrows starred,
Silently we went round and round
    The slippery asphalt yard;
Silently we went round and round,
    And no man spoke a word.

Silently we went round and round,
    And through each hollow mind
The Memory of dreadful things
    Rushed like a dreadful wind,
And Honour stalked before each man,
    And Terror crept behind.

The Warders strutted up and down,
  And kept their herd of brutes,
Their uniforms were spick and span,
  They wore their Sunday suits,
But we knew the work they had been at,
  By the quicklime on their boots.

For where a grave had opened wide,
  There was no grave at all:
Only a stretch of mud and sand
  By the hideous prison-wall,
And a little heap of burning lime,
  That the man should have his pall.

For he has a pall, this wretched man,
  Such as few men can claim:
Deep down below a prison-yard,
  Naked for greater shame,
He lies, with fetters on each foot,
  Wrapped in a sheet of flame!

And all the while the burning lime
  Eats flesh and bone away,
It eats the brittle bone by night,
  And the soft flesh by day,
It eats the flesh and bone by turns,
  But it eats the heart alway.

For three long years they will not sow
  Or root or seedling there;
For three long years the unblessed spot
  Will sterile be and bare,
And look upon the wondering sky
  With unreproachful stare.

They think a murderer's heart would taint
  Each simple seed they sow.
It is not true! God's kindly earth
  Is kindlier than men know,
And the red rose would but blow more red,
  The white rose whiter blow.

Out of his mouth a red, red rose!
 Out of his heart a white!
For who can say by what strange way
 Christ brings his will to light,
Since the barren staff the pilgrim bore
 Bloomed in the great Pope's sight?

But neither milk-white rose nor red
 May bloom in prison air;
The shard, the pebble, and the flint,
 Are what they give us there:
For flowers have been known to heal
 A common man's despair.

So never will wine-red rose or white
 Petal by petal, fall
On that stretch of mud and sand that lies
 By that hideous prison-wall,
To tell the men who tramp the yard
 That God's Son died for all.

Yet though the hideous prison-wall
 Still hems him round and round,
And a spirit may not walk by night
 That is with fetters bound,
And a spirit may but weep that lies
 In such unholy ground,

He is at peace—this wretched man—
 At peace, or will be soon:
There is no thing to make him mad,
 Nor does Terror walk at noon,
For the lampless Earth in which he lies
 Has neither Sun nor Moon.

They hanged him as a beast is hanged:
 They did not even toll
A requiem that might have brought
 Rest to his startled soul,
But hurriedly they took him out,
 And hid him in a hole.

They stripped him of his canvas clothes,
   And gave him to the flies:
They mocked the swollen purple throat,
   And the stark and staring eyes:
And with laughter loud they heaped the shroud
   In which their convict lies.

The Chaplain would not kneel to pray
   By his dishonoured grave:
Nor mark it with that blessed Cross
   That Christ for sinners gave,
Because the man was one of those
   Whom Christ came down to save.

Yet all is well; he has but passed
   To Life's appointed bourne:
And alien tears will fill for him
   Pity's long-broken urn,
For his mourners will be outcast men,
   And outcasts always mourn.

V

I know not whether Laws be right,
   Or whether Laws be wrong;
All that we know who lie in jail
   Is that the wall is strong;
And that each day is like a year,
   A year whose days are long.

But this I know, that every Law
   That men have made for Man,
Since first Man took his brother's life,
   And this sad world began,
But straws the wheat and saves the chaff
   With a most evil fan.

This too I know—and wise it were
   If each could know the same—
That every prison that men build
   Is built with bricks of shame,
And bound with bars lest Christ should see
   How men their brothers maim.

With bars they blur the gracious moon,
  And blind the goodly sun:
And they do well to hide their Hell,
  For in it things are done
That Son of God nor son of Man
  Ever should look upon!

The vilest deeds like poison weeds
  Bloom well in prison-air:
It is only what is good in Man
  That wastes and withers there:
Pale Anguish keeps the heavy gate,
  And the Warder is Despair.

For they starve the little frightened child,
  Till it weeps both night and day:
And they scourge the weak, and flog the fool,
  And gibe the old and grey,
And some grow mad, and all grow bad,
  And none a word may say.

Each narrow cell in which we dwell
  Is a foul and dark latrine,
And the fetid breath of living Death
  Chokes up each grated screen,
And all, but Lust, is turned to dust
  In Humanity's machine.

The brackish water that we drink
  Creeps with a loathsome slime,
And the bitter bread they weigh in scales
  Is full of chalk and lime,
And Sleep will not lie down, but walks
  Wild-eyed, and cries to Time.

But though lean Hunger and green Thirst
  Like asp with adder fight,
We have little care of prison fare,
  For what chills and kills outright
Is that every stone one lifts by day
  Becomes one's heart by night.

With midnight always in one's heart,
  And twilight in one's cell,
We turn the crank, or tear the rope,
  Each in his separate Hell,
And the silence is more awful far
  Than the sound of a brazen bell.

And never a human voice comes near
  To speak a gentle word:
And the eye that watches through the door
  Is pitiless and hard:
And by all forgot, we rot and rot,
  With soul and body marred.

And thus we rust Life's iron chain,
  Degraded and alone:
And some men curse, and some men weep,
  And some men make no moan:
But God's eternal Laws are kind
  And break the heart of stone.

And every human heart that breaks,
  In prison-cell or yard,
Is as that broken box that gave
  Its treasure to the Lord,
And filled the unclean leper's house
  With the scent of costliest nard.

Ah! happy they whose hearts can break
  And peace of pardon win!
How else may man make straight his plan
  And cleanse his soul from Sin?
How else but through a broken heart
  May Lord Christ enter in?

And he of the swollen purple throat,
  And the stark and staring eyes,
Waits for the holy hands that took
  The Thief to Paradise;
And a broken and a contrite heart
  The Lord will not despise.

The man in red who reads the Law
   Gave him three weeks of life,
Three little weeks in which to heal
   His soul of his soul's strife,
And cleanse from every blot of blood
   The hand that held the knife.

And with tears of blood he cleansed the hand,
   The hand that held the steel:
For only blood can wipe out blood,
   And only tears can heal:
And the crimson stain that was of Cain
   Became Christ's snow-white seal.

VI

In Reading gaol by Reading town
   There is a pit of shame,
And in it lies a wretched man
   Eaten by teeth of flame,
In a burning winding-sheet he lies,
   And his grave has got no name.

And there, till Christ call forth the dead,
   In silence let him lie:
No need to waste the foolish tear,
   Or heave the windy sigh:
The man had killed the thing he loved,
   And so he had to die.

And all men kill the thing they love,
   By all let this be heard,
Some do it with a bitter look,
   Some with a flattering word,
The coward does it with a kiss,
   The brave man with a sword!

JOHN DAVIDSON

A Runnable Stag

WHEN the pods went pop on the broom, green broom,
  And apples began to be golden-skinned,
We harboured a stag in the Priory coomb,
  And we feathered his trail up-wind, up-wind,
  We feathered his trail up-wind—
    A stag of warrant, a stag, a stag,
    A runnable stag, a kingly crop,
    Brow, bay and tray and three on top,
    A stag, a runnable stag.

Then the huntsman's horn rang yap, yap, yap,
  And "Forwards" we heard the harbourer shout;
But 'twas only a brocket that broke a gap
  In the beechen underwood, driven out,
  From the underwood antlered out
    By warrant and might of the stag, the stag,
    The runnable stag, whose lordly mind
    Was bent on sleep, though beamed and tined
    He stood, a runnable stag.

So we tufted the covert till afternoon
  With Tinkerman's Pup and Bell-of-the-North;
And hunters were sulky and hounds out of tune
  Before we tufted the right stag forth,
  Before we tufted him forth,
    The stag of warrant, the wily stag,
    The runnable stag with his kingly crop,
    Brow, bay and tray and three on top,
    The royal and runnable stag.

It was Bell-of-the-North and Tinkerman's Pup
  That stuck to the scent till the copse was drawn.
"Tally ho! tally ho!" and the hunt was up,
  The tufters whipped and the pack laid on,

The resolute pack laid on,
  And the stag of warrant away at last,
  The runnable stag, the same, the same,
  His hoofs on fire, his horns like flame,
  A stag, a runnable stag.

"Let your gelding be: if you check or chide
  He stumbles at once and you're out of the hunt;
For three hundred gentlemen, able to ride,
  On hunters accustomed to bear the brunt,
  Accustomed to bear the brunt,
    Are after the runnable stag, the stag,
    The runnable stag with his kingly crop,
    Brow, bay and tray and three on top,
    The right, the runnable stag."

By perilous paths in coomb and dell,
  The heather, the rocks, and the river-bed,
The pace grew hot, for the scent lay well,
  And a runnable stag goes right ahead,
  The quarry went right ahead—
    Ahead, ahead, and fast and far;
    His antlered crest, his cloven hoof,
    Brow, bay and tray and three aloof,
    The stag, the runnable stag.

For a matter of twenty miles and more,
  By the densest hedge and the highest wall,
Through herds of bullocks he baffled the lore
  Of harbourer, huntsman, hounds and all,
  Of harbourer, hounds and all—
    The stag of warrant, the wily stag,
    For twenty miles, and five and five,
    He ran, and he never was caught alive,
    This stag, this runnable stag.

When he turned at bay in the leafy gloom,
  In the emerald gloom where the brook ran deep,
He heard in the distance the rollers boom,
  And he saw in a vision of peaceful sleep,
  In a wonderful vision of sleep,

A stag of warrant, a stag, a stag,
A runnable stag in a jewelled bed,
Under the sheltering ocean dead,
A stag, a runnable stag.

So a fateful hope lit up his eye,
And he opened his nostrils wide again,
And he tossed his branching antlers high
As he headed the hunt down the Charlock glen,
As he raced down the echoing glen—
For five miles more, the stag, the stag,
For twenty miles, and five and five,
Not to be caught now, dead or alive,
The stag, the runnable stag.

Three hundred gentlemen, able to ride,
Three hundred horses as gallant and free,
Beheld him escape on the evening tide,
Far out till he sank in the Severn Sea,
Till he sank in the depths of the sea—
The stag, the buoyant stag, the stag
That slept at last in a jewelled bed
Under the sheltering ocean spread,
The stag, the runnable stag.

A Ballad of Hell

"A LETTER from my love today!
  Oh, unexpected, dear appeal!"
She struck a happy tear away,
  And broke the crimson seal.

"My love, there is no help on earth,
  No help in heaven; the dead-man's bell
Must toll our wedding; our first hearth
  Must be the well-paved floor of hell."

The color died from out her face,
  Her eyes like ghostly candles shone;
She cast dread looks about the place,
  Then clenched her teeth and read right on.

"I may not pass the prison door;
　Here must I rot from day to day,
Unless I wed whom I abhor,
　My cousin, Blanche of Valencay.

"At midnight with my dagger keen,
　I'll take my life; it must be so.
Meet me in hell tonight, my queen,
　For weal and woe."

She laughed, although her face was wan,
　She girded on her golden belt,
She took her jeweled ivory fan,
　And at her glowing missal knelt.

Then rose, "And am I mad?" she said:
　She broke her fan, her belt untied;
With leather girt herself instead,
　And stuck a dagger at her side.

She waited, shuddering in her room,
　Till sleep had fallen on all the house.
She never flinched; she faced her doom:
　They two must sin to keep their vows.

Then out into the night she went,
　And, stooping, crept by hedge and tree;
Her rose-bush flung a snare of scent,
　And caught a happy memory.

She fell, and lay a minute's space;
　She tore the sward in her distress;
The dewy grass refreshed her face;
　She rose and ran with lifted dress.

She started like a morn-caught ghost
　Once when the moon came out and stood
To watch; the naked road she crossed,
　And dived into the murmuring wood.

The branches snatched her streaming cloak;
　A live thing shrieked; she made no stay!

She hurried to the trysting-oak—
Right well she knew the way.

Without a pause she bared her breast,
 And drove her dagger home and fell,
And lay like one that takes her rest,
 And died and wakened up in hell.

She bathed her spirit in the flame,
 And near the center took her post;
From all sides to her ears there came
 The dreary anguish of the lost.

The devil started at her side,
 Comely, and tall, and black as jet.
"I am young Malespina's bride;
 Has he come hither yet?"

"My poppet, welcome to your bed."
 "Is Malespina here?"
"Not he! Tomorrow he must wed
 His cousin Blanche, my dear!"

"You lie, he died with me tonight."
 "Not he! it was a plot" . . . "You lie!"
"My dear, I never lie outright."
 "We died at midnight, he and I."

The devil went. Without a groan
 She, gathered up in one fierce prayer,
Took root in hell's midst all alone,
 And waited for him there.

She dared to make herself at home
 Amidst the wail, the uneasy stir.
The blood-stained flame that filled the dome,
 Scentless and silent, shrouded her.

How long she stayed I cannot tell;
 But when she felt his perfidy,
She marched across the floor of hell;
 And all the damned stood up to see.

The devil stopped her at the brink:
  She shook him off; she cried, "Away!"
"My dear, you have gone mad, I think."
  "I was betrayed: I will not stay."

Across the weltering deep she ran;
  A stranger thing was never seen:
The damned stood silent to a man;
  They saw the great gulf set between.

To her it seemed a meadow fair;
  And flowers sprang up about her feet.
She entered heaven; she climbed the stair
  And knelt down at the mercy-seat.

Seraphs and saints with one great voice
  Welcomed the soul that knew not fear.
Amazed to find it could rejoice,
  Hell raised a hoarse, half-human cheer.

FRANCIS THOMPSON

The Hound of Heaven

I FLED Him, down the nights and down the days;
  I fled Him, down the arches of the years;
I fled Him, down the labyrinthine ways
  Of my own mind; and in the mist of tears
I hid from Him, and under running laughter.
     Up vistaed hopes I sped;
     And shot, precipitated,
Adown Titanic glooms of chasmèd fears,
  From those strong Feet that followed, followed after.
     But with unhurrying chase,
     And unperturbèd pace,
  Deliberate speed, majestic instancy,
     They beat—and a Voice beat
     More instant than the Feet—
"All things betray thee, who betrayest Me."

I pleaded, outlaw-wise,
By many a hearted casement, curtained red,
  Trellised with intertwining charities;
(For, though I knew His love Who followèd,
        Yet was I sore adread
Lest, having Him, I must have naught beside);
But, if one little casement parted wide,
  The gust of His approach would clash it to.
  Fear wist not to evade, as Love wist to pursue.
Across the margent of the world I fled,
  And troubled the gold gateways of the stars,
  Smiting for shelter on their clangèd bars;
        Fretted to dulcet jars
And silvern chatter the pale ports o' the moon.
I said to Dawn: Be sudden—to Eve: Be soon;
  With thy young skiey blossoms heap me over
        From this tremendous Lover—
Float thy vague veil about me, lest He see!
I tempted all His servitors, but to find
My own betrayal in their constancy,
In faith to Him their fickleness to me,
  Their traitorous trueness, and their loyal deceit.
To all swift things for swiftness did I sue;
  Clung to the whistling mane of every wind.
    But whether they swept, smoothly fleet,
    The long savannahs of the blue;
        Or whether, Thunder-driven,
    They clanged his chariot 'thwart a heaven,
Plashy with flying lightnings round the spurn o' their feet:—
  Fear wist not to evade as Love wist to pursue.
        Still with unhurrying chase,
        And unperturbèd pace,
    Deliberate speed, majestic instancy,
        Came on the following Feet,
        And a Voice above their beat—
"Naught shelters thee, who wilt not shelter Me."

I sought no more that after which I strayed
        In face of man or maid;
But still within the little children's eyes
    Seems something, something that replies,
They at least are for me, surely for me!

I turned me to them very wistfully;
But just as their young eyes grew sudden fair
    With dawning answers there,
Their angel plucked them from me by the hair.
"Come then, ye other children, Nature's—share
With me" (said I) "your delicate fellowship;
    Let me greet you lip to lip,
    Let me twine with you caresses,
      Wantoning
    With our Lady-Mother's vagrant tresses,
      Banqueting
    With her in her wind-walled palace,
    Underneath her azured daïs,
    Quaffing, as your taintless way is,
      From a chalice
Lucent-weeping out of the dayspring."
    So it was done:
I in their delicate fellowship was one—
Drew the bolt of Nature's secrecies.
    I knew all the swift importings
    On the willful face of skies;
    I knew how the clouds arise
    Spumèd of the wild sea-snortings;
      All that 's born or dies
    Rose and drooped with; made them shapers
Of mine own moods, or wailful or divine;
    With them joyed and was bereaven.
    I was heavy with the even,
    When she lit her glimmering tapers
    Round the day's dead sanctities.
    I laughed in the morning's eyes.
I triumphed and I saddened with all weather,
    Heaven and I wept together,
And its sweet tears were salt with mortal mine.
Against the red throb of its sunset-heart
    I laid my own to beat,
    And share commingling heat;
But not by that, by that, was eased my human smart.
In vain my tears were wet on Heaven's gray cheek.
For ah! we know not what each other says,
    These things and I; in sound *I* speak—
Their sound is but their stir, they speak by silences.

Nature, poor stepdame, cannot slake my drouth;
    Let her, if she would owe me,
Drop yon blue bosom-veil of sky, and show me
    The breasts o' her tenderness:
Never did any milk of hers once bless
      My thirsting mouth.
      Nigh and nigh draws the chase,
      With unperturbèd pace,
    Deliberate speed, majestic instancy;
      And past those noisèd Feet
      A Voice comes yet more fleet—
    "Lo! naught contents thee, who content'st not Me."

Naked I wait Thy love's uplifted stroke!
My harness piece by piece Thou hast hewn from me,
      And smitten me to my knee;
    I am defenceless utterly.
    I slept, methinks, and woke,
And, slowly gazing, find me stripped in sleep.
In the rash lustihead of my young powers,
    I shook the pillaring hours
And pulled my life upon me; grimed with smears,
I stand amid the dust o' the mounded years—
My mangled youth lies dead beneath the heap.
My days have crackled and gone up in smoke,
Have puffed and burst as sun-starts on a stream.
    Yea, faileth now even dream
The dreamer, and the lute the lutanist;
Even the linked fantasies, in whose blossomy twist
I swung the earth a trinket at my wrist,
Are yielding; cords of all too weak account
For earth with heavy griefs so overplussed.
    Ah! is Thy love indeed
A weed, albeit an amaranthine weed,
Suffering no flowers except its own to mount?
    Ah! must—
    Designer infinite!—
Ah! must Thou char the wood ere Thou canst limn with it?
My freshness spent its wavering shower i' the dust;
And now my heart is as a broken fount,
Wherein tear-drippings stagnate, spilt down ever
    From the dank thoughts that shiver

Upon the sighful branches of my mind.
　　Such is; what is to be?
The pulp so bitter, how shall taste the rind?
I dimly guess what Time in mists confounds;
Yet ever and anon a trumpet sounds
From the hid battlements of Eternity;
Those shaken mists a space unsettle, then
Round the half-glimpsèd turrets slowly wash again.
　　But not ere him who summoneth
　　I first have seen, enwound
With glooming robes purpureal, cypress-crowned;
His name I know, and what his trumpet saith.
Whether man's heart or life it be which yields
　　The harvest, must Thy harvest-fields
　　Be dunged with rotten death?

　　　Now of that long pursuit
　　　Comes on at hand the bruit;
　　That Voice is round me like a bursting sea:
　　　"And is thy earth so marred,
　　　Shattered in shard on shard?
　　Lo, all things fly thee, for thou fliest Me!
　　Strange, piteous, futile thing!
Wherefore should any set thee love apart?
Seeing none but I makes much of naught" (He said),
"And human love needs human meriting:
　　How hast thou merited—
Of all man's clotted clay the dingiest clot?
　　Alack, thou knowest not
How little worthy of any love thou art!
Whom wilt thou find to love ignoble thee
　　Save Me, save only Me?
All which I took from thee I did but take,
　　Not for thy harms,
But just that thou might'st seek it in My arms.
　　All which thy child's mistake
Fancies as lost, I have stored for thee at home:
　　Rise, clasp My hand, and come!"

　　Halts by me that footfall:
　　Is my gloom, after all,
Shade of His hand, outstretched caressingly?

"Ah, fondest, blindest, weakest,
I am He Whom thou seekest!
Thou dravest love from thee, who dravest Me."

The Heart

II

O NOTHING, in this corporal earth of man,
   That to the imminent heaven of his high soul
Responds with colour and with shadow, can
   Lack correlated greatness. If the scroll
Where thoughts lie fast in spell of hieroglyph
   Be mighty through its mighty habitants;
If God be in His Name; grave potence if
   The sounds unbind of hieratic chants;
All's vast that vastness means. Nay, I affirm
   Nature is whole in her least things exprest,
Nor know we with what scope God builds the worm.
   Our towns are copies fragments from our breast;
      And all man's Babylons strive but to impart
      The grandeurs of his Babylonian heart.

Dream-Tryst

THE breaths of kissing night and day
   Were mingled in the eastern Heaven:
      Throbbing with unheard melody
Shook Lyra all its star-chord seven:
   When dusk shrunk cold, and light trod shy,
      And dawn's grey eyes were troubled grey;
   And souls went palely up the sky,
      And mine to Lucidé.

There was no change in her sweet eyes
   Since last I saw those sweet eyes shine;
There was no change in her deep heart
   Since last that deep heart knocked at mine.
      Her eyes were clear, her eyes were Hope's,
         Wherein did ever come and go

The sparkle of the fountain-drops
From her sweet soul below.

The chambers in the house of dreams
Are fed with so divine an air,
That Time's hoar wings grow young therein,
And they who walk there are most fair.
I joyed for me, I joyed for her,
Who with the Past meet girt about:
Where our last kiss still warms the air,
Nor can her eyes go out.

In No Strange Land

O WORLD invisible, we view thee,
O world intangible, we touch thee,
O world unknowable, we know thee,
Inapprehensible, we clutch thee!

Does the fish soar to find the ocean,
The eagle plunge to find the air—
That we ask of the stars in motion
If they have rumour of thee there?

Not where the wheeling systems darken,
And our benumbed conceiving soars!—
The drift of pinions, would we hearken,
Beats at our own clay-shuttered doors.

The angels keep their ancient places;—
Turn but a stone, and start a wing!
'Tis ye, 'tis your estrangèd faces,
That miss the many-splendoured thing.

But, when so sad thou canst not sadder,
Cry—and upon thy so sore loss
Shall shine the traffic of Jacob's ladder
Pitched betwixt Heaven and Charing Cross.

Yea, in the night, my Soul, my daughter,
Cry—clinging Heaven by the hems . . .
And lo, Christ walking on the water
Not of Gennesareth, but Thames!

A. E. HOUSMAN

II

LOVELIEST of trees, the cherry now
　Is hung with bloom along the bough,
And stands about the woodland ride
Wearing white for Eastertide.

Now, of my threescore years and ten,
Twenty will not come again,
And take from seventy springs a score,
It only leaves me fifty more.

And since to look at things in bloom
Fifty springs are little room,
About the woodlands I will go
To see the cherry hung with snow.

VII

When smoke stood up from Ludlow,
　And mist blew off from Teme,
And blithe afield to ploughing
　Against the morning beam
　I strode beside my team,

The blackbird in the coppice
　Looked out to see me stride,
And hearkened as I whistled
　The trampling team beside,
　And fluted and replied:

"Lie down, lie down, young yeoman;
　What use to rise and rise?
Rise man a thousand mornings
　Yet down at last he lies,
　And then the man is wise."

I heard the tune he sang me,
  And spied his yellow bill;
I picked a stone and aimed it
  And threw it with a will:
  Then the bird was still.

Then my soul within me
  Took up the blackbird's strain,
And still beside the horses
  Along the dewy lane
  It sang the song again:

"Lie down, lie down, young yeoman;
  The sun moves always west;
The road one treads to labour
  Will lead one home to rest,
  And that will be the best."

XII

When I watch the living meet,
  And the moving pageant file
Warm and breathing through the street
  Where I lodge a little while,

If the heats of hate and lust
  In the house of flesh are strong,
Let me mind the house of dust
  Where my sojourn shall be long.

In the nation that is not
  Nothing stands that stood before;
There revenges are forgot,
  And the hater hates no more;

Lovers lying two and two
  Ask not whom they sleep beside,
And the bridegroom all night through
  Never turns him to the bride.

XIII

When I was one-and-twenty
  I heard a wise man say,

"Give crowns and pounds and guineas
  But not your heart away;
Give pearls away and rubies
  But keep your fancy free."
But I was one-and-twenty,
  No use to talk to me.

When I was one-and-twenty
  I heard him say again,
"The heart out of the bosom
  Was never given in vain;
'Tis paid with sighs a plenty
  And sold for endless rue."
And I am two-and-twenty,
  And oh, 'tis true, 'tis true.

XLVIII

Be still, my soul, be still; the arms you bear are brittle,
  Earth and high heaven are fixt of old and founded strong
Think rather,—call to thought, if now you grieve a little
  The days when we had rest, O soul, for they were long.

Men loved unkindness then, but lightless in the quarry
  I slept and saw not; tears fell down, I did not mourn;
Sweat ran and blood sprang out and I was never sorry:
  Then it was well with me, in days ere I was born.

Now, I muse for why and never find the reason,
  I pace the earth, and drink the air, and feel the sun.
Be still, be still, my soul; it is but for a season:
  Let us endure an hour and see injustice done.

Ay, look: high heaven and earth ail from the prime foundation;
  All thoughts to rive the heart are here, and all are vain:
Horror and scorn and hate and fear and indignation—
  Oh why did I awake? when shall I sleep again?

LII

Far in a western brookland
  That bred me long ago
The poplars stand and tremble
  By pools I used to know.

There, in the windless night-time,
    The wanderer, marvelling why,
Halts on the bridge to hearken
    How soft the poplars sigh.

He hears: no more remembered:
    In fields where I was known,
Here I lie down in London
    And turn to rest alone.

There, by the starlit fences,
    The wanderer halts and hears
My soul that lingers sighing
    About the glimmering weirs.

LIV

With rue my heart is laden
    For golden friends I had,
For many a rose-lipt maiden
    And many a lightfoot lad.

By brooks too broad for leaping
    The lightfoot boys are laid;
The rose-lipt girls are sleeping
    In fields where roses fade.

FROM LAST POEMS

XXV

The Oracles

'TIS mute, the word they went to hear on high Dodona mountain
    When winds were in the oakenshaws and all the cauldrons tolled,
And mute's the midland navel-stone beside the singing fountain,
    And echoes list to silence now where gods told lies of old.

I took my question to the shrine that has not ceased from speaking,
    The heart within, that tells the truth and tells it twice as plain;

And from the cave of oracles I heard the priestess shrieking
  That she and I should surely die and never live again.

Oh priestess, what you cry is clear, and sound good sense I think it,
  But let the screaming echoes rest, and froth your mouth no more.
'Tis true there's better boose than brine, but he that drowns must
    drink it;
  And oh, my lass, the news is news that men have heard before.

The King with half the East at heel is marched from lands of
    morning;
  Their fighters drink the rivers up, their shafts benight the air.
And he that stands will die for nought, and home there's no re-
    turning.
  The Spartans on the sea-wet rock sat down and combed their hair.

XLI

Fancy's Knell

WHEN lads were home from labour
    At Abdon under Clee,
A man would call his neighbour
    And both would send for me.
And where the light in lances
    Across the mead was laid,
There to the dances
    I fetched my flute and played.

Ours were idle pleasures,
    Yet oh, content we were,
The young to wind the measures,
    The old to heed the air;
And I to lift with playing
    From tree and tower and steep
The light delaying,
    And flute the sun to sleep.

The youth toward his fancy
    Would turn his brow of tan,

And Tom would pair with Nancy
    And Dick step off with Fan;
The girl would lift her glances
    To his, and both be mute:
Well went the dances
    At evening to the flute.

Wenlock Edge was umbered,
    And bright was Abdon Burf,
And warm between them slumbered
    The smooth green miles of turf;
Until from grass and clover
    The upshot beam would fade,
And England over
    Advanced the lofty shade.

The lofty shade advances,
    I fetch my flute and play:
Come, lads, and learn the dances
    And praise the tune today.
Tomorrow, more's the pity,
    Away we both must hie,
To air the ditty,
    And to earth I.

SIR HENRY NEWBOLT

Drake's Drum

DRAKE, he's in his hammock an' a thousand mile away,
    (Capten, art tha sleepin' there below?)
Slung atween the round shot in Nombre Dios Bay,
    An' dreamin' arl the time o' Plymouth Hoe.
Yarnder lumes the Island, yarnder lie the ships,
    Wi' sailor lads a-dancin' heel-an'-toe,
An' the shore-lights flashin', an' the night-tide dashin',
    He sees et arl so plainly as he saw et long ago.

Drake he was a Devon man, an' ruled the Devon seas,
  (Capten, art tha sleepin' there below?)
Rovin' tho' his death fell, he went wi' heart at ease,
  An' dreamin' arl the time o' Plymouth Hoe.
"Take my drum to England, hang et by the shore,
  Strike et when your powder's runnin' low;
If the Dons sight Devon, I'll quit the port o' Heaven,
  And drum them up the Channel as we drummed them long ago."

Drake he's in his hammock till the great Armadas come,
  (Capten, art tha sleepin' there below?)
Slung atween the round shot, listenin' for the drum,
  An' dreamin' arl the time o' Plymouth Hoe.
Call him on the deep sea, call him up the Sound,
  Call him when ye sail to meet the foe;
Where the old trade's plyin' an' the old flag flyin',
  They shall find him ware an' wakin', as they found him long ago.

RUDYARD KIPLING

Danny Deever

"WHAT are the bugles blowin' for?" said Files-on-Parade.
  "To turn you out, to turn you out," the Colour-Sergeant
    said.
"What makes you look so white, so white?" said Files-on-Parade.
"I'm dreadin' what I've got to watch," the Colour-Sergeant said.
  For they're hangin' Danny Deever, you can hear the Dead March
    play,
  The regiment's in 'ollow square—they're hangin' him today;
  They've taken of his buttons off an' cut his stripes away,
  An' they're hangin' Danny Deever in the mornin'.

"What makes the rear-rank breathe so 'ard?" said Files-on-Parade.
"It's bitter cold, it's bitter cold," the Colour-Sergeant said.
"What makes that front-rank man fall down?" says Files-on-Parade.
"A touch o' sun, a touch o' sun," the Colour-Sergeant said.

They are hangin' Danny Deever, they are marchin' of 'im round,
They 'ave 'alted Danny Deever by 'is coffin on the ground;
An' 'e'll swing in 'arf a minute for a sneakin' shootin' hound—
O they're hangin' Danny Deever in the mornin'!

" 'Is cot was right-'and cot to mine," said Files-on-Parade.
" 'E's sleepin' out an' far tonight," the Colour-Sergeant said.
" 'I've drunk 'is beer a score o' times," said Files-on-Parade.
" 'E's drinkin' bitter beer alone," the Colour-Sergeant said.
They are hangin' Danny Deever, you must mark 'im to 'is place,
For 'e shot a comrade sleepin'—you must look 'im in the face;
Nine 'undred of 'is county an' the regiment's disgrace,
While they're hangin' Danny Deever in the mornin'.

"What's that so black agin the sun?" said Files-on-Parade.
"It's Danny fightin' 'ard for life," the Colour-Sergeant said.
"What's that that whimpers over'ead?" said Files-on-Parade.
"It's Danny's soul that's passing now," the Colour-Sergeant said.
For they're done with Danny Deever, you can 'ear the quickstep
   play,
The regiment's in column, an' they're marchin' us away;
Ho! the young recruits are shakin', an' they'll want their beer
   today,
After hangin' Danny Deever in the mornin'.

The Ballad of East and West

*OH, East is East, and West is West, and never the twain shall
   meet,
Till Earth and Sky stand presently at God's great Judgment Seat;
But there is neither East nor West, Border, nor Breed, nor Birth,
When two strong men stand face to face, though they come from the
   ends of the earth!*

Kamal is out with twenty men to raise the Border side,
And he has lifted the Colonel's mare that is the Colonel's pride.
He has lifted her out of the stable-door between the dawn and the
   day,
And turned the calkins upon her feet, and ridden her far away.
Then up and spoke the Colonel's son that led a troop of the Guides:
"Is there never a man of all my men can say where Kamal hides?"

Then up and spoke Mohammed Khan, the son of the Ressaldar:
"If ye know the track of the morning-mist, ye know where his
    pickets are.
At dusk he harries the Abazai—at dawn he is into Bonair,
But he must go by Fort Bukloh to his own place to fare.
So if ye gallop to Fort Bukloh as fast as a bird can fly,
By the favour of God ye may cut him off ere he win to the Tongue
    of Jagai.
But if he be past the Tongue of Jagai, right swiftly turn ye then,
For the length and the breadth of that grisly plain is sown with
    Kamal's men.
There is rock to the left, and rock to the right, and low lean thorn
    between,
And ye may hear a breech-bold snick where never a man is seen."
The Colonel's son has taken a horse, and a raw rough dun was he,
With the mouth of a bell and the heart of Hell and the head of a
    gallows-tree.
The Colonel's son to the Fort has won, they bid him stay to eat—
Who rides at the tail of a Border thief, he sits not long at his meat.
He's up and away from Fort Bukloh as fast as he can fly,
Till he was aware of his father's mare in the gut of the Tongue of
    Jagai,
Till he was aware of his father's mare with Kamal upon her back,
And when he could spy the white of her eye, he made the pistol
    crack.
He has fired once, he has fired twice, but the whistling ball went
    wide.
"Ye shoot like a soldier," Kamal said. "Show now if ye can ride!"
It's up and over the Tongue of Jagai, as blown dust-devils go,
The dun he fled like a stag of ten, but the mare like a barren doe.
The dun he leaned against the bit and slugged his head above,
But the red mare played with the snaffle-bars, as a maiden plays with
    a glove.
There was rock to the left and rock to the right, and low lean thorn
    between,
And thrice he heard a breech-bolt snick tho' never a man was seen.
They have ridden the low moon out of the sky, their hoofs drum up
    the dawn,
The dun he went like a wounded bull, but the mare like a new-
    roused fawn.
The dun he fell at a water-course—in a woeful heap fell he,
And Kamal has turned the red mare back, and pulled the rider free.

He has knocked the pistol out of his hand—small room was there
 to strive,
" 'Twas only by favour of mine," quoth he, "ye rode so long alive:
There was not a rock for twenty mile, there was not a clump of tree,
But covered a man of my own men with his rifle cocked on his knee.
If I had raised my bridle-hand, as I have held it low,
The little jackals that flee so fast were feasting all in a row.
If I had bowed my head on my breast, as I have held it high,
The kite that whistles above us now were gorged till she could not
 fly."
Lightly answered the Colonel's son: "Do good to bird and beast,
But count who come for the broken meats before thou makest a
 feast.
If there should follow a thousand swords to carry my bones away,
Belike the price of a jackal's meal were more than a thief could pay.
They will feed their horse on the standing crop, their men on the
 garnered grain,
The thatch of the byres will serve their fires when all the cattle are
 slain.
But if thou thinkest the price be fair,—thy brethren wait to sup,
The hound is kin to the jackal-spawn,—howl, dog, and call them up!
And if thou thinkest the price be high, in steer and gear and stack,
Give me my father's mare again, and I'll fight my own way back!"
Kamal has gripped him by the hand and set him upon his feet.
"No talk shall be of dogs," said he, "when wolf and grey wolf meet.
May I eat dirt if thou hast hurt of me in deed or breath;
What dam of lances brought thee forth to jest at the dawn with
 Death?"
Lightly answered the Colonel's son: "I hold by the blood of my clan:
Take up the mare for my father's gift—by God, she has carried a
 man!"
The red mare ran to the Colonel's son, and nuzzled against his
 breast;
"We be two strong men," said Kamal then, "but she loveth the
 younger best.
So she shall go with a lifter's dower, my turquoise-studded rein,
My 'broidered saddle and saddle-cloth, and silver stirrups twain."
The Colonel's son a pistol drew, and held it muzzle-end,
"Ye have taken the one from a foe," said he; "will ye take the mate
 from a friend?"
"A gift for a gift," said Kamal straight; "a limb for the risk of a
 limb.

Thy father has sent his son to me, I'll send my son to him!"
With that he whistled his only son, that dropped from a mountain-
crest—
He trod the ling like a buck in spring, and he looked like a lance
in rest.
"Now here is thy master," Kamal said, "who leads a troop of the
Guides,
And thou must ride at his left side as shield on shoulder rides.
Till Death or I cut loose the tie, at camp and board and bed,
Thy life is his—thy fate it is to guard him with thy head.
So thou must eat the White Queen's meat, and all her foes are thine,
And thou must harry thy father's hold for the peace of the Border-
line.
And thou must make a trooper tough and hack thy way to power—
Belike they will raise thee to Ressaldar when I am hanged in
Peshawur."

They have looked each other between the eyes, and there they found
no fault,
They have taken the Oath of the Brother-in-Blood on leavened bread
and salt:
They have taken the Oath of the Brother-in-Blood on fire and fresh-
cut sod,
On the hilt and the haft of the Khyber knife and the Wondrous
Names of God.
The Colonel's son he rides the mare and Kamal's boy the dun,
And two have come back to Fort Bukloh where there went forth
but one.
And when they drew to the Quarter-Guard, full twenty swords flew
clear—
There was not a man but carried his feud with the blood of the
mountaineer.
"Ha' done! ha' done!" said the Colonel's son. "Put up the steel at
your sides!
Last night ye had struck at a Border thief—tonight 'tis a man of the
Guides!"

Oh, East is East, and West is West, and never the twain shall meet,
Till Earth and Sky stand presently at God's great Judgment Seat;
But there is neither East nor West, Border, nor Breed, nor Birth,
When two strong men stand face to face, though they come from the
ends of the earth!

The Last Chantey

"And there was no more sea."

THUS said the Lord in the Vault above the Cherubim,
  Calling to the Angels and the Souls in their degree:
    "Lo! Earth has passed away
    On the smoke of Judgment Day.
That Our word may be established shall We gather up the sea?"

Loud sang the souls of the jolly, jolly mariners:
  "Plague upon the hurricane that made us furl and flee!
    But the war is done between us,
    In the deep the Lord hath seen us—
Our bones we'll leave the barracout', and God may sink the sea!"

Then said the soul of Judas that betrayèd Him:
  "Lord, hast Thou forgotten Thy covenant with me?
    How once a year I go
    To cool me on the floe?
And Ye take my day of mercy if Ye take away the sea!"

Then said the soul of the Angel of the Off-shore Wind:
  (He that bits the thunder when the bull-mouthed breakers flee):
    "I have watch and ward to keep
    O'er Thy wonders on the deep,
And Ye take mine honour from me if Ye take away the sea!"

Loud sang the souls of the jolly, jolly mariners:
  "Nay, but we were angry, and a hasty folk are we!
    If we worked the ship together
    Till she foundered in foul weather,
Are we babes that we should clamour for a vengeance on the sea?"

Then said the souls of the slaves that men threw overboard:
  "Kenneled in the picaroon a weary band were we;
    But Thy arm was strong to save,
    And it touched us on the wave,
  And we drowsed the long tides idle till Thy Trumpets tore the
    the sea."

Then cried the soul of the stout Apostle Paul to God:
  "Once we frapped a ship, and she labored woundily.
    There were fourteen score of these,
    And they blessed Thee on their knees,
  When they learned Thy Grace and Glory under Malta by the
    sea!"

Loud sang the souls of the jolly, jolly mariners,
  Plucking at their harps, and they plucked unhandily:
    "Our thumbs are rough and tarred,
    And the tune is something hard—
  May we lift a Deepsea Chantey such as seamen use at sea?"

Then said the souls of the gentlemen-adventurers—
  Fettered wrist to bar all for red iniquity:
    "Ho, we revel in our chains
    O'er the sorrow that was Spain's;
  Heave or sink it, leave or drink it, we were masters of the sea!"

Up spake the soul of a gray Gothavn 'speckshioner—
  (He that led the flenching in the fleets of fair Fundee):
    "Oh, the ice-blink white and near,
    And the bowhead breaching clear!
  Will Ye whelm them all for wantonness that wallow in the sea?"

Loud sang the souls of the jolly, jolly mariners,
  Crying: "Under Heaven, here is neither lead nor lea!
    Must we sing for evermore
    On the windless, glassy floor?
  Take back your golden fiddles and we'll beat to open sea!"

Then stooped the Lord, and He called the good sea up to Him,
  And 'stablished its borders unto all eternity,
    That such as have no pleasure
    For to praise the Lord by measure,
  They may enter into galleons and serve Him on the sea.

Sun, Wind, and Cloud shall fail not from the face of it,
  Stinging, ringing spindrift, nor the fulmar flying free;
    And the ships shall go abroad
    To the Glory of the Lord
  Who heard the silly sailor-folk and gave them back their sea!

Jobson's Amen

BLESSED be the English and all their ways and works.
   Cursed be the Infidels, Hereticks, and Turks!"
"Amen," quo' Jobson, "but where I used to lie
Was neither Candle, Bell nor Book to curse my brethren by:

"But a palm-tree in full bearing, bowing down, bowing down,
To a surf that drove unsparing at the brown-walled town—
Conches in a temple, oil-lamps in a dome—
And a low moon out of Africa said: 'This way home!' "

"Blessed be the English and all that they profess.
Cursed be the Savages that prance in nakedness!"
"Amen," quo' Jobson, "but where I used to lie
Was neither shirt nor pantaloons to catch my brethren by:

"But a well-wheel slowly creaking, going round, going round,
By a water-channel leaking over drowned, warm ground—
Parrots very busy in the trellised pepper-vine—
And a high sun over Asia shouting: 'Rise and shine!' "

"Blessed be the English and everything they own.
Cursed be the Infidels that bow to wood and stone!"
"Amen," quo' Jobson, "but where I used to lie
Was neither pew nor Gospelleer to save my brethren by:

"But a desert stretched and stricken, left and right, left and right,
Where the piled mirages thicken under white-hot light—
A skull beneath a sand-hill and a viper coiled inside—
And a red wind out of Libya roaring: 'Run and hide!' "

"Blessed be the English and all they make or do.
Cursed be the Hereticks who doubt that this is true!"
"Amen," quo' Jobson, "but where I mean to die
Is neither rule nor calliper to judge the matter by:

"But Himalaya heavenward-heading, sheer and vast, sheer and vast,
In a million summits bedding on the last world's past;
A certain sacred mountain where the scented cedars climb,
And—the feet of my Belovèd hurrying back through Time!"

HERBERT TRENCH

I Heard a Soldier

I HEARD a soldier sing some trifle
    Out in the sun-dried veldt alone:
He lay and cleaned his grimy rifle
    Idly, behind a stone.

"If after death, love, comes a waking,
    And in their camp so dark and still
The men of dust hear bugles breaking
    Their halt upon the hill,

"To me the slow and silver pealing
    That then the last high trumpet pours,
Shall softer than the dawn come stealing,
    For, with its call, comes yours!"

What grief of love had he to stifle,
    Basking so idly by his stone,
That grimy soldier with his rifle
    Out in the veldt, alone?

Old Anchor Chanty

First Voice.   With a long heavy heave, my very famous men . . . .
        (CHORUS. *Bring home! heave and rally!*)
Second Voice. And why do you, lad, look so pale? Is it for love,
        or lack of ale?
First Voice.   All hands bear a hand that have a hand to len'—
        And there never was a better haul than you gave
        then . . . .
        (CHORUS. *Bring home!*)

First Voice.   Heave hearty, my very famous men . . . .
     (Bring home! heave and rally!)
Second Voice.   Curl and scud, rack and squall—sea-clouds you shall
     know them all . . . .
First Voice.   For we're bound for Valparaiso and round the Horn
     again
     From Monte Desolado to the parish of Big Ben! . . . .
     (Bring home!)

First Voice.   Heave hearty, my very famous men . . . .
     (Bring home! heave and rally!)
Second Voice.   Bold through all or scuppers under, when shall we
     be back, I wonder?
First Voice.   From the green and chancy water we shall all come
     back again
     To the Lizard and the ladies—but who can say for
     when? . . . .
     (Bring home!)

First Voice.   Heave and she's a-trip, my very famous men . . . .
     (Bring home! heave and rally!)
Second Voice.   When your fair lass says farewell to you a fair wind
     I will sell to you . . . .
First Voice.   You may sell your soul's salvation, but I'll bet you
     two-pound-ten
     She's a-tripping on the ribs of the devil in his den . . . .
     (Bring home!)

First Voice.   Heave and she's a-peak, my very famous men . . . .
     (Bring home! heave and rally!)
Second Voice.   You shall tread for one cruzado, Fiddler's Green in
     El Dorado
First Voice.   Why, I've seen less lucky fellows pay for liquor with
     with doubloons
     And for 'baccy with ozellas, gold mohurs, and duca-
     toons!
     (Bring home!)

First Voice.   Heave and a-weigh, my very famous men . . . .
     (Bring home! heave and rally!)
Second Voice.   And drop her next in heat or cold, the flukes of
     England they shall hold! . . . .

First Voice.   Ring and shank, stock and fluke, she's coming into
      ken—
      Give a long and heavy heave, she's a-coming into
      ken . . . .
      (Bring home!)

First Voice.   Heave and in sight, my very famous men . . . .
      (Bring home! heave and rally!)
Second Voice. With her shells and tangle drippling she's a beauty we
      are shipping . . . .
First Voice.   And she likes a bed in harbour like a decent citizen,
      But her fancy for a hammock on the deep sea comes
      again . . . .
      (Bring home!)

First Voice.   Heave and she's a-wash, my very famous men . . .
      (Bring home! heave and rally!)
Second Voice. O never stop to write the news that we are off upon
      a cruise . . . .
First Voice.   For the Gulf of Californy's got a roller now and then
      But it's better to be sailing than a-sucking of a
      pen . . . .
      (Bring home!)

WILLIAM BUTLER YEATS

To a Friend Whose Work Has Come to Nothing

NOW all the truth is out,
  Be secret and take defeat
From any brazen throat,
For how can you compete,
Being honour bred, with one
Who, were it proved he lies,
Were neither shamed in his own
Nor in his neighbours' eyes?
Bred to a harder thing

Than Triumph, turn away
And like a laughing string
Whereon mad fingers play
Amid a place of stone,
Be secret and exult,
Because of all things known
That is most difficult.

Against Unworthy Praise

O HEART, be at peace, because
Nor knave nor dolt can break
What's not for their applause,
Being for a woman's sake.
Enough if the work has seemed,
So did she your strength renew,
A dream that a lion had dreamed
Till the wilderness cried aloud,
A secret between you two,
Between the proud and the proud.

What, still you would have their praise!
But here's a haughtier text,
The labyrinth of her days
That her own strangeness perplexed;
And how what her dreaming gave
Earned slander, ingratitude,
From self-same dolt and knave;
Aye, and worse wrong than these,
Yet she, singing upon her road,
Half lion, half child, is at peace.

Sailing to Byzantium

THAT is no country for old men. The young
In one another's arms, birds in the trees
(Those dying generations) at their song,
The salmon-falls, the mackerel-crowded seas,

Fish, flesh, or fowl, commend all summer long
Whatever is begotten, born, and dies.
Caught in that sensual music, all neglect
Monuments of unaging intellect.

An aged man is but a paltry thing,
A tattered coat upon a stick, unless
Soul clap its hands and sing, and louder sing
For every tatter in its mortal dress;
Nor is there singing school but studying
Monuments of its own magnificence;
And therefore I have sailed the seas and come
To the holy city of Byzantium.

O sages, standing in God's holy fire
As in the gold mosaic of a wall,
Come from the holy fire, perne in a gyre,
And be the singing-masters of my soul.
Consume my heart away—sick with desire
And fastened to a dying animal
It knows not what it is—and gather me
Into the artifice of eternity.

Once out of nature I shall never take
My bodily form from any natural thing,
But such a form as Grecian goldsmiths make
Of hammered gold and gold enamelling
To keep a drowsy emperor awake;
Or set upon a golden bough to sing
To lords and ladies of Byzantium
Of what is past, or passing, or to come.

For His Own Epitaph[1]

UNDER bare Ben Bulben's head
In Drumcliffe churchyard Yeats is laid.
An ancestor was rector there
Long years ago, a church stands near,

[1] The last lines were first sent to Dorothy Wellesley in a letter dated August 15, 1938. Yeats says that he wrote them on the margin of a book of essays about Rilke. They reappeared at the end of a long poem first entitled "His Convictions" and

By the road an ancient cross.
No marble, no conventional phrase;
On limestone quarried near the spot
By his command these words are cut:
    Cast a cold eye
    On life, on death.
    Horseman, pass by!

ERNEST DOWSON

Non sum qualis eram bonae sub regno Cynarae

LAST night, ah, yesternight, betwixt her lips and mine
   There fell thy shadow, Cynara! thy breath was shed
Upon my soul between the kisses and the wine;
And I was desolate and sick of an old passion,
    Yea, I was desolate and bowed my head:
I have been faithful to thee, Cynara! in my fashion.

All night upon mine heart I felt her warm heart beat,
Night-long within mine arms in love and sleep she lay;
Surely the kisses of her bought red mouth were sweet;
But I was desolate and sick of an old passion,
    When I awoke and found the dawn was gray:
I have been faithful to thee, Cynara! in my fashion.

I have forgot much, Cynara! gone with the wind,
Flung roses, roses riotously with the throng,
Dancing, to put thy pale, lost lilies out of mind;
But I was desolate and sick of an old passion,
    Yea, all the time, because the dance was long:
I have been faithful to thee, Cynara! in my fashion.

then, in *Last Poems & Plays,* "Under Ben-Bulben," with the date September 4, 1938.
The closing lines, says Dorothy Wellesley, "were chosen by Yeats for his own epitaph on his tombstone in Drumcliffe churchyard, Sligo." We reproduce here the
entire Section VI of "Under Ben Bulben."

I cried for madder music and for stronger wine,
But when the feast is finished and the lamps expire,
Then falls thy shadow, Cynara! the night is thine;
And I am desolate and sick of an old passion,
    Yea, hungry for the lips of my desire:
I have been faithful to thee, Cynara! in my fashion.

LIONEL JOHNSON

Bagley Wood

THE night is full of stars, full of magnificence:
   Nightingales hold the wood, and fragrance loads the dark.
Behold, what fires august, what lights eternal! Hark,
What passionate music poured in passionate love's defence!
Breathe but the wafting wind's nocturnal frankincense!
Only to feel this night's great heart, only to mark
The splendours and the glooms, brings back the patriarch,
Who on Chaldean wastes found God through reverence.

Could we but live at will upon this perfect height,
Could we but always keep the passion of this peace,
Could we but face unshamed the look of this pure light,
Could we but win earth's heart, and give desire release:
Then were we all divine, and then were ours by right
These stars, these nightingales, these scents: then shame would cease.

LAURENCE BINYON

For the Fallen

WITH proud thanksgiving, a mother for her children,
   England mourns for her dead across the sea,
Flesh of her flesh they were, spirit of her spirit,
Fallen in the cause of the free.

Solemn the drums thrill: Death august and royal
Sings sorrow up into immortal spheres,
There is music in the midst of desolation
And a glory that shines upon our tears.
They went with songs to the battle, they were young,
Straight of limb, true of eye, steady and aglow.
They were staunch to the end against odds uncounted,
They fell with their faces to the foe.

They shall grow not old, as we that are left grow old:
Age shall not weary them, nor the years condemn.
At the going down of the sun and in the morning
We will remember them.

They mingle not with their laughing comrades again;
They sit no more at familiar tables of home;
They have no lot in our labour of the day-time:
They sleep beyond England's foam.

But where our desires are and our hopes profound,
Felt as a well-spring that is hidden from sight,
To the innermost heart of their own land they are known
As the stars are known to the Night;

As the stars that shall be bright when we are dust
Moving in marches upon the heavenly plain,
As the stars that are starry in the time of our darkness,
To the end, to the end, they remain.

A Glimpse of Time

IN the shadow of a broken house,
    Down a deserted street,
Propt walls, cold hearths, and phantom stairs,
And the silence of dead feet—
Locked wildly in one another's arms
I saw two lovers meet.

And over the heartless house aghast
Rose from the mind's abyss
Lost stars and ruined, peering moons,

Worlds overshadowing this,—
Time's stony palace crumbled down
Before that instant kiss.

———— •-•-• ————

W. H. DAVIES

———— •-•-• ————

Leisure

WHAT is this life, if, full of care,
We have no time to stand and stare.

No time to stand beneath the boughs
And stare as long as sheep or cows.

No time to see, when woods we pass,
Where squirrels hide their nuts in grass.

No time to see, in broad daylight,
Streams full of stars, like skies at night.

No time to turn at Beauty's glance,
And watch her feet, how they can dance.

No time to wait till her mouth can
Enrich that smile her eyes began.

A poor life this if, full of care,
We have no time to stand and stare.

The Sleepers

AS I walked down the waterside
This silent morning, wet and dark;
Before the cocks in farmyards crowed,
Before the dogs began to bark;
Before the hour of five was struck
By old Westminster's mighty clock:

As I walked down the waterside
　This morning, in the cold damp air,
I saw a hundred women and men
　Huddled in rags and sleeping there:
These people have no work, thought I,
And long before their time they die.

That moment, on the waterside,
　A lighted car came at a bound;
I looked inside, and saw a score
　Of pale and weary men that frowned;
Each man sat in a huddled heap,
Carried to work while fast asleep.

Ten cars rushed down the waterside,
　Like lighted coffins in the dark;
With twenty dead men in each car,
　That must be brought alive by work:
These people work too hard, thought I,
And long before their time they die.

The Example

HERE'S an example from
　　A Butterfly;
That on a rough, hard rock
　Happy can lie;
Friendless and all alone
On this unsweetened stone.

Now let my bed be hard,
　No care take I;
I'll make my joy like this
　Small Butterfly;
Whose happy heart has power
To make a stone a flower.

A Great Time

SWEET Chance, that led my steps abroad,
 Beyond the town, where wild flowers grow—
A rainbow and a cuckoo, Lord!
 How rich and great the times are now!
  Know, all ye sheep
  And cows that keep
On staring that I stand so long
 In grass that's wet from heavy rain—
A rainbow and a cuckoo's song
 May never come together again;
  May never come
  This side the tomb.

T. STURGE MOORE

The Faun Tells of the Rout of the Amazons

IT was for beauty like a fleet at sea,
 Or like an hundred swans
Sailing before the breeze across a lake!
Their vests of daffodil, or pallid pink
Or milky violet! their saffron caps
And hoods like birds for sudden wing-like flaps!
Their white and piebald mounts! the rich green sward,
The morning light, the blossoming hawthorn trees!
The zephyr's music in the holts that crown
With delicate fern-like trees, each soft knoll's top!
I thought the night had borne me heavenward
And in Olympus I had waked from sleep;
And when their war-song rose
Long tears of rapture ran across my face:
Apollo made it, or, if 'twas not he,
Why, Marsyas died for nought.

Then heard I shouts, male voices,
And turning round I saw them come,

The men of Attica;
With archers on the hills
In bands of twenty strong,
And horsemen in the plain,
And infantry drawn up in branching glens
Which sloped from either side down to the meads;
I knew their stations had been ta'en with care;
And soon the women would have turned the range,
And both those armies in each other's view
Must stand opposed.

In the boughs of an oak I have quaked, where four roads met,
To watch upon either hand draw near to the cross
A boy and a girl both lovely and light of foot,
With life escaping out of unhindering eyes;
My heart has ached for fear that they should not laugh,
Not utter the kindly word when they met, but withstand
The power of either's beauty, and shamefac'd pass,
Fighting desire in their breasts for lack of a heart
Gallant with daring and sense; my pulse stood still.
But, for fearing the thing that those nearing armies might do,
When they met in the widening meads at the foot of the hills,
My blood it grew cold, so long a time it stood still.
For now a silence settled on both their hosts,
As a wistness fell on those children, when they heard,
Each unseen, the other's approaching step on the road;
For scouts had sighted and made to both sides report.
Ah, that hush was like a December night in my soul,
And dull the sound of the hooves as the dismal sound
In the winter forest that wakes one upon a thaw.

Ahi, ahi, ahi, it was shrewd pain!
And not with a radiant welcome and hearty laugh
Each fronted each; but with a shout like a curse,
With a yell that had stricken a lion's heart with fear,
They on to each other rushed.
Ah! the eyes, that saw it, bleed;
And my ear is a wounded sense!
These were men, that their terrible spears
Hurled at the female breast:
These were men, who the well-aimed arrow
Let fly in the eyes of a girl.

RALPH HODGSON

Eve

EVE, with her basket, was
Deep in the bells and grass,
Wading in bells and grass
Up to her knees,
Picking a dish of sweet
Berries and plums to eat,
Down in the bells and grass
Under the trees.

Mute as a mouse in a
Corner the cobra lay,
Curled round a bough of the
Cinnamon tall. . . .
Now to get even and
Humble proud heaven and
Now was the moment or
Never at all.

"Eva!" Each syllable
Light as a flower fell;
"Eva!" he whispered the
Wondering maid;
Soft as a bubble sung
Out of a linnet's lung,
Soft and most silverly
"Eva!" he said.

Picture that orchard sprite,
Eve, with her body white,
Supple and smooth to her
Slim finger tips,
Wondering, listening,
Listening, wondering,
Eve with a berry
Half-way to her lips.

Oh, had our simple Eve
Seen through the make-believe!
Had she but known the
Pretender he was!
Out of the boughs he came,
Whispering still her name,
Tumbling in twenty rings
Into the grass.

Here was the strangest pair
In the world anywhere,
Eve in the bells and grass
Kneeling, and he
Telling his story low. . . .
Singing birds saw them go
Down the dark path to
The Blasphemous Tree.

Oh, what a clatter when
Titmouse and Jenny Wren
Saw him successful and
Taking his leave!
How the birds rated him,
How they all hated him!
How they all pitied
Poor motherless Eve!

Picture her crying
Outside in the lane,
Eve, with no dish of sweet
Berries and plums to eat,
Haunting the gate of the
Orchard in vain. . . .
Picture the lewd delight
Under the hill to-night—
"Eva!" the toast goes round,
"Eva!" again.

The Bull

SEE an old unhappy bull,
  Sick in soul and body both,
Slouching in the undergrowth
Of the forest beautiful,
Banished from the herd he led,
Bulls and cows a thousand head.

Cranes and gaudy parrots go
Up and down the burning sky;
Tree-top cats purr drowsily
In the dim-day green below;
And troops of monkeys, nutting, some,
All disputing, go and come;

And things abominable sit
Picking offal buck or swine,
On the mess and over it
Burnished flies and beetles shine,
And spiders big as bladders lie
Under hemlocks ten foot high;

And a dotted serpent curled
Round and round and round a tree,
Yellowing its greenery,
Keeps a watch on all the world,
All the world and this old bull
In the forest beautiful.

Bravely by his fall he came:
One he led, a bull of blood
Newly come to lustihood,
Fought and put his prince to shame,
Snuffed and pawed the prostrate head
Tameless even while it bled.

There they left him, every one,
Left him there without a lick,
Left him for the birds to pick,

Left him there for carrion,
Vilely from their bosom cast
Wisdom, worth and love at last.

When the lion left his lair
And roared his beauty through the hills,
And the vultures pecked their quills
And flew into the middle air,
Then this prince no more to reign
Came to life and lived again.

He snuffed the herd in far retreat,
He saw the blood upon the ground,
And snuffed the burning airs around
Still with beevish odours sweet,
While the blood ran down his head
And his mouth ran slaver red.

Pity him, this fallen chief,
All his splendour, all his strength,
All his body's breadth and length
Dwindled down with shame and grief,
Half the bull he was before,
Bones and leather, nothing more.

See him standing dewlap-deep
In the rushes at the lake,
Surly, stupid, half asleep,
Waiting for his heart to break
And the birds to join the flies
Feasting at his bloodshot eyes;

Standing with his head hung down
In a stupor, dreaming things:
Green savannas, jungles brown,
Battlefields and bellowings,
Bulls undone and lions dead
And vultures flapping overhead.

Dreaming things: of days he spent
With his mother gaunt and lean
In the valley warm and green,

Full of baby wonderment,
Blinking out of silly eyes
At a hundred mysteries;

Dreaming over once again
How he wandered with a throng
Of bulls and cows a thousand strong,
Wandered on from plain to plain,
Up the hill and down the dale,
Always at his mother's tail;

How he lagged behind the herd,
Lagged and tottered, weak of limb,
And she turned and ran to him
Blaring at the loathly bird
Stationed always in the skies,
Waiting for the flesh that dies.

Dreaming maybe of a day
When her drained and drying paps
Turned him to the sweets and saps,
Richer fountains by the way,
And she left the bull she bore
And he looked to her no more;

And his little frame grew stout,
And his little legs grew strong,
And the way was not so long;
And his little horns came out,
And he played at butting trees
And boulder-stones and tortoises,

Joined a game of knobby skulls
With the youngsters of his year,
All the other little bulls,
Learning both to bruise and bear,
Learning how to stand a shock
Like a little bull of rock.

Dreaming of a day less dim,
Dreaming of a time less far,
When the faint but certain star

Of destiny burned clear for him,
And a fierce and wild unrest
Broke the quiet of his breast,

And the gristles of his youth
Hardened in his comely pow,
And he came to fighting growth,
Beat his bull and won his cow,
And flew his tail and trampled off
Past the tallest, vain enough,

And curved about in splendour full
And curved again and snuffed the airs
As who should say Come out who dares!
And all beheld a bull, a Bull,
And knew that here was surely one
That backed for no bull, fearing none.

And the leader of the herd
Looked and saw, and beat the ground,
And shook the forest with his sound,
Bellowed at the loathly bird
Stationed always in the skies,
Waiting for the flesh that dies.

Dreaming, this old bull forlorn,
Surely dreaming of the hour
When he came to sultan power,
And they owned him master-horn,
Chiefest bull of all among
Bulls and cows a thousand strong;

And in all the tramping herd
Not a bull that barred his way,
Not a cow that said him nay,
Not a bull or cow that erred
In the furnace of his look
Dared a second, worse rebuke;

Not in all the forest wide,
Jungle, thicket, pasture, fen,
Not another dared him then,

Dared him and again defied;
Not a sovereign buck or boar
Came a second time for more;

Not a serpent that survived
Once the terrors of his hoof
Risked a second time reproof,
Came a second time and lived,
Not a serpent in its skin
Came again for discipline;

Not a leopard bright as flame,
Flashing fingerhooks of steel
That a wooden tree might feel,
Met his fury once and came
For a second reprimand,
Not a leopard in the land;

Not a lion of them all,
Not a lion of the hills,
Hero of a thousand kills,
Dared a second fight and fall,
Dared that ram terrific twice,
Paid a second time the price.

Pity him, this dupe of dream,
Leader of the herd again
Only in his daft old brain,
Once again the bull supreme
And bull enough to bear the part
Only in his tameless heart.

Pity him that he must wake;
Even now the swarm of flies
Blackening his bloodshot eyes
Bursts and blusters round the lake,
Scattered from the feast half-fed,
By great shadows overhead;

And the dreamer turns away
From his visionary herds
And his splendid yesterday,

Turns to meet the loathly birds
Flocking round him from the skies,
Waiting for the flesh that dies.

───── ·•·•· ─────

WALTER DE LA MARE

───── ·•·•· ─────

The Listeners

I S there anybody there?" said the Traveller,
   Knocking on the moonlit door;
And his horse in the silence champed the grasses
   Of the forest's ferny floor:
And a bird flew up out of the turret,
   Above the Traveller's head:
And he smote upon the door again a second time;
   "Is there anybody there?" he said.
But no one descended to the Traveller;
   No head from the leaf-fringed sill
Leaned over and looked into his grey eyes,
   Where he stood perplexed and still.
But only a host of phantom listeners
   That dwelt in the lone house then
Stood listening in the quiet of the moonlight
   To that voice from the world of men:
Stood thronging the faint moonbeams on the dark stair,
   That goes down to the empty hall,
Hearkening in an air stirred and shaken
   By the lonely Traveller's call.
And he felt in his heart their strangeness,
   Their stillness answering his cry,
While his horse moved, cropping the dark turf,
   'Neath the starred and leafy sky;
For he suddenly smote on the door, even
   Louder, and lifted his head:—
"Tell them I came, and no one answered,
   That I kept my word," he said.

Never the least stir made the listeners,
  Though every word he spake
Fell echoing through the shadowiness of the still house
  From the one man left awake:
Ay, they heard his foot upon the stirrup,
  And the sound of iron on stone,
And how the silence surged softly backward,
  When the plunging hoofs were gone.

All That's Past

VERY old are the woods;
  And the buds that break
Out of the brier's boughs,
  When March winds wake,
So old with their beauty are—
  Oh, no man knows
Through what wild centuries
  Roves back the rose.
Very old are the brooks;
  And the rills that rise
Where snow sleeps cold beneath
  The azure skies
Sing such a history
  Of come and gone,
Their every drop is as wise
  As Solomon.

Very old are we men;
  Our dreams are tales
Told in dim Eden
  By Eve's nightingales;
We wake and whisper awhile,
  But, the day gone by,
Silence and sleep like fields
  Of amaranth lie.

The Scribe

WHAT lovely things
   Thy hand hath made:
The smooth-plumed bird
   In its emerald shade,
The seed of the grass,
   The speck of stone
Which the wayfaring ant
   Stirs—and hastes on!

Though I should sit
   By some tarn in thy hills,
Using its ink
   As the spirit wills
To write of Earth's wonders,
   Its live, willed things,
Flit would the ages
   On soundless wings
Ere unto Z
   My pen drew nigh;
Leviathan told,
   And the honey-fly:

And still would remain
   My wit to try—
My worn reeds broken,
   The dark tarn dry,
All words forgotten—
   Thou, Lord, and I.

An Epitaph

HERE lies a most beautiful lady,
   Light of step and heart was she;
I think she was the most beautiful lady
That ever was in the West Country.
But beauty vanishes; beauty passes;
However rare—rare it be;
And when I crumble, who will remember
This lady of the West Country?

GILBERT KEITH CHESTERTON

Lepanto

WHITE founts falling in the courts of the sun,
  And the Soldan of Byzantium is smiling as they run;
There is laughter like the fountains in that face of all men feared,
It stirs the forest darkness, the darkness of his beard,
It curls the blood-red crescent, the crescent of his lips,
For the inmost sea of all the earth is shaken with his ships.
They have dared the white republics up the capes of Italy,
They have dashed the Adriatic round the Lion of the Sea,
And the Pope has cast his arms abroad for agony and loss,
And called the kings of Christendom for swords about the Cross,
The cold queen of England is looking in the glass;
The shadow of the Valois is yawning at the Mass:
From evening isles fantastical rings faint the Spanish gun,
And the Lord upon the Golden Horn is laughing in the sun.
Dim drums throbbing, in the hills half heard,
Where only on a nameless throne a crownless prince has stirred,
Where, risen from a doubtful seat and half-attainted stall,
The last knight of Europe takes weapons from the wall,
The last and lingering troubadour to whom the bird has sung,
That once went singing southward when all the world was young,
In that enormous silence, tiny and unafraid,
Comes up along a winding road the noise of the Crusade.
Strong gongs groaning as the guns boom far,
Don John of Austria is going to the war,
Stiff flags straining in the night-blasts cold
In the gloom black-purple, in the glint old-gold,
Torchlight crimson on the copper kettle-drums,
Then the tuckets, then the trumpets, then the cannon, and he comes.
Don John laughing in the brave beard curled,
Spurning of his stirrups like the thrones of all the world,
Holding his head up for a flag of all the free.
Love-light of Spain—hurrah!
Death-light of Africa!

Don John of Austria
Is riding to the sea.

Mahound is in his paradise above the evening star,
(*Don John of Austria is going to the war.*)
He moves a mighty turban on the timeless houri's knees,
His turban that is woven of the sunset and the seas.
He shakes the peacock gardens as he rises from his ease,
And he strides among the tree-tops and is taller than the trees,
And his voice through all the garden is a thunder sent to bring
Black Azrael and Ariel and Ammon on the wing.
Giants and the Genii,
Multiplex of wing and eye,
Whose strong obedience broke the sky
When Solomon was king.

They rush in red and purple from the red clouds of the morn,
From temples where the yellow gods shut up their eyes in scorn;
They rise in green robes roaring from the green hells of the sea
Where fallen skies and evil hues and eyeless creatures be;
On them the sea-valves cluster and the grey sea-forests curl,
Splashed with a splendid sickness, the sickness of the pearl;
They swell in sapphire smoke out of the blue cracks to the ground,—
They gather and they wonder and give worship to Mahound.
And he saith, "Break up the mountains where the hermit-folk may
      hide,
And sift the red and silver sands lest bone of saint abide,
And chase the Giaours flying night and day, not giving rest,
For that which was our trouble comes again out of the west.
We have set the seal of Solomon on all things under sun,
Of knowledge and of sorrow and endurance of things done,
But a noise is in the mountains, in the mountains, and I know
The voice that shook our palaces—four hundred years ago:
It is he that saith not "Kismet"; it is he that knows not Fate;
It is Richard, it is Raymond, it is Godfrey in the gate!
It is he whose loss is laughter when he counts the wager worth.
Put down your feet upon him, that our peace be on the earth."
For he heard drums groaning and he heard guns jar,
(*Don John of Austria is going to the war.*)
Sudden and still—hurrah!
Bolt from Iberia!

Don. John of Austria
Is gone by Alcalar.

St. Michael's on his Mountain in the sea-roads of the north
(*Don John of Austria is girt and going forth.*)
Where the grey seas glitter and the sharp tides shift
And the sea folk labour and the red sails lift.
He shakes his lance of iron and he claps his wings of stone;
    The noise is gone through Normandy; the noise is gone alone;
The North is full of tangled things and texts and aching eyes
And dead is all the innocence of anger and surprise,
And Christian killeth Christian in a narrow dusty room,
And Christian dreadeth Christ that hath a newer face of doom,
And Christian hateth Mary that God kissed in Galilee,
But Don John of Austria is riding to the sea.
Don John calling through the blast and the eclipse
Crying with the trumpet, with the trumpet of his lips,
Trumpet that sayeth ha!
    Domino gloria!
Don John of Austria
Is shouting to the ships.

King Philip's in his closet with the Fleece about his neck
(*Don John of Austria is armed upon the deck.*)
The walls are hung with velvet that is black and soft as sin,
And little dwarfs creep out of it and little dwarfs creep in.
He holds a crystal phial that has colours like the moon,
He touches, and it tingles, and he trembles very soon,
And his face is as a fungus of a leprous white and grey
Like plants in the high houses that are shuttered from the day,
And death is in the phial, and the end of noble work,
But Don John of Austria has fired upon the Turk.
Don John's hunting, and his hounds have bayed—
Booms away past Italy the rumour of his raid.
Gun upon gun, ha! ha!
Gun upon gun, hurrah!
Don John of Austria
Has loosed the cannonade.

The Pope was in his chapel before day or battle broke,
(*Don John of Austria is hidden in the smoke.*)

The hidden room in a man's house where God sits all the year,
The secret window whence the world looks small and very dear.
He sees as in a mirror on the monstrous twilight sea
The crescent of his cruel ships whose name is mystery;
They fling great shadows foe-wards, making Cross and Castle dark,
They veil the plumèd lions on the galleys of St. Mark;
And above the ships are palaces of brown, black-bearded chiefs,
And below the ships are prisons, where with multitudinous griefs,
Christian captives sick and sunless, all a labouring race repines
Like a race in sunken cities, like a nation in the mines.
They are lost like slaves that swat, and in the skies of morning hung
The stairways of the tallest gods when tyranny was young.
They are countless, voiceless, hopeless as those fallen or fleeing on
Before the high Kings' horses in the granite of Babylon.
And many a one grows witless in his quiet room in hell
Where a yellow face looks inward through the lattice of his cell,
And he finds his God forgotten, and he seeks no more a sign—
(*But Don John of Austria has burst the battle-line!*)
Don John pounding from the slaughter-painted poop,
Purpling all the ocean like a bloody pirate's sloop,
Scarlet running over on the silvers and the golds,
Breaking of the hatches up and bursting of the holds,
Thronging of the thousands up that labour under sea
White for bliss and blind for sun and stunned for liberty.
Vivat Hispania!
Domino Gloria!
Don John of Austria
Has set his people free!

Cervantes on his galley sets the sword back in the sheath
(*Don John of Austria rides homeward with a wreath.*)
And he sees across a weary land a straggling road in Spain,
Up which a lean and foolish knight forever rides in vain,
And he smiles, but not as Sultans smile, and settles back the
    blade. . . .
(*But Don John of Austria rides home from the Crusade.*)

EDWARD THOMAS

Haymaking

AFTER night's thunder far away had rolled
The fiery day had a kernel sweet of cold,
And in the perfect blue the clouds uncurled,
Like the first gods before they made the world
And misery, swimming the stormless sea
In beauty and in divine gaiety.
The smooth white empty road was lightly strewn
With leaves—the holly's Autumn falls in June—
And fir cones standing stiff up in the heat.
The mill-foot water tumbled white and lit
With tossing crystals, happier than any crowd
Of children pouring out of school aloud.
And in the little thickets where a sleeper
For ever might lie lost, the nettle-creeper
And garden warbler sang unceasingly;
While over them shrill shrieked in his fierce glee
The swift with wings and tail as sharp and narrow
As if the bow had flown off with the arrow.
Only the scent of woodbine and hay new-mown
Travelled the road. In the field sloping down,
Park-like, to where its willows showed the brook,
Haymakers rested. The tosser lay forsook
Out in the sun: and the long waggon stood
Without its team, it seemed it never would
Move from the shadow of that single yew.
The team, as still, until their task was due,
Beside the labourers enjoyed the shade
That three squat oaks mid-field together made
Upon a circle of grass and weed uncut,
And on the hollow, once a chalk-pit, but
Now brimmed with nut and elder-flower so clean.
The men leaned on their rakes, about to begin,
But still. And all were silent. All was old,
This morning time, with a great age untold,

Older than Clare and Cobbett, Morland and Crome,
Than, at the field's far edge, the farmer's home,
A white house crouched at the foot of a great tree.
Under the heavens that know not what years be
The men, the beasts, the trees, the implements
Uttered even what they will in times far hence—
All of us gone out of the reach of change—
Immortal in a picture of an old grange.

JOHN MASEFIELD

From *Dauber*

(SECTION VI)

ALL through the windless night the clipper rolled
In a great swell with oily gradual heaves
Which rolled her down until her time-bells tolled,
Clang, and the weltering water moaned like beeves.
The thundering rattle of slatting shook the sheaves,
Startles of water made the swing ports gush,
The sea was moaning and sighing and saying "Hush!"

It was all black and starless. Peering down
Into the water, trying to pierce the gloom,
One saw a dim, smooth, oily glitter of brown
Heaving and dying away and leaving room
For yet another. Like the march of doom
Came those great powers of marching silences;
Then fog came down, dead-cold, and hid the seas.

They set the Dauber to the foghorn. There
He stood upon the poop, making to sound
Out of the pump the sailor's nasal blare,
Listening lest ice should make the note resound.
She bayed there like a solitary hound
Lost in a covert; all the watch she bayed.
The fog, come closelier down, no answer made.

Denser it grew, until the ship was lost.
The elemental hid her; she was merged
In mufflings of dark death, like a man's ghost,
New to the change of death, yet thither urged.
Then from the hidden waters something surged—
Mournful, despairing, great, greater than speech,
A noise like one slow wave on a still beach.

Mournful, and then again mournful, and still
Out of the night that mighty voice arose;
The Dauber at his foghorn felt the thrill.
Who rode that desolate sea? What forms were those?
Mournful, from things defeated, in the throes
Of memory of some conquered hunting-ground,
Out of the night of death arose the sound.

"Whales!" said the Mate. They stayed there all night long
Answering the horn. Out of the night they spoke,
Defeated creatures who had suffered wrong,
But were still noble underneath the stroke.
They filled the darkness when the Dauber woke;
The men came peering to the rail to hear,
And the sea sighed, and the fog rose up sheer.

A wall of nothing at the world's last edge,
Where no life came except defeated life.
The Dauber felt shut in within a hedge,
Behind which form was hidden and thought was rife,
And that a blinding flash, a thrust, a knife
Would sweep the hedge away and make all plain,
Brilliant beyond all words, blinding the brain.

So the night passed, but then no morning broke—
Only a something showed that night was dead.
A sea-bird, cackling like a devil, spoke,
And the fog drew away and hung like lead.
Like mighty cliffs it shaped, sullen and red;
Like glowering gods at watch it did appear,
And sometimes drew away, and then drew near.

Then came the cry of "Call all hands on deck!"
The Dauber knew its meaning; it was come:

Cape Horn, that tramples beauty into wreck,
And crumples steel and smites the strong man dumb.
Down clattered flying kites and staysails: some
Sang out in quick, high calls: the fair-leads skirled,
And from the south-west came the end of the world.

"Caught in her ball-dress," said the Bosun, hauling;
"Lee-ay, lee-ay!" quick, high, come the men's call;
It was all wallop of sails and startled calling.
"Let fly!" "Let go!" "Clew up!" and "Let go all!"
"Now up and make them fast!" "Here, give us a haul!"
"Now up and stow them! Quick! By God! we're done!"
The blackness crunched all memory of the sun.

"Up!" said the Mate. "Mizen top-gallants. Hurry!"
The Dauber ran, the others ran, the sails
Slatted and shook; out of the black a flurry
Whirled in fine lines, tattering the edge to trails.
Painting and art and England were old tales
Told in some other life to that pale man,
Who struggled with white fear and gulped and ran.

He struck a ringbolt in his haste and fell—
Rose, sick with pain, half-lamed in his left knee;
He reached the shrouds where clambering men pell-mell
Hustled each other up and cursed him; he
Hurried aloft with them: then from the sea
Came a cold, sudden breath that made the hair
Stiff on the neck, as though Death whispered there.

A man below him punched him in the side.
"Get up, you Dauber, or let me get past."
He saw the belly of the skysail skied,
Gulped, and clutched tight, and tried to go more fast.
Sometimes he missed his ratline and was grassed,
Scraped his shin raw against the rigid line;
The clamberers reached the futtock-shrouds' incline.

Cursing they came; one, kicking out behind,
Kicked Dauber in the mouth, and one below
Punched at his calves; the futtock-shrouds inclined;
It was a perilous path for one to go.

"Up, Dauber, up!" A curse followed a blow.
He reached the top and gasped, then on, then on.
And one voice yelled "Let go!" and one "All gone!"

Fierce clamberers, some in oilskins, some in rags,
Hustling and hurrying up, up the steep stairs.
Before the windless sails, were blown to flags,
And whirled like dirty birds athwart great airs,
Ten men in all, to get this mast of theirs
Snugged to the gale in time. "Up! Damn you, run!"
The mizzen topmast head was safely won.

"Lay out!" the Bosun yelled. The Dauber laid
Out on the yard, gripping the yard and feeling
Sick at the mighty space of air displayed
Below his feet, where mewing birds were wheeling.
A giddy fear was on him; he was reeling.
He bit his lip half through, clutching the jack.
A cold sweat glued the shirt upon his back.

The yard was shaking, for a brace was loose.
He felt that he would fall; he clutched, he bent,
Clammy with natural terror to the shoes
While idiotic promptings came and went.
Snow fluttered on a wind-flaw and was spent;
He saw the water darken. Someone yelled,
"Frap it; don't stay to furl! Hold on!" He held.

Darkness came down—half darkness—in a whirl;
The sky went out, the waters disappeared.
He felt a shocking pressure of blowing hurl
The ship upon her side. The darkness speared
At her with wind; she staggered, she careered,
Then down she lay. The Dauber felt her go;
He saw his yard tilt downwards. Then the snow

Whirled all about—dense, multitudinous, cold—
Mixed with the wind's one devilish thrust and shriek,
Which whiffled out men's tears, deafened, took hold,
Flattening the flying drift against the cheek.
The yards buckled and bent, man could not speak.
The ship lay on her broadside; the wind's sound
Had devilish malice at having got her downed.

How long the gale had blown he could not tell,
Only the world had changed, his life had died.
A moment now was everlasting hell.
Nature, an onslaught from the weather side,
A withering rush of death, a frost that cried,
Shrieked, till he withered at the heart; a hail
Plastered his oilskins with an icy mail.

"Cut!" yelled his mate. He looked—the sail was gone,
Blown into rags in the first furious squall;
The tatters drummed the devil's tattoo. On
The buckling yard a block thumped like a mall.
The ship lay—the sea smote her, the wind's bawl
Came, "loo, loo, loo!" The devil cried his hounds
On to the poor spent stag strayed in his bounds.

"Cut! Ease her!" yelled his mate; the Dauber heard.
His mate wormed up the tilted yard and slashed,
A rag of canvas skimmed like a darting bird.
The snow whirled, the ship bowed to it, the gear lashed,
The sea-tops were cut off and flung down smashed;
Tatters of shouts were flung, the rags of yells—
And clang, clang, clang, below beat the two bells.

"O God!" the Dauber moaned. A roaring rang,
Blasting the royals like a cannonade;
The backstays parted with a crackling clang,
The upper spars were snapped like twigs decayed—
Snapped at their heels, their jagged splinters splayed,
Like white and ghastly hairs erect with fear.
The Mate yelled, "Gone, by God, and pitched them clear!"

"Up!" yelled the Bosun; "up and clear the wreck!"
The Dauber followed where he led: below
He caught one giddy glimpsing of the deck
Filled with white water, as though heaped with snow.
He saw the streamers of the rigging blow
Straight out like pennons from the splintered mast,
Then, all sense dimmed, all was an icy blast,

Roaring from nether hell and filled with ice,
Roaring and crashing on the jerking stage,

An utter bridle given to utter vice,
Limitless power mad with endless rage
Withering the soul; a minute seemed an age.
He clutched and hacked at ropes, at rags of sail,
Thinking that comfort was a fairy-tale

Told long ago—long, long ago—long since
Heard of in other lives—imagined, dreamed—
There where the basest beggar was a prince
To him in torment where the tempest screamed.
Comfort and warmth and ease no longer seemed
Things that a man could know: soul, body, brain,
Knew nothing but the wind, the cold, the pain.

The Passing Strange

OUT of the earth to rest or range
Perpetual in perpetual change
The unknown passing through the strange.

Water and saltness held together
To tread the dust and stand the weather
And plough the field and stretch the tether.

To pass the wine cup and be witty,
Water the sands and build the city,
Slaughter like devils and have pity;

Be red with rage and pale with lust,
Make beauty come, make peace, make trust,
Water and saltness mixed with dust;

Drive over earth, swim under sea,
Fly in the eagle's secrecy,
Guess where the hidden comets be;

Know all the deathy seeds that still
Queen Helen's beauty, Cæsar's will,
And slay them even as they kill;

Fashion an altar for a rood,
Defile a continent with blood,
And watch a brother starve for food;

Love like a madman, shaking, blind,
Till self is burnt into a kind
Possession of another mind;

Brood upon beauty till the grace
Of beauty with the holy face
Brings peace into the bitter place;

Probe in the lifeless granites, scan
The stars for hope, for guide, for plan,
Live as a woman or a man;

Fasten to lover or to friend
Until the heart break at the end
The break of death that cannot mend.

Then to lie useless, helpless, still
Down in the earth, in dark, to fill
The roots of grass or daffodil.

Down in the earth, in dark, alone,
A mockery of the ghost in bone,
The strangeness, passing the unknown.

Time will go by, that outlasts clocks,
Dawn in the thorps will rouse the cocks
Sunset be glory on the rocks.

But it, the thing, will never heed
Even the rootling from the seed
Thrusting to suck it for its need.

Since moons decay and suns decline
How else should end this life of mine?
Water and saltness are not wine.

But in the darkest hour of night
When even the foxes peer for sight
The byre-cock crows; he feels the light.

So, in this water mixed with dust,
The byre-cock spirit crows from trust

That death will change because it must,

For all things change, the darkness changes,
The wandering spirits change their ranges,
The corn is gathered to the granges.

The corn is sown again, it grows;
The stars burn out, the darkness goes.
The rhythms change, they do not close.

They change, and we, who pass like foam,
Like dust blown through the streets of Rome,
Change ever, too; we have no home,

Only a beauty, only a power,
Sad in the fruit, bright in the flower,
Endlessly erring for its hour

But gathering, as we stray, a sense
Of Life, so lovely and intense,
It lingers when we wander hence.

That those who follow feel behind
Their backs, when all before is blind,
Our joy, a rampart to the mind.

WILFRED WILSON GIBSON

The Vindictive Staircase

OR

The Reward of Industry

IN a doomed and empty house in Houndsditch
All night long I lie awake and listen,
While all night the ghost of Mrs. Murphy
Tiptoes up and down the wheezy staircase,
Sweeling ghostly grease of quaking candles.

Mrs. Murphy, timidest of spectres,
You who were the cheeriest of charers,
With the heart of innocence and only
Torn between a zest for priests and porter,
Mrs. Murphy of the ample bosom—
Suckler of a score or so of children
("Children? Bless you! Why, I've buried six, sir.")
Who in forty years wore out three husbands,
And one everlasting, shameless bonnet,
Which I've little doubt was coffined with you—
Mrs. Murphy, wherefor do you wander,
Sweeling ghostly grease of quaking candles,
Up and down the stairs you scrubbed so sorely,
Scrubbed till they were naked, dank, and aching?

Now that you are dead, is this their vengeance?
Recollecting all you made them suffer
With your bristled brush and soapy water
When you scrubbed them naked, dank, and aching,
Have they power to hold your ghostly footsteps
Chained as to an everlasting treadmill?

Mrs. Murphy, think you 'twould appease them
If I rose now in my shivering nightshirt,
Rose and told them how you, too, had suffered—
You, their seeming tyrant, but their bondslave—
Toiling uncomplaining in their service
Till your knuckles and your knees were knotted
Into writhing fires of red rheumatics,
And how, in the end, 'twas they who killed you?

Even should their knots still harden to you,
Bow your one and all-enduring bonnet
Till your ear is level with my keyhole,
While I whisper ghostly consolation:
Know this house is marked out for the spoiler,
Doomed to fall to Hobnails with his pickaxe;
And its crazy staircase chopped to firewood,
Splintered, bundled, burned to smoke and ashes,
Soon shall perish, scattered to the four winds.
Then, God rest your spirit, Mrs. Murphy!

Yet, who knows! A staircase . . . Mrs. Murphy,
God forbid that you be doomed to tiptoe
Through eternity, a timid spectre,
Sweeling ghostly grease of quaking candles,
Up and down the spectre of a staircase,
While all night I lie awake and listen
In a damned and ghostly house in Houndsditch!

A Catch for Singing

SAID the Old Young Man to the Young Old Man—
Alack and well-a-day!
Said the Young Old Man to the Old Young Man—
The cherry tree's in flourish!

Said the Old Young Man to the Young Old Man—
The world is growing gray.
Said the Young Old Man to the Old Young Man—
The cherry tree's in flourish!

Said the Old Young Man to the Young Old Man—
Both flower and fruit decay.
Said the Young Old Man to the Old Young Man—
The cherry tree's in flourish!

Said the Old Young Man to the Young Old Man—
Alack and well-a-day!
The world is growing grey,
And flower and fruit decay.
Beware Old Man, beware Old Man!
For the end of life is nearing
And the grave yawns by the way. . . .
Said the Young Old Man to the Old Young Man—
I'm a trifle hard of hearing
And can't catch a word you say . . .
But the cherry tree's in flourish!

ALFRED NOYES

Forty Singing Seamen

"In our lands be Beeres and Lyons of dyvers colours as ye redd, grene, black, and white. And in our land be also unicornes and these Unicornes slee many Lyons. . . . Also there dare no man make a lye in our lande, for if he dyde he sholde incontynent be sleyn."

Mediaeval Epistle, of Pope Prester John.

I

ACROSS the seas of Wonderland to Mogadore we plodded,
　　Forty singing seamen in an old black barque,
And we landed in the twilight where a Polyphemus nodded
　　With his battered moon-eye winking red and yellow through the
　　　　dark!
　　　　For his eye was growing mellow,
　　　　Rich and ripe and red and yellow,
　　As was time, since old Ulysses made him bellow in the dark!
Cho.—Since Ulysses bunged his eye up with a pine-torch in the dark!

II

Were they mountains in the gloaming or the giant's ugly shoulders
　　Just beneath the rolling eyeball, with its bleared and vinous glow,
Red and yellow o'er the purple of the pines among the boulders
　　And the shaggy horror brooding on the sullen slopes below,
　　　　Were they pines among the boulders
　　　　Or the hair upon his shoulders?
　　We were only simple seamen, so of course we didn't know.
Cho.—We were simple singing seamen, so of course we couldn't
　　know.

III

But we crossed a plain of poppies, and we came upon a fountain
　　Not of water, but of jewels, like a spray of leaping fire;

And behind it, in an emerald glade, beneath a golden mountain
  There stood a crystal palace, for a sailor to admire;
    For a troop of ghosts came round us,
    Which with leaves of bay they crowned us,
  Then with grog they well nigh drowned us, to the depth of our
    desire!
Cho.—And 'twas very friendly of them, as a sailor can admire!

IV

There was music all about us, we were growing quite forgetful
  We were only singing seamen from the dirt of London-town,
Though the nectar that we swallowed seemed to vanish half regretful
  As if we wasn't good enough to take such vittles down,
    When we saw a sudden figure,
    Tall and black as any nigger,
  Like the devil—only bigger—drawing near us with a frown!
Cho.—Like the devil—but much bigger—and he wore a golden
    crown!

V

And "What's all this?" he growls at us! With dignity we chaunted,
  "Forty singing seamen, sir, as won't be put upon!"
"What? Englishmen?" he cries, "Well, if ye don't mind being
    haunted,
    Faith you're welcome to my palace; I'm the famous Prester John!
    Will ye walk into my palace?
    I don't bear 'ee any malice!
  One and all ye shall be welcome in the halls of Prester John!"
Cho.—So we walked into the palace and the halls of Prester John!

VI

Now the door was one great diamond and the hall a hollow ruby—
  Big as Beachy Head, my lads, nay bigger by a half!
And I sees the mate wi' mouth agape, a-staring like a booby,
  And the skipper close behind him, with his tongue out like a calf!
    Now the way to take it rightly
    Was to walk along politely
  Just as if you didn't notice—so I couldn't help but laugh!
Cho.—For they both forgot their manners and the crew was bound to
    laugh!

VII

But he took us through his palace and, my lads, as I'm a sinner,
　　We walked into an opal like a sunset-colored cloud—
"My dining-room," he says, and, quick as light we saw a dinner
　　Spread before us by the fingers of a hidden fairy crowd;
　　　　And the skipper, swaying gently
　　　　After dinner, murmurs faintly,
　　"I looks to-wards you, Prester John, you've done us very proud!"
Cho.—And we drank his health with honors, for he *done* us *very*
　　proud!

VIII

Then he walks us to his garden where we sees a feathered demon
　　Very splendid and important on a sort of spicy tree!
"That's the Phœnix," whispers Prester, "which all eddicated seamen
　　Knows the only one existent, and *he's* waiting for to flee!
　　　　When his hundred years expire
　　　　Then he'll set hisself a-fire
　　And another from his ashes rise most beautiful to see!"
Cho.—With wings of rose and emerald most beautiful to see!

IX

Then he says, "In younder forest there's a little silver river,
　　And whosoever drinks of it, his youth shall never die!
The centuries go by, but Prester John endures for ever
　　With his music in the mountains and his magic on the sky!
　　　　While *your* hearts are growing colder,
　　　　While your world is growing older,
　　There's a magic in the distance, where the sea-line meets the sky."
Cho.—It shall call to singing seamen till the fount o' song is dry!

X

So we thought we'd up and seek it, but that forest fair defied us,—
　　First a crimson leopard laughs at us most horrible to see,
Then a sea-green lion came and sniffed and licked his chops and eyed
　　us,
　　While a red and yellow unicorn was dancing round a tree!
　　　　We was trying to look thinner,
　　　　Which was hard, because our dinner
　　Must ha' made us very tempting to a cat o' high degree!
Cho.—Must ha' made us very tempting to the whole menarjeree!

XI

So we scuttled from that forest and across the poppy meadows
  Where the awful shaggy horror brooded o'er us in the dark!
And we pushes out from shore again a-jumping at our shadows,
  And pulls away most joyful to the old black barque!
     And home again we plodded
     While the Polyphemus nodded
With his battered moon-eye winking red and yellow through the
    dark.
Cho.—Oh, the moon above the mountains, red and yellow through
    the dark!

XII

Across the seas of Wonderland to London-town we blundered,
  Forty singing seamen as was puzzled for to know
If the visions that we saw was caused by—here again we pondered—
  A tiple in a vision forty thousand years ago.
     Could the grog we *dreamt* we swallowed
     Make us *dream* of all that followed?
We were only simple seamen, so of course we didn't know!
Cho.—We were simple singing seamen, so of course we could not
    know!

PADRAIC COLUM

The Plougher

SUNSET and silence! A man: around him earth savage, earth
    broken;
Beside him two horses—a plough!

Earth savage, earth broken, the brutes, the dawn man there in the
    sunset,
And the Plough that is twin to the Sword, that is founder of cities!

*Brute-tamer, plough-maker, earth-breaker! Can'st hear? There are
    ages between us.
Is it praying you are as you stand there alone in the sunset?

"Surely our sky-born gods can be naught to you, earth child and earth
    master?
Surely your thoughts are of Pan, or of Wotan, or Dana?

"Yet why give thought to the gods? Has Pan led your brutes where
    they stumble?
Has Dana numbed pain of the child-bed, or Wotan put hands to
    your plough?

"What matter your foolish reply! O, man, standing lone and bowed
    earthward,
Your task is a day near its close. Give thanks to the night-giving
    God."

. . . .

Slowly the darkness falls, the broken lands blend with the savage;
The brute-tamer stands by the brutes, a head's breadth only above
    them.

A head's breadth? Ay, but therein is hell's depth, and the height up
    to heaven,
And the thrones of the gods and their halls, their chariots, purples
    and splendors.

Shall I Go Bound and You Go Free?

SHALL I go bound and you go free,
  And love one so removed from me?
Not so; the falcon o'er my brow
Hath better quest, I dare avow!

And must I run where you will ride,
And must I stay where you abide?
Not so; the feather that I wear
Is from an eyrie in the air!

And must I climb a broken stair,
And must I pace a chamber bare?
Not so; the Brenny plains are wide
And there are banners where I ride!

No Child

I HEARD in the night the pigeons
    Stirring within their nest:
The wild pigeons' stir was tender,
Like a child's hand at the breast.

I cried "O stir no more!
(My breast was touched with tears).
O pigeons, make no stir—
A childless woman hears."

Monkeys

TWO little creatures
    With faces the size of
A pair of pennies
Are clasping each other.
"Ah, do not leave me,"
One says to the other,
In the high monkey-
Cage in the beast-shop.

There are no people
To gape at them now,
For people are loth to
Peer in the dimness;
Have they not builded
Streets and playhouses,
Sky-signs and bars,
To lose the loneliness
Shaking the hearts
Of the two little Monkeys?

Yes. But who watches
The penny-small faces
Can hear the voices:
"Ah, do not leave me;

Suck I will give you,
Warmth and clasping,
And if you slip from
This beam I can never
Find you again."

Dim is the evening,
And chill is the weather;
There, drawn from their coloured
Hemisphere,
The apes lilliputian
With faces the size of
A pair of pennies,
And voices as low as
The flow of my blood.

———•—•—•———

LASCELLES ABERCROMBIE

———•—•—•———

Epilogue

FROM EMBLEMS OF LOVE

WHAT shall we do for Love these days?
    How shall we make an altar-blaze
To smite the horny eyes of men
With the renown of our Heaven,
And to the unbelievers prove
Our service to our dear god, Love?
What torches shall we lift above
The crowd that pushes through the mire,
To amaze the dark heads with strange fire?
I should think I were much to blame,
If never I held some fragrant flame
Above the noises of the world,
And openly 'mid men's hurrying stares,
Worshipped before the sacred fears
That are like flashing curtains furled
Across the presence of our lord Love.

Nay, would that I could fill the gaze
Of the whole earth with some great praise
Made in a marvel for men's eyes,
Some tower of glittering masonries,
Therein such a spirit flourishing
Men should see what my heart can sing:
All that Love hath done to me
Built into stone, a visible glee;
Marble carried to gleaming height
As moved aloft by inward delight;
Not as with toil of chisels hewn,
But seeming poised in a mighty tune.
For of all those who have been known
To lodge with our kind host, the sun,
I envy one for just one thing:
In Cordova of the Moors
There dwelt a passion-minded King,
Who set great bands of marble-hewers
To fashion his heart's thanksgiving
In a tall palace, shapen so
All the wondering world might know
The joy he had of his Moorish lass.
His love, that brighter and larger was
Than the starry places, into firm stone
He sent, as if the stone were glass
Fired and into beauty blown.
  Solemn and invented gravely
In its bulk the fabric stood,
Even as Love, that trusteth bravely
In its own exceeding good
To be better than the waste
Of time's devices; grandly spaced,
Seriously the fabric stood.
But over it all a pleasure went
Of carven delicate ornament,
Wreathing up like ravishment,
Mentioning in sculptures twined
The blitheness Love hath in his mind;
And like delighted senses were
The windows, and the columns there
Made the following sight to ache
As the heart that did them make.

Well I can see that shining song
Flowering there, the upward throng
Of porches, pillars and windowed walls,
Spires like piercing panpipe calls,
Up to the roof's snow-cloud flight;
All glancing in the Spanish light
White as water of arctic tides,
Save an amber dazzle on sunny sides.
You had said, the radiant sheen
Of that palace might have been
A young god's fantasy, ere he came
His serious worlds and suns to frame;
Such an immortal passion
Quivered among the slim hewn stone.
And in the nights it seemed a jar
Cut in the substance of a star,
Wherein a wine, that will be poured
Some time for feasting Heaven, was stored.
   But within this fretted shell,
The wonder of Love made visible,
The King a private gentle mood
There placed, of pleasant quietude.
For right amidst there was a court,
Where always muskèd silences
Listened to water and to trees;
And herbage of all fragrant sort,—
Lavender, lad's-love, rosemary,
Basil, tansy, centaury,—
Was the grass of that orchard, hid
Love's amazements all amid.
Jarring the air with rumour cool,
Small fountains played into a pool
With sound as soft as the barley's hiss
When its beard just sprouting is;
Whence a young stream, that trod on moss,
Prettily rimpled the court across.
And in the pool's clear idleness,
Moving like dreams through happiness,
Shoals of small bright fishes were;
In and out weed-thickets bent
Perch and carp, and sauntering went
With mounching jaws and eyes a-stare;

Or on a lotus leaf would crawl
A brindled loach to bask and sprawl,
Tasting the warm sun ere it dipped
Into the water; but quick as fear
Back his shining brown head slipped
To crouch on the gravel of his lair,
Where the cooled sunbeams, broke in wrack,
Spilt shattered gold about his back.

  So within that green-veiled air,
Within that white-walled quiet, where
Innocent water thought aloud,—
Childish prattle that must make
The wise sunlight with laughter shake
On the leafage overbowed,—
Often the King and his love-lass
Let the delicious hours pass.
All the outer world could see
Graved and sawn amazingly
Their love's delighted riotise,
Fixed in marble for all men's eyes;
But only these twain could abide
In the cool peace that withinside
Thrilling desire and passion dwelt;
They only knew the still meaning spelt
By Love's flaming script, which is
God's word written in ecstasies.

  And where is now that palace gone,
All the magical skilled stone,
All the dreaming towers wrought
By Love as if no more than thought
The unresisting marble was?
How could such a wonder pass?
Ah, it was but built in vain
Against the stupid horns of Rome,
That pushed down into the common loam
The loveliness that shone in Spain.
But we have raised it up again!
A loftier palace, fairer far,
Is ours, and one that fears no war.
Safe in marvellous walls we are;
Wondering sense like builded fires,
High amazement of desires,

Delight and certainty of love,
Closing around, roofing above
Our unapproached and perfect hour
Within the splendours of love's power.

· · ·

JAMES STEPHENS

· · ·

What Tomas an Buile Said in a Pub

I SAW God! Do you doubt it?
Do you dare to doubt it?
I saw the Almighty Man! His hand
Was resting on a mountain! And
He looked upon the World, and all about it:
I saw Him plainer than you see me now
—You mustn't doubt it!

He was not satisfied;
His look was all dissatisfied!
His beard swung on a wind, far out of sight
Behind the world's curve! And there was light
Most fearful from His forehead! And he sighed
—That star went always wrong, and from the start
I was dissatisfied!—

He lifted up His hand!
I say He heaved a dreadful hand
Over the spinning earth! Then I said,—Stay,
You must not strike it, God! I'm in the way!
And I will never move from where I stand!—
He said,—Dear child, I feared that you were dead,—
. . . And stayed His hand!

On a Lonely Spray

UNDER a lonely sky a lonely tree
 Is beautiful! All that is loneliness
Is beautiful! A feather, lost at sea;
A staring owl; a moth; a yellow tress
Of seaweed on a rock, is beautiful!

The night-lit moon, wide-wandering in sky!
A blue-bright spark, where ne'er a cloud is up!
A wing, where no wing is, it is so high!
A bee in winter! and a buttercup,
Late blown! are lonely, and are beautiful!

She, whom you saw but once, and saw no more!
That he, who startled you, and went away!
The eye that watched you from a cottage door!
The first leaf, and the last! The break of day!
The mouse, the cuckoo, and the cloud, are beautiful!

For all that is, is lonely! All that may
Will be as lonely as is that you see!
The lonely heart sings on a lonely spray!
The lonely soul swings lonely in the sea;
And all that loneliness is beautiful!

All: all alone: and all without a part
Is beautiful! for beauty is all where!
Where is an eye, is beauty! Where an heart,
Is beauty, brooding out, on empty air,
All that is lonely, and is beautiful!

The Pit of Bliss

WHEN I was young
 I dared to sing
Of everything,
And anything!
Of joy, and woe, and fate, and God!

Of dreaming cloud, and teeming sod!
Of hill, that thrust an amber spear
Into the sunset! And the sheer
Precipice that shakes the soul
To its black gape—I sang the whole
Of God and Man, nor sought to know
Man, or God, or Joy, or Woe!
And, though an older wight I be,
My soul hath still such Ecstasy
That, on a pulse, I sing and sing
Of Everything, and Anything!

There is a Light
Shines in the head:
It is not gold,
It is not red,
But, as the lightning's blinding light,
It is a stare of silver white
That one surmise might fancy blue!
On that mind-blinding hue I gaze
An instant, and am in a maze
Of thinking—could one call it so?
It is no thinking that I know!
—An hurricane of Knowing, that
Could whelm the soul that was not pat
To flinch, and lose the deadly thing;
—And Sing, and Sing again, and Sing
Of Everything, and Anything!

An Eagle
Whirling up the sky;
Sunblind! Dizzy!
Urging high,
And higher beating yet a wing,
Until he can no longer cling,
Or hold; or do a thing, but fall,
And sink, and whirl, and scream, through all
His dizzy, heaven-hell of Pit,
In mile-a-minute flight from It
That he had dared! From height of height,
So the Poet takes his flight
And tumble in the Pit of Bliss!

And, in the roar of that Abyss,
And falling, he will Sing and Sing
Of Everything, and Anything!
What is Knowing?
'Tis to see!
What is Feeling?
'Tis to be!
What is Love? But, more and more,
To See and Be! To be a Pour
And Avalanche of Being, till
Being ceases, and is still
For very motion—What is Joy?
—Being, past all earthly cloy
And intermixture! Being spun
Of Itself is Being won
That is Joy—And this is God,
To be That, in cloud and clod!
And, in cloud, and clod, to Sing
Of Everything, and Anything!

A Glass of Beer

THE lanky hank of a she in the inn over there
   Nearly killed me for asking the loan of a glass of beer;
May the devil grip the whey-faced slut by the hair,
And beat bad manners out of her skin for a year.

That parboiled ape, with the toughest jaw you will see
On virtue's path, and a voice that would rasp the dead,
Came roaring and raging the minute she looked at me,
And threw me out of the house on the back of my head!

If I asked her master he'd give me a cask a day;
But she, with the beer at hand, not a gill would arrange!
May she marry a ghost and bear him a kitten, and may
The High King of Glory permit her to get the mange.

JAMES ELROY FLECKER

The Old Ships

I HAVE seen old ships sail like swans asleep
Beyond the village which men still call Tyre,
With leaden age o'ercargoed, dipping deep
For Famagusta and the hidden sun
That rings black Cyprus with a lake of fire;
And all those ships were certainly so old
Who knows how oft with squat and noisy gun,
Questing brown slaves or Syrian oranges,
The pirate Genoese
Hell-raked them till they rolled
Blood, water, fruit and corpses up the hold.
But now through friendly seas they softly run,
Painted the mid-sea blue or shore-sea green,
Still patterned with the vine and grapes in gold.

But I have seen,
Pointing her shapely shadows from the dawn
And image tumbled on a rose-swept bay,
A drowsy ship of some yet older day;
And, wonder's breath indrawn,
Thought I—who knows—who knows—but in that same
(Fished up beyond Ææa, patched up new
—Stern painted brighter blue—)
That talkative, bald-headed seaman came
(Twelve patient comrades sweating at the oar)
From Troy's doom-crimson shore,
And with great lies about his wooden horse
Set the crew laughing, and forgot his course.

It was so old a ship—who knows, who knows?
—And yet so beautiful, I watched in vain
To see the mast burst open with a rose,
And the whole deck put on its leaves again.

Gates of Damascus

FOUR great gates has the city of Damascus,
  And four Grand Wardens, on their spears reclining,
All day long stand like tall stone men
  And sleep on the towers when the moon is shining.

This is the song of the East Gate Warden
When he locks the great gate and smokes in his garden.

Postern of Fate, the Desert Gate, Disaster's Cavern, Fort of Fear,
The Portal of Bagdad am I, the Doorway of Diarbekir.

The Persian Dawn with new desires may net the flushing mountain
    spires:
But my gaunt buttress still rejects the suppliance of those mellow
    fires.

Pass not beneath, O Caravan, or pass not singing. Have you heard
That silence where the birds are dead yet something pipeth like a
    bird?

Pass not beneath! Men say there blows in stony deserts still a rose
But with no scarlet to her leaf—and from whose heart no perfume
    flows.

Wilt thou bloom red where she buds pale, thy sister rose? Wilt thou
    not fail
When noonday flashes like a flail? Leave nightingale the caravan!

Pass then, pass all! "Bagdad!" ye cry, and down the billows of blue
    sky
Ye beat the bell that beats to hell, and who shall thrust ye back?
    Not I.

The Sun who flashes through the head and paints the shadows green
    and red,—
The Sun shall eat thy fleshless dead, O Caravan, O Caravan!

And one who licks his lips for thirst with fevered eyes shall face in
    fear

The palms that wave, the streams that burst, his last mirage, O
  Caravan!

And one—the bird-voiced Singing-man—shall fall behind thee,
  Caravan!
And God shall meet him in the night, and he shall sing as best
  he can.

And one the Bedouin shall slay, and one, sand-stricken on the way
Go dark and blind; and one shall say—"How lonely is the Caravan!"

Pass out beneath, O Caravan, Doom's Caravan, Death's Caravan!
I had not told ye, fools, so much, save that I heard your Singing-
  man.

> *This was sung by the West Gate's keeper*
> *When heaven's hollow dome grew deeper.*

I am the gate toward the sea: O sailor men, pass out from me!
I hear you high on Lebanon, singing the marvels of the sea.

The dragon-green, the luminous, the dark, the serpent-haunted sea,
The snow-besprinkled wine of earth, the white-and-blue-flower
  foaming sea.

Beyond the sea are towns with towers, carved with lions and lily
  flowers,
And not a soul in all those lonely streets to while away the hours.

Beyond the towns, an isle where, bound, a naked giant bites the
  ground:
The shadow of a monstrous wing looms on his back: and still no
  sound.

Beyond the isle a rock that screams like madmen shouting in their
  dreams,
From whose dark issues night and day blood crashes in a thousand
  streams.

Beyond the rock is Restful Bay, where no wind breathes or ripple
  stirs,
And there on Roman ships, they say, stand rows of metal mariners.

Beyond the bay in utmost West old Solomon the Jewish King
Sits with his beard upon his breast, and grips and guards his magic
   ring:

And when that ring is stolen, he will rise in outraged majesty,
And take the World upon his back, and fling the World beyond the
   sea.

> *This is the song of the North Gate's master,*
> *Who singeth fast, but drinketh faster.*

I am the gay Aleppo Gate: a dawn, a dawn and thou art there:
Eat not thy heart with fear and care, O brother of the beast we
   hate!

Thou hast not many miles to tread, nor other foes than fleas to
   dread;
Homs shall behold thy morning meal and Hama see thee safe in
   bed.

Take to Aleppo filigrane, and take them paste of apricots,
And coffee tables botched with pearl, and little beaten brassware
   pots:

And thou shalt sell thy wares for thrice the Damascene retailers'
   price,
And buy a fat Armenian slave who smelleth odorous and nice.

Some men of noble stock were made: some glory in the murder-
   blade:
Some praise a Science or an Art, but I like honourable Trade!

Sell them the rotten, buy the ripe! Their heads are weak; their
   pockets burn.
Aleppo men are mighty fools. Salaam Aleikum! Safe return!

> *This is the song of the South Gate Holder,*
> *A silver man, but his song is older.*

I am the Gate that fears no fall: the Mihrab of Damascus wall,
The bridge of booming Sinai: the Arch of Allah all in all.

O spiritual pilgrim rise: the night has grown her single horn:
The voices of the souls unborn are half adream with Paradise.

To Meccah thou hast turned in prayer with aching heart and eyes
    that burn:
Ah Hajji, whither wilt thou turn when thou art there, when thou art
    there?

God be thy guide from camp to camp: God be thy shade from well
    to well;
God grant beneath the desert stars thou hear the Prophet's camel
    bell.

And God shall make thy body pure, and give thee knowledge to
    endure
This ghost-life's piercing phantom-pain, and bring thee out to Life
    again.

And God shall make thy soul a Glass where eighteen thousand
    Æons pass,
And thou shalt see the gleaming Worlds as men see dew upon the
    grass.

And son of Islam, it may be that thou shalt learn at journey's end
Who walks thy garden eve on eve, and bows his head, and calls thee
    Friend.

----•-•-•----

SIEGFRIED SASSOON

----•-•-•----

Everyone Sang

EVERYONE suddenly burst out singing;
    And I was filled with such delight
As prisoned birds must find in freedom,
Winging wildly across the white
Orchards and dark-green fields; on—on—and out of sight.

Everyone's voice was suddenly lifted;
And beauty came like the setting sun:
My heart was shaken with tears; and horror
Drifted away . . . O, but Everyone
Was a bird; and the song was wordless; the singing will never be
    done.

Aftermath

*H*AVE you forgotten yet? . . .
    For the world's events have rumbled on since those gagged
        days,
Like traffic checked awhile at the crossing of city ways:
And the haunted gap in your mind has filled with thoughts that
    flow
Like clouds in the lit heavens of life; and you're a man reprieved
    to go
Taking your peaceful share of Time, with joy to spare.
But the past is just the same,—and War's a bloody game. . . .
Have you forgotten yet? . . .
*Look down, and swear by the slain of the War that you'll never
    forget.*

Do you remember the dark months you held the sector at Mametz,—
The nights you watched and wired and dug and piled sandbags on
    parapets?
Do you remember the rats; and the stench
Of corpses rotting in front of the front-line trench,—
And dawn coming dirty-white, and chill with a hopeless rain?
Do you ever stop and ask, "Is it all going to happen again?"

Do you remember that hour of din before the attack,—
And the anger, the blind compassion that seized and shook you
    then
As you peered at the doomed and haggard faces of your men?
Do you remember the stretcher-cases lurching back
With dying eyes and lolling heads, those ashen-gray
Masks of the lads who once were keen and kind and gay?

Have you forgotten yet? . . .
*Look up, and swear by the green of the Spring that you'll never
    forget!*

Grandeur of Ghosts

WHEN I have heard small talk about great men
        I climb to bed; light my two candles; then
Consider what was said; and put aside
What Such-a-one remarked and Someone-else replied.

They have spoken lightly of my deathless friends,
(Lamps for my gloom, hands guiding where I stumble,)
Quoting, for shallow conversational ends,
What Shelley shrilled, what Blake once wildly muttered. . . .

How can they use such names and be not humble?
I have sat silent; angry at what they uttered.
The dead bequeathed them life; the dead have said
What these can only memorize and mumble.

RUPERT BROOKE

The Soldier

IF I should die, think only this of me;
        That there's some corner of a foreign field
That is for ever England. There shall be
        In that rich earth a richer dust concealed;
A dust whom England bore, shaped, made aware,
        Gave, once, her flowers to love, her ways to roam,
A body of England's breathing English air,
        Washed by the rivers, blest by suns of home.

And think, this heart, all evil shed away,
        A pulse in the eternal mind, no less
                Gives somewhere back the thoughts by England given;
Her sights and sounds; dreams happy as her day;
        And laughter, learnt of friends; and gentleness,
                In hearts at peace, under an English heaven.

The Dead

THESE hearts were woven of human joys and cares,
  Washed marvellously with sorrow, swift to mirth.
The years had given them kindness. Dawn was theirs,
And sunset, and the colours of the earth.
These had seen movement, and heard music; known
Slumber and waking; loved; gone proudly friended;
Felt the quick stir of wonder; sat alone;
Touched flowers and furs and cheeks. All this is ended.
There are waters blown by changing winds to laughter
And lit by the rich skies, all day. And after,
Frost, with a gesture, stays the waves that dance
And wandering loveliness. He leaves a white
Unbroken glory, a gathered radiance,
A width, a shining peace, under the night.

Heaven

FISH (fly-replete, in depth of June
  Dawdling away their wat'ry noon)
Ponder deep Wisdom, dark or clear,
Each secret fishy hope or fear.
Fish say, they have their Stream and Pond:
But is there anything Beyond?
This life cannot be All, they swear,
For how unpleasant, if it were!
One may not doubt that, somehow, good
Shall come of Water and of Mud:
And, sure, the reverent eye must see
A Purpose in Liquidity.
We darkly know, by Faith we cry,
The future is not Wholly Dry.
Mud unto Mud!—Death eddies near—
Not here the appointed End, not here!
But somewhere, beyond Space and Time,
Is wetter water, slimier slime!
And there (they trust) there swimmeth One
Who swam ere rivers were begun,

Immense, of fishy form and mind,
Squamous, omnipotent and kind:
And under that Almighty Fin
The littlest fish may enter in.
Oh! never fly conceals a hook,
Fish say, in the Eternal Brook,
But more than mundane weeds are there,
And mud, celestially fair;
Fat caterpillars drift around,
And Paradisal grubs are found;
Unfading moths, immortal flies,
And the worm that never dies.
And in that Heaven of all their wish,
There shall be no more land, say fish.

EDITH SITWELL

Colonel Fantock

THUS spoke the lady underneath the trees:
I was a member of a family
Whose legend was of hunting—(all the rare
And unattainable brightness of the air)—
A race whose fabled skill in falconry
Was used on the small song-birds and a winged
And blinded Destiny. . . . I think that only
Winged ones know the highest eyrie is so lonely.
There in a land, austere and elegant,
The castle seemed an arabesque in music;
We moved in an hallucination born
Of silence, which like music gave us lotus
To eat, perfuming lips and our long eyelids
As we trailed over the sad summer grass,
Or sat beneath a smooth and mournful tree.

And Time passed, suavely, imperceptibly.

But Dagobert and Peregrine and I
Were children then; we walked like shy gazelles

Among the music of the thin flower-bells.
And life still held some promise,—never ask
Of what,—but life seemed less a stranger, then,
Than ever after in this cold existence.
I always was a little outside life,—
And so the things we touch could comfort me;
I loved the shy dreams we could hear and see—
For I was like one dead, like a small ghost,
A little cold air wandering and lost.
All day within the straw-roofed arabesque
Of the towered castle and the sleepy gardens wandered
We; those delicate paladins the waves
Told us fantastic legends that we pondered.

And the soft leaves were breasted like a dove,
Crooning old mournful tales of untrue love.
When night came, sounding like the growth of trees,
My great-grandmother bent to say good night,
And the enchanted moonlight seemed transformed
Into the silvery tinkling of an old
And gentle music-box that played a tune
Of Circean enchantments and far seas;
Her voice was lulling like the splash of these.
When she had given me her good-night kiss,
There, in her lengthened shadow, I saw this
Old military ghost with mayfly whiskers,—
Poor harmless creature, blown by the cold wind,
Boasting of unseen unreal victories
To a harsh unbelieving world unkind,—
For all the battles that this warrior fought
Were with cold poverty and helpless age—
His spoils were shelters from the winter's rage.
And so for ever through his braggart voice,
Through all that martial trumpet's sound, his soul
Wept with a little sound so pitiful,
Knowing that he is outside life for ever
With no one that will warm or comfort him. . . .
He is not even dead, but Death's buffoon
On a bare stage, a shrunken pantaloon.
His military banner never fell,
Nor his account of victories, the stories
Of old apocryphal misfortunes, glories

Which comforted his heart in later life
When he was the Napoleon of the schoolroom
And all the victories he gained were over
Little boys who would not learn to spell.

All day within the sweet and ancient gardens
He had my childish self for audience—
Whose body flat and strange, whose pale straight hair
Made me appear as though I had been drowned—
(We all have the remote air of a legend)—
And Dagobert my brother whose large strength,
Great body and grave beauty still reflect
The Angevin dead kings from whom we spring;
And sweet as the young tender winds that stir
In thickets when the earliest flower-bells sing
Upon the boughs, was his just character;
And Peregrine the youngest with a naïve
Shy grace like a faun's, whose slant eyes seemed
The warm green light beneath eternal boughs.
His hair was like the fronds of feathers, life
In him was changing ever, springing fresh
As the dark songs of birds . . . the furry warmth
And purring sound of fires was in his voice
Which never failed to warm and comfort me.

And there were haunted summers in Troy Park
When all the stillness budded into leaves;
We listened, like Ophelia drowned in blond
And fluid hair, beneath stag-antlered trees;
Then, in the ancient park the country-pleasant
Shadows fell as brown as any pheasant,
And Colonel Fantock seemed like one of these.
Sometimes for comfort in the castle kitchen
He drowsed, where with a sweet and velvet lip
The snapdragons within the fire
Of their red summer never tire.
And Colonel Fantock liked our company;
For us he wandered over each old lie,
Changing the flowering hawthorn, full of bees,
Into the silver helm of Hercules,
For us defended Troy from the top stair
Outside the nursery, when the calm full moon

Was like the sound within the growth of trees.
But then came one cruel day in deepest June,
When pink flowers seemed a sweet Mozartian tune,
And Colonel Fantock pondered o'er a book.
A gay voice like a honeysuckle nook,—
So sweet,—said, "It is Colonel Fantock's age
Which makes him babble.". . . Blown by winter's rage
The poor old man then knew his creeping fate,
The darkening shadow that would take his sight
And hearing; and he thought of his saved pence
Which scarce would rent a grave . . . that youthful voice
Was a dark bell which ever clanged "Too late"—
A creeping shadow that would steal from him
Even the little boys who would not spell,—
His only prisoners. . . . On that June day
Cold Death had taken his first citadel.

OSBERT SITWELL

Elegy for Mr. Goodbeare

DO you remember Mr. Goodbeare, the carpenter,
Godfearing and bearded Mr. Goodbeare,
Who worked all day
At his carpenter's tray,
Do you remember Mr. Goodbeare?
Mr. Goodbeare, that Golconda of gleaming fable,
Lived thin-ground between orchard and stable,
Pressed thus close against Alfred, his rival—
Mr. Goodbeare, who had never been away.

Do you remember Mr. Goodbeare,
Mr. Goodbeare, who never touched a cup?
Do you remember Mr. Goodbeare,
Who remembered a lot?
Mr. Goodbeare could remember
When things were properly kept up:

Mr. Goodbeare could remember
  The christening and the coming-of-age:
Mr. Goodbeare could remember
  The entire and roasted ox:
Mr. Goodbeare could remember
  When the horses filled the stable,
And the port-wine-coloured gentry rode after the tawny fox,
Mr. Goodbeare could remember
  The old lady in her eagle rage,
    Which knew no bounds:
Mr. Goodbeare could remember
  When the escaped and hungering tiger
Flickered lithe and fierce through Foxton Wood,
When old Sir Nigel took his red-tongued, clamouring hounds,
And hunted it then and there,
  As a Gentleman should.

Do you remember Mr. Goodbeare,
Mr. Goodbeare who never forgot?
Do you remember Mr. Goodbeare,
That wrinkled and golden apricot,
Dear, bearded, godfearing Mr. Goodbeare
Who remembered remembering such a lot?

Oh, do you remember, do you remember,
As *I* remember and deplore,
That day in drear and far-away December
When dear, godfearing, bearded Mr. Goodbeare
Could remember
No more?

WILFRED OWEN

Strange Meeting

IT seemed that out of the battle I escaped
Down some profound dull tunnel, long since scooped
Through granites which Titanic wars had groined.
Yet also there encumbered sleepers groaned,
Too fast in thought or death to be bestirred.
Then, as I probed them, one sprang up and stared
With piteous recognition in fixed eyes,
Lifting distressful hands as if to bless.
And by his smile I knew that sullen hall:
With a thousand fears that vision's face was grained;
Yet no blood reached there from the upper ground,
And no guns thumped, or down the flues made moan.
"Strange friend," I said, "here is no cause to mourn."
"None," said the other, "but the undone years,
The hopelessness. Whatever hope is yours
Was my life also; I went hunting wild
After the wildest beauty in the world,
Which lies not calm in eyes, or braided hair,
But mocks the steady running of the hour,
And if it grieves, grieves richlier than here.
For by my glee might many men have laughed,
And of my weeping something has been left
Which must die now. I mean the truth untold,
The pity of war, the pity war distilled.
Now men will go content with what we spoiled,
Or, discontent, boil bloody, and be spilled.
They will be swift with swiftness of the tigress,
None will break ranks, though nations trek from progress.
Courage was mine, and I had mystery;
Wisdom was mine, and I had mastery;
To miss the march of this retreating world
Into vain citadels that are not walled.
Then, when much blood had clogged their chariot-wheels,

I would go up and wash them from sweet wells,
Even with truths that lie too deep for taint.
I would have poured my spirit without stint,
But not through wounds; not on the cess of war.
Foreheads of men have bled where no wounds were.
I am the enemy you killed, my friend.
I knew you in this dark; for so you frowned
Yesterday through me as you jabbed and killed.
I parried; but my hands were loath and cold.
Let us sleep now. . . ."

Dulce et Decorum Est

BENT double, like old beggars under sacks,
Knock-kneed, coughing like hags, we cursed through sludge,
Till on the haunting flares we turned our backs,
And towards our distant rest began to trudge.
Men marched asleep. Many had lost their boots,
But limped on, blood-shod. All went lame, all blind;
Drunk with fatigue; deaf even to the hoots
Of gas-shells dropping softly behind.

Gas! Gas! Quick, boys!—An ecstasy of fumbling,
Fitting the clumsy helmets just in time,
But some one still was yelling out and stumbling
And flound'ring like a man in fire or lime.
Dim through the misty panes and thick green light,
As under a green sea, I saw him drowning.

In all my dreams before my helpless sight
He plunges at me, guttering, choking, drowning.

If in some smothering dreams, you too could pace
Behind the wagon that we flung him in,
And watch the white eyes wilting in his face,
His hanging face, like a devil's sick of sin,
If you could hear, at every jolt, the blood
Come gargling from the froth-corrupted lungs
Bitten as the cud
Of vile, incurable sores on innocent tongues,—

My friend, you would not tell with such high zest
To children ardent for some desperate glory,
The old Lie: *Dulce et decorum est
Pro patria mori.*

Anthem for Doomed Youth

WHAT passing-bells for these who die as cattle?
    Only the monstrous anger of the guns.
Only the stuttering rifles' rapid rattle
Can patter out their hasty orisons.
No mockeries for them; no prayers nor bells,
Nor any voice of mourning save the choirs,—
The shrill, demented choirs of wailing shells;
And bugles calling for them from sad shires.
What candles may be held to speed them all?
Not in the hands of boys, but in their eyes
Shall shine the holy glimmers of good-bys.
The pallor of girls' brows shall be their pall;
Their flowers the tenderness of patient minds,
And each slow dusk a drawing-down of blinds.

EDMUND BLUNDEN

The Waggoner

THE old waggon drudges through the miry lane
    By the skulking pond where the pollards frown,
Notched dumb surly images of pain;
On a dulled earth the night droops down.

Wincing to slow and wistful airs,
The leaves on the shrubbed oaks know their hour,
And the unknown wandering spoiler bares
The thorned black hedge of a mournful shower.

Small bodies fluster in the dead brown wrack
As the stumbling shaft-horse jingles past,
And the waggoner flicks his whip a crack;
The odd light flares on shadows vast

Over the lodges and oasts and byres
Of the darkened farm; the moment hangs wan
As though nature flagged and all desires.
But in the dim court the ghost is gone

From the hug-secret yew to the penthouse wall,
And stooping there seems to listen to
The waggoner leading the gray to stall,
As centuries past itself would do.

Thiepval Wood

THE tired air groans as the heavies swing over, the river-hollows
    boom;
The shell-fountains leap from the swamps, and with wildfire and
    fume
  The shoulder of the chalkdown convulses.
Then jabbering echoes stampede in the slatting wood,
Ember-black the gibbet trees like bones or thorns protrude
  From the poisonous smoke—past all impulses.
To them these silvery dews can never again be dear,
Nor the blue javelin-flame of thunderous noons strike fear.

The Pike

FROM shadows of rich oaks outpeer
  The moss-green bastions of the weir,
    Where the quick dipper forages
    In elver-peopled crevices.
And a small runlet trickling down the sluice
Gossamer music tires not to unloose.

  Else round the broad pool's hush
    Nothing stirs.
Unless sometime a straggling heifer crush

Through the thronged spinny whence the pheasant whirs;
  Or martins in a flash
Come with wild mirth to dip their magical wings,
While in the shallow some doomed bulrush swings
  At whose hid root the diver vole's teeth gnash.

And nigh this toppling reed, still as the dead
  The great pike lies, the murderous patriarch,
  Watching the waterpit shelving and dark
Where through the plash his lithe bright vassals thread.

    The rose-finned roach and bluish bream
    And staring ruffe steal up the stream
    Hard by their glutted tyrant, now
    Still as a sunken bough.

    He on the sandbank lies,
      Sunning himself long hours
    With stony gorgon eyes:
      Westward the hot sun lowers.

Sudden the gray pike changes, and quivering poises for slaughter;
Intense terror wakens around him, the shoals scud awry, but there
    chances
A chub unsuspecting; the prowling fins quicken, in fury he lances;
And the miller that opens the hatch stands amazed at the whirl in
    the water.

RUTH PITTER

Digdog

ROOTING in packing case of
  dirty straw hurling
lumps of it overboard moaning desire
moaning desire of vermin lovely rat
ineffable mouse attar of felicity
BUT there is nothing

nothing but dirt and darkness
but strawdirt chaffdust smellillusion ALAS.
BRAVE CHIEN ANGLAIS
NOBLE RENARDEARTHER
DIGDOG

Alas I also
root in earth desiring
something for nothing digging down to peace.
Follow the mole and not the lark
bet with the bloke who knows
peace lies there whence from the dark
arise the lily and the rose,
peace rains down in rivers of gold
and there great nuggets of sleep
wait for the seeker, ever been sold
sit on your tail and weep
for there is nothing
nothing but dust and darkness
but strawdirt chaffdust smellillusion ALAS.
LACHE ESPRIT ANGLAIS
POLTRON DE RENARDEARTHER
DIGDOG

O Come Out of the Lily

O COME out of the lily to me,
    Come out of the morning-glory's bell,
Out of the rose and the peony,
You that made them, made so well
Leaf and flower and the spiral shell,
And the weed that waves in coves of the sea.

O look out of the ermine's eye,
And look down with the eye of the bird,
And ride the air with the butterfly
Whose wings are written with many a word,
Read and beloved but never heard,
The secret message, the silent cry.

O leap out of another's mind,
Come from the toils of the terrible brain:
Sleep no longer, nor lurk behind
Hate and anger and woeful pain:
As once in the garden, walk again,
Centre and spirit of human kind.

ROY CAMPBELL

Mazeppa

HELPLESS, condemned, yet still for mercy croaking
    Like a trussed rooster swinging by the claws,
They hoisted him: they racked his joints asunder;
They lashed his belly to a thing of thunder—
A tameless brute, with hate and terror smoking,
    That never felt the bit between its jaws.

So when his last vain struggle had subsided,
    His gleeful butchers wearied of the fun:
Looping the knots about his thighs and back,
With lewd guffaws they heard his sinews crack,
And laughed to see his lips with foam divided,
    His eyes too glazed with blood to know the sun.

A whip cracked, they were gone: alone they followed
    The endless plain: the long day volleyed past
With only the white clouds above them speeding
And the grey steppe into itself receding,
Where each horizon, by a vaster swallowed,
    Repeated but the bareness of the last.

Out of his trance he wakened: on they flew:
    The blood ran thumping down into his brain:
With skull a-dangle, facing to the sky
That like a great black wind went howling by,

Foaming, he strove to gnash the tethers through
That screwed his flesh into a knot of pain.

To him the earth and sky were drunken things—
Bucked from his senses, jolted to and fro,
He only saw them reeling hugely past,
As sees a sailor soaring at the mast,
Who retches as his sickening orbit swings
The sea above him and the sky below.

Into his swelling veins and open scars
The pythin cords bit deeper than before,
And the great beast, to feel their sharpened sting,
Looping his body in a thundrous sling
As if to jolt his burden to the stars,
Recoiled, and reared, and plunged ahead once more.

Three days had passed, yet could not check nor tire
That cyclone whirling in its spire of sand;
Charged with resounding cordite, as they broke
In sudden flashes through the flying smoke,
The fusillading hoofs in rapid fire
Rumbled a dreary volley through the land.

Now the dark sky with gathering ravens hums:
And vultures, swooping down on his despair,
Struck at the loose and lolling head whereunder
The flying coffin sped, the hearse of thunder
Whose hoof-beats with the roll of muffled drums
Led on the black processions of the air.

The fourth sun saw the great black wings descending
Where crashed in blood and spume the charger lay:
From the snapped cords a shapeless bundle falls—
Scarce human now, like a cut worm he crawls
Still with a shattered arm his face defending
As inch by inch he drags himself away.

Who'd give a penny for that strip of leather?
Go, set him flapping in a field of wheat,
Or take him as a pull-through for your gun,
Or hang him up to kipper in the sun,

Or leave him here, a strop to hone the weather
And whet the edges of the wind and sleet.

Who on that brow foresees the gems aglow?
Who, in that shrivelled hand, the sword that swings
Wide as a moonbeam through the farthest regions,
To crop the blood-red harvest of the legions,
Making amends to every cheated crow
And feasting vultures on the fat of kings?

This is that Tartar prince, superbly pearled,
Whose glory soon on every wind shall fly,
Whose arm shall wheel the nations into battle,
Whose warcry, rounding up the tribes like cattle,
Shall hurl his cossacks rumbling through the world
As thunder hurls the hail-storm through the sky.

And so it is whenever some new god,
Boastful, and young, and avid of renown,
Would make his presence known upon the earth—
Choosing some wretch from those of mortal birth,
He takes his body like a helpless clod
And on the croup of genius straps it down.

With unseen hand he knots the cord of pain,
Unseen the winged courser strains for flight:
He leads it forth into some peopled space
Where the dull eyes of those who throng the place
See not the wings that wave, the thews that strain,
But only mark the victim of their might.

Left for the passing rabble to admire,
He fights for breath, he chokes, and rolls his eyes:
They mime his agonies with loud guffaws,
They pelt him from the place with muddy paws,
Nor do they hear the sudden snort of fire
To which the tether snaps, the great wings rise. . . .

Vertiginously through the heavens rearing,
Plunging through chasms of eternal pain,
Splendours and horrors open on his view,
And wingèd fiends like fiercer kites pursue,

With hateful patience at his side careering,
To hook their claws of iron on his brain.

Beyond the limits of the world we know
He sees what none have ever dared to dream—
Glories that have no name in mortal breath
And terrors starker than the self of death,
Heavens of song, and hells of endless woe—
And Solitude, above all else supreme.

Out of his pain, perhaps, some god-like thing
Is born. A god has touched him, though with whips:
We only know that, hooted from our walls,
He hurtles on his way, he reels, he falls,
And staggers up to find himself a king
With truth a silver trumpet at his lips.

The Zebras

FROM the dark woods that breathe of fallen showers,
Harnessed with level rays in golden reins,
The zebras draw the dawn across the plains
Wading knee-deep among the scarlet flowers.
The sunlight, zithering their flanks with fire,
Flashes between the shadows as they pass
Barred with electric tremors through the grass
Like wind along the gold strings of a lyre.

Into the flushed air snorting rosy plumes
That smoulder round their feet in drifting fumes,
With dove-like voices call the distant fillies,
While round the herds the stallion wheels his flight,
Engine of beauty volted with delight,
To roll his mare among the trampled lilies.

On Some South African Novelists

YOU praise the firm restraint with which they write—
I'm with you there, of course:
They use the snaffle and the curb all right,
But where's the bloody horse?

LOUIS MACNEICE

The Glacier

JUST as those who gaze get higher than those who climb
A paradox unfolds on any who can tamper with time.
Where bus encumbers upon bus and fills its slot
Speed up the traffic in a quick motion film of thought
Till bus succeeds bus so identically sliding through
That you cannot catch the fraction of a chink between the two;
But they all go so fast, bus after bus, day after day,
Year after year, that you cannot mark any headway,
But the whole stream of traffic seems to crawl
Carrying its dead boulders down a glacier wall
And we who have always been haunted by the fear of becoming stone
Cannot bear to watch that catafalque creep down.
Therefore turn we away to seemingly slower things
And rejoice there to have found the speed of fins and wings
In the minnow-twistings of the latinist who alone
Nibbles and darts through the shallows of the lexicon
Or among plate-glass cases in sombre rooms where
Eyes appraise the glazen life of majolica ware
Or where a gardener with trowel and rheumatic pains
Pumps up the roaring sap of vegetables through their veins.

The Death-Wish

IT being in this life forbidden to move
Too lightly, people, over-cautious, contrive
To save their lives by weighting them with dead
Habits, hopes, beliefs, anything not alive,
Till all this ballast of unreality sinks
The boat and all our thinking gurgles down
Into the deep sea that never thinks.

Which being so, it is not surprising that
Some in their impatience jump the rails,

Refusing to wait the communal failure, preferring
The way the madman or the meteor fails,
Deceiving themselves to think their death uncommon,
Avid to possess the unpossessable sea
As a man in spring desires to die in woman.

W. H. AUDEN

O What Is That Sound

O WHAT is that sound which so thrills the ear
    Down in the valley drumming, drumming?
Only the scarlet soldiers, dear,
    The soldiers coming.

O what is that light I see flashing so clear
    Over the distance brightly, brightly?
Only the sun on their weapons, dear,
    As they step lightly.

O what are they doing with all that gear;
    What are they doing this morning, this morning?
Only the usual manoeuvres, dear,
    Or perhaps a warning.

O why have they left the road down there;
    Why are they suddenly wheeling, wheeling?
Perhaps a change in the orders, dear;
    Why are you kneeling?

O haven't they stopped for the doctor's care;
    Haven't they reined their horses, their horses?
Why, they are none of them wounded, dear,
    None of these forces.

O is it the parson they want with white hair;
    Is it the parson, is it, is it?
No, they are passing his gateway, dear,
    Without a visit.

O it must be the farmer who lives so near;
  It must be the farmer so cunning, so cunning?
They have passed the farm already, dear,
    And now they are running.

O where are you going? stay with me here!
  Were the vows you swore me deceiving, deceiving?
No, I promised to love you, dear,
    But I must be leaving.

O it's broken the lock and splintered the door,
  O it's the gate where they're turning, turning;
Their feet are heavy on the floor
    And their eyes are burning.

Song

(TUNE: FRANKIE & JOHNNY)

VICTOR was a little baby,
  Into this world he came;
His father took him on his knee and said:
"Don't dishonour the family name."

Victor looked up at his father
Looked up with big round eyes:
His father said; "Victor, my only son,
Don't you ever ever tell lies."

Victor and his father went riding
Out in a little dog-cart;
His father took a Bible from his pocket and read;
"Blessed are the pure in heart."

It was a frosty December,
It wasn't the season for fruits;
His father fell dead of heart disease
While lacing up his boots.

It was a frosty December
When into his grave he sank;

His uncle found Victor a post as cashier
In the Midland Counties Bank.

It was a frosty December
Victor was only eighteen,
But his figures were neat and his margins straight
And his cuffs were always clean.

He took a room at the Peveril,
A respectable boarding-house;
And Time watched Victor day after day
As a cat will watch a mouse.

The clerks slapped Victor on the shoulder;
"Have you ever had a woman?" they said,
"Come down town with us on Saturday night."
Victor smiled and shook his head.

The manager sat in his office,
Smoked a Corona cigar:
Said, "Victor's a decent fellow but
He's too mousey to go far."

Victor went up to his bedroom,
Set the alarum bell;
Climbed into bed, took his Bible and read
Of what happened to Jezebel.

It was the First of April,
Anna to the Peveril came;
Her eyes, her lips, her breasts, her hips
And her smile set men aflame.

She looked as pure as a schoolgirl
On her First Communion day,
But her kisses were like the best champagne
When she gave herself away.

It was the Second of April,
She was wearing a coat of fur;
Victor met her upon the stairs
And he fell in love with her.

The first time he made his proposal,
She laughed, said; "I'll never wed";
The second time there was a pause;
Then she smiled and shook her head.

Anna looked into her mirror,
Pouted and gave a frown:
Said; "Victor's as dull as a wet afternoon
But I've got to settle down."

The third time he made his proposal,
As they walked by the Reservoir:
She gave him a kiss like a blow on the head,
Said; "You are my heart's desire."

They were married early in August,
She said; "Kiss me, you funny boy":
Victor took her in his arms and said;
"O my Helen of Troy."

It was the middle of September,
Victor came to the office one day;
He was wearing a flower in his buttonhole,
He was late but he was gay.

The clerks were talking of Anna,
The door was just ajar:
One said, "Poor old Victor, but where ignorance
Is bliss, etcetera."

Victor stood still as a statue,
The door was just ajar:
One said; "God, what fun I had with her
In that Baby Austin car."

Victor walked out into the High Street,
He walked to the edge of the town;
He came to the allotments and the rubbish heaps
And his tears came tumbling down.

Victor looked up at the sunset
As he stood there all alone;

Cried: "Are you in Heaven, Father?"
But the sky said "Address not known."

Victor looked up at the mountains,
The mountains all covered with snow:
Cried; "Are you pleased with me, Father?"
And the answer came back, "No."

Victor came to the forest,
Cried: "Father, will she ever be true?"
And the oaks and the beeches shook their heads
And they answered: "Not to you."

Victor came to the meadow
Where the wind went sweeping by:
Cried; "O Father, I love her so,"
But the wind said, "She must die."

Victor came to the river
Running so deep and so still:
Crying; "O Father, what shall I do?"
And the river answered, "Kill."

Anna was sitting at table,
Drawing cards from a pack;
Anna was sitting at table
Waiting for her husband to come back.

It wasn't the Jack of Diamonds
Nor the Joker she drew at first;
It wasn't the King or the Queen of Hearts
But the Ace of Spades reversed.

Victor stood in the doorway,
He didn't utter a word:
She said; "What's the matter, darling?"
He behaved as if he hadn't heard.

There was a voice in his left ear,
There was a voice in his right,
There was a voice at the base of his skull
Saying, "She must die tonight."

Victor picked up a carving-knife,
His features were set and drawn,
Said; "Anna, it would have been better for you
If you had not been born."

Anna jumped up from the table,
Anna started to scream,
But Victor came slowly after her
Like a horror in a dream.

She dodged behind the sofa,
She tore down a curtain rod,
But Victor came slowly after her:
Said; "Prepare to meet thy God."

She managed to wrench the door open,
She ran and she didn't stop.
But Victor followed her up the stairs
And he caught her at the top.

He stood there above the body,
He stood there holding the knife;
And the blood ran down the stairs and sang,
"I'm the Resurrection and the Life."

They tapped Victor on the shoulder,
They took him away in a van;
He sat as quiet as a lump of moss
Saying, "I am the Son of Man."

Victor sat in a corner
Making a woman of clay:
Saying; "I am Alpha and Omega, I shall come
To judge the earth one day."

Chorus

FROM "FOR THE TIME BEING"

HE is the Way.
Follow Him through the Land of Unlikeness;
You will see rare beasts, and have unique adventures.

He is the Truth.
Seek Him in the Kingdom of Anxiety;
You will come to a great city that has expected your return for years.

He is the Life.
Love Him in the World of the Flesh;
And at your marriage all its occasions shall dance for joy.

STEPHEN SPENDER

The Express

AFTER the first powerful plain manifesto
The black statement of pistons, without more fuss
But gliding like a queen, she leaves the station.
Without bowing and with restrained unconcern
She passes the houses which humbly crowd outside,
The gasworks and at last the heavy page
Of death, printed by gravestones in the cemetery.
Beyond the town there lies the open country
Where, gathering speed, she acquires mystery,
The luminous self-possession of ships on ocean.
It is now she begins to sing—at first quite low
Then loud, and at last with a jazzy madness—
The song of her whistle screaming at curves,
Of deafening tunnels, brakes, innumerable bolts.
And always light, aerial, underneath
Goes the elate metre of her wheels.
Steaming through metal landscape on her lines
She plunges new eras of wild happiness
Where speed throws up strange shapes, broad curves
And parallels clean like the steel of guns.
At last, further than Edinburgh or Rome,
Beyond the crest of the world, she reaches night
Where only a low streamline brightness
Of phosphorous on the tossing hills is white.

Ah, like a comet through flame she moves entranced
Wrapt in her music no bird song, no, nor bough
Breaking with honey buds, shall never equal.

I THINK continually of those who were truly great.
  Who, from the womb, remembered the soul's history
Through corridors of light where the hours are suns
Endless and singing. Whose lovely ambition
Was that their lips, still touched with fire,
Should tell of the Spirit clothed from head to foot in song.
And who hoarded from the Spring branches
The desires falling across their bodies like blossoms.

What is precious is never to forget
The essential delight of the blood drawn from ageless springs
Breaking through rocks in worlds before our earth.
Never to deny its pleasure in the morning simple light
Nor its grave evening demand for love.
Never to allow gradually the traffic to smother
With noise and fog the flowering of the spirit.

Near the snow, near the sun, in the highest fields
See how these names are fêted by the waving grass
And by the streamers of white cloud
And whispers of wind in the listening sky.
The names of those who in their lives fought for life
Who wore at their hearts the fire's centre.
Born of the sun they travelled a short while towards the sun,
And left the vivid air signed with their honour.

Landscape Near an Aerodrome

MORE beautiful and soft than any moth
    With burring furred antennae feeling its huge path
Through dusk, the air-liner with shut-off engines
Glides over suburbs and the sleeves set trailing tall
To point the wind. Gently, broadly, she falls
Scarcely disturbing charted currents of air.

Lulled by descent, the travellers across sea
And across feminine land indulging its easy limbs
In miles of softness, now let their eyes trained by watching
Penetrate through dusk the outskirts of this town
Here where industry shows a fraying edge.
Here they may see what is being done.

Beyond the winking masthead light
And the landing-ground, they observe the outposts
Of work: chimneys like lank black fingers
Or figures frightening and mad: and squat buildings
With their strange air behind trees, like women's faces
Shattered by grief. Here where few houses
Moan with faint light behind their blinds
They remark the unhomely sense of complaint, like a dog
Shut out and shivering at the foreign moon.

In the last sweep of love, they pass over fields
Behind the aerodrome, where boys play all day
Hacking dead grass: whose cries, like wild birds,
Settle upon the nearest roofs
But soon are hid under the loud city.

Then, as they land, they hear the tolling bell
Reaching across the landscape of hysteria
To where, larger than all the charcoaled batteries
And imaged towers against that dying sky,
Religion stands, the church blocking the sun.

C. DAY LEWIS

Tempt Me No More

TEMPT me no more; for I
Have known the lightning's hour,
The poet's inward pride,
The certainty of power.

Bayonets are closing round.
I shrink; yet I must wring
A living from despair
And out of steel a song.

Though song, though breath be short,
I'll share not the disgrace
Of those that ran away
Or never left the base.

Comrades, my tongue can speak
No comfortable words,
Calls to a forlorn hope,
Gives work and not rewards.

Oh keep the sickle sharp
And follow still the plough:
Others may reap, though some
See not the winter through.

Father, who endest all,
Pity our broken sleep;
For we lie down with tears
And waken but to weep.

And if our blood alone
Will melt this iron earth,
Take it. It is well spent
Easing a saviour's birth.

In Me Two Worlds

IN me two worlds at war
   Trample the patient flesh,
This lighted ring of sense where clinch
Heir and ancestor.

This moving point of dust
Where past and future meet
Traces their battle-line and shows
Each thrust and counterthrust.

The armies of the dead
Are trenched within my bones,
My blood's their semaphore, their wings
Are watchers overhead.

Their captains stand at ease
As on familiar ground;
The veteran longings of the heart
Serve them for mercenaries.

Conscious of power and pride
Imperially they move
To pacify an unsettled zone—
The life for which they died.

But see, from vision's height
March down the men to come,
And in my body rebel cells
Look forward to the fight.

The insolence of the dead
Breaks on their solid front:
They tap my nerves for power, my veins
To stain their banners red.

These have the spirit's range,
The measure of the mind:
Out of the dawn their fire comes fast
To conquer and to change.

So heir and ancestor
Pursue the inveterate feud,
Making my senses' darkened fields
A theatre of war.

American Poetry

INTRODUCTION

AMERICAN POETRY has been extensively anthologized; but so far as I am aware there has been no attempt hitherto to present a selection which shall represent the whole range of it, from its beginnings down to the present day. In a few textbooks, it is true, one may find, along with prose selections also, a fairly adequate survey. But for some curious reason the notion of a compact and comprehensive anthology of the verse alone has not found expression. That such a thing should be useful goes without saying. That it should be difficult is obvious, too—almost as obvious as that the editor who undertakes it will inevitably make mistakes in judgment and will inevitably be reproached for them. At the very outset he faces the formidable question of proportion. How much space shall he give to "early" American poetry—the poetry of the seventeenth and eighteenth centuries? How much, in this regard, shall he allow himself to be weighed upon by purely historical considerations? Should the Connecticut wits—for example—be represented, simply on the ground that they existed, and that they enjoyed for a time a kind of popularity? Or should he frankly admit to himself that their work was almost wholly without esthetic value, and ruthlessly exclude them?

The present editor has felt that the esthetic judgment (whatever that may be, and however we may define it) is the only sound basis for procedure; and if now and then he has momentarily compromised with this principle, admitting here and there a poem merely because it has achieved an immense popularity, he has, on the whole, done this reluctantly and seldom. American poetry, if one takes it as a whole, is not yet a great or rich poetry, though it has shown not infrequently the elements of greatness and richness; it has been provincial, uneven, tentative, brilliant; but if one cannot as yet say that it takes a very high place in the poetry of the world, as the expression of a national soul or culture, one can at least say emphatically that the time has come for a firm revision of our critical attitude toward it. We are too much accustomed, I fear, to what one might term a high protective tariff in this matter. We are a little too willing to suspend or modify judgment, on the ground that too much was not to be expected of a pioneer people in a new continent. Insensibly, we have got into the habit of accepting the second-best; and by closing our eyes to the best—by which I mean the best poetry of the world—have found it not too difficult to persuade ourselves of the excellence of the native product.

It is time, I think, to give up this rather childish habit, and to regard American poetry as severely as we would regard Greek or Chinese or English poetry. For if American poetry is not yet great, it has at least reached that point at which one may say that it is mature. It has a history of nearly three hundred years. In sheer quantity, if one keeps in mind all the minor poets and poetasters of the eighteenth and nineteenth centuries, it is enormous: few people, unless we except librarians, can have any idea of it. And if we admit cheerfully enough that the first two-thirds of its history is pretty barren, nevertheless one can also say with some assurance that it now comprises names of which no country need be ashamed, and that it is beginning to wear the dignity that goes with a tradition.

In view of this, it has been the present editor's intention to be somewhat severer with his material than his predecessors have been, in order that the process of clarification of this tradition might take a step forward. He has been rather hard on certain national favorites; it will be thought by some that he has been too drastic with Longfellow and Holmes and Whittier and Lowell and Lanier; that he has been too generous with Poe and Whitman and Dickinson; and that he has perhaps erred in proportion by giving to the poetry of the last twenty years so much more space than has been given to that of any preceding era. To such an objection he can only reply that in his opinion the poetry which begins, roughly, with Emily Dickinson has been the richest which America has produced; and that our so-called classics have been very seriously overestimated. If he can disturb prevailing notions about these things, and set in motion a revaluation of American poetry, which will find perhaps a higher place for comparatively unknown poets like Anne Bradstreet or Thomas Chivers or Trumbull Stickney than for Longfellow or Lowell or Bryant—not, be it understood, in point of range, but in point of sheer excellence or intensity—he will consider that he has been of some small service to American criticism. He has tried to eliminate, as far as possible, those things which embody the faults which so cursed American poetry in the nineteenth century—excessive sentimentality, sententiousness, easy dactylic exoticism—in order that the present movement in American poetry toward severer outline, both in idea and expression, might be more visible. If he has at all succeeded in this, he will have made one degree easier the ultimate compilation of a first-rate anthology by his successors.

Almost a literary generation has passed since this anthology was first published in another format; but in now revising and amplifying it, and bringing it up to date, I have cast back even further than that. Perspective changes; the critic's eye changes; poetry changes too. One finds that one had too much of X, too little of Y, none at all of Z—nor is it even as simple as that. For there arises also the question of the relation of X with Y, and then, further, the relation of each with the whole mass and current of his day. One's own view of the mass and current, meanwhile, has been imperceptibly changing with the changing times; the shadows and lights fall now in other places; what seemed formerly only a tendency, and the vaguest and most tentative at that, now reveals itself as a quite definite and accomplished direction; what formerly seemed to be a direction has now become vestigial, stopped off: one of Nature's little experiments which, alas, has failed.

But in adding (and to a very small extent subtracting) I believe I have only sharpened, not changed, the character of this collection. The aim has been to be rid of excess baggage, particularly of the more sentimental sort, even if (such are one's bad habits) one cannot hope to be wholly successful. I have been blamed by some anthologists for being too "abstract" in my taste; if by this it is meant that I have tried to avoid the pretty, on the one hand, or the oratorical and politically tendentious, on the other, I take it as a compliment. Sentiment, whether it is for privileged classes, or for the flowers that bloom in the spring, can never excuse inadequacy of statement. For if poetry can very nearly do without meaning (witness the miracles of nonsense verse) it plainly cannot do without excellence of statement. The "greatness" of a poet will, of course, in the end, always depend, and precisely, on his range and richness of meaning: do we perceive him as an island, a peninsula, a continent? But without that *first* prerequisite of poetry, clarity and excellence of statement, he will never have been perceived by us at all, even as an islet.

It remains to add that every anthology, and this is no exception, is a collaboration, a collaboration between the anthologist, the poets and the public. It is also, however, a collaboration in experiment. Which way will taste go? Which way will poetry go? Will these yellows keep their luminosity, the reds turn gray? Even now new poets are working at this, competitively, and for survival; new ideas and fashions are competing too, if more bloodlessly, for a share in the evolving consciousness of man. The anthologist is an interpreter in all this, with perhaps a little, just a *little,* unconscious *parti pris;* and the public, the public awareness, itself grinding out its own conflicting complex of wants and fears, is the slow-working arbiter and perpetuator. The whole fascinating confusion, with its involved differentials, is simply a process of communal growing. . . . And no doubt, in another twenty years, we shall know into what.

CONRAD AIKEN

Brewster, Massachusetts

ANNE BRADSTREET

The Flesh and the Spirit

IN secret place where once I stood,
Close by the banks of lacrym flood,
I heard two sisters reason on
Things that are past and things to come.
One Flesh was called, who had her eye
On worldly wealth and vanity;
The other Spirit, who did rear
Her thoughts unto a higher sphere.
"Sister," quoth Flesh, "what livest thou on—
Nothing but meditation?
Doth contemplation feed thee, so
Regardlessly to let earth go?
Can speculation satisfy
Notion without reality?
Dost dream of things beyond the moon,
And dost thou hope to dwell there soon?
Hast treasures there laid up in store
That all in the world thou countest poor?
Art fancy sick, or turned a sot,
To catch at shadows which are not?
Come, come, I'll show unto thy sense
Industry hath its recompense.
What canst desire but thou mayst see
True substance in variety?
Dost honor like? Acquire the same,
As some to their immortal fame,
And trophies to thy name erect
Which wearing time shall ne'er deject.
For riches dost thou long full sore?
Behold enough of precious store;
Earth hath more silver, pearls, and gold
Than eyes can see or hands can hold.
Affectest thou pleasure? Take thy fill;
Earth hath enough of what you will.

Then let not go what thou mayst find
For things unknown, only in mind."

SPIRIT

"Be still, thou unregenerate part;
Disturb no more my settled heart,
For I have vowed, and so will do,
Thee as a foe still to pursue,
And combat with thee will and must
Until I see thee laid in the dust.
Sisters we are, yea, twins we be,
Yet deadly feud 'twixt thee and me;
For from one father are we not.
Thou by old Adam was begot,
But my arise is from above,
Whence my dear Father I do love.
Thou speakest me fair, but hatest me sore;
Thy flattering shows I'll trust no more.
How oft thy slave hast thou me made
When I believed what thou hast said,
And never had more cause of woe
Than when I did what thou bad'st do.
I'll stop mine ears at these thy charms,
And count them for my deadly harms.
Thy sinful pleasures I do hate,
Thy riches are to me no bait,
Thine honors do nor will I love,
For my ambition lies above.
My greatest honor it shall be
When I am victor over thee,
And triumph shall, with laurel head,
When thou my captive shalt be led.
How I do live thou needst not scoff,
For I have meat thou knowst not of:
The hidden manna I do eat,
The word of life it is my meat.
My thoughts do yield me more content
Than can thy hours in pleasure spent.
Nor are they shadows which I catch,
Nor fancies vain at which I snatch,
But reach at things that are so high
Beyond thy dull capacity.

Eternal substance I do see,
With which enrichéd I would be;
Mine eye doth pierce the heavens, and see
What is invisible to thee.
My garments are not silk or gold,
Nor such like trash which earth doth hold,
But royal robes I shall have on,
More glorious than the glistering sun.
My crown not diamonds, pearls, and gold,
But such as angels' heads enfold.
The city where I hope to dwell
There's none on earth can parallel:
The stately walls, both high and strong,
Are made of precious jasper stone;
The gates of pearl both rich and clear,
And angels are for porters there;
The streets thereof transparent gold,
Such as no eye did e'er behold;
A crystal river there doth run,
Which doth proceed from the Lamb's throne;
Of life there are the waters sure,
Which shall remain for ever pure;
Of sun or moon they have no need,
For glory doth from God proceed—
No candle there, nor yet torch-light,
For there shall be no darksome night.
From sickness and infirmity
For evermore they shall be free,
Nor withering age shall e'er come there,
But beauty shall be bright and clear.
This city pure is not for thee,
For things unclean there shall not be.
If I of Heaven may have my fill,
Take thou the world, and all that will."

Contemplations

SOME time now past in the Autumnal Tide,
When *Phœbus* wanted but one hour to bed,
The trees all richly clad, yet void of pride,
Were gilded o'er by his rich golden head;

Their leaves & fruits seem'd painted, but was true
Of green, of red, of yellow, mixed hew;
Rapt were my senses at this delectable view.

I wist not what to wish; "yet sure," thought I,
"If so much excellence abide below,
How excellent is he that dwells on high,
Whose power and beauty by his works we know!
Sure he is goodness, wisdome, glory, light,
That hath this under-world so richly dight."
More Heaven then Earth was here, no winter & no night.

Then on a stately Oak I cast mine Eye,
Whose ruffling top the Clouds seem'd to aspire:
"How long since thou wast in thine Infancy?
Thy strength and stature, more thy years admire.
Hath hundred winters past since thou wast born,
Or thousand since thou brakest thy shell of horn?
If so, all these as nought Eternity doth scorn."

Then higher on the glistering Sun I gaz'd,
Whose beams was shaded by the leavie Tree.
The more I look'd the more I grew amaz'd,
And softly said: "What glory 's like to thee,
Soul of this world, this Universes Eye?
No wonder some made thee a Deity:
Had I not better known, alas, the same had I.

"Thou as a Bridegroom from thy Chamber rushes,
And as a strong man joyes to run a race;
The morn doth usher thee with smiles & blushes,
The Earth reflects her glances in thy face;
Birds, insects, Animals, with Vegative,
Thy heart from death and dulness doth revive,
And in the darksome womb of fruitful nature dive.

"Thy swift Annual and diurnal Course,
Thy daily streight and yearly oblique path,
Thy pleasing fervor and thy scorching force,
All mortals here the feeling knowledge hath.
Thy presence makes it day, thy absence night;

Quaternal Seasons caused by thy might.
Hail, Creature full of sweetness, beauty, & delight!

"Art thou so full of glory that no Eye
Hath strength thy shining Rayes once to behold?
And is thy splendid Throne erect so high
As to approach it can no earthly mould?
How full of glory, then, must thy Creator be
Who gave this bright light luster unto thee:
Admir'd, ador'd for ever be that Majesty!"

Silent, alone, where none or saw or heard,
In pathless paths I lead my wandring feet,
My humble Eyes to lofty Skyes I rear'd:
To sing some Song my mazed Muse thought meet;
My great Creator I would magnifie,
That nature had thus decked liberally;
But Ah, and Ah again, my imbecility!

I heard the merry grasshopper then sing,
The black-clad Cricket bear a second part;
They kept one tune and plaid on the same string
Seeming to glory in their little Art.
Shall Creatures abject thus their voices raise,
And in their kind resound their makers praise,
Whilst I as mute can warble forth no higher layes!

When present times look back to Ages past,
And men in being fancy those are dead,
It makes things gone perpetually to last,
And calls back moneths and years that long since fled;
It makes a man more aged in conceit
Then was *Methuselah* or 's grand-sire great,
While of their persons & their acts his mind doth treat.

Sometimes in *Eden* fair he seems to be;
Sees glorious *Adam* there made Lord of all;
Fancyes the Apple dangle on the Tree,
That turn'd his Sovereign to a naked thral,
Who like a miscreant's driven from that place,
To get his bread with pain and sweat of face,
A penalty impos'd on his backsliding Race.

Here sits our Grandame in retired place,
And in her lap her bloody *Cain* new born;
The weeping Imp oft looks her in the face,
Bewails his unknown hap and fate forlorn:
His Mother sighs to think of Paradise,
And how she lost her bliss to be more wise,
Believing him that was and is Father of lyes.

Here *Cain* and *Abel* come to sacrifice;
Fruits of the Earth and Fatlings each do bring:
On *Abel's* gift the fire descends from Skies,
But no such sign on false *Cain's* offering.
With sullen hateful looks he goes his wayes,
Hath thousand thoughts to end his brother's dayes,
Upon whose blood his future good he hopes to raise.

There *Abel* keeps his sheep, no ill he thinks;
His brother comes, then acts his fratricide:
The Virgin Earth of blood her first draught drinks,
But since that time she often hath been cloy'd.
The wretch, with ghastly face and dreadful mind,
Thinks each he sees will serve him in his kind,
Though none on Earth but kindred near then could he find.

Who fancyes not his looks now at the Barr?
His face like death, his heart with horror fraught,
Nor Male-factor ever felt like warr
When deep dispair with wish of life hath fought.
Branded with guilt and crusht with treble woes,
A Vagabond to Land of *Nod* he goes;
A City builds, that wals might him secure from foes.

Who thinks not oft upon the Fathers' ages?
Their long descent; how nephews sons they saw;
The starry observations of those Sages,
And how their precepts to their sons were law;
How Adam sigh'd to see his Progeny
Cloath'd all in his black sinfull Livery,
Who neither guilt nor yet the punishment could fly.

Our Life compare we with their length of dayes;
Who to the tenth of theirs doth now arrive?

And though thus short, we shorten many wayes,
Living so little while we are alive:
In eating, drinking, sleeping, vain delight,
So unawares comes on perpetual night,
And puts all pleasures vain unto eternal flight.

When I behold the heavens as in their prime,
And then the earth, though old, stil clad in green
The stones and trees insensible of time,
Nor age nor wrinkle on their front are seen;
If winter come and greeness then do fade,
A Spring returns and they more youthfull made;
But Man grows old, lies down, remains where once he's laid.

By birth more noble then those creatures all,
Yet seems by nature and by custome curs'd:
No sooner born but grief and care makes fall,
That state obliterate he had at first;
Nor youth nor strength nor wisdom spring again,
Nor habitations long their names retain,
But in oblivion to the final day remain.

Shall I, then, praise the heavens, the trees, the earth,
Because their beauty and their strength last longer?
Shall I wish there or never to had birth,
Because they 're bigger, & their bodyes stronger?
Nay, they shall darken, perish, fade, and dye,
And when unmade so ever shall they lye;
But man was made for endless immortality.

Under the cooling shadow of a stately Elm,
Cose sate I by a goodly River's side,
Where gliding streams the Rocks did overwhelm;
A lonely place, with pleasures dignifi'd.
I once that lov'd the shady woods so well
Now thought the rivers did the trees excel;
And if the sun would ever shine, there would I dwell.

While on the stealing stream I fixt mine eye,
Which to the long'd for Ocean held its course,
I markt nor crooks nor rubs that there did lye
Could hinder ought, but still augment its force:

"Oh happy Flood," quoth I, "that holds thy race
  Till thou arrive at thy beloved place,
  Nor is it rocks or shoals that can obstruct thy pace.

"Nor is 't enough that thou alone may'st slide,
  But hundred brooks in thy cleer waves do meet;
  So hand in hand along with thee they glide
  To *Thetis* house, where all imbrace and greet:
  Thou Emblem true of what I count the best,
  O could I lead my Rivolets to rest,
  So may we press to that vast mansion ever blest!

"Ye Fish which in this liquid Region 'bide,
  That for each season have your habitation,
  Now salt, now fresh, where you think best to glide
  To unknown coasts to give a visitation,
  In Lakes and ponds you leave your numerous fry;
  So nature taught, and yet you know not why,
  You watry folk that know not your felicity.

"Look how the wantons frisk to tast the air,
  Then to the colder bottome streight they dive;
  Eftsoon to *Neptune's* glassie Hall repair,
  To see what trade they great ones there do drive,
  Who forage o'er the spacious sea-green field
  And take the trembling prey before it yield,
  Whose armour is their scales, their spreading fins their shield."

While musing thus, with contemplation fed,
  And thousand fancies buzzing in my brain,
  The sweet-tongu'd Philomel percht ore my head,
  And chanted forth a most melodious strain;
  Which rapt me so with wonder and delight
  I judg'd my hearing better then my sight,
  And wisht me wings with her a while to take my flight.

"O merry Bird," said I, "that fears no snares,
  That neither toyles nor hoards up in thy barn,
  Feels no sad thoughts, nor cruciating cares
  To gain more good or shun what might thee harm;
  Thy cloaths ne're wear, thy meat is every where,

Thy bed a bough, thy drink the water cleer;
Reminds not what is past, nor what's to come dost fear.

"The dawning morn with songs thou dost prevent,
Sets hundred notes unto thy feathered crew,
So each one tunes his pretty instrument
And, warbling out the old, begin anew;
And thus they pass their youth in summer season,
Then follow thee into a better Region,
Where winter 's never felt by that sweet airy legion."

Man at the best a creature frail and vain,
In knowledg ignorant, in strength but weak,
Subject to sorrows, losses, sickness, pain,
Each storm his state, his mind, his body break;
From some of these he never finds cessation,
But day or night, within, without, vexation,
Troubles from foes from friends, from dearest, near'st **Relation**.

And yet this sinfull creature, frail and vain,
This lump of wretchedness, of sin and sorrow,
This weather-beaten vessel wrackt with pain,
Joyes not in hope of an eternal morrow;
Nor all his losses, crosses, and vexation,
In weight, in frequency and long duration,
Can make him deeply groan for that divine Translation.

The Mariner that on smooth waves doth glide
Sings merrily and steers his Barque with ease,
As if he had command of wind and tide,
And now become great Master of the seas;
But suddenly a storm spoiles all the sport,
And makes him long for a more quiet port,
Which 'gainst all adverse winds may serve for fort.

So he that saileth in this world of pleasure,
Feeding on sweets, that never bit of th' sowre,
That 's full of friends, of honour, and of treasure,
Fond fool, he takes this earth ev'n for heav'ns bower.
But sad affliction comes & makes him see
Here's neither honour, wealth, nor safety:
Only above is found all with security.

O Time, the fatal wrack of mortal things,
That draws oblivion's curtains over kings,
Their sumptuous monuments, men know them not,
Their names without a Record are forgot,
Their parts, their ports, their pomp's all laid in th' dust,
Nor wit nor gold nor guildings scape times rust:
But he whose name is grav'd in the white stone
Shall last and shine when all of these are gone.

A Letter to Her Husband

PHŒBUS, make haste: the day 's too long; be gone;
The silent night 's the fittest time for moan
But stay this once, unto my suit give ear,
And tell my griefs in either Hemisphere;
And if the whirling of thy wheels don't drown'd
The woful accents of my doleful sound,
If in thy swift Carrier thou canst make stay,
I crave this boon, this Errand by the way:
Commend me to the man more lov'd then life;
Shew him the sorrows of his widdowed wife,
My dumpish thoughts, my groans, my brakish tears,
My sobs, my longing hopes, my doubting fears;
And if he love, how can he there abide?
My interest 's more then all the world beside.
He that can tell the starrs or Ocean sand,
Or all the grass that in the Meads do stand,
The leaves in th' woods, the hail or drops of rain,
Or in a corn-field number every grain,
Or every mote that in the sun-shine hops,
May count my sighs and number all my drops.
Tell him the countless steps that thou dost trace
That once a day thy Spouse thou mayst imbrace;
And when thou canst not treat by loving mouth,
Thy rayes afar salute her from the south.
But for one moneth I see no day, poor soul,
Like those far scituate under the pole,
Which day by day long wait for thy arise:
O how they joy when thou dost light the skyes.
O *Phœbus,* hadst thou but thus long from thine
Restrain'd the beams of thy beloved shine,

At thy return, if so thou could'st or durst,
Behold a Chaos blacker then the first.
Tell him here 's worse than a confused matter—
His little world 's a fathom under water;
Nought but the fervor of his ardent beams
Hath power to dry the torrent of these streams.
Tell him I would say more, but cannot well:
Oppressed minds abruptest tales do tell.
Now post with double speed, mark what I say;
By all our loves conjure him not to stay.

Longing for Heaven

AS weary pilgrim now at rest
   Hugs with delight his silent nest,
His wasted limbes now lye full soft
   That myrie steps have troden oft,
Blesses himself to think upon
   his dangers past and travailes done;
The burning sun no more shall heat,
   Nor stormy raines on him shall beat;
The bryars and thornes no more shall scratch,
   nor hungry wolves at him shall catch;
He erring pathes no more shall tread,
   nor wild fruits eate in stead of bread;
For waters cold he doth not long,
   for thirst no more shall parch his tongue;
No rugged stones his feet shall gaule,
   nor stumps nor rocks cause him to fall;
All cares and feares he bids farwell,
   and meanes in safity now to dwell:
A pilgrim I on earth perplext,
   with sinns, with cares and sorrows vext,
By age and paines brought to decay,
   and my Clay house mouldring away,
Oh how I long to be at rest
   and soare on high among the blest!
This body shall in silence sleep,
   Mine eyes no more shall ever weep,
No fainting fits shall me assaile,
   nor grinding paines my body fraile,

With cares and fears ne'r cumbred be,
    Nor losses know nor sorrowes see.
What tho my flesh shall there consume?
    it is the bed Christ did perfume;
And when a few years shall be gone,
    this mortall shall be cloth'd upon:
A Corrupt Carcasse downe it lyes,
    a glorious body it shall rise;
In weakness and dishonour sowne,
    in power 't is rais'd by Christ alone.
Then soule and body shall unite,
    and of their maker have the sight.
Such lasting joyes shall there behold
    as eare ne'r heard nor tongue e'er told.
Lord, make me ready for that day:
    then Come, deare bridgrome, Come away!

THOMAS GODFREY

The Invitation

DAMON. Haste, Sylvia, haste, my charming maid!
    Let 's leave these fashionable toys:
Let's seek the shelter of some shade,
    And revel in ne'er fading joys.
See, *Spring* in liv'ry gay appears,
    And winter's chilly blasts are fled;
Each grove its leafy honours rears,
    And meads their lovely verdure spread.

SYLVIA. Yes, Damon, glad I'll quit the town:
    Its gaieties now languid seem:
Then sweets to luxury unknown
    We'll taste, and sip th' untainted stream.
In *Summer's* sultry noon-tide heat
    I'll lead thee to the shady grove,
There hush thy cares, or pleas'd repeat
    Those vows that won my soul to love.

DAMON. When o'er the mountain peeps the dawn,
 And round her ruddy beauties play,
I'll wake my love to view the lawn,
 Or hear the warblers hail the day.
But without thee the rising morn
 In vain awakes the cooling breeze;
In vain does nature's face adorn—
 Without my Sylvia nought can please.

SYLVIA. At night, when universal gloom
 Hides the bright prospects from our view,
When the gay groves give up their bloom
 And verdant meads their lovely hue,
Tho' fleeting spectres round me move,
 When in thy circling arms I 'm prest,
I 'll hush my rising fears with love,
 And sink in slumber on thy Breast.

DAMON. The new-blown rose, whilst on its leaves
 Yet the bright scented dew-drop 's found,
Pleas'd on thy bosom whilst it heaves,
 Shall shake its heav'nly fragrance round.
Then mingled sweets the sense shall raise,
 Then mingled beauties catch the eye:
What pleasure on such charms to gaze,
 What rapture 'mid such sweets to lie!

SYLIVA. How sweet thy words! But, Damon, cease,
 Nor strive to fix me ever here;
Too well you know these accents please,
 That oft have fill'd my ravish'd ear.
Come, lead me to these promis'd joys
 That dwelt so lately on thy tongue;
Direct me by thy well-known voice,
 And calm my transports with thy song!

PHILIP FRENEAU

FROM "THE HOUSE OF NIGHT"

TREMBLING I write my dream, and recollect
    A fearful vision at the midnight hour;
So late, death o'er me spreads his signal wings,
Painted with fancies of malignant power!

Such was the dream the sage Chaldean saw
Disclos'd to him that felt heaven's vengeful rod,
Such was the ghost, who through deep silence cry'd,
Shall mortal man—be juster than his God?

Let others draw from smiling skies their theme,
And tell of climes that boast unfading light,
I draw a darker scene, replete with gloom,
I sing the horrors of the *House of Night*.

Stranger, believe the truth experience tells,
Poetic dreams are of a finer cast
Than those which o'er the sober brain diffused,
Are but a repetition of some action past.

Fancy, I own thy power—when sunk in sleep
Thou play'st thy wild delusive part so well
You lift me into immortality,
Depict new heavens, or draw the scenes of hell.

By some sad means, when Reason holds no sway,
Lonely I rov'd at midnight o'er a plain
Where murmuring streams and mingling rivers flow
Far to their springs or seek the sea again.

Sweet vernal May! tho' then thy woods in bloom
Flourish'd, yet nought of this could Fancy see;
No wild pinks bless'd the meads, no green the fields,
And naked seem'd to stand each lifeless tree.

Dark was the sky, and not one friendly star
Shone from the zenith or horizon, clear;
Mist sate upon the woods, and darkness rode
In her black chariot with a wild career.

And from the woods the late-resounding note
Issued of the loquacious *Whip-poor-will;*
Hoarse, howling dogs and nightly roving wolves
Clamour'd from far-off clifts invisible.

Rude from the wide-extended *Chesapeke*
I heard the winds the dashing waves assail,
And saw from far, by picturing fancy form'd,
The black ship travelling through the noisy gale.

At last, by chance and guardian fancy led,
I reach'd a noble dome rais'd fair and high,
And saw the light from upper windows flame,
Presage of mirth and hospitality.

And by that light around the dome appear'd
A mournful garden of autumnal hue;
Its lately pleasing flowers all drooping stood
Amidst high weeds that in rank plenty grew.

The Primrose there, the violet darkly blue,
Daisies and fair Narcissus ceas'd to rise;
Gay spotted pinks their charming bloom withdrew,
And Polyanthus quench'd its thousand dyes.

No pleasant fruit or blossom gaily smil'd;
Nought but unhappy plants and trees were seen:
The yew, the myrtle, and the church-yard elm,
The cypress with its melancholy green.

There cedars dark, the osier, and the pine,
Shorn tamarisks, and weeping willows grew,
The poplar tall, the lotos, and the lime;
And pyracantha did her leaves renew.

The poppy there, companion to repose,
Display'd her blossoms that began to fall;

And here the purple amaranthus rose,
With mint strong-scented, for the funeral.

And here and there, with laurel shrubs between,
A tombstone lay, inscrib'd with strains of woe;
And stanzas sad, throughout the dismal green,
Lamented for the dead that slept below.

Peace to this awful dome!—when strait I heard
The voice of men in a secluded room;
Much did they talk of death and much of life,
Of coffins, shrouds, and horrors of a tomb. . . .

Then up three winding stairs my feet were brought
To a high chamber, hung with mourning sad;
The unsnuff'd candles glar'd with visage dim,
'Midst grief in ecstasy of woe run mad.

A wide-leaf'd table stood on either side,
Well fraught with phials, half their liquids spent;
And from a couch behind the curtain's veil
I heard a hollow voice of loud lament.

Turning to view the object whence it came,
My frighted eyes a horrid form survey'd
(*Fancy, I own thy power*): Death on the couch,
With fleshless limbs, at rueful length, was laid.

And o'er his head flew jealousies and cares,
Ghosts, imps, and half the black Tartarian crew,
Arch-angels damn'd; nor was their Prince remote,
Borne on the vaporous wings of Stygian dew.

Around his bed, by the dull flambeaux' glare,
I saw pale phantoms: Rage to madness vext,
Wan, wasting grief, and ever-musing care,
Distressful pain, and poverty perplext.

Sad was his countenance—if we can call
That *countenance* where only bones were seen—
And eyes sunk in their sockets, dark and low,
And teeth that only show'd themselves to grin.

Reft was his scull of hair, and no fresh bloom
Of chearful mirth sate on his visage hoar:
Sometimes he rais'd his head, while deep-drawn groans
Were mixt with words that did his fate deplore.

Oft did he wish to see the daylight spring;
And often toward the window lean'd to hear,
Fore-runner of the scarlet-mantled morn,
The early note of wakeful *Chanticleer.* . . .

Then with a hollow voice thus went he on:
"Get up and search, and bring, when found, to me
Some cordial, potion, or some pleasant draught,
Sweet, slumb'rous poppy or the mild Bohea.

"But hark, my pitying friend!—and if you can,
Deceive the grim physician at the door—
Bring half the mountain springs—ah, hither bring
The cold rock-water from the shady bower;

"For till this night such thirst did ne'er invade,
A thirst provok'd by heav'n's avenging hand:
Hence bear me, friends, to quaff and quaff again
The cool wave bubbling from the yellow sand.

"To these dark walls with stately step I came,
Prepar'd your drugs and doses to defy;
Smit with the love of never-dying fame,
I came, alas! to conquer—not to die!"

Glad, from his side I sprang and fetch'd the draught,
Which down his greedy throat he quickly swills;
Then on a second errand sent me strait,
To search in some dark corner for his pills.

Quoth he, "These pills have have long compounded been
Of dead men's bones and bitter roots, I trow;
But that I may to wonted health return
Throughout my lank veins shall their substance go."

So down they went.—He rais'd his fainting head,
And oft in feeble tone essay'd to talk:

Quoth he, "Since remedies have small avail,
Assist unhappy Death once more to walk."

Then, slowly rising from his loathsome bed,
On wasted legs the meagre monster stood,
Gap'd wide, and foam'd, and hungry seem'd to ask,
Tho' sick, an endless quantity of food.

Said he, "The sweet melodious flute prepare,
The anthem, and the organ's solemn sound,
Such as may strike my soul with ecstasy,
Such as may from yon' lofty walls rebound.

"Sweet music can the fiercest pains assuage:
She bids the soul to heav'n's blest mansions rise;
She calms despair, controuls infernal rage;
And deepest anguish, when it hears her, dies.

"And see, the mizzling, misty midnight reigns,
And no soft dews are on my eye-lids sent:
Here, stranger, lend thy hand, assist me, pray,
To walk a circuit of no large extent."

On my prest shoulders leaning, round he went,
And could have made the boldest spectre flee.
I led him up stairs, and I led him down,
But not one moment's rest from pain got he. . . .

Up rush'd a band, with compasses and scales
To measure his slim carcase, long and lean.
"Be sure," said he, "to frame my coffin strong,
You, master workman, and your men, I mean;

"For if the Devil, so late my trusty friend,
Should get one hint where I am laid, from you,
Not with my soul content, he 'd seek to find
That mouldering mass of bones, my body, too!

"Of hardest ebon let the plank be found,
With clamps and ponderous bars secur'd around,
That if the box by Satan should be storm'd
It may be able for resistance found."

"Yes," said the master workman, "noble Death,
Your coffin shall be strong—that leave to me;
But who shall these your funeral dues discharge?
Nor friends nor pence you have, that I can see."

To this said Death, "You might have ask'd me, too,
Base caitiff, who are my executors,
Where my estate, and who the men that shall
Partake my substance and be call'd my heirs.

"Know, then, that hell is my inheritance;
The devil himself my funeral dues must pay:
Go—since you must be paid—go ask of him,
For he has gold, as fabling poets say."

Strait they retir'd—when thus he gave me charge,
Pointing from the light window to the west:
"Go three miles o'er the plain, and you shall see
A burying-yard of sinners dead, unblest.

"Amid the graves a spiry building stands,
Whose solemn knell resounding through the gloom
Shall call thee o'er the circumjacent lands
To the dull mansion destin'd for my tomb.

"There, since 't is dark, I 'll plant a glimmering light
Just snatch'd from hell, by whose reflected beams
Thou shalt behold a tomb-stone, full eight feet,
Fast by a grave replete with ghosts and dreams.

"And on that stone engrave this epitaph,
Since Death, it seems, must die like mortal men;
Yes, on that stone engrave this epitaph,
Though all hell's furies aim to snatch the pen:—

"Death in this tomb his weary bones hath laid,
Sick of dominion o'er the human kind:
Behold what devastations he hath made;
Survey the millions by his arm confin'd.

"Six thousand years has sovereign sway been mine;
None but myself can real glory claim:

Great Regent of the world I reign'd alone,
And princes trembled when my mandate came.

"Vast and unmatch'd throughout the world, my fame
Takes place of gods, and asks no mortal date—
No, by myself and by the heavens I swear
Not Alexander's name is half so great.

"Nor swords nor darts my prowess could withstand;
All quit their arms and bow'd to my decree:
Even mighty JULIUS *died beneath my hand,*
For slaves and Cæsars were the same to me.

"Traveller, wouldst thou his noblest trophies seek,
Search in no narrow spot obscure for those;
The sea profound, the surface of all land,
Is moulded with the myriads of his foes." . . .

O'er a dark field I held my dubious way,
Where Jack-a-lanthorn walk'd his lonely round;
Beneath my feet substantial darkness lay,
And screams were heard from the distemper'd ground.

Nor look'd I back, till to a far-off wood,
Trembling with fear, my weary feet had sped:
Dark was the night, but at the inchanted dome
I saw the infernal windows flaming red.

And from within the howls of Death I heard,
Cursing the dismal night that gave him birth,
Damning his ancient sire and mother sin,
Who at the gates of hell, accursed, brought him forth.

(For fancy gave to my enraptur'd soul
An eagle's eye, with keenest glance to see;
And bade those distant sounds distinctly roll,
Which, waking, never had affected me.)

Oft his pale breast with cruel hand he smote,
And, tearing from his limbs a winding-sheet,
Roar'd to the black skies, while the woods around,
As wicked as himself, his words repeat.

Thrice tow'rd the skies his meagre arms he rear'd,
Invok'd all hell and thunders on his head,
Bid light'nings fly, earth yawn, and tempests roar,
And the sea wrap him in its oozy bed.

"My life for one cool draught! O, fetch your springs!
Can one unfeeling to my woes be found?
No friendly visage comes to my relief,
But ghosts impend and spectres hover round.

"Though humbled now, dishearten'd, and distrest,
Yet, when admitted to the peaceful ground,
With heroes, kings, and conquerors I shall rest,
Shall sleep as safely and perhaps as sound."

Dim burnt the lamp; and now the phantom Death
Gave his last groans in horror and despair:
"All hell demands me hence!" he said, and threw
The red lamp hissing through the midnight air.

Trembling, across the plain my course I held,
And found the grave-yard, loitering through the gloom,
And in the midst a hell-red, wandering light,
Walking in fiery circles round the tomb. . . .

At distance far, approaching to the tomb,
By lamps and lanthorns guided through the shade,
A coal-black chariot hurried through the gloom,
Spectres attending, in black weeds array'd,

Whose woeful forms yet chill my soul with dread:
Each wore a vest in Stygian chambers wove,
Death's kindred all—Death's horses they bestrode,
And gallop'd fiercely, as the chariot drove.

Each horrid face a grizly mask conceal'd;
Their busy eyes shot terror to my soul
As now and then, by the pale lanthorn's glare,
I saw them for their parted friend condole.

Before the herse Death's chaplain seem'd to go,
Who strove to comfort, what he could, the dead;

Talk'd much of *Satan* and the land of woe,
And many a chapter from the scriptures read.

At last he rais'd the swelling anthem high;
In dismal numbers seem'd he to complain:
The captive tribes that by *Euphrates* wept,
Their song was jovial to his dreary strain.

That done, they plac'd the carcase in the tomb,
To dust and dull oblivion now resign'd;
Then turn'd the chariot tow'rd the House of Night,
Which soon flew off and left no trace behind.

The Indian Burying Ground

IN spite of all the learned have said,
    I still my old opinion keep:
The *posture* that *we* give the dead
    Points out the soul's eternal sleep.

Not so the ancients of these lands:
    The Indian, when from life released,
Again is seated with his friends,
    And shares again the joyous feast.

His imaged birds and painted bowl,
    And venison for a journey dressed,
Bespeak the nature of the soul—
    ACTIVITY that knows no rest.

His bow for action ready bent,
    And arrows with a head of stone,
Can only mean that life is spent,
    And not the old ideas gone.

Thou, stranger, that shalt come this way,
    No fraud upon the dead commit:
Observe the swelling turf, and say,
    "They do not *lie*, but here they *sit*."

Here still a lofty rock remains,
    On which the curious eye may trace

(Now wasted, half, by wearing rains)
    The fancies of a ruder race.

Here still an aged elm aspires,
    Beneath whose far-projecting shade
(And which the shepherd still admires)
    The children of the forest played.

There oft a restless Indian queen,
    Pale *Shebah,* with her braided hair,
And many a barbarous form is seen,
    To chide the man that lingers there.

By midnight moons, o'er moistening dews,
    In habit for the chase arrayed,
The hunter still the deer pursues,
    The hunter and the deer a shade.

And long shall timorous fancy see
    The painted chief and pointed spear,
And Reason's self shall bow the knee
    To shadows and delusions here.

Song of Thyrsis

THE turtle on yon withered bough,
    That lately mourned her murdered mate,
Has found another comrade now—
Such changes all await!
Again her drooping plume is drest,
Again she's willing to be blest
And takes her lover to her nest.

If nature has decreed it so
With all above, and all below,
Let us like them forget our woe,
    And not be killed with sorrow.
If I should quit your arms tonight
And chance to die before 't was light,
I would advise you—and you might—
    Love again tomorrow.

RICHARD HENRY DANA

The Little Beach-Bird

THOU little bird, thou dweller by the sea,
　　Why takest thou its melancholy voice,
　　　　And with that boding cry
　　　　Why o'er the waves dost fly?
O, rather, bird, with me
　　Through the fair land rejoice!

Thy flitting form comes ghostly dim and pale,
　　As driven by a beating storm at sea;
　　　　Thy cry is weak and scared,
　　　　As if thy mates had shared
The doom of us. Thy wail,—
　　What doth it bring to me?

Thou call'st along the sand, and haunt'st the surge
　　Restless and sad; as if, in strange accord
　　　　With the motion and the roar
　　　　Of waves that drive to shore,
One spirit did ye urge—
　　The Mystery—the Word.

Of thousands, thou, both sepulcher and pall,
　　Old Ocean! A requiem o'er the dead,
　　　　From out thy gloomy cells,
　　　　A tale of mourning tells,—
Tells of man's woe and fall,
　　His sinless glory fled.

Then turn thee, little bird, and take thy flight
　　Where the complaining sea shall sadness bring
　　　　Thy spirit nevermore.
　　　　Come, quit with me the shore,
For gladness and the light,
　　Where birds of summer sing.

WILLIAM CULLEN BRYANT

To a Waterfowl

WHITHER, midst falling dew,
  While glow the heavens with the last steps of day,
Far, through their rosy depths, dost thou pursue
  Thy solitary way?

Vainly the fowler's eye
Might mark thy distant flight to do thee wrong,
As, darkly painted on the crimson sky,
  Thy figure floats along.

Seek'st thou the plashy brink
Of weedy lake, or marge of river wide,
Or where the rocking billows rise and sink
  On the chafed ocean-side?

There is a Power whose care
Teaches thy way along that pathless coast,—
The desert and illimitable air,—
  Lone wandering, but not lost.

All day thy wings have fanned
At that far height, the cold, thin atmosphere,
Yet stoop not, weary, to the welcome land,
  Though the dark night is near.

And soon that toil shall end;
Soon shalt thou find a summer home, and rest,
And scream among thy fellows; reeds shall bend
  Soon, o'er thy sheltered nest.

Thou'rt gone, the abyss of heaven
Hath swallowed up thy form; yet, on my heart
Deeply hath sunk the lesson thou hast given,
  And shall not soon depart.

He who, from zone to zone,
Guides through the boundless sky thy certain flight,
In the long way that I must tread alone,
Will lead my steps aright.

Thanatopsis

TO him who in the love of nature holds
Communion with her visible forms, she speaks
A various language; for his gayer hours
She has a voice of gladness, and a smile
And eloquence of beauty, and she glides
Into his darker musings, with a mild
And healing sympathy, that steals away
Their sharpness, ere he is aware. When thoughts
Of the last bitter hour come like a blight
Over thy spirit, and sad images
Of the stern agony, and shroud, and pall,
And breathless darkness, and the narrow house,
Make thee to shudder and grow sick at heart;—
Go forth, under the open sky, and list
To Nature's teachings, while from all around—
Earth and her waters, and the depths of air—
Comes a still voice:—

Yet a few days, and thee
The all-beholding sun shall see no more
In all his course; nor yet in the cold ground,
Where thy pale form was laid, with many tears,
Nor in the embrace of ocean, shall exist
Thy image. Earth, that nourished thee, shall claim
Thy growth, to be resolved to earth again,
And, lost each human trace, surrendering up
Thine individual being, shalt thou go
To mix forever with the elements,
To be a brother to the insensible rock
And to the sluggish clod, which the rude swain
Turns with his share, and treads upon. The oak
Shall send his roots abroad and pierce thy mold.

Yet not to thine eternal resting-place
Shalt thou retire alone, nor couldst thou wish
Couch more magnificent. Thou shalt lie down
With patriarchs of the infant world—with kings,
The powerful of the earth—the wise, the good,
Fair forms, and hoary seers of ages past,
All in one mighty sepulcher. The hills,
Rock-ribbed and ancient as the sun,—the vales
Stretching in pensive quietness between;
The venerable woods—rivers that move
In majesty, and the complaining brooks
That make the meadows green; and, poured round all,
Old Ocean's gray and melancholy waste,—
Are but the solemn decorations all
Of the great tomb of man. The golden sun,
The planets, all the infinite host of heaven,
Are shining on the sad abodes of death
Through the still lapse of ages. All that tread
The globe are but a handful to the tribes
That slumber in its bosom.—Take the wings
Of morning, pierce the Barcan wilderness,
Or lose thyself in the continuous woods
Where rolls the Oregon, and hears no sound
Save his own dashings—yet the dead are there:
And millions in those solitudes, since first
The flight of years began, have laid them down
In their last sleep—the dead reign there alone.

So shalt thou rest, and what if thou withdraw
In silence from the living, and no friend
Take note of thy departure? All that breathe
Will share thy destiny. The gay will laugh
When thou art gone, the solemn brood of care
Plod on, and each one as before will chase
His favorite phantom; yet all these shall leave
Their mirth and their employments, and shall come
And make their bed with thee. As the long train
Of ages glides away, the sons of men—
The youth in life's fresh spring, and he who goes
In the full strength of years, matron and maid,
The speechless babe, and the gray-headed man—

Shall one by one be gathered to thy side,
By those who in their turn shall follow them.

So live, that when thy summons comes to join
The innumerable caravan, which moves
To that mysterious realm, where each shall take
His chamber in the silent halls of death,
Thou go not, like the quarry-slave at night,
Scourged to his dungeon, but, sustained and soothed
By an unfaltering trust, approach thy grave
Like one who wraps the drapery of his couch
About him, and lies down to pleasant dreams.

"Oh Fairest of the Rural Maids"

OH fairest of the rural maids!
   Thy birth was in the forest shades;
Green boughs, and glimpses of the sky,
Were all that met thine infant eye.

Thy sports, thy wanderings, when a child,
Were ever in the sylvan wild;
And all the beauty of the place
Is in thy heart and on thy face.

The twilight of the trees and rocks
Is in the light shade of thy locks;
Thy step is as the wind, that weaves
Its playful way among the leaves.

Thine eyes are springs, in whose serene
And silent waters heaven is seen;
Their lashes are the herbs that look
On their young figures in the brook.

The forest depths, by foot unpressed,
Are not more sinless than thy breast;
The holy peace, that fills the air
Of those calm solitudes, is there.

To the Fringed Gentian

THOU blossom bright with autumn dew,
  And colored with the heaven's own blue,
That openest when the quiet light
Succeeds the keen and frosty night,

Thou comest not when violets lean
O'er wandering brooks and springs unseen,
Or columbines, in purple dressed,
Nod o'er the ground-bird's hidden nest.

Thou waitest late and com'st alone,
When woods are bare and birds are flown,
And frosts and shortening days portend
The aged year is near his end.

Then doth thy sweet and quiet eye
Look through its fringes to the sky,
Blue—blue—as if that sky let fall
A flower from its cerulean wall.

I would that thus, when I shall see
The hour of death draw near to me,
Hope, blossoming within my heart,
May look to heaven as I depart.

EDGAR ALLAN POE

Sonnet—To Science

SCIENCE, true daughter of Old Time thou art!
  Who alterest all things with thy peering eyes.
Why preyest thou thus upon the poet's heart,
  Vulture, whose wings are dull realities?
How should he love thee, or how deem thee wise,
  Who wouldst not leave him in his wandering
To seek for treasure in the jewelled skies,

Albeit he soared with an undaunted wing?
Hast thou not dragged Diana from her car,
  And driven the Hamadryad from the wood
To seek a shelter in some happier star?
  Hast thou not torn the Naiad from her flood,
The Elfin from the green grass, and from me
The summer dream beneath the tamarind tree?

Song from "All Aaraaf"

NEATH blue-bell or streamer,
    Or tufted wild spray
That keeps from the dreamer
    The moonbeam away,
Bright beings that ponder,
    With half-closing eyes,
On the stars which your wonder
    Hath drawn from the skies,
'Till they glance thro' the shade and
    Come down to your brow
Like eyes of the maiden
    Who calls on you now,—
Arise from your dreaming
    In violet bowers,
To duty beseeming
    These star-litten hours,
And shake from your tresses
    Encumber'd with dew
The breath of those kisses
    That cumber them too
(Oh, how, without you, Love,
    Could angels be blest?)—
Those kisses of true love
    That lull'd ye to rest!
Up! shake from your wing
    Each hindering thing:
The dew of the night—
    It would weigh down your flight;
And true-love caresses—
    O, leave them apart;

They are light on the tresses,
But lead on the heart.
Ligeia! Ligeia!
My beautiful one!
Whose harshest idea
Will to melody run,
O, is it thy will
On the breezes to toss?
Or, capriciously still,
Like the lone Albatross,
Incumbent on night
(As she on the air)
To keep watch with delight
On the harmony there?
Ligeia, wherever
Thy image may be,
No magic shall sever
Thy music from thee!
Thou hast bound many eyes
In a dreamy sleep;
But the strains still arise
Which *thy* vigilance keep:
The sound of the rain
Which leaps down to the flower,
And dances again
In the rhythm of the shower,
The murmur that springs
From the growing of grass,
Are the music of things—
But are modell'd, alas!
Away, then, my dearest,
O, hie thee away
To springs that lie clearest
Beneath the moon-ray;
To lone lake that smiles,
In its dream of deep rest,
At the many star-isles
That enjewel its breast.
Where wild flowers, creeping,
Have mingled their shade,
On its margin is sleeping
Full many a maid;

Some have left the cool glade, and
  Have slept with the bee:
Arouse them, my maiden,
  On the moorland and lea;
Go, breathe on their slumber,
  All softly in ear,
The musical number
  They slumber'd to hear;
For what can awaken
  An angel so soon,
Whose sleep hath been taken
  Beneath the cold moon,
As the spell which no slumber
  Of witchery may test,
The rhythmical number
  Which lull'd him to rest?

To Helen

HELEN, thy beauty is to me
  Like those Nicean barks of yore,
That gently, o'er a perfumed sea,
  The weary, way-worn wanderer bore
  To his own native shore.

On desperate seas long wont to roam,
  Thy hyacinth hair, thy classic face,
Thy Naiad airs have brought me home
  To the glory that was Greece
  And the grandeur that was Rome.

Lo, in yon brilliant window-niche
  How statue-like I see thee stand,
The agate lamp within thy hand!
  Ah, Psyche, from the regions which
  Are Holy Land!

Israfel

IN Heaven a spirit doth dwell
  Whose heart-strings are a lute:
None sing so wildly well

As the angel Israfel,
And the giddy stars (so legends tell),
Ceasing their hymns, attend the spell
  Of his voice, all mute.

Tottering above
  In her highest noon,
  The enamoured moon
Blushes with love,
  While, to listen, the red levin
  (With the rapid Pleiades, even,
  Which were seven)
  Pauses in Heaven.

And they say (the starry choir
  And the other listening things)
That Israfeli's fire
Is owing to that lyre
  By which he sits and sings—
The trembling living wire
  Of those unusual strings.

But the skies that angel trod,
  Where deep thoughts are a duty,
Where Love 's a grown-up God,
  Where the Houri glances are
Imbued with all the beauty
  Which we worship in a star.

Therefore thou art not wrong,
  Israfeli, who despisest
An unimpassioned song:
To thee the laurels belong,
  Best bard because the wisest;
Merrily live, and long!

The ecstasies above
  With thy burning measures suit—
Thy grief, thy joy, thy hate, thy love,
  With the fervour of thy lute:
  Well may the stars be mute!

Yes, Heaven is thine; but this
Is a world of sweets and sours:
Our flowers are merely—flowers,
And the shadow of thy perfect bliss
Is the sunshine of ours.

If I could dwell
Where Israfel
Hath dwelt, and he where I,
He might not sing so wildly well
A mortal melody,
While a bolder note than this might swell
From my lyre within the sky.

The City in the Sea

LO, Death has reared himself a throne
In a strange city lying alone
Far down within the dim West,
Where the good and the bad and the worst and the best
Have gone to their eternal rest.
There shrines and palaces and towers
(Time-eaten towers that tremble not!)
Resemble nothing that is ours.
Around, by lifting winds forgot,
Resignedly beneath the sky
The melancholy waters lie.
   No rays from the holy heaven come down
On the long night-time of that town;
But light from out the lurid sea
Streams up the turrets silently—
Gleams up the pinnacles far and free—
Up domes—up spires—up kingly halls—
Up fanes—up Babylon-like walls—
Up shadowy long-forgotten bowers
Of sculptured ivy and stone flowers—
Up many and many a marvellous shrine
Whose wreathèd friezes intertwine
The viol, the violet, and the vine.
Resignedly beneath the sky
The melancholy waters lie.

So blend the turrets and shadows there
That all seem pendulous in air,
While from a proud tower in the town
Death looks gigantically down.
  There open fanes and gaping graves
Yawn level with the luminous waves;
But not the riches there that lie
In each idol's diamond eye,
Not the gaily-jewelled dead
Tempt the waters from their bed:
For no ripples curl, alas,
Along that wilderness of glass;
No swellings tell that winds may be
Upon some far-off happier sea;
No heavings hint that winds have been
On scenes less hideously serene.
  But, lo, a stir is in the air!
The wave—there is a movement there,
As if the towers had thrust aside,
In slightly sinking, the dull tide,
As if their tops had feebly given
A void within the filmy Heaven!
The waves have now a redder glow;
The hours are breathing faint and low;
And when, amid no earthly moans,
Down, down that town shall settle hence,
Hell, rising from a thousand thrones,
Shall do it reverence.

The Sleeper

AT midnight, in the month of June,
  I stand beneath the mystic moon.
An opiate vapour, dewy, dim,
Exhales from out her golden rim,
And softly dripping, drop by drop,
Upon the quiet mountain top,
Steals drowsily and musically
Into the universal valley.
The rosemary nods upon the grave;
The lily lolls upon the wave;

Wrapping the fog about its breast,
The ruin moulders into rest;
Looking like Lethe, see, the lake
A conscious slumber seems to take,
And would not, for the world, awake.
All Beauty sleeps! And, lo, where lies
Irene, with her Destinies!
Oh, lady bright, can it be right—
This window open to the night?
The wanton airs, from the tree-top,
Laughingly through the lattice drop—
The bodiless airs, a wizard rout,
Flit through thy chamber in and out,
And wave the curtain canopy
So fitfully—so fearfully—
Above the closed and fringèd lid
'Neath which thy slumb'ring soul lies hid,
That, o'er the floor and down the wall,
Like ghosts the shadows rise and fall!
Oh, lady dear, hast thou no fear?
Why and what art thou dreaming here?
Sure thou art come o'er far-off seas,
A wonder to these garden trees!
Strange is thy pallor! strange thy dress!
Strange, above all, thy length of tress,
      And this all solemn silentness!
      The lady sleeps! Oh, may her sleep,
Which is enduring, so be deep!
Heaven have her in its sacred keep!
This chamber changed for one more holy,
This bed for one more melancholy,
I pray to God that she may lie
Forever with unopened eye,
While the pale sheeted ghosts go by!
      My love, she sleeps! Oh, may her sleep,
As it is lasting, so be deep!
Soft may the worms about her creep!
Far in the forest, dim and old,
For her may some tall vault unfold—
Some vault that oft hath flung its black
And wingèd panels fluttering back,
Triumphant, o'er the crested palls,

Of her grand family funerals—
Some sepulchre, remote, alone,
Against whose portal she hath thrown,
In childhood, many an idle stone—
Some tomb from out whose sounding door
She ne'er shall force an echo more,
Thrilling to think, poor child of sin,
It was the dead who groaned within.

To One in Paradise

THOU wast all that to me, love,
    For which my soul did pine—
A green isle in the sea, love,
    A fountain and a shrine,
All wreathed with fairy fruits and flowers,
    And all the flowers were mine.

Ah, dream too bright to last!
    Ah, starry Hope, that didst arise
But to be overcast!
    A voice from out the Future cries,
"On! on!"—but o'er the Past
    (Dim gulf!) my spirit hovering lies
Mute, motionless, aghast!

For, alas, alas, with me
    The light of Life is o'er!
"No more—no more—no more—"
    (Such language holds the solemn sea
To the sands upon the shore)
    Shall bloom the thunder-blasted tree,
Or the stricken eagle soar!

And all my days are trances,
    And all my nightly dreams
Are where thy grey eye glances,
    And where thy footstep gleams—
In what ethereal dances,
    By what eternal streams.

The Haunted Palace

IN the greenest of our valleys
  By good angels tenanted,
Once a fair and stately palace—
  Radiant palace—reared its head.
In the monarch Thought's dominion,
  It stood there;
Never seraph spread a pinion
  Over fabric half so fair!

Banners yellow, glorious, golden,
  On its roof did float and flow
(This—all this—was in the olden
  Time long ago);
And every gentle air that dallied,
  In that sweet day,
Along the ramparts plumed and pallid,
  A wingèd odor went away.

Wanderers in that happy valley,
  Through two luminous windows, saw
Spirits moving musically,
  To a lute's well-tunèd law,
Round about a throne where, sitting
  (Porphyrogene!)
In state his glory well befitting,
  The ruler of the realm was seen.

And all with pearl and ruby glowing
  Was the fair palace door,
Through which came flowing, flowing,
    flowing,
  And sparkling evermore,
A troop of Echoes, whose sweet duty
  Was but to sing,
In voices of surpassing beauty,
  The wit and wisdom of their king.

But evil things, in robes of sorrow,
  Assailed the monarch's high estate.

(Ah, let us mourn! for never morrow
  Shall dawn upon him desolate!)
And round about his home the glory
  That blushed and bloomed
Is but a dim-remembered story
  Of the old time entombed.

And travellers now, within that valley,
  Through the red-litten windows see
Vast forms, that move fantastically
  To a discordant melody;
While, like a ghastly rapid river,
  Through the pale door
A hideous throng rush out forever
  And laugh—but smile no more.

The Conqueror Worm

LO, 'tis a gala night
  Within the lonesome latter years;
An angel throng, bewinged, bedight
  In veils, and drowned in tears,
Sit in a theater, to see
  A play of hopes and fears,
While the orchestra breathes fitfully
  The music of the spheres.

Mimes, in the form of God on high,
  Mutter and mumble low,
And hither and thither fly—
  Mere puppets they, who come and go
At bidding of vast formless things
  That shift the scenery to and fro,
Flapping from out their Condor wings
  Invisible woe!

That motley drama, oh, be sure
  It shall not be forgot!
With its Phantom chased for evermore
  By a crowd that seize it not,
Through a circle that ever returneth in
  To the self-same spot,

And much of Madness, and more of Sin,
  And Horror the soul of the plot.

But see, amid the mimic rout
  A crawling shape intrude!
A blood-red thing that writhes from out
  · The scenic solitude!
It writhes! it writhes! with mortal pangs
  The mimes become its food,
And seraphs sob at vermin fangs
  In human gore imbued.

Out, out are the lights—out all!
  And over each quivering form
The curtain, a funeral pall,
  Comes down with the rush of a storm;
While the angels, all pallid and wan,
  Uprising, unveiling, affirm
That the play is the tragedy "Man,"
  And its hero the Conqueror Worm.

The Raven

ONCE upon a midnight dreary, while I pondered, weak and
    weary,
Over many a quaint and curious volume of forgotten lore,
While I nodded, nearly napping, suddenly there came a tapping,
As of some one gently rapping, rapping at my chamber door.
" 'T is some visitor," I muttered, "tapping at my chamber door—
                      Only this and nothing more."

Ah, distinctly I remember it was in the bleak December,
And each separate dying ember wrought its ghost upon the floor.
Eagerly I wished the morrow; vainly I had sought to borrow
From my books surcease of sorrow—sorrow for the lost Lenore,
For the rare and radiant maiden whom the angels name Lenore—
                      Nameless *here* for evermore.

And the silken, sad, uncertain rustling of each purple curtain
Thrilled me—filled me with fantastic terrors never felt before;
So that now, to still the beating of my heart, I stood repeating,

" 'T is some visitor entreating entrance at my chamber door—
Some late visitor entreating entrance at my chamber door—
   This it is and nothing more."

Presently my soul grew stronger: hesitating then no longer,
"Sir," said I, "or Madam, truly your forgiveness I implore;
But the fact is I was napping, and so gently you came rapping,
And so faintly you came tapping, tapping at my chamber door,
That I scarce was sure I heard you"—here I opened wide the door—
   Darkness there and nothing more.

Deep into that darkness, peering, long I stood there, wondering,
 fearing,
Doubting, dreaming dreams no mortal ever dared to dream before;
But the silence was unbroken, and the stillness gave no token,
And the only word there spoken was the whispered word "Le-
 nore!"
This I whispered, and an echo murmured back the word "Lenore!"
   Merely this and nothing more.

Back into the chamber turning, all my soul within me burning,
Soon again I heard a tapping, somewhat louder than before.
"Surely," said I, "surely that is something at my window lattice;
Let me see, then, what thereat is, and this mystery explore,—
Let my heart be still a moment and this mystery explore—
   'T is the wind and nothing more."

Open here I flung the shutter, when, with many a flirt and flutter,
In there stepped a stately Raven of the saintly days of yore.
Not the least obeisance made he, not a minute stopped or stayed he,
But with mien of lord or lady perched above my chamber door—
Perched upon a bust of Pallas just above my chamber door—
   Perched and sat, and nothing more.

Then, this ebony bird beguiling my sad fancy into smiling
By the grave and stern decorum of the countenance it wore,
"Though thy crest be shorn and shaven, thou," I said, "art sure no
 craven,
Ghastly, grim, and ancient Raven, wandering from the Nightly
 shore:
Tell me what thy lordly name is on the Night's Plutonian shore!"
   Quoth the Raven, "Nevermore."

Much I marvelled this ungainly fowl to hear discourse so plainly,
Though its answer little meaning, little relevancy, bore;
For we cannot help agreeing that no living human being
Ever yet was blessed with seeing bird above his chamber door—
Bird or beast upon the sculptured bust above his chamber door—
  With such name as "Nevermore."

But the Raven, sitting lonely on the placid bust, spoke only
That one word, as if his soul in that one word he did outpour.
Nothing farther then he uttered, not a feather then he fluttered;
Till I scarcely more than muttered, "Other friends have flown before;
On the morrow *he* will leave me, as my Hopes have flown before."
  Then the bird said, "Nevermore."

Startled at the stillness broken by reply so aptly spoken,
"Doubtless," said I, "what it utters is its only stock and store,
Caught from some unhappy master whom unmerciful Disaster
Followed fast and followed faster till his songs one burden bore,
Till the dirges of his Hope that melancholy burden bore
  Of 'Never—nevermore.'"

But the Raven still beguiling my sad fancy into smiling,
Straight I wheeled a cushioned seat in front of bird and bust and door;
Then, upon the velvet sinking, I betook myself to linking
Fancy unto fancy, thinking what this ominous bird of yore,
What this grim, ungainly, ghastly, gaunt, and ominous bird of yore,
  Meant in croaking "Nevermore."

This I sat engaged in guessing, but no syllable expressing
To the fowl whose fiery eyes now burned into my bosom's core;
This and more I sat divining, with my head at ease reclining
On the cushion's velvet lining that the lamp-light gloated o'er,
But whose velvet violet lining, with the lamp-light gloating o'er,
  She shall press, ah, nevermore!

Then, methought, the air grew denser, perfumed from an unseen censer
Swung by seraphim whose footfalls tinkled on the tufted floor.
"Wretch!" I cried, "thy God hath lent thee, by these angels he hath sent thee,

Respite—respite and nepenthe from thy memories of Lenore!
Quaff, oh quaff this kind nepenthe, and forget this lost Lenore!"
                    Quoth the Raven, "Nevermore."

"Prophet!" said I, "thing of evil! prophet still, if bird or devil!
Whether Tempter sent, or whether tempest tossed thee here ashore,
Desolate yet all undaunted, on this desert land enchanted—
On this home by Horror haunted—tell me truly, I implore,
Is there—*is* there balm in Gilead?—tell me—tell me, I implore!"
                    Quoth the Raven, "Nevermore."

"Prophet!" said I, "thing of evil! prophet still, if bird or devil!
By that Heaven that bends above us—by that God we both adore—
Tell this soul with sorrow laden if, within the distant Aidenn,
It shall clasp a sainted maiden whom the angels name Lenore—
Clasp a rare and radiant maiden whom the angels name Lenore."
                    Quoth the Raven, "Nevermore."

"Be that word our sign of parting, bird or fiend!" I shrieked, up-
    starting;
"Get thee back into the tempest and the Night's Plutonian shore!
Leave no black plume as a token of that lie thy soul hath spoken!
Leave my loneliness unbroken!—quit the bust above my door!
Take thy beak from out my heart, and take thy form from off my
    door!"
                    Quoth the Raven, "Nevermore."

And the Raven, never flitting, still is sitting, *still* is sitting
On the pallid bust of Pallas just above my chamber door;
And his eyes have all the seeming of a demon's that is dreaming,
And the lamp-light o'er him streaming throws his shadow on the
    floor;
And my soul from out that shadow that lies floating on the floor
                    Shall be lifted—nevermore!

Ulalume

THE skies they were ashen and sober,
    The leaves they were crispèd and sere—
    The leaves they were withering and sere;
It was night in the lonesome October
    Of my most immemorial year;

It was hard by the dim lake of Auber,
    In the misty mid region of Weir—
It was down by the dank tarn of Auber,
    In the ghoul-haunted woodland of Weir.

Here once, through an alley Titanic
    Of cypress, I roamed with my Soul—
    Of cypress, with Psyche, my Soul.
These were days when my heart was volcanic
    As the scoriac rivers that roll—
    As the lavas that restlessly roll
Their sulphurous currents down Yaanek,
    In the ultimate climes of the pole—
That groan as they roll down Mount Yaanek,
    In the realms of the boreal pole.

Our talk had been serious and sober,
    But our thoughts they were palsied and sere—
    Our memories were treacherous and sere,—
For we knew not the month was October,
    And we marked not the night of the year
(Ah, night of all nights in the year!)—
We noted not the dim lake of Auber
    (Though once we had journeyed down here)—
Remembered not the dank tarn of Auber,
    Nor the ghoul-haunted woodland of Weir.

And now, as the night was senescent
    And star-dials pointed to morn—
    As the star-dials hinted of morn,—
At the end of our path a liquescent
    And nebulous lustre was born,
Out of which a miraculous crescent
    Arose with a duplicate horn—
Astarte's bediamonded crescent
    Distinct with its duplicate horn.

And I said: "She is warmer than Dian:
    She rolls through an ether of sighs—
    She revels in a region of sighs;
She has seen that the tears are not dry on
    These cheeks, where the worm never dies,

And has come past the stars of the Lion
    To point us the path to the skies—
    To the Lethean peace of the skies,—
Come up, in despite of the Lion,
    To shine on us with her bright eyes—
Come up through the lair of the Lion,
    With love in her luminous eyes."

But Psyche, uplifting her finger,
    Said: "Sadly this star I mistrust—
    Her pallor I strangely mistrust:—
Oh, hasten!—oh, let us not linger!
    Oh, fly! let us fly!—for we must."
In terror she spoke, letting sink her
    Wings until they trailed in the dust—
In agony sobbed, letting sink her
    Plumes till they trailed in the dust—
    Till they sorrowfully trailed in the dust.

I replied: "This is nothing but dreaming:
    Let us on by this tremulous light!
    Let us bathe in this crystalline light!
Its Sibyllic splendor is beaming
    With Hope and in Beauty tonight—
    See! it flickers up the sky through the night!
Ah, we safely may trust to its gleaming,
    And be sure it will lead us aright—
We safely may trust to a gleaming
    That cannot but guide us aright,
    Since it flickers up to Heaven through the night."

Thus I pacified Psyche, and kissed her,
    And tempted her out of her gloom—
    And conquered her scruples and gloom;
And we passed to the end of the vista,
    But were stopped by the door of a tomb—
    By the door of a legended tomb;
And I said: "What is written, sweet sister,
    On the door of this legended tomb?"
    She replied: "Ulalume—Ulalume—
    'T is the vault of thy lost Ulalume!"

Then my heart it grew ashen and sober
 As the leaves that were crispèd and sere—
 As the leaves that were withering and sere;
And I cried: "It was surely October
 On *this* very night of last year
 That I journeyed—I journeyed down here,—
 That I brought a dread burden down here:
 On this night of all nights in the year,
 Ah, what demon has tempted me here?
Well I know, now, this dim lake of Auber—
 This misty mid region of Weir,—
Well I know, now, this dank tarn of Auber—
 This ghoul-haunted woodland of Weir."

Annabel Lee

IT was many and many a year ago,
 In a kingdom by the sea,
That a maiden there lived whom you may know
 By the name of ANNABEL LEE;
And this maiden she lived with no other thought
 Than to love and be loved by me.

I was a child and *she* was a child,
 In this kingdom by the sea;
But we loved with a love that was more than love—
 I and my ANNABEL LEE—
With a love that the wingèd seraphs of heaven
 Coveted her and me.

And this was the reason that, long ago,
 In this kingdom by the sea,
A wind blew out of a cloud, chilling
 My beautiful ANNABEL LEE;
So that her high-born kinsmen came
 And bore her away from me,
To shut her up in a sepulchre
 In this kingdom by the sea.

The angels, not half so happy in heaven,
 Went envying her and me—

Yes! that was the reason (as all men know,
　　In this kingdom by the sea)
That the wind came out of the cloud by night,
　　Chilling and killing my ANNABEL LEE.

But our love it was stronger by far than the love
　　Of those who were older than we—
　　Of many far wiser than we;
And neither the angels in heaven above,
　　Nor the demons down under the sea,
Can ever dissever my soul from the soul
　　Of the beautiful ANNABEL LEE:

For the moon never beams without bringing me dreams
　　Of the beautiful ANNABEL LEE;
And the stars never rise but I feel the bright eyes
　　Of the beautiful ANNABEL LEE;
And so, all the night-tide, I lie down by the side
Of my darling—my darling—my life and my bride,
　　In the sepulchre there by the sea,
　　In her tomb by the sounding sea.

Eldorado

GAILY bedight,
　　A gallant knight,
In sunshine and in shadow,
　　Had journeyed long,
　　Singing a song,
In search of Eldorado.

　　But he grew old—
　　This knight so bold,—
And o'er his heart a shadow
　　Fell as he found
　　No spot of ground
That looked like Eldorado.

　　And, as his strength
　　Failed him at length,
He met a pilgrim shadow.

"Shadow," said he,
"Where can it be—
This land of Eldorado?"

"Over the mountains
Of the Moon,
Down the Valley of the Shadow,
Ride, boldly ride,"
The shade replied,
"If you seek for Eldorado!"

Romance

ROMANCE, who loves to nod and sing,
With drowsy head and folded wing,
Among the green leaves as they shake
Far down within some shadowy lake,
To me a painted paroquet
Hath been—a most familiar bird—
Taught me my alphabet to say—
To lisp my very earliest word
While in the wild wood I did lie,
A child—with a most knowing eye.

Of late, eternal Condor years
So shake the very Heaven on high
With tumult as they thunder by,
I have no time for idle cares
Through gazing on the unquiet sky.
And when an hour with calmer wings
Its down upon my spirit flings—
That little time with lyre and rhyme
To while away—forbidden things!
My heart would feel to be a crime
Unless it trembled with the strings.

A Dream Within a Dream

TAKE this kiss upon the brow!
And, in parting from you now,
This much let me avow—

You are not wrong, who deem
That my days have been a dream;
Yet if hope has flown away
In a night, or in a day,
In a vision, or in none,
Is it therefore the less *gone?*
All that we see or seem
Is but a dream within a dream.

I stand amid the roar
Of a surf-tormented shore,
And I hold within my hand
Grains of the golden sand—
How few! yet how they creep
Through my fingers to the deep,
While I weep—while I weep!
O God! can I not grasp
Them with a tighter clasp?
O God! can I not save
One from the pitiless wave?
Is *all* that we see or seem
But a dream within a dream?

Lenore

AH, broken is the golden bowl! the spirit flown forever!
Let the bell toll!—a saintly soul floats on the Stygian river,
And, Guy De Vere, hast *thou* no tear?—weep now or never more!
See! on yon drear and rigid bier low lies thy love, Lenore!
Come! let the burial rite be read—the funeral song be sung!—
An anthem for the queenliest dead that ever died so young—
A dirge for her the doubly dead in that she died so young.

"Wretches! ye loved her for her wealth and hated her for her pride,
And when she fell in feeble health, ye blessed her—that she died!
How *shall* the ritual, then, be read?—the requiem how be sung
By you—by yours, the evil eye,—by yours, the slanderous tongue
That did to death the inocence that died, and died so young?"

Peccavimus; but rave not thus! and let a Sabbath song
Go up to God so solemnly the dead may feel no wrong!

The sweet Lenore hath "gone before," with Hope, that flew beside,
Leaving thee wild for the dear child that should have been thy
  bride—
For her, the fair and *debonair,* that now so lowly lies,
The life upon her yellow hair but not within her eyes—
The life still there, upon her hair—the death upon her eyes.

'Avaunt! tonight my heart is light. No dirge will I upraise.
But waft the angel on her flight with a pæan of old days!
Let *no* bell toll!—lest her sweet soul, amid its hallowed mirth,
Should catch the note, as it doth float up from the damnèd Earth.
To friends above, from fiends below, the indignant ghost is riven—
From Hell unto a high estate far up within the Heaven—
From grief and groan, to a golden throne, beside the King of
  Heaven."

Dream-Land

BY a route obscure and lonely,
  Haunted by ill angels only,
Where an Eidolon, named NIGHT,
On a black throne reigns upright,
I have reached these lands but newly
From an ultimate dim Thule—
From a wild weird clime that lieth, sublime,
    Out of SPACE—out of TIME.

Bottomless vales and boundless floods,
And chasms, and caves, and Titan woods,
With forms that no man can discover
For the tears that drip all over;
Mountains toppling evermore
Into seas without a shore;
Seas that restlessly aspire,
Surging, unto skies of fire;
Lakes that endlessly outspread
Their lone waters—lone and dead,—
Their still waters—still and chilly
With the snows of the lolling lily.

By the lakes that thus outspread
Their lone waters, lone and dead,—

Their sad waters, sad and chilly
With the snows of the lolling lily,—
By the mountains—near the river
Murmuring lowly, murmuring ever,—
By the grey woods,—by the swamp
Where the toad and the newt encamp,—
By the dismal tarns and pools
    Where dwell the Ghouls,—
By each spot the most unholy—
In each nook most melancholy,—
There the traveller meets, aghast,
Sheeted Memories of the Past—
Shrouded forms that start and sigh
As they pass the wanderer by—
White-robed forms of friends long given,
In agony, to the Earth—and **Heaven.**

For the heart whose woes are legion
'Tis a peaceful, soothing region—
For the spirit that walks in shadow
'Tis—oh 'tis an Eldorado!
But the traveller, travelling through it,
May not—dare not openly view it;
Never its mysteries are exposed
To the weak human eye unclosed;
So wills its King, who hath forbid
The uplifting of the fringèd lid;
And thus the sad Soul that here passes
Beholds it but through darkened glasses.

By a route obscure and lonely,
Haunted by ill angels only,
Where an Eidolon, named NIGHT,
On a black throne reigns upright,
I have wandered home but newly
From this ultimate dim Thule.

For Annie

THANK Heaven! the crisis—
    The danger is past,
And the lingering illness
    Is over at last—
And the fever called "Living"
    Is conquered at last.

Sadly, I know
    I am shorn of my strength,
And no muscle I move
    As I lie at full length—
But no matter!—I feel
    I am better at length.

And I rest so composedly
    Now, in my bed,
That any beholder
    Might fancy me dead—
Might start at beholding me,
    Thinking me dead.

The moaning and groaning,
    The sighing and sobbing,
Are quieted now,
    With that horrible throbbing
At heart:—ah that horrible,
    Horrible throbbing!

The sickness—the nausea—
    The pitiless pain—
Have ceased with the fever
    That maddened my brain—
With the fever called "Living"
    That burned in my brain.

And oh! of all tortures
    That torture the worst
Has abated—the terrible
    Torture of thirst

For the napthaline river
    Of Passion accurst:—
I have drunk of a water
    That quenches all thirst:—

Of a water that flows,
    With a lullaby sound,
From a spring but a very few
    Feet under ground—
From a cavern not very far
    Down under ground.

And ah! let it never
    Be foolishly said
That my room it is gloomy
    And narrow my bed;
For a man never slept
    In a different bed—
And, to sleep, you must slumber
    In just such a bed.

My tantalized spirit
    Here blandly reposes,
Forgetting, or never
    Regretting, its roses—
Its old agitations
    Of myrtles and roses:

For now, while so quietly
    Lying, it fancies
A holier odor
    About it, of pansies—
A rosemary odor,
    Commingled with pansies—
With rue and the beautiful
    Puritan pansies.

And so it lies happily,
    Bathing in many
A dream of the truth
    And the beauty of Annie—
Drowned in a bath
    Of the tresses of Annie.

She tenderly kissed me,
    She fondly caressed,
And then I fell gently
    To sleep on her breast—
Deeply to sleep
    From the heaven of her breast.

When the light was extinguished,
    She covered me warm,
And she prayed to the angels
    To keep me from harm—
To the queen of the angels
    To shield me from harm.

And I lie so composedly,
    Now, in my bed,
(Knowing her love)
    That you fancy me dead—
And I rest so contentedly,
    Now, in my bed,
(With her love at my breast)
    That you fancy me dead—
That you shudder to look at me,
    Thinking me dead:—

But my heart it is brighter
    Than all of the many
Stars of the sky,
    For it sparkles with Annie—
It glows with the light
    Of the love of my Annie—
With the thought of the light
    Of the eyes of my Annie.

EDWARD COATE PINKNEY

A Serenade

LOOK out upon the stars, my love,
    And shame them with thine eyes,
On which, than on the lights above,
    There hang more destinies.
Night's beauty is the harmony
    Of blending shades and light;
Then, lady, up,—look out, and be
    A sister to the night!

Sleep not! thine image wakes for aye
    Within my watching breast:
Sleep not! from her soft sleep should fly
    Who robs all hearts of rest.
Nay, lady, from thy slumbers break,
    And make this darkness gay
With looks, whose brightness well might make
    Of darker nights a day.

Votive Song

I BURN no incense, hang no wreath,
    On this thine early tomb:
Such cannot cheer the place of death,
    But only mock its gloom.
Here odorous smoke and breathing flower
    No grateful influence shed;
They lose their perfume and their power,
    When offered to the dead.

And if, as is the Afghan's creed,
    The spirit may return,
A disembodied sense to feed,
    On fragrance, near its urn,—

It is enough that she, whom thou
　　Didst love in living years,
Sits desolate beside it now,
　　And fall these heavy tears.

T. H. CHIVERS

Avalon

DEATH'S pale cold orb has turned to an eclipse
　　My Son of Love!
The worms are feeding on thy lily-lips,
　　My milk-white Dove!
Pale purple tinges thy soft finger-tips!
While nectar thy pure soul in glory sips,
As Death's cold frost mine own forever nips!
　　　　Where thou art lying
　　　　Beside the beautiful undying
In the Valley of the pausing of the Moon,
Oh! Avalon! my son! my son!

Wake up, oh! Avalon! my son! my son!
　　And come from Death!
Heave off the clod that lies so heavy on
　　Thy breast beneath
In that cold grave, my more than Precious One!
And come to me! for I am here alone—
With none to comfort me!—my hopes are gone
　　　　Where thou art lying
　　　　Beside the beautiful undying
In the Valley of the pausing of the Moon,
Oh! Avalon! my son! my son!

Forever more must I, on this damp sod,
　　Renew and keep
My Covenant of Sorrows with my God,
　　And weep, weep, weep!
Writhing in pain beneath Death's iron rod!

Till I shall go to that Divine Abode—
Treading the path that thy dear feet have trod—
    Where thou art lying
    Beside the beautiful undying
In the Valley of the pausing of the Moon,
Oh! Avalon! my son! my son!

Oh! precious Saviour! gracious heavenly Lord!
    Refresh my soul!
Here, with the healings of thy heavenly Word,
  Make my heart whole!
My little Lambs are scattered now abroad
In Death's dark Valley, where they bleat unheard!
Dear Shepherd! give their Shepherd his reward
    Where they are lying
    Beside the beautiful undying
In the Valley of the pausing of the Moon,
With Avalon! my son! my son!

For thou didst tread with fire-ensandaled feet,
  Star-crowned, forgiven,
The burning diapason of the stars so sweet,
  To God in Heaven!
And, walking on the sapphire-paven street,
Didst take upon the highest Sill thy seat—
Waiting in glory there my soul to meet,
    When I am lying
    Beside the beautiful undying
In the Valley of the pausing of the Moon,
Oh! Avalon! my son! my son!

Thou wert my Micro-Uranos below—
  My Little Heaven!
My Micro-Cosmos in this world of wo,
  From morn till even!
A living Lyre of God who charmed me so
With thy sweet songs, that I did seem to go
Out of this world where thou art shining now,
    But without lying
    Beside the beautiful undying
In the Valley of the pausing of the Moon,
Oh! Avalon! my son! my son!

Thou wert my son of Melody alway,
    Oh! Child Divine!
Whose golden radiance filled the world with Day!
    For thou didst shine
A lustrous Diadem of Song for aye,
Whose Divertisements, through Heaven's Holyday,
Now ravish Angel's ears—as well they may—
        While I am crying
        Beside the beautiful undying
In the Valley of the pausing of the Moon,
Oh! Avalon! my son! my son!

Thy soul did soar up to the Gates of God,
    Oh! Lark-Like Child!
And through Heaven's Bowers of Bliss, by Angels trod,
    Poured Wood-notes wild!
In emulation of that Bird, which stood,
In solemn silence, listening to thy flood
Of golden Melody deluge the wood
        Where thou art lying
        Beside the beautiful undying
In the Valley of the pausing of the Moon,
Oh! Avalon! my son! my son!

The redolent quintessence of thy tongue,
    Oh! Avalon!
Embowered by Angels Heaven's sweet Bowers among—
    Many in one—
Is gathered from the choicest of the throng,
In an Æonian Hymn forever young,
Thou Philomelian Eclecticist of Song!
        While I am sighing
        Beside the beautiful undying
In the Valley of the pausing of the Moon,
For Avalon! my son! my son!

Thou wert like Taleisin, "full of eyes,"
    Bardling of Love!
My beautiful Divine Eumenides!
    My gentle Dove!
Thou silver Swan of Golden Elegies!
Whose Mendelssohnian Songs now fill the skies!

While I am weeping where my Lily lies!
  Where thou art lying
  Beside the beautiful undying
In the Valley of the pausing of the Moon,
Oh! Avalon! my son! my son!

Kindling the high-uplifted stars at even
  With thy sweet song,
The Angels, on the Sapphire Sills of Heaven,
  In Rapturous throng,
Melted to milder meekness, with the Seven
Bright Lamps of God to glory given,
Leant down to hear thy voice roll up the leven,
  Where thou art lying
  Beside the beautiful undying
In the Valley of the pausing of the Moon,
Oh! Avalon! my son! my son!

Can any thing that Christ has ever said,
  Make my heart whole?
Can less than bringing back the early dead,
  Restore my soul?
No! this alone can make my Heavenly bread—
Christ's Bread of Life brought down from Heaven, instead
Of this sad Song, on which my soul has fed,
  Where thou art lying
  Beside the beautiful undying
In the Valley of the pausing of the Moon,
Oh! Avalon! my son! my son!

Have I not need to weep from Morn till Even
  Far bitterer tears
Than cruel Earth, the unforgiven,
  Through his long years—
Inquisitorial Hell, or strictest Heaven,
Wrung from Christ's bleeding heart when riven?
Thus from one grief unto another driven,
  Where thou art lying
  Beside the beautiful undying
In the Valley of the pausing of the Moon,
Oh! Avalon! my son! my son!

JOHN GREENLEAF WHITTIER

The Eternal Goodness

O FRIENDS! with whom my feet have trod
    The quiet aisles of prayer,
Glad witness to your zeal for God
    And love of man I bear.

I trace your lines of argument;
    Your logic linked and strong
I weigh as one who dreads dissent,
    And fears a doubt as wrong.

But still my human hands are weak
    To hold your iron creeds:
Against the words ye bid me speak
    My heart within me pleads.

Who fathoms the Eternal Thought?
    Who talks of scheme and plan?
The Lord is God! He needeth not
    The poor device of man.

I walk with bare, hushed feet the ground
    Ye tread with boldness shod;
I dare not fix with mete and bound
    The love and power of God.

Ye praise His justice; even such
    His pitying love I deem:
Ye seek a king; I fain would touch
    The robe that hath no seam.

Ye see the curse which overbroods
    A world of pain and loss;
I hear our Lord's beatitudes
    And prayer upon the cross.

More than your schoolmen teach, within
    Myself, alas! I know:
Too dark ye cannot paint the sin,
    Too small the merit show.

I bow my forehead to the dust,
    I veil mine eyes for shame,
And urge, in trembling self-distrust,
    A prayer without a claim.

I see the wrong that round me lies,
    I feel the guilt within;
I hear, with groan and travail-cries,
    The world confess its sin.

Yet, in the maddening maze of things,
    And tossed by storm and flood,
To one fixed trust my spirit clings;
    I know that God is good!

Not mine to look where cherubim
    And seraphs may not see,
But nothing can be good in Him
    Which evil is in me.

The wrong that pains my soul below
    I dare not throne above,
I know not of His hate,—I know
    His goodness and His love.

I dimly guess from blessings known
    Of greater out of sight,
And, with the chastened Psalmist, own
    His judgments too are right.

I long for household voices gone,
    For vanished smiles I long,
But God hath led my dear ones on,
    And He can do no wrong.

I know not what the future hath
    Of marvel or surprise,
Assured alone that life and death
    His mercy underlies.

And if my heart and flesh are weak
    To bear an untried pain,
The bruisèd reed He will not break,
    But strengthen and sustain.

No offering of my own I have,
    Nor works my faith to prove;
I can but give the gifts He gave,
    And plead His love for love.

And so beside the Silent Sea
    I wait the muffled oar;
No harm from Him can come to me
    On ocean or on shore.

I know not where His islands lift
    Their fronded palms in air;
I only know I cannot drift
    Beyond His love and care.

O brothers! if my faith is vain,
    If hopes like these betray,
Pray for me that my feet may gain
    The sure and safer way.

And Thou, O Lord! by whom are seen
    Thy creatures as they be,
Forgive me if too close I lean
    My human heart on Thee!

Ichabod

SO fallen, so lost! the light withdrawn
    Which once he wore!
The glory from his gray hairs gone
    Forevermore!

Revile him not—the Tempter hath
    A snare for all;
And pitying tears, not scorn and wrath,
    Befit his fall.

Oh dumb be passion's stormy rage
　　When he who might
Have lighted up and led his age
　　Falls back in night.

Scorn? would the angels laugh to mark
　　A bright soul driven,
Fiend-goaded, down the endless dark,
　　From hope and heaven?

Let not the land once proud of him
　　Insult him now,
Nor brand with deeper shame his dim,
　　Dishonored brow.

But let its humbled sons, instead,
　　From sea to lake,
A long lament as for the dead
　　In sadness make.

Of all we loved and honored, nought
　　Save power remains—
A fallen angel's pride of thought,
　　Still strong in chains.

All else is gone; from those great eyes
　　The soul has fled:
When faith is lost, when honor dies,
　　The man is dead.

Then pay the reverence of old days
　　To his dead fame;
Walk backward, with averted gaze,
　　And hide the shame.

My Playmate

THE pines were dark on Ramoth hill,
　　Their song was soft and low;
The blossoms in the sweet May wind
　　Were falling like the snow.

The blossoms drifted at our feet,
    The orchard birds sang clear;
The sweetest and the saddest day
    It seemed of all the year.

For, more to me than birds or flowers,
    My playmate left her home,
And took with her the laughing spring,
    The music and the bloom.

She kissed the lips of kith and kin,
    She laid her hand in mine:
What more could ask the bashful boy,
    Who fed her father's kine?

She left us in the bloom of May:
    The constant years told o'er
Their seasons with as sweet May morns,
    But she came back no more.

I walk, with noiseless feet, the round
    Of uneventful years;
Still o'er and o'er I sow the spring
    And reap the autumn ears.

She lives where all the golden year
    Her summer roses blow;
The dusky children of the sun
    Before her come and go.

There haply with her jewelled hands
    She smooths her silken gown—
No more the homespun lap wherein
    I shook the walnuts down.

The wild grapes wait us by the brook,
    The brown nuts on the hill,
And still the May-day flowers make sweet
    The woods of Follymill.

The lilies blossom in the pond,
    The bird builds in the tree,

The dark pines sing on Ramoth hill
The slow song of the sea.

I wonder if she thinks of them,
And how the old time seems;
If ever the pines of Ramoth wood
Are sounding in her dreams.

I see her face, I hear her voice:
Does she remember mine?
And what to her is now the boy
Who fed her father's kine?

What cares she that the orioles build
For other eyes than ours;
That other hands with nuts are filled,
And other laps with flowers?

O playmate in the golden time,
Our mossy seat is green,
Its fringing violets blossom yet,
The old trees o'er it lean.

The winds so sweet with birch and fern
A sweeter memory blow;
And there in spring the veeries sing
The song of long ago.

And still the pines of Ramoth wood
Are moaning like the sea—
The moaning of the sea of change
Between myself and thee!

OLIVER WENDELL HOLMES

The Last Leaf

I SAW him once before,
As he passed by the door,
      And again
The pavement stones resound,
As he totters o'er the ground
      With his cane.

They say that in his prime,
Ere the pruning-knife of Time
      Cut him down,
Not a better man was found
By the Crier on his round
      Through the town.

But now he walks the streets,
And he looks at all he meets
      Sad and wan,
And he shakes his feeble head,
That it seems as if he said,
      "They are gone."

The mossy marbles rest
On the lips that he has prest
      In their bloom,
And the names he loved to hear
Have been carved for many a year
      On the tomb.

My grandmama has said,—
Poor old lady, she is dead
      Long ago,—
That he had a Roman nose,
And his cheek was like a rose
      In the snow;

But now his nose is thin,
And it rests upon his chin
            Like a staff,
And a crook is in his back,
And a melancholy crack
            In his laugh.

I know it is a sin
For me to sit and grin
            At him here;
But the old three-cornered hat,
And the breeches, and all that,
            Are so queer!

And if I should live to be
The last leaf upon the tree,
            In the spring,
Let them smile, as I do now,
At the old forsaken bough
            Where I cling.

----- • • • -----

JAMES RUSSELL LOWELL

----- • • • -----

Hebe

I SAW the twinkle of white feet,
  I saw the flash of robes descending;
Before her ran an influence fleet,
  That bow'd my heart like barley bending.

As, in bare fields, the searching bees
  Pilot to blooms beyond our finding,
It led me on,—by sweet degrees,
  Joy's simple honey-cells unbinding.

Those graces were that seem'd grim fates;
  With nearer love the sky lean'd o'er me;

The long-sought secret's golden gates
On musical hinges swung before me.

I saw the brimm'd bowl in her grasp
Thrilling with godhood; like a lover,
I sprang the proffer'd life to clasp:
The beaker fell, the luck was over.

The earth has drunk the vintage up;
What boots it patch the goblet's splinters?
Can Summer fill the icy cup
Whose treacherous crystal is but Winter's?

O spendthrift haste! Await the gods;
Their nectar crowns the lips of Patience.
Haste scatters on unthankful sods
The immortal gift in vain libations.

Coy Hebe flies from those that woo,
And shuns the hands would seize upon her;
Follow thy life, and she will sue
To pour for thee the cup of honour!

Auspex

MY heart, I cannot still it,
    Nest that had song-birds in it;
And when the last shall go,
The dreary days to fill it,
Instead of lark or linnet,
Shall whirl dead leaves and snow.

Had they been swallows only,
Without the passion stronger
That skyward longs and sings,—
Woe 's me, I shall be lonely
When I can feel no longer
The impatience of their wings!

A moment, sweet delusion,
Like birds the brown leaves hover;

But it will not be long
Before their wild confusion
Fall wavering down to cover
The poet and his song.

St. Michael the Weigher

STOOD the tall Archangel weighing
    All man's dreaming, doing, saying,
All the failure and the pain,
All the triumph and the gain,
In the unimagined years,
Full of hopes, more full of tears,
Since old Adam's hopeless eyes
Backward searched for Paradise,
And, instead, the flame-blade saw
Of inexorable Law.

Waking, I beheld him there,
With his fire-gold, flickering hair,
In his blinding armor stand,
And the scales were in his hand:
Mighty were they, and full well
They could poise both heaven and hell.

"Angel," asked I humbly then,
"Weighest thou the souls of men?
That thine office is, I know."
"Nay," he answered me, "not so;
But I weigh the hope of Man
Since the power of choice began,
In the world, of good or ill."
Then I waited and was still.

In one scale I saw him place
All the glories of our race,
Cups that lit Belshazzar's feast,
Gems, the lightning of the East,
Kublai's sceptre, Cæsar's sword,
Many a poet's golden word,
Many a skill of science, vain
To make men as gods again.

In the other scale he threw
Things regardless, outcast, few,
Martyr-ash, arena sand,
Of St. Francis' cord a strand,
Beechen cups of men whose need
Fasted that the poor might feed,
Disillusions and despairs
Of young saints with grief-grayed hairs,
Broken hearts that brake for Man.

Marvel through my pulses ran
Seeing then the beam divine
Swiftly on this hand decline,
While Earth's splendor and renown
Mounted light as thistle-down.

MARIA WHITE LOWELL

An Opium Fantasy

SOFT hangs the opiate in the brain,
    And lulling soothes the edge of pain,
Till harshest sound, far off or near,
Sings floating in its mellow sphere.

What wakes me from my heavy dream?
    Or am I still asleep?
Those long and soft vibrations seem
    A slumberous charm to keep.

The graceful play, a moment stopt,
    Distance again unrolls,
Like silver balls, that, softly dropt,
    Ring into golden bowls.

I question of the poppies red,
    The fairy flaunting band,

While I, a weed with drooping head,
    Within their phalanx stand:—

"Some airy one, with scarlet cap,
    The name unfold to me
Of this new minstrel who can lap
    Sleep in his melody!"

Bright grew their scarlet-kerchief'd heads,
    As freshening winds had blown,
And from their gently-swaying beds
    They sang in undertone:—

"Oh he is but a little owl,
    The smallest of his kin,
Who sits beneath the midnight's cowl
    And makes this airy din."

"Deceitful tongues of fiery tints!
    Far more than this ye know,
That he is your enchanted prince
    Doom'd as an owl to go;—

"Nor his fond play for years hath stopt,
    But nightly he unrolls
His silver balls, that, softly dropt,
    Ring into golden bowls."

RALPH WALDO EMERSON

The Rhodora

ON BEING ASKED, WHENCE IS THE FLOWER?

IN May, when sea-winds pierced our solitudes,
  I found the fresh Rhodora in the woods,
Spreading its leafless blooms in a damp nook,
To please the desert and the sluggish brook.

The purple petals, fallen in the pool,
Made the black water with their beauty gay;
Here might the red-bird come his plumes to cool,
And court the flower that cheapens his array.
Rhodora! if the sages ask thee why
This charm is wasted on the earth and sky,
Tell them, dear, that if eyes were made for seeing,
Then Beauty is its own excuse for being:
Why thou wert there, O rival of the rose!
I never thought to ask, I never knew;
But, in my simple ignorance, suppose
The self-same Power that brought me there brought you.

Compensation

WHY should I keep holiday
　　When other men have none?
Why but because, when these are gay,
　　I sit and mourn alone?

And why, when mirth unseals all tongues,
　　Should mine alone be dumb?
Ah! late I spoke to silent throngs,
　　And now their hour is come.

Give All to Love

GIVE all to love;
　Obey thy heart;
Friends, kindred, days,
Estate, good-fame,
Plans, credit, and the Muse,—
Nothing refuse.

'Tis a brave master;
Let it have scope:
Follow it utterly,
Hope beyond hope:
High and more high
It dives into noon,

With wing unspent,
Untold intent;
But it is a god,
Knows its own path,
And the outlets of the sky.

It was never for the mean;
It requireth courage stout,
Souls above doubt,
Valor unbending;
It will reward,—
They shall return
More than they were,
And ever ascending

Leave all for love;
Yet, hear me, yet,
One word more thy heart behoved,
One pulse more of firm endeavor,—
Keep thee today
Tomorrow, forever,
Free as an Arab
Of thy beloved.

Cling with life to the maid;
But when the surprise,
First vague shadow of surmise
Flits across her bosom young
Of a joy apart from thee,
Free be she, fancy-free;
Nor thou detain her vesture's hem,
Nor the palest rose she flung
From her summer diadem.

Though thou loved her as thyself,
As a self of purer clay,
Though her parting dims the day,
Stealing grace from all alive;
Heartily know,
When half-gods go,
The gods arrive.

Bacchus

BRING me wine, but wine which never grew
　　In the belly of the grape,
Or grew on vine whose tap-roots, reaching through
Under the Andes to the Cape,
Suffer no savor of the earth to scape.

Let its grapes the morn salute
From a nocturnal root,
Which feels the acrid juice
Of Styx and Erebus;
And turns the woe of Night,
By its own craft, to a more rich delight.

We buy ashes for bread;
We buy diluted wine;
Give me of the true,—
Whose ample leaves and tendrils curled
Among the silver hills of heaven,
Draw everlasting dew;
Wine of wine,
Blood of the world,
Form of forms, and mould of statures,
That I intoxicated,
And by the draught assimilated,
May float at pleasure through all natures;
The bird-language rightly spell,
And that which roses say so well.

Wine that is shed
Like the torrents of the sun
Up the horizon walls,
Or like the Atlantic streams, which run
When the South Sea calls.

Water and bread,
Food which needs no transmuting,
Rainbow-flowering, wisdom-fruiting,
Wine which is already man,
Food which teach and reason can.

Wine which Music is,—
Music and wine are one,—
That I, drinking this,
Shall hear far Chaos talk with me;
Kings unborn shall walk with me;
And the poor grass shall plot and plan
What it will do when it is man.
Quickened so, will I unlock
Every crypt of every rock.

I thank the joyful juice
For all I know;—
Winds of remembering
Of the ancient being blow,
And seeming-solid walls of use
Open and flow.

Pour, Bacchus! the remembering wine;
Retrieve the loss of me and mine!
Vine for vine be antidote,
And the grape requite the lote!
Haste to cure the old despair,—
Reason in Nature's lotus drenched,
The memory of ages quenched;
Give them again to shine;
Let wine repair what this undid;
And where the infection slid,
A dazzling memory revive;
Refresh the faded tints,
Recut the aged prints,
And write my old adventures with the pen
Which on the first day drew,
Upon the tablets blue,
The dancing Pleiads and eternal men.

Brahma

IF the red slayer think he slays,
  Or if the slain think he is slain,
They know not well the subtle ways
  I keep, and pass, and turn again.

Far or forgot to me is near;
    Shadow and sunlight are the same;
The vanquished gods to me appear;
    And one to me are shame and fame.

They reckon ill who leave me out;
    When me they fly, I am the wings;
I am the doubter and the doubt,
    And I the hymn the Brahmin sings.

The strong gods pine for my abode,
    And pine in vain the sacred Seven;
But thou, meek lover of the good!
    Find me, and turn thy back on heaven.

Merops

WHAT care I, so they stand the same,—
    Things of the heavenly mind,—
How long the power to give them name
    Tarries yet behind?

Thus far to-day your favors reach,
    O fair, appeasing presences!
Ye taught my lips a single speech,
    And a thousand silences.

Space grants beyond his fated road
    No inch to the god of day;
And copious language still bestowed
    One word, no more, to say.

Uriel

IT fell in the ancient periods
    Which the brooding soul surveys,
Or ever the wild Time coined itself
    Into calendar months and days.

This was the lapse of Uriel,
Which in Paradise befell.
Once, among the Pleiads walking,
Seyd overhead the young gods talking;
And the treason, too long pent,
To his ears was evident.
The young deities discussed
Laws of form, and metre just,
Orb, quintessence, and sunbeams,
What subsisteth, and what seems.
One, with low tones that decide,
And doubt and reverend use defied,
With a look that solved the sphere,
And stirred the devils everywhere,
Gave his sentiment divine
Against the being of a line.
"Line in nature is not found;
Unit and universe are round;
In vain produced, all rays return;
Evil will bless, and ice will burn."
As Uriel spoke with piercing eye,
A shudder ran around the sky;
The stern old war-gods shook their heads,
The seraphs frowned from myrtle-beds;
Seemed to the holy festival
The rash word boded ill to all;
The balance-beam of Fate was bent;
The bounds of good and ill were rent;
Strong Hades could not keep his own,
But all slid to confusion.

A sad self-knowledge, withering, fell
On the beauty of Uriel;
In heaven once eminent, the god
Withdrew, that hour, into his cloud;
Whether doomed to long gyration
In the sea of generation,
Or by knowledge grown too bright
To hit the nerve of feebler sight.
Straightway, a forgetting wind
Stole over the celestial kind,

And their lips the secret kept,
If in ashes and fire-seed slept.
But now and then, truth-speaking things
Shamed the angels' veiling wings;
And, shrilling from the solar course,
Or from fruit of chemic force,
Procession of a soul in matter,
Or the speeding change of water,
Or out of the good of evil born,
Came Uriel's voice of cherub scorn,
And a blush tinged the upper sky,
And the gods shook, they knew not why.

Days

DAUGHTERS of Time, the hypocritic Days,
Muffled and dumb like barefoot dervishes,
And marching single in an endless file,
Bring diadems and fagots in their hands.
To each they offer gifts after his will,
Bread, kingdoms, stars, and sky that holds them all.
I, in my pleached garden, watched the pomp,
Forgot my morning wishes, hastily
Took a few herbs and apples, and the Day
Turned and departed silent. I, too late,
Under her solemn fillet saw the scorn.

Character

THE sun set, but set not his hope:
Stars rose; his faith was earlier up:
Fixed on the enormous galaxy,
Deeper and older seemed his eye;
And matched his sufferance sublime
The taciturnity of time.
He spoke, and words more soft than rain
Brought the Age of Gold again:
His action won such reverence sweet
As hid all measure of the feat.

HENRY DAVID THOREAU

Inspiration

IF with light head erect I sing,
  Though all the Muses lend their force,
From my poor love of anything,
The verse is weak and shallow as its source.

But if with bended neck I grope
Listening behind me for my wit,
With faith superior to hope,
More anxious to keep back than forward it,—

Making my soul accomplice there
Unto the flame my heart hath lit,
Then will the verse forever wear,—
Time cannot bend the line which God has writ.

I hearing get, who had but ears,
And sight, who had but eyes before;
I moments live, who lived for years,
And truth discern, who knew but learning's lore.

Now chiefly is my natal hour,
And only now my prime of life;
Of manhood's strength it is the flower,
'T is peace's end, and war's beginning strife.

It comes in summer's broadest noon,
By a gray wall, or some chance place,
Unseasoning time, insulting June,
And vexing day with its presuming face.

I will not doubt the love untold
Which not my worth nor want hath bought,
Which wooed me young, and woos me old,
And to this evening hath me brought.

Smoke

LIGHT-WINGED Smoke! Icarian bird,
　　Melting thy pinions in thy upward flight,
Lark without song, and messenger of dawn,
Circling above the hamlets as thy nest;
Or else, departing dream, and shadowy form
Of midnight vision, gathering up thy skirts;
By night star-veiling, and by day
Darkening the light and blotting out the sun;
Go thou my incense upward from this hearth,
And ask the gods to pardon this clear flame.

JULIA WARD HOWE

The Battle-Hymn of the Republic

MINE eyes have seen the glory of the coming of the Lord;
　　He is trampling out the vintage where the grapes of wrath
　　　　are stored;
He hath loosed the fateful lightning of His terrible swift sword;
　　His truth is marching on.

I have seen Him in the watch-fires of a hundred circling camps;
They have builded Him an altar in the evening dews and damps;
I can read His righteous sentence by the dim and flaring lamps;
　　His day is marching on.

I have read a fiery gospel, writ in burnished rows of steel:
"As ye deal with my contemners, so with you my grace shall deal;
Let the Hero, born of woman, crush the serpent with his heel,
　　Since God is marching on."

He has sounded forth the trumpet that shall never call retreat;
He is sifting out the hearts of men before His judgment-seat:
Oh, be swift, my soul, to answer Him! be jubilant, my feet!
　　Our God is marching on.

In the beauty of the lilies Christ was born across the sea,
With a glory in His bosom that transfigures you and me:
As He died to make men holy, let us die to make men free,
    While God is marching on.

HENRY WADSWORTH LONGFELLOW

Hymn to the Night

'Ασπασίη, τρίλλιστος

I HEARD the trailing garments of the Night
    Sweep through her marble halls;
I saw her sable skirts all fringed with light
    From the celestial walls.

I felt her presence, by its spell of might,
    Stoop o'er me from above—
The calm, majestic presence of the Night,
    As of the one I love.

I heard the sounds of sorrow and delight,
    The manifold, soft chimes,
That fill the haunted chambers of the Night,
    Like some old poet's rhymes.

From the cool cisterns of the midnight air
    My spirit drank repose;
The fountain of perpetual peace flows there,
    From those deep cisterns flows.

O holy Night! from thee I learn to bear
    What man has borne before;
Thou layest thy finger on the lips of Care,
    And they complain no more.

Peace! Peace! Orestes-like I breathe this prayer;
    Descend with broad-winged flight,
The welcome, the thrice-prayed for, the most fair,
    The best-beloved Night!

My Lost Youth

OFTEN I think of the beautiful town
    That is seated by the sea,
Often in thought go up and down
The pleasant streets of that dear old town,
    And my youth comes back to me.
        And a verse of a Lapland song
        Is haunting my memory still:
    "A boy's will is the wind's will,
And the thoughts of youth are long, long thoughts."

I can see the shadowy lines of its trees,
    And catch, in sudden gleams,
The sheen of the far-surrounding seas,
And islands that were the Hesperides
    Of all my boyish dreams.
        And the burden of that old song,
        It murmurs and whispers still:
    "A boy's will is the wind's will,
And the thoughts of youth are long, long thoughts."

I remember the black wharves and the slips,
    And the sea-tides tossing free,
And Spanish sailors with bearded lips,
And the beauty and mystery of the ships,
    And the magic of the sea.
        And the voice of that wayward song
        Is singing and saying still:
    "A boy's will is the wind's will,
And the thoughts of youth are long, long thoughts."

I remember the bulwarks by the shore,
    And the fort upon the hill;
The sunrise gun, with its hollow roar,
The drum-beat repeated o'er and o'er,
    And the bugle wild and shrill.
        And the music of that old song
        Throbs in my memory still:
    "A boy's will is the wind's will,
And the thoughts of youth are long, long, thoughts."

I remember the sea-fight far away,
  How it thundered o'er the tide!
And the dead captains, as they lay
In their graves, o'erlooking the tranquil bay,
  Where they in battle died.
      And the sound of that mournful song
      Goes through me with a thrill:
    "A boy's will is the wind's will,
And the thoughts of youth are long, long thoughts."

I can see the breezy dome of groves,
  The shadows of Deering's Woods;
And the friendships old and the early loves
Come back with a sabbath sound, as of doves
  In quiet neighborhoods.
      And the verse of that sweet old song,
      It flutters and murmurs still:
    "A boy's will is the wind's will,
And the thoughts of youth are long, long thoughts."

I remember the gleams and glooms that dart
  Across the school-boy's brain;
The song and the silence in the heart,
That in part are prophecies and in part
  Are longings wild and vain.
      And the voice of that fitful song
      Sings on, and is never still:
    "A boy's will is the wind's will,
And the thoughts of youth are long, long thoughts."

There are things of which I may not speak;
  There are dreams that cannot die;
There are thoughts that make the strong heart weak,
And bring a pallor into the cheek
  And a mist before the eye.
      And the words of that fatal song
      Come over me like a chill:
    "A boy's will is the wind's will,
And the thoughts of youth are long, long thoughts."

Strange to me now are the forms I meet
  When I visit the dear old town;

But the native air is pure and sweet,
And the trees that o'ershadow each well-known street,
   As they balance up and down,
     Are singing the beautiful song,
     Are sighing and whispering still:
"A boy's will is the wind's will,
And the thoughts of youth are long, long thoughts."

And Deering's Woods are fresh and fair;
   And with joy that is almost pain
My heart goes back to wander there,
And among the dreams of the days that were
   I find my lost youth again.
     And the strange and beautiful song,
     The groves are repeating it still:
"A boy's will is the wind's will,
And the thoughts of youth are long, long thoughts."

The Three Silences of Molinos

TO JOHN GREENLEAF WHITTIER

THREE Silences there are: the first of speech,
   The second of desire, the third of thought;
This is the lore a Spanish monk, distraught
With dreams and visions, was the first to teach.
These Silences, commingling each with each,
Made up the perfect Silence that he sought
And prayed for, and wherein at times he caught
Mysterious sounds from realms beyond our reach.
O thou, whose daily life anticipates
The life to come, and in whose thought and word
The spiritual world preponderates,
Hermit of Amesbury! thou too hast heard
Voices and melodies from beyond the gates,
And speakest only when thy soul is stirred!

The Sound of the Sea

THE sea awoke at midnight from its sleep,
   And round the pebbly beaches far and wide
I heard the first wave of the rising tide
Rush onward with uninterrupted sweep;
A voice out of the silence of the deep,
A sound mysteriously multiplied
As of a cataract from the mountain's side,
Or roar of winds upon a wooded steep.
So comes to us at times, from the unknown
And inaccessible solitudes of being,
The rushing of the sea-tides of the soul;
And inspirations, that we deem our own,
Are some divine foreshadowing and foreseeing
Of things beyond our reason or control.

Divina Commedia

I

OFT have I seen at some cathedral door
   A laborer, pausing in the dust and heat,
   Lay down his burden, and with reverent feet
   Enter, and cross himself, and on the floor
Kneel to repeat his paternoster o'er;
   Far off the noises of the world retreat;
   The loud vociferations of the street
   Become an undistinguishable roar.
So, as I enter here from day to day,
   And leave my burden at this minster gate,
   Kneeling in prayer, and not ashamed to pray,
The tumult of the time disconsolate
   To inarticulate murmurs dies away,
   While the eternal ages watch and wait.

II

How strange the sculptures that adorn these towers!
   This crowd of statues, in whose folded sleeves

Birds build their nests; while canopied with leaves
　　Parvis and portal bloom like trellised bowers,
And the vast minster seems a cross of flowers!
　　But fiends and dragons of the gargoyled eaves
　　Watch the dead Christ between the living thieves,
　　And, underneath, the traitor Judas lowers!
Ah! from what agonies of heart and brain,
　　What exultations trampling on despair,
　　What tenderness, what tears, what hate of wrong,
What passionate outcry of a soul in pain,
　　Uprose this poem of the earth and air,
　　This mediæval miracle of song!

III

I enter, and I see thee in the gloom
　　Of the long aisles, O poet saturnine!
　　And strive to make my steps keep pace with thine.
The air is filled with some unknown perfume;
　　The congregation of the dead make room
　　For thee to pass; the votive tapers shine;
　　Like rooks that haunt Ravenna's groves of pine
　　The hovering echoes fly from tomb to tomb.
From the confessionals I hear arise
　　Rehearsals of forgotten tragedies,
　　And lamentations from the crypts below;
And then a voice celestial that begins
　　With the pathetic words, "Although your sins
　　As scarlet be," and ends with "as the snow."

IV

With snow-white veil and garments as of flame,
　　She stands before thee, who so long ago
　　Filled thy young heart with passion and the woe
　　From which thy song and all its splendors came;
And while with stern rebuke she speaks thy name,
　　The ice about thy heart melts as the snow
　　On the mountain heights, and in swift overflow
　　Comes gushing from thy lips in sobs of shame.
Thou makest full confession; and a gleam,
　　As of the dawn on some dark forest cast,
　　Seems on thy lifted forehead to increase;

Lethe and Eunoë—the remembered dream
    And the forgotten sorrow—bring at last
    That perfect pardon which is perfect peace.

V

I lift mine eyes, and all the windows blaze
    With forms of Saints and holy men who died,
    Here martyred and hereafter glorified;
    And the great Rose upon its leaves displays
Christ's Triumph, and the angelic roundelays,
    With splendor upon splendor multiplied;
    And Beatrice again at Dante's side
    No more rebukes, but smiles her words of praise.
And then the organ sounds, and unseen choirs
    Sing the old Latin hymns of peace and love
    And benedictions of the Holy Ghost;
And the melodious bells among the spires
    O'er all the house-tops and through heaven above
    Proclaim the elevation of the Host!

VI

O star of morning and of liberty!
    O bringer of the light, whose splendor shines
    Above the darkness of the Apennines,
    Forerunner of the day that is to be!
The voices of the city and the sea,
    The voices of the mountains and the pines,
    Repeat thy song, till the familiar lines
    Are footpaths for the thought of Italy!
Thy flame is blown abroad from all the heights,
    Through all the nations, and a sound is heard,
    As of a mighty wind, and men devout,
Strangers of Rome, and the new proselytes,
    In their own language hear thy wondrous word,
    And many are amazed and many doubt.

HERMAN MELVILLE

L'Envoi

THE RETURN OF THE SIRE DE NESLE
A.D. 16—

MY towers at last! These rovings end,
  Their thirst is slaked in larger dearth:
The yearning infinite recoils,
  For terrible is earth.

Kaf thrusts his snouted crags through fog:
Araxes swells beyond his span,
And knowledge poured by pilgrimage
Overflows the banks of man.

But thou, my stay, thy lasting love
One lonely good, let this but be!
Weary to view the wide world's swarm,
  But blest to fold but thee.

Southern Cross

EMBLAZONED bleak in austral skies—
  A heaven remote, whose starry swarm
Like Science lights but cannot warm—
Translated Cross, hast thou withdrawn,
Dim paling too at every dawn,
With symbols vain once counted wise,
And gods declined to heraldries?

Estranged, estranged: can friend prove so?
Aloft, aloof, a frigid sign:
How far removed, thou Tree divine,
Whose tender fruit did reach so low—

Love apples of New-Paradise!
About the wide Australian sea
The planted nations yet to be—

When, ages hence, they lift their eyes,
Tell, what shall they retain of thee?
But class thee with Orion's sword?
In constellations unadored,
Christ and the Giant equal prize?
The atheist cycles—*must* they be?
Fomentors as forefathers we?

Monody

TO have known him, to have loved him
    After loneness long;
And then to be estranged in life,
    And neither in the wrong;
And now for death to set his seal—
    Ease me, a little ease, my song!

By wintry hills his hermit-mound
    The sheeted snow-drifts drape,
And houseless there the snow-bird flits
    Beneath the fir-trees' crape;
Glazed now with ice the cloistral vine
    That hid the shyest grape.

Of Rama

THAT Rama whom the Indian sung—
    A god he was, but knew it not;
Hence vainly puzzled at the wrong
Misplacing him in human lot.
Curtailment of his right he bare
Rather than wrangle; but no less
Was taunted for his tameness there.
A fugitive without redress,
He never the Holy Spirit grieved,

Nor the divine in him bereaved,
Though what that was he might not guess.

Live they who, like to Rama, led
Unspotted from the world aside,
Like Rama are discredited—
Like him, in outlawry abide?
May life and fable so agree?—
The innocent if lawless elf,
Ethereal in virginity,
Retains the consciousness of self.
Though black frost nip, though white frost chill,
Nor white frost nor the black may kill
The patient root, the vernal sense
Surviving hard experience
As grass the winter. Even that curse
Which is the wormwood mixed with gall—
Better dependent on the worse—
Divine upon the animal—
That can not make such natures fall.
Though yielding easy rein, indeed,
To impulse which the fibers breed,
Nor quarreling with indolence;
Shall these the cup of grief dispense
Deliberate to any heart?
Not craft they know, nor envy's smart.
Theirs be the thoughts that dive and skim,
Theirs the spiced tears that overbrim,
And theirs the dimple and the lightsome whim.

The Night-March

WITH banners furled, the clarions mute,
An army passes in the night;
And beaming spears and helms salute
The dark with bright.

In silence deep the legions stream,
With open ranks, in order true;
Over boundless plains they stream and gleam—
No chief in view!

Afar, in twinkling distance lost,
    (So legends tell) he lonely wends
And back through all that shining host
    His mandate sends.

Lone Founts

THOUGH fast youth's glorious fable flies,
    View not the world with worldling's eyes;
Nor turn with weather of the time.
Foreclose the coming of surprise:
Stand where Posterity shall stand;
Stand where the Ancients stood before,
And, dipping in lone founts thy hand,
Drink of the never-varying lore:
Wise once, and wise thence evermore.

WALT WHITMAN

The Last Invocation

AT the last, tenderly,
    From the walls of the powerful, fortressed house,
From the clasp of the knitted locks—from the keep of the well-closed
    doors.
Let me be wafted.

Let me glide noiselessly forth;
With the key of softness unlock the locks—with a whisper
Set ope the doors, O Soul!

      Tenderly! be not impatient!
      (Strong is your hold, O mortal flesh!
      Strong is your hold, O love.)

Out of the Cradle Endlessly Rocking

OUT of the cradle endlessly rocking,
  Out of the mocking-bird's throat, the musical shuttle,
Out of the Ninth-month midnight,
Over the sterile sands and the fields beyond, where the child leaving
  his bed wandered alone, bareheaded, barefoot,
Down from the showered halo,
Up from the mystic play of shadows twining and twisting as if they
  were alive,
Out from the patches of briers and blackberries,
From the memories of the bird that chanted to me,
From your memories, sad brother, from the fitful risings and fallings
  I heard,
From under that yellow half-moon late-risen and swollen as if with
  tears,
From those beginning notes of yearning and love there in the mist,
From the thousand responses of my heart never to cease.
From the myriad thence-aroused words,
From the word stronger and more delicious than any,
From such as now they start the scene revisiting,
As a flock, twittering, rising, or overhead passing,
Borne hither, ere all eludes me, hurriedly,
A man, yet by these tears a little boy again,
Throwing myself on the sand, confronting the waves,
I, chanter of pains and joys, uniter of here and hereafter,
Taking all hints to use them, but swiftly leaping beyond them,
A reminiscence sing.
Once Paumanok,
When the lilac-scent was in the air and Fifth-month grass was
  growing,
Up this seashore in some briers,
Two feathered guests from Alabama, two together,
And their nest, and four light-green eggs spotted with brown,
And every day the he-bird to and fro near at hand,
And every day the she-bird crouched on her nest, silent, with bright
  eyes,
And every day I, a curious boy, never too close, never disturbing
  them,
Cautiously peering, absorbing, translating.

Shine! shine! shine!
Pour down your warmth, great sun!
While we bask, we two together.

Two together!
Winds blow south, or winds blow north,
Day come white, or night come black,
Home, or rivers and mountains from home,
Singing all time, minding no time,
While we two keep together.

Till of a sudden,
Maybe killed, unknown to her mate,
One forenoon the she-bird crouched not on the nest,
Nor returned that afternoon, nor the next,
Nor ever appeared again.

And thenceforward all summer in the sound of the sea,
And at night under the full of the moon in calmer weather,
Over the hoarse surging of the sea,
Or flitting from brier to brier by day,
I saw, I heard at intervals the remaining one, the he-bird,
The solitary guest from Alabama.

Blow! blow! blow!
Blow up sea-winds along Paumanok's shore;
I wait and I wait till you blow my mate to me.

Yes, when the stars glistened,
All night long on the prong of a moss-scalloped stake,
Down almost amid the slapping waves,
Sat the lone singer, wonderful, causing tears.

He called on his mate,
He poured forth the meanings which I of all men know.

Yes, my brother, I know,—
The rest might not, but I have treasured every note,
For more than once dimly down to the beach gliding,
Silent, avoiding the moonbeams, blending myself with the shadows,
Recalling now the obscure shapes, the echoes, the sounds and sights
     after their sorts,

The white arms out in the breakers tirelessly tossing,
I, with bare feet, a child, the wind wafting my hair,
Listened long and long.

Listened to keep, to sing, now translating the notes,
Following you, my brother.

Soothe! soothe! soothe!
Close on its wave soothes the wave behind,
And again another behind embracing and lapping, every one close,
But my love soothes not me, not me.

Low hangs the moon, it rose late,
It is lagging—O I think it is heavy with love, with love.

O madly the sea pushes upon the land,
With love, with love.

O night! do I not see my love fluttering out among the breakers?
What is that little black thing I see there in the white?

Loud! loud! loud!
Loud I call to you, my love!

High and clear I shoot my voice over the waves,
Surely you must know who is here, is here,
You must know who I am, my love.

Low-hanging moon!
What is that dusky spot in your brown yellow?
O it is the shape, the shape of my mate!
O moon, do not keep her from me any longer.

Land! land! O land!
Whichever way I turn, O, I think you could give me my mate back
again if you only would,
For I am almost sure I see her dimly whichever way I look.

O rising stars!
Perhaps the one I want so much will rise, will rise with some of you.

O throat! O trembling throat!
Sound clearer through the atmosphere!
Pierce the woods, the earth,
Somewhere listening to catch you must be the one I want.

Shake out carols!
Solitary here, the night's carols!
Carols of lonesome love! death's carols!
Carols under that lagging, yellow, waning moon!
O under that moon where she droops almost down into the sea!
O reckless despairing carols!

But soft! sink low!
Soft! let me just murmur,
And do you wait a moment, you husky-noised sea,
For somewhere I believe I heard my mate responding to me,
So faint, I must be still, be still to listen,
But not altogether still, for then she might not come immediately
    to me.

Hither, my love!
Here I am! here!
With this just-sustained note I announce myself to you,
This gentle call is for you, my love, for you.

Do not be decoyed elsewhere:
That is the whistle of the wind, it is not my voice,
That is the fluttering, the fluttering of the spray,
Those are the shadows of leaves.

O darkness! O in vain!
O I am very sick and sorrowful.
O brown halo in the sky near the moon, drooping upon the sea!
O troubled reflection in the sea!
O throat! O throbbing heart!
And I singing uselessly! uselessly all the night.

O past! O happy life; O songs of joy!
In the air, in the woods, over fields,
Loved! loved! loved! loved! loved!
But my mate no more, no more with me!
We two together no more.

The aria sinking,
All else continuing, the stars shining,
The winds blowing, the notes of the bird continuous echoing,
With angry moans the fierce old mother incessantly moaning,
On the sands of Paumanok's shore gray and rustling,
The yellow half-moon enlarged, sagging down, drooping, the face
    of the sea almost touching,
The boy ecstatic, with his bare feet the waves, with his hair the
    atmosphere dallying,
The love in the heart long pent, now loose, now at last tumultuously
    bursting,
The aria's meaning, the ears, the soul, swiftly depositing,
The strange tears down the cheeks coursing,
The colloquy there, the trio, each uttering,
The undertone, the savage old mother incessantly crying,
To the boy's soul's questions sullenly timing, some drown'd secret
    hissing,
To the outsetting bard.
Demon or bird! (said the boy's soul)
Is it indeed toward your mate you sing? or is it really to me?
For I, that was a child, my tongue's use sleeping, now I have heard
    you,
Now in a moment I know what I am for, I awake,
And already a thousand singers, a thousand songs, clearer, louder
    and more sorrowful than yours,
A thousand warbling echoes have started to life within me, never to
    die.

O you singers solitary, singing by yourself, projecting me,
O solitary me listening, never more shall I cease perpetuating you,
Never more shall I escape, never more the reverberations,
Never more the cries of unsatisfied love be absent from me,
Never again leave me to be the peaceful child I was before what
    there in the night,
By the sea under yellow and sagging moon,
The messenger there aroused, the fire, the sweet hell within,
The unknown want, the destiny of me.
O give me the clew! (it lurks in the night here somewhere)
O if I am to have so much, let me have more!

A word then, (for I will conquer it)
The word final, superior to all,

Subtle, sent up—what is it?—I listen;
Are you whispering it, and have been all the time, you sea-waves?
Is that it from your liquid rims and wet sands?
Whereto answering, the sea,
Delaying not, hurrying not,
Whispered me through the night, and very plainly before daybreak,
Lisped to me the low and delicious word death,
And again death, death, death, death,
Hissing melodious, neither like the bird nor like my aroused child's
     heart,
But edging near as privately for me, rustling at my feet,
Creeping thence steadily up to my ears and laving me softly all over,
Death, death, death, death, death.

Which I do not forget,
But fuse the song of my dusky demon and brother,
That he sang to me in the moonlight on Paumanok's gray beach,
With the thousand responsive songs at random,
My own songs awaked from that hour,
And with them the key, the word up from the waves,
The word of the sweetest song and all songs,
That strong and delicious word which, creeping to my feet,
(Or like some old crone rocking the cradle, swathed in sweet gar-
     ments, bending aside)
The sea whispered me.

Death Carol

(FROM "WHEN LILACS LAST IN THE DOOR-YARD BLOOMED")

COME, lovely and soothing Death,
     Undulate round the world, serenely arriving, arriving,
In the day, in the night, to all, to each,
Sooner or later, delicate Death.

Praised be the fathomless universe,
For life and joy, and for objects and knowledge curious;
And for love, sweet love—But praise! praise! praise!
For the sure-enwinding arms of cool-enfolding Death.

Dark Mother, always gliding near, with soft feet,
Have none chanted for thee a chant of fullest welcome?

Then I chant it for thee—I glorify thee above all;
I bring thee a song that when thou must indeed come, come un-
    falteringly.

Approach, strong deliveress!
When it is so—when thou hast taken them, I joyously sing the
    dead,
Lost in the loving, floating ocean of thee,
Laved in the flood of thy bliss, O Death.

From me to thee glad serenades,
Dances for thee I propose, saluting thee—adornments and feastings
    for thee;
And the sights of the open landscape, and the high-spread sky, are
    fitting,
And life and the fields, and the huge and thoughtful night.

The night, in silence, under many a star;
The ocean shore, and the husky whispering wave, whose voice I
    know;
And the soul turning to thee, O vast and well-veiled Death,
And the body gratefully nestling close to thee.

Over the tree-tops I float thee a song!
Over the rising and sinking waves—over the myriad fields, and the
    prairies wide;
Over the dense-packed cities all, and the teeming wharves and ways,
I float this carol with joy, with joy to thee, O Death!

A Noiseless, Patient Spider

A NOISELESS, patient spider,
    I marked, where, on a little promontory, it stood isolated;
Marked how, to explore the vacant, vast surrounding,
It launched forth filament, filament, filament, out of itself;
Ever unreeling them—ever tirelessly speeding them.

And you, O my Soul, where you stand,
Surrounded, surrounded, in measureless oceans of space,
Ceaselessly musing, venturing, throwing,—seeking the spheres, to
    connect them;

Till the bridge you will need, be formed—till the ductile anchor
  hold;
Till the gossamer thread you fling, catch somewhere, O my Soul.

Song of Myself

1

I CELEBRATE myself, and I sing myself,
  And what I assume you shall assume,
For every atom belonging to me as good belongs to you.

I loafe and invite my soul,
I lean and loafe at my ease observing a spear of summer grass.

My tongue, every atom of my blood, form'd from this soil, this air,
Born here of parents born here from parents the same, and their
  parents the same,
I, now thirty-seven years old in perfect health begin,
Hoping to cease not till death.

Creeds and schools in abeyance,
Retiring back a while sufficed at what they are, but never forgotten,
I harbor for good or bad, I permit to speak at every hazard,
Nature without check with original energy.

2

Houses and rooms are full of perfumes, the shelves are crowded
  with perfumes,
I breathe the fragrance myself and know it and like it,
The distillation would intoxicate me also, but I shall not let it.

The atmosphere is not a perfume, it has no taste of the distillation,
  it is odorless,
It is for my mouth forever, I am in love with it,
I will go to the bank by the wood and become undisguised and
  naked,
I am mad for it to be in contact with me.

The smoke of my own breath,
Echoes, ripples, buzz'd whispers, love-root, silk-thread, crotch and
  vine,

My respiration and inspiration, the beating of my heart, the passing
    of blood and air through my lungs,
The sniff of green leaves and dry leaves, and of the shore and dark-
    color'd sea-rocks, and of hay in the barn,
The sound of the belch'd words of my voice loos'd to the eddies of
    the wind,
A few light kisses, a few embraces, a reaching around of arms,
The play of shine and shade on the trees as the supple boughs wag,
The delight alone or in the rush of the streets, or along the fields
    and hill-sides,
The feeling of health, the full-moon trill, the song of me rising from
    bed and meeting the sun.

Have you reckon'd a thousand acres much? have you reckon'd the
    earth much?
Have you practis'd so long to learn to read?
Have you felt so proud to get at the meaning of poems?

Stop this day and night with me and you shall possess the origin
    of all poems,
You shall possess the good of the earth and sun, (there are millions
    of suns left,)
You shall no longer take things at second or third hand, nor look
    through the eyes of the dead, nor feed on the spectres in books,
You shall not look through my eyes either, nor take things from me,
You shall listen to all sides and filter them from your self.

3

I have heard what the talkers were talking, the talk of the begin-
    ning and the end,
But I do not talk of the beginning or the end.

There was never any more inception than there is now,
Nor any more youth or age than there is now,
And will never be any more perfection than there is now,
Nor any more heaven or hell than there is now.

Urge and urge and urge,
Always the procreant urge of the world.
Out of the dimness opposite equals advance, always substance and
    increase, always sex,
Always a knit of identity, always distinction, always a breed of life.

To elaborate is no avail, learn'd and unlearn'd feel that it is so.

Sure as the most certain sure, plumb in the uprights, well entretied,
    braced in the beams,
Stout as a horse, affectionate, haughty, electrical,
I and this mystery here we stand.

Clear and sweet is my soul, and clear and sweet is all that is not my
    soul.

Lack one lacks both, and the unseen is proved by the seen,
Till that becomes unseen and receives proof in its turn.

Showing the best and dividing it from the worst age vexes age,
Knowing the perfect fitness and equanimity of things, while they
    discuss I am silent, and go bathe and admire myself.

Welcome is every organ and attribute of me, and of any man hearty
    and clean,
Not an inch nor a particle of an inch is vile, and none shall be less
    familiar than the rest.

I am satisfied—I see, dance, laugh, sing;
As the hugging and loving bed-fellow sleeps at my side through the
    night, and withdraws at the peep of the day with stealthy tread,
Leaving me baskets cover'd with white towels swelling the house
    with their plenty,
Shall I postpone my acceptation and realization and scream at my
    eyes,
That they turn from gazing after and down the road,
And forthwith cipher and show me to a cent,
Exactly the value of one and exactly the value of two, and which
    is ahead?

4

Trippers and askers surround me,
People I meet, the effect upon me of my early life or the ward and
    city I live in, or the nation,
The latest dates, discoveries, inventions, societies, authors old and
    new,
My dinner, dress, associates, looks, compliments, dues,
The real or fancied indifference of some man or woman I love,

The sickness of one of my folks or of myself, or ill-doing or loss or
  lack of money, or depressions or exaltations,
Battles, the horrors of fratricidal war, the fever of doubtful news,
  the fitful events;
These come to me days and nights and go from me again,
But they are not the Me myself.

Apart from the pulling and hauling stands what I am,
Stands amused, complacent, compassionating, idle, unitary,
Looks down, is erect, or bends an arm on an impalpable certain rest,
Looking with side-curved head curious what will come next,
Both in and out of the game and watching and wondering at it.

Backward I see in my own days where I sweated through fog with
  linguists and contenders,
I have no mockings or arguments, I witness and wait.

5

I believe in you my soul, the other I am must not abase itself to you,
And you must not be abased to the other.

Loafe with me on the grass, loose the stop from your throat,
Not words, nor music or rhyme I want, not custom or lecture, not
  even the best,
Only the lull I like, the hum of your valvèd voice.
I mind how once we lay such a transparent summer morning,
How you settled your head athwart my hips and gently turn'd over
  upon me,
And parted the shirt from my bosom-bone, and plunged your tongue
  to my bare-stript heart,
And reach'd till you felt my beard, and reach'd till you held my feet.

Swiftly arose and spread around me the peace and knowledge that
  pass all the argument of the earth,
And I know that the hand of God is the promise of my own,
And I know that the spirit of God is the brother of my own,
And that all the men ever born are also my brothers, and the women
  my sisters and lovers,
And that a kelson of the creation is love,
And limitless are leaves stiff or drooping in the fields,
And brown ants in the little wells beneath them,

And mossy scabs of the worm fence, heap'd stones, elder, mullein
    and poke-weed.

6

A child said *What is the grass?* fetching it to me with full hands,
How could I answer the child? I do not know what it is any more
    than he.

I guess it must be the flag of my disposition, out of hopeful green
    stuff woven.

Or I guess it is the handkerchief of the Lord,
A scented gift and remembrancer designedly dropt,
Bearing the owner's name some way in the corners, that we may see
    and remark, and say *Whose?*

Or I guess the grass is itself a child, the produced babe of the vegeta-
    tion.

Or I guess it is a uniform hieroglyphic,
And it means, Sprouting alike in broad zones and narrow zones,
Growing among black folks as among white,
Kanuck, Tuckahoe, Congressman, Cuff, I give them the same, I
    receive them the same.

And now it seems to me the beautiful uncut hair of graves.

Tenderly will I use you curling grass,
It may be you transpire from the breasts of young men,
It may be if I had known them I would have loved them,
It may be you are from old people, or from offspring taken soon
    out of their mothers' laps,
And here you are the mothers' laps.

This grass is very dark to be from the white heads of old mothers,
Darker than the colorless beards of old men,
Dark to come from under the faint red roofs of mouths.

O I perceive after all so many uttering tongues,
And I perceive they do not come from the roofs of mouths for
    nothing.

I wish I could translate the hints about the dead young men and
    women,
And the hints about old men and mothers, and the offspring taken
    soon out of their laps.

What do you think has become of the young and old men?
And what do you think has become of the women and children?

They are alive and well somewhere,
The smallest sprout shows there is really no death,
And if ever there was it led forward life, and does not wait at the
    end to arrest it,
And ceas'd the moment life appear'd.

All goes onward and outward, nothing collapses,
And to die is different from what any one supposed, and luckier.

7

Has any one supposed it lucky to be born?
I hasten to inform him or her it is just as lucky to die, and I know it.

I pass death with the dying and birth with the new-wash'd babe,
    and am not contain'd between my hat and boots,
And peruse manifold objects, no two alike and every one good,
The earth good and the stars good, and their adjuncts all good.

I am not an earth nor an adjunct of an earth,
I am the mate and companion of people, all just as immortal and
    fathomless as myself,
(They do not know how immortal, but I know.)

Every kind for itself and its own, for me mine male and female,
For me those that have been boys and that love women,
For me the man that is proud and feels how it stings to be slighted,
For me the sweet-heart and the old maid, for me mothers and the
    mothers of mothers,
For me lips that have smiled, eyes that have shed tears,
For me children and the begetters of children.

Undrape! you are not guilty to me, nor stale nor discarded,
I see through the broadcloth and gingham whether or no,

And am around, tenacious, acquisitive, tireless, and cannot be shaken
away.

8

The little one sleeps in its cradle,
I lift the gauze and look a long time, and silently brush away flies
with my hand.

The youngster and the red-faced girl turn aside up the bushy hill,
I peeringly view them from the top.

The suicide sprawls on the bloody floor of the bedroom,
I witness the corpse with its dabbled hair, I note where the pistol
has fallen.

The blab of the pave, tires of carts, sluff of boot-soles, talk of the
promenaders,
The heavy omnibus, the driver with his interrogating thumb, the
clank of the shod horses on the granite floor,
The snow-sleighs, clinking, shouted jokes, pelts of snow-balls,
The hurrahs for popular favorites, the fury of rous'd mobs,
The flap of the curtain'd litter, a sick man inside borne to the
hospital,
The meeting of enemies, the sudden oath, the blows and fall,
The excited crowd, the policeman with his star quickly working
his passage to the centre of the crowd,
The impassive stones that receive and return so many echoes,
What groans of over-fed or half-starv'd who fall sunstruck or in fits,
What exclamations of women taken suddenly who hurry home and
give birth to babes,
What living and buried speech is always vibrating here, what howls
restrain'd by decorum,
Arrests of criminals, slights, adulterous offers made, acceptances,
rejections with convex lips,
I mind them or the show or resonance of them—I come and I depart

9

The doors of the country barn stand open and ready,
The dried grass of the harvest-time loads the slow-drawn wagon,
The clear light plays on the brown gray and green intertinged,
The armfuls are pack'd to the sagging mow.

I am there, I help, I came stretch'd atop of the load,
I felt its soft jolts, one leg reclined on the other,
I jump from the cross-beams and seize the clover and timothy,
And roll head over heels and tangle my hair full of wisps.

10

Alone far in the wilds and mountains I hunt,
Wandering amazed at my own lightness and glee,
In the late afternoon choosing a safe spot to pass the night,
Kindling a fire and broiling the fresh-kill'd game,
Falling asleep on the gather'd leaves with my dog and gun by my
    side.

The Yankee clipper is under her sky-sails, she cuts the sparkle and
    scud,
My eyes settle the land, I bend at her prow or shout joyously from
    the deck.

The boatmen and clam-diggers arose early and stopt for me,
I tuck'd my trowser-ends in my boots and went and had a good
    time;
You should have been with us that day round the chowder-kettle.

I saw the marriage of the trapper in the open air in the far west,
    the bride was a red girl,
Her father and his friends sat near cross-legged and dumbly smok-
    ing, they had moccasins to their feet and large thick blankets
    hanging from their shoulders,
On a bank lounged the trapper, he was drest mostly in skins, his
    luxuriant beard and curls protected his neck, he held his bride
    by the hand,
She had long eyelashes, her head was bare, her coarse straight locks
    descended upon her voluptuous limbs and reach'd to her feet.

The runaway slave came to my house and stopt outside,
I heard his motions crackling the twigs of the woodpile,
Through the swung half-door of the kitchen I saw him limpsy and
    weak,
And went where he sat on a log and led him in and assured him,
And brought water and fill'd a tub for his sweated body and bruis'd
    feet,

And gave him a room that enter'd from my own, and gave him
    some coarse clean clothes,
And remember perfectly well his revolving eyes and his awkward-
    ness,
And remember putting plasters on the galls of his neck and ankles;
He staid with me a week before he was recuperated and pass'd north,
I had him sit next to me at table, my fire-lock lean'd in the corner.

II

Twenty-eight young men bathe by the shore,
Twenty-eight young men and all so friendly;
Twenty-eight years of womanly life and all so lonesome.

She owns the fine house by the rise of the bank,
She hides handsome and richly drest aft the blinds of the window.

Which of the young men does she like the best?
Ah the homeliest of them is beautiful to her.

Where are you off to, lady? for I see you,
You splash in the water there, yet stay stock still in your room.

Dancing and laughing along the beach came the twenty-ninth
    bather,
The rest did not see her, but she saw them and loved them.

The beards of the young men glisten'd with wet, it ran from their
    long hair,
Little streams pass'd all over their bodies.

An unseen hand also pass'd over their bodies,
It descended tremblingly from their temples and ribs.

The young men float on their backs, their white bellies bulge to the
    sun, they do not ask who seizes fast to them,

They do not know who puffs and declines with pendant and bending
    arch,
They do not think whom they souse with spray.

12

The butcher-boy puts off his killing-clothes, or sharpens his knife at
    the stall in the market,
I loiter enjoying his repartee and his shuffle and break-down.

Blacksmiths with grimed and hairy chests environ the anvil,
Each has his main-sledge, they are all out, there is a great heat in
    the fire.

From the cinder-strew'd threshold I follow their movements,
The lithe sheer of their waists plays even with their massive arms,
Overhand the hammers swing, overhand so slow, overhand so sure,
They do not hasten, each man hits in his place.

13

The Negro holds firmly the reins of his four horses, the block swags
    underneath on its tied-over chain,
The Negro that drives the long dray of the stone-yard, steady and
    tall he stands pois'd on one leg on the string-piece,
His blue shirt exposes his ample neck and breast and loosens over
    his hip-band,
His glance is calm and commanding, he tosses the slouch of his
    hat away from his forehead,
The sun falls on his crispy hair and mustache, falls on the black of
    his polish'd and perfect limbs.

I behold the picturesque giant and love him, and I do not stop there,
I go with the team also.

In me the caresser of life wherever moving, backward as well as
    forward sluing,
To niches aside and junior bending, not a person or object missing,
Absorbing all to myself and for this song.

Oxen that rattle the yoke and chain or halt in the leafy shade, what
    is that you express in your eyes?
It seems to me more than all the print I have read in my life.

My tread scares the wood-drake and wood-duck on my distant and
    day-long ramble,
They rise together, they slowly circle around.

I believe in those wing'd purposes,
And acknowledge red, yellow, white, playing within me,
And consider green and violet and the tufted crown intentional,
And do not call the tortoise unworthy because she is not something
    else,
And the jay in the woods never studied the gamut, yet trills pretty
    well to me,
And the look of the bay mare shames silliness out of me.

14

The wild gander leads his flock through the cool night,
Ya-honk he says, and sounds it down to me like an invitation,
The pert may suppose it meaningless, but I listening close,
Find its purpose and place up there toward the wintry sky.

The sharp-hoof'd moose of the north, the cat on the house-sill, the
    chickadee, the prairie-dog,
The litter of the grunting sow as they tug at her teats,
The brood of the turkey-hen and she with her half-spread wings.
I see in them and myself the same old law.

The press of my foot to the earth springs a hundred affections,
They scorn the best I can do to relate them.

I am enamour'd of growing out-doors,
Of men that live among cattle or taste of the ocean or woods,
Of the builders and steerers of ships and the wielders of axes and
    mauls, and the drivers of horses,
I can eat and sleep with them week in and week out.

What is commonest, cheapest, nearest, easiest, is Me,
Me going in for my chances, spending for vast returns,
Adorning myself to bestow myself on the first that will take me,
Not asking the sky to come down to my good will,
Scattering it freely forever.

15

The pure contralto sings in the organ loft,
The carpenter dresses his plank, the tongue of his foreplane whistles
    its wild ascending lisp,
The married and unmarried children ride home to their Thanks-
    giving dinner,

The pilot seizes the king-pin, he heaves down with a strong arm,
The mate stands braced in the whale-boat, lance and harpoon are
ready,
The duck-shooter walks by silent and cautious stretches,
The deacons are ordain'd with cross'd hands at the altar,
The spinning-girl retreats and advances to the hum of the big wheel,
The farmer stops by the bars as he walks on a First-day loafe and
looks at the oats and rye,
The lunatic is carried at last to the asylum a confirm'd case,
(He will never sleep any more as he did in the cot in his mother's
bed-room;)
The jour printer with gray head and gaunt jaws works at his case,
He turns his quid of tobacco while his eyes blurr with the manu-
script;
The malform'd limbs are tied to the surgeon's table,
What is removed drops horribly in a pail;
The quadroon girl is sold at the auction-stand, the drunkard nods
by the bar-room stove,
The machinist rolls up his sleeves, the policeman travels his beat,
the gate-keeper marks who pass,
The young fellow drives the express wagon, (I love him, though I do
not know him;)
The half-breed straps on his light boots to compete in the race,
The western turkey-shooting draws old and young, some lean on
their rifles, some sit on logs,
Out from the crowds steps the marksman, takes his position, levels
his piece;
The groups of newly-come immigrants cover the wharf or levee,
As the woolly-pates hoe in the sugar-field, the overseer views them
from his saddle,
The bugle calls in the ball-room, the gentlemen run for their part-
ners, the dancers bow to each other,
The youth lies awake in the cedar-roof'd garret and harks to the
musical rain,
The Wolverine sets traps on the creek that helps fill the Huron,
The squaw wrapt in her yellow-hemm'd cloth is offering moccasins
and bead-bags for sale,
The connoisseur peers along the exhibition-gallery with half-shut
eyes bent sideways,
As the deck-hands make fast the steamboat the plank is thrown for
the shore-going passengers,

The young sister holds out the skein while the elder sister winds it
off in a ball, and stops now and then for the knots,

The one-year wife is recovering and happy having a week ago borne
her first child,

The clean-hair'd Yankee girl works with her sewing-machine or in
the factory or mill,

The paving man leans on his two-handed rammer, the reporter's
lead flies swiftly over the note-book, the sign-painter is lettering
with blue and gold,

The canal boy trots on the tow-path, the book-keeper counts at his
desk, the shoemaker waxes his thread,

The conductor beats time for the band and all the performers follow
him,

The child is baptized, the convert is making his first professions,

The regatta is spread on the bay, the race is begun, (how the white
sails sparkle!)

The drover watching his drove sings out to them that would stray,

The peddler sweats with his pack on his back, (the purchaser hig-
gling about the odd cent;)

The bride unrumples her white dress, the minute-hand of the clock
moves slowly,

The opium-eater reclines with rigid head and just-open'd lips,

The prostitute draggles her shawl, her bonnet bobs on her tipsy and
pimpled neck,

The crowd laugh at her blackguard oaths, the men jeer and wink to
each other,

(Miserable! I do not laugh at your oaths nor jeer you;)

The President holding a cabinet council is surrounded by the great
Secretaries,

On the piazza walk three matrons stately and friendly with twined
arms,

The crew of the fish-smack pack repeated layers of halibut in the
hold,

The Missourian crosses the plains toting his wares and his cattle,

As the fare-collector goes through the train he gives notice by the
jingling of loose change,

The floor-men are laying the floor, the tinners are tinning the roof,
the masons are calling for mortar,

In single file each shouldering his hod pass onward the laborers;

Seasons pursuing each other the indescribable crowd is gather'd, it
is the fourth of Seventh-month, (what salutes of cannon and
small arms!)

Seasons pursuing each other the plougher ploughs, the mower mows,
and the winter-grain falls in the ground;
Off on the lakes the pike-fisher watches and waits by the hole in the
frozen surface,
The stumps stand thick round the clearing, the squatter strikes deep
with his axe,
Flatboatmen make fast towards dusk near the cotton-wood or pecan-
trees,
Coon-seekers go through the regions of the Red river or through
those drain'd by the Tennessee, or through those of the Arkansas,
Torches shine in the dark that hangs on the Chattahooche or Al-
tamahaw,
Patriarchs sit at supper with sons and grandsons and great-grandsons
around them,
In walls of adobe, in canvas tents, rest hunters and trappers after
their day's sport,
The city sleeps and the country sleeps,
The living sleep for their time, the dead sleep for their time,
The old husband sleeps by his wife and the young husband sleeps by
his wife;
And these tend inward to me, and I tend outward to them,
And such as it is to be of these more or less I am,
And of these one and all I weave the song of myself.

16

I am of old and young, of the foolish as much as the wise,
Regardless of others, ever regardful of others,
Maternal as well as paternal, a child as well as a man,
Stuff'd with the stuff that is coarse and stuff'd with the stuff that
is fine,
One of the Nation of many nations, the smallest the same and the
largest the same,
A Southerner soon as a Northerner, a planter nonchalant and hospi-
table down by the Oconee I live,
A Yankee bound my own way ready for trade, my joints the lim-
berest joints on earth and the sternest joints on earth,
A Kentuckian walking the vale of the Elkhorn in my deerskin
leggings, a Louisianian or Georgian,
A boatman over lakes or bays or along coasts, a Hoosier, Badger,
Buckeye;
At home on Kanadian snow-shoes or up in the bush, or with fisher-
men off Newfoundland,

At home in the fleet of ice-boats, sailing with the rest and tacking,
At home on the hills of Vermont or in the woods of Maine, or the
    Texan ranch,
Comrade of Californians, comrade of free North-Westerners, (loving
    their big proportions,)
Comrade of raftsmen and coalmen, comrade of all who shake hands
    and welcome to drink and meat,
A learner with the simplest, a teacher of the thoughtfullest,
A novice beginning yet experient of myriads of seasons,
Of every hue and caste am I, of every rank and religion,
A farmer, mechanic, artist, gentleman, sailor, quaker,
Prisoner, fancy-man, rowdy, lawyer, physician, priest.

I resist any thing better than my own diversity,
Breathe the air but leave plenty after me,
And am not stuck up, and am in my place.

(The moth and the fish-eggs are in their place,
The bright suns I see and the dark suns I cannot see are in their
    place,
The palpable is in its place and the impalpable is in its place.)

17

These are really the thoughts of all men in all ages and lands, they
    are not original with me,
If they are not yours as much as mine they are nothing, or next to
    nothing,
If they are not the riddle and the untying of the riddle they are
    nothing,
If they are not just as close as they are distant they are nothing.
This is the grass that grows wherever the land is and the water is,
This is the common air that bathes the globe.

18

With music strong I come, with my cornets and my drums,
I play not marches for accepted victors only, I play marches for con-
    quer'd and slain persons.
Have you heard that it was good to gain the day?
I also say it is good to fall, battles are lost in the same spirit in which
    they are won.

I beat and pound for the dead,
I blow through my embouchures my loudest and gayest for them.

Vivas to those who have fail'd!
And to those whose war-vessels sank in the sea!
And to those themselves who sank in the sea!
And to all generals that lost engagements, and all overcome heroes!
And the numberless unknown heroes equal to the greatest heroes
    known!

19

This is the meal equally set, this the meat for natural hunger,
It is for the wicked just the same as the righteous, I make appoint-
    ments with all,
I will not have a single person slighted or left away,
The kept-woman, sponger, thief, are hereby invited,
The heavy-lipp'd slave is invited, the venerealee is invited;
There shall be no difference between them and the rest.

This is the press of a bashful hand, this the float and odor of hair,
This is the touch of my lips to yours, this the murmur of yearning,
This the far-off depth and height reflecting my own face,
This the thoughful merge of myself, and the outlet again.
Do you guess I have some intricate purpose?
Well I have, for the Fourth-month showers have, and the mica on
    the side of a rock has.

Do you take it I would astonish?
Does the daylight astonish? does the early redstart twittering through
    the woods?
Do I astonish more than they?

This hour I tell things in confidence,
I might not tell everybody, but I will tell you.

20

Who goes there? hankering, gross, mystical, nude;
How is it I extract strength from the beef I eat?

What is a man anyhow? what am I? what are you?

All I mark as my own you shall offset it with your own,
Else it were time lost listening to me.

I do not snivel that snivel the world over,
That months are vacuums and the ground but wallow and filth.

Whimpering and truckling fold with powders for invalids, conformity goes to the fourth-remov'd,
I wear my hat as I please indoors or out.

Why should I pray? why should I venerate and be ceremonious?

Having pried through the strata, analyzed to a hair, counsel'd with
doctors and calculated close,
I find no sweeter fat than sticks to my own bones.

In all people I see myself, none more and not one a barley-corn less,
And the good or bad I say of myself I say of them.

I know I am solid and sound,
To me the converging objects of the universe perpetually flow,
All are written to me, and I must get what the writing means.

I know I am deathless,
I know this orbit of mine cannot be swept by a carpenter's compass,
I know I shall not pass like a child's carlacue cut with a burnt stick
at night.

I know I am august,
I do not trouble my spirit to vindicate itself or be understood,
I see that the elementary laws never apologize,
(I reckon I behave no prouder than the level I plant my house by,
after all.)

I exist as I am, that is enough,
If no other in the world be aware I sit content,
And if each and all be aware I sit content.

One world is aware and by far the largest to me, and that is myself,
And whether I come to my own today or in ten thousand or ten
million years,
I can cheerfully take it now, or with equal cheerfulness I can wait.

My foothold is tenon'd and mortis'd in granite,
I laugh at what you call dissolution,
And I know the amplitude of time.

21

I am the poet of the Body and I am the poet of the Soul,
The pleasures of heaven are with me and the pains of hell are with
    me,
The first I graft and increase upon myself, the latter I translate into
    a new tongue.

I am the poet of the woman the same as the man,
And I say it is as great to be a woman as to be a man,
And I say there is nothing greater than the mother of men.

I chant the chant of dilation or pride,
We have had ducking and deprecating about enough,
I show that size is only development.

Have you outstript the rest? are you the President?
It is a trifle, they will more than arrive there every one, and still
    pass on.
I am he that walks with the tender and growing night,
I call to the earth and sea half-held by the night.

Press close bare-bosom'd night—press close magnetic nourishing
    night!
Night of south winds—night of the large few stars!
Still nodding night—mad naked summer night.

Smile O voluptuous cool-breath'd earth!
Earth of the slumbering and liquid trees!

Earth of departed sunset—earth of the mountains misty-topt!
Earth of the vitreous pour of the full moon just tinged with blue!
Earth of shine and dark mottling the tide of the river!
Earth of the limpid gray of clouds brighter and clearer for my sake!
Far-swooping elbow'd earth—rich apple-blossom'd earth!
Smile, for your lover comes.

Prodigal, you have given me love—therefore I to you give love!
O unspeakable passionate love.

22

You sea! I resign myself to you also—I guess what you mean,
I behold from the beach your crooked inviting fingers,
I believe you refuse to go back without feeling of me,
We must have a turn together, I undress, hurry me out of sight of
    the land,
Cushion me soft, rock me in billowy drowse,
Dash me with amorous wet, I can repay you.

Sea of stretch'd ground-swells,
Sea breathing broad and convulsive breaths,
Sea of the brine of life and of unshovell'd yet always-ready graves,
Howler and scooper of storms, capricious and dainty sea,
I am integral with you, I too am of one phase and of all phases.

Partaker of influx and efflux, I, extoller of hate and conciliation,
Extoller of amies and those that sleep in each other's arms.

I am he attesting sympathy,
(Shall I make my list of things in the house and skip the house that
    supports them?)

I am not the poet of goodness only, I do not decline to be the poet
    of wickedness also.

What blurt is this about virtue and about vice?
Evil propels me and reform of evil propels me, I stand indifferent,
My gait is no fault-finder's or rejector's gait,
I moisten the roots of all that has grown.

Did you fear some scrofula out of the unflagging pregnancy?
Did you guess the celestial laws are yet to be work'd over and
    rectified?

I find one side a balance and the antipodal side a balance,
Soft doctrine as steady help as stable doctrine,
Thoughts and deeds of the present our rouse and early start.

This minute that comes to me over the past decillions,
There is no better than it and now.

What behaved well in the past or behaves well today is not such a
   wonder,
The wonder is always and always how there can be a mean man or
   an infidel.

23

Endless unfolding of words of ages!
And mine a word of the modern, the word En-Masse.

A word of the faith that never balks,
Here or henceforward it is all the same to me, I accept Time ab-
   solutely.
It alone is without flaw, it alone rounds and completes all,
That mystic baffling wonder alone completes all.

I accept Reality and dare not question it,
Materialism first and last imbuing.

Hurrah for positive science! long live exact demonstration!
Fetch stonecrop mixt with cedar and branches of lilac,
This is the lexicographer, this the chemist, this made a grammar of
   the old cartouches,
These mariners put the ship through dangerous unknown seas,
This is the geologist, this works with the scalpel, and this is a
   mathematician.

Gentlemen, to you the first honors always!
Your facts are useful, and yet they are not my dwelling,
I but enter by them to an area of my dwelling.

Less the reminders of properties told my words,
And more the reminders they of life untold, and of freedom and
   extrication,
And make short account of neuters and geldings, and favor men
   and women fully equipt,
And beat the gong of revolt, and stop with fugitives and them that
   plot and conspire.

24

Walt Whitman, a kosmos, of Manhattan the son,
Turbulent, fleshy, sensual, eating, drinking and breeding,

No sentimentalist, no stander above men and women or apart from
    them,
No more modest than immodest.
Unscrew the locks from the doors!
Unscrew the doors themselves from their jambs!

Whoever degrades another degrades me,
And whatever is done or said returns at last to me.
Through me the afflatus surging and surging, through me the
    current and index.

I speak the pass-word primeval, I give the sign of democracy,
By God! I will accept nothing which all cannot have their counter-
    part of on the same terms.

Through me many long dumb voices,
Voices of the interminable generations of prisoners and slaves,
Voices of the diseas'd and despairing and of thieves and dwarfs,
Voices of cycles of preparation and accretion,
And of the threads that connect the stars, and of wombs and of the
    father-stuff,
And of the rights of them the others are down upon,
Of the deform'd, trivial, flat, foolish, despised,
Fog in the air, beetles rolling balls of dung.

Through me forbidden voices,
Voices of sexes and lusts, voices veil'd and I remove the veil,
Voices indecent by me clarified and transfigur'd.

I do not press my fingers across my mouth,
I keep as delicate around the bowels as around the head and heart,
Copulation is no more rank to me than death is.
I believe in the flesh and the appetites,
Seeing, hearing, feeling, are miracles, and each part and tag of me is
    a miracle.

Divine am I inside and out, and I make holy whatever I touch or am
    touch'd from,
The scent of these arm-pits aroma finer than prayer,
This head more than churches, bibles, and all the creeds.

If I worship one thing more than another it shall be the spread of my
　　own body, or any part of it,
Translucent mould of me it shall be you!
Shaded ledges and rests it shall be you!
Firm masculine colter it shall be you!
Whatever goes to the tilth of me it shall be you!
You my rich blood! your milky stream pale strippings of my life!
Breast that presses against other breasts it shall be you!
My brain it shall be your occult convolutions!
Root of wash'd sweet-flag! timorous pond-snipe! nest of guarded
　　duplicate eggs! it shall be you!
Mix'd tussled hay of head, beard, brawn, it shall be you!
Trickling sap of maple, fibre of manly wheat, it shall be you!
Sun so generous it shall be you!
Vapors lighting and shading my face it shall be you!
You sweaty brooks and dews it shall be you!
Winds whose soft-tickling genitals rub against me it shall be you!
Broad muscular fields, branches of live oak loving lounger in my
　　winding paths, it shall be you!
Hands I have taken, face I have kiss'd, mortal I have ever touch'd,
　　it shall be you.

I dote on myself, there is that lot of me and all so luscious,
Each moment and whatever happens thrills me with joy,
I cannot tell how my ankles bend, nor whence the cause of my
　　faintest wish,
Nor the cause of the friendship I emit, nor the cause of the friendship
　　I take again.

That I walk up my stoop, I pause to consider if it really be,
A morning-glory at my window satisfies me more than the meta-
　　physics of books.

To behold the day-break!
The little light fades the immense and diaphanous shadows,
The air tastes good to my palate.
Hefts of the moving world at innocent gambols silently rising,
　　freshly exuding,
Scooting obliquely high and low.
Something I cannot see puts upward libidinous prongs,
Seas of bright juice suffuse heaven.

The earth by the sky staid with, the daily close of their junction,
The heav'd challenge from the east that moment over my head,
The mocking taunt, See then whether you shall be master!

25

Dazzling and tremendous how quick the sun-rise would kill me,
If I could not now and always send sun-rise out of me.

We also ascend dazzling and tremendous as the sun,
We found our own O my soul in the calm and cool of the daybreak.

My voice goes after what my eyes cannot reach,
With the twirl of my tongue I encompass worlds and volumes of
    worlds.

Speech is the twin of my vision, it is unequal to measure itself,
It provokes me forever, it says sarcastically,
Walt you contain enough, why don't you let it out then?

Come now I will not be tantalized, you conceive too much of articu-
    lation,
Do you not know O speech how the buds beneath you are folded?
Waiting in gloom, protected by frost,
The dirt receding before my prophetical screams,
I underlying causes to balance them at last,
My knowledge my live parts, it keeping tally with the meaning of
    all things,
Happiness, (which whoever hears me let him or her set out in search
    of this day.)

My final merit I refuse you, I refuse putting from me what I really
    am,
Encompass worlds, but never try to encompass me,
I crowd your sleekest and best by simply looking toward you.

Writing and talk do not prove me,
I carry the plenum of proof and every thing else in my face,
With the hush of my lips I wholly confound the skeptic.

26

Now I will do nothing but listen,
To accrue what I hear into this song, to let sounds contribute toward it.

I hear bravuras of birds, bustle of growing wheat, gossip of flames, clack of sticks cooking my meals,
I hear the sound I love, the sound of the human voice,
I hear all sounds running together, combined, fused or following,
Sounds of the city and sounds out of the city, sounds of the day and night,
Talkative young ones to those that like them, the loud laugh of work-people at their meals,
The angry base of disjointed friendship, the faint tones of the sick,
The judge with hands tight to the desk, his pallid lips pronouncing a death-sentence,
The heave'e'yo of stevedores unlading ships by the wharves, the refrain of the anchor-lifters,
The ring of alarm-bells, the cry of fire, the whir of swift-streaking engines and hose-carts with premonitory tinkles and color'd lights,
The steam-whistle, the solid roll of the train of approaching cars,
The slow march play'd at the head of the association marching two and two,
(They go to guard some corpse, the flag-tops are draped with black muslin.)

I hear the violoncello, ('tis the young man's heart's complaint,)
I hear the key'd cornet, it glides quickly in through my ears,
It shakes mad-sweet pangs through my belly and breast.
I hear the chorus, it is a grand opera,
Ah this indeed is music—this suits me.

A tenor large and fresh as the creation fills me,
The orbic flex of his mouth is pouring and filling me full.

I hear the train'd soprano (what work with hers is this?)
The orchestra whirls me wider than Uranus flies,
It wrenches such ardors from me I did not know I possess'd them,
It sails me, I dab with bare feet, they are lick'd by the indolent waves,
I am cut by bitter and angry hail, I lose my breath,

Steep'd amid honey'd morphine, my windpipe throttled in fakes of
    death,
At length let up again to feel the puzzle of puzzles,
And that we call Being.

27

To be in any form, what is that?
(Round and round we go, all of us, and ever come back thither,)
If nothing lay more develop'd the quahaug in its callous shell were
    enough.

Mine is no callous shell,
I have instant conductors all over me whether I pass or stop,
They seize every object and lead it harmlessly through me.

I merely stir, press, feel with my fingers, and am happy,
To touch my person to some one else's is about as much as I can
    stand.

28

Is this then a touch? quivering me to a new identity,
Flames and ether making a rush for my veins,
Treacherous tip of me reaching and crowding to help them,
My flesh and blood playing out lightning to strike what is hardly
    different from myself,
On all sides prurient provokers stiffening my limbs,
Straining the udder of my heart for its withheld drip,
Behaving licentious toward me, taking no denial,
Depriving me of my best as for a purpose,
Unbuttoning my clothes, holding me by the bare waist,
Deluding my confusion with the calm of the sunlight and pasture-
    fields,
Immodestly sliding the fellow-senses away,
They bribed to swap off with touch and go and graze at the edges
    of me,
No consideration, no regard for my draining strength or my anger,
Fetching the rest of the herd around to enjoy them a while,
Then all uniting to stand on a headland and worry me.

The sentries desert every other part of me,
They have left me helpless to a red marauder,
They all come to the headland to witness and assist against me.

I am given up by traitors,
I talk wildly, I have lost my wits, I and nobody else am the greatest
    traitor,
I went myself first to the headland, my own hands carried me there.
You villain touch! what are you doing? my breath is tight in its
    throat,
Unclench your floodgates, you are too much for me.

29

Blind loving wrestling touch, sheath'd hooded sharp-tooth'd touch!
Did it make you ache so, leaving me?

Parting track'd by arriving, perpetual payment of perpetual loan,
Rich showering rain, and recompense richer afterward.

Sprouts take and accumulate, stand by the curb prolific and vital,
Landscapes projected masculine, full-sized and golden.

30

All truths wait in all things,
They neither hasten their own delivery nor resist it,
They do not need the obstetric forceps of the surgeon,
The insignificant is as big to me as any,
(What is less or more than a touch?)

Logic and sermons never convince,
The damp of the night drives deeper into my soul.

(Only what proves itself to every man and woman is so,
Only what nobody denies is so.)
A minute and a drop of me settle my brain,
I believe the soggy clods shall become lovers and lamps,
And a compend of compends is the meat of a man or woman.
And a summit and flower there is the feeling they have for each
    other,
And they are to branch boundlessly out of that lesson until it becomes
    omnific,
And until one and all shall delight us, and we them.

31

I believe a leaf of grass is no less than the journey-work of the stars,
And the pismire is equally perfect, and a grain of sand, and the
egg of the wren,
And the tree-toad is a chef-d'œuvre for the highest,
And the running blackberry would adorn the parlors of heaven,
And the narrowest hinge in my hand puts to scorn all machinery,
And the cow crunching with depress'd head surpasses any statue,
And a mouse is miracle enough to stagger sextillions of infidels.

I find I incorporate gneiss, coal, long-threaded moss, fruits, grains,
esculent roots,
And am stucco'd with quadrupeds and birds all over,
And have distanced what is behind me for good reasons,
But call any thing back again when I desire it.

In vain the speeding or shyness,
In vain the plutonic rocks send their old heat against my approach,
In vain the mastodon retreats beneath its own powder'd bones,
In vain objects stand leagues off and assume manifold shapes,
In vain the ocean settling in hollows and the great monsters lying
low,
In vain the buzzard houses herself with the sky,
In vain the snake slides through the creepers and logs,
In vain the elk takes to the inner passes of the woods,
In vain the razor-bill'd auk sails far north to Labrador,
I follow quickly, I ascend to the nest in the fissure of the cliff.

32

I think I could turn and live with animals, they are so placid and
self-contain'd,
I stand and look at them long and long.

They do not sweat and whine about their condition,
They do not lie awake in the dark and weep for their sins,
They do not make me sick discussing their duty to God,
Not one is dissatisfied, not one is demented with the mania of own-
ing things,
Not one kneels to another, nor to his kind that lived thousands of
years ago,
Not one is respectable or unhappy over the whole earth.

So they show their relations to me and I accept them,
They bring me tokens of myself, they evince them plainly in their
    possession.

I wonder where they get those tokens,
Did I pass that way huge times ago and negligently drop them?
Myself moving forward then and now and forever,
Gathering and showing more always and with velocity,
Infinite and omnigenous, and the like of these among them,
Not too exclusive toward the reachers of my remembrancers,
Picking out here one that I love, and now go with him on brotherly
    terms.

A gigantic beauty of a stallion, fresh and responsive to my caresses,
Head high in the forehead, wide between the ears,
Limbs glossy and supple, tail dusting the ground,
Eyes full of sparkling wickedness, ears finely cut, flexibly moving.

His nostrils dilate as my heels embrace him,
His well-built limbs tremble with pleasure as we race around and
    return.
I but use you a minute, then I resign you, stallion,
Why do I need your paces when I myself out-gallop them?
Even as I stand or sit passing faster than you.

33

Space and Time! now I see it is true, what I guess'd at,
What I guess'd when I loaf'd on the grass,
What I guess'd while I lay alone in my bed,
And again as I walk'd the beach under the paling stars of the
    morning.

My ties and ballasts leave me, my elbows rest in sea-gaps,
I skirt sierras, my palms cover continents,
I am afoot with my vision.

By the city's quadrangular houses—in log huts, camping with lum-
    bermen,
Along the ruts of the turnpike, along the dry gulch and rivulet bed,
Weeding my onion-patch or hoeing rows of carrots and parsnips,
    crossing savannas, trailing in forests,
Prospecting, gold-digging, girdling the trees of a new purchase,

Scorch'd ankle-deep by the hot sand, hauling my boat down the
shallow river,
Where the panther walks to and fro on a limb overhead, where the
buck turns furiously at the hunter,
Where the rattlesnake suns his flabby length on a rock, where the
otter is feeding on fish,
Where the alligator in his tough pimples sleeps by the bayou,
Where the black bear is searching for roots or honey, where the
beaver pats the mud with his paddle-shaped tail;
Over the growing sugar, over the yellow-flower'd cotton plant, over
the rice in its low moist field,
Over the sharp-peak'd farm house, with its scallop'd scum and
slender shoots from the gutters,
Over the western persimmon, over the long-leav'd corn, over the
delicate blue-flower flax,
Over the white and brown buckwheat, a hummer and buzzer there
with the rest,
Over the dusky green of the rye as it ripples and shades in the
breeze;
Scaling mountains, pulling myself cautiously up, holding on by low
scragged limbs,
Walking the path worn in the grass and beat through the leaves
of the brush,
Where the quail is whistling betwixt the woods and the wheatlot,
Where the bat flies in the Seventh-month eve, where the great gold-
bug drops through the dark,
Where the brook puts out of the roots of the old tree and flows to
the meadow,
Where cattle stand and shake away flies with the tremulous shudder-
ing of their hides,
Where the cheese-cloth hangs in the kitchen, where andirons straddle
the hearth-slab, where cobwebs fall in festoons from the rafters;
Where trip-hammers crash, where the press is whirling its cylinders,
Wherever the human heart beats with terrible throes under its ribs,
Where the pear-shaped balloon is floating aloft, (floating in it myself
and looking composedly down,)
Where the life-car is drawn on the slip-noose, where the heat hatches
pale-green eggs in the dented sand,
Where the she-whale swims with her calf and never forsakes it,
Where the steam-ship trails hind-ways its long pennant of smoke,
Where the fin of the shark cuts like a black chip out of the water,
Where the half-burn'd brig is riding on unknown currents,

Where shells grow to her slimy deck, where the dead are corrupting
　　below;
Where the dense-starr'd flag is born at the head of the regiments,
Approaching Manhattan up by the long-stretching island,
Under Niagara, the cataract falling like a veil over my countenance,
Upon a door-step, upon the horse-block of hard wood outside,
Upon the race-course, or enjoying picnics or jigs or a good game of
　　base-ball,
At he-festivals, with blackguard gibes, ironical license, bull-dances,
　　drinking, laughter,
At the cider-mill tasting the sweets of the brown mash, sucking the
　　juice through a straw,
At apple-peelings wanting kisses for all the red fruit I find,
At musters, beach-parties, friendly bees, huskings, house-raisings;
Where the mocking-bird sounds his delicious gurgles, cackles,
　　screams, weeps,
Where the hay-rick stands in the barn-yard, where the dry stalks
　　are scatter'd, where the brood-cow waits in the hovel,
Where the bull advances to do his masculine work, where the stud
　　to the mare, where the cock is treading the hen,
Where the heifers browse, where geese nip their food with short
　　jerks,
Where sun-down shadows lengthen over the limitless and lonesome
　　prairie,
Where herds of buffalo make a crawling spread of the square miles
　　far and near,
Where the humming-bird shimmers, where the neck of the long-
　　lived swan is curving and winding,
Where the laughing-gull scoots by the shore, where she laughs her
　　near-human laugh,
Where bee-hives range on a gray bench in the garden half hid by
　　the high weeds,
Where band-neck'd partridges roost in a ring on the ground with
　　their heads out,
Where burial coaches enter the arch'd gates of a cemetery,
Where winter wolves bark amid wastes of snow and icicled trees,
Where the yellow-crown'd heron comes to the edge of the marsh at
　　night and feeds upon small crabs,
Where the splash of swimmers and divers cools the warm moon,
Where the katy-did works her chromatic reed on the walnut-tree
　　over the well,
Through patches of citrons and cucumbers with silver-wired leaves,

Through the salt-lick or orange glade, or under conical firs,
Through the gymnasium, through the curtain'd saloon, through the
    office or public hall;
Pleas'd with the native and pleas'd with the foreign, pleas'd with the
    new and old,
Pleas'd with the homely woman as well as the handsome,
Pleas'd with the quakeress as she puts off her bonnet and talks
    melodiously,
Pleas'd with the tune of the choir of the whitewash'd church,
Pleas'd with the earnest words of the sweating Methodist preacher,
    impress'd seriously at the camp-meeting;
Looking in at the shop-windows of Broadway the whole forenoon,
    flatting the flesh of my nose on the thick plate glass,
Wandering the same afternoon with my face turn'd up to the clouds,
    or down a lane or along the beach,
My right and left arms around the sides of two friends, and I in the
    middle;
Coming home with the silent and dark-cheek'd bush-boy, (behind
    me he rides at the drape of the day,)
Far from the settlements studying the print of animals' feet, or the
    moccasin print,
By the cot in the hospital reaching lemonade to a feverish patient,
Nigh the coffin'd corpse when all is still, examining with a candle;
Voyaging to every port to dicker and adventure,
Hurrying with the modern crowd as eager and fickle as any,
Hot toward one I hate, ready in my madness to knife him,
Solitary at midnight in my back yard, my thoughts gone from me a
    long while,
Walking the old hills of Judæa with the beautiful gentle God by my
    side,
Speeding through space, speeding through heaven and the stars,
Speeding amid the seven satellites and the broad ring, and the di-
    ameter of eighty thousand miles,
Speeding with tail'd meteors, throwing fire-balls like the rest,
Carrying the crescent child that carries its own full mother in its
    belly,
Storming, enjoying, planning, loving, cautioning,
Backing and filling, appearing and disappearing,
I tread day and night such roads.

I visit the orchards of spheres and look at the product,
And look at quintillions ripen'd and look at quintillions green.

I fly those flights of a fluid and swallowing soul,
My course runs below the soundings of plummets.

I help myself to material and immaterial,
No guard can shut me off, no law prevent me.

I anchor my ship for a little while only,
My messengers continually cruise away or bring their returns to me.

I go hunting polar furs and the seal, leaping chasms with a pike-
    pointed staff, clinging to topples of brittle and blue.
I ascend to the foretruck,
I take my place at night in the crow's-nest,
We sail the arctic sea, it is plenty light enough,
Through the clear atmosphere I stretch around on the wonderful
    beauty,
The enormous masses of ice pass me and I pass them, the scenery
    is plain in all directions,
The white-topt mountains show in the distance, I fling out my fancies
    toward them,
We are approaching some great battle-field in which we are soon to
    be engaged,
We pass the colossal outposts of the encampment, we pass with still
    feet and caution,
Or we are entering by the suburbs some vast and ruin'd city,
The blocks and fallen architecture more than all the living cities of
    the globe.

I am a free companion, I bivouac by invading watchfires,
I turn the bridegroom out of bed and stay with the bride myself,
I tighten her all night to my thighs and lips.

My voice is the wife's voice, the screech by the rail of the stairs,
They fetch my man's body up dripping and drown'd.

I understand the large hearts of heroes,
The courage of present times and all times,
How the skipper saw the crowded and rudderless wreck of the
    steam-ship, and Death chasing it up and down the storm,
How he knuckled tight and gave not an inch, and was faithful of
    days and faithful of nights,

And chalk'd in large letters on a board, *Be of good cheer, we will
    not desert you;*
How we follow'd with them and tack'd with them three days and
    would not give it up,
How he saved the drifting company at last,
How the lank loose-gown'd women look'd when boated from the
    side of their prepared graves,
How the silent old-faced infants and the lifted sick, and the sharp-
    lipp'd unshaven men;
All this I swallow, it tastes good, I like it well, it becomes mine,
I am the man, I suffer'd, I was there.

The disdain and calmness of martyrs,
The mother of old, condemn'd for a witch, burnt with dry wood,
    her children gazing on,
The hounded slave that flags in the race, leans by the fence,
    blowing, cover'd with sweat.
The twinges that sting like needles his legs and neck, the murderous
    buckshot and the bullets,
All these I feel or am.

I am the hounded slave, I wince at the bite of the dogs,
Hell and despair are upon me, crack and again crack the marksmen,
I clutch the rails of the fence, my gore dribs, thinn'd with the ooze
    of my skin,
I fall on the weeds and stones,
The riders spur their unwilling horses, haul close,
Taunt my dizzy ears and beat me violently over the head with whip-
    stocks.

Agonies are one of my changes of garments,
I do not ask the wounded person how he feels, I myself become the
    wounded person,
My hurts turn livid upon me as I lean on a cane and observe.

I am the mash'd fireman with breast-bone broken,
Tumbling walls buried me in their debris,
Heat and smoke I inspired, I heard the yelling shouts of my com-
    rades,
I heard the distant click of their picks and shovels,
They have clear'd the beams away, they tenderly lift me forth.

I lie in the night air in my red shirt, the pervading hush is for my
 sake,
Painless after all I lie exhausted but not so unhappy,
White and beautiful are the faces around me, the heads are bared
 of their fire-caps,
The kneeling crowd fades with the light of the torches.

Distant and dead resuscitate,
They show as the dial or move as the hands of me, I am the clock
 myself.

I am an old artillerist, I tell of my fort's bombardment,
I am there again.
Again the long roll of the drummers,
Again the attacking cannon, mortars,
Again to my listening ears the cannon responsive.

I take part, I see and hear the whole,
The cries, curses, roar, the plaudits for well-aim'd shots,
The ambulanza slowly passing trailing its red drip,
Workmen searching after damages, making indispensable repairs,
The fall of grenades through the rent roof, the fan-shaped explosion,
The whizz of limbs, heads, stone, wood, iron, high in the air.

Again gurgles the mouth of my dying general, he furiously waves
 with his hand,
He gasps through the clot *Mind not me—mind—the entrenchments.*

34

Now I tell what I knew in Texas in my early youth,
(I tell not the fall of Alamo,
Not one escaped to tell the fall of Alamo,
The hundred and fifty are dumb yet at Alamo,)
'Tis the tale of the murder in cold blood of four hundred and twelve
 young men.

Retreating they had form'd in a hollow square with their baggage
 for breastworks,
Nine hundred lives out of the surrounding enemy's, nine times their
 number, was the price they took in advance,
Their colonel was wounded and their ammunition gone,

They treated for an honorable capitulation, receiv'd writing and
    seal, gave up their arms and march'd back prisoners of war.

They were the glory of the race of rangers,
Matchless with horse, rifle, song, supper, courtship,
Large, turbulent, generous, handsome, proud, and affectionate,
Bearded, sunburnt, drest in the free costume of hunters,
Not a single one over thirty years of age.
The second First-day morning they were brought out in squads and
    massacred, it was beautiful early summer,
The work commenced about five o'clock and was over by eight.

None obey'd the command to kneel,
Some made a mad and helpless rush, some stood stark and straight,
A few fell at once, shot in the temple or heart, the living and dead
    lay together,
The maim'd and mangled dug in the dirt, the new-comers saw them
    there,
Some half-kill'd attempted to crawl away,
These were despatch'd with bayonets or batter'd with the blunts of
    muskets,
A youth not seventeen years old seiz'd his assassin till two more
    came to release him,
The three were all torn and cover'd with the boy's blood.

At eleven o'clock began the burning of the bodies;
That is the tale of the murder of the four hundred and twelve young
    men.

35

Would you hear of an old-time sea-fight?
Would you learn who won by the light of the moon and stars?
List to the yarn, as my grandmother's father the sailor told it to me.

Our foe was no skulk in his ship I tell you, (said he,)
His was the surly English pluck, and there is no tougher or truer,
    and never was, and never will be;
Along the lower'd eve he came horribly raking us.

We closed with him, the yards entangled, the cannon touch'd,
My captain lash'd fast with his own hands.

We had receiv'd some eighteen pound shots under the water,
On our lower-gun-deck two large pieces had burst at the first fire,
    killing all around and blowing up overhead.
Fighting at sun-down, fighting at dark,
Ten o'clock at night, the full moon well up, our leaks on the gain,
    and five feet of water reported,
The master-at-arms loosing the prisoners confined in the afterhold
    to give them a chance for themselves.

The transit to and from the magazine is now stopt by the sentinels,
They see so many strange faces they do not know whom to trust.

Our frigate takes fire,
The other asks if we demand quarter?
If our colors are struck and the fighting done?

Now I laugh content, for I hear the voice of my little captain,
We have not struck, he composedly cries, *we have just begun our
    part of the fighting.*

Only three guns are in use,
One is directed by the captain himself against the enemy's main-
    mast,
Two well serv'd with grape and canister silence his musketry and
    clear his decks.

The tops alone second the fire of this little battery, especially the
    main-top,
They hold out bravely during the whole of the action.

Not a moment's cease,
The leaks gain fast on the pumps, the fire eats toward the powder-
    magazine.
One of the pumps has been shot away, it is generally thought we are
    sinking.

Serene stands the little captain,
He is not hurried, his voice is neither high nor low,
His eyes give more light to us than our battle-lanterns.

Toward twelve there in the beams of the moon they surrender to us.

36

Stretch'd and still lies the midnight,
Two great hulls motionless on the breast of the darkness,
Our vessel riddled and slowly sinking, preparations to pass to the
    one we have conquer'd,
The captain on the quarter-deck coldly giving his orders through
    a countenance white as a sheet,
Near by the corpse of the child that serv'd in the cabin,
The dead face of an old salt with long white hair and carefully
    curl'd whiskers,
The flames spite of all that can be done flickering aloft and below,
The husky voices of the two or three officers yet fit for duty,
Formless stacks of bodies and bodies by themselves, dabs of flesh
    upon the masts and spars,
Cut of cordage, dangle of rigging, slight shock of the soothe of waves,
Black and impassive guns, litter of powder parcels, strong scent,
A few large stars overhead, silent and mournful shining,
Delicate sniffs of sea-breeze, smells of sedgy grass and fields by the
    shore, death-messages given in charge to survivors.
The hiss of the surgeon's knife, the gnawing teeth of his saw,
Wheeze, cluck, swash of falling blood, short wild scream, and long,
    dull, tapering groan,
These so, these irretrievable.

37

You laggards there on guard! look to your arms!
In at the conquer'd doors they crowd! I am possess'd!
Embody all presences outlaw'd or suffering,
See myself in prison shaped like another man,
And feel the dull unintermitted pain.

For me the keepers of convicts shoulder their carbines and keep
    watch,
It is I let out in the morning and barr'd at night.

Not a mutineer walks handcuff'd to jail but I am handcuff'd to him
    and walk by his side,
(I am less the jolly one there, and more the silent one with sweat
    on my twitching lips.)

Not a youngster is taken for larceny but I go up too, and am tried
and sentenced.

Not a cholera patient lies at the last gasp but I also lie at the last
gasp,
My face is ash-color'd, my sinews gnarl, away from me people retreat.

Askers embody themselves in me and I am embodied in them,
I project my hat, sit shame-faced, and beg.

38

Enough! enough! enough!
Somehow I have been stunn'd. Stand back!
Give me a little time beyond my cuff'd head, slumbers, dreams, gap-
ing,
I discover myself on the verge of a usual mistake.
That I could forget the mockers and insults!
That I could forget the trickling tears and the blows of the bludgeons
and hammers!
That I could look with a separate look on my own crucifixion and
bloody crowning.

I remember now,
I resume the overstaid fraction,
The grave of rock multiplies what has been confided to it, or to any
graves,
Corpses rise, gashes heal, fastenings roll from me.

I troop forth replenish'd with supreme power, one of an average
unending procession,
Inland and sea-coast we go, and pass all boundary lines,
Our swift ordinances on their way over the whole earth,
The blossoms we wear in our hats the growth of thousands of years.

Eleves, I salute you! come forward!
Continue your annotations, continue your questionings.

39

The friendly and flowing savage, who is he?
Is he waiting for civilization, or past it and mastering it?

Is he some Southwesterner rais'd out-doors? is he Kanadian?
Is he from the Mississippi country? Iowa, Oregon, California?
The mountains? prairie-life, bush-life? or sailor from the sea?

Wherever he goes men and women accept and desire him,
They desire he should like them, touch them, speak to them, stay
    with them.

Behavior lawless as snow-flakes, words simple as grass, uncomb'd
    head, laughter, and naiveté,
Slow-stepping feet, common features, common modes and emana-
    tions,
They descend in new forms from the tips of his fingers,
They are wafted with the odor of his body or breath, they fly out of
    the glance of his eyes.

40

Flaunt of the sunshine I need not your bask—lie over!
You light surfaces only, I force surfaces and depths also.

Earth! you seem to look for something at my hands,
Say, old top-knot, what do you want?

Man or woman, I might tell how I like you, but cannot,
And might tell what it is in me and what it is in you, but cannot,
And might tell that pining I have, that pulse of my nights and days.

Behold, I do not give lectures or a little charity,
When I give I give myself.

You there, impotent, loose in the knees,
Open your scarf'd chops till I blow grit within you,
Spread your palms and lift the flaps of your pockets,
I am not to be denied, I compel, I have stores plenty and to spare,
And any thing I have I bestow.

I do not ask who you are, that is not important to me,
You can do nothing and be nothing but what I will infold you.

To cotton-field drudge or cleaner of privies I lean,
On his right cheek I put the family kiss,
And in my soul I swear I never will deny him.

On women fit for conception I start bigger and nimbler babes,
(This day I am jetting the stuff of far more arrogant republics.)

To any one dying, thither I speed and twist the knob of the door,
Turn the bed-clothes toward the foot of the bed,
Let the physician and the priest go home.

I seize the descending man and raise him with resistless will,
O despairer, here is my neck,
By God, you shall not go down! hang your whole weight upon me.

I dilate you with tremendous breath, I buoy you up,
Every room of the house do I fill with an arm'd force,
Lovers of me, bafflers of graves.

Sleep—I and they keep guard all night,
Not doubt, not decease shall dare to lay finger upon you,
I have embraced you, and henceforth possess you to myself,
And when you rise in the morning you will find what I tell you is
    so.

41

I am he bringing help for the sick as they pant on their backs,
And for strong upright men I bring yet more needed help.

I heard what was said of the universe,
Heard it and heard it of several thousand years;
It is middling well as far as it goes—but is that all?

Magnifying and applying come I,
Outbidding at the start the old cautious hucksters,
Taking myself the exact dimensions of Jehovah,
Lithographing Kronos, Zeus his son, and Hercules his grandson,
Buying drafts of Osiris, Isis, Belus, Brahma, Buddha,
In my portfolio placing Manito loose, Allah on a leaf, the crucifix
    engraved,
With Odin and the hideous-faced Mexitli and every idol and image,
Taking them all for what they are worth and not a cent more,
Admitting they were alive and did the work of their days,
(They bore mites as for unfledg'd birds who have now to rise and
    fly and sing for themselves,)

Accepting the rough deific sketches to fill out better in myself, bestowing them freely on each man and woman I see,
Discovering as much or more in a framer framing a house,
Putting higher claims for him there with his roll'd-up sleeves driving the mallet and chisel,
Not objecting to special revelations, considering a curl of smoke or a hair on the back of my hand just as curious as any revelation,
Lads ahold of fire-engines and hook-and-ladder ropes no less to me than the gods of the antique wars,
Minding their voices' peal through the crash of destruction,
Their brawny limbs passing safe over charr'd laths, their white foreheads whole and unhurt out of the flames;
By the mechanic's wife with her babe at her nipple interceding for every person born,
Three scythes at harvest whizzing in a row from three lusty angels with shirts bagg'd out at their waists,
The snag-tooth'd hostler with red hair redeeming sins past and to come,
Selling all he possesses, travelling on foot to fee lawyers for his brother and sit by him while he is tried for forgery;
What was strewn in the amplest strewing the square rod about me, and not filling the square rod then,
The bull and the bug never worshipp'd half enough,
Dung and dirt more admirable than was dream'd,
The supernatural of no account, myself waiting my time to be one of the supremes,
The day getting ready for me when I shall do as much good as the best, and be as prodigious;
By my life-lumps! becoming already a creator,
Putting myself here and now to the ambush'd womb of the shadows.

42

A call in the midst of the crowd,
My own voice, orotund, sweeping and final.

Come my children,
Come my boys and girls, my women, household and intimates,
Now the performer launches his nerve, he has pass'd his prelude on the reeds within.

Easily written loose-finger'd chords—I feel the thrum of your climax and close.

My head slues round on my neck,
Music rolls, but not from the organ,
Folks are around me, but they are no household of mine.

Ever the hard unsunk ground,
Ever the eaters and drinkers, ever the upward and downward sun,
    ever the air and the ceaseless tides,
Ever myself and my neighbors, refreshing, wicked, real,
Ever the old inexplicable query, ever that thorn'd thumb, that breath
    of itches and thirsts,
Ever the vexer's *hoot! hoot!* till we find where the sly one hides and
    bring him forth,

Ever love, ever the sobbing liquid of life,
Ever the bandage under the chin, ever the trestles of death.

Here and there with dimes on the eyes walking,
To feed the greed of the belly the brains liberally spooning,
Tickets buying, taking, selling, but in to the feast never once going,
Many sweating, ploughing, thrashing, and then the chaff for pay-
    ment receiving,
A few idly owning, and they the wheat continually claiming.

This is the city and I am one of the citizens,
Whatever interests the rest interests me, politics, wars, markets, news-
    papers, schools,
The mayor and councils, banks, tariffs, steamships, factories, stocks,
    stores, real estate and personal estate.

The little plentiful manikins skipping around in collars and tail'd
    coats,
I am aware who they are, (they are positively not worms or fleas,)
I acknowledge the duplicates of myself, the weakest and shallowest
    is deathless with me,
What I do and say the same waits for them,
Every thought that flounders in me the same flounders in them.

I know perfectly well my own egotism,
Know my omnivorous lines and must not write any less,
And would fetch you whoever you are flush with myself.

Not words of routine this song of mine,
But abruptly to question, to leap beyond yet nearer bring;
This printed and bound book—but the printer and the printing-
   office boy?
The well-taken photographs—but your wife or friend close and
   solid in your arms?
The black ship mail'd with iron, her mighty guns in her turrets—
   but the pluck of the captain and engineers?
In the houses the dishes and fare and furniture—but the host and
   hostess, and the look out of their eyes?
The sky up there—yet here or next door, or across the way?
The saints and sages in history—but you yourself?
Sermons, creeds, theology—but the fathomless human brain,
And what is reason? and what is love? and what is life?

43

I do not despise you priests, all time, the world over,
My faith is the greatest of faiths and the least of faiths,
Enclosing worship ancient and modern and all between ancient and
   modern,
Believing I shall come again upon the earth after five thousand years,
Waiting responses from oracles, honoring the gods, saluting the sun,
Making a fetich of the first rock or stump, powowing with sticks in
   the circle of obis,
Helping the lama or brahmin as he trims the lamps of the idols,
Dancing yet through the streets in a phallic procession, rapt and
   austere in the woods a gymnosophist,
Drinking mead from the skull-cup, to Shastas and Vedas admirant,
   minding the Koran,
Walking the Teokallis, spotted with gore from the stone and knife,
   beating the serpent-skin drum,
Accepting the Gospels, accepting him that was crucified, knowing
   assuredly that he is divine,
To the mass kneeling or the puritan's prayer rising, or sitting pa-
   tiently in a pew,
Ranting and frothing in my insane crisis, or waiting dead-like till
   my spirit arouses me,
Looking forth on pavement and land, or outside of pavement and
   land,
Belonging to the winders of the circuit of circuits.

One of that centripetal and centrifugal gang I turn and talk like a
    man leaving charges before a journey.
Down-hearted doubters dull and excluded,
Frivolous, sullen, moping, angry, affected, dishearten'd, atheistical,
I know every one of you, I know the sea of torment, doubt, despair
    and unbelief.

How the flukes splash!
How they contort rapid as lightning, with spasms and spouts of
    blood!

Be at peace bloody flukes of doubters and sullen mopers,
I take my place among you as much as among any,
The past is the push of you, me, all, precisely the same,
And what is yet untried and afterward is for you, me, all, precisely
    the same.

I do not know what is untried and afterward,
But I know it will in its turn prove sufficient, and cannot fail.

Each who passes is consider'd, each who stops is consider'd, not a
    single one can it fail.

It cannot fail the young man who died and was buried,
Nor the young woman who died and was put by his side,
Nor the little child that peep'd in at the door, and then drew back
    and was never seen again,
Nor the old man who has lived without purpose, and feels it with
    bitterness worse than gall,
Nor him in the poor house tubercled by rum and the bad disorder,
Nor the numberless slaughter'd and wreck'd, nor the brutish koboo
    call'd the ordure of humanity,
Nor the sacs merely floating with open mouths for food to slip in,
Nor any thing in the earth, or down in the oldest graves of the earth,
Nor any thing in the myriads of spheres, nor the myriads of myriads
    that inhabit them,
Nor the present, nor the least wisp that is known.

44

It is time to explain myself—let us stand up.

What is known I strip away,
I launch all men and women forward with me into the Unknown.

The clock indicates the moment—but what does eternity indicate?

We have thus far exhausted trillions of winters and summers,
There are trillions ahead, and trillions ahead of them.

Births have brought us richness and variety,
And other births will bring us richness and variety.

I do not call one greater and one smaller,
That which fills its period and place is equal to any.

Were mankind murderous or jealous upon you, my brother, my
  sister?
I am sorry for you, they are not murderous or jealous upon me,
All has been gentle with me, I keep no account with lamentation,
(What have I to do with lamentation?)

I am an acme of things accomplish'd, and I an encloser of things
  to be.

My feet strike an apex of the apices of the stairs,
On every step bunches of ages, and larger bunches between the
  steps,
All below duly travel'd, and still I mount and mount.

Rise after rise bow the phantoms behind me,
Afar down I see the huge first Nothing, I know I was even there,
I waited unseen and always, and slept through the lethargic mist,
And took my time, and took no hurt from the fetid carbon.

Long I was hugg'd close—long and long.

Immense have been the preparations for me,
Faithful and friendly the arms that have help'd me.

Cycles ferried my cradle, rowing and rowing like cheerful boatmen,
For room to me stars kept aside in their own rings,
They sent influences to look after what was to hold me.

Before I was born out of my mother generations guided me,
My embryo has never been torpid, nothing could overlay it.

For it the nebula cohered to an orb,
The long slow strata piled to rest it on,
Vast vegetables gave it sustenance,
Monstrous sauroids transported it in their mouths and deposited it
with care.

All forces have been steadily employ'd to complete and delight me,
Now on this spot I stand with my robust soul.

45

O span of youth! ever-push'd elasticity.
O manhood, balanced, florid and full.

My lovers suffocate me,
Crowding my lips, thick in the pores of my skin,
jostling me through streets and public halls, coming naked to me at
night,
Crying by day *Ahoy!* from the rocks of the river, swinging and
chirping over my head,
Calling my name from flower-beds, vines, tangled underbrush,
Lighting on every moment of my life,
Bussing my body with soft balsamic busses,
Noiselessly passing handfuls out of their hearts and giving them to
be mine.

Old age superbly rising! O welcome, ineffable grace of dying days!
Every condition promulges not only itself, it promulges what grows
after and out of itself,
And the dark hush promulges as much as any.

I open my scuttle at night and see the far-sprinkled systems,
And all I see multiplied as high as I can cipher edge but the rim of
the farther systems.

Wider and wider they spread, expanding, always expanding,
Outward and outward and forever outward.

My sun has his sun and round him obediently wheels,
He joins with his partners a group of superior circuit,
And greater sets follow, making specks of the greatest inside them.

There is no stoppage and never can be stoppage,
If I, you, and the worlds, and all beneath or upon their surfaces,
    were this moment reduced back to a pallid float, it would not
    avail in the long run,
We should surely bring up again where we now stand,
And surely go as much farther, and then farther and farther.

A few quadrillions of eras, a few octillions of cubic leagues, do not
    hazard the span or make it impatient,
They are but parts, any thing is but a part.

See ever so far, there is limitless space outside of that,
Count ever so much, there is limitless time around that.

My rendezvous is appointed, it is certain,
The Lord will be there and wait till I come on perfect terms,
The great Camerado, the lover true for whom I pine will be there.

46

I know I have the best of time and space, and was never measured
    and never will be measured.

I tramp a perpetual journey, (come listen all!)
My signs are a rain-proof coat, good shoes, and a staff cut from the
    woods,
No friend of mine takes his ease in my chair,
I have no chair, no church, no philosophy,
I lead no man to a dinner-table, library, exchange,
But each man and each woman of you I lead upon a knoll,
My left hand hooking you round the waist,
My right hand pointing to landscapes of continents and the public
    road.

Not I, not any one else can travel that road for you,
You must travel it for yourself.

It is not far, it is within reach,
Perhaps you have been on it since you were born and did not know,
Perhaps it is everywhere on water and on land.

Shoulder your duds dear son, and I will mine, and let us hasten forth,
Wonderful cities and free nations we shall fetch as we go.

If you tire, give me both burdens, and rest the chuff of your hand on my hip,
And in due time you shall repay the same service to me,
For after we start we never lie by again.

This day before dawn I ascended a hill and look'd at the crowded heaven,
And I said to my spirit *When we become the enfolders of those orbs, and the pleasure and knowledge of every thing in them, shall we be fill'd and satisfied then?*
And my spirit said *No, we but level that lift to pass and continue beyond.*

You are also asking me questions and I hear you,
I answer that I cannot answer, you must find out for yourself.

Sit a while dear son,
Here are biscuits to eat and here is milk to drink,
But as soon as you sleep and renew yourself in sweet clothes, I kiss you with a good-by kiss and open the gate for your egress hence.

Long enough have you dream'd contemptible dreams,
Now I wash the gum from your eyes,
You must habit yourself to the dazzle of the light and of every moment of your life.

Long have you timidly waded holding a plank by the shore,
Now I will you to be a bold swimmer,
To jump off in the midst of the sea, rise again, nod to me, shout, and laughingly dash with your hair.

47

I am the teacher of athletes,
He that by me spreads a wider breast than my own proves the width of my own,
He most honors my style who learns under it to destroy the teacher.

The boy I love, the same becomes a man not through derived power,
    but in his own right,
Wicked rather than virtuous out of conformity or fear,
Fond of his sweetheart, relishing well his steak,
Unrequited love or a slight cutting him worse than sharp steel cuts,
First-rate to ride, to fight, to hit the bull's eye, to sail a skiff, to sing
    a song or play on the banjo,
Preferring scars and the beard and faces pitted with small-pox over
    all latherers,
And those well-tann'd to those that keep out of the sun.

I teach straying from me, yet who can stray from me?
I follow you whoever you are from the present hour,
My words itch at your ears till you understand them.

I do not say these things for a dollar or to fill up the time while I
    wait for a boat,
(It is you talking just as much as myself, I act as the tongue of you,
Tied in your mouth, in mine it begins to be loosen'd.)

I swear I will never again mention love or death inside a house,
And I swear I will never translate myself at all, only to him or her
    who privately stays with me in the open air.

If you would understand me go to the heights or water-shore,
The nearest gnat is an explanation, and a drop or motion of waves
    a key,
The maul, the oar, the hand-saw, second my words.

No shutter'd room or school can commune with me,
But roughs and little children better than they.

The young mechanic is closest to me, he knows me well,
The woodman that takes his axe and jug with him shall take me
    with him all day,
The farm-boy ploughing in the field feels good at the sound of my
    voice,
In vessels that sail my words sail, I go with fishermen and seamen
    and love them.

The soldier camp'd or upon the march is mine,
On the night ere the pending battle many seek me, and I do not fail
    them,

On that solemn night (it may be their last) those that know me seek
me.

My face rubs to the hunter's face when he lies down alone in his
blanket,
The driver thinking of me does not mind the jolt of his wagon,
The young mother and old mother comprehend me,
The girl and the wife rest the needle a moment and forget where
they are,
They and all would resume what I have told them.

48

I have said that the soul is not more than the body,
And I have said that the body is not more than the soul,
And nothing, not God, is greater to one than one's self is,
And whoever walks a furlong without sympathy walks to his own
funeral drest in his shroud,
And I or you pocketless of a dime may purchase the pick of the
earth,
And to glance with an eye or show a bean in its pod confounds the
learning of all times,
And there is no trade or employment but the young man following
it may become a hero,
And there is no object so soft but it makes a hub for the wheel'd
universe,
And I say to any man or woman, Let your soul stand cool and
composed before a million universes.

And I say to mankind, Be not curious about God,
For I who am curious about each am not curious about God,
(No array of terms can say how much I am at peace about God and
about death.)

I hear and behold God in every object, yet understand God not in
the least,
Nor do I understand who there can be more wonderful than myself.

Why should I wish to see God better than this day?
I see something of God each hour of the twenty-four, and each moment then,
In the faces of men and women I see God, and in my own face in
the glass,

I find letters from God dropt in the street, and every one is sign'd
    by God's name,
And I leave them where they are, for I know that wheresoe'er I go,
Others will punctually come for ever and ever.

49

And as to you Death, and you bitter hug of mortality, it is idle to
    try to alarm me.

To his work without flinching the accoucheur comes,
I see the elder-hand pressing receiving supporting,
I recline by the sills of the exquisite flexible doors,
And mark the outlet, and mark the relief and escape.

And as to you Corpse I think you are good manure, but that does
    not offend me,
I smell the white roses sweet-scented and growing,
I reach to the leafy lips, I reach to the polish'd breasts of melons.

And as to you Life I reckon you are the leavings of many deaths,
(No doubt I have died myself ten thousand times before.)
I hear you whispering there O stars of heaven,
O suns—O grass of graves—O perpetual transfers and promotions,
If you do not say any thing how can I say any thing?

Of the turbid pool that lies in the autumn forest,
Of the moon that descends the steeps of the soughing twilight,
Toss, sparkles of day and dusk—toss on the black stems that decay
    in the muck,
Toss to the moaning gibberish of the dry limbs.

I ascend from the moon, I ascend from the night,
I perceive that the ghastly glimmer is noonday sunbeams reflected,
And debouch to the steady and central from the offspring great or
    small.

50

There is that in me—I do not know what it is—but I know it is in
    me.

Wrench'd and sweaty—calm and cool then my body becomes,
I sleep—I sleep long.

I do not know it—it is without name—it is a word unsaid,
It is not in any dictionary, utterance, symbol.

Something it swings on more than the earth I swing on,
To it the creation is the friend whose embracing awakes me.

Perhaps I might tell more. Outlines! I plead for my brothers and
  sisters.
Do you not see O my brothers and sisters?
It is not chaos or death—it is form, union, plan—it is eternal life—
  it is Happiness.

51

The past and present wilt—I have fill'd them, emptied them,
And proceed to fill my next fold of the future.

Listener up there! what have you to confide to me?
Look in my face while I snuff the sidle of evening,
(Talk honestly, no one else hears you, and I stay only a minute
  longer.)

Do I contradict myself?
Very well then I contradict myself,
(I am large, I contain multitudes.)

I concentrate toward them that are nigh, I wait on the door-slab.

Who has done his day's work? who will soonest be through with
  his supper?
Who wishes to walk with me?

Will you speak before I am gone? will you prove already too late?

52

The spotted hawk swoops by and accuses me, he complains of my
  gab and my loitering.

I too am not a bit tamed, I too am untranslatable,
I sound my barbaric yawp over the roofs of the world.

The last scud of day holds back for me,
It flings my likeness after the rest and true as any on the shadow'd
  wilds,
It coaxes me to the vapor and the dusk.

I depart as air, I shake my white locks at the runaway sun,
I effuse my flesh in eddies, and drift it in lacy jags.

I bequeath myself to the dirt to grow from the grass I love,
If you want me again look for me under your boot-soles.

You will hardly know who I am or what I mean,
But I shall be good health to you nevertheless,
And filter and fibre your blood.

Failing to fetch me at first keep encouraged,
Missing me one place search another,
I stop somewhere waiting for you.

· To Think of Time

1

TO think of time—of all that retrospection,
  To think of today, and the ages continued henceforward.

Have you guess'd you yourself would not continue?
Have you dreaded these earth-beetles?
Have you fear'd the future would be nothing to you?

Is today nothing? is the beginningless past nothing?
If the future is nothing they are just as surely nothing.

To think that the sun rose in the east—that men and women were
    flexible, real, alive—that every thing was alive,
To think that you and I did not see, feel, think, nor bear our part,
To think that we are now here and bear our part.

2

Not a day passes, not a minute or second without an accouchement,
Not a day passes, not a minute or second without a corpse.

The dull nights go over and the dull days also,
The soreness of lying so much in bed goes over,
The physician after long putting off gives the silent and terrible look
    for an answer,
The children come hurried and weeping, and the brothers and sisters
    are sent for,
Medicines stand unused on the shelf, (the camphor-smell has long
    pervaded the rooms,)
The faithful hand of the living does not desert the hand of the dying,
The twitching lips press lightly on the forehead of the dying,
The breath ceases and the pulse of the heart ceases,
The corpse stretches on the bed and the living look upon it,
It is palpable as the living are palpable.

The living look upon the corpse with their eyesight,
But without eyesight lingers a different living and looks curiously
    on the corpse.

3

To think the thought of death merged in the thought of materials,
To think of all these wonders of city and country, and others taking
    great interest in them, and we taking no interest in them.

To think how eager we are in building our houses,
To think others shall be just as eager, and we quite indifferent.

(I see one building the house that serves him a few years, or seventy
    or eighty years at most,
I see one building the house that serves him longer than that.)

Slow-moving and black lines creep over the whole earth—they never
    cease—they are the burial lines,
He that was President was buried, and he that is now President shall
    surely be buried.

4

A reminiscence of the vulgar fate,
A frequent sample of the life and death of workmen,

Each after his kind.

Cold dash of waves at the ferry-wharf, posh and ice in the river, half-
frozen mud in the streets,

A gray discouraged sky overhead, the short last daylight of December,

A hearse and stages, the funeral of an old Broadway stage-driver,
the cortege mostly drivers.

Steady the trot to the cemetery, duly rattles the death-bell,

The gate is pass'd, the new-dug grave is halted at, the living alight,
the hearse uncloses,

The coffin is pass'd out, lower'd and settled, the whip is laid on the
coffin, the earth is swiftly shovel'd in,

The mound above is flatted with the spades—silence,

A minute—no one moves or speaks—it is done,

He is decently put away—is there any thing more?

He was a good fellow, free-mouth'd, quick-temper'd, not bad-look-
ing,

Ready with life or death for a friend, fond of women, gambled, ate
hearty, drank hearty,

Had known what it was to be flush, grew low-spirited toward the
last, sicken'd, was help'd by a contribution,

Died, aged forty-one years—and that was his funeral.

Thumb extended, finger uplifted, apron, cape, gloves, strap, wet-
weather clothes, whip carefully chosen,

Boss, spotter, starter, hostler, somebody loafing on you, you loafing
on somebody, headway, man before and man behind,

Good day's work, bad day's work, pet stock, mean stock, first out,
last out, turning-in at night,

To think that these are so much and so nigh to other drivers, and
he there takes no interest in them.

Good-Bye, My Fancy

GOOD-BYE, my Fancy!
Farewell, dear mate, dear love!
I'm going away, I know not where,
Or to what fortune, or whether I may ever see you again,
So Good-bye, my Fancy.

Now for my last—let me look back a moment;
The slower fainter ticking of the clock is in me,
Exit, nightfall, and soon the heart-thud stopping.
Long have we lived, joy'd, caress'd together;
Delightful!—now separation—Good-bye, my Fancy.

Yet let me not be too hasty:
Long indeed have we lived, slept, filter'd, become really blended
  into one;
Then if we die we die together (yes, we'll remain one),
If we go anywhere we'll go together to meet what happens,
May-be we'll be better off and blither, and learn something,
May-be it is yourself now really ushering me to the true songs (who
  knows?),
May-be it is you the mortal knob really undoing, turning—so now
  finally,
Good-bye—and hail! my Fancy.

Whispers of Heavenly Death

WHISPERS of heavenly death murmur'd I hear,
  Labial gossip of night, sibilant chorals,
Footsteps gently ascending, mystical breezes wafted soft and low,
Ripples of unseen rivers, tides of a current flowing, forever flowing
(Or is it the plashing of tears? the measureless waters of human
  tears?)

I see, just see skyward, great cloud-masses;
Mournfully, slowly they roll, silently swelling and mixing,
With at times a half-dimm'd sadden'd far-off star,
Appearing and disappearing.

(Some parturition rather, some solemn immortal birth;
On the frontiers to eyes impenetrable,
Some soul is passing over.)

O Captain! My Captain!

O CAPTAIN! my Captain, our fearful trip is done,
   The ship has weathered every rack, the prize we sought is
      won,
The port is near, the bells I hear, the people all exulting,
While follow eyes the steady keel, the vessel grim and daring;
   But O heart! heart! heart!
    O the bleeding drops of red,
      Where on the deck my Captain lies,
       Fallen cold and dead.

O Captain! my Captain! rise up and hear the bells;
Rise up—for you the flag is flung—for you the bugle trills,
For you bouquets and ribboned wreaths—for you the shores acrowd-
     ing,
For you they call, the swaying mass, their eager faces turning;
   Here Captain! dear father!
    This arm beneath your head!
      It is some dream that on the deck
       You've fallen cold and dead.

My Captain does not answer, his lips are pale and still,
My father does not feel my arm, he has no pulse nor will,
The ship is anchored safe and sound, its voyage closed and done,
From fearful trip the victor ship comes in with object won;
   Exult O shores, and ring O bells!
    But I, with mournful tread,
      Walk the deck my Captain lies,
       Fallen cold and dead.

LOUISE CHANDLER MOULTON

Hic Jacet

SO Love is dead that has been quick so long!
   Close, then, his eyes, and bear him to his rest,
With eglantine and myrtle on his breast,
   And leave him there, their pleasant scents among;
And chant a sweet and melancholy song
   About the charms whereof he was possessed,
And how of all things he was loveliest,
   And to compare with aught were him to wrong.
Leave him beneath the still and solemn stars,
   That gather and look down from their far place
With their long calm our brief woes to deride,
   Until the Sun the Morning's gate unbars
And mocks, in turn, our sorrows with his face;—
   And yet, had Love been Love, he had not died.

RICHARD REALF

Indirection

FAIR are the flowers and the children, but their subtle suggestion
   is fairer;
Rare is the roseburst of dawn, but the secret that clasps it is rarer;
Sweet the exultance of song, but the strain that precedes it is sweeter;
And never was poem yet writ, but the meaning outmastered the
   metre.
Never a daisy that grows, but a mystery guideth the growing;
Never a river that flows, but a majesty sceptres the flowing;
Never a Shakespeare that soared, but a stronger than he did enfold
   him,
Nor ever a prophet foretells, but a mightier seer hath foretold him.

Back of the canvas that throbs the painter is hinted and hidden;
Into the statue that breathes the soul of the sculptor is bidden;
Under the joy that is felt lie the infinite issues of feeling;
Crowning the glory revealed is the glory that crowns the revealing.

Great are the symbols of being, but that which is symboled is greater;
Vast the create and beheld, but vaster the inward creator;
Back of the sound broods the silence, back of the gift stands the
    giving;
Back of the hand that receives thrill the sensitive nerves of receiving.

Space is as nothing to spirit, the deed is outdone by the doing;
The heart of the wooer is warm, but warmer the heart of the woo-
    ing;
And up from the pits where these shiver, and up from the heights
    where those shine,
Twin voices and shadows swim starward, and the essence of life is
    divine.

EMILY DICKINSON

I

I Found the Phrase

I FOUND the phrase to every thought
    I ever had, but one;
And that defies me,—as a hand

Did try to chalk the sun
To races nurtured in the dark:—
How would your own begin?
Can blaze be done in cochineal,
Or noon in mazarin?

II

Parting

MY life closed twice before its close;
 It yet remains to see
If Immortality unveil
A third event to me,
So huge, so hopeless to conceive,
 As these that twice befell:
Parting is all we know of heaven,
 And all we need of hell.

III.

Called Back

JUST lost when I was saved!
 Just felt the world go by!
Just girt me for the onset with eternity,
When breath blew back,
And on the other side
I heard recede the disappointed tide;

Therefore, as one returned, I feel,
Odd secrets of the line to tell!
Some sailor, skirting foreign shores,
Some pale reporter from the awful doors
Before the seal!

Next time, to stay!
Next time, the things to see
By ear unheard,
Unscrutinized by eye.

Next time, to tarry,
While the ages steal,—
Slow tramp the centuries,
And the cycles wheel.

IV

Choice

OF all the souls that stand create
I have elected one.
When sense from spirit files away,
And subterfuge is done;

When that which is and that which was
Apart, intrinsic, stand,
And this brief tragedy of flesh
Is shifted like a sand;

When figures show their royal front
And mists are carved away,—
Behold the atom I preferred
To all the lists of clay!

V

To Hear an Oriole

TO hear an oriole sing
May be a common thing,
Or only a divine.

It is not of the bird
Who sings the same, unheard,
As unto crowd.

The fashion of the ear
Attireth that it hear
In dun or fair.

So whether it be rune,
Or whether it be none,
Is of within;

The "tune is in the tree,"
The sceptic showeth me;
"No, sir! In thee!"

VI

There's a Certain Slant of Light

THERE'S a certain slant of light,
On winter afternoons,
That oppresses, like the weight
Of cathedral tunes.

Heavenly hurt it gives us;
We can find no scar,
But internal difference
Where the meanings are.

None may teach it anything
'Tis the seal, despair,—
An imperial affliction
Sent us of the air.

When it comes, the landscape listens,
Shadows hold their breath;
When it goes, 'tis like the distance
On the look of death.

VII

Apparently with No Surprise

APPARENTLY with no surprise
To any happy flower,
The frost beheads it at its play
In accidental power.
The blond assassin passes on,
The sun proceeds unmoved
To measure off another day
For an approving God.

VIII

The Last Night

THE last night that she lived,
  It was a common night,
Except the dying; this to us
Made nature different.

We noticed smallest things,—
Things overlooked before,
By this great light upon our minds
Italicized, as 'twere.

That others could exist
While she must finish quite,
A jealousy for her arose
So nearly infinite.

We waited while she passed;
It was a narrow time,
Too jostled were our souls to speak,
At length the notice came.

She mentioned, and forgot;
Then lightly as a reed
Bent to the water, shivered scarce,
Consented, and was dead.

And we, we placed the hair,
And drew the head erect;
And then an awful leisure was,
Our faith to regulate.

IX

The Bustle in a House

THE bustle in a house
  The morning after death
Is solemnest of industries
Enacted upon earth,—

The sweeping up the heart,
And putting love away
We shall not want to use again
Until eternity.

x

I Know That He Exists

I KNOW that he exists
   Somewhere, in silence.
He has hid his rare life
From our gross eyes.

'Tis an instant's play,
'Tis a fond ambush,
Just to make bliss
Earn her own surprise!

But should the play
Prove piercing earnest,
Should the glee glaze
In death's stiff stare,

Would not the fun
Look too expensive?
Would not the jest
Have crawled too far?

xi

We Never Know How High

WE never know how high we are
   Till we are called to rise;
And then, if we are true to plan,
   Our statures touch the skies.

The heroism we recite
   Would be a daily thing,

Did not ourselves the cubits warp
For fear to be a king.

XII

The Soul Selects

THE soul selects her own society,
   Then shuts the door;
On her divine majority
Obtrude no more.

Unmoved, she notes the chariot's pausing
At her low gate;
Unmoved, an emperor is kneeling
Upon her mat.
I've known her from an ample nation
Choose one;
Then close the valves of her attention
Like stone.

XIII

A Thought Went Up My Mind

A THOUGHT went up my mind today
   That I have had before,
But did not finish,—some way back,
I could not fix the year,

Nor where it went, nor why it came
The second time to me,
Nor definitely what it was,
Have I the art to say.

But somewhere in my soul, I know
I've met the thing before;
It just reminded me—'twas all—
And came my way no more.

XIV

Dying

I HEARD a fly buzz when I died;
　　The stillness round my form
Was like the stillness in the air
　　Between the heaves of storm.

The eyes beside had wrung them dry,
　　And breaths were gathering sure
For that last onset, when the king
　　Be witnessed in his power.

I willed my keepsakes, signed away
　　What portion of me I
Could make assignable—and then
　　There interposed a fly,

With blue, uncertain, stumbling buzz,
　　Between the light and me;
And then the windows failed, and then
　　I could not see to see.

XV

A Clock Stopped

A CLOCK stopped—not the mantel's;
　　Geneva's farthest skill
Can't put the puppet bowing
　　That just now dangled still.

An awe came on the trinket!
　　The figures hunched with pain,
Then quivered out of decimals
　　Into degreeless noon.

It will not stir for doctors,
　　This pendulum of snow;

The shopman importunes it,
    While cool, concernless No

Nods from the gilded pointers,
    Nods from the seconds slim,
Decades of arrogance between
    The dial life and him.

XVI

Not Any Sunny Tone

NOT any sunny tone
    From any fervent zone
Finds entrance there.
Better a grave of Balm
Toward human nature's home,
    And Robins near,
Then a stupendous Tomb
Proclaiming to the gloom
    How dead we are.

XVII

I Felt a Funeral

I FELT a funeral in my brain,
    And mourners, to and fro,
Kept treading, treading, till it seemed
    That sense was breaking through.

And when they all were seated,
    A service like a drum
Kept beating, beating, till I thought
    My mind was going numb.

And then I heard them lift a box,
    And creak across my soul
With those same boots of lead, again.
    Then space began to toll.

As all the heavens were a bell,
　And Being but an ear,
And I and silence some strange race,
　Wrecked, solitary, here.

XVIII

To My Quick Ear

TO my quick ear the leaves conferred;
　The bushes they were bells;
I could not find a privacy
From Nature's sentinels.

In cave if I presumed to hide,
The walls began to tell;
Creation seemed a mighty crack
To make me visible.

XIX

In the Garden

A BIRD came down the walk:
　He did not know I saw;
He bit an angle-worm in halves
And ate the fellow raw.

And then he drank a dew
From a convenient grass,
And then hopped sidewise to the wall
To let a beetle pass.

He glanced with rapid eyes
That hurried all abroad—
They looked like frightened beads, I thought;
He stirred his velvet head

Like one in danger; cautious,
I offered him a crumb,

And he unrolled his feathers
And rowed him softer home

Than oars divide the ocean,
Too silver for a seam,
Or butterflies, off banks of noon,
Leap, plashless, as they swim.

XX

Safe in Their Alabaster Chambers

SAFE in their alabaster chambers,
  Untouched by morning and untouched by noon,
Sleep the meek members of the resurrection,
Rafter of satin, and roof of stone.

Light laughs the breeze in her castle of sunshine;
Babbles the bee in a stolid ear;
Pipe the sweet birds in ignorant cadence—
Ah, what sagacity perished here!

Grand go the years in the crescent above them;
Worlds scoop their arcs, and firmaments row,
Diadems drop and Doges surrender,
Soundless as dots on a disk of snow.

XXI

The Wind

OF all the sounds despatched abroad,
  There's not a charge to me
Like that old measure in the boughs,
That phraseless melody

The wind does, working like a hand
Whose fingers brush the sky,
Then quiver down, with tufts of tune
Permitted gods and me.

When winds go round and round in bands,
And thrum upon the door,
And birds take places overhead,
To bear them orchestra,

I crave him grace, of summer boughs,
If such an outcast be,
He never heard that fleshless chant
Rise solemn in the tree,

As if some caravan of sound
On deserts, in the sky,
Had broken rank,
Then knit, and passed
In seamless company.

XXII

The Chariot

BECAUSE I could not stop for Death,
He kindly stopped for me;
The carriage held but just ourselves
And Immortality.

We slowly drove, we knew no haste,
And I had put away
My labour, and my leisure too,
For his civility.

We passed the school where children played
Their lessons scarcely done;
We passed the fields of gazing grain,
We passed the setting sun.

We paused before a house that seemed
A swelling on the ground;
The roof was scarcely visible,
The cornice but a mound.

Since then 'tis centuries; but each
Feels shorter than the day
I first surmised the horses' heads
Were toward eternity.

XXIII

I Died for Beauty

I DIED for beauty, but was scarce
Adjusted in the tomb,
When one who died for truth was lain
In an adjoining room.

He questioned softly why I failed?
"For beauty," I replied.
"And I for truth—the two are one;
We brethren are," he said.

And so, as kinsmen met a-night,
We talked between the rooms,
Until the moss had reached our lips,
And covered up our names.

XXIV

Mysteries

THE murmur of a bee
A Witchcraft yieldeth me.
If any ask me why,
'Twere easier to die
Than tell.

The red upon the hill
Taketh away my will;
If anybody sneer,
Take care, for God is here,
That's all.

The breaking of the day
Addeth to my degree;
If any ask me how,
Artist, who drew me so,
Must tell!

HELEN HUNT JACKSON

Emigravit

WITH sails full set, the ship her anchor weighs.
    Strange names shine out beneath her figure head.
What glad farewells with eager eyes are said!
What cheer for him who goes, and him who stays!
Fair skies, rich lands, new homes, and untried days
Some go to seek: the rest but wait instead,
Watching the way wherein their comrades led,
Until the next stanch ship her flag doth raise.
Who knows what myriad colonies there are
Of fairest fields, and rich, undreamed-of gains
Thick planted in the distant shining plains
Which we call sky because they lie so far?
Oh, write of me, not "Died in bitter pains,"
But "Emigrated to another star!"

A Dream

I DREAMED that I was dead and crossed heavens,—
    Heavens after heavens with burning feet and swift,—
And cried: "O God, where art Thou? I left one
    On earth, whose burden I would pray Thee lift."

I was so dead I wondered at no thing,—
    Not even that the angels slowly turned
Their faces, speechless, as I hurried by
    (Beneath my feet the golden pavements burned);

Nor, at the first, that I could not find God,
　Because the heavens stretched endlessly like space.
At last a terror seized my very soul;
　I seemed alone in all the crowded place.

Then, sudden, one compassionate cried out,
　Though like the rest his face from me he turned,
As I were one no angel might regard
　(Beneath my feet the golden pavements burned):

"No more in heaven than earth will he find God
　Who does not know his loving mercy swift
But waits the moment consummate and ripe,
　Each burden from each human soul to lift."

Though I was dead, I died again for shame;
　Lonely, to flee from heaven again I turned;
The ranks of angels looked away from me
　(Beneath my feet the golden pavements burned).

Danger

WITH what a childish and short-sighted sense
　Fear seeks for safety; reckons up the days
Of danger and escape, the hours and ways
Of death; it breathless flies the pestilence;
It walls itself in towers of defence;
By land, by sea, against the storm it lays
Down barriers; then, comforted, it says:
"This spot, this hour is safe." Oh, vain pretence!
Man born of man knows nothing when he goes;
The winds blow where they list, and will disclose
To no man which brings safety, which brings risk.
The mighty are brought low by many a thing
Too small to name. Beneath the daisy's disk
Lies hid the pebble for the fatal sling.

EDWARD ROWLAND SILL

Five Lives

FIVE mites of monads dwelt in a round drop
That twinkled on a leaf by a pool in the sun.
To the naked eye they lived invisible;
Specks, for a world of whom the empty shell
Of a mustard-seed had been a hollow sky.

One was a meditative monad, called a sage;
And, shrinking all his mind within, he thought:
"Tradition, handed down for hours and hours,
Tells that our globe, this quivering crystal world,
Is slowly dying. What if, seconds hence,
When I am very old, yon shimmering dome
Come drawing down and down, till all things end?"
Then with a weazen smirk he proudly felt
No other mote of God had ever gained
Such giant grasp of universal truth.

One was a transcendental monad; thin
And long and slim in the mind; and thus he mused:
"Oh, vast, unfathomable monad-souls!
Made in the image"—a hoarse frog croaks from the pool—
"Hark! 't was some god, voicing his glorious thought
In thunder music! Yea, we hear their voice,
And we may guess their minds from ours, their work.
Some taste they have like ours, some tendency
To wriggle about, and munch a trace of scum."
He floated up on a pin-point bubble of gas
That burst, pricked by the air, and he was gone.

One was a barren-minded monad, called
A positivist; and he knew positively:
"There is no world beyond this certain drop.
Prove me another! let the dreamers dream

Of their faint dreams, and noises from without,
And higher and lower; life is life enough."
Then swaggering half a hair's breadth, hungrily
He seized upon an atom of bug, and fed.

One was a tattered monad, called a poet;
And with shrill voice ecstatic thus he sang:
"Oh, the little female monad's lips!
Oh, the little female monad's eyes:
Ah, the little, little, female, female monad!"

The last was a strong-minded monadess,
Who dashed amid the infusoria,
Danced high and low, and wildly spun and dove
Till the dizzy others held their breath to see.

But while they led their wondrous little lives
Aeonian moments had gone wheeling by,
The burning drop had shrunk with fearful speed;
A glistening film—'t was gone; the leaf was dry.
The little ghost of an inaudible squeak
Was lost to the frog that goggled from his stone;
Who, at the huge, slow tread of a thoughtful ox
Coming to drink, stirred sideways fatly, plunged,
Launched backward twice, and all the pool was still.

JOHN TOWNSEND TROWBRIDGE

Midwinter

THE speckled sky is dim with snow,
The light flakes falter and fall slow;
Athwart the hill-top, rapt and pale,
Silently drops a silvery veil;
And all the valley is shut in
By flickering curtains gray and thin.

But cheerily the chickadee
Singeth to me on fence and tree;
The snow sails round him as he sings,
White as the down of angels' wings.

I watch the slow flakes as they fall
On bank and brier and broken wall;
Over the orchard, waste and brown,
All noiselessly they settle down,
Tipping the apple-boughs, and each
Light quivering twig of plum and peach.

On turf and curb and bower-roof
The snow-storm spreads its ivory woof;
It paves with pearl the garden-walk;
And lovingly round tattered stalk
And shivering stem its magic weaves
A mantle fair as lily-leaves.

The hooded beehive, small and low,
Stands like a maiden in the snow;
And the old door-slab is half-hid
Under an alabaster lid.

All day it snows: the sheeted post
Gleams in the dimness like a ghost;
All day the blasted oak has stood
A muffled wizard of the wood;

Garland and airy cap adorn
The sumach and the wayside thorn,
And clustering spangles lodge and shine
In the dark tresses of the pine.

The ragged bramble, dwarfed and old,
Shrinks like a beggar in the cold;
In surplice white the cedar stands,
And blesses him with priestly hands.

Still cheerily the chickadee
Singeth to me on fence and tree:
But in my inmost ear is heard

The music of a holier bird;
And heavenly thoughts as soft and white
As snow-flakes, on my soul alight,
Clothing with love my lonely heart,
Healing with peace each bruisëd part,
Till all my being seems to be
Transfigured by their purity.

GEORGE HENRY BOKER

Dirge for a Soldier

CLOSE his eyes; his work is done!
    What to him is friend or foeman,
Rise of moon, or set of sun,
    Hand of man, or kiss of woman?
        Lay him low, lay him low,
        In the clover or the snow!
        What cares he? he cannot know:
            Lay him low!

As man may, he fought his fight,
    Proved his truth by his endeavor;
Let him sleep in solemn night,
    Sleep forever and forever.
        Lay him low, lay him low,
        In the clover or the snow!
        What cares he? he cannot know:
            Lay him low!

Fold him in his country's stars,
    Roll the drum and fire the volley!
What to him are all our wars,
    What but death bemocking folly?
        Lay him low, lay him low,
        In the clover or the snow!
        What cares he? he cannot know:
            Lay him low!

Leave him to God's watching eye,
 Trust him to the hand that made him
Mortal love weeps idly by:
 God alone has power to aid him.
  Lay him low, lay him low,
  In the clover or the snow!
  What cares he? he cannot know:
   Lay him low!

MAURICE THOMPSON

Wild Honey

WHERE hints of racy sap and gum
 Out of the old dark forest come;

Where birds their beaks like hammers wield,
And pith is pierced and bark is peeled;

Where the green walnut's outer rind
Gives precious bitterness to the wind;

There lurks the sweet creative power,
As lurks the honey in the flower.

In winter's bud that bursts in spring,
In nut of autumn's ripening,

In acrid bulb beneath the mold,
Sleeps the elixir, strong and old,

That Rosicrucians sought in vain,—
Life that renews itself again!

What bottled perfume is so good
As fragrance of split tulip-wood?

What fabled drink of God or muse
Was rich as purple mulberry juice?

And what school-polished gem of thought
Is like the rune from Nature caught?

He is a poet strong and true
Who loves wild thyme and honey-dew;

And like a brown bee works and sings
With morning freshness on his wings,

And a gold burden on his thighs,—
The pollen-dust of centuries!

JOHN VANCE CHENEY

The Happiest Heart

WHO drives the horses of the sun
    Shall lord it but a day;
Better the lowly deed were done,
And kept the humble way.

The rust will find the sword of fame,
The dust will hide the crown;
Ay, none shall nail so high his name
Time will not tear it down.

The happiest heart that ever beat
Was in some quiet breast
That found the common daylight sweet,
And left to Heaven the rest.

STEPHEN COLLINS FOSTER

My Old Kentucky Home

THE sun shines bright in the old Kentucky home;
 'Tis summer, the darkies are gay;
The corn-top's ripe, and the meadow's in the bloom,
 While the birds make music all the day.
The young folks roll on the little cabin floor,
 All merry, all happy and bright;
By-'n'-by hard times comes a-knocking at the door:—
 Then my old Kentucky home, good-night!

    Weep no more, my lady,
     O, weep no more today!
   We will sing one song for the old Kentucky home,
    For the old Kentucky home, far away.

They hunt no more for the possum and the coon,
 On the meadow, the hill, and the shore;
They sing no more by the glimmer of the moon,
 On the bench by the old cabin door.
The day goes by like a shadow o'er the heart,
 With sorrow, where all was delight;
The time has come when the darkies have to part:—
 Then my old Kentucky home, good-night!

The head must bow, and the back will have to bend
 Wherever the darky may go;
A few more days, and the trouble all will end,
 In the field where the sugar-canes grow.
A few more days for to tote the weary load,—
 No matter, 'twill never be light;
A few more days till we totter on the road:—
 Then my old Kentucky home, good-night!

Weep no more, my lady,
O, weep no more today!
We will sing one song for the old Kentucky home,
For the old Kentucky home, far away.

THOMAS BAILEY ALDRICH

Memory

MY mind lets go a thousand things,
　　Like dates of wars and deaths of kings,
And yet recalls the very hour—
'Twas noon by yonder village tower,
And on the last blue noon in May
The wind came briskly up this way,
Crisping the brook beside the road;
Then, pausing here, set down its load
Of pine-scents, and shook listlessly
Two petals from that wild-rose tree.

Enamored Architect of Airy Rhyme

ENAMORED architect of airy rhyme,
　　Build as thou wilt; heed not what each man says:
Good souls, but innocent of dreamers' ways,
Will come, and marvel why thou wastest time;
Others, beholding how thy turrets climb
'Twixt theirs and heaven, will hate thee all thy days;
But most beware of those who come to praise.
O Wondersmith, O worker in sublime
And heaven-sent dreams, let art be all in all;
Build as thou wilt, unspoiled by praise or blame,
Build as thou wilt, and as thy light is given:
Then, if at last the airy structure fall,
Dissolve, and vanish—take thyself no shame.
They fail, and they alone, who have not striven.

JOHN BURROUGHS

Waiting

SERENE, I fold my hands and wait,
    Nor care for wind, or tide, or sea;
I rave no more 'gainst time or fate,
    For, lo! my own shall come to me.

I stay my haste, I make delays,
    For what avails this eager pace?
I stand amid the eternal ways,
    And what is mine shall know my face.

Asleep, awake, by night or day,
    The friends I seek are seeking me;
No wind can drive my bark astray,
    Nor change the tide of destiny.

What matter if I stand alone?
    I wait with joy the coming years;
My heart shall reap where it has sown,
    And garner up its fruit of tears.

The waters know their own and draw
    The brook that springs in yonder height;
So flows the good with equal law
    Unto the soul of pure delight.

The stars come nightly to the sky;
    The tidal wave unto the sea;
Nor time, nor space, nor deep, nor high,
    Can keep my own away from me.

JOAQUIN MILLER

At the Grave of Walker

HE lies low in the levelled sand,
  Unsheltered from the tropic sun,
And now of all he knew not one
Will speak him fair in that far land.
Perhaps 'twas this that made me seek,
Disguised, his grave one winter-tide;
A weakness for the weaker side,
A siding with the helpless weak.

A palm not far held out a hand,
Hard by a long green bamboo swung,
And bent like some great bow unstrung,
And quivered like a willow wand;
Perched on its fruits that crooked hand,
Beneath a broad banana's leaf,
A bird in rainbow splendor sang
A low, sad song, tempered grief.

No sod, no sign, no cross nor stone,
But at his side a cactus green
Upheld its lances long and keen;
It stood in sacred sands alone,
Flat-palmed and fierce with lifted spears;
One bloom of crimson crowned its head,
A drop of blood, so bright, so red,
Yet redolent as roses' tears.

In my left hand I held a shell,
All rosy lipped and pearly red;
I laid it by his lowly bed,
For he did love so passing well
The grand songs of the solemn sea.
O shell! sing well, wild, with a will,

When storms blow loud and birds be still,
The wildest sea-song known to thee!

I said some things with folded hands,
Soft whispered in the dim sea-sound,
And eyes held humbly to the ground,
And frail knees sunken in the sands.
He had done more than this for me,
And yet I could not well do more:
I turned me down the olive shore,
And set a sad face to the sea.

———— • • • ————

SIDNEY LANIER

———— • • • ————

The Marshes of Glynn

GLOOMS of the live-oaks, beautiful-braided and woven
   With intricate shades of the vines that myriad-cloven
Clamber the forks of the multiform boughs,—
      Emerald twilights,—
      Virginal shy lights,
Wrought of the leaves to allure to the whisper of vows,
When lovers pace timidly down through the green colonnades
Of the dim sweet woods, of the dear dark woods,
   Of the heavenly woods and glades,
That run to the radiant marginal sand-beach within
      The wide sea-marshes of Glynn;—

Beautiful glooms, soft dusks in the noon-day fire,—
Wildwood privacies, closets of lone desire,
Chamber from chamber parted with wavering arras of leaves,—
Cells for the passionate pleasure of prayer to the soul that grieves,
Pure with a sense of the passing of saints through the wood,
Cool for the dutiful weighing of ill with good;—
O braided dusks of the oak and woven shades of the vine,
While the riotous noon-day sun of the June-day long did shine
Ye held me fast in your heart and I held you fast in mine;

But now when the noon is no more, and riot is rest,
And the sun is a-wait at the ponderous gate of the West,
And the slant yellow beam down the wood-aisle doth seem
Like a lane into heaven that leads from a dream,—
Ay, now, when my soul all day hath drunken the soul of the oak,
And my heart is at ease from men, and the wearisome sound of the
      stroke
  Of the scythe of time and the trowel of trade is low,
  And belief overmasters doubt, and I know that I know,
  And my spirit is grown to a lordly great compass within,
That the length and the breadth and the sweep of the marshes of
    Glynn
Will work me no fear like the fear they have wrought me of yore
When length was fatigue, and when breadth was but bitterness sore,
And when terror and shrinking and dreary unnamable pain
Drew over me out of the merciless miles of the plain,—

Oh, now, unafraid, I am fain to face
  The vast sweet visage of space.
To the edge of the wood I am drawn, I am drawn,   ·
Where the gray beach glimmering runs, as a belt of the dawn,
  For a mete and a mark
    To the forest-dark:—
      So:
Affable live-oak, leaning low,—
Thus—with your favor—soft, with a reverent hand
(Not lightly touching your person, Lord of the land!),
Bending your beauty aside, with a step I stand
On the firm-packed sand,
    Free
By a world of marsh that borders a world of sea.
  Sinuous southward and sinuous northward the shimmering band
  Of the sand-beach fastens the fringe of the marsh to the folds of
    the land.
Inward and outward to northward and southward the beach-lines
    linger and curl
As a silver-wrought garment that clings to and follows the firm sweet
    limbs of a girl.
Vanishing, swerving, evermore curving again into sight,
Softly the sand-beach wavers away to a dim grap looping of light.
And what if behind me to westward the wall of the woods stands
    high?

The world lies east: how ample, the marsh and the sea and the sky!
A league and a league of marsh-grass, waist-high, broad in the blade,
Green, and all of a height, and unflecked with a light or a shade,
Stretch leisurely off, in a pleasant plain,
To the terminal blue of the main.

Oh, what is abroad in the marsh and the terminal sea?
   Somehow my soul seems suddenly free
From the weighing of fate and the sad discussion of sin,
By the length and the breadth and the sweep of the marshes of
   Glynn.

Ye marshes, how candid and simple and nothing-withholding and
      free
Ye publish yourselves to the sky and offer yourselves to the sea!
Tolerant plains, that suffer the sea and the rains and the sun,
Ye spread and span like the catholic man who hath mightily won
God out of knowledge and good out of infinite pain
And sight out of blindness and purity out of a stain.

As the marsh-hen secretly builds on the watery sod,
Behold I will build me a nest on the greatness of God:
I will fly in the greatness of God as the marsh-hen flies
In the freedom that fills all the space 'twixt the marsh and the skies:
By so many roots as the marsh-grass sends in the sod
I will heartily lay me a-hold on the greatness of God:
Oh, like to the greatness of God is the greatness within
The range of the marshes, the liberal marshes of Glynn.

And the sea lends large, as the marsh: lo, out of his plenty the sea
Pours fast: full soon the time of the flood-tide must be:
Look how the grace of the sea doth go
About and about through the intricate channels that flow
      Here and there,
         Everywhere,
Till his waters have flooded the uttermost creeks and the low-lying
   lanes,
And the marsh is meshed with a million veins,
That like as with rosy and silvery essences flow
   In the rose-and-silver evening glow.
         Farewell, my lord Sun!
The creeks overflow: a thousand rivulets run

'Twixt the roots of the sod; the blades of the marsh-grass stir;
Passeth a hurrying sound of wings that westward whir;
Passeth, and all is still; and the currents cease to run;
And the sea and the marsh are one.

How still the plains of the waters be!
The tide is in his ecstasy.
The tide is at his highest height:
 And it is night.

And now from the Vast of the Lord will the waters of sleep
Roll in on the souls of men,
But who will reveal to our waking ken
The forms that swim and the shapes that creep
 Under the waters of sleep?

Opposition

OF fret, of dark, of thorn, of chill,
 Complain no more; for these, O heart,
Direct the random of the will
 As rhymes direct the rage of art.

The lute's fixt fret, that runs athwart
 The strain and purpose of the string,
For governance and nice consort
 Doth bar his wilful wavering.

The dark hath many dear avails;
 The dark distils divinest dews;
The dark is rich with nightingales,
 With dreams, and with the heavenly Muse.

Bleeding with thorns of petty strife,
 I'll ease (as lovers do) my smart
With sonnets to my lady Life
 Writ red in issues from the heart.

What grace may lie within the chill
 Of favor frozen fast in scorn!
When Good's a-freeze, we call it Ill!
 This rosy Time is glacier-born.

Of fret, of dark, of thorn, of chill,
　　Complain thou not, O heart; for these
Bank-in the current of the will
　　To uses, arts, and charities.

* * *

HENRY AUGUSTIN BEERS

* * *

Ecce in Deserto

THE wilderness a secret keeps
　　Upon whose guess I go:
Eye hath not seen, ear hath not heard;
　　And yet I know, I know,

Some day the viewless latch will lift,
　　The door of air swing wide
To one lost chamber of the wood
　　Where those shy mysteries hide,—

One yet unfound, receding depth,
　　From which the wood-thrush sings,
Still luring in to darker shades,
　　In—in to colder springs.

There is no wind abroad today.
　　But hark!—the pine-tops' roar,
That sleep and in their dreams repeat
　　The music of the shore.

What wisdom in their needles stirs?
　　What song is that they sing?
Those airs that search the forest's heart,
　　What rumor do they bring?

A hushed excitement fills the gloom,
　　And, in the stillness, clear
The vireo's tell-tale warning rings:
　　" 'Tis near—'tis near—'tis near!"

As, in the fairy-tale, more loud
    The ghostly music plays
When, toward the enchanted bower, the prince
    Draws closer through the maze.

Nay—nay. I track a fleeter game,
    A wilder than ye know,
To lairs beyond the inmost haunt
    Of thrush or vireo.

This way it passed: the scent lies fresh;
    The ferns still lightly shake.
Ever I follow hard upon,
    But never overtake.

To other woods the trail leads on,
    To other worlds and new,
Where they who keep the secret here
    Will keep the promise too.

JOHN BANISTER TABB

Clover

LITTLE masters, hat in hand
    Let me in your presence stand,
Till your silence solve for me
This your threefold mystery.

Tell me—for I long to know—
How, in darkness there below,
Was your fairy fabric spun,
Spread and fashioned, three in one.

Did your gossips gold and blue,
Sky and Sunshine, choose for you,
Ere your triple forms were seen,
Suited liveries of green?

Can ye,—if ye dwelt indeed
Captives of a prison seed,—
Like the Genie, once again
Get you back into the grain?

Little masters, may I stand
In your presence, hat in hand,
Waiting till you solve for me
This your threefold mystery?

EDWIN MARKHAM

The Man with the Hoe

GOD MADE MAN IN HIS OWN IMAGE
IN THE IMAGE OF GOD HE MADE HIM.—GENESIS.

BOWED by the weight of centuries he leans
Upon his hoe and gazes on the ground,
The emptiness of ages in his face,
And on his back the burden of the world.
Who made him dead to rapture and despair,
A thing that grieves not and that never hopes,
Stolid and stunned, a brother to the ox?
Who loosened and let down this brutal jaw?
Whose was the hand that slanted back this brow?
Whose breath blew out the light within this brain?

Is this the Thing the Lord God made and gave
To have dominion over sea and land;
To trace the stars and search the heavens for power;
To feel the passion of Eternity?
Is this the dream He dreamed who shaped the suns
And markt their ways upon the ancient deep?
Down all the caverns of Hell to their last gulf
There is no shape more terrible than this—
More tongued with censure of the world's blind greed—

More filled with signs and portents for the soul—
More packt with danger to the universe.

What gulfs between him and the seraphim!
Slave of the wheel of labor, what to him
Are Plato and the swing of Pleiades?
What the long reaches of the peaks of song,
The rift of dawn, the reddening of the rose?
Through this dread shape the suffering ages look;
Time's tragedy is in that aching stoop;
Through this dread shape humanity betrayed,
Plundered, profaned and disinherited,
Cries protest to the Powers that made the world,
A protest that is also prophecy.

O masters, lords and rulers in all lands,
Is this the handiwork you give to God,
This monstrous thing distorted and soul-quencht?
How will you ever straighten up this shape;
Touch it again with immortality;
Give back the upward looking and the light;
Rebuild in it the music and the dream;
Make right the immemorial infamies,
Perfidious wrongs, immedicable woes?

O masters, lords and rulers in all lands,
How will the future reckon with this Man?
How answer his brute question in that hour
When whirlwinds of rebellion shake all shores?
How will it be with kingdoms and with kings—
With those who shaped him to the thing he is—
When this dumb Terror shall rise to judge the world,
After the silence of the centuries?

WILLIAM VAUGHN MOODY

A Grey Day

GREY drizzling mists the moorlands drape,
Rain whitens the dead sea,
From headland dim to sullen cape
Grey sails creep wearily.
I know not how that merchantman
Has found the heart; but 'tis her plan
Seaward her endless course to shape.

Unreal as insects that appall
A drunkard's peevish brain,
O'er the grey deep the dories crawl,
Four-legged, with rowers twain:
Midgets and minims of the earth,
Across old ocean's vasty girth
Toiling—heroic, comical!

I wonder how that merchant's crew
Have ever found the will!
I wonder what the fishers do
To keep them toiling still!
I wonder how the heart of man
Has patience to live out its span,
Or wait until its dreams come true.

Pandora Song

I STOOD within the heart of God;
It seemed a place that I had known:
(I was blood-sister to the clod,
Blood-brother to the stone.)

I found my love and labor there,
My house, my raiment, meat and wine,

My ancient rage, my old despair,—
Yea, all things that were mine.

I saw the spring and summer pass,
The trees grow bare, and winter come;
All was the same as once it was
Upon my hills at home.

Then suddenly in my own heart
I felt God walk and gaze about;
He spoke; his words seemed held apart
With gladness and with doubt.

"Here is my meat and wine," He said,
"My love, my toil, my ancient care;
Here is my cloak, my book, my bed,
And here my old despair.

"Here are my seasons: winter, spring,
Summers the same, and autumn spills
The fruits I look for; everything
As on my heavenly hills."

An Ode in Time of Hesitation

I

BEFORE the solemn bronze Saint Gaudens made
To thrill the heedless passer's heart with awe,
And set here in the city's talk and trade
To the good memory of Robert Shaw,
This bright March morn I stand,
And hear the distant spring come up the land;
Knowing that what I hear is not unheard
Of this boy soldier and his Negro band,
For all their gaze is fixed so stern ahead,
For all the fatal rhythm of their tread.
The land they died to save from death and shame
Trembles and waits, hearing the spring's great name
And by her pangs these resolute ghosts are stirred.

II

Through street and mall the tides of people go
Heedless; the trees upon the Common show
No hint of green; but to my listening heart.
The still earth doth impart
Assurance of her jubilant emprise,
And it is clear to my long-searching eyes
That love at last has might upon the skies.
The ice is runneled on the little pond;
A telltale patter drips from off the trees;
The air is touched with Southland spiceries,
As if but yesterday it tossed the frond
Of pendent mosses where the live-oaks grow
Beyond Virginia and the Carolines,
Or had its will among the fruits and vines
Of aromatic isles asleep beyond
Florida and the Gulf of Mexico.

III

Soon shall the Cape Ann children shout in glee,
Spying the arbutus, spring's dear recluse;
Hill lads at dawn shall hearken the wild goose
Go hanking northward over Tennessee;
West from Oswego to Sault Sainte-Marie,
And on to where the Pictured Rocks are hung,
And yonder where, gigantic, wilful, young,
Chicago sitteth at the northwest gates,
With restless violent hands and casual tongue
Moulding her mighty fates,
The Lakes shall robe them in ethereal sheen;
And like a larger sea, the vital green
Of springing wheat shall vastly be outflung
Over Dakota and the prairie states.
By desert people immemorial
On Arizonian mesas shall be done
Dim rites unto the thunder and the sun;
Nor shall the primal gods lack sacrifice
More splendid, when the white Sierras call
Unto the Rockies straightway to arise
And dance before the unveiled ark of the year.
Sounding their windy cedars as for shawms,

Unrolling rivers clear
For flutter of broad phylacteries;
While Shasta signals to Alaskan seas
That watch old sluggish glaciers downward creep
To fling their icebergs thundering from the steep,
And Mariposa through the purple calms
Gazes at far Hawaii crowned with palms
Where East and West are met,—
A rich seal on the ocean's bosom set
To say that East and West are twain,
With different loss and gain:
The Lord hath sundered them; let them be sundered yet.

IV

Alas! what sounds are these that come
Sullenly over the Pacific seas,—
Sounds of ignoble battle, striking dumb
The season's half-awakened ecstasies?
Must I be humble, then,
Now when my heart hath need of pride?
Wild love falls on me from these sculptured men;
By loving much the land for which they died
I would be justified.
My spirit was away on pinions wide
To soothe in praise of her its passionate mood
And ease it of its ache of gratitude.
Too sorely heavy is the debt they lay
On me and the companions of my day.
I would remember now
My country's goodliness, make sweet her name.
Alas! what shade art thou
Of sorrow or of blame
Liftest the lyric leafage from her brow,
And pointest a slow finger at her shame?

V

Lies! lies! It cannot be! The wars we wage
Are noble, and our battles still are won
By justice for us, ere we lift the gage.
We have not sold our loftiest heritage.
The proud republic hath not stooped to cheat

And scramble in the market-place of war;
Her forehead weareth yet its solemn star.
Here is her witness: this, her perfect son,
This delicate and proud New England soul
Who leads despisèd men, with just-unshackled feet,
Up the large ways where death and glory meet,
To show all peoples that our shame is done,
That once more we are clean and spirit-whole.

VI

Crouched in the sea-fog on the moaning sand
All night he lay, speaking some simple word
From hour to hour to the slow minds that heard,
Holding each poor life gently in his hand
And breathing on the base rejected clay
Till each dark face shone mystical and grand
Against the breaking day;
And lo, the shard the potter cast away
Was grown a fiery chalice crystal-fine,
Fulfilled of the divine
Great wine of battle wrath by God's ring-finger stirred.
Then upward, where the shadowy bastion loomed
Huge on the mountain in the wet sea light,
Whence now, and now, infernal flowerage bloomed,
Bloomed, burst, and scattered down its deadly seed,—
They swept, and died like freemen on the height,
Like freemen, and like men of noble breed;
And when the battle fell away at night
By hasty and contemptuous hands were thrust
Obscurely in a common grave with him
The fair-haired keeper of their love and trust.
Now limb doth mingle with dissolvèd limb
In nature's busy old democracy
To flush the mountain laurel when she blows
Sweet by the Southern sea,
And heart with crumbled heart climbs in the rose:—
The untaught hearts with the high heart that knew
This mountain fortress for no earthly hold
Of temporal quarrel, but the bastion old
Of spiritual wrong,
Built by an unjust nation sheer and strong,

Expugnable but by a nation's rue
And bowing down before that equal shrine
By all men held divine,
Whereof his band and he were the most holy sign.

VII

O bitter, bitter shade!
Wilt thou not put the scorn
And instant tragic question from thine eye?
Do thy dark brows yet crave
That swift and angry stave—
Unmeet for this desirous morn—
That I have striven, striven to evade?
Gazing on him, must I not deem they err
Whose careless lips in street and shop aver
As common tidings, deeds to make his cheek
Flush from the bronze, and his dead throat to speak?
Surely some elder singer would arise,
Whose harp hath leave to threaten and to mourn
Above this people when they go astray.
Is Whitman, the strong spirit, overworn?
Has Whittier put his yearning wrath away?
I will not and I dare not yet believe!
Though furtively the sunlight seems to grieve,
And the spring-laden breeze
Out of the gladdening west is sinister
With sounds of nameless battle overseas;
Though when we turn and question in suspense
If these things be indeed after these ways,
And what things are to follow after these,
Our fluent men of place and consequence
Fumble and fill their mouths with hollow phrase,
Or for the end-all of deep arguments
Intone their dull commercial liturgies—
I dare not yet believe! My ears are shut!
I will not hear the thin satiric praise
And muffled laughter of our enemies,
Bidding us never sheathe our valiant sword
Till we have changed our birthright for a gourd
Of wild pulse stolen from a barbarian's hut;
Showing how wise it is to cast away

The symbols of our spiritual sway,
That so our hands with better ease
May wield the driver's whip and grasp the jailer's keys.

VIII

Was it for this our fathers kept the law?
This crown shall crown their struggle and their ruth?
Are we the eagle nation Milton saw
Mewing its mighty youth,
Soon to possess the mountain winds of truth,
And be a swift familiar of the sun
Where aye before God's face his trumpets run?
Or have we but the talons and the maw,
And for the abject likeness of our heart
Shall some less lordly bird be set apart?
Some gross-billed wader where the swamps are fat?
Some gorger in the sun? Some prowler with the bat?

IX

Ah, no!
We have not fallen so.
We are our fathers' sons: let those who lead us know!
'T was only yesterday sick Cuba's cry
Came up the tropic wind, "Now help us, for we die!"
Then Alabama heard,
And rising, pale, to Maine and Idaho
Shouted a burning word.
Proud state with proud impassioned state conferred,
And at the lifting of a hand sprang forth,
East, west, and south, and north,
Beautiful armies. Oh, by the sweet blood and young
Shed on the awful hill slope at San Juan,
By the unforgotten names of eager boys
Who might have tasted girl's love and been stung
With the old mystic joys
And starry griefs, now the spring nights come on,
But that the heart of youth is generous,—
We charge you, ye who lead us,
Breathe on their chivalry no hint of stain!
Turn not their new-world victories to gain!
One least leaf plucked for chaffer from the bays

Of their dear praise,
One jot of their pure conquest put to hire,
The implacable republic will require;
With clamor, in the glare and gaze of noon,
Or subtly, coming as a thief at night,
But surely, very surely, slow or soon
That insult deep we deeply will requite.
Tempt not our weakness, our cupidity!
For save we let the island men go free,
Those baffled and dislaureled ghosts
Will curse us from the lamentable coasts
Where walk the frustrate dead.
The cup of trembling shall be drainèd quite,
Eaten the sour bread of astonishment,
With ashes of the hearth shall be made white
Our hair, and wailing shall be in the tent;
Then on your guiltier head
Shall our intolerable self-disdain
Wreak suddenly its anger and its pain;
For manifest in that disastrous light
We shall discern the right
And do it, tardily.—O ye who lead,
Take heed!
Blindness we may forgive, but baseness we will smite.

STEPHEN CRANE

War Is Kind

DO not weep, maiden, for war is kind.
 Because your lover threw wild hands toward the sky
And the affrighted steed ran on alone,
Do not weep.
War is kind.

 Hoarse, booming drums of the regiment,
 Little souls who thirst for fight, .

These men were born to drill and die.
The unexplained glory flies above them,
Great is the battle-god, great, and his kingdom—
A field where a thousand corpses lie.

Do not weep, babe, for war is kind.
Because your father tumbled in the yellow trenches,
Raged at his breast, gulped and died,
Do not weep.
War is kind.

Swift blazing flag of the regiment,
Eagle with crest of red and gold,
These men were born to drill and die.
Point for them the virtue of slaughter,
Make plain to them the excellence of killing
And a field where a thousand corpses lie.

Mother whose heart hung humble as a button
On the bright splendid shroud of your son,
Do not weep.
War is kind.

GEORGE CABOT LODGE

Day and Dark

NOW the golden fields of sunset rose on rose to me-ward fall,
   Down the dark reverberate beaches clear and far the sea-birds
   call,
Blue across the fire-stained waters, eastward thrusts the chuckling
   tide,
Fresh as when the immortal impulse took the lifeless world for
   bride.

Now the shore's thin verge of shallows keep the tense and tender
   light,

Now the stars hang few and faultless, diademed on the brows of
    night,
Now the moon's unstinted silver falls like dew along the sea
While from far a friendly casement softly fills with light for me.

So it ends! I reaped the harvest, lived the long and lavish day,
Saw the earliest sunlight shiver thro' the breakers' endless play,
Felt the noonday's warm abundance, shared the hours of large repose,
While the stately sun descended thro' the twilight's sumptuous close.

Now the night-fall—Ah! I guess the immortal secret, glimpse the
    goal,
Know the hours have scanted nothing, know each fragment hints
    the whole,
While the Soul in power and freedom dares and wills to claim its
    own,
Star over star, a larger, lovelier unknown heaven beyond the known!

GEORGE SANTAYANA

On the Death of a Metaphysician

UNHAPPY dreamer, who outwinged in flight
    The pleasant region of the things I love,
And soared beyond the sunshine, and above
The golden cornfields and the dear and bright
Warmth of the hearth,—blasphemer of delight,
Was your proud bosom not at peace with Jove,
That you sought, thankless for his guarded grove,
The empty horror of abysmal night?
Ah, the thin air is cold above the moon!
I stood and saw you fall, befooled in death,
As, in your numbèd spirit's fatal swoon,
You cried you were a god, or were to be;
I heard with feeble moan your boastful breath
Bubble from depths of the Icarian sea.

"As in the Midst of Battle There Is Room"

AS in the midst of battle there is room
    For thoughts of love, and in foul sin for mirth,
    As gossips whisper of a trinket's worth
Spied by the death-bed's flickering candle-gloom;
As in the crevices of Cæsar's tomb
    The sweet herbs flourish on a little earth:
    So in this great disaster of our birth
We can be happy, and forget our doom.

For morning, with a ray of tenderest joy
    Gilding the iron heaven, hides the truth,
And evening gently woos us to employ
    Our grief in idle catches. Such is youth;
Till from that summer's trance we wake, to find
Despair before us, vanity behind.

Solipsism

I COULD believe that I am here alone,
    And all the world my dream;
The passion of the scene is all my own,
    And things that seem but seem.

Perchance an exhalation of my sorrow
    Hath raised this vaporous show,
For whence but from my soul should all things borrow
    So deep a tinge of woe?

I keep the secret doubt within my breast
    To be the gods' defence,
To ease the heart by too much ruth oppressed
    And drive the horror hence.

O sorrow that the patient brute should cower
    And die, not having sinned!
O pity that the wild and fragile flower
    Should shiver in the wind!

Then were I dreaming dreams I know not of,
　　For that is part of me
That feels the piercing pang of grief and love
　　And doubts eternally.

But whether all to me the vision come
　　Or break in many beams,
The pageant ever shifts, and being's sum
　　Is but the sum of dreams.

Odes

WHAT god will choose me from this labouring nation
　　To worship him afar, with inward gladness,
At sunset and at sunrise, in some Persian
　　　　Garden of roses;

Or under the full moon, in rapturous silence,
Charmed by the trickling fountain, and the moaning
Of the death-hallowed cypress, and the myrtle
　　　　Hallowed by Venus?

O for a chamber in an eastern tower,
Spacious and empty, roofed in odorous cedar,
A silken soft divan, a woven carpet
　　　　Rich, many-coloured;

A jug that, poised on her firm head, a Negress
Fetched from the well; a window to the ocean,
Lest of the stormy world too deep seclusion
　　　　Make me forgetful!

Thence I might watch the vessel-bearing waters
Beat the slow pulses of the life eternal,
Bringing of nature's universal travail
　　　　Infinite echoes;

And there at even I might stand and listen
To thrum of distant lutes and dying voices

Chanting the ditty an Arabian captive
  Sang to Darius.

So would I dream awhile, and ease a little
The soul long stifled and the straitened spirit,
Tasting new pleasures in a far-off country
  Sacred to beauty.

II

My heart rebels against my generation,
That talks of freedom and is slave to riches,
And, toiling 'neath each day's ignoble burden,
  Boasts of the morrow.

No space for noonday rest or midnight watches,
No purest joy of breathing under heaven!
Wretched themselves, they heap, to make them happy,
  Many possessions.

But thou, O silent Mother, wise, immortal,
To whom our toil is laughter,—take, divine one,
This vanity away, and to thy lover
  Give what is needful:—

III

Gathering the echoes of forgotten wisdom,
And mastered by a proud, adventurous purpose,
Columbus sought the golden shores of India
  Opposite Europe.

He gave the world another world, and ruin
Brought upon blameless, river-loving nations,
Cursed Spain with barren gold, and made the Andes
  Fiefs of Saint Peter;

While in the cheerless North the thrifty Saxon
Planted his corn, and, narrowing his bosom,
Made covenant with God, and by keen virtue
  Trebled his riches.

What venture hast thou left us, bold Columbus?
What honour left thy brothers, brave Magellan?

Daily the children of the rich for pastime
    Circle the planet.

And what good comes to us of all your dangers?
A smaller earth and a smaller hope of heaven.
Ye have but cheapened gold, and, measuring ocean,
    Counted the islands.

No Ponce de Leon shall drink in fountains,
On any flowering Easter, youth eternal;
No Cortes look upon another ocean;
    No Alexander

Found in the Orient dim a boundless kingdom,
And, clothing his Greek strength with barbarous splendour,
Build by the sea his throne, while Sacred Egypt
    Honours his godhead.

The earth, the mother once of godlike Theseus
And mighty Heracles, at length is weary,
And now brings forth a spawn of antlike creatures,
    Blackening her valleys,

Inglorious in their birth and in their living,
Curious and querulous, afraid of battle,
Rummaging earth for coals, in camps of hovels
    Crouching from winter,

As if grim fate, amid our boastful prating,
Made us the image of our brutish fathers,
When from their caves they issued, crazed with terror,
    Howling and hungry.

For all things come about in sacred cycles,
And life brings death, and light eternal darkness,
And now the world grows old apace; its glory
    Passes for ever.

Perchance the earth will yet for many ages
Bear her dead child, her moon, around her orbit;
Strange craft may tempt the ocean streams, new forests
    Cover the mountains.

If in those latter days men still remember
Our wisdom and our travail and our sorrow,
They never can be happy, with that burden
    Heavy upon them,

Knowing the hideous past, the blood, the famine,
The ancestral hate, the eager faith's disaster,
All ending in their little lives, and vulgar
    Circle of troubles.

But if they have forgot us, and the shifting
Of sands has buried deep our thousand cities,
Fell superstition then will seize upon them;
    Protean error

Will fill their panting heart with sickly phantoms
Of sudden blinding good and monstrous evil;
There will be miracles again, and torment,
    Dungeon and fagot,—

Until the patient earth, made dry and barren,
Sheds all her herbage in a final winter,
And the gods turn their eyes to some far distant
    Bright constellation.

IV

Slowly the black earth gains upon the yellow,
And the caked hill-side is ribbed soft with furrows.
Turn now again, with voice and staff, my ploughman,
    Guiding thy oxen.

Lift the great ploughshare, clear the stones and brambles,
Plant it the deeper, with thy foot upon it,
Uprooting all the flowering weeds that bring not
    Food to thy children.

Patience is good for man and beast, and labour
Hardens to sorrow and the frost of winter,
Turn then, again, in the brave hope of harvest,
    Singing to heaven.

V

Of thee the Northman by his beachèd galley
Dreamt, as he watched the never-setting Ursa
And longed for summer and thy light, O sacred
      Mediterranean.

Unseen he loved thee; for the heart within him
Knew earth had gardens where he might be blessed,
Putting away long dreams and aimless, barbarous
      Hunger for battle.

The foretaste of thy languors thawed his bosom;
A great need drove him to thy caverned islands
From the gray, endless reaches of the outer
      Desert of Ocean.

He saw thy pillars, saw thy sudden mountains
Wrinkled and stark, and in their crooked gorges,
'Neath peeping pine and cypress, guessed the torrent
      Smothered in flowers.

Thine incense to the sun, thy gathered vapours,
He saw suspended on the flanks of Taurus,
Or veiling the snowed bosom of the virgin
      Sister of Atlas.

He saw the luminous top of wide Olympus,
Fit for the happy gods; he saw the pilgrim
River, with rains of Ethiopia flooding
      Populous Egypt.

And having seen, he loved thee. His racked spirit,
By thy breath tempered and the light that clothes thee,
Forgot the monstrous gods, and made of Nature
      Mistress and mother.

The more should I, O fatal sea, before thee
Of alien words make echoes to thy music;
For I was born where first the rills of Tagus
      Turn to the westward.

And wandering long, alas! have need of drinking
Deep of the patience of thy perfect sadness,
O thou that constant through the change of ages,
    Beautiful ever,

Never wast wholly young and void of sorrows,
Nor ever canst be old, while yet the morning
Kindles thy ripples, or the golden evening
    Dyes thee in purple.

Thee, willing to be tamed but still untamable,
The Roman called his own until he perished,
As now the busy English hover o'er thee,
    Stalwart and noble;

But all is naught to thee, while no harsh winter
Congeals thy fountains, and the blown Sahara
Chokes not with dreadful sand thy deep and placid
    Rock-guarded havens.

Thou carest not what men may tread thy margin;
Nor I, while from some heather-scented headland
I may behold thy beauty, the eternal
    Solace of mortals.

TRUMBULL STICKNEY

Be Still. The Hanging Gardens Were a Dream

BE still. The Hanging Gardens were a dream
  That over Persian roses flew to kiss
The curlèd lashes of Semiramis.
Troy never was, nor green Skamander stream.
Provence and Troubadour are merest lies,
The glorious hair of Venice was a beam
Made within Titian's eye. The sunsets seem,
The world is very old and nothing is.
Be still. Thou foolish thing, thou canst not wake,

Nor thy tears wedge thy soldered lids apart,
But patter in the darkness of thy heart.
Thy brain is plagued. Thou art a frighted owl
Blind with the light of life thou'ldst not forsake,
And error loves and nourishes thy soul.

Live Blindly

LIVE blindly and upon the hour. The Lord,
Who was the Future, died full long ago.
Knowledge which is the Past is folly. Go,
Poor child, and be not to thyself abhorred.
Around thine earth sun-wingèd winds do blow
And planets roll; a meteor draws his sword;
The rainbow breaks his seven-coloured chord
And the long strips of river-silver flow:
Awake! Give thyself to the lovely hours.
Drinking their lips, catch thou the dream in flight
About their fragile hairs' aërial gold.
Thou art divine, thou livest,—as of old
Apollo springing naked to the light,
And all his island shivered into flowers.

He Said: "If in His Image I Was Made"

HE said: "If in his image I was made,
I am his equal and across the land
We two should make our journey hand in hand
Like brothers dignified and unafraid."
And God that day was walking in the shade.
To whom he said: "The world is idly planned,
We cross each other, let us understand
Thou who thou art, I who I am," he said.
Darkness came down. And all that night was heard
Tremendous clamour and the broken roar
Of things in turmoil driven down before.
Then silence. Morning broke, and sang a bird.
He lay upon the earth, his bosom stirred;
But God was seen no longer any more.

On Some Shells Found Inland

THESE are my murmur-laden shells that keep
A fresh voice tho' the years lie very gray.
The wave that washed their lips and tuned their lay
Is gone, gone with the faded ocean sweep,
The royal tide, gray ebb and sunken neap
And purple midday,—gone! To this hot clay
Must sing my shells, where yet the primal day,
Its roar and rhythm and splendour will not sleep.
What hand shall join them to their proper sea
If all be gone? Shall they forever feel
Glories undone and worlds that cannot be?—
'T were mercy to stamp out this agèd wrong,
Dash them to earth and crunch them with the heel
And make a dust of their seraphic song.

In Ampezzo

ONLY once more and not again—the larches
Shake to the wind their echo, "Not again,"—
We see, below the sky that over-arches
Heavy and blue, the plain

Between Tofana lying and Cristallo
In meadowy earths above the ringing stream:
Whence interchangeably desire may follow,
Hesitant as in dream,

At sunset, south, by lilac promontories
Under green skies to Italy, or forth
By calms of morning beyond Lavinores
Tyrolward and to north:

As now, this last of latter days, when over
The brownish field by peasants are undone
Some widths of grass, some plots of mountain clover
Under the autumn sun.

With honey-warm perfume that risen lingers
In mazes of low heat, or takes the air,
Passing delicious as a woman's fingers
Passing amid the hair;

When scythes are swishing and the mower's muscle
Spans a repeated crescent to and fro,
Or in dry stalks of corn the sickles rustle,
Tangle, detach and go,

Far thro' the wide blue day and greening meadow
Whose blots of amber beaded are with sheaves,
Wherever pallidly a cloud-shadow
Deadens the earth and leaves:

Whilst high around and near, their heads of iron
Sunken in sky whose azure overlights
Ravines and edges, stand the gray and maron
Desolate Dolomites,—

And older than decay from the small summit
Unfolds a stream of pebbly wreckage down
Under the suns of midday, like some comet
Struck into gravel stone.

Faintly across this gold and amethystine
September, images of summer fade;
And gentle dreams now freshen on the pristine
Viols, awhile unplayed,

Of many a place where lovingly we wander,
More dearly held that quickly we forsake,—
A pine by sullen coasts, an oleander
Reddening on the lake.

And there, each year with more familiar motion,
From many a bird and windy forestries,
Or along shaking fringes of the ocean
Vapours of music rise.

From many easts the morning gives her splendour;
The shadows fill with colours we forget;

Remembered tints at evening grow tender,
Tarnished with violet.

Let us away! soon sheets of winter metal
On this discoloured mountain-land will close,
While elsewhere Spring-time weaves a crimson petal,
Builds and perfumes a rose.

Away! for here the mountain sinks in gravel.
Let us forget the unhappy site with change,
And go, if only happiness be travel
After the new and strange:—

Unless 'twere better to be very single,
To follow some diviner monotone,
And in all beauties, where ourselves commingle,
Love but a love, but one,

Across this shadowy minute of our living,
What time our hearts so magically sing,
To mitigate our fever, simply giving
All in a little thing?

Just as here, past yon dumb and melancholy
Sameness of ruin, while the mountains ail,
Summer and sunset-coloured autumn slowly
Dissipate down the vale;

And all these lines along the sky that measure,
Sorapis and the rocks of Mezzodi
Crumble by foamy miles into the azure
Mediterranean sea:

Whereas today at sunrise, under brambles,
A league above the moss and dying pines
I picked this little—in my hand that trembles—
Parcel of columbines.

Mt. Lykaion

ALONE on Lykaion since man hath been
Stand on the height two columns, where at rest
Two eagles hewn of gold sit looking East
Forever; and the sun goes up between.
Far down around the mountain's oval green
An order keeps the falling stones abreast.
Below within the chaos last and least
A river like a curl of light is seen.
Beyond the river lies the even sea,
Beyond the sea another ghost of sky,—
O God, support the sickness of my eye
Lest the far space and long antiquity
Suck out my heart, and on this awful ground
The great wind kill my little shell with sound.

Near Helikon

BY such an all-embalming summer day
As sweetens now among the mountain pines
Down to the cornland yonder and the vines,
To where the sky and sea are mixed in gray,
How do all things together take their way
Harmonious to the harvest, bringing wines
And bread and light and whatsoe'er combines
In the large wreath to make it round and gay.
To me my troubled life doth now appear
Like scarce distinguishable summits hung
Around the blue horizon: places where
Not even a traveller purposeth to steer,—
Whereof a migrant bird in passing sung,
And the girl closed her window not to hear.

Fidelity

NOT lost or won but above all endeavour
Thy life like heaven circles around mine;
Thy eyes it seems upon my eyes did shine
Since forever.

For aught he summon up his earliest hour
No man remembers the surprise of day,
Nor where he saw with virgin wonder play
          The first flower.

And o'er the imagination's last horizon
No brain has leaning descried nothing more:
Still there are stars and in the night before
          More have arisen.

Not won or lost is unto thee my being;
Our eyes were always so together met.
If mine should close, if ever thine forget,
          Time is dying.

                    •

Mnemosyne

IT'S autumn in the country I remember.

How warm a wind blew here about the ways!
And shadows on the hillside lay to slumber
During the long sun-sweetened summer-days.

It's cold abroad the country I remember.

The swallows veering skimmed the golden grain
At midday with a wing aslant and limber;
And yellow cattle browsed upon the plain.

It's empty down the country I remember.

I had a sister lovely in my sight:
Her hair was dark, her eyes were very sombre;
We sang together in the woods at night.

It's lonely in the country I remember.

The babble of our children fills my ears,
And on our hearth I stare the perished ember
To flames that show all starry thro' my tears.

It's dark about the country I remember.

Now in the Palace Gardens

NOW in the palace gardens warm with age,
  On lawn and flower-bed this afternoon
The thin November-coloured foliage
Just as last year unfastens lilting down,

And round the terrace in gray attitude
The very statues are becoming sere
With long presentiment of solitude.
Most of the life that I have lived is here,

Here by the path and autumn's earthly grass
And chestnuts standing down the breadths of sky:
Indeed I know not how it came to pass,
The life I lived here so unhappily.

Yet blessing over all! I do not care
What wormwood I have ate to cups of gall;
I care not what despairs are buried there
Under the ground, no, I care not at all.

Nay, if the heart have beaten, let it break!
I have not loved and lived but only this
Betwixt my birth and grave. Dear Spirit, take
The gratitude that pains so deep it is.

When Spring shall be again, and at your door
You stand to feel the mellower evening wind,
Remember if you will my heart is pure,
Perfectly pure and altogether kind;

How much it aches to linger in these things!
I thought the perfect end of love was peace
Over the long-forgiven sufferings.
But something else, I know not what it is,

The words that came so nearly and then not,
The vanity, the error of the whole,
The strong cross-purpose, oh, I know not what
Cries dreadfully in the distracted soul.

The evening fills the garden, hardly red;
And autumn goes away, like one alone.
Would I were with the leaves that thread by thread
Soften to soil, I would that I were one.

SHAEMAS O'SHEEL

They Went Forth to Battle, but They Always Fell

THEY went forth to battle, but they always fell;
   Their eyes were fixed above the sullen shields;
Nobly they fought and bravely, but not well,
And sank heart-wounded by a subtle spell.
   They knew not fear that to the foeman yields,
   They were not weak, as one who vainly wields
A futile weapon; yet the sad scrolls tell
How on the hard-fought field they always fell.

It was a secret music that they heard,
   A sad sweet plea for pity and for peace;
And that which pierced the heart was but a word,
Though the white breast was red-lipped where the sword
   Pressed a fierce cruel kiss, to put surcease
   On its hot thirst, but drank a hot increase.
Ah, they by some strange troubling doubt were stirred,
And died for hearing what no foeman heard.

They went forth to battle, but they always fell;
   Their might was not the might of lifted spears;
Over the battle-clamor came a spell
Of troubling music, and they fought not well.
   Their wreaths are willows and their tribute, tears;
   Their names are old sad stories in men's ears;
Yet they will scatter the red hordes of Hell,
Who went to battle forth and always fell.

ADELAIDE CRAPSEY

Vendor's Song

MY songs to sell, good sir!
    I pray you buy.
Here's one will win a lady's tears,
    Here's one will make her gay,
Here's one will charm your true love true
    Forever and a day;
Good sir, I pray you buy!

Oh, no, he will not buy.

My songs to sell, sweet maid!
    I pray you buy.
This one will teach you Lilith's lore,
    And this what Helen knew,
And this will keep your gold hair gold,
    And this your blue eyes blue;
Sweet maid, I pray you buy!

Oh, no, she will not buy.

If I'd as much money as I could tell,
I never would cry my songs to sell.
I never would cry my songs to sell.

The Lonely Death

IN the cold I will rise, I will bathe
    In waters of ice; myself
Will shiver, and shrive myself,
Alone in the dawn, and anoint
Forehead and feet and hands;

I will shutter the windows from light,
I will place in their sockets the four
Tall candles and set them aflame
In the grey of the dawn; and myself
Will lay myself straight in my bed,
And draw the sheet under my chin.

EDWIN ARLINGTON ROBINSON

Eros Turannos

SHE fears him, and will always ask
   What fated her to choose him;
She meets in his engaging mask
   All reasons to refuse him;
But what she meets and what she fears
Are less than are the downward years,
Drawn slowly to the foamless weirs
   Of age, were she to lose him.

Between a blurred sagacity
   That once had power to sound him,
And Love, that will not let him be
   The Judas that she found him,
Her pride assuages her almost,
As if it were alone the cost.—
He sees that he will not be lost,
   And waits and looks around him.

A sense of ocean and old trees
   Envelops and allures him;
Tradition, touching all he sees,
   Beguiles and reassures him;
And all her doubts of what he says
Are dimmed with what she knows of days—
Till even prejudice delays
   And fades, and she secures him.

The falling leaf inaugurates
    The reign of her confusion;
The pounding wave reverberates
    The dirge of her illusion;
And home, where passion lived and died,
Becomes a place where she can hide,
While all the town and harbour side
    Vibrate with her seclusion.

We tell you, tapping on our brows,
    The story as it should be—
As if the story of a house
    Were told, or ever could be;
We'll have no kindly veil between
Her visions and those we have seen—
As if we guessed what hers have been,
    Or what they are or would be.

Meanwhile we do no harm; for they
    That with a god have striven,
Not hearing much of what we say,
    Take what the god has given;
Though like waves breaking it may be,
Or like a changed familiar tree,
Or like a stairway to the sea
    Where down the blind are driven.

For a Dead Lady

NO more with overflowing light
    Shall fill the eyes that now are faded,
Nor shall another's fringe with night
Their woman-hidden world as they did.
No more shall quiver down the days
The flowing wonder of her ways,
Whereof no language may requite
The shifting and the many-shaded.

The grace, divine, definitive,
Clings only as a faint forestalling;
The laugh that love could not forgive

Is hushed, and answers to no calling;
The forehead and the little ears
Have gone where Saturn keeps the years;
The breast where roses could not live
Has done with rising and with falling.

The beauty, shattered by the laws
That have creation in their keeping,
No longer trembles at applause,
Or over children that are sleeping;
And we who delve in beauty's lore
Know all that we have known before
Of what inexorable cause
Makes Time so vicious in his reaping.

ANNA HEMPSTEAD BRANCH

The Monk in the Kitchen

I

ORDER is a lovely thing;
　On disarray it lays its wing,
Teaching simplicity to sing.
It has a meek and lowly grace,
Quiet as a nun's face.
Lo—I will have thee in this place!
Tranquil well of deep delight,
All things that shine through thee appear
As stones through water, sweetly clear.
Thou clarity,
That with angelic charity
Revealest beauty where thou art,
Spread thyself like a clean pool,
Then all the things that in thee are,
Shall seem more spiritual and fair,
Reflection from serener air—

Sunken shapes of many a star
In the high heavens set afar.

II

Ye stolid, homely, visible things,
Above you all brood glorious wings
Of your deep entities, set high,
Like slow moons in a hidden sky.
But you, their likenesses, are spent
Upon another element.
Truly ye are but seemings—
The shadowy cast-off gleamings
Of bright solidities. Ye seem
Soft as water, vague as dream;
Image, cast in a shifting stream.

III

What are ye?
I know not.
Brazen pan and iron pot,
Yellow brick and gray flag-stone
That my feet have trod upon—
Ye seem to me
Vessels of bright mystery.
For ye do bear a shape, and so
Though ye were made by man, I know
An inner Spirit also made,
And ye his breathings have obeyed.

IV

Shape, the strong and awful spirit,
Laid his ancient hand on you.
He waste chaos doth inherit;
He can alter and subdue.
Verily, he doth lift up
Matter, like a sacred cup,
Into deep substance he reached, and lo
Where ye were not, ye were; and so
Out of useless nothing, ye
Groaned and laughed and came to be.

And I use you, as I can,
Wonderful uses, made for man,
Iron pot and brazen pan.

V

What are ye?
I know not;
Nor what I really do
When I move and govern you.
There is no small work unto God.
He required of us greatness;
Of His last creature
A high angelic nature,
Stature superb and bright completeness,
He sets to us no humble duty.
Each act that He would have us do
Is haloed round with strangest beauty;
Terrific deeds and cosmic tasks
Of His plainest child He asks.
When I polish the brazen pan
I hear a creature laugh afar
In the gardens of a star,
And from his burning presence run
Flaming wheels of many a sun.
Whoever makes a thing more bright,
He is an angel of all light.
When I cleanse this earthen floor
My spirit leaps to see
Bright garments trailing over it,
A cleanness made by me.
Purger of all men's thoughts and ways,
With labour do I sound Thy praise,
My work is done for Thee.
Whoever makes a thing more bright,
He is an angel of all light.
Therefore let me spread abroad
The beautiful cleanness of my God.

VI

One time in the cool of dawn
Angels came and worked with me.

The air was soft with many a wing.
They laughed amid my solitude
And cast bright looks on everything.
Sweetly of me did they ask
That they might do my common task.
And all were beautiful—but One
With garments whiter than the sun
Had such a face
Of deep, remembered grace;
That when I saw I cried—"Thou art
The great Blood-Brother of my heart.
Where have I seen Thee?"—And He said,
"When we are dancing round God's throne,
How often thou art there.
Beauties from thy hands have flown
Like white doves wheeling in mid air.
Nay—thy soul remembers not?
Work on, and cleanse thy iron pot."

VII

What are we? I know not.

Ere the Golden Bowl Is Broken

HE gathered for His own delight
    The sparkling waters of my soul.
A thousand creatures, bubbling bright—
    He set me in a golden bowl.

From the deep cisterns of the earth
    He bade me up—the shining daughter—
And I am exquisite with mirth,
    A brightening and a sunlit water.

The wild, the free, the radiant one,
    A happy bubble I did glide.
I poised my sweetness to the sun
    And there I sleeked my silver side.

Sometimes I lifted up my head
    And globed the moonlight with my hands,

Or thin as flying wings I spread
  Angelic wildness through the sands.

Then, woven into webs of light,
  I breathed, I sighed, I laughed aloud,
And lifting up my pinions bright
  I shone in Heaven, a bird-white cloud.

Then did I dance above the mead,
  And through the crystal fields would run,
And from my scarlet splendours breed
  The golden thunders of the sun.

Beneath the whitening stars I flew
  And floated moon-like on the breeze,
Or my frail heart was piercèd through
  With sharp sweet flowers of the trees.

Of giant crags I bear the scars,
  And I have swept along the gale,
Such multitudes as are the stars,
  My myriad faces rapt and pale.

As savage creatures strong and free
  Make wild the jungle of the wood,
The starry powers that sport in me
  Habit my silver solitude.

From out my smallness, soft as dew,
  That utter fastness, stern and deep,
Terrible meanings look at you
  Like vision from the eyes of sleep.

I cannot leap—I cannot run—
  I only glimmer, soft and mild,
A limpid water in the sun,
  A sparkling and a sunlit child.

What stranger ways shall yet be mine
  When I am spilled, you cannot see.
But now you laugh to watch me shine,
  And smooth the hidden stars in me.

Lightly you stroke my silver wing—
   The folded carrier of my soul.
A soft, a shy, a silent thing,
   A water in a golden bowl.

AMY LOWELL

Little Ivory Figures Pulled with String

IS it the tinkling of mandolins which disturbs you?
   Or the dropping of bitter-orange petals among the coffee-cups?
Or the slow creeping of the moonlight between the olive-trees?
   *Drop! drop! the rain
   Upon the thin plates of my heart.*

String your blood to chord with this music,
Stir your heels upon the cobbles to the rhythm of a dance-tune.
They have slim thighs and arms of silver;
The moon washes away their garments;
They make a pattern of fleeing feet in the branch shadows,
And the green grapes knotted about them
Burst as they press against one another.
   *The rain knocks upon the plates of my heart,
   They are crumpled with its beating.*

Would you drink only from your brains, Old Man?
See, the moonlight has reached your knees,
It falls upon your head in an accolade of silver.
Rise up on the music,
Fling against the moon-drifts in a whorl of young light bodies:
Leaping grape-clusters,
Vine leaves tearing from a grey wall.
You shall run, laughing, in a braid of women,
And weave flowers with the frosty spines of thorns.
Why do you gaze into your glass,
And jar the spoons with your finger-tapping?
   *The rain is rigid on the plates of my heart.
   The murmur of it is loud—loud.*

Patterns

I WALK down the garden paths,
And all the daffodils
Are blowing, and the bright blue squills.
I walk down the patterned garden paths
In my stiff, brocaded gown.
With my powdered hair and jewelled fan,
I too am a rare
Pattern. As I wander down
The garden paths,
My dress is richly figured,
And the train
Makes a pink and silver stain
On the gravel, and the thrift
Of the borders.
Just a plate of current fashion,
Tripping by in high-heeled, ribboned shoes.
Not a softness anywhere about me,
Only whalebone and brocade.
And I sink on a seat in the shade
Of a lime tree. For my passion
Wars against the stiff brocade.
The daffodils and squills
Flutter in the breeze
As they please.
And I weep;
For the lime tree is in blossom
And one small flower has dropped upon my bosom.
And the plashing of waterdrops
In the marble fountain
Comes down the garden paths.
The dripping never stops.
Underneath my stiffened gown
Is the softness of a woman bathing in a marble basin,
A basin in the midst of hedges grown
So thick, she cannot see her lover hiding,
But she guesses he is near,
And the sliding of the water

Seems the stroking of a dear
Hand upon her.
What is Summer in a fine brocaded gown!
I should like to see it lying in a heap upon the ground.
All the pink and silver crumpled up on the ground.

I would be the pink and silver as I ran along the paths,
And he would stumble after,
Bewildered by my laughter.
I should see the sun flashing from his sword-hilt and the buckles
    on his shoes.
I would choose
To lead him in a maze along the patterned paths,
A bright and laughing maze for my heavy-booted lover.
Till he caught me in the shade,
And the buttons of his waistcoat bruised my body as he clasped me,
Aching, melting, unafraid.
With the shadows of the leaves and the sundrops,
And the plopping of the waterdrops,
All about us in the open afternoon—
I am very like to swoon
With the weight of this brocade,
For the sun sifts through the shade.

Underneath the fallen blossom
In my bosom,
Is a letter I have hid.
It was brought to me this morning by a rider from the Duke.
"Madam, we regret to inform you that Lord Hartwell
Died in action Thursday se'nnight."
As I read it in the white, morning sunlight,
The letters squirmed like snakes.
"Any answer, Madam," said my footman.
"No," I told him.
"See that the messenger takes some refreshment.
No, no answer."
And I walked into the garden,
Up and down the patterned paths,
In my stiff, correct brocade.
The blue and yellow flowers stood up proudly in the sun,
Each one.

I stood upright too,
Held rigid to the pattern
By the stiffness of my gown.
Up and down I walked,
Up and down.

In a month he would have been my husband.
In a month, here, underneath this lime,
We would have broke the pattern;
He for me, and I for him,
He as Colonel, I as Lady,
On this shady seat.
He had a whim
That sunlight carried blessing.
And I answered, "It shall be as you have said."
Now he is dead.

In Summer and in Winter I shall walk
Up and down
The patterned garden paths
In my stiff, brocaded gown.
The squills and daffodils
Will give place to pillared roses, and to asters, and to snow.
I shall go
Up and down,
In my gown.
Gorgeously arrayed,
Boned and stayed.
And the softness of my body will be guarded from embrace
By each button, hook, and lace.
For the man who should loose me is dead,
Fighting with the Duke in Flanders,
In a pattern called a war.
Christ! What are patterns for?

EDGAR LEE MASTERS

(FROM "SPOON RIVER ANTHOLOGY")

Thomas Trevelyan

READING in Ovid the sorrowful story of Itys,
Son of the love of Tereus and Procne, slain
For the guilty passion of Tereus for Philomela,
The flesh of him served to Tereus by Procne,
And the wrath of Tereus, the murderess pursuing
Till the gods made Philomela a nightingale,
Lute of the rising moon, and Procne a swallow!
Oh livers and artists of Hellas centuries gone,
Sealing in little thuribles dreams and wisdom,
Incense beyond all price, forever fragrant,
A breath whereof makes clear the eyes of the soul!
How I inhaled its sweetness here in Spoon River!
The thurible opening when I had lived and learned
How all of us kill the children of love, and all of us,
Knowing not what we do, devour their flesh;
And all of us change to singers, although it be
But once in our lives, or change—alas!—to swallows,
To twitter amid cold winds and falling leaves!

Edmund Pollard

I WOULD I had thrust my hands of flesh
Into the disk-flowers bee-infested,
Into the mirror-like core of fire
Of the light of life, the sun of delight.
For what are anthers worth or petals
Or halo-rays? Mockeries, shadows
Of the heart of the flower, the central flame!
All is yours, young passer-by;
Enter the banquet room with the thought;

Don't sidle in as if you were doubtful
Whether you're welcome—the feast is yours!
Nor take but a little, refusing more
With a bashful "Thank you," when you're hungry.
Is your soul alive? Then let it feed!
Leave no balconies where you can climb;
Nor milk-white bosoms where you can rest;
Nor golden heads with pillows to share;
Nor wine cups while the wine is sweet;
Nor ecstasies of body or soul,
You will die, no doubt, but die while living
In depths of azure, rapt and mated,
Kissing the queen-bee, Life!

Bert Kessler

I WINGED my bird,
Though he flew toward the setting sun;
But just as the shot rang out, he soared
Up and up through the splinters of golden light,
Till he turned right over, feathers ruffled,
With some of the down of him floating near,
And fell like a plummet into the grass.
I tramped about, parting the tangles,
Till I saw a splash of blood on a stump,
And the quail lying close to the rotten roots.
I reached my hand, but saw no brier,
But something pricked and stung and numbed it.
And then, in a second, I spied the rattler—
The shutters wide in his yellow eyes,
The head of him arched, sunk back in the rings of him,
A circle of filth, the color of ashes,
Or oak leaves bleached under layers of leaves.
I stood like a stone as he shrank and uncoiled
And started to crawl beneath the stump,
When I fell limp in the grass.

Petit, the Poet

SEEDS in a dry pod, tick, tick, tick,
  Tick, tick, tick, like mites in a quarrel—
Faint iambics that the full breeze wakens—
But the pine tree makes a symphony thereof.
Triolets, villanelles, rondels, rondeaus,
Ballades by the score with the same old thought:
The snows and the roses of yesterday are vanished;
And what is love but a rose that fades?
Life all around me here in the village:
Tragedy, comedy, valor and truth,
Courage, constancy, heroism, failure—
All in the loom, and oh what patterns!
Woodlands, meadows, streams and rivers—
Blind to all of it all my life long.
Triolets, villanelles, rondels, rondeaus,
Seeds in a dry pod, tick, tick, tick,
Tick, tick, tick, what little iambics,
While Homer and Whitman roared in the pines?

ROBERT FROST

Desert Places

SNOW falling and night falling fast oh fast
  In a field I looked into going past,
And the ground almost covered smooth in snow,
But a few weeds and stubble showing last.

The woods around it have it—it is theirs.
All animals are smothered in their lairs.
I am too absent-spirited to count;
The loneliness includes me unawares.

And lonely as it is that loneliness
Will be more lonely ere it will be less—
A blanker whiteness of benighted snow
With no expression, nothing to express.

They cannot scare me with their empty spaces
Between stars—on stars where no human race is.
I have it in me so much nearer home
To scare myself with my own desert places.

Bereft

WHERE had I heard this wind before
Change like this to a deeper roar?
What would it take my standing there for,
Holding open a restive door,
Looking down hill to a frothy shore?
Summer was past and day was past.
Sombre clouds in the west were massed.
Out in the porch's sagging floor,
Leaves got up in a coil and hissed,
Blindly struck at my knee and missed.
Something sinister in the tone
Told me my secret must be known:
Word I was in the house alone
Somehow must have gotten abroad,
Word I was in my life alone,
Word I had no one left but God.

For Once, Then, Something

OTHERS taunt me with having knelt at well-curbs
Always wrong to the light, so never seeing
Deeper down in the well than where the water
Gives me back in a shining surface picture
Me myself in the summer heaven godlike
Looking out of a wreath of fern and cloud puffs.
Once, when trying with chin against a well-curb
I discerned, as I thought, beyond the picture,

Through the picture, a something white, uncertain,
Something more of the depths—and then I lost it.
Water came to rebuke the too clear water.
One drop fell from a fern, and lo, a ripple
Shook whatever it was lay there at bottom,
Blurred it, blotted it out. What was that whiteness?
Truth? A pebble of quartz? For once, then, something.

Once by the Pacific

THE shattered water made a misty din.
   Great waves looked over others coming in,
And thought of doing something to the shore
That water never did to land before.
The clouds were low and hairy in the skies,
Like locks blown forward in the gleam of eyes.
You could not tell, and yet it looked as if
The shore was lucky in being backed by cliff,
The cliff in being backed by continent;
It looked as if a night of dark intent
Was coming, and not only a night, an age.
Someone had better be prepared for rage.
There would be more than ocean-water broken
Before God's last *Put out the Light* was spoken.

The Telephone

WHEN I was just as far as I could walk
   From here today,
There was an hour
All still
When leaning with my head against a flower
I heard you talk.
Don't say I didn't, for I heard you say—
You spoke from that flower on the window sill—
Do you remember what it was you said?"

"First tell me what it was you thought you heard."

"Having found the flower and driven a bee away,
I leaned my head,
And holding by the stalk,
I listened and I thought I caught the word—
What was it? Did you call me by my name?
Or did you say—
Someone said 'Come'—I heard it as I bowed."

"I may have thought as much, but not aloud."

"Well, so I came."

The Road Not Taken

TWO roads diverged in a yellow wood,
And sorry I could not travel both
And be one traveler, long I stood
And looked down one as far as I could
To where it bent in the undergrowth;

Then took the other, as just as fair,
And having perhaps the better claim,
Because it was grassy and wanted wear;
Though as for that the passing there
Had worn them really about the same,

And both that morning equally lay
In leaves no step had trodden black.
Oh, I kept the first for another day!
Yet knowing how way leads on to way,
I doubted if I should ever come back.

I shall be telling this with a sigh
Somewhere ages and ages hence:
Two roads diverged in a wood, and I—
I took the one less traveled by,
And that has made all the difference.

My November Guest

MY sorrow, when she's here with me,
    Thinks these dark days of autumn rain
Are beautiful as days can be;
She loves the bare, the withered tree;
    She walks the sodden pasture lane.

Her pleasure will not let me stay.
    She talks and I am fain to list:
She's glad the birds are gone away,
She's glad her simple worsted grey
    Is silver now with clinging mist.

The desolate, deserted trees,
    The faded earth, the heavy sky,
The beauties she so truly sees,
She thinks I have no eye for these,
    And vexes me for reason why.

Not yesterday I learned to know
    The love of bare November days
Before the coming of the snow;
But it were vain to tell her so,
    And they are better for her praise.

Home Burial

HE saw her from the bottom of the stairs
    Before she saw him. She was starting down,
Looking back over her shoulder at some fear.
She took a doubtful step and then undid it
To raise herself and look again. He spoke
Advancing toward her: "What is it you see
From up there always—for I want to know."
She turned and sank upon her skirts at that,
And her face changed from terrified to dull.
He said to gain time: "What is it you see?"
Mounting until she cowered under him,
"I will find out now—you must tell me, dear."

She, in her place, refused him any help
With the least stiffening of her neck and silence.
She let him look, sure that he wouldn't see,
Blind creature; and a while he didn't see.
But at last he murmured, "Oh," and again,
    "Oh."
"What is it—what?" she said.

                        "Just that I see."
"You don't," she challenged. "Tell me what it is."

"The wonder is I didn't see at once.
I never noticed it from here before.
I must be wonted to it—that's the reason.
The little graveyard where my people are!
So small the window frames the whole of it.
Not so much larger than a bedroom, is it?
There are three stones of slate and one of marble,
Broad-shouldered little slabs there in the sunlight
On the sidehill. We haven't to mind *those*.
But I understand: it is not the stones,
But the child's mound—"

      "Don't, don't, don't, don't," she cried.
She withdrew shrinking from beneath his arm
That rested on the banister, and slid downstairs;
And turned on him with such a daunting look,
He said twice over before he knew himself:
"Can't a man speak of his own child he's lost?"

"Not you! Oh, where's my hat? Oh, I don't need it!
I must get out of here. I must get air.
I don't know rightly whether any man can."

"Amy! Don't go to someone else this time.
Listen to me. I won't come down the stairs."
He sat and fixed his chin between his fists.
"There's something I should like to ask you, dear."

"You don't know how to ask it."

                          "Help me, then."

Her fingers moved the latch for all reply.

"My words are nearly always an offence.
I don't know how to speak of anything
So as to please you. But I might be taught
I should suppose. I can't say I see how.
A man must partly give up being a man
With women-folk. We could have some arrangement
By which I'd bind myself to keep hands off
Anything special you're a mind to name.
Though I don't like such things 'twixt those that love.
Two that don't love can't live together without them.
But two that do can't live together with them."
She moved the latch a little. "Don't, don't go.
Don't carry it to someone else this time.
Tell me about it if it's something human.
Let me into your grief. I'm not so much
Unlike other folks as your standing there
Apart would make me out. Give me my chance.
I do think, though, you overdo it a little.
What was it brought you up to think it the thing
To take your mother-loss of a first child
So inconsolably—in the face of love.
You'd think his memory might be satisfied—"

"There you go sneering now!"

                                    "I'm not, I'm not!
You make me angry. I'll come down to you.
God, what a woman! And it's come to this,
A man can't speak of his own child that's dead."

"You can't because you don't know how.
If you had any feelings, you that dug
With your own hand—how could you?—his little grave;
I saw you from that very window there,
Making the gravel leap and leap in air,
Leap up, like that, like that, and land so lightly
And roll down the mound beside the hole.
I thought, who is that man? I don't know you.
And I crept down the stairs and up the stairs
To look again, and still your spade kept lifting.
Then you came in. I heard your rumbling voice
Out in the kitchen, and I don't know why,

But I went near to see with my own eyes.
You could sit there with the stains on your shoes
Of the fresh earth from your own baby's grave
And talk about your everyday concerns.
You had stood the spade up against the wall
Outside there in the entry, for I saw it."

"I shall laugh the worst laugh I ever laughed.
I'm cursed. God, if I don't believe I'm cursed."

"I can repeat the very words you were saying.
'Three foggy mornings and one rainy day
Will rot the best birch fence a man can build.'
Think of it, talk like that at such a time!
What had how long it takes a birch to rot
To do with that was in the darkened parlour.
You *couldn't* care! The nearest friends can go
With any one to death, comes so far short
They might as well not try to go at all.
No, from the time when one is sick to death,
One is alone, and he dies more alone.

Friends make pretence of following to the grave,
But before one is in it, their minds are turned
And making the best of their way back to life
And living people, and things they understand.
But the world's evil. I won't have my grief so
If I can change it. Oh, I won't, I won't!"

"There, you have said it all and you feel better.
You won't go now. You're crying. Close the door.
The heart's gone out of it: why keep it up.
Amy! There's someone coming down the road!"

"*You*—oh, you think the talk is all. I must go—
Somewhere out of this house. How can I make you—"

"If—you—do!" She was opening the door wider.
"Where do you mean to go? First tell me that.
I'll follow and bring you back by force. I *will!*—"

The Sound of the Trees

I WONDER about the trees
 Why do we wish to bear
Forever the noise of these
More than another noise
So close to our dwelling place?
We suffer them by the day
Till we lose all measure of pace,
And fixity in our joys,
And acquire a listening air.
They are that that talks of going
But never gets away;
And that talks no less for knowing,
As it grows wiser and older,
That now it means to stay.
My feet tug at the floor
And my head sways to my shoulder
Sometimes when I watch trees sway,
From the window or the door.
I shall set forth for somewhere,
I shall make the reckless choice
Some day when they are in voice
And tossing so as to scare
The white clouds over them on.
I shall have less to say,
But I shall be gone.

Hyla Brook

BY June our brook's run out of song and speed.
 Sought for much after that, it will be found
Either to have gone groping underground
(And taken with it all the Hyla breed
That shouted in the mist a month ago,
Like ghost of sleigh-bells in a ghost of snow)—
Or flourished and come up in jewel-weed,
Weak foliage that is blown upon and bent
Even against the way its waters went.

Its bed is left a faded paper sheet
Of dead leaves stuck together by the heat—
A brook to none but who remember long.
This as it will be seen is other far
Than with brooks taken otherwhere in song.
We love the things we love for what they are.

Mowing

THERE was never a sound beside the wood but one,
And that was my long scythe whispering to the ground.
What was it it whispered? I knew not well myself;
Perhaps it was something about the heat of the sun,
Something, perhaps, about the lack of sound—
And that was why it whispered and did not speak.
It was no dream of the gift of idle hours,
Or easy gold at the hand of fay or elf:
Anything more than the truth would have seemed too weak
To the earnest love that laid the swale in rows,
Not without feeble-pointed spikes of flowers
(Pale orchises), and scared a bright green snake.
The fact is the sweetest dream that labor knows.
My long scythe whispered and left the hay to make.

To Earthward

LOVE at the lips was touch
As sweet as I could bear;
And once that seemed too much;
I lived on air

That crossed me from sweet things,
The flow of—was it musk
From hidden grapevine springs
Down hill at dusk?

I had the swirl and ache
From spray of honeysuckle
That when they're gathered shake
Dew on the knuckle.

I craved strong sweets, but those
Seemed strong when I was young;
The petal of the rose
It was that stung.

Now no joy but lacks salt
That is not dashed with pain
And weariness and fault;
I crave the stain

Of tears, the aftermark
Of almost too much love,
The sweet of bitter bark
And burning clove.

When stiff and sore and scarred
I take away my hand
From leaning on it hard
In grass and sand,

The hurt is not enough:
I long for weight and strength
To feel the earth as rough
To all my length.

Fire and Ice

SOME say the world will end in fire,
  Some say in ice.
From what I've tasted of desire
I hold with those who favor fire.
But if it had to perish twice,
I think I know enough of hate
To say that for destruction ice
Is also great
And would suffice.

Stopping by Woods on a Snowy Evening

WHOSE woods these are I think I know.
His house is in the village though;
He will not see me stopping here
To watch his woods fill up with snow.

My little horse must think it queer
To stop without a farmhouse near
Between the woods and frozen lake
The darkest evening of the year.

He gives his harness bells a shake
To ask if there is some mistake.
The only other sound's the sweep
Of easy wind and downy flake.

The woods are lovely, dark and deep,
But I have promises to keep,
And miles to go before I sleep,
And miles to go before I sleep.

WILLIAM ELLERY LEONARD

The Image of Delight

O HOW came I that loved stars, moon, and flame,
And unimaginable wind and sea,
All inner shrines and temples of the free,
Legends and hopes and golden books of fame;
I that upon the mountain carved my name
With cliffs and clouds and eagles over me,
O how came I to stoop to loving thee—
I that had never stooped before to shame?

O 'twas not thee! Too eager of a white
Far beauty and a voice to answer mine,
Myself I built an image of delight,
Which all one purple day I deemed divine—
And when it vanished in the fiery night,
I lost not thee, nor any shape of thine.

CARL SANDBURG

Cool Tombs

WHEN Abraham Lincoln was shoveled into the tombs, he forgot the copperheads and the assassin . . . in the dust, in the
cool tombs.

And Ulysses Grant lost all thought of con men and Wall Street,
cash and collateral turned ashes . . . in the dust, in the cool
tombs.

Pocahontas' body, lovely as a poplar, sweet as a red haw in November or a pawpaw in May, did she wonder? does she remember?
. . . in the dust, in the cool tombs?

Take any streetful of people buying clothes and groceries, cheering
a hero or throwing confetti and blowing tin horns . . . tell me
if the lovers are losers . . . tell me if any get more than the
lovers . . . in the dust . . . in the cool tombs.

Four Preludes on Playthings of the Wind

"THE PAST IS A BUCKET OF ASHES"

I

THE woman named Tomorrow
sits with a hairpin in her teeth
and takes her time
and does her hair the way she wants it

and fastens at last the last braid and coil
and puts the hairpin where it belongs
and turns and drawls: Well, what of it?
My grandmother, Yesterday, is gone.
What of it? Let the dead be dead.

2

The doors were cedar
and the panel strips of gold
and the girls were golden girls
and the panels read and the girls chanted:
> We are the greatest city,
> and the greatest nation:
> nothing like us ever was.

The doors are twisted on broken hinges,
Sheets of rain swish through on the wind
> where the golden girls ran and the panels read:
> We are the greatest city,
> the greatest nation,
> nothing like us ever was.

3

It has happened before.
Strong men put up a city and got
> a nation together,
And paid singers to sing and women
> to warble: We are the greatest city,
> the greatest nation,
> nothing like us ever was.

And while the singers sang
and the strong men listened
and paid the singers well,
> there were rats and lizards who listened
> . . . and the only listeners left now
> . . . are . . . the rats . . . and the lizards.
> And there are black crows
> crying, "Caw, caw,"
> bringing mud and sticks
> building a nest
> over the words carved

on the doors where the panels were cedar
and the strips on the panels were gold
and the golden girls came singing:
>We are the greatest city,
>the greatest nation:
>nothing like us ever was.

The only singers now are crows crying, "Caw, caw,"
And the sheets of rain whine in the wind and doorways.
And the only listeners now are . . . the rats . . . and the lizards.

4

The feet of the rats
scribble on the doorsills;
the hieroglyphs of the rat footprints
chatter the pedigrees of the rats
and babble of the blood
and gabble of the breed
of the grandfathers and the great-grandfathers
of the rats.

And the wind shifts
and the dust on a doorsill shifts
and even the writing of the rat footprints
tells us nothing, nothing at all
>about the greatest city, the greatest nation
>where the strong men listened
>and the women warbled: Nothing like us ever was.

Jazz Fantasia

DRUM on your drums, batter on your banjos, sob on the long
cool winding saxophones. Go to it, O jazzmen.

Sling your knuckles on the bottoms of the happy tim pans, let your
trombones ooze, and go husha-husha-hush with the slippery
sandpaper.

Moan like an autumn wind high in the lonesome treetops, moan
soft like you wanted somebody terrible, cry like a racing car

slipping away from a motorcycle-cop, bang-bang! you jazzmen, bang altogether drums, traps, banjos, horns, tin cans—make two people fight on the top of a stairway and scratch each other's eyes in a clinch tumbling down the stairs.

Can the rough stuff. . . . Now a Mississippi steamboat pushes up the night river with a hoo-hoo-hoo-oo . . . and the green lanterns calling to the high soft stars . . . a red moon rides on the humps of the low river hills. . . . Go to it, O jazzmen.

Gone

EVERYBODY loved Chick Lorimer in our town
     Far off.
  Everybody loved her.
So we all love a wild girl keeping a hold
    On a dream she wants.
Nobody knows now where Chick Lorimer went.
Nobody knows why she packed her trunk . . . a few old things
And is gone,
    Gone with her little chin
    Thrust ahead of her
    And her soft hair blowing careless
    From under a wide hat,
Dancer, singer, a laughing passionate lover.

Were there ten men or a hundred hunting Chick?
Were there five men or fifty with aching hearts?
    Everybody loved Chick Lorimer.
    Nobody knows where she's gone.

VACHEL LINDSAY

Abraham Lincoln Walks at Midnight

(IN SPRINGFIELD, ILLINOIS)

IT is portentous, and a thing of state
That here at midnight, in our little town
A mourning figure walks, and will not rest,
Near the old court-house pacing up and down,

Or by his homestead, or in shadowed yards
He lingers where his children used to play,
Or through the market, on the well-worn stones
He stalks until the dawn-stars burn away.

A bronzed, lank man! His suit of ancient black,
A famous high top-hat and plain worn shawl
Make him the quaint great figure that men love,
The prairie-lawyer, master of us all.

He cannot sleep upon his hillside now.
He is among us:—as in times before!
And we who toss and lie awake for long
Breathe deep, and start, to see him pass the door.

His head is bowed. He thinks on men and kings.
Yes, when the sick world cries, how can he sleep?
Too many peasants fight, they know not why,
Too many homesteads in black terror weep.

The sins of all the war-lords burn his heart.
He sees the dreadnoughts scouring every main.
He carries on his shawl-wrapped shoulders now
The bitterness, the folly and the pain.

He cannot rest until a spirit-dawn
Shall come;—the shining hope of Europe free:
The league of sober folk, the Workers' Earth,
Bringing long peace to Cornland, Alp and Sea.

It breaks his heart that kings must murder still,
That all his hours of travail here for men
Seem yet in vain. And who will bring white peace
That he may sleep upon his hill again?

The Eagle That Is Forgotten

[JOHN P. ALTGELD. BORN DECEMBER 30, 1847; DIED MARCH 12, 1902]

SLEEP softly . . . eagle forgotten . . . under the stone,
Time has its way with you there, and the clay has its own.
"We have buried him now," thought your foes, and in secret rejoiced.
They made a brave show of their mourning, their hatred unvoiced,
They had snarled at you, barked at you, foamed at you, day after
day,
Now you were ended. They praised you, . . . and laid you away.

The others that mourned you in silence and terror and truth,
The widow bereft of her pittance, the boy without youth,
The mocked and the scorned and the wounded, the lame and the
poor
That should have remembered forever, . . . remember no more.

Where are those lovers of yours, on what name do they call
The lost, that in armies wept over your funeral pall?
They call on the names of a hundred high-valiant ones,
A hundred white eagles have risen, the sons of your sons,
The zeal in their wings is a zeal that your dreaming began,
The valor that wore out your soul in the service of man.

Sleep softly, . . . eagle forgotten, . . . under the stone,
Time has its way with you there, and the clay has its own.
Sleep on, O brave hearted, O wise man, that kindled the flame—
To live in mankind is far more than to live in a name,
To live in mankind, far, far more . . . than to live in a name.

Aladdin and the Jinn

BRING me soft song," said Aladdin.
   "This tailor-shop sings not at all.
Chant me a word of the twilight,
Of roses that mourn in the fall.
Bring me a song like hashish
That will comfort the stale and the sad,
For I would be mending my spirit,
Forgetting these days that are bad,
Forgetting companions too shallow,
Their quarrels and arguments thin,
Forgetting the shouting Muezzin:"—
"I AM YOUR SLAVE," said the Jinn.

"Bring me old wines," said Aladdin.
"I have been a starved pauper too long.
 Serve them in vessels of jade and of shell,
 Serve them with fruit and with song:—
 Wines of pre-Adamite Sultans
 Digged from beneath the black seas:—
 New-gathered dew from the heavens
 Dripped down from Heaven's sweet trees,.
 Cups from the angels' pale tables
 That will make me both handsome and wise,
 For I have beheld her, the princess,
 Firelight and starlight her eyes.
 Pauper I am, I would woo her.
 And—let me drink wine, to begin,
 Though the Koran expressly forbids it."
"I AM YOUR SLAVE," said the Jinn.

"Plan me a dome," said Aladdin,
"That is drawn like the dawn of the MOON,
 When the sphere seems to rest on the mountains,
 Half-hidden, yet full-risen soon.
 Build me a dome," said Aladdin,
"That shall cause all young lovers to sigh,
 The fullness of life and of beauty,

Peace beyond peace to the eye—
A palace of foam and of opal,
Pure moonlight without and within,
Where I may enthrone my sweet lady."
"I AM YOUR SLAVE," said the Jinn.

WALLACE STEVENS

Domination of Black

AT night, by the fire,
  The colors of the bushes
And of the fallen leaves,
Repeating themselves,
Turned in the room,
Like the leaves themselves
Turning in the wind.
Yes: but the color of the heavy hemlocks
Came striding.
And I remembered the cry of the peacocks.

The colors of their tails
Were like the leaves themselves
Turning in the wind,
In the twilight wind.
They swept over the room,
Just as they flew from the boughs of the hemlocks
Down to the ground.

I heard them cry—the peacocks.
Was it a cry against the twilight
Or against the leaves themselves
Turning in the wind,
Turning as the flames
Turned in the fire,
Turning as the tails of the peacocks
Turned in the loud fire,

Loud as the hemlocks
Full of the cry of the peacocks?
Or was it a cry against the hemlocks?

Out of the window,
I saw how the planets gathered
Like the leaves themselves
Turning in the wind.
I saw how the night came,
Came striding like the color of the heavy hemlocks.
I felt afraid.
And I remembered the cry of the peacocks.

Sea Surface Full of Clouds

I

IN that November off Tehuantepec,
The slopping of the sea grow still one night
And in the morning summer hued the deck

And made one think of rosy chocolate
And gilt umbrellas. Paradisal green
Gave suavity to the perplexed machine

Of ocean, which like limpid water lay.
Who, then, in that ambrosial latitude
Out of the light evolved the moving blooms,

Who, then, evolved the sea-blooms from the clouds
Diffusing balm in that Pacific calm?
C'était mon enfant, mon bijou, mon âme.

The sea-clouds whitened far below the calm
And moved, as blooms move, in the swimming green
And in its watery radiance, while the hue

Of heaven in an antique reflection rolled
Round those flotillas. And sometimes the sea
Poured brilliant iris on the glistening blue.

II

In that November off Tehuantepec
The slopping of the sea grew still one night.
At breakfast jelly yellow streaked the deck

And made one think of chop-house chocolate
And sham umbrellas. And a sham-like green
Capped summer-seeming on the tense machine

Of ocean, which in sinister flatness lay.
Who, then, beheld the rising of the clouds
That strode submerged in that malevolent sheen,

Who saw the mortal massives of the blooms
Of water moving on the water-floor?
C'était mon frère du ciel, ma vie, mon or.

The gongs rang loudly as the windy blooms
Hoo-hooed it in the darkened ocean-blooms.
The gongs grew still. And then blue heaven spread

Its crystalline pendentives on the sea
And the macabre of the water-glooms.
In an enormous undulation fled.

III

In that November off Tehuantepec,
The slopping of the sea grew still one night,
And a pale silver patterned on the deck

Made one think of porcelain chocolate
And pied umbrellas. An uncertain green,
Piano-polished, held the tranced machine

Of ocean, as a prelude holds and holds.
Who, seeing silver petals of white blooms
Unfolding in the water, feeling sure

Of the milk within the saltiest spurge, heard, then,
The sea unfolding in the sunken clouds?
Oh! C'était mon extase et mon amour.

So deeply sunken were they that the shrouds,
The shrouding shadows, made the petals black
Until the rolling heaven made them blue,

A blue beyond the rainy hyacinth,
And smiting the crevasses of the leaves
Deluged the ocean with a sapphire hue.

IV

In that November off Tehuantepec
The night-long slopping of the sea grew still.
A mallow morning dozed upon the deck

And made one think of musky chocolate
And frail umbrellas. A too-fluent green
Suggested malice in the dry machine

Of ocean, pondering dank stratagem.
Who then beheld the figures of the clouds,
Like blooms secluded in the thick marine?

Like blooms? Like damasks that were shaken off
From the loosed girdles in the spangling must.
C'était ma foi, la nonchalance divine.

The nakedness would rise and suddenly turn
Salt masks of beard and mouths of bellowing,
Would— But more suddenly the heaven rolled

Its bluest sea-clouds in the thinking green
And the nakedness became the broadest blooms,
Mile-mallows that a mallow sun cajoled.

V

In that November off Tehuantepec
Night stilled the slopping of the sea. The day
Came, bowing and voluble, upon the deck,

Good clown. . . . One thought of Chinese chocolate
And large umbrellas. And a motley green
Followed the drift of the obese machine

Of ocean, perfected in indolence.
What pistache one, ingenious and droll,
Beheld the sovereign clouds as jugglery

And the sea as turquoise-turbaned Sambo, neat
At tossing saucers—cloudy-conjuring sea?
C'était mon esprit batard, l'ignominie.

The sovereign clouds came clustering. The conch
Of loyal conjuration trumped. The wind
Of green blooms turning crisped the motley hue

To clearing opalescence. Then the sea
And heaven rolled as one and from the two
Came fresh transfigurings of freshest blue.

To the One of Fictive Music

SISTER and mother and diviner love,
And of the sisterhood of the living dead
Most near, most clear, and of the clearest bloom,
And of the fragrant mothers the most dear
And queen, and of diviner love the day
And flame and summer and sweet fire, no thread
Of cloudy silver sprinkles in your gown
Its venom of renown, and on your head
No crown is simpler than the simple hair.

Now, of the music summoned by the birth
That separates us from the wind and sea,
Yet leaves us in them, until earth becomes,
By being so much of the things we are,
Gross effigy and simulacrum, none
Gives motion to perfection more serene
Than yours, out of our imperfections wrought,
Most rare, or ever of more kindred air
In the laborious weaving that you wear.

For so retentive of themselves are men
That music is intensest which proclaims
The near, the clear, and vaunts the clearest bloom,

And of all vigils musing the obscure,
That apprehends the most which sees and names,
As in your name, an image that is sure,
Among the arrant spices of the sun,
O bough and bush and scented vine, in whom
We give ourselves our likest issuance.

Yet not too like, yet not so like to be
Too near, too clear, saving a little to endow
Our feigning with the strange unlike, whence springs
The difference that heavenly pity brings.
For this, musician, in your girdle fixed
Bear other perfumes. On your pale head wear
A band entwining, set with fatal stones.
Unreal, give back to us what once you gave:
The imagination that we spurned and crave.

Peter Quince at the Clavier

I

JUST as my fingers on these keys
     Make music, so the self-same sounds
On my spirit make a music too.

Music is feeling then, not sound;
And thus it is that what I feel,
Here in this room, desiring you,

Thinking of your blue-shadowed silk,
Is music. It is like the strain
Waked in the elders by Susanna:

Of a green evening, clear and warm,
She bathed in her still garden, while
The red-eyed elders, watching, felt

The basses of their being throb
In witching chords, and their thin blood
Pulse pizzicati of Hosanna.

II

In the green evening, clear and warm,
Susanna lay.
She searched
The touch of springs,
And found
Concealed imaginings.
She sighed
For so much melody.

Upon the bank she stood
In the cool
Of spent emotions.
She felt, among the leaves,
The dew
Of old devotions.

She walked upon the grass,
Still quavering.
The winds were like her maids,
On timid feet,
Fetching her woven scarves,
Yet wavering.

A breath upon her hand
Muted the night.
She turned—
A cymbal clashed,
And roaring horns.

III

Soon, with a noise like tambourines,
Came her attendant Byzantines.

They wondered why Susanna cried
Against the elders by her side:

And as they whispered, the refrain
Was like a willow swept by rain.

Anon their lamps' uplifted flame
Revealed Susanna and her shame.

And then the simpering Byzantines,
Fled, with a noise like tambourines.

IV

Beauty is momentary in the mind—
The fitful tracing of a portal;
But in the flesh it is immortal.

The body dies; the body's beauty lives.
So evenings die, in their green going,
A wave, interminably flowing.

So gardens die, their meek breath scenting
The cowl of Winter, done repenting.
So maidens die to the auroral
Celebration of a maiden's choral.

Susanna's music touched the bawdy strings
Of those white elders; but, escaping,
Left only Death's ironic scraping.
Now in its immortality, it plays
On the clear viol of her memory,
And makes a constant sacrament of praise.

Sunday Morning

I

COMPLACENCIES of the peignoir, and late
   Coffee and oranges in a sunny chair,
And the green freedom of a cockatoo
Upon a rug, mingle to dissipate
The holy hush of ancient sacrifice.
She dreams a little, and she feels the dark
Encroachment of that old catastrophe,
As a calm darkens among water-lights.
The pungent oranges and bright green wings
Seem things in some procession of the dead,
Winding across wide water, without sound.
The day is like wide water, without sound,
Stilled for the passing of her dreaming feet

Over the seas, to silent Palestine,
Dominion of the blood and sepulchre.

II

She hears, upon that water without sound,
A voice that cries: "The tomb in Palestine
Is not the porch of spirits lingering;
It is the grave of Jesus, where He lay."
We live in an old chaos of the sun,
Or old dependency of day and night,
Or island solitude, unsponsored, free,
Of that wide water, inescapable.
Deer walk upon our mountains, and the quail
Whistle about us their spontaneous cries;
Sweet berries ripen in the wilderness;
And in the isolation of the sky,
At evening, casual flocks of pigeons make
Ambiguous undulations as they sink,
Downward to darkness, on extended wings.

III

She says: "I am content when wakened birds,
Before they fly, test the reality
Of misty fields, by their sweet questionings;
But when the birds are gone, and their warm fields
Return no more, where, then, is paradise?"
There is not any haunt of prophecy,
Nor any old chimera of the grave,
Neither the golden underground, nor isle
Melodious, where spirits gat them home,
Nor visionary South, nor cloudy palm
Remote on heaven's hill, that has endured
As April's green endures; or will endure
Like her remembrance of awakened birds,
Or her desire for June and evening, tipped
By the consummation of the swallow's wings.

IV

She says, "But in contentment I still feel
The need of some imperishable bliss."

Death is the mother of beauty; hence from her,
Alone, shall come fulfilment to our dreams
And our desires. Although she strews the leaves
Of sure obliteration on our paths—
The path sick sorrow took, the many paths
Where triumph rang its brassy phrase, or love
Whispered a little out of tenderness—
She makes the willow shiver in the sun
For maidens who were wont to sit and gaze
Upon the grass, relinquished to their feet.
She causes boys to bring sweet-smelling pears
And plums in ponderous piles. The maidens taste
And stray impassioned in the littering leaves.

                           V

Supple and turbulent, a ring of men
Shall chant in orgy on a summer morn
Their boisterous devotion to the sun—
Not as a god, but as a god might be,
Naked among them, like a savage source.
Their chant shall be a chant of paradise,
Out of their blood, returning to the sky;
And in their chant shall enter, voice by voice,
The windy lake wherein their lord delights,
The trees, like seraphim, and echoing hills,
That choir among themselves long afterward.
They shall know well the heavenly fellowship
Of men that perish and of summer morn—
And whence they came and whither they shall go,
The dew upon their feet shall manifest.

Le Monocle de Mon Oncle

                           I

MOTHER of heaven, regina of the clouds,
    O sceptre of the sun, crown of the moon,
There is not nothing, no, no, never nothing,
Like the clashed edges of two words that kill."
And so I mocked her in magnificent measure.

Or was it that I mocked myself alone?
I wish that I might be a thinking stone.
The sea of spuming thoughts foists up again
The radiant bubble that she was. And then
A deep up-pouring from some saltier well
Within me, bursts its watery syllable.

II

A red bird flies across the golden floor.
It is a red bird that seeks out his choir
Among the choirs of wind and wet and wing.
A torrent will fall from him when he finds.
Shall I uncrumple this much-crumpled thing?
I am a man of fortune greeting heirs;
For it has come that thus I greet the Spring.
These choirs of welcome choir for me farewell.
No Spring can follow past meridian.
Yet you persist with anecdotal bliss
To make believe a starry *connaissance*.

III

Is it for nothing, then, that old Chinese
Sat titivating by their mountain pools
Or in the Yangtse studied out their beards?
I shall not play the flat historic scale.
You know how Utamaro's beauties sought
The end of love in their all-speaking braids.
You know the mountainous coiffures of Bath.
Alas! Have all the barbers lived in vain
That not one curl in Nature has survived?
Why, without pity on these studious ghosts,
Do you come dripping in your hair from sleep?

IV

This luscious and impeccable fruit of life
Falls, it appears, of its own weight to earth.
When you were Eve, its acrid juice was sweet,
Untasted, in its heavenly, orchard air—
An apple serves as well as any skull
To be the book in which to read a round,

And is as excellent, in that it is composed
Of what, like skulls, comes rotting back to ground.
But it excels in this that as the fruit
Of love, it is a book too mad to read
Before one merely reads to pass the time.

V

In the high West there burns a furious star.
It is for fiery boys that star.was set
And for sweet-smelling virgins close to them.
The measure of the intensity of love
Is measure, also, of the verve of earth.
For me, the firefly's quick, electric stroke
Ticks tediously the time of one more year.
And you? Remember how the crickets came
Out of their mother grass, like little kin . . .
In the pale nights, when your first imagery
Found inklings of your bond to all that dust.

VI

If men at forty will be painting lakes
The ephemeral blues must merge for them in one,
The basic slate, the universal hue.
There is a substance in us that prevails.
But in our amours amorists discern
Such fluctuations that their scrivening
Is breathless to attend each quirky turn.
When amorists grow bald, then amours shrink
Into the compass and curriculum
Of introspective exiles, lecturing.
It is a theme for Hyacinth alone.

VII

The mules that angels ride come slowly down
The blazing passes, from beyond the sun.
Descensions of their tinkling bells arrive.
These muleteers are dainty of their way.
Meantime centurions guffaw and beat
Their shrilling tankards on the table-boards.
This parable, in sense, amounts to this:

The honey of heaven may or may not come,
But that of earth both comes and goes at once.
Suppose these couriers brought amid their train
A damsel heightened by eternal bloom. . . .

VIII

Like a dull scholar, I behold, in love,
An ancient aspect touching a new mind.
It comes, it blooms, it bears its fruit and dies.
This trivial trope reveals a way of truth.
Our bloom is gone. We are the fruit thereof.
Two golden gourds distended on our vines,
We hang like warty squashes, streaked and rayed,
Into the Autumn weather, splashed with frost,
Distorted by hale fatness, turned grotesque.
The laughing sky will see the two of us
Washed into rinds by rotting winter rains.

IX

In verses wild with motion, full of din,
Loudened by cries, by clashes, quick and sure
As the deadly thought of men accomplishing
Their curious fates in war, come, celebrate
The faith of forty, ward of Cupido.
Most venerable heart, the lustiest conceit
Is not too lusty for your broadening.
I quiz all sounds, all thoughts, all everything
For the music and manner of the paladins
To make oblation fit. Where shall I find
Bravura adequate to this great hymn?

X

The fops of fancy in their poems leave
Memorabilia of the mystic sprouts,
Spontaneously watering their gritty soils.
I am a yeoman, as such fellows go.
I know no magic trees, no balmy boughs,
No silver-ruddy, gold-vermilion fruits.
But, after all, I know a tree that bears
A semblance to the thing I have in mind.

It stands gigantic, with a certain tip
To which all birds come sometime in their time.
But when they go that tip still tips the tree.

XI

If sex were all, then every trembling hand
Could make us speak, like dolls, the wished-for words.
But note the unconscionable treachery of fate,
That makes us weep, laugh, grunt and groan, and shout
Doleful heroics, pinching gestures forth
From madness or delight, without regard
To that first foremost law. Anguishing hour!
Last night, we sat beside a pool of pink,
Clippered with lilacs, scudding the bright chromes,
Keen to the point of starlight, while a frog
Boomed from his very belly, odious chords.

XII

A blue pigeon it is, that circles the blue sky,
On side-long wing, around and round and round.
A white pigeon it is, that flutters to the ground,
Grown tired of flight. Like a dark rabbi, I
Observed, when young, the nature of mankind,
In lordly study. Every day, I found
Man proved a gobbet in my mincing world.
Like a rose rabbi, later, I pursued,
And still pursue, the origin and course
Of love, but until now I never knew
That fluttering things have so distinct a shade.

Tattoo

THE light is like a spider.
    It crawls over the water.
It crawls over the edges of the snow.
It crawls under your eyelids
And spreads its webs there—
Its two webs.

The webs of your eyes
Are fastened

To the flesh and bones of you
As to rafters or grass.

There are filaments of your eyes
On the surface of the water
And in the edges of the snow.

The Bird with the Coppery, Keen Claws

ABOVE the forest of the parakeets,
　A parakeet of parakeets prevails,
A pip of life amid a mort of tails.

(The rudiments of tropics are around,
Aloe of ivory, pear of rusty rind.)
His lids are white because his eyes are blind.

He is not paradise of parakeets,
Of his gold ether, golden alguazil.
Except because he broods there and is still,

Panache upon panache, his tails deploy
Upward and outward, in green-vented forms,
His tip a drop of water full of storms.

But though the turbulent tinges undulate
As his pure intellect applies its laws,
He moves not on his coppery, keen claws.

He munches a dry shell while he exerts
His will, yet never ceases, perfect cock,
To flare, in the sun-pallor of his rock.

Of Heaven Considered as a Tomb

WHAT word have you, interpreters, of men
　Who in the tomb of heaven walk by night,
The darkened ghosts of our old comedy?
Do they believe they range the gusty cold,
With lanterns borne aloft to light the way,

Freemen of death, about and still about
To find whatever it is they seek? Or does
That burial, pillared up each day as porte
And spiritous passage into nothingness,
Foretell each night the one abysmal night,
When the host shall no more wander, nor the light
Of the steadfast lanterns creep across the dark?
Make hue among the dark comedians,
Halloo them in the topmost distances
For answer from their icy Elysée.

Of the Manner of Addressing Clouds

GLOOMY grammarians in golden gowns,
Meekly you keep the mortal rendezvous,
Eliciting the still sustaining pomps
Of speech which are like music so profound
They seem an exaltation without sound.
Funest philosophers and ponderers,
Their evocations are the speech of clouds.
So speech of your processionals returns
In the casual evocations of your tread
Across the stale, mysterious seasons. These
Are the music of meet resignation; these
The responsive, still sustaining pomps for you
To magnify, if in that drifting waste
You are to be accompanied by more
Than mute bare splendors of the sun and moon.

WITTER BYNNER

Spouse

NOW this Ophelia was a wiser woman,—
She wanted all his life and all his worth;
And yet she said, Since he is only human,
I can lie down upon my lonely earth.

I can allow him Tuesdays, if he chooses,
To stay away from me and let me nurse
My sentimental madnesses and bruises.
I have six days of him. It might be worse.
The others come, the others go, she said,
But I can madden only upon him.
So let me moan along the river-bed,
That he is absent from the river-brim
And weave these flowers in my hair for sorrow,
For this is Tuesday,—Wednesday is tomorrow.

Ghost

HE rises from his guests, abruptly leaves,
    Because of memory that long moons ago
Others now dead had dined with him, and grieves
Because these newer persons he must know
Might not have loved his ghosts, his unknown dead.
There are new smiles, new answers to his quips;
But there are intervals when, having said
His dinner-table say, he hears dead lips . . .
The dead have ways of mingling in the uses
Of life they leave behind, the dead can rise
When dinner's done. But one of them refuses
To go away and gazes with dead eyes
Piercing him deeper than a rain can reach,
Leaving him only motion, only speech.

Correspondent

WORDS, words and words! What else, when men are dead,
    Their small lives ended and their sayings said,
Is left of them? Their children go to dust,
As also all their children's children must,
And their belongings are of paltry worth
Against the insatiable consuming earth . . .
I knew a man and almost had forgot
The wisdom of the letters that he wrote;
But words, if words are wise, go on and on

To make a longer note of unison
With man and man than living persons make
With one another for whatever sake.
Therefore I wept tonight when quick words rose
Out of a dead man's grave, whom no one knows.

Ganymede

WHEN love begins with Ganymede, he gathers
All blossoms that a cloudy rain can bring
And, heedless of the warning of his fathers,
Folds in his arms the elements of spring.
This is a world that vernal things should count in,
There should be only happiness to know,—
A breath of wild-flowers carried from the mountain
And changed, along the waves, to falling snow.
Shade may be cool and comfortable for lovers;
But what great shadow darkening in the sky
Circles and distances, then nears and hovers
As though a vulturous bird of death were by? . . .
Ganymede feels the talon in his spine
Lift him Olympian to lustier wine.

Captain's Table

CASSANDRA, treading the Titanic deck,
Her eye still proud, although the boat may sink,
What shall she do against the coming wreck
But wrap her pride within a cloak of mink?
She hears an ominous whisper in the sky
But hides with gaiety her guessing heart.
She is as willing as a ghost to die
But—willing still to play a social part—
Pretends to think that dinners are the Lord,
Though the last supper happen every day.
Others than she are travelling aboard,
But not inured, like her, to tragic play.
And so she sits at everybody's right
A female Oedipus with half his sight.

Charioteer

HERE is a woman whom a man can greet
Equal to equal, which is something said;
For seldom will a man forego conceit
And grant a woman room, till she is dead.
But here's a woman different: a young mind
In a body aging with no age at all.
She's like a living portrait whom you find
Some rainy night in your ancestral hall,
The spark within her eye aware and human . . .
Having Athena's mind, Achilles' heel,
She's mythological, this modern woman.
Torn from the chariot, a loosened wheel
Which kept the chariot upon its course,
She runs ahead, beyond the fallen horse.

————•—•—————

ELINOR WYLIE

————•—•—————

This Corruptible

THE Body, long oppressed
And pierced, then prayed for rest
(Being but apprenticed to the other Powers);
And kneeling in that place
Implored the thrust of grace
Which makes the dust lie level with the flowers.

Then did that fellowship
Of three, the Body strip;
Beheld his wounds, and none among them mortal;
The Mind severe and cool;
The Heart still half a fool;
The fine-spun Soul, a beam of sun can startle.

These three, a thousand years
Had made adventurers

Amid all villainies the earth can offer,
Applied them to resolve
From the universal gulph
What pangs the poor material flesh may suffer.

"This is a pretty pass;
To hear the growing grass
Complain; the clay cry out to be translated;
Will not this grosser stuff
Receive reward enough
If stabled after labouring, and baited?"

Thus spoke the Mind in scorn:
The Heart, which had outworn
The Body, and was weary of its fashion,
Preferring to be dressed
In skin of bird or beast,
Replied more softly, in a feigned compassion.

"Anatomy most strange
Crying to chop and change;
Inferior copy of a higher image;
While I, the noble guest,
Sick of your second-best
Sigh for embroidered archangelic plumage:

"For shame, thou fustian cloak!"
And then the Spirit spoke;
Within the void it swung securely tethered
By strings composed of cloud;
It spoke both low and loud
Above a storm no lesser star had weathered.

"O lodging for the night!
O house of my delight!
O lovely hovel builded for my pleasure!
Dear tenement of clay
Endure another day
As coffin sweetly fitted to my measure.

"Take Heart, and call to Mind
Although we are unkind;

Although we steal your shelter, strength, and clothing;
'Tis you who shall escape
In some enchanting shape
Or be dissolved to elemental nothing.

"You, the unlucky slave,
Are the lily on the grave;
The wave that runs above the bones a-whitening;
You are the new-mown grass;
And the wheaten bread of the Mass;
And the fabric of the rain, and the lightning.

"If one of us elect
To leave the poor suspect
Imperfect bosom of the earth our parent;
And from the world avert
The Spirit or the Heart
Upon a further and essential errand;

"His chain he cannot slough
Nor cast his substance off;
He bears himself upon his flying shoulder;
The Heart, infirm and dull;
The Mind, in any skull;
Are captive still, and wearier and colder.

" 'Tis you who are the ghost,
Disintegrated, lost;
The burden shed; the dead who need not bear it;
O grain of God in power,
Endure another hour!
It is but for an hour," said the Spirit.

The Eagle and the Mole

AVOID the reeking herd,
　　Shun the polluted flock,
Live like that stoic bird,
The eagle of the rock.

The huddled warmth of crowds
Begets and fosters hate;

He keeps, above the clouds,
His cliff inviolate.

When flocks are folded warm,
And herds to shelter run,
He sails above the storm,
He stares into the sun.

If in the eagle's track
Your sinews cannot leap,
Avoid the lathered pack,
Turn from the steaming sheep.

If you would keep your soul
From spotted sight or sound,
Live like the velvet mole;
Go burrow under ground.

And there hold intercourse
With roots of trees and stones,
With rivers at their source,
And disembodied bones.

Escape

WHEN foxes eat the last gold grape,
    And the last white antelope is killed,
I shall stop fighting and escape
Into a little house I'll build.

But first I'll shrink to fairy size,
With a whisper no one understands,
Making blind moons of all your eyes,
And muddy roads of all your hands.

And you may grope for me in vain
In hollows under the mangrove root,
Or where, in apple-scented rain,
The silver wasp-nests hang like fruit.

Confession of Faith

I LACK the braver mind
   That dares to find
The lover friend, and kind.

I fear him to the bone;
   I lie alone
By the beloved one,

And, breathless for suspense,
   Erect defense
Against love's violence

Whose silences portend
   A bloody end
For lover never friend.

But, in default of faith,
   In futile breath,
I dream no ill of Death.

Address to My Soul

MY soul, be not disturbed
   By planetary war;
Remain securely orbed
In this contracted star.

Fear not, pathetic flame;
   Your sustenance is doubt:
Glassed in translucent dream
They cannot snuff you out.

Wear water, or a mask
   Of unapparent cloud;
Be brave and never ask
A more defunctive shroud.

The universal points
Are shrunk into a flower;
Between its delicate joints
Chaos keeps no power.

The pure integral form,
Austere and silver-dark,
Is balanced on the storm
In its predestined arc.

Small as a sphere of rain
It slides along the groove
Whose path is furrowed plain
Among the suns that move.

The shapes of April buds
Outlive the phantom year:
Upon the void at odds
The dewdrop falls severe.

Five-petalled flame, be cold:
Be firm, dissolving star;
Accept the stricter mould
That makes you singular.

True Vine

THERE is a serpent in perfection tarnished
   The thin shell pierced, the purity grown fainter,
The virgin silver shield no longer burnished,
The pearly fruit with ruin at its centre.

The thing that sits expectant in our bosoms
Contriving heaven out of very little
Demands such delicate immaculate blossoms
As no malicious verity makes brittle.

This wild fastidious hope is quick to languish;
Its smooth diaphanous escape is swifter
Than the pack of truth; no mortal can distinguish
Its trace upon the durable hereafter.

Not so the obdurate and savage lovely
Whose roots are set profoundly upon trouble;
This flower grows so fiercely and so bravely
It does not even know that it is noble.

This is the vine to love, whose balsams flourish
Upon a living soil corrupt and faulty,
Whose leaves have drunk the skies, and stooped to nourish
The earth again with honey sweet and salty.

EZRA POUND*

Envoi (1919)

GO, dumb-born book,
Tell her that sang me once that song of Lawes:
Hadst thou but song
As thou hast subjects known,
Then were there cause in thee that should condone
Even my faults that heavy upon me lie,
And build her glories their longevity.

Tell her that sheds
Such treasure in the air,
Recking naught else but that her graces give
Life to the moment,
I would bid them live
As roses might, in magic amber laid,
Red overwrought with orange and all made
One substance and one colour
Braving time.

*After the publishers of the Modern Library omitted the poems of Ezra Pound from the first edition of this volume, a veritable avalanche of praise and blame, equally divided, descended upon them.

Nothing could have been farther from the intention of the publishers than to exercise arbitrary rights of censorship. We now have decided to include these poems of Ezra Pound in order to remove any possible hint of suppression, and because we concede that it may be wrong to confuse Pound the poet with Pound the man.

Tell her that goes
With song upon her lips
But sings not out the song, nor knows
The maker of it, some other mouth,
May be as fair as hers,
Might, in new ages, gain her worshippers,
When our two dusts with Waller's shall be laid,
Siftings on siftings in oblivion,
Till change hath broken down
All things save Beauty alone.

The Tree

I STOOD still and was a tree amid the wood,
Knowing the truth of things unseen before;
Of Daphne and the laurel bough
And that god-feasting couple old
That grew elm-oak amid the wold.
'Twas not until the gods had been
Kindly entreated, and been brought within
Unto the hearth of their heart's home
That they might do this wonder thing;
Nathless I have been a tree amid the wood
And many a new thing understood
That was rank folly to my head before.

The Tomb at Akr Çaar

"I AM thy soul, Nikoptis. I have watched
These five millennia, and thy dead eyes
Moved not, nor ever answer my desire,
And thy light limbs, wherethrough I leapt aflame,
Burn not with me nor any saffron thing.
See, the light grass sprang up to pillow thee,
And kissed thee with a myriad grassy tongues;
But not thou me.
I have read out the gold upon the wall,

And wearied out my thought upon the signs.
And there is no new thing in all this place.

I have been kind. See, I have left the jars sealed,
Lest thou shouldst wake and whimper for thy wine.
And all thy robes I have kept smooth on thee.

O thou unmindful! How should I forget!
—Even the river many days ago,
The river? thou wast over young.
And three souls came upon Thee—
And I came.
And I flowed in upon thee, beat them off;
I have been intimate with thee, known thy ways.
Have I not touched thy palms and finger-tips,
Flowed in, and through thee and about thy heels?
How 'came I in'? Was I not thee and Thee?

And no sun comes to rest me in this place,
And I am torn against the jagged dark,
And no light beats upon me, and you say
No word, day after day.

Oh! I could get me out, despite the marks
And all their crafty work upon the door,
Out through the glass-green fields. . . .

   .   .   .   .   .   .

Yet it is quiet here:

I do not go."

Portrait d'une Femme

YOUR mind and you are our Sargasso Sea,
   London has swept about you this score years
And bright ships left you this or that in fee:
Ideas, old gossip, oddments of all things,
Strange spars of knowledge and dimmed wares of price.
Great minds have sought you—lacking someone else.

You have been second always. Tragical?
No. You preferred it to the usual thing:
One dull man, dulling and uxorious,
One average mind—with one thought less, each year.
Oh, you are patient, I have seen you sit
Hours, where something might have floated up.
And now you pay one. Yes, you richly pay.
You are a person of some interest, one comes to you
And takes strange gain away:
Trophies fished up; some curious suggestion;
Fact that leads nowhere; and a tale or two,
Pregnant with mandrakes, or with something else
That might prove useful and yet never proves,
That never fits a corner or shows use,
Or finds its hour upon the loom of days:
The tarnished, gaudy, wonderful old work;
Idols and ambergris and rare inlays,
These are your riches, your great store; and yet
For all this sea-hoard of deciduous things,
Strange woods half sodden, and new brighter stuff:
In the slow float of differing light and deep,
No! there is nothing! In the whole and all,
Nothing that's quite your own.
              Yet this is you.

Apparuit

GOLDEN rose the house, in the portal I saw
     thee, a marvel, carven in subtle stuff, a
portent. Life died down in the lamp and flickered,
     caught at the wonder.

Crimson, frosty with dew, the roses bend where
thou afar, moving in the glamorous sun,
drinkst in life of earth, of the air, the tissue
     golden about thee.

Green the ways, the breath of the fields is thine there,
open lies the land, yet the steely going
darkly hast thou dared and the dreaded æther
    parted before thee.

Swift at courage thou in the shell of gold, casting a-loose the cloak of the body, camest
straight, then shone thine oriel and the stunned light
    faded about thee.

Half the graven shoulder, the throat aflash with
strands of light inwoven about it, loveliest of all things, frail alabaster, ah me!
    swift in departing.

Clothed in goldish weft, delicately perfect,
gone as wind! The cloth of the magical hands:
Thou a slight thing, thou in access of cunning
    dar'dst to assume this?

A Virginal

NO, no! Go from me. I have left her lately.
    I will not spoil my sheath with lesser brightness.
For my surrounding air hath a new lightness;
Slight are her arms, yet they have bound me straitly
And left me cloaked as with a gauze of æther;
As with sweet leaves; as with subtle clearness.
Oh, I have picked up magic in her nearness
To sheathe me half in half the things that sheathe her.
No, no! Go from me. I have still the flavour,
Soft as spring wind that's come from birchen bowers.
Green come the shoots, aye April in the branches,
As winter's wound with her sleight hand she staunches,
Hath of the trees a likeness of the savour:
As white their bark, so white this lady's hours.

The Return

SEE, they return; ah, see the tentative
Movements, and the slow feet,
The trouble in the pace and the uncertain
Wavering!

See, they return, one, and by one,
With fear, as half-awakened;
As if the snow should hesitate
And murmur in the wind,
            and half turned back;
These were the "Wing'd-with-Awe,"
            Inviolable.

Gods of the wingèd shoe!
With them the silver hounds,
            sniffing the trace of air!

Haie! Haie!
      These were the swift to harry;
These the keen-scented;
These were the souls of blood.

Slow on the leash,
            pallid the leash-men!

The River-Merchant's Wife:

A Letter

WHILE my hair was still cut straight across my forehead
I played about the front gate, pulling flowers.
You came by on bamboo stilts, playing horse,
You walked about my seat, playing with blue plums.
And we went on living in the village of Chokan:
Two small people, without dislike or suspicion.

At fourteen I married My Lord you.
I never laughed, being bashful.
Lowering my head, I looked at the wall.
Called to, a thousand times, I never looked back.

At fifteen I stopped scowling,
I desired my dust to be mingled with yours
Forever and forever and forever.
Why should I climb the look out?

At sixteen you departed,
You went into far Ku-to-yen, by the river of swirling eddies,
And you have been gone five months.
The monkeys make sorrowful noise overhead.

You dragged your feet when you went out.
By the gate now, the moss is grown, the different mosses,
Too deep to clear them away!
The leaves fall early this autumn, in wind.
The paired butterflies are already yellow with August
Over the grass in the West garden;
They hurt me. I grow older.
If you are coming down through the narrows of the river Kiang,
Please let me know beforehand,
And I will come out to meet you
          As far as Cho-fu-Sa.

Rihaku

The Flame

'TIS not a game that plays at mates and mating,
  Provençe knew;
'Tis not a game of barter, lands and houses,
Provençe knew.
We who are wise beyond your dream of wisdom,
Drink our immortal moments; we "pass through."
We have gone forth beyond your bonds and borders,
Provençe knew;
And all the tales of Oisin say but this:

That man doth pass the net of days and hours.
Where time is shrivelled down to time's seed corn
We of the Ever-living, in that light
Meet through our veils and whisper, and of love.

O smoke and shadow of a darkling world,
These, and the rest, and all the rest we knew.

'Tis not a game that plays at mates and mating,
'Tis not a game of barter, lands and houses,
'Tis not "of days and nights" and troubling years,
Of cheeks grown sunken and glad hair gone gray;
There *is* the subtler music, the clear light
Where time burns back about the eternal embers.
We are not shut from all the thousand heavens:
Lo, there are many gods whom we have seen,
Folk of unearthly fashion, places splendid,
Bulwarks of beryl and of chrysoprase.

Sapphire Benacus, in thy mists and thee
Nature herself's turned metaphysical,
Who can look on that blue and not believe?

Thou hooded opal, thou eternal pearl,
O thou dark secret with a shimmering floor,
Through all thy various mood I know thee mine;
If I have merged my soul, or utterly
Am solved and bound in, through aught here on earth,
There canst thou find me, O thou anxious thou,
Who call'st about my gates for some lost me;
I say my soul flowed back, became translucent.
Search not my lips, O Love, let go my hands,
This thing that moves as man is no more mortal.
If thou hast seen my shade sans character,
If thou hast seen that mirror of all moments,
That glass to all things that o'ershadow it,
Call not that mirror me, for I have slipped
Your grasp, I have eluded.

Dance Figure

FOR THE MARRIAGE IN CANA OF GALILEE

Dark eyed,
O woman of my dreams,
Ivory sandaled,
There is none like thee among the dancers,
None with swift feet.

I have not found thee in the tents,
In the broken darkness.
I have not found thee at the well-head
Among the women with pitchers.

Thine arms are as a young sapling under the bark;
Thy face as a river with lights.

White as an almond are thy shoulders;
As new almonds stripped from the husk.
They guard thee not with eunuchs;
Not with bars of copper.

Gilt turquoise and silver are in the place of thy rest.
A brown robe, with threads of gold woven in patterns,
        hast thou gathered about thee,
O Nathat-Ikanaie, "Tree-at-the-river."

As a rillet among the sedge are thy hands upon me;
Thy fingers a frosted stream.

Thy maidens are white like pebbles;
Their music about thee!

There is none like thee among the dancers;
None with swift feet.

Lament of the Frontier Guard

BY the North Gate, the wind blows full of sand,
   Lonely from the beginning of time until now!
Trees fall, the grass goes yellow with autumn.
I climb the towers and towers
            to watch out the barbarous land:
Desolate castle, the sky, the wide desert.
There is no wall left to this village.
Bones white with a thousand frosts,
High heaps, covered with trees and grass;
Who brought this to pass?
Who has brought the flaming imperial anger?
Who has brought the army with drums and with
            kettle-drums?
Barbarous kings.
A gracious spring, turned to blood-ravenous autumn,
A turmoil of wars-men, spread over the middle kingdom,
Three hundred and sixty thousand,
And sorrow, sorrow like rain.
Sorrow to go, and sorrow, sorrow returning.
Desolate, desolate fields,
And no children of warfare upon them,
            No longer the men for offence and defence.
Ah, how shall you know the dreary sorrow at the
            North Gate,
With Rihaku's name forgotten,
And we guardsmen fed to the tigers.

                                        Rihaku

Taking Leave of a Friend

BLUE mountains to the north of the walls,
   White river winding about them;
Here we must make separation
And go out through a thousand miles of dead grass.

Mind like a floating wide cloud,
Sunset like the parting of old acquaintances
Who bow over their clasped hands at a distance.
Our horses neigh to each other
            as we are departing.

Rihaku

ALFRED KREYMBORG

Nun Snow

A Pantomime of Beads

Earth Voice

IS she
    Thoughtless of life,
A lover of imminent death,
Nun Snow
Touching her strings of white beads?
Is it her unseen hands
Which urge the beads to tremble?
Does Nun Snow,
Aware of the death she must die alone,
Away from the nuns
Of the green beads,
Of the ochre and brown,
Of the purple and black—
Does she improvise
Along those soundless strings
In the worldly hope
That the answering, friendly tune,
The faithful, folk-like miracle,
Will shine in a moment or two?

Moon Voice

> Or peradventure,
> Are the beads merely wayward,
> On an evening so soft,
> And One Wind
> Is so gentle a mesmerist
> As he draws them and her with his hand?

Earth Voice

> Was it Full Moon,
> Who contrives tales of this order,
> And himself loves the heroine,
> Nun Snow—

Wind Voice

> Do you see his beads courting hers?—
> Lascivious monk!—

Earth Voice

> Was it Full Moon,
> Slyly innocent of guile,
> Propounder of sorrowless whimseys,
> Who breathed that suspicion?
> Is it One Wind,
> The wily, scholarly pedant—
> Is it he who retorts—

Wind Voice

> Like olden allegros
> In olden sonatas,
> All tales have two themes,
> *She is beautiful,*
> *He is beautiful,*
> With the traditional movement,
> *Their beads court each other,*
> Revealing a cadence as fatally true
> As the sum which follows a one-plus-one—
> So, why inquire further?
> Nay, inquire further,
> Deduce it your fashion!

Nun Snow,
As you say,
Touches her strings of white beads,
Full Moon,
Let you add,
His lute of yellow strings;
And, our Night
Is square, nay,
Our Night
Is round, nay
Our Night
Is a blue balcony—
And therewith close your inquisition!

Earth Voice

Who urged the beads to tremble?
They're still now!
Fallen, or cast over me!
Nun, Moon, and Wind are gone!
Are they betraying her?—

Moon Voice

Ask our Night—

Earth Voice

Did the miracle appear?—

Moon Voice

Ask our night,
Merely a child on a balcony,
Letting down her hair and
Black beads, a glissando—
Ask her what she means,
Dropping the curtain so soon!

JOHN GOULD FLETCHER

Irradiations

I

THE spattering of the rain upon pale terraces
   Of afternoon is like the passing of a dream
Amid the roses shuddering 'gainst the wet green stalks
Of the streaming trees—the passing of the wind
Upon the pale lower terraces of my dream
Is like the crinkling of the wet grey robes
Of the hours that come to turn over the urn
Of the day and spill its rainy dream.
Vague movement over the puddled terraces:
Heavy gold pennons—a pomp of solemn gardens
Half hidden under the liquid veil of spring:
Far trumpets like a vague rout of faded roses
Burst 'gainst the wet green silence of distant forests:
A clash of cymbals—then the swift swaying footsteps
Of the wind that undulates along the languid terraces.
Pools of rain—the vacant terraces
Wet, chill and glistening
Towards the sunset beyond the broken doors of today.

II

The iridescent vibrations of midsummer light
Dancing, dancing suddenly flickering and quivering
Like little feet or the movement of quick hands clapping,
Or the rustle of furbelows or the clash of polished gems.
The palpitant mosaic of the midday light
Colliding, sliding, leaping and lingering:
O, I could lie on my back all day,
And mark the mad ballet of the midsummer sky.

III

Over the roof-tops race the shadows of clouds;
Like horses the shadows of clouds charge down the street.

Whirlpools of purple and gold,
Winds from the mountains of cinnabar,
Lacquered mandarin moments, palanquins swaying and balancing
Amid the vermilion pavilions, against the jade balustrades.
Glint of the glittering wings of dragon-flies in the light:
Silver filaments, golden flakes settling downwards,
Rippling, quivering flutters, repulse and surrender,
The sun broidered upon the rain,
The rain rustling with the sun.

Over the roof-tops race the shadows of clouds;
Like horses the shadows of clouds charge down the street.

IV

The balancing of gaudy broad pavilions
Of summer against the insolent breeze:
The bellying of the sides of striped tents,
Swelling taut, shuddering in quick collapse,
Silent under the silence of the sky.

Earth is streaked and spotted
With great splashes and dapples of sunlight:
The sun throws an immense circle of hot light upon the world,
Rolling slowly in ponderous rhythm
Darkly, musically forward.
All is silent under the steep cone of afternoon:
The sky is imperturbably profound.
The ultimate divine union seems about to be accomplished,
All is troubled at the attainment
Of the inexhaustible infinite.

The rolling and the tossing of the sides of immense pavilions
Under the whirling wind that screams up the cloudless sky.

V

Flickering of incessant rain
On flashing pavements:
Sudden scurry of umbrellas:
Bending, recurved blossoms of the storm.

The winds came clanging and clattering
From long white highroads whipping in ribbons up summits:
They strew upon the city gusty wafts of apple-blossom,
And the rustling of innumerable translucent leaves.
Uneven tinkling, the lazy rain
Dripping from the eaves.

VI

The fountain blows its breathless spray
From me to you and back to me.

Whipped, tossed, curdled,
Crashing, quivering:
I hurl kisses like blows upon your lips.
The dance of a bee drunken with sunlight:
Irradiant ecstasies, white and gold,
Sigh and relapse.

The fountain tosses pallid spray
Far in the sorrowful, silent sky.

Green Symphony

I

THE glittering leaves of the rhododendrons
    Balance and vibrate in the cool air;
While in the sky above them
White clouds chase each other.

Like scampering rabbits,
Flashes of sunlight sweep the lawn;
They fling in passing
Patterns of shadow,
Golden and green.

With long cascades of laughter,
The mating birds dart and swoop to the turf:
'Mid their mad trillings
Glints the gay sun behind the trees.

Down there are deep blue lakes:
Orange blossom droops in the water.
In the tower of the winds,
All the bells are set adrift:
Jingling
For the dawn.

Thin fluttering streamers
Of breeze lash through the swaying boughs,
Palely expectant
The earth receives the slanting rain.

I am a glittering raindrop
Hugged close by the cool rhododendron.
I am a daisy starring
The exquisite curves of the close-cropped turf.

The glittering leaves of the rhododendron
Are shaken like blue-green glades of grass,
Flickering, cracking, falling:
Splintering in a million fragments.
The wind runs laughing up the slope
Stripping off handfuls of wet green leaves,
To fling in peoples' faces.
Wallowing on the daisy-powdered turf,
Clutching at the sunlight,
Cavorting in the shadow.

Like baroque pearls,
Like cloudy emeralds,
The clouds and the trees clash together;
Whirling and swirling,
In the tumult
Of the spring,
And the wind.

II

The trees splash the sky with their fingers,
A restless green rout of stars.

With whirling movement
They swing their boughs

About their stems:
Planes on planes of light and shadow
Pass among them,
Opening fan-like to fall.

The trees are like a sea;
Tossing,
Trembling,
Roaring,
Wallowing,
Darting their long green flickering fronds up at the sky,
Spotted with white blossom-spray.

The trees are roofs:
Hollow caverns of cool blue shadow,
Solemn arches
In the afternoons.
The whole vast horizon
In terrace beyond terrace,
Pinnacle above pinnacle,
Lifts to the sky
Serrated ranks of green on green.

They caress the roofs with their fingers,
They sprawl about the river to look into it;
Up the hill they come
Gesticulating challenge:
They cower together
In dark valleys;
They yearn out over the fields.
Enamelled domes
Tumble upon the grass,
Crashing in ruin
Quiet at last.

The trees lash the sky with their leaves,
Uneasily shaking their dark green manes.

III

Far let the voices of the mad wild birds be calling me,
I will abide in this forest of pines.

When the wind blows
Battling through the forest,
I hear it distantly,
The crash of a perpetual sea.

When the rain falls,
I watch silver spears slanting downwards
From pale river-pools of sky,
Enclosed in dark fronds.

When the sun shines,
I weave together distant branches till they enclose mighty circles,
I sway to the movement of hooded summits,
I swim leisurely in deep blue seas of air.

I hug the smooth bark of stately red pillars
And with cones carefully scattered
I mark the progression of dark dial-shadows
Flung diagonally downwards through the afternoon.

This turf is not like turf:
It is a smooth dry carpet of velvet,
Embroidered with brown patterns of needles and cones.
These trees are not like trees:
They are innumerable feathery pagoda-umbrellas,
Stiffly ungracious to the wind,
Teetering on red-lacquered stems.

In the evening I listen to the winds' lisping,
While the conflagrations of the sunset flicker and clash behind me,
Flamboyant crenellations of glory amid the charred ebony boles.

In the night the fiery nightingales
Shall clash and trill through the silence:
Like the voices of mermaids crying
From the sea.

Long ago has the moon whelmed this uncompleted temple.
Stars swim like gold fish far above the black arches.

Far let the timid feet of dawn fly to catch me:
I will abide in this forest of pines:

For I have unveiled naked beauty,
And the things that she whispered to me in the darkness,
Are buried deep in my heart.

Now let the black tops of the pine-trees break like a spent wave,
Against the grey sky:
These are tombs and memorials and temples and altars sun-kindled
for me.

White Symphony

I

FORLORN and white,
Whorls of purity about a golden chalice,
Immense the peonies
Flare and shatter their petals over my face.

They slowly turn paler,
They seem to be melting like blue-grey flakes of ice,
Thin greyish shivers
Fluctuating 'mid the dark green lance-thrust of the leaves.

Like snowballs tossed,
Like soft white butterflies,
The peonies poise in the twilight.
And their narcotic insinuating perfume
Draws me into them
Shivering with the coolness,
Aching with the void.
They kiss the blue chalice of my dreams
Like a gesture seen for an instant and then lost forever.

Outwards the petals
Thrust to embrace me,
Pale daggers of coldness
Run through my aching breast.

Outwards, still outwards,
Till on the brink of twilight

They swirl downwards silently,
Flurry of snow in the void.

Outwards, still outwards,
Till the blue walls are hidden,
And in the blinding white radiance
Of a whirlpool of clouds, I awake.

Like spraying rockets
My peonies shower
Their glories on the night.
Wavering perfumes,
Drift about the garden;
Shadows of the moonlight,
Drift and ripple over the dew-gemmed leaves.

Soar, crash, and sparkle,
Shoal of stars drifting
Like silver fishes,
Through the black sluggish boughs.
Towards the impossible,
Towards the inaccessible,
Towards the ultimate,
Towards the silence,
Towards the eternal,
These blossoms go.

The peonies spring like rockets in the twilight,
And out of them all I rise.

II

Downwards through the blue abyss it slides,
The white snow-water of my dreams,
Downwards crashing from slippery rock
Into the boiling chasm:
In which no eye dare look, for it is the chasm of death.
Upwards from the blue abyss it rises,
The chill water-mist of my dreams;
Upwards to greyish weeping pines,
And to skies of autumn ever about my heart,
It is blue at the beginning,
And blue-white against the grey-greenness;

It wavers in the upper air,
Catching unconscious sparkles, a rainbow-glint of sunlight,
And fading in the sad depths of the sky.

Outwards rush the strong pale clouds,
Outwards and ever outwards;
The blue-grey clouds indistinguishable one from another:
Nervous, sinewy, tossing their arms and brandishing,
Till on the blue serrations of the horizon
They drench with their black rain a great peak of changeless snow.

As evening came on, I climbed the tower,
To gaze upon the city far beneath:
I was not weary of day; but in the evening
A white mist assembled and gathered over the earth
And blotted it from sight.
But to escape:
To chase with the golden clouds galloping over the horizon:
Arrows of the northwest wind
Singing amid them,
Ruffling up my hair!

As evening came on the distance altered,
Pale wavering reflections rose from out the city,
Like sighs of the beckoning of half-invisible hands.
Monotonously and sluggishly they crept upwards
A river that had spent itself in some chasm,
And dwindled and foamed at last at my weary feet.

Autumn! Golden fountains,
And the winds neighing
Amid the monotonous hills:
Desolation of the old gods,
Rain that lifts and rain that moves away;
In the green-black torrent
Scarlet leaves.

It was now perfectly evening:
And the tower loomed like a gaunt peak in mid-air
Above the city: its base was utterly lost.
It was slowly coming on to rain,
And the immense columns of white mist
Wavered and broke before the faint-hurled spears.

I will descend the mountains like a shepherd,
And in the folds of tumultuous misty cities,
I will put all my thoughts, all my old thoughts, safely to sleep.
For it is already autumn,
O whiteness of the pale southwestern sky!
O wavering dream that was not mine to keep!
In midnight, in mournful moonlight,
By paths I could not trace,
I walked in the white garden,
Each flower had a white face.

Their perfume intoxicated me: thus I began my dream.

I was alone; I had no one to guide me,
But the moon was like the sun:
It stooped and kissed each waxen petal,
One after one.
Green and white was that garden: diamond rain hung in the
    branches,
You will not believe it!

In the morning, at the dayspring,
I wakened, shivering; lo,
The white garden that blossomed at my feet
Was a garden hidden in snow.

It was my sorrow to see that all this was a dream.

III

Blue, clogged with purple,
Mists uncoil themselves:
Sparkling to the horizon,
I see the snow alone.

In the deep blue chasm,
Boats sleep under gold thatch;
Icicle-like trees fret
Faintly rose-touched sky.

Under their heaped snow-eaves,
Leaden houses shiver.

Through thin blue crevasses,
Trickles an icy stream.

The pines groan white-laden,
The waves shiver, struck by the wind;
Beyond from treeless horizons,
Broken snow-peaks crawl to the sea.

Wearily the snow glares,
Through the grey silence, day after day,
Mocking the colourless cloudless sky
With the reflection of death.

There is no smoke through the pine tops,
No strong red boatmen in pale green reeds,
No herons to flicker an instant,
No lanterns to glow with gay ray.

No sails beat up to the harbour,
With creaking cordage and sailors' song.
Somnolent, bare-poled, indifferent,
They sleep, and the city sleeps.

Mid-winter about them casts
Its dreary fortifications:
Each day is a gaunt grey rock,
And death is the last of them all.

Over the sluggish snow,
Drifts now a pallid weak shower of bloom:
Boredom of fresh creation,
Death-weariness of old returns.

White, white blossom,
Fall of the shattered cups day on day:
Is there anything here that is not ancient,
That has not bloomed a thousand years ago?

Under the glare of the white-hot day,
Under the restless wind-rakes of the winter,
White blossom or white snow scattered,
And beneath them, dark, the graves.

Dark graves never changing,
White dream, drifting, never changing above them:
O that the white scroll of heaven might be rolled up,
And the naked red lightning thrust at the smouldering earth!

H. D.

At Baia

I SHOULD have thought
In a dream you would have brought
Some lovely perilous thing,
Orchids piled in a great sheath,
As who would say (in a dream)
I send you this,
Who left the blue veins
Of your throat unkissed.
Why was it that your hands
(That never took mine)
Your hands that I could see
Drift over the orchid heads
So carefully,
Your hands, so fragile, sure to lift
So gently, the fragile flower stuff—
Ah, ah, how was it

You never sent (in a dream)
The very form, the very scent,
Not heavy, not sensuous.
But perilous—perilous—
Of orchids, piled in a great sheath,
And folded underneath on a bright scroll
Some word:
Flower sent to flower;
For white hands, the lesser white,
Less lovely of flower leaf,

Or

Lover to lover, no kiss,
No touch, but forever and ever this.

"Not Honey"

NOT honey,
Not the plunder of the bee
From meadow or sand-flower
Or mountain bush;
From winter-flower or shoot
Born of the later heat:
Not honey, not the sweet
Stain on the lips and teeth:
Not honey, not the deep
Plunge of soft belly
And the clinging of the gold-edged
Pollen-dusted feet.

Not so—
Though rapture blind my eyes,
And hunger crisp
Dark and inert my mouth,
Not honey, not the south,
Not the tall stalk
Of red twin-lilies,
Nor light branch of fruit tree
Caught in flexible light branch.

Not honey, not the south;
Ah, flower of purple iris,
Flower of white,
Or of the iris, withering the grass—
For fleck of the sun's fire,
Gathers such heat and power,
That shadow-print is light,
Cast through the petals
Of the yellow iris flower.

Not iris—old desire—old passion—
Old forgetfulness—old pain—
Not this, nor any flower,

But if you turn again,
Seek strength of arm and throat,
Touch as the god:
Neglect the lyre-note;
Knowing that you shall feel,
About the frame,
No trembling of the string
But heat more passionate
Of bone and the white shell
And fiery tempered steel.

Song

YOU are as gold
     As the half-ripe grain
That merges to gold again,
As white as the white rain
That beats through
The half-opened flowers
Of the great flower tufts
Thick on the black limbs
Of an Illyrian apple bough.

Can honey distil such fragrance
As your bright hair—
For your face is as fair as rain,
Yet as rain that lies clear
On white honey-comb,
Lends radiance to the white wax,
So your hair on your brow
Casts light for a shadow.

The Garden

I

YOU are clear,
     O rose, cut in rock.

I could scrape the colour
From the petals,
Like spilt dye from a rock.

If I could break you
I could break a tree.

If I could stir
I could break a tree,
I could break you.

II

O wind, rend open the heat,
Cut apart the heat,
Slit it to tatters.

Fruit cannot drop
Through this thick air;
Fruit cannot fall into heat
That presses up and blunts
The points of pears,
And rounds grapes.

Cut the heat:
Plough through it,
Turning it on either side
Of your path.

Orchard

I SAW the first pear
as it fell—
the honey-seeking, golden banded,
the yellow swarm,
was not more fleet than I,
(spare us from loveliness!)
and I fell prostrate,
crying:
you have flayed us with your blossoms,
spare us the beauty
of fruit-trees!

The honey-seeking
paused not;
the air thundered their song,
and I alone was prostrate.

O rough-hewn
god of the orchard,
I bring you an offering—
do you, alone unbeautiful,
son of the god,
spare us from loveliness:
these fallen hazel-nuts,
stripped late of their green sheaths,
grapes, red-purple,
their berries
dripping with wine;
pomegranates already broken,
and shrunken figs,
and quinces untouched,
I bring you as offering.

LOUIS UNTERMEYER

Long Feud

WHERE, without bloodshed, can there be
A more relentless enmity
Than the long feud fought silently

Between man and the growing grass?
Man's the aggressor, for he has
Weapons to humble and harass

The impudent spears that charge upon
His sacred privacy of lawn,
He mows them down, and they are gone

Only to lie in wait, although
He builds above and digs below
Where never a root would dare to go.

His are the triumphs till the day
There's no more grass to cut away,
And, tired of labor, tired of play,

Having exhausted every whim,
He stretches out each conquering limb.
And then the small grass covers him.

———•••———

JOHN HALL WHEELOCK

———•••———

Earth

GRASSHOPPER, your fairy song
And my poem alike belong
To the dark and silent earth
From which all poetry has birth;
All we say and all we sing
Is but as the murmuring
Of that drowsy heart of hers
When from her deep dream she stirs:
If we sorrow, or rejoice,
You and I are but her voice.

Deftly does the dust express
In mind her hidden loveliness,
And from her cool silence stream
The cricket's cry and Dante's dream;
For the earth that breeds the trees
Breeds cities too, and symphonies.

Equally her beauty flows
Into a savior, or a rose—
Looks down in dream, and from above

Smiles at herself in Jesus' love.
Christ's love and Homer's art
Are but the workings of her heart;
Through Leonardo's hand she seeks
Herself, and through Beethoven speaks
In holy thunderings around
The awful message of the ground.

The serene and humble mold
Does in herself all selves enfold—
Kingdoms, destinies, and creeds,
Great dreams, and dauntless deeds,
Science that metes the firmament,
The high, inflexible intent
Of one for many sacrificed—
Plato's brain, the heart of Christ;
All love, all legend, and all lore
Are in the dust forevermore.

Even as the growing grass,
Up from the soil religions pass,
And the field that bears the rye
Bears parables and prophecy.
Out of the earth the poem grows
Like the lily, or the rose;
And all man is, or yet may be,
Is but herself in agony
Toiling up the steep ascent
Toward the complete accomplishment
When all dust shall be, the whole
Universe, one conscious soul.
Yea, the quiet and cool sod
Bears in her breast the dream of God.

If you would know what earth is, scan
The intricate, proud heart of man,
Which is the earth articulate,
And learn how holy and how great,
How limitless and how profound
Is the nature of the ground—
How without terror or demur
We may entrust ourselves to her

When we are wearied out and lay
Our faces in the common clay.

For she is pity, she is love,
All wisdom, she, all thoughts that move
About her everlasting breast
Till she gathers them to rest:
All tenderness of all the ages,
Seraphic secrets of the sages,
Vision and hope of all the seers,
All prayer, all anguish, and all tears
Are but the dust that from her dream
Awakes, and knows herself supreme—
Are but earth, when she reveals
All that her secret heart conceals
Down in the dark and silent loam,
Which is ourselves, asleep, at home.

Yea, and this, my poem, too,
Is part of her as dust and dew,
Wherein herself she doth declare
Through my lips, and say her prayer.

CALE YOUNG RICE

Chanson of the Bells of Osenèy

THIRTEENTH CENTURY

THE bells of Osenèy
  (Hautclère, Doucement, Austyn)
Chant sweetly every day,
And sadly, for our sin.
The bells of Osenèy
(John, Gabriel, Marie)
Chant lowly,
        Chant slowly,
Chant wistfully and holy
Of Christ, our Paladin.

Hautclère chants to the East
(His tongue is silvery high),
And Austyn like a priest
Sends west a weighty cry.
But Doucement set between
(Like an appeasive nun)
Chants cheerly,
　　　Chants clearly,
As if Christ heard her nearly,
A plea to every sky.

A plea that John takes up
(He is the evangelist)
Till Gabriel's angel cup
Pours sound to sun or mist.
And last of all Marie
(The virgin-voice of God)
Peals purely,
　　　Demurely,
And with a tone so surely
Divine, that all must hear.

The bells of Osenèy
(Doucement, Austyn, Hautclère)
Pour ever day by day
Their peals on the rapt air;
And with their mellow mates
(John, Gabriel, Marie)
Tell slowly,
　　　Tell lowly,
Of Christ the High and Holy,
Who makes the whole world fair.

MARIANNE MOORE

The Fish

WADE
　　through black jade
Of the crow-blue mussel shells, one
　　keeps
　　　adjusting the ash heaps;
opening and shutting itself like

an
injured fan.
　　The barnacles which encrust the
　　　side
　　　of the wave, cannot hide
there for the submerged shafts of the

sun,
split like spun
　　glass, move themselves with spotligh
　　　swiftness
　　　into the crevices—
in and out, illuminating

the
turquoise sea
　　of bodies. The water drives a
　　　wedge
　　　of iron through the iron edge
of the cliff, whereupon the stars,

pink
rice grains, ink
　　bespattered jelly-fish, crabs like
　　　green
　　　lilies and submarine
toadstools, slide each on the other.

All
external
        marks of abuse are present on
                this
                        defiant edifice—
        all the physical features of

ac-
cident—lack
        of cornice, dynamite grooves, burns
                and
                        hatchet strokes, these things stand
        out on it; the chasm side is

dead.
Repeated
        evidence has proved that it can
                live
                        on what cannot revive
        its youth. The sea grows old in it.

My Apish Cousins

WINKED too much and were afraid of snakes. The zebras,
        supreme in
their abnormality; the elephants with their fog-colored skin
        and strictly practical appendages
                were there, the small cats; and the parakeet—
                        trivial and humdrum on examination, destroying
        bark and portions of the food it could not eat.

I recall their magnificence, now not more magnificent
than it is dim. It is difficult to recall the ornament,
        speech, and precise manner of what one might
                call the minor acquaintances twenty
                        years back; but I shall not forget him—that
                                Gilgamesh among
                the hairy carnivora—that cat with the

wedge-shaped, slate-gray marks on its forelegs and the resolute tail,
astringently remarking: "They have imposed on us with their pale

half-fledged protestations, trembling about
    in articulate frenzy, saying
        it is not for us to understand art; finding it
    all so difficult, examining the thing

as if it were inconceivably arcanic, as symmet-
rically frigid as if it had been carved out of chrysoprase
  or marble—strict with tension, malignant
        in its power over us and deeper
           than the sea when it proffers flattery in exchange for
           hemp,
  rye, flax, horses, platinum, timber, and fur."

Poetry

I TOO, dislike it: there are things that are important beyond all
   this fiddle.
Reading it, however, with a perfect contempt for it, one discovers
        that there is in
it after all, a place for the genuine.
Hands that can grasp, eyes
that can dilate, hair that can rise
    if it must, these things are important not because a
high sounding interpretation can be put upon them but because they
        are
    useful; when they become so derivative as to become unintelli-
        gible,
  the same thing may be said for all of us, that we
    do not admire what
    we cannot understand: the bat,
        holding on upside down or in quest of something to
eat, elephants pushing, a wild horse taking a roll, a tireless wolf
    under
  a tree, the immovable critic twitching his skin like a horse that
      feels a flea, the base-
  ball fan, the statistician—
    nor is it valid
      to discriminate against "business documents and

school-books"; all these phenomena are important. One must make
   a distinction

however: when dragged into prominence by half poets, the
　　　result is not poetry,
nor till the poets among us can be
　　"literalists of
　　　the imagination"—above
　　　　insolence and triviality and can present

for inspection, imaginary gardens with real toads in them, shall we
　　　have
　it. In the meantime, if you demand on one hand,
　the raw material of poetry in
　　all its rawness and
　　that which is on the other hand
　　　genuine, then you are interested in poetry.

A Talisman

UNDER a splintered mast,
　　Torn from the ship and cast
　　Near her hull,

A stumbling shepherd found
Embedded in the ground,
　　A seagull

Of lapis lazuli,
A scarab of the sea,
　　With wings spread—

Curling its coral feet,
Parting its beak to greet
　　Men long dead.

Roses Only

YOU do not seem to realize that beauty is a liability rather than
　　an asset—that in view of the fact that spirit creates form we
　　are justified in supposing
　　　that you must have brains. For you, a symbol of the unit,
　　stiff and sharp,

conscious of surpassing by dint of native superiority and liking
for everything
self-dependent, anything an

ambitious civilization might produce: for you, unaided, to attempt
through sheer
reserve, to confuse presumptions resulting from observation, is
idle. You cannot make us
think you a delightful happen-so. But rose, if you are brilliant, it
is not because your petals are the without-which-nothing of pre-
eminence. Would you not, minus
thorns, be a what-is-this, a mere

peculiarity? They are not proof against a worm, the elements, or
mildew;
but what about the predatory hand? What is brilliance without
co-ordination? Guarding the
infinitesimal pieces of your mind, compelling audience to
the remark that it is better to be forgotten than to be remembered too violently,
your thorns are the best part of you.

ROBINSON JEFFERS

Continent's End

AT the equinox when the earth was veiled in a late rain, wreathed
with wet poppies, waiting spring,
The ocean swelled for a far storm and beat its boundary, the ground-
swell shook the beds of granite.

I gazing at the boundaries of granite and spray, the established sea-
marks, felt behind me
Mountain and plain, the immense breadth of the continent, before
me the mass and doubled stretch of water.

I said: You yoke the Aleutian seal-rocks with the lava and coral sowings that flower the south,
Over your flood the life that sought the sunrise faces ours that has followed the evening star.

The long migrations meet across you and it is nothing to you, you have forgotten us, mother.
You were much younger when we crawled out of the womb and lay in the sun's eye on the tideline.

It was long and long ago; we have grown proud since then and you have grown bitter; life retains
Your mobile soft unquiet strength; and envies hardness, the insolent quietness of stone.

The tides are in our veins, we still mirror the stars, life is your child, but there is in me
Older and harder than life and more impartial, the eye that watched before there was an ocean.

That watched you fill your beds out of the condensation of thin vapor and watched you change them,
That saw you soft and violent wear your boundaries down, eat rock, shift places with the continents.

Mother, though my song's measure is like your surf-beat's ancient rhythm I never learned it of you.
Before there was any water there were tides of fire, both our tones flow from the older fountain.

Apology for Bad Dreams

I

IN the purple light, heavy with redwood, the slopes drop seaward,
Headlong convexities of forest, drawn in together to the steep ravine. Below, on the sea-cliff,
A lonely clearing; a little field of corn by the streamside; a roof under spared trees. Then the ocean
Like a great stone someone has cut to a sharp edge and polished to shining. Beyond it, the fountain

And furnace of incredible light flowing up from the sunk sun. In
     the little clearing a woman
Was punishing a horse; she had tied the halter to a sapling at the
     edge of the wood; but when the great whip
Clung to the flanks the creature kicked so hard she feared he would
     snap the halter; she called from the house
The young man her son; who fetched a chain tie-rope, they working
     together
Noosed the small rusty links round the horse's tongue
And tied him by the swollen tongue to the tree.
Seen from this height they are shrunk to insect size,
Out of all human relation. You cannot distinguish
The blood dripping from where the chain is fastened,
The beast shuddering; but the thrust neck and the legs
Far apart. You can see the whip fall on the flanks. . . .
The gesture of the arm. You cannot see the face of the woman.
The enormous light beats up out of the west across the cloud-bars of
     the trade-wind. The ocean
Darkens, the high clouds brighten, the hills darken together.
Unbridled and unbelievable beauty
Covers the evening world . . . not covers, grows apparent out of it,
     as Venus down there grows out
From the lit sky. What said the prophet? "I create good: and I
     create evil: I am the Lord."

II

This coast crying out for tragedy like all beautiful places,
(The quiet ones ask for quieter suffering; but here the granite cliff
     the gaunt cypresses' crown
Demands what victim? The dykes of red lava and black what Titan?
     The hills like pointed flames
Beyond Soberanes, the terrible peaks of the bare hills under the sun,
     what immolation?)
This coast crying out for tragedy like all beautiful places: and like
     the passionate spirit of humanity
Pain for its bread: God's, many victims', the painful deaths, the hor-
     rible transfigurements: I said in my heart,
"Better invent than suffer: imagine victims
Lest your own flesh be chosen the agonist, or you
Martyr some creature to the beauty of the place." And I said,
"Burn sacrifices once a year to magic

Horror away from the house, this little house here
You have built over the ocean with your own hands
Beside the standing boulders: for what are we,
The beast that walks upright, with speaking lips
And little hair, to think we should always be fed,
Sheltered, intact, and self-controlled? We sooner more liable
Than the other animals. Pain and terror, the insanities of desire; not
   accidents, but essential,
And crowd up from the core." I imagined victims for those wolves,
   I made the phantoms to follow.
They have hunted the phantoms and missed the house. It is not
   good to forget over what gulls the spirit
Of the beauty of humanity, the petal of a lost flower blown seaward
   by the night-wind, floats to its quietness.

III

Boulders blunted like an old bear's teeth break up from the head-
   land; below them
All the soil is thick with shells, the tide-rock feasts of a dead people.
Here the granite flanks are scarred with ancient fire, the ghosts of
   the tribe
Crouch in the nights beside the ghost of a fire, they try to remember
   the sunlight,
Light has died out of their skies. These have paid something for the
   future
Luck of the country, while we living keep old griefs in memory:
   though God's
Envy is not a likely fountain of ruin, to forget evil calls down
Sudden reminders from the cloud: remembered deaths be our re-
   deemers;
Imagined victims our salvation: white as the half moon at midnight
Someone flamelike passed me, saying, "I am Tamar Cauldwell, I
   have my desire,"
Then the voice of the sea returned, when she had gone by, the stars
   to their towers.
. . . Beautiful country, burn again, Point Pinos down to the Sur
   Rivers
Burn as before with bitter wonders, land and ocean and the Carmel
   water.

IV

He brays humanity in a mortar to bring the savor
From the bruised root: a man having bad dreams, who invents vic-
  tims, is only the ape of that God.
He washes it out with tears and many waters, calcines it with fire
  in the red crucible,
Deforms it, makes it horrible to itself: the spirit flies out and stands
  naked, he sees the spirit.
He takes it in the naked ecstasy; it breaks in his hand, the atom is
  broken, the power that massed it
Cries to the power that moves the stars, "I have come home to my-
  self, behold me.
I bruised myself in the flint mortar and burnt me
In the red shell, I tortured myself, I flew forth,
Stood naked of myself and broke me in fragments,
And here am I moving the stars that are me."
I have seen these ways of God: I know of no reason
For fire and change and torture and the old returnings.
He being sufficient might be still. I think they admit no reason; they
  are the ways of my love.
Unmeasured power, incredible passion, enormous craft: no thought
  apparent but burns darkly
Smothered with its own smoke in the human brain-vault: no thought
  outside: a certain measure in phenomena:
The fountains of the boiling stars, the flowers on the foreland, the
  ever-returning roses of dawn.

Love the Wild Swan

I HATE my verses, every line, every word.
  Oh pale and brittle pencils ever to try
One grass-blade's curve, or the throat of one bird
That clings to twig, ruffled against white sky.
Oh cracked and twilight mirrors ever to catch
One color, one glinting flash, of the splendor of things.
Unlucky hunter, Oh bullets of wax,
The lion beauty, the wild-swan wings, the storm of the wings."
—This wild swan of a world is no hunter's game.
Better bullets than yours would miss the white breast,
Better mirrors than yours would crack in the flame.

Does it matter whether you hate your . . . self? At least
Love your eyes that can see, your mind that can
Hear the music, the thunder of the wings. Love the wild swan.

MARSDEN HARTLEY

Confidence

WE'LL have the sun now,"
    the quaking sea gulls said—
"We've run the gamut of the thundering sea,
one by one—one by one,
and though the wave is full of bread
a wing is often tendon-weary
of a thing so varied-vast;
we do our geodetic surveillance,
for herring are a shining thing,
a shape of sleek imagining,
a pretty circumstance.
The shiver of an ash leaf and of pine
makes other music for a day's determining,
even sea gulls love the shape of roses
ere day closes."

Warblers

AN hundred warblers in the nearest aching gap,
    it seems as though it loved its aching
filled with hyper-ikonistic misery.
I did not expect such staggering wealth
to come to me by dawn-delivered stealth,
though morning is the time—and spring
the way love knows of its best being.

All through the leaves a burning
rush of gilded, swift, whirling wing.

All warblers of the world have come
to me, and are in me living—
I only cool retreat and humble shade
giving,
my leaves with excess of sun
trampled.

I said an hundred warblers came
to me,
and now that I am clear, what it
was, was very near—
it was but two, or three,
But—how they fastened me.

In Robin Hood Cove

THE tide comes in, and out goes tide;
    it skirts the cliffs, and in their shadow sees
the remnants of the days that fall
between a seagull's and a robin's call.
There is the bridge, and under flows
the rests of evening with its primulous
shows—
it is a river made of listless sea
after it has explained its fierce integrity;
no thunder makes, or on rock heaves—
it learns the place for plain humility,
and keeps reflection of some mindless
leaves.

These evening greens
that gather wistfully among
the ripening coronals of summer
when rain has done its streaming
and the sea has washed back
its waters into these little cities
made of whispered wish
and gentle, seabird thought, homely consecration;
airs—vibrant with the felt glimmer of a day
gone down to glory of a sunken yesterday;
night stepping in, soft-shod and separate

in her smooth design;
these evening greens
that gather wistfully, making melody
of nothings in their tuneful
prime.

T. S. ELIOT

The Love Song of J. Alfred Prufrock

*S'io credesse che mia risposta fosse
A persona che mai tornasse al mondo,
Questa fiamma staria senza piu scosse.
Ma perciocche giammai di questo fondo
Non torno vivo alcun s'i'odo il vero,
Senza tema d'infamia ti rispondo.*

LET us go then, you and I,
   When the evening is spread out against the sky
Like a patient etherized upon a table;
Let us go, through certain half-deserted streets,
The muttering retreats
Of restless nights in one-night cheap hotels
And sawdust restaurants with oyster-shells:
Streets that follow like a tedious argument
Of insidious intent
To lead you to an overwhelming question. . . .
Oh, do not ask, "What is it?"
Let us go and make our visit.
In the room the women come and go
Talking of Michelangelo.

The yellow fog that rubs its back upon the window-panes,
The yellow smoke that rubs its muzzle on the window-panes,
Licked its tongue into the corners of the evening,
Lingered upon the pools that stand in drains,
Let fall upon its back the soot that falls from chimneys.

Slipped by the terrace, made a sudden leap,
And seeing that it was a soft October night,
Curled once about the house, and fell asleep.

And indeed there will be time
For the yellow smoke that slides along the street,
Rubbing its back upon the window-panes;
There will be time, there will be time
To prepare a face to meet the faces that you meet;
There will be time to murder and create,
And time for all the works and days of hands
That lift and drop a question on your plate;
Time for you and time for me,
And time yet for a hundred indecisions,
And for a hundred visions and revisions,
Before the taking of a toast and tea.
In the room the women come and go
Talking of Michelangelo.

And indeed there will be time
To wonder, "Do I dare?" and, "Do I dare?"
Time to turn back and descend the stair,
With a bald spot in the middle of my hair—
(They will say: "How his hair is growing thin!")
My morning coat, my collar mounting firmly to the chin,
My necktie rich and modest, but asserted by a simple pin—
(They will say: "But how his arms and legs are thin!")
Do I dare
Disturb the universe?
In a minute there is time
For decisions and revisions which a minute will reverse.

For I have known them all already, known them all:
Have known the evenings, mornings, afternoons,
I have measured out my life with coffee spoons;
I know the voices dying with a dying fall
Beneath the music from a farther room.
    So how should I presume?

And I have known the eyes already, known them all—
The eyes that fix you in a formulated phrase,
And when I am formulated, sprawling on a pin,

When I am pinned and wriggling on the wall,
Then how should I begin
To spit out all the butt-ends of my days and ways?
    And how should I presume?

And I have known the arms already, known them all—
Arms that are braceleted and white and bare
(But in the lamplight, downed with light brown hair!)
Is it perfume from a dress
That makes me so digress?
Arms that lie along a table, or wrap about a shawl.
    And should I then presume?
    And how should I begin?

Shall I say, I have gone at dusk through narrow streets
And watched the smoke that rises from the pipes
Of lonely men in shirt-sleeves, leaning out of windows? . . .
I should have been a pair of ragged claws
Scuttling across the floors of silent seas.

And the afternoon, the evening, sleeps so peacefully!
Smoothed by long fingers,
Asleep . . . tired . . . or it malingers,
Stretched on the floor, here beside you and me.
Should I, after tea and cakes and ices,
Have the strength to force the moment to its crisis?
But though I have wept and faster, wept and prayed,
Though I have seen my head (grown slightly bald) brought in upon
        a platter,
I am no prophet—and here's no great matter;
I have seen the moment of my greatness flicker,
And I have seen the eternal Footman hold my coat, and snicker,
And in short, I was afraid.

And would it have been worth it, after all,
After the cups, the marmalade, the tea,
Among the porcelain, among some talk of you and me,
Would it have been worth while,
To have bitten off the matter with a smile,
To have squeezed the universe into a ball
To roll it toward some overwhelming question,
To say: "I am Lazarus, come from the dead,

Come back to tell you all, I shall tell you all"—
If one, settling a pillow by her head,
    Should say: "That was not what I meant at all;
    That is not it, at all."

And would it have been worth it, after all,
Would it have been worth while,
After the sunsets and the dooryards and the sprinkled streets,
After the novels, after the teacups, after the skirts that trail along the
      floor—
And this, and so much more?—
It is impossible to say just what I mean!
But as if a magic lantern threw the nerves in patterns on a screen:
Would it have been worth while
If one, settling a pillow or throwing off a shawl,
And turning toward the window, should say:
    "That is not it at all,
    That is not what I meant at all."

No! I am not Prince Hamlet, nor was meant to be;
Am an attendant lord, one that will do
To swell a progress, start a scene or two,
Advise the prince; no doubt, an easy tool,
Deferential, glad to be of use,
Politic, cautious, and meticulous;
Full of high sentence, but a bit obtuse;
At times, indeed, almost ridiculous—
Almost, at times, the Fool.

I grow old . . . I grow old . . .
I shall wear the bottoms of my trousers rolled.

Shall I part my hair behind? Do I dare to eat a peach?
I shall wear white flannel trousers, and walk upon the beach.
I have heard the mermaids singing, each to each.

I do not think that they will sing to me.
I have seen them riding seaward on the waves
Combing the white hair of the waves blown back
When the wind blows the water white and black.
We have lingered in the chambers of the sea

By sea-girls wreathed with seaweed red and brown
Till human voices wake us, and we drown.

Sweeney Among the Nightingales

ὤμοι πέπληγμαι καιρίαν πληγὴν ἔσω.

*Why should I speak of the nightingale? The nightingale sings of
adulterous wrong.*

APENECK SWEENEY spreads his knees
Letting his arms hang down to laugh,
The zebra stripes along his jaw
Swelling to maculate giraffe.

The circles of the stormy moon
Slide westward to the River Plate,
Death and the Raven drift above
And Sweeney guards the hornèd gate.

Gloomy Orion and the Dog
Are veiled; and hushed the shrunken seas;
The person in the Spanish cape
Tries to sit on Sweeney's knees

Slips and pulls the table cloth
Overturns a coffee cup,
Reorganized upon the floor
She yawns and draws a stocking up;

The silent man in mocha brown
Sprawls at the window-sill and gapes;
The waiter brings in oranges,
Bananas, figs and hot-house grapes;

The silent vertebrate exhales,
Contracts and concentrates, withdraws;
Rachel *née* Rabinovitch
Tears at the grapes with murderous paws;

She and the lady in the cape
Are suspect, thought to be in league;

Therefore the man with heavy eyes
Declines the gambit, shows fatigue,

Leaves the room and reappears
Outside the window, leaning in,
Branches of wistaria
Circumscribe a golden grin;

The host with someone indistinct
Converses at the door apart,
The nightingales are singing near
The Convent of the Sacred Heart,

And sang within the bloody wood
When Agamemnon cried aloud,
And let their liquid siftings fall
To stain the stiff dishonoured shroud.

Gerontion

*Thou hast nor youth nor age
But as it were an after dinner sleep
Dreaming of both.*

HERE I am, an old man in a dry month,
       Being read to by a boy, waiting for rain.
I was neither at the hot gates
Nor fought in the warm rain
Nor knee deep in the salt marsh, heaving a cutlass,
Bitten by flies, fought.
My house is a decayed house,
And the Jew squats on the window sill, the owner,
Spawned in some estaminet of Antwerp,
Blistered in Brussels, patched and peeled in London.
The goat coughs at night in the field overhead;
Rocks, moss, stonecrop, iron, merds.
The woman keeps the kitchen, makes tea,
Sneezes at evening, poking the peevish gutter.

                              I an old man,
A dull head among windy spaces.

Signs are taken for wonders. "We would see a sign!"
The word within a word, unable to speak a word,
Swaddled with darkness. In the juvescence of the year
Came Christ the tiger.

In depraved May, dogwood and chestnut, flowering judas,
To be eaten, to be divided, to be drunk
Among whispers; by Mr. Silvero
With caressing hands, at Limoges
Who walked all night in the next room;
By Hakagawa, bowing among the Titians;
By Madame de Tornquist, in the dark room
Shifting the candles; Fraulein von Kulp
Who turned in the hall, one hand on the door. Vacant shuttles
Weave the wind. I have no ghosts,
An old man in a draughty house
Under a windy knob.

After such knowledge, what forgiveness? Think now
History has many cunning passages, contrived corridors
And issues, deceives with whispering ambitions,
Guides us by vanities. Think now
She gives when our attention is distracted
And what she gives, gives with such supple confusions
That the giving famishes the craving. Gives too late
What's not believed in, or if still believed,
In memory only, reconsidered passion. Gives too soon
Into weak hands, what's thought can be dispensed with
Till the refusal propagates a fear. Think
Neither fear nor courage saves us. Unnatural vices
Are fathered by our heroism. Virtues
Are forced upon us by our impudent crimes.
These tears are shaken from the wrath-bearing tree.

The tiger springs in the new year. Us he devours.
    Think at last
We have not reached conclusion, when I
Stiffen in a rented house. Think at last
I have not made this show purposelessly
And it is not by any concitation
Of the backward devils.
I would meet you upon this honestly.

I that was near your heart was removed therefrom
To lose beauty in terror, terror in inquisition.
I have lost my passion: why should I need to keep it
Since what is kept must be adulterated?
I have lost my sight, smell, hearing, taste and touch:
How should I use it for your closer contact?

These with a thousand small deliberations
Protract the profit, of their chilled delirium,
Excite the membrane, when the sense has cooled,
With pungent sauces, multiply variety
In a wilderness of mirrors. What will the spider do,
Suspend its operations, will the weevil
Delay? De Bailhache, Fresca, Mrs. Cammell, whirled
Beyond the circuit of the shuddering Bear
In fractured atoms. Gull against the wind, in the windy straits
Of Belle Isle, or running on the Horn,
White feathers in the snow, the Gulf claims,
And an old man driven by the Trades
To a sleepy corner.

                    Tenants of the house,
Thoughts of a dry brain in a dry season.

Burnt Norton

I

TIME present and time past
Are both perhaps present in time future,
And time future contained in time past.
If all time is eternally present
All time is unredeemable.
What might have been is an abstraction
Remaining a perpetual possibility
Only in a world of speculation.
What might have been and what has been
Point to one end, which is always present.
Footfalls echo in the memory
Down the passage which we did not take
Towards the door we never opened

Into the rose-garden. My words echo
Thus, in your mind.
                              But to what purpose
Disturbing the dust on a bowl of rose-leaves
I do not know.
                              Other echoes
Inhabit the garden. Shall we follow?
Quick, said the bird, find them, find them,
Round the corner. Through the first gate,
Into our first world, shall we follow
The deception of the thrush? Into our first world.
There they were, dignified, invisible,
Moving without pressure, over the dead leaves,
In the autumn heat, through the vibrant air,
And the bird called, in response to
The unheard music hidden in the shrubbery,
And the unseen eyebeam crossed, for the roses
Had the look of flowers that are looked at.
There they were as our guests, accepted and accepting.
So we moved, and they, in a formal pattern,
Along the empty alley, into the box circle,
To look down into the drained pool.
Dry the pool, dry concrete, brown edged,
And the pool was filled with water out of sunlight,
And the lotos rose, quietly, quietly,
The surface glittered out of heart of light,
And they were behind us, reflected in the pool.
Then a cloud passed, and the pool was empty.
Go, said the bird, for the leaves were full of children,
Hidden excitedly, containing laughter.
Go, go, go, said the bird: human kind
Cannot bear very much reality.
Time past and time future
What might have been and what has been
Point to one end, which is always present.

II

Garlic and sapphires in the mud
Clot the bedded axle-tree.
The trilling wire in the blood
Sings below inveterate scars
And reconciles forgotten wars.

The dance along the artery
The circulation of the lymph
Are figured in the drift of stars
Ascend to summer in the tree
We move above the moving tree
In light upon the figured leaf
And hear upon the sodden floor
Below, the boarhound and the boar
Pursue their pattern as before
But reconciled among the stars.

At the still point of the turning world. Neither flesh nor fleshless;
Neither from nor towards; at the still point, there the dance is,
But neither arrest nor movement. And do not call it fixity,
Where past and future are gathered. Neither movement from nor
        towards,
Neither ascent nor decline. Except for the point, the still point,
There would be no dance, and there is only the dance.
I can only say, *there* we have been: but I cannot say where.
And I cannot say, how long, for that is to place it in time.

The inner freedom from the practical desire,
The release from action and suffering, release from the inner
And the outer compulsion, yet surrounded
By a grace of sense, a white light still and moving,
Erhebung without motion, concentration
Without elimination, both a new world
And the old made explicit, understood
In the completion of its partial ecstasy,
The resolution of its partial horror.
Yet the enchainment of past and future
Woven in the weakness of the changing body,
Protects mankind from heaven and damnation
Which flesh cannot endure.
                        Time past and time future
Allow but a little consciousness.
To be conscious is not to be in time
But only in time can the moment in the rose-garden,
The moment in the arbour where the rain beat,
The moment in the draughty church at smokefall
Be remembered; involved with past and future.
Only through time time is conquered.

III

Here is a place of disaffection
Time before and time after
In a dim light: neither daylight
Investing form with lucid stillness
Turning shadow into transient beauty
With slow rotation suggesting permanence
Nor darkness to purify the soul
Emptying the sensual with deprivation
Cleansing affection from the temporal.
Neither plenitude nor vacancy. Only a flicker
Over the strained time-ridden faces
Distracted from distraction by distraction
Filled with fancies and empty of meaning
Tumid apathy with no concentration
Men and bits of paper, whirled by the cold wind
That blows before and after time,
Wind in and out of unwholesome lungs
Time before and time after.
Eructation of unhealthy souls
Into the faded air, the torpid
Driven on the wind that sweeps the gloomy hills of London,
Hampstead and Clerkenwell, Campden and Putney,
Highgate, Primrose and Ludgate. Not here
Not here the darkness, in this twittering world.
Descend lower, descend only
Into the world of perpetual solitude,
World not world, but that which is not world,
Internal darkness, deprivation
And destitution of all property,
Desiccation of the world of sense,
Evacuation of the world of fancy,
Inoperancy of the world of spirit;
This is the one way, and the other
Is the same, not in movement
But abstention from movement; while the world moves
In appetency, on its metalled ways
Of time past and time future.

IV

Time and the bell have buried the day,
The black cloud carries the sun away.
Will the sunflower turn to us, will the clematis
Stray down, bend to us; tendril and spray
Clutch and cling?
Chill
Fingers of yew be curled
Down on us? After the kingfisher's wing
Has answered light to light, and is silent, the light is still
At the still point of the turning world.

V

Words move, music moves
Only in time; but that which is only living
Can only die. Words, after speech, reach
Into the silence. Only by the form, the pattern,
Can words or music reach
The stillness, as a Chinese jar still
Moves perpetually in its stillness.
Not the stillness of the violin, while the note lasts,
Not that only, but the co-existence,
Or say that the end precedes the beginning,
And the end and the beginning were always there
Before the beginning and after the end.
And all is always now. Words strain,
Crack and sometimes break, under the burden,
Under the tension, slip, slide, perish,
Decay with imprecision, will not stay in place,
Will not stay still. Shrieking voices
Scolding, mocking, or merely chattering,
Always assail them. The Word in the desert
Is most attacked by voices of temptation,
The crying shadow in the funeral dance,
The loud lament of the disconsolate chimera.

The detail of the pattern is movement,
As in the figure of the ten stairs.
Desire itself is movement
Not in itself desirable;
Love is itself unmoving,

Only the cause and end of movement,
Timeless, and undesiring
Except in the aspect of time
Caught in the form of limitation
Between un-being and being.
Sudden in a shaft of sunlight
Even while the dust moves
There rises the hidden laughter
Of children in the foliage
Quick now, here, now, always—
Ridiculous the waste sad time
Stretching before and after.

Ash Wednesday

I

BECAUSE I do not hope to turn again
   Because I do not hope
Because I do not hope to turn
Desiring this man's gift and that man's scope
I no longer strive to strive towards such things
(Why should the aged eagle stretch its wings?)
Why should I mourn
The vanished power of the usual reign?

Because I do not hope to know again
The infirm glory of the positive hour
Because I do not think
Because I know I shall not know
The one veritable transitory power
Because I cannot drink
There, where trees flower, and springs flow, for there is nothing again

Because I know that time is always time
And place is always and only place
And what is actual is actual only for one time
And only for one place
I rejoice that things are as they are and
I renounce the blessèd face
And renounce the voice

Because I cannot hope to turn again
Consequently I rejoice, having to construct something
Upon which to rejoice

And pray to God to have mercy upon us
And I pray that I may forget
These matters that with myself I too much discuss
Too much explain
Because I do not hope to turn again
Let these words answer
For what is done, not to be done again,
May the judgment not be too heavy upon us

Because these wings are no longer wings to fly
But merely vans to beat the air
The air which is now thoroughly small and dry
Smaller and dryer than the will
Teach us to care and not to care
Teach us to sit still.

Pray for us sinners now and at the hour of our death
Pray for us now and at the hour of our death.

II

Lady, three white leopards sat under a juniper-tree
In the cool of the day, having fed to satiety
On my legs my heart my liver and that which had been contained
In the hollow round of my skull. And God said
Shall these bones live? shall these
Bones live? And that which had been contained
In the bones (which were already dry) said chirping:
Because of the goodness of this Lady
And because of her loveliness, and because
She honors the Virgin in meditation,
We shine with brightness. And I who am here dissembled
Proffer my deeds to oblivion, and my love
To the posterity of the desert and the fruit of the gourd.
It is this which recovers
My guts the strings of my eyes and the indigestible portions
Which the leopards reject. The Lady is withdrawn
In a white gown, to contemplation, in a white gown.

Let the whiteness of bones atone to forgetfulness.
There is no life in them. As I am forgotten
And would be forgotten, so I would forget
Thus devoted, concentrated in purpose. And God said
Prophesy to the wind, to the wind only, for only
The wind will listen. And the bones sang chirping
With the burden of the grasshopper, saying

Lady of silences
Calm and distressed
Torn and most whole
Rose of memory
Rose of forgetfulness
Exhausted and life-giving
Worried reposeful
The single Rose
Is now the Garden
Where all loves end
Terminate torment
Of love unsatisfied
The greater torment
Of love satisfied
End of the endless
Journey to no end
Conclusion of all that
Is inconclusible
Speech without word and
Word of no speech
Grace to the Mother
For the Garden
Where all love ends.

Under a juniper-tree the bones sang, scattered and shining
We are glad to be scattered, we did little good to each other,
Under a tree in the cool of the day, with the blessing of sand,
Forgetting themselves and each other, united
In the quiet of the desert. This is the land which ye
Shall divide by lot. And neither division nor unity
Matters. This is the land. We have our inheritance.

III

At the first turning of the second stair
I turned and saw below
The same shape twisted on the banister
Under the vapor in the fetid air
Struggling with the devil of the stairs who wears
The deceitful face of hope and of despair.

At the second turning of the second stair
I left them twisting, turning below;
There were no more faces and the stair was dark,
Damp, jaggèd, like an old man's mouth drivelling, beyond repair,
Or the toothed gullet of an agèd shark.

At the first turning of the third stair
Was a slotted window bellied like the fig's fruit
And beyond the hawthorn blossom and a pasture scene
The broadbacked figure drest in blue and green
Enchanted the maytime with an antique flute.

Blown hair is sweet, brown hair over the mouth blown,
Lilac and brown hair;
Distraction, music of the flute, stops and steps of the mind over the
    third stair,
Fading, fading; strength beyond hope and despair
Climbing the third stair.
Lord, I am not worthy
Lord, I am not worthy

        but speak the word only.

IV

Who walked between the violet and the violet
Who walked between
The various ranks of varied green
Going in white and blue, in Mary's color,
Talking of trivial things
In ignorance and in knowledge of eternal dolour
Who moved among the others as they walked,
Who then made strong the fountains and made fresh the springs

Made cool the dry rock and made firm the sand
In blue of larkspur, blue of Mary's color,
Sovegna vos

Here are the years that walk between, bearing
Away the fiddles and the flutes, restoring
One who moves in the time between sleep and waking, wearing

White light folded, sheathed about her, folded.
The new years walk, restoring
Through a bright cloud of tears, the years, restoring
With a new verse the ancient rhyme. Redeem
The time. Redeem
The unread vision in the higher dream
While jewelled unicorns draw by the gilded hearse.

The silent sister veiled in white and blue
Between the yews, behind the garden god,
Whose flute is breathless, bent her head and sighed but spoke no
  word

But the fountain sprang up and the bird sang down
Redeem the time, redeem the dream
The token of the word unheard, unspoken

Till the wind shake a thousand whispers from the yew

And after this our exile

v

If the lost word is lost, if the spent word is spent
If the unheard, unspoken
Word is unspoken, unheard;
Still is the unspoken word, the Word unheard,
The Word without a word, the Word within
The world and for the world;
And the light shone in darkness and
Against the Word the unstilled world still whirled
About the center of the silent Word.

O my people, what have I done unto thee.

Where shall the word be found, where will the word
Resound? Not here, there is not enough silence,
Not on the sea or on the islands, not
On the mainland, in the desert or the rain land,
For those who walk in darkness
Both in the day time and in the night time
The right time and the right place are not here
No place of grace for those who avoid the face
No time to rejoice for those who walk among noise and deny the
 voice

Will the veiled sister pray for
Those who walk in darkness, who chose thee and oppose thee,
Those who are torn on the horn between season and season, time
 and time, between
Hour and hour, word and word, power and power, those who wait
In darkness? Will the veiled sister pray
For children at the gate
Who will not go away and cannot pray:
Pray for those who chose and oppose

   O my people, what have I done unto thee.

Will the veiled sister between the slender
Yew trees pray for those who offend her
And are terrified and cannot surrender
And affirm before the world and deny between the rocks
In the last desert between the last blue rocks
The desert in the garden the garden in the desert
Of drouth, spitting from the mouth the withered apple-seed.

   O my people.

     VI

Although I do not hope to turn again
Although I do not hope
Although I do not hope to turn

Wavering between the profit and the loss
In this brief transit where the dreams cross
The dreamcrossed twilight between birth and dying

(Bless me father) though I do not wish to wish these things
From the wide window towards the granite shore
The white sails still fly seaward, seaward flying
Unbroken wings
And the lost heart stiffens and rejoices
In the lost lilac and the lost sea voices
And the weak spirit quickens to rebel
For the bent golden-rod and the lost sea smell
Quickens to recover
The cry of quail and the whirling plover
And the blind eye creates
The empty forms between the ivory gates
And smell renews the salt savor of the sandy earth
This is the time of tension between dying and birth
The place of solitude where three dreams cross
Between blue rocks
But when the voices shaken from the yew-tree drift away
Let the other yew be shaken and reply.

Blessed sister, holy mother, spirit of the fountain, spirit of the garden,
Suffer us not to mock ourselves with falsehood
Teach us to care and not to care
Teach us to sit still
Even among these rocks,
Our peace in His will
And even among these rocks
Sister, mother,
And spirit of the river, spirit of the sea,
Suffer me not to be separated

And let my cry come unto Thee.

JOHN CROWE RANSOM

Blue Girls

TWIRLING your blue skirts, travelling the sward
    Under the towers of your seminary,
Go listen to your teachers old and contrary
    Without believing a word.

Tie the white fillets then about your lustrous hair
    And think no more of what will come to pass
Than bluebirds that go walking on the grass
    And chattering on the air.

Practise your beauty, blue girls, before it fail;
    And I will cry with my loud lips and publish
Beauty which all our power shall never establish,
    It is so frail.

For I could tell you a story which is true:
    I know a lady with a terrible tongue,
Blear eyes fallen from blue,
    All her perfections tarnished—and yet it is not long
Since she was lovelier than any of you.

Antique Harvesters

(SCENE: OF THE MISSISSIPPI THE BANK SINISTER, AND OF THE OHIO THE
BANK SINISTER.)

TAWNY are the leaves turned, but they still hold.
    It is the harvest; what shall this land produce?
A meager hill of kernels, a runnel of juice.
Declension looks from our land, it is old.
Therefore let us assemble, dry, grey, spare,
And mild as yellow air.

"I hear the creak of a raven's funeral wing."
The young men would be joying in the song
Of passionate birds; their memories are not long.
What is it thus rehearsed in sable? "Nothing."
Trust not but the old endure, and shall be older
Than the scornful beholder.

We pluck the spindling ears and gather the corn.
One spot has special yield? "On this spot stood
Heroes and drenched it with their only blood."
And talk meets talk, as echoes from the horn
Of the hunter—echoes are the old men's arts,
Ample are the chambers of their hearts.

Here come the hunters, keepers of a rite.
The horn, the hounds, the lank mares coursing by
Under quaint archetypes of chivalry;
And the fox, lovely ritualist, in flight
Offering his unearthly ghost to quarry;
And the fields, themselves to harry.

Resume, harvesters. The treasure is full bronze
Which you will garner for the Lady, and the moon
Could tinge it no yellower than does this noon;
But the grey will quench it shortly—the fields, men, stones.
Pluck fast, dreamers; prove as you rumble slowly
Not less than men, not wholly.

Bare the arm too, dainty youths, bend the knees
Under bronze burdens. And by an autumn tone
As by a grey, as by a green, you will have known
Your famous Lady's image; for so have these.
And if one say that easily will your hands
More prosper in other lands,

Angry as wasp-music be your cry then:
"Forsake the Proud Lady, of the heart of fire,
The look of snow, to the praise of a dwindled choir,
Song of degenerate specters that were men?
The sons of the fathers shall keep her, worthy of
What these have done in love."

True, it is said of our Lady, she ageth.
But see, if you peep shrewdly, she hath not stooped;
Take no thought of her servitors that have drooped,
For we are nothing; and if one talk of death—
Why, the ribs of the earth subsist frail as a breath
If but God wearieth.

Captain Carpenter

CAPTAIN CARPENTER rose up in his prime
Put on his pistols and went riding out
But had got wellnigh nowhere at that time
Till he fell in with ladies in a rout.

It was a pretty lady and all her train
That played with him so sweetly but before
An hour she'd taken a sword with all her main
And twined him of his nose for evermore.

Captain Carpenter mounted up one day
And rode straightway into a strange rogue
That looked unchristian but be that as may
The Captain did not wait upon prologue.

But drew upon him out of his great heart
The other swung against him with a club
And cracked his two legs at the shinny part
And let him roll and stick like any tub.

Captain Carpenter rode many a time
From male and female took he sundry harms
He met the wife of Satan crying "I'm
The she-wolf bids you shall bear no more arms."

Their strokes and counters whistled in the wind
I wish he had delivered half his blows
But where she should have made off like a hind
The bitch bit off his arms at the elbows.

And Captain Carpenter parted with his ears
To a black devil that used him in this wise

O jesus ere his threescore and ten years
Another had plucked out his sweet blue eyes.

Captain Carpenter got up on his roan
And sallied from the gate in hell's despite
I heard him asking in the grimmest tone
If any enemy yet there was to fight?

"To any adversary it is fame
If he risk to be wounded by my tongue
Or burnt in two beneath my red heart's flame
Such are the perils he is cast among.

"But if he can he has a pretty choice
From an anatomy with little to lose
Whether he cut my tongue and take my voice
Or whether it be my round red heart he choose."

It was the neatest knave that ever was seen
Stepping in perfume from his lady's bower
Who at this word put in his merry mien
And fell on Captain Carpenter like a tower.

I would not knock old fellows in the dust
But there lay Captain Carpenter on his back
His weapons were the old heart in his bust
And a blade shook between rotten teeth alack.

The rogue in scarlet and grey soon knew his mind
He wished to get his trophy and depart
With gentle apology and touch refined
He pierced him and produced the Captain's heart.

God's mercy rest on Captain Carpenter now
I thought him Sirs and honest gentleman
Citizen husband soldier and scholar enow
Let jangling kites eat of him if they can.

But God's deep curses follow after those
That shore him of his goodly nose and ears
His legs and strong arms at the two elbows
And eyes that had not watered seventy years.

The curse of hell upon the sleek upstart
Who got the Captain finally on his back
And took the red red vitals of his heart
And made the kites to whet their beaks clack clack.

Bells for John Whiteside's Daughter

THERE was such speed in her little body,
    And such lightness in her footfall,
It is no wonder that her brown study
Astonishes us all.

Her wars were bruited in our high window.
We looked among orchard trees and beyond,
Where she took arms against her shadow,
Or harried unto the pond

The lazy geese, like a snow cloud
Dripping their snow on the green grass,
Tricking and stopping, sleepy and proud,
Who cried in goose, Alas,

For the tireless heart within the little
Lady with rod that made them rise
From their noon apple-dreams, and scuttle
Goose-fashion under the skies:

But now go the bells, and we are ready;
In one house we are sternly stopped
To say we are vexed at her brown study,
Lying so primly propped.

Lady Lost

THIS morning, there flew up the lane
    A timid lady-bird to our bird-bath
And eyed her image dolefully as death;
This afternoon, knocked on our windowpane
To be let in from the rain.

And when I caught her eye
She looked aside, but at the clapping thunder
And sight of the whole earth blazing up like tinder
Looked in on us again most miserably,
Indeed as if she would cry.

So I will go out into the park and say,
"Who has lost a delicate brown-eyed lady
In the West End Section? Or has anybody
Injured some fine woman in some dark way,
Last night or yesterday?

"Let the owner come and claim possession,
No questions will be asked. But stroke her gently
With loving words, and she will evidently
Resume her full soft-haired white-breasted fashion,
And her right home and her right passion."

Here Lies a Lady

HERE lies a lady of beauty and high degree.
Of chills and fever she died, of fever and chills,
The delight of her husband, her aunts, an infant of three,
And of medicos marveling sweetly on her ills.

For either she burned, and her confident eyes would blaze,
And her fingers fly in a manner to puzzle their heads—
What was she making? Why, nothing; she sat in a maze
Of old scraps of laces, snipped into curious shreds—

Or this would pass, and the light of her fire decline
Till she lay discouraged and cold as a thin stalk white and blown,
And would not open her eyes, to kisses, to wine.
The sixth of these states was her last; the cold settled down.

Sweet ladies, long may ye bloom, and toughly I hope ye may thole,
But was she not lucky? In flowers and lace and mourning,
In love and great honor we bade God rest her soul
After six little spaces of chill, and six of burning.

EDNA ST. VINCENT MILLAY

Elegy Before Death

THERE will be rose and rhododendron
   When you are dead and under ground;
Still will be heard from white syringas
   Heavy with bees, a sunny sound.

Still will the tamaracks be raining
   After the rain has ceased, and still
Will there be robins in the stubble,
   Brown sheep upon the warm green hill.

Spring will not ail nor autumn falter;
   Nothing will know that you are gone,
Saving alone some sullen plough-land
   None but yourself set foot upon;

Saving the may-weed and the pig-weed
   Nothing will know that you are dead,—
These, and perhaps a useless wagon
   Standing beside some tumbled shed.

Oh, there will pass with your great passing
   Little of beauty not your own,—
Only the light from common water,
   Only the grace from simple stone.

What Lips My Lips Have Kissed

WHAT lips my lips have kissed, and where, and why,
   I have forgotten, and what arms have lain
Under my head till morning; but the rain
Is full of ghosts tonight, that tap and sigh
Upon the glass and listen for reply;
And in my heart there stirs a quiet pain

For unremembered lads that not again
Will turn to me at midnight with a cry.

Thus in the winter stands the lonely tree,
Nor knows what birds have vanished one by one,
Yet knows its boughs more silent than before:
I cannot say what loves have come and gone;
I only know that summer sang in me
A little while, that in me sings no more.

------ • • • ------

ARCHIBALD MACLEISH

------ • • • ------

L'An Trentiesme de Mon Âge

AND I have come upon this place
By lost ways, by a nod, by words,
By faces, by an old man's face
At Morlaix lifted to the birds,

By hands upon the tablecloth
At Aldebori's, by the thin
Child's hands that opened to the moth
And let the flutter of the moonlight in,

By hands, by voices, by the voice
Of Mrs. Husman on the stair,
By Margaret's "If we had the choice
To choose or not"—through her thick hair,

By voices, by the creak and fall
Of footsteps on the upper floor,
By silence waiting in the hall
Between the doorbell and the door,

By words, by voices, a lost way—
And here above the chimney stack
The unknown constellations sway—
And by what way shall I go back?

The Too-Late Born

WE too, we too, descending once again
   The hills of our own land, we too have heard
Far off—Ah, que ce cor a longue haleine—
The horn of Roland in the passages of Spain,
The first, the second blast, the failing third,
And with the third turned back and climbed once more
The steep road southward, and heard faint the sound
Of swords, of horses, the disastrous war,
And crossed the dark defile at last, and found
At Ronçevaux upon the darkening plain
The dead against the dead and on the silent ground
The silent slain—

Einstein

STANDING between the sun and moon preserves
   A certain secrecy. Or seems to keep
Something inviolate if only that
His father was an ape.
                        Sweet music makes
All of his walls sound hollow and he heard
Sighs in the panelling and underfoot
Melancholy voices. So there is a door
Behind the seamless arras and within
A living something:—but no door that will
Admit the sunlight nor no windows where
The mirror moon can penetrate his bones
With cold deflection. He is small and tight
And solidly contracted into space
Opaque and perpendicular which blots
Earth with its shadow. And he terminates
In shoes which bearing up against the sphere
Attract his concentration,
                        for he ends
If there why then no farther, as, beyond
Extensively the universe itself,
Or chronologically the two dates
Original and ultimate of time,

Einstein upon a public bench Wednesday the ninth contemplates finity

Nor could Jehovah and the million stars
Staring within their solitudes of light,
Nor all night's constellations be contained
Between his boundaries,
                              nor could the sun
Receive him nor his groping roots run down
Into the loam and steaming sink of time
Where coils the middle serpent and the ooze
Breeds maggots.
                              But it seems assured he ends
Precisely at his shoes in proof whereof
He can revolve in orbits opposite
The orbit of the earth and so refuse
All planetary converse. And he wears
Clothes that distinguish him from what is not
His own circumference, as first a coat
Shaped to his back or modelled in reverse
Of the surrounding cosmos and below
Trousers preserving his detachment from
The revolutions of the stars.

Einstein descends the Hartmannsweiler-strasse

                              His hands
And face go naked and alone converse
With what encloses him, as rough and smooth
And sound and silence and the intervals
Of rippling ether and the swarming motes
Clouding a privy: move to them and make
Shadows that mirror them within his skull
In perpendiculars and curves and planes
And bodiless significances blurred
As figures undersea and images
Patterned from eddies of the air.

Einstein ultimately before a mirror accepts the hypothesis of exterior reality

                              Which are
Perhaps not shadows but the thing itself
And may be understood.
                              Decorticate
The petals of the enfolding world and leave
A world in reason which is in himself
And has his own dimensions. Here do trees
Adorn the hillsides and hillsides enrich
The hazy marches of the sky and skies
Kindle and char to ashes in the wind,
And winds blow toward him from the verge, and suns

Rise on his dawn and on his dusk go down
And moons prolong his shadow. And he moves
Here as within a garden in a close
And where he moves the bubble of the world
Takes centre and there circle round his head
Like golden flies in summer the gold stars.

Disintegrates.

              For suddenly he feels
The planet plunge beneath him, and a flare
Falls from the upper darkness to the dark
And awful shadows loom across the sky
That have no life from him and suns go out
And livid as a drowned man's face the moon
Floats to the lapsing surface of the night
And sinks discolored under.

                    So he knows
Less than a world and must communicate
Beyond his knowledge.

Einstein unsuccessfully after lunch attempts to enter, essaying synthesis with what's not he, the Bernese Oberland

              Outstretched on the earth
He plunges both his arms into the swirl
Of what surrounds him but the yielding grass
Excludes his finger tips and the soft soil
Will not endure confusion with his hands,
Nor will the air receive him nor the light
Dissolve their difference but recoiling turns
Back from his touch. By which denial he can
Crawl on the earth and sense the opposing sun
But not make answer to them.

                  Put out leaves
And let the old remembering wind think through
A green intelligence, or under sea
Float out long filaments of amber in
The numb and wordless revery of tides.

In autumn the black branches dripping rain
Bruise his uncovered bones and in the spring
His swollen tips are gorged with aching blood
That bursts the laurel.

              But although they seize

His sense he has no name for them, no word
To give them meaning and no utterance
For what they say. Feel the new summer's sun
Crawl up the warmed relaxing hide of earth
And weep for his lost youth, his childhood home
And a wide water on an inland shore!
Or to the night's mute asking in the blood
Give back a girl's name and three notes together!

He cannot think the smell of after rain
Nor close his thought around the long smooth lag
And falter of a wind, nor bring to mind
Dusk and the whippoorwill.
              But violins
Split out of trees and strung to tone can sing
Strange nameless words that image to the ear
What has no waiting image in the brain.
She plays in darkness and the droning wood
Dissolves to reverberations of a world
Beating in waves against him, till his sense
Trembles to rhythm and his naked brain
Feels without utterance in form the flesh
Of dumb and incommunicable earth,
And knows at once, and without knowledge how,
The stroke of the blunt rain, and blind receives
The sun.
           When he a moment occupies
The hollow of himself and like an air
Pervades all other.
           But the violin
Presses its dry insistence through the dream
That swims above it, shivering its speech
Back to a rhythm that becomes again
Music and vaguely ravels into sound.
So then there is no speech that can resolve
Their texture to clear thought and enter them.

Einstein dissolved in violins invades the molecular structure of F. P. Paepke's Sommergarten. Is repulsed

To Einstein asking at the gate of stone none opens

The Virgin of Chartres whose bleaching bones still wear
The sapphires of her glory knew a word—
That now is three round letters like the three
Round empty staring punctures in a skull.
And there were words in Rome once and one time

Words at Eleusis.
                     Now there are no words
Nor names to name them and they will not speak
But grope against his groping touch and throw
The long unmeaning shadows of themselves
Across his shadow and resist his sense.

Einstein hearing behind the wall of the Grand Hôtel du Nord the stars discovers the Back Stair

Why then if they resist destroy them. Dumb
Yet speak them in their elements. Whole,
Break them to reason.
                     He lies upon his bed
Exerting on Arcturus and the moon
Forces proportional inversely to
The squares of their remoteness, and conceives
The universe.
          Atomic.
                     He can count
Ocean in atoms and weigh out the air
In multiples of one and subdivide
Light to its numbers.
                     If they will not speak
Let them be silent in their particles.
Let them be dead and he will lie among
Their dust and cipher them,—undo the signs
Of their unreal identities and free
The pure and single factor of all sums,—
Solve them to unity.
          Democritus
Scooped handfuls out of stones and like the sea
Let earth run through his fingers. Well, he too,
He can achieve obliquity and learn
The cold distortion of the winter's sun
That breaks the surfaces of summer.

Einstein on the terrasse of The Acacias forces the secret door

                     Stands
Facing the world upon a windy slope
And with his mind relaxes the stiff forms
Of all he sees so that the heavy hills
Impend like rushing water and the earth
Hangs on the steep and momentary crest
Of overflowing ruin.
          Overflow!

Sweep over into movement and dissolve
All differences in the indifferent flux!
Crumble to eddyings of dust and drown
In change the thing that changes!
　　　　　　　　　　　　There begins
A vague unquiet in the fallow ground,
A seething in the grass, a bubbling swirl
Over the surface of the fields that spreads
Around him gathering until the green
Boils and beneath the frothy loam the rocks
Ferment and simmer and like thinning smoke
The trees melt into nothing.
　　　　　　　　　　Still he stands
Watching the vortex widen and involve
In swirling dissolution the whole earth
And circle through the skies till swaying time
Collapses crumpling into dark the stars
And motion ceases and the sifting world
Opens beneath.
　　　　　　　When he shall feel infuse
His flesh with the rent body of all else
And spin within his opening brain the motes
Of suns and worlds and spaces.

　　　　　　　　　　　　　　　　Einstein enters

　　　　　　　Like a foam
His flesh is withered and his shrivelling
And ashy bones are scattered on the dark.
But still the dark denies him. Still withstands
The dust his penetration and flings back
Himself to answer him.
　　　　　　　　　Which seems to keep
Something inviolate. A living something.

You, Andrew Marvell

AND here face down beneath the sun,
　　And here upon earth's noonward height,
To feel the always coming on,
The always rising of the night.

To feel creep up the curving east
The earthly chill of dusk and slow
Upon those under lands the vast
And ever-climbing shadow grow,

And strange at Ecbatan the trees
Take leaf by leaf the evening, strange,
The flooding dark about their knees,
The mountains over Persia change,

And now at Kermanshah the gate,
Dark, empty, and the withered grass,
And through the twilight now the late
Few travellers in the westward pass.

And Baghdad darken and the bridge
Across the silent river gone,
And through Arabia the edge
Of evening widen and steal on,

And deepen on Palmyra's street
The wheel rut in the ruined stone,
And Lebanon fade out and Crete
High through the clouds and overblown,

And over Sicily the air
Still flashing with the landward gulls,
And loom and slowly disappear
The sails above the shadowy hulls,

And Spain go under and the shore
Of Africa, the gilded sand,
And evening vanish and no more
The low pale light across that land,

Nor now the long light on the sea—

And here face downward in the sun
To feel how swift, how secretly,
The shadow of the night comes on. . . .

Memorial Rain

AMBASSADOR PUSER the ambassador
Reminds himself in French, the felicitous tongue,
What these (young men no longer) lie here for
In rows that once, and somewhere else, were young—

    All night in Brussels the wind had tugged at my door:
I had heard the wind at my door and the trees strung
Taut, and to me who had never been before
In that country it was a strange wind blowing
Steadily, stiffening the walls, the floor,
The roof of my room. I had not slept for knowing
He too, dead, was a stranger in that land
And felt beneath the earth in the wind's flowing
A tightening of roots and would not understand,
Remembering lake winds in Illinois,
That strange wind. I had felt his bones in the sand
Listening.

        —Reflects that these enjoy
Their country's gratitude, that deep repose,
That peace no pain can break, no hurt destroy,
That rest, that sleep—

        At Ghent the wind rose.
There was a smell of rain and a heavy drag
Of wind in the hedges but not as the wind blows
Over fresh water when the waves lag
Foaming and the willows huddle and it will rain:
I felt him waiting.

        —Indicates the flag
Which (may he say) enisles in Flanders' plain
This little field these happy, happy dead
Have made America—

        In the ripe grain
The wind coiled glistening, darted, fled,
Dragging its heavy body: at Waereghem

The wind coiled in the grass above his head:
Waiting—listening—

                    —Dedicates to them
This earth their bones have hallowed, this last gift
A grateful country—

                    Under the dry grass stem
The words are blurred, are thickened, the words sift
Confused by the rasp of the wind, by the thin grating
Of ants under the grass, the minute shift
And tumble of dusty sand separating
From dusty sand. The roots of the grass strain,
Tighten, the earth is rigid, waits—he is waiting—
And suddenly, and all at once, the rain!

The people scatter, they run into houses, the wind
Is trampled under the rain, shakes free, is again
Trampled. The rain gathers, running in thinned
Spurts of water that ravel in the dry sand
Seeping into the sand under the grass roots, seeping
Between cracked boards to the bones of a clenched hand:
The earth relaxes, loosens; he is sleeping,
He rests, he is quiet, he sleeps in a strange land.

MARK VAN DOREN

No Faith

WHAT held the bones together? Not belief,
     Not anything he could probe, no ligament god.
Why was the world so one for him yet many,
So woman and yet so speechless? Then the odd,
The furtive, ashamed security. We wondered.
But there was no faith in him that sang or thundered.

There was no understanding in this man
Of his own simplest secret: of the way
Earth's air kept warm for him, and how there shone
Always another light outdoors of day.
He would have chosen darkness; he denied
What was so strange, so palpable, inside;

He said he could be unhappy. But we knew.
There was this sweet continuum, this flesh;
There were these bones, articulated so—
A web they were, with music up the mesh,
A frame of hidden wires too deep for tone,
A skeleton wholeness, humming up to him alone.

He must have heard the harmony, but he swore
Time talked to him in separated sounds.
He took them as they came and loved them singly—
Each one, he parried, perfect within its bounds.
As for the burden's end, the tune's direction—
He smiled; he was content with disconnection.

Yet who could smile and mean it? Who could rest,
As this man did, midway the million things?
Who else could be serene at truth's circumference
When only the known center of it sings?
Who else but he?—submissive to each part
Till it became the all, the homeless heart.

His Trees

ONLY when he was old enough, and silent:
    Not breaking-old; time-coated; that was it;
Only when he was dry enough: but seasoned;
Time-guarded against all weather-warp and split;
Time-roughened, with years of ridges down his bark:
Then only grew he worthy of their remark.

They did not move; but watched him as he came,
Man-tired, and paused and peered among their shade.
No magical advancing; each emerged
Only as slow acquaintance thus was made:

The oaks and he confronted, that was all;
Save that his leaves of ignorance could fall.

They fell, and filled the temperate aging air
With a crisp rustle, flake on flake descending;
Till in some month it ceased, and trunk on trunk
Acknowledged him, in rows without an ending.
The lesser with the greater shadows wove:
He there with them, companions of the grove.

The ash was proud to show him in its side
How narrowly and coldly time had cut:
A flank of iron; and how its sharpened leaves
Stood out too stiff for any wind to shut:
Stubborn; yet some antiquity of grace
Still kept it king, still proved the priestly face.

That maple there, the old man of the wood:
Shaggy, with clefts of shadow in its rind;
Like a deep-bearded deity, becloaked,
Shed down upon him, slowly, what of its mind
Went floating: lightly, lightly; though of late
Time pressed it under centuries of weight.

He touched them all, and moved among their shapes
Like a blind child whom giants might despise.
Yet he was their true copy; so they leaned,
Indulgent to his autumn; met his eyes;
And uttered as much, responding to his hands,
As ever a second childhood understands.

Exaggerator

THE truth for him was like a tree,
Was like a funnel; like a fan;
Like any point from which a cone
Spreads upside down until the span
From base to base across the top
Cannot be guessed by any man.

The truth for him was not the seed,
Was not the apex, handle, spout;
Was not the particle or germ,
Or what grew thence so wild and stout;
Was not the great, the upper end.
It was the joy of starting out;

Of feeling something in him rise
And widen instantly—and swell,
As if the wind and he were one,
And blew upon each other well;
As if the sky and he were single:
Clapper there and flangèd bell.

The truth for him was hearing quick
The cordage whistle, and the whine
Of wakened metal; something bronze;
Something moaning thin and fine,
Something low; until it burst,
And all was plangent with word-shine.

The truth for him was leaving earth
Between two beams that sloped and rose;
And never joined—the angle's bound
Was all of distance at the close;
Whence he descended, narrowing down
And resting gently where he chose.

The Whisperer

BE extra careful by this door,
No least, least sound, she said.
It is my brother Oliver's,
And he would strike you dead.

Come on. It is the top step now,
And carpet all the way.
But wide enough for only one,
Unless you carry me.

I love your face as hot as this.
Put me down, though, and creep.
My father! He would strangle you,
I think, like any sheep.

Now take me up again, again;
We're at the landing post.
You hear her saying Hush, and Hush?
It is my mother's ghost.

She would have loved you, loving me.
She had a voice as fine—
I love you more for such a kiss,
And here is mine, is mine.

And one for her—Oh, quick, the door!
I cannot bear it so.
The vestibule, and out; for now
Who passes that would know?

Here we could stand all night and let
Strange people smile and stare.
But you must go, and I must lie
Alone up there, up there.

Remember? But I understand.
More with a kiss is said.
And do not mind it if I cry,
Passing my mother's bed.

E. E. CUMMINGS

Love Is More Thicker Than Forget

LOVE is more thicker than forget
more thinner than recall
more seldom than a wave is wet
more frequent than to fail

it is most mad and moonly
and less it shall unbe
than all the sea which only
is deeper than the sea

love is less always than to win
less never than alive
less bigger than the least begin
less littler than forgive

it is most sane and sunly
and more it cannot die
than all the sky which only
is higher than the sky

My Father Moved Through Dooms of Love

MY father moved through dooms of love
through sames of am through haves of give,
singing each morning out of each night
my father moved through depths of height

this motionless forgetful where
turned at his glance to shining here;
that if (so timid air is firm)
under his eyes would stir and squirm

newly as from unburied which
floats the first who, his april touch
drove sleeping selves to swarm their fates
woke dreamers to their ghostly roots

and should some why completely weep
my father's fingers brought her sleep:
vainly no smallest voice might cry
for he could feel the mountains grow.

Lifting the valleys of the sea
my father moved through griefs of joy;
praising a forehead called the moon
singing desire into begin

joy was his song and joy so pure
a heart of star by him could steer
and pure so now and now so yes
the wrists of twilight would rejoice

keen as midsummer's keen beyond
conceiving mind of sun will stand,
so strictly (over utmost him
so hugely) stood my father's dream

his flesh was flesh his blood was blood:
no hungry man but wished him food;
no cripple wouldn't creep one mile
uphill to only see him smile.

Scorning the pomp of must and shall
my father moved through dooms of feel;
his anger was as right as rain
his pity was as green as grain

septembering arms of year extend
less humbly wealth to foe and friend
than he to foolish and to wise
offered immeasurable is

proudly and (by octobering flame
beckoned) as earth will downward climb,
so naked for immortal work
his shoulders marched against the dark

his sorrow was as true as bread:
no liar looked him in the head;
if every friend became his foe
he'd laugh and build a world with snow.

My father moved through theys of we,
singing each new leaf out of each tree
(and every child was sure that spring
danced when she heard my father sing)

then let men kill which cannot share,
let blood and flesh be mud and mire,

scheming imagine, passion willed,
freedom a drug that's bought and sold

giving to steal and cruel kind,
a heart to fear, to doubt a mind,
to differ a disease of same,
conform the pinnacle of am

though dull were all we taste as bright,
bitter all utterly things sweet,
maggoty minus and dumb death
all we inherit, all bequeath

and nothing quite so least as truth
—i say though hate were why men breathe—
because my father lived his soul
love is the whole and more than all

As Freedom Is a Breakfastfood

As freedom is a breakfastfood
     or truth can live with right and wrong
or molehills are from mountains made
—long enough and just so long
will being pay the rent of seem
and genius please the talentgang
and water most encourage flame

as hatracks into peachtrees grow
or hopes dance best on bald men's hair
and every finger is a toe
and any courage is a fear
—long enough and just so long
will the impure think all things pure
and hornets wail by children stung

or as the seeing are the blind
and robins never welcome spring
nor flatfolk prove their world is round
nor dingsters die at break of dong
and common's rare and millstones float

—long enough and just so long
tomorrow will not be too late

worms are the words but joy's the voice
down shall go which and up come who
breasts will be breasts thighs will be thighs
deeds cannot dream what dreams can do
—time is a tree (this life one leaf)
but love is the sky and i am for you
just so long and long enough

Always Before Your Voice My Soul

ALWAYS before your voice my soul
   half-beautiful and wholly droll
is as some smooth and awkward foal,
whereof young moons begin
the newness of his skin,

so of my stupid sincere youth
the exquisite failure uncouth
discovers a trembling and smooth
Unstrength, against the strong
silences of your song;

or as a single lamb whose sheen
of full unsheared fleece is mean
beside its lovelier friends, between
your thoughts more white than wool
My thought is sorrowful:

but my heart smote in trembling thirds
of anguish quivers to your words,
As to a flight of thirty birds
shakes with a thickening fright
the sudden fooled light.

it is the autumn of a year:
When through the thin air stooped with fear,
across the harvest whitely peer
empty of surprise
death's faultless eyes

(whose hand my folded soul shall know
while on faint hills do fraily go
The peaceful terrors of the snow,
and before your dead face
which sleeps, a dream shall pass)

and these my days their sounds and flowers
Fall in a pride of petaled hours,
like flowers at the feet of mowers
whose bodies strong with love
through meadows hugely move.

yet what am i that such and such
mysteries very simply touch
me, whose heart-wholeness overmuch
Expects of your hair pale,
a terror musical?

while in an earthless hour my fond
soul seriously yearns beyond
this fern of sunset frond on frond
opening in a rare
Slowness of gloried air . . .

The flute of morning stilled in noon—
noon the implacable bassoon—
now Twilight seeks the thrill of moon,
washed with a wild and thin
despair of violin

H. PHELPS PUTNAM

Hasbrouck and the Rose

HASBROUCK was there and so were Bill
And Smollet Smith the poet, and Ames was there.
After his thirteenth drink, the burning Smith,
Raising his fourteenth trembling in the air,

Said, "Drink with me, Bill, drink up to the Rose."
But Hasbrouck laughed like old men in a myth,
Inquiring, "Smollet, are you drunk? What rose?"
And Smollet said, "I drunk? It may be so;
Which comes from brooding on the flower, the flower
I mean toward which mad hour by hour
I travel brokenly; and I shall know,
With Hermes and the alchemists—but, hell,
What use is it talking that way to you?
Hard-boiled, unbroken egg, what can you care
For the enfolded passion of the Rose?"
Then Hasbrouck's voice rang like an icy bell:

"Arcane romantic flower, meaning what?
Do you know what is meant? Do I?
We do not know.
Unfolding pungent rose, the glowing bath
Of ecstasy and clear forgetfulness;
Closing and secret bud one might achieve
By long debauchery—
Except that I have eaten it, and so
There is no call for further lunacy.
In Springfield, Massachusetts, I devoured
The mystic, the improbable, the Rose.
For two nights and a day, rose and rosette,
And petal after petal and the heart,
I had my banquet by the beams
Of four electric stars which shone
Weakly into my room, for there,
Drowning their light and gleaming at my side,
Was the incarnate star
Whose body bore the stigma of the Rose.
And that is all I know about the flower;
I have eaten it—it has disappeared.
There is no Rose."

Young Smollet Smith let fall his glass; he said
"Oh Jesus, Hasbrouck, am I drunk or dead?"

About Women

FAIR golden thoughts and lovely words—
    Away, away from her they call,
For women are the silly birds,
And perching on a sunny wall
They chirp the answer and the all;
They hold for true all futile things—
Life, death, and even love—they fall
To dreaming over jeweled rings.

Their bodies are uncouthly made,
And heavy swollen like a pear,
And yet their conquered, undismayed
And childish lovers call them fair.
Their honor fills them full of care,
Their honor that is nothingness,
The mystery of empty air,
The veil of vain delightfulness.

Their subtleties are thin and pale,
Their hearts betray them in their eyes:
They are a simple flute, and frail,
With triple stops for playing lies.
These poor machines of life are wise
To scorn the metaphysic glow,
The careless game that laughs and dies,
The heady grace they cannot know.

Well, give them kisses, scatter flowers,
And whisper that you cannot stay;
We shall have clarity and hours
Which women shall not take away.

ROBERT HILLYER

Letter to a Teacher of English

JAMES B. MUNN

YOUR learning, James, in classics and romance,
  Sits lightlier than most men's ignorance;
But often do I see in our profession
Learning a mere extraneous possession,
An undigested mass of dates and sources
Roll'd round in academe's diurnal courses,
Where scholars prepare scholars, not for life,
But gaudy footnotes and a threadbare wife,—
Keen eyes for errors in a worthless text,
But none at all for this world or the next.
Your modesty, that even tops your learning,
Forbids what I would say of you, so turning
Not, as I hope, from Ghibelline to Guelph,
I will discuss, as is the vogue, myself.

I fall between two stools—I can't say Chairs—
A bard too learn'd, a scholar in arrears.
The critical reviewers, week by week,
Damn poets who command their own technique.
Professor is a title that to them
Begins in laughter and concludes in phlegm.
A careful rhyme, a spondee nobly planned
Is academic, and the work unmanned.
Would that these critics lived in houses fashioned
By carpenters congenially impassioned.
I'd love to see the rooftree fall on . . . no,
The name is Legion; let us leave it so.
But as a teacher I have equal luck,—
In ponds a chicken and on shore a duck.
My wretched memory, for all my pains,
Drops tons for every ounce that it retains;
Far wiser now, I have less factual knowledge
At forty-one than when I was in college. . . .

Yet there is recompense for knowing well
One language, if it be incomparable.
Disdainful, the Athenian would speak
No other language than his native Greek.
Now his provincial literature is prized
In every barbarous tongue that he despised.
The learned Roman, who knew Greek by heart,
Had twice the scholarship, and half the art.
The great Elizabethans' education
Thrived less on lore than on superb translation.
Our scholars, to whom every root is known,
Command all languages, except their own.
For confirmation, but consult the theses
That year by year bankrupt the college presses.

When poets go, grammarians arrive.
Is Virgil dead? Let commentators thrive.
The gift of tongues without the Holy Ghost
Becomes a Babel, not a Pentecost.
In short, dear James, by now you plainly see
I find no virtue in philology;
At best a sterile hobby, often worse,
The plumes, when language dies, upon its hearse. . . .

Now, James, I stop complaining, I will plan
An education to produce a man.
Make no mistake, I do not want this done,—
My limitations are the cornerstone.
Plato's *Republic* may have served some use
In manuscript, but not in Syracuse,
So let my dream Academy remain
A dream;—I'm sure I do not ask in vain.
First would I have my scholar learn the tongue
He never learned to speak when he was young;
Then would I have him read therein, but merely
In the great books, to understand them clearly.
O that our living literature could be
Our sustenance, not archæology!
Time is the wisest judge, who folds away
The surplus of a too-abundant day.
My scholar shall be brilliantly forbidden
To dig old garbage from a kitchen midden.

Far better Alexandria in flames
Than buried beneath unimportant names,
And even Sappho, glory that was Greece's,
Lives best, I blasphemously think, in pieces.
Surely our sprite, who over Amherst hovered,
Would gain if no more poems were discovered.
That Chinese emperor who burned the books
Succumbed to madness shrewder than it looks;
The minor poets and the minor sages
Went up in smoke; the great shine down the ages.
The Harvard Library's ungainly porch
Has often made me hunger for a torch,
But this not more to simplify a lecture
Than to appease the Muse of architecture.

When music and sweet poetry agree,
Who would be thinking of a Ph.D.?
O who would Ablauts bear, when Brahms's First
Is soon to be performed or but rehearsed?
My scholar must have music in his heart,
Bach and Beethoven, Schumann and Mozart,
Franck and Sibelius, and more like these,
Their works, if not their names, sweet symphonies.
Ah, James, I missed my calling; I would turn
To that one art toward which the others yearn,—
But I observe my neighbor's cow, who leaves
Her fertile pasture for my barren sheaves.
The field next door, the next-door art, will thus
Always attract the mildly covetous.
Yet some day I will play you the main theme
Of the immortal counterpoint I dream:
Clear melody in fugue and canon rises
On strings, with many structural surprises.
No letter, but a prelude, for your sake
I would compose beside this tranquil lake.
Its line should rise toward heaven until it broke
Halfway between the sky and the great oak;
Then waver, like a flock of homing birds,
In slow descending flights of minor thirds.
Music alone can set the spirit free
From the dark past and darker things to be.
Could Man be judged by music, then the Lord

Would quench the angel of the flaming sword.
Alas, the final tones so soon disperse
Their echoes through the empty universe,
And hearers, weak from following Beethoven,
Relax with Gershwin, Herbert, and de Koven.

But to return to Polyhymnia,
And incidentally to my student. Ah,
Where is the creature? No, but is that he?
A saxophone is nuzzling on his knee!
His eyes pop out, his bellied cheeks expand,
His foot taps "Alexander's Ragtime Band."
Ungraceful and unpardonable wretch!
Was it for you my eager pen would sketch
A new, a sensible curriculum?
Burst with your Panpipes! and we'll both be dumb.
I was about to urge philosophy,
Especially the Greek, I was to be
Your godfather in recommending Faith
To you, fit godson for a Sigmund Spaeth!
Of history and time I was to tell,
Things visible and things invisible,
But what to you are echoes from Nicea,
Who never prayed nor cherished an idea?
And what have you to gain from education,
Blown bellows for unceasing syncopation?
Learning and life are too far wrenched apart,
I cannot reconcile, for all my art,
Studies that go one way and life another,
Tastes that demoralize, and tests that smother.

James, what is this I find? an angry scowl
Sits on my brow like a Palladian owl!
Let me erase it, lest it should transform
The soft horizon with a thunderstorm.
I would you were beside me now, to share
The sound of falling water, the sweet air.
Under the yew a vacant easy chair
Awaits your coming; and long-planted seeds
Begin to bloom amid the encircling weeds.
I bade my student an abrupt adieu
But find it harder to take leave of you.

May we not some day have a mild carouse
In Pontefract instead of Warren House?
The distance nothing—in two hours' time
Another land where that word's but a rhyme.
Would I were Marvell, then you could not harden
Your heart against a visit to my garden.
I'd write those happy lines about the green
Annihilation, and you'd soon be seen
Hatless and coatless, bootless,—well, my soul!
He's in the lake with nothing on at all!
To sink, to swim, that is the only question:
Thus ends my treatise on—was it digestion?
Farewell, and yours sincerely, and yours ever,
The time has come for the initial shiver.
When into lakes, as into life, we dive,
We're fortunate if we come up alive.

EDMUND WILSON

Riverton

HERE am I among elms again—ah, look
How, high above low windows hung with white,
Dark on white dwellings, rooted among rock,
They rise like iron ribs that pillar night!
The stars are high again; the night is clear;
The bed rolls with the old uneven floor;
The air is still again—I lie and hear
The river always falling at the door.

—O elms! O river! aid me at this turn—
Their passing makes my late imperative:
They flicker now who frightfully did burn,
And I must tell their beauty while I live.
Changing their grace as water in its flight,
And gone like water; give me then the art,
Firm as night-frozen ice found silver-bright,
That holds the splendor though the days depart.

A House of the Eighties

NO more in dreams as once it draws me there,
    All fungus-grown and sunken in damp ground—
No more as once when waking I gazed down
On elms like water-weeds in moonlit air
Or heard the August downpour with its dull full sound—
Drenched hedges and the hillside and the night,
The largest house in sight—
And thought it sunken out of time or drowned
As hulks in Newark Bay are soaked and slowly drown.

—The ugly stained-glass window on the stair,
Dark-panelled dining-room, the guinea fowl's fierce clack,
The great gray cat that on the oven slept—
My father's study with its books and birds,
His scornful tone, his eighteenth-century words,
His green door sealed with baize
—Today I travel back
To find again that one fixed point he kept
And left me for the day
In which this other world of theirs grows dank, decays,
And founders and goes down.

———•••———

LOUISE BOGAN

———•••———

Summer Wish

That cry's from the first cuckoo of the year.
I wished before it ceased.

FIRST VOICE

WE call up the green to hide us
    This hardened month, by no means the beginning
Of the natural year, but of the shortened span
Of leaves upon the earth. We call upon
The weed as well as the flower: groundsel, stellaria.

It is the month to make the summer wish;
It is time to ask
The wish from summer as always: *It will be,
It will be.*
        That tool we have used
So that its haft is smooth; it knows the hand.
Again we lift the wish to its expert uses,
Tired of the bird that calls one long note downward,
And the forest in cast-iron. No longer, no longer,
The season of the lying equinox
Wherein false cock-crow sounds!

SECOND VOICE

In March the shadow
Already falls with a look of summer, fuller
Upon the snow, because the sun at last
Is almost centered. Later, the sprung moss
Is the tree's shadow; under the black spruces
It lies where lately snow lay, bred green from the cold
Cast down from melting branches.

FIRST VOICE

A wish like a hundred others.
You cannot, as once, yearn forward. The blood now never
Stirs hot to memory, or to the fantasy
Of love, with which, both early and late, one lies
As with a lover.
Now do you suddenly envy
Poor praise you told long since to keep its tongue,
Of pride's acquired accent,—pomposity, arrogance,
That trip in their latinity? With these at heart
You could make a wish, crammed with the nobility
Of error. It would be no use. You cannot
Take yourself in.

SECOND VOICE

Count over what these days have: lilies
Returned in little to an earth unready,
To the sun not accountable;
The hillside mazed and leafless, but through the ground
The leaf from the bulb, the unencouraged green

Heaving the metal earth, presage of thousand
Shapes of young leaves—lanceolate, trefoil,
Peach, willow, plum, the lilac like a heart.

FIRST VOICE

Memory long since put by,—to what end the dream
That drags back lived-out life with the wrong words,
The substitute meaning?
Those that you once knew there play out false time,
Elaborate yesterday's words, that they were deaf to,
Being dead ten years.—Call back in anguish
The anger in childhood that defiled the house
In walls and timber with its violence?
Now must you listen again
To your own tears, shed as a child, hold the bruise
With your hand, and weep, fallen against the wall,
And beg, *Don't, don't,* while the pitiful rage goes on
That cannot stem itself?
Or, having come into woman's full estate,
Enter the rich field, walk between the bitter
Bowed grain, being compelled to serve,
To heed unchecked in the heart the reckless fury
That tears fresh day from day, destroys its traces,—
Now bear the blow too young?

SECOND VOICE

In early April
At six o'clock the sun has not set; on the walls
It shines with scant light, pale, dilute, misplaced,
Light there's no use for. At overcast noon
The sun comes out in a flash, and is taken
Slowly back to the cloud.

FIRST VOICE

Not memory, and not the renewed conjecture
Of passion that opens the breast, the unguarded look
Flaying clean the raped defence of the body,
Breast, bowels, throat, now pulled to the use of the eyes
That see and are taken. The body that works and sleeps,
Made vulnerable, night and day, to delight that changes
Upon the lips that taste it, to the lash of jealousy

Struck on the face, so the betraying bed
Is gashed clear, cold on the mind, together with
Every embrace that agony dreads but sees
Open as the love of dogs.

SECOND VOICE

The cloud shadow flies up the bank, but does not
Blow off like smoke. It stops at the bank's edge.
In the field by trees two shadows come together.
The trees and the cloud throw down their shadow upon
The man who walks there. Dark flows up from his feet
To his shoulders and throat, then has his face in its mask,
Then lifts.

FIRST VOICE

Will you turn to yourself, proud breast,
Sink to yourself, to an ingrained, pitiless
Rejection of voice and touch not your own, press sight
Into a myth no eye can take the gist of;
Clot up the bone of phrase with the black conflict
That claws it back from sense?
                                    Go into the breast . . .
You have traced that lie, before this, out to its end,
Heard bright wit headstrong in the beautiful voice
Changed to a word mumbled across the shoulder
To one not there; the gentle self split up
Into a yelling fiend and a soft child.
You have seen the ingrown look
Come at last upon a vision too strong
Ever to turn away.

The breast's six madnesses repeat their dumb-show.

SECOND VOICE

In the bright twilight children call out in the fields.
The evening takes their cry. How late it is!
Around old weeds worn thin and bleached to their pith
The field has leaped to stalk and strawberry blossom.
The orchard by the road
Has the pear-tree full at once of flowers and leaves,
The cherry with flowers only.

FIRST VOICE

The mind for refuge, the grain of reason, the will,
Pulled by a wind it thinks to point and name?
Malicious symbol, key for rusty wards,
The crafty knight in the game, with its mixed move,
Prey to an end not evident to craft. . . .

SECOND VOICE

Fields are ploughed inward
From edge to center; furrows squaring off
Make dark lines far out in irregular fields,
On hills that are builded like great clouds that over them
Rise, to depart.
Furrow within furrow, square within a square,
Draw to the center where the team turns last.
Horses in half-ploughed fields
Make earth they walk upon a changing color.

FIRST VOICE

The year's begun; the share's again in the earth.

Speak out the wish like music, that has within it
The horn, the string, the drum pitched deep as grief.
Speak it like laughter, outward. O brave, O generous
Laughter that pours from the well of the body and draws
The bane that cheats the heart: aconite, nightshade,
Hellebore, hyssop, rue,—symbols and poisons
We drink, in fervor, thinking to gain thereby
Some difference, some distinction.
Speak it, as that man said, *as though the earth spoke,*
By the body of rock, shafts of heaved strata, separate,
Together.
            Though it be but for sleep at night,
Speak out the wish.
The vine we pitied is in leaf; the wild
Honeysuckle blows by the granite.

SECOND VOICE

See now
Open above the field, stilled in wing-stiffened flight,
The stretched hawk fly.

MALCOLM COWLEY

The Long Voyage

NOT that the pines were darker there,
    nor mid-May dogwood brighter there,
nor swifts more swift in summer air;
        it was my own country.

having its thunderclap of spring,
its long midsummer ripening,
its corn hoar-stiff at harvesting,
        almost like any country.

yet being mine; its face, its speech,
its hills bent low within my reach,
its river birch and upland beech
        were mine, of my own country.

Now the dark waters at the bow
fold back, like earth against the plow;
foam brightens like the dogwood now
        at home, in my own country.

THEODORE SPENCER

Song

I WHO love you bring
    Against our cherishing
These faults I daren't deny
Lest love should prove a lie.
        But Oh, if you love me, forgive me,
        And none of this is true.

A too resilient mind
That seeking fact, must find
Reasons on every side
Why fact should be denied.
　　　But Oh, if you love me, forgive me,
　　　And none of this is true.

A body that has wooed
More pleasure than it should,
And for that pleasure sought
What it had thrived without.
　　　But Oh, if you love me, forgive me,
　　　And none of this is true.

And until now, a soul
That could find no goal
Beyond body and mind;
And so turned blind.
　　　But Oh, if you love me, forgive me,
　　　And none of this is true.

Spring Song

I HAVE come again, gentlemen and ladies,
　Whatever you call me, ladies, gentlemen;
Dancing, dancing down, sweet ladies,
And up with a dance I come, kind gentlemen;
I am here; we are dancing again.

Brown leaf on a dust-hill, ladies, ladies;
A running ant from the dust-hill, gentlemen;
Look out of the window; here I am;
Look back to the bedroom; here I am.
Sleep; and we'll fall together, gentlemen—
Falling towers and crumpled gowns
To a dust, a most sleepy dust, ladies,
From towers and golden gowns. But sleep,
Oh sleep again, and I'll promise you green,
A green, shattering sun-blade green,
With a daffodil prance like forever, gentlemen,
Forever a tower of gold like a daffodil.

I have come again, gentlemen and ladies;
Whatever you call me, a leaf and a dust-hill;
Dancing up, gentlemen, sweet ladies;
And dancing down, ladies, kind gentlemen.
I am here; we are dancing again.

R. P. BLACKMUR

Half-Tide Ledge

SUNDAY the sea made morning worship, sang
Venite, Kyrie, and a long Amen,
over a flowing cassock did put on
glittering blindness, surplice of the sun.
Towards high noon her eldest, high-run tide
rebelled at formal song and in the Sanctus
made heavy mockery of God,
and I, almost before I knew it, saw
the altar ledges of the Lord awash.
These are the obsequies I think on most.

Scarabs for the Living

I

O SAILOR sailor tell me why
though in the seawine of your eye
I see nothing dead and nothing die
I know from the stillness seething there
my heart's hope is my soul's despair.

II

To meditate upon the tiger, turn
your human eyes from his past-human stare;
beyond his cage a pigeon tops an urn,

beyond the pigeon falls the twilight air,
and there, steadfast, he sees a viewless lair.

III

Lay down one hand before you like a tool
and let the other, in your mind, grow strange;
then let the strangers meet. Who but a fool
or a passionate man, thinks loss is blood-exchange,
if the cold hand should warm and the hot cool!

IV

Within this windless covert silence drops
leaf by leaf and birches make bare bones;
a startled woodcock's whistling flight new-stops
the wind beyond the woods, and I, alone,
feel my still flight trembling into stone.

V

There is, besides the warmth, in this new love—
besides the radiance, the spring—the chill
that in the old had seemed the slow, the still
amounting up of that indifferent will
in which we die. I keep last winter's glove.

VI

Oh, I was honest in the womb
where I had neither time nor room
nor any secret hope to hide.
Now there are love and work this side
of honesty, two hopes that lied.

VII

The chickadee-dee-dee is not a bird
like stilted heron fishing minnie pools
that in their fleeing shriek the sky like fools;
the chickadee (dee-dee) is most a word
to keep the thicket warm when summer cools.

VIII

It is the slow encroachment, word by word,
of sleep upon the wakened mind, the slow
manoeuvre of unseemly vertigo,
whereby disease in order is inferred;
and in the sleep a blotting fall of snow.

IX

Quiet the self, and silence brims like spring:
the soaking in of light, the gathering
of shadow up, after each passing cloud,
the green life eating into death aloud,
the hum of seasons; all on beating wing.

YVOR WINTERS

Sir Gawaine and the Green Knight

REPTILIAN green the wrinkled throat,
  Green as a bough of yew the beard;
He bent his head, and so I smote;
Then for a thought my vision cleared.

The head dropped clean; he rose and walked;
He fixed his fingers in the hair;
The head was unabashed and talked;
I understood what I must dare.

His flesh, cut down, arose and grew.
He bade me wait the season's round,
And then, when he had strength anew,
To meet him on his native ground.

The year declined; and in his keep
I passed in joy a thriving yule;
And whether waking or in sleep,
I lived in riot like a fool.

He beat the woods to bring me meat.
His lady, like a forest vine,
Grew in my arms; the growth was sweet;
And yet what thoughtless force was mine!

By practice and conviction formed,
With ancient stubbornness ingrained,
Although her body clung and swarmed,
My own identity remained.

Her beauty, lithe, unholy, pure
Took shapes that I had never known;
And had I once been insecure,
Had grafted laurel in my bone.

And then, since I had kept the trust,
Had loved the lady, yet was true,
The knight withheld his giant thrust
And let me go with what I knew.

I left the green bark and the shade,
Where growth was rapid, thick, and still;
I found a road that men had made
And rested on a drying hill.

JOHN WHEELWRIGHT

Train Ride

AFTER rain, through afterglow, the unfolding fan
of railway landscape sidled on the pivot
of a larger arc into the green of evening;
I remembered that noon I saw a gradual bud
still white; though dead in its warm bloom;
always the enemy is the foe at home.
And I wondered what surgery could recover
our lost, long stride of indolence and leisure

which is labor in reverse; what physic recalls the smile
not of lips, but of eyes as of the sea bemused.

We, when we disperse from common sleep to several
tasks, we gather to despair; we, who assembled
once for hopes from common toil to dreams
or sickish and hurting or triumphal rapture;
always the enemy is our foe at home.

We, deafened with far scattered city rattles
to the hubbub of forest birds (never having
"had time" to grieve or to hear through vivid sleep
the sea knock on its cracked and hollow stones)
so that the stars, almost, and birds comply,
and the garden-wet; the trees retire; We are
a scared patrol, fearing the guns behind;
always the enemy is the foe at home.

What wonder that we fear our own eyes' look
and fidget to be at home alone, and pitifully
put off age by some change in brushing the hair
and stumble to our ends like smothered runners at their tape;

Then (as while the stars herd to the great trough
the blind, in the always-only-outward of their dismantled
archways, awake at the smell of warmed stone
or to the sound of reeds, lifting from the dim
into their segment of green dawn) *always
our enemy is our foe at home,* more
certainly than through spoken words or from grief-
twisted writing on paper, unblotted by tears
the thought came:
                 There is no physic
for the world's ill, nor surgery; it must
(hot smell of tar on wet salt air)
burn in a fever forever, an incense pierced
with arrows, whose name is Love and another name
Rebellion (the twinge, the gulf, split seconds,
the very raindrop, render, and instancy
of Love).

All Poetry to this not-to-be-looked-upon sun
of Passion is the moon's cupped light; all
Politics to this moon, a moon's reflected
cupped light, like the moon of Rome, after
the deep wells of Grecian light sank low;
always the enemy is the foe at home.

But these three are friends whose arms twine
without words; as, in a still air,
the great grove leans to wind, past and to come.

Fish Food

An Obituary to Hart Crane

AS you drank deep as Thor, did you think of milk or wine?
Did you drink blood, while you drank the salt deep?
Or see through the film of light, that sharpened your rage with its
   stare,
a shark, dolphin, turtle? Did you not see the Cat
who, when Thor lifted her, unbased the cubic ground?
You would drain fathomless flagons to be slaked with vacuum—
The sea's teats have suckled you, and you are sunk far
in bubble-dreams, under swaying translucent vines
of thundering interior wonder. Eagles can never now
carry parts of your body, over cupped mountains
as emblems of their anger, embers to fire self-hate
to other wonders, unfolding white flaming vistas.

Fishes now look upon you, with eyes which do not gossip.
Fishes are never shocked. Fishes will kiss you, each
fish tweak you; every kiss takes bits of you away,
till your bones alone will roll, with the Gulf Stream's swell.
So has it been already, so have the carpers and puffers
nibbled your carcass of fame, each to his liking. Now
in tides of noon, the bones of your thought-suspended structures
gleam as you intended. Noon pulled your eyes with small
magnetic headaches; the will seeped from your blood. Seeds
of meaning popped from the pods of thought. And you fall.
      And the unseen
churn of Time changes the pearl-hued ocean;
like a pearl-shaped drop, in a huge water-clock
falling; from *came* to *go,* from *come* to *went.* And you fell.
Waters received you. Waters of our Birth in Death dissolve you.
Now you have willed it, may the Great Wash take you.
As the Mother-Lover takes your woe away, and cleansing
grief and you away, you sleep, you do not snore.
Lie still. Your rage is gone on a bright flood

away; as, when a bad friend held out his hand
you said, "Do not talk any more. I know you meant no harm."
What was the soil whence your anger sprang, who are deaf
as the stones to the whispering flight of the Mississippi's rivers?
What did you see as you fell? What did you hear as you sank?
Did it make you drunken with hearing?
I will not ask any more. You saw or heard no evil.

ALLEN TATE

Ode to the Confederate Dead

ROW after row with strict impunity
　　The headstones yield their names to the element,
The wind whirrs without recollection;
In the riven troughs the splayed leaves
Pile up, of nature the casual sacrament
To the seasonal eternity of death;
Then driven by the fierce scrutiny
Of heaven to their election in the vast breath,
They sough the rumor of mortality.

Autumn is desolation in the plot
Of a thousand acres where these memories grow
From the inexhaustible bodies that are not
Dead, but feed the grass row after rich row.
Think of the autumns that have come and gone!—
Ambitious November with the humors of the year,
With a particular zeal for every slab,
Staining the uncomfortable angels that rot
On the slabs, a wing chipped here, an arm there:
The brute curiosity of an angel's stare
Turns you, like them, to stone,
Transforms the heaving air
Till plunged to a heavier world below
You shift your sea-space blindly
Heaving, turning like the blind crab.

> Dazed by the wind, only the wind
> The leaves flying, plunge

You know who have waited by the wall
The twilight certainty of an animal,
Those midnight restitutions of the blood
You know—the immitigable pines, the smoky frieze
Of the sky, the sudden call: you know the rage,
The cold pool left by the mounting flood,
Of muted Zeno and Parmenides.
You who have waited for the angry resolution
Of those desires that should be yours tomorrow,

You know the unimportant shrift of death
And praise the vision
And praise the arrogant circumstance
Of those who fall
Rank upon rank, hurried beyond decision—
Here by the sagging gate, stopped by the wall.

> Seeing, seeing only the leaves
> Flying, plunge and expire

Turn your eyes to the immoderate past,
Turn to the inscrutable infantry rising
Demons out of the earth—they will not last.
Stonewall, Stonewall, and the sunken fields of hemp,
Shiloh, Antietam, Malvern Hill, Bull Run.
Lost in that orient of the thick and fast
You will curse the setting sun.

> Cursing only the leaves crying
> Like an old man in a storm

You hear the shout, the crazy hemlocks point
With troubled fingers to the silence which
Smothers you, a mummy, in time.

> The hound bitch
Toothless and dying, in a musty cellar
Hears the wind only.

                    Now that the salt of their blood
Stiffens the saltier oblivion of the sea,
Seals the malignant purity of the flood,
What shall we who count our days and bow
Our heads with a commemorial woe
In the ribboned coats of grim felicity,
What shall we say of the bones, unclean,
Whose verdurous anonymity will grow?

The ragged arms, the ragged heads and eyes
Lost in these acres of the insane green?
The gray lean spiders come, they come and go;
In a tangle of willows without light
The singular screech-owl's tight
Invisible lyric seeds the mind
With the furious murmur of their chivalry.

       We shall say only the leaves
       Flying, plunge and expire

We shall say only the leaves whispering
In the improbable mist of nightfall
That flies on multiple wing:
Night is the beginning and the end
And in between the ends of distraction
Waits mute speculation, the patient curse
That stones the eyes, or like the jaguar leaps
For his own image in a jungle pool, his victim.

What shall we say who have knowledge
Carried to the heart? Shall we take the act
To the grave? Shall we, more hopeful, set up the grave
In the house? The ravenous grave?

                                    Leave now
The shut gate and the decomposing wall:
The gentle serpent, green in the mulberry bush,
Riots with his tongue through the hush—
Sentinel of the grave who counts us all!

HART CRANE

AND yet this great wing of eternity,
Of rimless floods, unfettered leewardings,
Samite sheeted and processioned where
Her undinal vast belly moonward bends,
Laughing the wrapt inflections of our love;

Take this Sea, whose diapason knells
On scrolls of silver snowy sentences,
The sceptered terror of whose sessions rends
As her demeanors motion well or ill,
All but the pieties of lovers' hands.

And onward, as bells off San Salvador
Salute the crocus lusters of the stars,
In these poinsettia meadows of her tides,—
Adagios of islands, O my Prodigal,
Complete the dark confessions her veins spell.

Mark how her turning shoulders wind the hours,
And hasten while her penniless rich palms
Pass superscription of bent foam and wave,—
Hasten, while they are true,—sleep, death, desire,
Close round one instant in one floating flower.

Bind us in time, O seasons clear, and awe.
O minstrel galleons of Carib fire,
Bequeath us to no earthly shore until
Is answered in the vortex of our grave
The seal's wide spindthrift gaze toward paradise.

Where icy and bright dungeons lift
Of swimmers their lost morning eyes,

And ocean rivers, churning, shift
Green borders under stranger skies,

Steadily as a shell secretes
Its beating leagues of monotone,
Or as many waters trough the sun's
Red kelson past the cape's wet stone;

O rivers mingling toward the sky
And harbor of the phoenix' breast—
My eyes pressed black against the prow,
—Thy derelict and blinded guest

Waiting, afire, what name, unspoke,
I cannot claim: let thy waves rear
More savage than the death of kings,
Some splintered garland for the seer.

Beyond siroccos harvesting
The solstice thunders, crept away,
Like a cliff swinging or a sail
Flung into April's inmost day—

Creation's blithe and petaled word
To the lounged goddess when she rose
Conceding dialogue with eyes
That smile unsearchable repose—

Still fervid convenant, Bell Isle,
—Unfolded floating dais before
Which rainbows twine continual hair—
Bell Isle, white echo of the oar!

The imaged word, it is, that holds
Hushed willows anchored in its glow.
It is the unbetrayable reply
Whose accent no farewell can know.

Praise for an Urn

IT was a kind and northern face
That mingled in such exile guise
The everlasting eyes of Pierrot
And, of Gargantua, the laughter.

His thoughts, delivered to me
From the white coverlet and pillow,
I see now, were inheritances—
Delicate riders of the storm.

The slant moon on the slanting hill
Once moved us toward presentiments
Of what the dead keep, living still,
And such assessments of the soul

As, perched in the crematory lobby,
The insistent clock commented on,
Touching as well upon our praise
Of glories proper to the time.

Still, having in mind gold hair,
I cannot see that broken brow
And miss the dry sound of bees
Stretching across a lucid space.

Scatter these well-meant idioms
Into the smoky spring that fills
The suburbs, where they will be lost.
They are no trophies of the sun.

The River

(FROM "THE BRIDGE")

STICK your patent name on a signboard
brother—all over—going west—young man
Tintex—Japalac—Certain-teed Overalls ads
and lands sakes! under the new playbill ripped
in the guaranteed corner—see Bert Williams what?

Minstrels when you steal a chicken just
save me the wing, for if it isn't
Erie it ain't for miles around a
Mazda—and the telegraphic night coming on Thomas

a Ediford—and whistling down the tracks
a headlight rushing with the sound—can you
imagine—while an EXPRESS makes time like
SCIENCE—COMMERCE and the HOLYGHOST
RADIO ROARS IN EVERY HOME WE HAVE THE NORTHPOLE
WALLSTREET AND VIRGINBIRTH WITHOUT STONES OR
WIRES OR EVEN RUNNing brooks connecting ears
and no more sermons windows flashing roar
Breathtaking—as you like it . . . eh?

                                    So the 20th Century—so
whizzed the Limited—roared by and left
three men, still hungry on the tracks, ploddingly
watching the tail lights wizen and converge, slip-
ping gimleted and neatly out of sight.
The last bear, shot drinking in the Dakotas,
Loped under wires that span the mountain stream.
Keen instruments, strung to a vast precision
Bind town to town and dream to ticking dream.
But some men take their liquor slow—and count
—Though they'll confess no rosary nor clue—
The river's minute by the far brook's year.
Under a world of whistles, wires and steam
Caboose-like they go ruminating through
Ohio, Indiana—blind baggage—
To Cheyenne tagging . . . Maybe Kalamazoo.
Time's renderings, time's blendings they construe
As final reckonings of fire and snow;
Strange bird-wit, like the elemental gist
Of unwalled winds they offer, singing low
My Old Kentucky Home and Casey Jones,
Some Sunny Day. I heard a road-gang chanting so.
And afterwards, who had a colt's eyes—one said,
"Jesus! Oh I remember watermelon days!" And sped
High in a cloud of merriment, recalled
"—And when my Aunt Sally Simpson smiled," he drawled—
"It was almost Louisiana, long ago."

"There's no place like Booneville though, Buddy,'
One said, excising a last burr from his vest,
"—For early trouting." Then peering in the can,
"—But I kept on the tracks." Possessed, resigned,
He trod the fire down pensively and grinned,
Spreading dry shingles of a beard. . . .

Behind
My father's cannery works I used to see
Rail-squatters ranged in nomad raillery,
The ancient men—wifeless or runaway
Hobo-trekkers that forever search
An empire wilderness of freight and rails.
Each seemed a child, like me, on a loose perch,
Holding to childhood like some termless play.
John, Jake, or Charley, hopping the slow freight
—Memphis to Tallahassee—riding the rods,
Blinding fists of nothing, humpty-dumpty clods.

Yet they touch something like a key perhaps.
From pole to pole across the hills, the states
—They know a body under the wide rain;
Youngsters with eyes like fjords, old reprobates
With racetrack jargon,—dotting immensity
They lurk across her, knowing her yonder breast
Snow-silvered, sumac-stained or smoky blue,
Is past the valley-sleepers, south or west.
—As I have trod the rumorous midnights, too.
And past the circuit of the lamp's thin flame
(O Nights that brought me to her body bare!)
Have dreamed beyond the print that bound her **name**.
Trains sounding the long blizzards out—I heard
Wail into distances I knew were hers.
Papooses crying on the wind's long mane
Screamed redskin dynasties that fled the brain,
—Dead echoes! But I knew her body there,
Time like a serpent down her shoulder, dark,
And space, an eaglet's wing, laid on her hair.

Under the Ozarks, domed by Iron Mountain,
The old gods of the rain lie wrapped in pools
Where eyeless fish curvet a sunken fountain

And re-descend with corn from querulous crows.
Such pilferings make up their timeless eatage,
Propitiate them for their timber torn
By iron, iron—always the iron dealt cleavage!
They doze now, below axe and powder horn.

And Pullman breakfasters glide glistening steel
From tunnel into field—iron strides the dew—
Straddles the hill, a dance of wheel on wheel.
You have a half-hour's wait at Siskiyou,
Or stay the night and take the next train through.
Southward, near Cairo passing, you can see
The Ohio merging,—borne down Tennessee;
And if it's summer and the sun's in dusk
Maybe the breeze will lift the River's musk
—As though the waters breathed that you might know
Memphis Johnny, Steamboat Bill, Missouri Joe.
Oh, lean from the window, if the train slows down,
As though you touched hands with some ancient clown,
—A little while gaze absently below
And hum *Deep River* with them while they go.

Yes, turn again and sniff once more—look see,
O Sheriff, Brakeman and Authority—
Hitch up your pants and crunch another quid,
For you, too, feed the River timelessly.

And few evade full measure of their fate;
Always they smile out eerily what they seem.
I could believe he joked at heaven's gate—
Dan Midland—jolted from the cold brake-beam.

Down, down—born pioneers in time's despite,
Grimed tributaries to an ancient flow—
They win no frontier by their wayward plight,
But drift in stillness, as from Jordan's brow.

You will not hear it as the sea; even stone
Is not more hushed by gravity . . . But slow,
As loth to take more tribute—sliding prone
Like one whose eyes were buried long ago

The River, spreading, flows—and spends your dream.
What are you, lost within this tideless spell?
You are your father's father, and the stream—
A liquid theme that floating niggers swell.

Damp tonnage and alluvial march of days—
Nights turbid, vascular with silted shale
And roots surrendered down of moraine clays:
The Mississippi drinks the farthest dale.

O quarrying passion, undertowed sunlight!
The basalt surface drags a jungle grace
Ochreous and lynx-barred in lengthening might;
Patience! and you shall reach the biding place!

Over De Soto's bones the freighted floors
Throb past the City storied of three thrones.
Down two more turns the Mississippi pours
(Anon tall ironsides up from salt lagoons)

And flows within itself, heaps itself free.
All fades but one thin skyline 'round . . . Ahead
No embrace opens but the stinging sea;
The River lifts itself from its long bed,

Poised wholly on its dream, a mustard glow,
Tortured with history, its one will—flow!
—The Passion spreads in wide tongues, choked and slow,
Meeting the Gulf, hosannas silently below.

The Dance

(FROM "THE BRIDGE")

THE swift red flesh, a winter king—
    Who squired the glacier woman down the sky?
She ran the neighing canyons all the spring;
She spouted arms; she rose with maize—to die.

And in the autumn drouth, whose burnished hands
With mineral wariness found out the stone

Where prayers, forgotten, streamed the mesa sands?
He holds the twilight's dim, perpetual throne.

Mythical brows we saw retiring—loth,
Disturbed and destined, into denser green.
Greeting they sped us, on the arrow's oath:
Now lie incorrigibly what years between. . . .

There was a bed of leaves, and broken play;
There was a veil upon you, Pocahontas, bride—
O Princess whose brown lap was virgin May;
And bridal flanks and eyes hid tawny pride.

I left the village for dogwood. By the canoe
Tugging below the mill-race, I could see
Your hair's keen crescent running, and the blue
First moth of evening take wing stealthily.

What laughing chains the water wove and threw!
I learned to catch the trout's moon whisper; I
Drifted how many hours I never knew,
But, watching, saw that fleet young crescent die,—

And one star, swinging, take its place, alone,
Cupped in the larches of the mountain pass—
Until, immortally, it bled into the dawn.
I left my sleek boat nibbling margin grass. . . .

I took the portage climb, then chose
A further valley-shed; I could not stop.
Feet nozzled watery webs of upper flows;
One white veil gusted from the very top.

O Appalachian Spring! I gained the ledge;
Steep, inaccessible smile that eastward bends
And northward reaches in that violet wedge
Of Adirondack!—wisped of azure wands,

Over how many bluffs, tarns, streams I sped!
—And knew myself within some boding shade:
Grey tepees tufting the blue knolls ahead,
Smoke swirling through the yellow chestnut glade. . . .

A distant cloud, a thunder-bud—it grew,
That blanket of the skies: the padded foot
Within,—I hear it; 'til its rhythm drew,
—Siphoned the black pool from the heart's hot root!

A cyclone threshes in the turbine crest,
Swooping in eagle feathers down your back;
Know, Maquokeeta, greeting; know death's best;
—Fall, Sachem, strictly as the tamarack!

A birch kneels. All her whistling fingers fly.
The oak grove circles in a crash of leaves;
The long moan of a dance is in the sky.
Dance, Maquokeeta: Pocahontas grieves. . . .

And every tendon scurries toward the twangs
Of lightning deltaed down your saber hair.
Now snaps the flint in every tooth; red fangs
And splay tongues thinly busy the blue air. . . .

Dance, Maquokeeta! snake that lives before,
That casts his pelt, and lives beyond! Sprout, horn!
Spark, tooth! Medicine-man, relent, restore—
Lie to us—dance us back the tribal morn!

Spears and assemblies: black drums thrusting on—
O yelling battlements,—I, too, was liege
To rainbows currying each pulsant bone:
Surpassed the circumstance, danced out the siege!

And buzzard-circleted, screamed from the stake;
I could not pick the arrows from my side.
Wrapped in that fire, I saw more escorts wake—
Flickering, sprint up the hill, groins like a tide.

I heard the hush of lava wrestling your arms,
And stag teeth foam about the raven throat;
Flame cataracts of heaven in seething swarms
Fed down your anklets to the sunset's moat.

Oh, like the lizard in the furious noon,
That drops his legs and colors in the sun,

—And laughs, pure serpent, Time itself, and moon
Of his own fate, I saw thy change begun!

And saw thee dive to kiss that destiny
Like one white meteor, sacrosanct and blent
At last with all that's consummate and free
There, where the first and last gods keep thy tent.

Thewed of the levin, thunder-shod and lean,
Lo, through what infinite seasons dost thou gaze—
Across what bivouacs of thine angered slain,
And see'st thy bride immortal in the maize!

Totem and fire-gall, slumbering pyramid—
Though other calendars now stack the sky,
Thy freedom is her largesse, Prince, and hid
On paths thou knewest best to claim her by.

High unto Labrador the sun strikes free
Her speechless dream of snow, and stirred again,
She is the torrent and the singing tree;
And she is virgin to the last of men. . . .

West, west and south! winds over Cumberland
And winds across the llano grass resume
Her hair's warm sibilance. Her breasts are fanned—
O stream by slope and vineyard—into bloom!

And when the caribou slant down for salt
Do arrows thirst and leap? Do antlers shine
Alert, star-triggered in the listening vault
Of dusk?—And are her perfect brows to thine?

We danced, O Brave, we danced beyond their farms,
In cobalt desert closures made our vows . . .
Now is the strong prayer folded in thine arms,
The serpent with the eagle in the boughs.

Indiana

(FROM "THE BRIDGE")

. . . and read her in a mother's farewell gaze.

THE morning-glory, climbing the morning long
   Over the lintel on its wiry vine,
Closes before the dusk, furls in its song
    As I close mine . . .

And bison thunder rends my dreams no more
   As once my womb was torn, my boy, when you
Yielded your first cry at the prairie's door . . .
    Your father knew

Then, though we'd buried him behind us, far
   Back on the gold trail—then his lost bones stirred . . .
But you who drop the scythe to grasp the oar
    Knew not, nor heard.

How we, too, Prodigal, once rode off, too—
   Waved Seminary Hill a gay good-bye . . .
We found God lavish there in Colorado
    But passing sly.

The pebbles sang, the firecat slunk away
   And glistening through the sluggard freshets came
In golden syllables loosed from the clay
    His gleaming name.

A dream called Eldorado was his town,
   It rose up shambling in the nuggets' wake,
It had no charter but a promised crown
    Of claims to stake.

But we,—too late, too early, howsoever—
   Won nothing out of fifty-nine—those years—
But gilded promise, yielded to us never,
    And barren tears . . .

The long trail back! I huddled in the shade
  Of wagon-tenting looked out once and saw
Bent westward, passing on a stumbling jade
      A homeless squaw—

Perhaps a halfbreed. On her slender back
  She cradled a babe's body, riding without rein.
Her eyes, strange for an Indian's, were not black
      But sharp with pain

And like twin stars. They seemed to shun the gaze
  Of all our silent men—the long team line—
Until she saw me—when their violet haze
      Lit with love shine . . .

I held you up—I suddenly the bolder,
  Knew that mere words could not have brought us nearer.
She nodded—and that smile across her shoulder
      Will still endear her

As long as Jim, your father's memory, is warm.
  Yes, Larry, now you're going to sea, remember
You were the first—before Ned and this farm,—
      First-born, remember—

And since then—all that's left to me of Jim
  Whose folks, like mine, came out of Arrowhead.
And you're the only one with eyes like him—
      Kentucky bred!

I'm standing still, I'm old, I'm half of stone!
  Oh, hold me in those eyes' engaging blue;
There's where the stubborn years gleam and atone,—
      Where gold is true!

Down the dim turnpike to the river's edge—
  Perhaps I'll hear the mare's hoofs to the ford . . .
Write me from Rio . . . and you'll keep your pledge;
      I know your word!

Come back to Indiana—not too late!
  (Or will you be a ranger to the end?)

Good-bye . . . Good-bye . . . oh, I shall always wait
 You, Larry, traveller—
                        stranger,
                        son,
                                —my friend—

Atlantis

(FROM "THE BRIDGE")

*Music is then the knowledge of that which relates to
love in harmony and system.*
                                        —*Plato*

THROUGH the bound cable strands, the arching path
   Upward, veering with light, the flight of strings,—
Taut miles of shuttling moonlight syncopate
The whispered rush, telepathy of wires.
Up the index of night, granite and steel—
Transparent meshes—fleckless the gleaming staves—
Sibylline voices flicker, waveringly stream
As though a god were issue of the strings. . . .

And through that cordage, threading with its call
One arc synoptic of all tides below—
Their labyrinthine mouths of history
Pouring reply as though all ships at sea
Complighted in one vibrant breath made cry,—
"Make thy love sure—to weave whose song we ply!"
—From black embankments, moveless soundings hailed,
So seven oceans answer from their dream.

And on, obliquely up bright carrier bars
New octaves trestle the twin monoliths
Beyond whose frosted capes the moon bequeaths
Two worlds of sleep (O arching strands of song!)—
Onward and up the crystal-flooded aisle
White tempest nets file upward, upward ring
With silver terraces the humming spars,
The loft of vision, palladium helm of stars.

Sheerly the eyes, like seagulls stung with rime—
Slit and propelled by glistening fins of light—

Pick biting way up towering looms that press
Sidelong with flight of blade on tendon blade
—Tomorrows into yesteryear—and link
What cipher-script of time no traveller reads
But who, through smoking pyres of love and death,
Searches the timeless laugh of mythic spears.

Like hails, farewells—up planet-sequined heights
Some trillion whispering hammers glimmer Tyre:
Serenely, sharply up the long anvil cry
Of inchling æons silence rivets Troy.
And you, aloft there—Jason! hesting Shout!
Still wrapping harness to the swarming air!
Silvery the rushing wake, surpassing call,
Beams yelling Æolus! splintered in the straits!

From gulfs unfolding, terrible of drums,
Tall Vision-of-the-Voyage, tensely spare—
Bridge, lifting night to cycloramic crest
Of deepest day—O choir, translating time
Into what multitudinous Verb the suns
And synergy of waters ever fuse, recast
In myriad syllables,—Psalm of Cathay!
O Love, thy white, pervasive Paradigm . . . !

We left the haven hanging in the night—
Sheened harbor lanterns backward fled the keel.
Pacific here at time's end, bearing corn,—
Eyes stammer through the pangs of dust and steel.
And still the circular, indubitable frieze
Of heaven's meditation, yoking wave
To kneeling wave, one song devoutly binds—
The vernal strophe chimes from deathless strings!

O Thou steeled Cognizance whose leap commits
The agile precincts of the lark's return;
Within whose lariat sweep encinctured sing
In single chrysalis the many twain,—
Of stars Thou art the stitch and stallion glow
And like an organ, Thou, with sound of doom—
Sight, sound and flesh Thou leadest from time's realm
As love strikes clear direction for the helm.

Swift peal of secular light, intrinsic Myth
Whose fell unshadow is death's utter wound,—
O River-throated—iridescently upborne
Through the bright drench and fabric of our veins;
With white escarpments swinging into light,
Sustained in tears the cities are endowed
And justified conclamant with ripe fields
Revolving through their harvests in sweet torment.
Forever Deity's glittering Pledge, O Thou

Whose canticle fresh chemistry assigns
To rapt inception and beatitude,—
Always through blinding cables, to our joy,
Of thy white seizure springs the prophecy:
Always through spiring cordage, pyramids
Of silver sequel, Deity's young name
Kinetic of white choiring wings . . . ascends.

Migrations that must needs void memory,
Inventions that cobblestone the heart,—
Unspeakable Thou Bridge to Thee, O Love.
Thy pardon for this history, whitest Flower,
O Answerer of all,—Anemone,—
Now while thy petals spend the suns about us, hold—
(O Thou whose radiance doth inherit me)
Atlantis,—hold thy floating singer late!

So to thine Everpresence, beyond time,
Like spears ensanguined of one tolling star
That bleeds infinity—the orphic strings,
Sidereal phalanxes, leap and converge:
—One Song, one Bridge of Fire! Is it Cathay,
Now pity steeps the grass and rainbows ring
The serpent with the eagle in the leaves . . . ?
Whispers antiphonal in azure swing.

OSCAR WILLIAMS

The Man Coming Toward You

THE man coming toward you is falling forward on all fronts:
　　He has just come in from the summer hot box of circumstance,
His obedient arm pulls a ticket from the ticket machine,
A bell announces to the long tables his presence on the scene;
The room is crowded with Last Suppers and the air is angry;
The halleluiahs lift listless heads; the man is hungry.

He looks at the people, the rings of lights, the aisles, the chairs,
They mass and attack his eyes and they take him unawares,
But in a moment it is over and the immense hippopotamus cries
And swims away to safety in the vast past of his eyes;
The weeks recoil before the days, the years before the months;
The man is hungry and keeps moving forward on all fronts.

His hair is loosening, his teeth are at bay, he breathes fear,
His nails send futile tendrils into the belly of the atmosphere;
Every drop of his blood is hanging loose in the universe;
His children's faces everywhere bring down the college doors;
He is growing old on all fronts; his foes and his friends
Are bleeding behind invisible walls bedecked with dividends;

His wife is aging, and his skin puts on its anonymous gloves;
The man is helpless, surrounded by two billion hates and loves;
Look at him squirm inside his clothes, the harpies around his ears,
In just one minute his brothers will have aged four thousand years.
Who records his stupendous step on the delicate eardrum of Chance?
The man coming toward you is marching forward on all fronts.

The Leg in the Subway

WHEN I saw the woman's leg on the floor of the subway train,
　　Protrude beyond the panel (while her body overflowed my
mind's eye),

When I saw the pink stocking, black shoe, curve bulging with
    warmth,
The delicate etching of the hair behind the flesh-colored gauze,
When I saw the ankle of Mrs. Nobody going nowhere for a nickel,
When I saw this foot motionless on the moving motionless floor, .
My mind caught on a nail of a distant star, I was wrenched out
Of the reality of the subway ride, I hung in a socket of distance:
And this is what I saw:

The long tongue of the earth's speed was licking the leg,
Upward and under and around went the long tongue of speed:
It was made of a flesh invisible, it dripped the saliva of miles:
It drank moment, lit shivers of insecurity in niches between bones:
It was full of eyes, it stopped licking to look at the passengers:
It was as alive as a worm, and busier than anybody in the train:

It spoke saying: To whom does this leg belong? Is it a bonus leg
For the rush hour? Is it a forgotten leg? Among the many
Myriads of legs did an extra leg fall in from the Out There?
O Woman, sliced off bodily by the line of the panel, shall I roll
Your leg into the abdominal nothing, among the digestive teeth?
Or shall I fit it in with the pillars that hold up the headlines?
But nobody spoke, though all the faces were talking silently,
As the train zoomed, a zipper closing up swiftly the seam of time.

Alas, said the long tongue of the speed of the earth quite faintly,
What is one to do with an incorrigible leg that will not melt—
But everybody stopped to listen to the train vomiting cauldrons
Of silence, while somebody's jolted-out afterthought trickled down
The blazing shirt-front solid with light bulbs, and just then
The planetary approach of the next station exploded atoms of light,
And when the train stopped, the leg had grown a surprising mate,
And the long tongue had slipped hurriedly out through a window:

I perceived through the hole left by the nail of the star in my mind
How civilization was as dark as a wood and dimensional with things
And how birds dipped in chromium sang in the crevices of our deeds.

ROBERT PENN WARREN

Bearded Oaks

THE oaks, how subtle and marine,
Bearded, and all the layered light
Above them swims; and thus the scene,
Recessed, awaits the positive night.

So, waiting, we in the grass now lie
Beneath the langorous tread of light:
The grasses, kelp-like, satisfy
The nameless motions of the air.

Upon the floor of light, and time,
Unmurmuring, of polyp made
We rest; we are, as light withdraws,
Twin atolls on a shelf of shade.

Ages to our construction went,
Dim architecture, hour by hour:
And violence, forgot now, lent
The present stillness all its power.

The storm of noon above us rolled,
Of light the fury, furious gold,
The long drag troubling us, the depth:
Dark is unrocking, unrippling, still.

Passion and slaughter, ruth, decay
Descend, minutely whispering down,
Silted down swaying streams, to lay
Foundation for our voicelessness.

All our debate is voiceless here,
As all our rage, the rage of stone;
If hope is hopeless, then fearless fear,
And history is thus undone.

Our feet once wrought the hollow street
With echo when the lamps were dead
At windows, once our headlight glare
Disturbed the doe that, leaping, fled.

I do not love you less that now
The caged heart makes iron stroke,
Or less that all that light once gave
The graduate dark should now revoke.

We live in time so little time
And we learn all so painfully,
That we may spare this hour's term
To practice for eternity.

Revelation

BECAUSE he had spoken harshly to his mother,
The day became astonishingly bright,
The enormity of distance crept to him like a dog now,
And earth's own luminescence seemed to repel the night.

Roof was rent like the loud paper tearing to admit
Sun-sulphurous splendor where had been before
But the submarine glimmer by kindly countenances lit,
As slow, phosphorescent dignities light the ocean floor.

By walls, by walks, chrysanthemum and aster,
All hairy, fat-petalled species, lean, confer,
And his ears, and heart, should burn at that insidious whisper
Which concerns him so, he knows; but he cannot make out the
    words.

The peacock screamed, and his feathered fury made
Legend shake, all day, while the sky ran pale as milk;
That night, all night, the buck rabbit stamped in the moonlit glade,
And the owl's brain glowed like a coal in the grove's combustible
    dark.

When Sulla smote and Rome was rent, Augustine
Recalled how Nature, shuddering, tore her gown,

And kind changed kind, and the blunt herbivorous tooth dripped
    blood;
At Duncan's death, at Dunsinane, chimneys blew down.

But, oh! his mother was kinder than ever Rome,
Dearer than Duncan—no wonder, then, Nature's frame
Thrilled in voluptuous hemispheres far off from his home;
But not in terror: only as the bride, as the bride.

In separateness only does love learn definition,
Though Brahma smiles beneath the dappled shade,
Though tears, that night, wet the pillow where the boy's head was
    laid
Dreamless of splendid antipodal agitation;

And though across what tide and tooth Time is,
He was to lean back toward that recalcitrant face,
He would think, than Sulla more fortunate, how once he had learned
Something important about love, and about love's grace.

KENNETH PATCHEN

At the New Year

IN the shape of this night, in the still fall of snow, Father
    In all that is cold and tiny, these little birds and children
In everything that moves tonight, the trolleys and the lovers, Father
In the great hush of country, in the ugly noise of our cities
In this deep throw of stars, in those trenches where the dead are,
    Father
In all the wide land waiting, and in the liners out on the black water
In all that has been said bravely, in all that is mean anywhere in the
    world, Father
In all that is good and lovely, in every house where sham and hatred
    are
In the name of those who wait, in the sound of angry voices, Father
Before the bells ring, before this little point in time has rushed us on
Before this clean moment has gone, before this night turns to face
    tomorrow, Father

There is this high singing in the air
Forever this sorrowful human face in eternity's window
And there are other bells that we would ring, Father
Other bells that we would ring.

DELMORE SCHWARTZ

"Mentrechè il Vento, Come Fa, Si Tace"

WILL you perhaps consent to be
 Now that a little while is still
(Ruth of sweet wind) now that a little while
My mind's continuing and unreleasing wind
Touches this single of your flowers, this one only,
Will you perhaps consent to be
My many-branchéd, small and dearest tree?

My mind's continuing and unreleasing wind
—The wind which is wild and restless, tired and asleep,
The wind which is tired, wild and still continuing,
The wind which is chill, and warm, wet, soft, in every influence,
Lusts for Paris, Crete and Pergamus,
Is suddenly off for Paris and Chicago,
Judaea, San Francisco, the Midi,
—May I perhaps return to you
Wet with an Attic dust and chill from Norway
My dear, so-many-branchéd smallest tree?

Would you perhaps consent to be
The very rack and crucifix of winter, winter's wild
Knife-edged, continuing and unreleasing,
Intent and stripping, ice-caressing wind?
My dear, most dear, so-many-branchéd smallest tree
My mind's continuing and unreleasing wind
Touches this single of your flowers, faith in me,
Wide as the—sky!—accepting as the (air)!
—Consent, consent, consent to be
My many-branchéd, small and dearest tree.

Socrates' Ghost Must Haunt Me Now

SOCRATES' ghost must haunt me now,
　Notorious death has let him go,
He comes to me with a clumsy bow,
Saying in his disuséd voice,
That I do not know I do not know,
The mechanical whims of appetite
Are all that I have of conscious choice,
The butterfly caged in electric light
Is my only day in the world's great night,
Love is not love, it is a child
Sucking his thumb and biting his lip,
But grasp it all, there may be more!
From the topless sky to the bottomless floor
With the heavy head and the finger tip:
All is not blind, obscene, and poor.
Socrates stands by me stockstill,
Teaching hope to my flickering will,
Pointing to the sky's inexorable blue
—Old Noumenon, come true, come true!

RICHARD EBERHART

The Groundhog

IN June, amid the golden fields,
　I saw a groundhog lying dead.
Dead lay he; my senses shook,
And mind outshot our naked frailty.
There lowly in the vigorous summer
His form began its senseless change,
And made my senses waver dim
Seeing nature ferocious in him.
Inspecting close his maggots' might
And seething cauldron of his being,

Half with loathing, half with a strange love,
I poked him with an angry stick.
The fever arose, became a flame
And Vigour circumscribed the skies,
Immense energy in the sun,
And through my frame a sunless trembling.
My stick had done nor good nor harm.
Then stood I silent in the day
Watching the object, as before;
And kept my reverence for knowledge
Trying for control, to be still,
To quell the passion of the blood;
Until I had bent down on my knees
Praying for joy in the sight of decay.
And so I left; and I returned
In Autumn strict of eye, to see
The sap gone out of the groundhog,
But the bony sodden hulk remained.
But the year had lost its meaning,
And in intellectual chains
I lost both love and loathing,
Mured up in the wall of wisdom.
Another summer took the fields again
Massive and burning, full of life,
But when I chanced upon the spot
There was only a little hair left,
And bones bleaching in the sunlight
Beautiful as architecture;
I watched them like a geometer,
And cut a walking stick from a birch.
It has been three years, now.
There is no sign of the groundhog.
I stood there in the whirling summer,
My hand capped a withered heart,
And thought of China and of Greece,
Of Alexander in his tent;
Of Montaigne in his tower,
Of Saint Theresa in her wild lament.

KARL JAY SHAPIRO

Poet

Il arrive que l'esprit demande la poesie

LEFT leg flung out, head cocked to the right,
    Tweed coat or army uniform, with book,
Beautiful eyes, who is this walking down?
Who, glancing at the pane of glass looks sharp
And thinks it is not he—as when a poet
Comes swiftly on some half-forgotten poem
And loosely holds the page, steady of mind,
        Thinking it is not his?

And when will *you* exist?—Oh, it is I,
Incredibly skinny, stooped, and neat as pie,
Ignorant as dirt, erotic as an ape,
Dreamy as puberty—with dirty hair!
Into the room like kangaroo he bounds,
Ears flopping like the most expensive hound's;
His chin received all questions as he bows
        Mouthing a green bon-bon.

Has no more memory than rubber. Stands
Waist-deep in heavy mud of thought and broods
At his own wetness. When he would get out,
To his surprise he lifts in air a phrase
As whole and clean and silvery as a fish.
Which jumps and dangles on his damned hooked grin,
But like a name-card on a man's lapel
        Calls him a conscious fool.

And childlike he remembers all his life
And cannily constructs it, fact by fact,
As boys paste postage stamps in careful books,
Denoting pence and legends and profiles,

Nothing more valuable.—And like a thief,
His eyes glassed over and concealed with guilt,
Fondles his secrets like a case of tools,
    And waits in empty doors.

By men despised for knowing what he is,
And by himself. But he exists for women.
As dolls to girls, as perfect wives to men,
So he to women. And to himself a thing,
All ages, epicene, without a trade.
To girls and wives always alive and fated;
To men and scholars always dead like Greek
    And always mistranslated.

Towards exile and towards shame he lures himself,
Tongue winding on his arm, and thinks like Eve
By biting apple will become most wise.
Sentio ergo sum: he feels his way
And words themselves stand up for him like Braille
And punch and perforate his parchment ear.
All language falls like Chinese on his soul,
    Image of song unsounded.

This is the coward's coward that in his dreams
Sees shapes of pain grow tall. Awake at night
He peers at sounds and stumbles at a breeze.
And none holds life less dear. For as a youth
Who by some accident observes his love
Naked and in some natural ugly act,
He turns with loathing and with flaming hands,
    Seared and betrayed by sight.

He is the business man, on beauty trades,
Dealer in arts and thoughts who, like the Jew,
Shall rise from slums and hated dialects
A tower of bitterness. Shall be always strange,
Hunted and then sought after. Shall be sat
Like an ambassador from another race
At tables rich with music. He shall eat flowers,
Chew honey and spit out gall. They shall all smile
    And love and pity him.

His death shall be by drowning. In that hour
When the last bubble of pure heaven's air
Hovers within his throat, safe on his bed,
A small eternal figurehead in terror,
He shall cry out and clutch his days of straw
Before the blackest wave. Lastly, his tomb
Shall list and founder in the troughs of grass.
        And none shall speak his name.

The Twins

LIKENESS has made them animal and shy.
    See how they turn their full gaze left and right,
Seeking the other, yet not moving close;
Nothing in their relationship is gross,
But soft, conspicuous, like giraffes. And why
Do they not speak except by sudden sight?

Sisters kiss freely and unsubtle friends
Wrestle like lovers; brothers loudly laugh:
These in a dreamier bondage dare not touch.
Each is the other's soul and hears too much
The heartbeat of the other; each apprehends
The sad duality and the imperfect half.

The one lay sick, the other wandered free,
But like a child to a small plot confined
Walked a short way and dumbly reappeared.
Is it not all-in-all of what they feared,
The single death, the obvious destiny
That maims the miracle their will designed?

For they go emptily from face to face,
Keeping the instinctive partnership of birth
A ponderous marriage and a sacred name;
Theirs is the pride of shouldering each the same
The old indignity of Esau's race
And Dromio's denouement of tragic mirth.

Travelogue for Exiles

LOOK and remember. Look upon this sky;
    Look deep and deep into the sea-clean air,
The unconfined, the terminus of prayer.
Speak now and speak into the hallowed dome.
What do you hear? What does the sky reply?
The heavens are taken: this is not your home.

Look and remember. Look upon this sea;
Look down and down into the tireless tide.
What of a life below, a life inside,
A tomb, a cradle in the curly foam?
The waves arise; sea-wind and sea agree
The waters are taken: this is not your home.

Look and remember. Look upon this land,
Far, far across the factories and the grass.
Surely, there, surely, they will let you pass.
Speak then and ask the forest and the loam.
What do you hear? What does the land command?
The earth is taken: this is not your home.

Nostalgia

MY soul stands at the window of my room,
    And I ten thousand miles away;
My days are filled with Ocean's sound of doom,
    Salt and cloud and the bitter spray.
Let the wind blow, for many a man shall die.

My selfish youth, my books with gilded edge,
    Knowledge and all gaze down the street;
The potted plants upon the window ledge
    Gaze down with selfish lives and sweet,
Let the wind blow, for many a man shall die.

My night is now her day, my day her night,
    So I lie down, and so I rise;

The sun burns close, the star is losing height,
    The clock is hunted down the skies.
Let the wind blow, for many a man shall die.

Truly a pin can make the memory bleed,
    A world explode the inward mind
And turn the skulls and flowers never freed
    Into the air, no longer blind.
Let the wind blow, for many a man shall die.

Laughter and grief join hands. Always the heart
    Clumps in the breast with heavy stride;
The face grows lined and wrinkled like a chart,
    The eyes bloodshot with tears and tide.
Let the wind blow, for many a man shall die.

JOHN MALCOLM BRINNIN

Islands: A Song

ISLANDS are subtle places, still,
    Lonely and shining;
Islands of grief refuse to tell
Their separating difference ever;
Feudally they stand, nor cry
"I wait for your discovery!"
    Breakers go over,
    Sympathy never.

Furious my island city,
    Treeless and steepled,
Ample its flashing pity,
Touchable, eager, sweet to wear;
Come, lover, to your radio,
Put fingers to your wrist-veins, so:
    Sea-parted, share
    This quickening fear.

LLOYD FRANKENBERG

The Sea

IN the midmost of ocean
  the water lifts its arms dreaming of spars;
the world is very round, projects its roundness
past all the poles, beyond the one horizon
on that bald ocean overhead, the sky
where swim the worlds like fish in soundless waters.

Imposing its single structure on the sky
and drawing thence its variable mood
of bright confusion, gloom and equable
conformity, the ocean goes scotfree
of other obligation but to pay
the moon its due respects, discharged like spouse.

Left to its own enormous devices the sea
in timeless reverie conceives of life,
being itself the world in pantomime.

Predicting past and future in one long
drawn breath it blends its tides with dawn,
rolls in panoramic sleight-of-hand
creation out of chaos endlessly;

all forms revealed in fluid architecture
flowing like time as if time were turned back:
undreamed-of wars all happening at once
(what rage pent up in atoms: do the drops
take toll of one another? no the sea
had not dreamed this)

                         but like a savage plays
archaic symmetries and simple shapes:
builds promontories, houses lakes, holds out
mirages of itself, erects straw cliffs
hurdled with ease;

or lolling all its length
coiled and Niled, in coat of mail tilts evil
complete with scale and hiss, smitten to sculpture,
to iron leaves, to flame, to birds flying
in and out of fluted, spandreled, spired
buildings out of all time swaying, crumpling
in scaffoldings of spray.

And then the flowers
all petal and no stem; then finned and ferned,
the leaping swordfish an effrontery
to all its backs, all life presumptuous
and those looking too long upon its wake
who thought to make themselves immortal too,
taking it at its word, instruct it now

(old moonface cratered and sunksocketed,
seamywrinkled, picked and pocked with waves,
the waves all faces lifted looking around,
hair dripping across their foreheads or flung back
for a last despairing gasp before they drown)

for now the last least vestige of the air
that gave the ocean its free hand with space,
gave fins wings roots and legs to walk the sky,
withdraws and leaves it still.

Now on its sleeve
it wears the heart that every shipwreck finds;
lies flat, unworked by other element

and in this state of utter unbelief
that keeps it what it is, like nothing else,
smoother than glass, stiller than the dead,
its natural supine and spineless self
that never will arise but from without
(yet even now protests the least intrusion)

believing not that all its mimicry
has ever come to pass, how perfectly
mirrors God's face, the workings of his mind.

Hide in the Heart

I

HERE is no shadow but cloudshadow and nightshadow
     Moving across and rolling away and leaving
Only the purple avenues the ant
Drags his weight across from here to there
Between the leaning towers of his town.

Here are no voices but the gull's hard lot
Easing his discontent with all the beach,
Abusive tongues of terns, rheumatic crows'
Dry commentaries concerning tomorrow's weather
And pipers fleeing the sound of their own lament.

And the wind's singing is before all music
Picking the strings of grass and thumping the roof
And all the stops of the ocean to be pulled out
When anger is the howling of the wind
And all armies the marches of the sea.

And mornings bringing the white lies of peace,
The rags of truce upon the sea and sky,
Ambassadorial breeze from cloud to wave,
All solved and settled under a smiling sun
Blandly agreeing his hands to everything.

Until the fog with sidelong stratagem
Confers in huddled whispers with the earth—
And ships and birds are asking their way about
Of the whistling buoy that keeps its courage up
Through the long dark and vistas of the mist—

Then lifts again, its mission otherwhere
And leaves us this again our isle of quiet:
Surrounded with seas of grass and the glassy sea
Here in the sweet unreasonable weather
We think us safe, we think us housed in peace.

II

All day the storm stood off from about our door.
The tongues of sand lay panting in the sun,
We listening to the sounds of listless water
With wisps of ragtime over the dunes from town
And scraps of headline: BOMBING ALMERIA.

Who brought this newspaper in like contraband
To poison the horizons of our minds?
All day the sun was stored serenity
Before the cloud fulfilled its promised rain.
Now seeing the fire-edged cloud our thought is of war.

Our sea was water where we drowned our thoughts.
We plunged and lay like time—not like this time.
Our sea was not an endless belt of bullets
Round after round transmitted to the breech
To riddle time to tatters and red teeth.

Now more than ever we do not know how long
This little space of peace will be our own.
The nations run like nightmare toward the repeated
Dream's end and beyond the end and beyond,
Toward the waking up screaming and it's true! it's true!

III

Nations perpetuate the fatal motion
Letting their anger go from them with no
Power to retract, to make amends and an end.
The people standing under the balconies
Look up and become part of what they see.

The cannon standing at stiff-armed salute
Discharge their duties in the innocent air.
The bleak and bankrupt bones are all there is
To pay revenge its dividend and hate
Its pebble dropped, its circle widening.

IV

There is no hiding in these island seas.
The air is full of forebodings of disaster

The gulls come up dead on the tide. It is one to them
Whether the world hold fish. The sandfleas dance
Burning alive on the phosphorescent beach.

The stars are a regiment of fixed bayonets;
The steelgrey seas a rank upon rank of helmets.
Clouds march and countermarch. Winds marshal them;
Roll on their spokes guncarriages of thunder.
The army of grass is led in all directions.

A large drop falls and that is all. The storm
Wheels to the skyline; leaves a sunspace; waits.
These little silly bombardments are but a device
To larger ends; rally the peace-protectors
About false standards, his eye upon another.

V

All day the storm stood off in a rift of cloud.
We thought us safe, we thought us housed in peace,
Ringed in by sun, chalked off by grass, passed by
In a lull of the storm, in a quiet isle. Till night
Darkened our door and the storm broke and the sea

Moving in fury upon the enduring beach
We put our windows against the rain, we drew
Bolts on the wind and shuttered out the storm.
At night the four walls shook like a heart in the gale
Shedding a light like blood on the troubled darkness.

Four walls in the wind are the wind's mouse and we
The heart in the mouse. The lightning lifts a paw,
Purrs in its throat and lets the paw fall slack.
The tail of the wind stirs lazily, shakes the floor
And we are alone with the taste of mouth on mouth.

VI

Hide in the heart. There is no help without.
The strong winds ramp about the world tonight.
The heart is wide enough to move about.
The heart is tall. In a world too small for flight
This is the only border out of doubt.

The light comes in as through the hand's devotion.
The world is held in the hollow of this hand.
Its own sea with its own moon-made motion
Rolls upon the shores of its own land.
Before all singing is the music of this ocean.

Find out this music pounding through the wrists.
Stop out the sounds of the feet tramping the roof.
Let the rain beat with all its mailed fists.
The heart is the only timber to be proof
Against all thunderclaps and lightningtwists.

Hide in this roof until the storm has been;
Till fear leaves us under the eaves of the blood
And one by one arising let them in
Disarming at the door the roaring flood,
The infantry of rain and the strong wind.

JOSÉ GARCIA VILLA

Be Beautiful, Noble, Like the Antique Ant

BE beautiful, noble, like the antique ant,
　Who bore the storms as he bore the sun,
Wearing neither gown nor helmet,
Though he was archbishop and soldier:
Wore only his own flesh.

Salute characters with gracious dignity:
Though what these are is left to
Your own terms. Exact: the universe is
Not so small but these will be found
Somewhere. Exact: they will be found.

Speak with great moderation: but think
With great fierceness, burning passion:
Though what the ant thought

No annals reveal, nor his descendants
Break the seal.

Trace the tracelessness of the ant,
Every ant has reached this perfection.
As he comes, so he goes,
Flowing as water flows,
Essential but secret like a rose.

God Said, "I Made a Man"

GOD said, "I made a man
Out of clay—
But so bright he, he spun
Himself to brightest Day

Till he was all shining gold,
And oh,
He was lovely to behold!
But in his hands held he a bow

Aimed at me who created
Him. And I said,
'Wouldst murder me
Who am thy Fountainhead!'

Then spoke he the man of gold:
'I will not
Murder thee: I do but
Measure thee. Hold

Thy peace!' And this I did.
But I was curious
Of this so regal head.
'Give thy name!'—'Sir! Genius.'"

Now, If You Will Look in My Brain

NOW, if you will look in my brain
You will see not Because
But Cause—

The strict Rose whose clean
Light utters all my pain.
Dwelleth there my God
With a strict Rod
And a most luminous mien.
And He whippeth! lo how
He whippeth! O see
The rod's velocity
In utterest unmercy
Carve, inflict upon this brow
The majesty of its doomèd Now

My Mouth Is Very Quiet

MY mouth is very quiet
Reverencing the luminance of my brain:
If words must find an outlet
They must work with jewelled pain.

They must cut a way immaculate
To leave the brain incorrupt:
They must repay their Debt
Like archangels undropt.

The miracle of a word is to my mouth
The miracle of God in my brain:
Archangels holding to His North and South,
His East and West by an inviolable chain.

An archangel upon my mouth
May blow his silver trumpet:
But he holds to his North or South
Blows—and again is quiet.

The Way My Ideas Think Me

THE way my ideas think me
Is the way I unthink God.
As in the name of heaven I make hell
That is the way the Lord says me.

And all is adventure and danger
And I roll Him off cliffs and mountains
But fast as I am to push Him off
Fast am I to reach Him below.

And it may be then His turn to push me off,
I wait breathless for that terrible second:
And if He push me not, I turn around in anger:
"O art thou the God I would have!"

Then He pushes me and I plunge down, down!
And when He comes to help me up
I put my arms around Him, saying, "Brother,
Brother." . . . This is the way we are.

Saw God Dead but Laughing

SAW God dead but laughing.
Uttered the laugh for Him.
Heard my skull crack with doom
Tragedian laughing!

Peered into the cracked skull—
Saw the tragic monkhood
In the shape of God's deathhead
Laughter upon its mouth a jewel.

Jewel bright, O Jewel bright,
Laughter of the Lord.
Laughter with eternity immured
O laugh bright, laugh bright.

Then did the Lord laugh louder
I laughing for Him,
I from the heart's honeycomb
Feeding braver, braver,

Till all the universe was Laughter
But the Laughter of the Lord
O the Laughter of His Word
That could laugh only—after His murder.

INDEX OF POETS

ACKNOWLEDGMENTS

FOR the right to reprint the copyrighted poems in this volume, the editors are indebted to the following poets, agents and publishers:

Mrs. George Bambridge for "Danny Deever," "The Ballad of East and West," "The Last Chantey" and "Jobson's Amen" by Rudyard Kipling.

R. P. Blackmur for "Half-Tide Ledge," "Scarabs for the Living" (Nos. I–IX) by R. P. Blackmur.

Brandt & Brandt for "Love Is More Thicker Than Forget," "My Father Moved Through Dooms of Love," "As Freedom Is a Breakfast-food," "Always Before Your Voice My Soul" from *Fifty Poems* by E. E. Cummings, published by Duell, Sloan & Pearce, copyright, 1939, 1940, by E. E. Cummings; "What Lips My Lips Have Kissed" from *The Harpweaver and Other Poems,* published by Harper & Brothers, copyright, 1920, by Edna St. Vincent Millay and "Elegy Before Death" from *Second April,* published by Harper & Brothers, copyright, 1920, by Edna St. Vincent Millay.

Chatto & Windus "Strange Meeting," "Dulce et Decorum Est," "Anthem for Doomed Youth" by Wilfred Owen.

Citizens Fidelity Bank and Trust Company of Louisville, Ky. for "Chanson of the Bells of Oseney" by Cale Young Rice.

Malcolm Cowley for "The Long Voyage" by Malcolm Cowley.

Dial Press, Inc. for "Mazeppa," "The Zebras," "On Some South African Novelists" by Roy Campbell.

Dodd, Mead & Company, Inc. for "Lepanto" by G. K. Chesterton; "The Soldier," "Heaven," "The Dead" by Rupert Brooke.

Doubleday, Doran and Company, Inc., for "Danny Deever," "The Ballad of East and West" from *Departmental Ditties* by Rudyard Kipling, copyright, 1899, by Rudyard Kipling, reprinted by permission of Mrs. Bambridge and Doubleday, Doran and Company, Inc., "The Last Chantey" from *A Diversity of Creatures* by Rudyard Kipling, copyright, 1904, by Rudyard Kipling, reprinted by permission of Mrs. Bambridge and Doubleday, Doran and Company, Inc., "Jobson's Amen" from *Seven Seas* by Rudyard Kipling, copyright, 1896, by Rudyard Kipling, reprinted by permission of Mrs. Bambridge and Doubleday, Doran and Company, Inc.; "Elegy for Mr. Goodbeare" from *England Reclaimed* by Osbert Sitwell, reprinted by permission of Doubleday, Doran and Company, Inc.

Farrar & Rinehart, Inc., for "The Sea," "Hide in the Heart" from *The Red Kite* by Lloyd Frankenberg.

John Gould Fletcher for "Irradiations I–VI," "Green Symphony," "White Symphony" by John Gould Fletcher.

Harcourt, Brace and Company, Inc., "Four Preludes on Playthings of the Wind," "Jazz Fantasia" from *Smoke and Steel* by Carl Sandburg, copyright, 1920, by Harcourt, Brace and Company, Inc.; "Long Feud" from *Burning Bush* by Louis Untermeyer, copyright, 1928, by Harcourt, Brace and Company, Inc.; "Sweeney Among the Nightingales," "The Love Song of J. Alfred Prufrock," "Gerontion," "Burnt Norton," "Ash Wednesday" from *Collected Poems of T. S. Eliot,* copyright, 1936, by Harcourt, Brace and Company, Inc.

Henry Holt and Company, Inc. for Poems II, VII, XII, XIII, XLVIII, LII, LIV from *A Shropshire Lad* and "The Oracles," "Fancy's Knell" from *Last Poems* by A. E. Housman; "Gone" from *Chicago Poems* and "Cool Tombs" from *Cornhuskers* by Carl Sandburg; "No Faith," "His Trees," "Exaggerator," "The Whisper" by Mark Van Doren; "Desert Places," "Bereft," "For Once, Then Something," "Once by the Pacific," "The Telephone," "The Road Not Taken," "My November Guest," "Home Burial," "The Sound of the Trees," "Hyla Brook," "Mowing," "To Earthward," "Fire and Ice," "Stopping by Woods on a Snowy Evening" by Robert Frost; "The Listeners," "All That's Past," "The Scribe," "An Epitaph" by Walter de la Mare; "I Heard a Soldier," "Old Anchor Chanty" by Herbert Trench.

Houghton Mifflin Company for "The Battle-Hymn of the Republic" by Julia Ward Howe; "Five Lives" by E. R. Sill; "Memory," "Enamored Architect of Airy Rhyme" by T. B. Aldrich. "The Eternal Goodness," "Ichabod," "My Playmate" by John Greenleaf Whittier; "The Last Leaf" by Oliver Wendell Holmes; "Hebe," "Auspex," "St. Michael the Weigher" by James Russell Lowell; "Inspiration," "Smoke" by Henry David Thoreau "Hymn to the Night," "My Last Youth," "The Three Silences of Molinos," "The Sound of the Sea," "Divina Commedia" by Henry W. Longfellow; "The Rhodora," "Compensation," "Give All to Love," "Bacchus," "Brahma," "Merops," "Uriel," "Days," "Character" by Ralph Waldo Emerson; "Waiting" by John Burroughs; "Day and Dark" by George Cabot Lodge; "A Grey Day," "Pandora Song," "An Ode in Time of Hesitation" by William Vaughn Moody; "Little Ivory Figures Pulled with String," "Patterns," by Amy Lowell. "Midwinter" by John Townsend Trowbridge; "The Monk in the Kitchen," "Ere the Golden Bowl Is Broken" by Anna Hempstead Branch; "At Baia," " 'Not Honey,' " "Song," "The Garden," "Orchard" by H. D.; "L'An Trentiesme de Mon Age," "The Too-Late Born," "Einstein," "You, Andrew Marvell," "Memorial Rain" by Archibald MacLeish.

Alfred A. Knopf, Inc., for "War Is Kind" from *Black Riders and Other Lines* by Stephen Crane, copyright, 1895, 1922, by William H. Crane; "Vendor's Song," "The Lonely Death" from *Verse* by Adelaide Crapsey, copyright, 1915, 1922, by Algernon S. Crapsey; "Domination of Black," "Sea Surface Full of Clouds," "To the One of Fictive Music,"

"Peter Quince at the Clavier," "Sunday Morning," "Le Monocle de Mon Oncle," "Tattoo," "The Bird with the Coppery, Keen Claws," "Of Heaven Considered as a Tomb," "Of the Manner of Addressing Clouds," from *Harmonium* by Wallace Stevens, copyright, 1923, 1931, by Alfred A. Knopf, Inc.; "Spouse," "Ganymede," "Ghost," "Correspondent," "Captain's Table," "Charioteer" from *Guest Book* by Witter Bynner, copyright, 1935, by Alfred A. Knopf, Inc.; "This Corruptible," "The Eagle and the Mole," "Escape," "Confession of Faith," "Address to My Soul," "True Vine" from *Collected Poems of Elinor Wylie*, copyright, 1932, by Alfred A. Knopf, Inc.; "Blue Girls," "Antique Harvesters," "Captain Carpenter," "Bells for John Whiteside's Daughter," "Lady Lost," "Here Lies a Lady" from *Two Gentlemen in Bonds* and *Chills and Fever* by John Crowe Ransom, copyright, 1927, 1932, by Alfred A. Knopf, Inc.; "Letter to a Teacher of English" ("A Letter to James B. Munn") from *Letter to Robert Frost and Others* by Robert Hillyer, copyright, 1936, by Robert Hillyer.

Alfred Kreymborg for "Nun Snow" by Alfred Kreymborg.

J. B. Lippincott Company for "Forty Singing Seamen" from *Collected Poems* (Vol. I) by Alfred Noyes, copyright, 1906, by J. B. Lippincott Company.

Little, Brown & Company for "I Found the Phrase," "Parting," "Called Back," "Choice," "To Hear an Oriole," "There's a Certain Slant of Light," "Apparently with No Surprise," "The Last Night," "The Bustle in a House," "I Know That He Exists," "We Never Know How High," "The Soul Selects," "A Thought Went Up My Mind," "Dying," "A Clock Stopped," "Not Any Sunny Tone," "I Felt a Funeral," "To My Quick Ear," "In the Garden," "Safe in Their Alabaster Chambers," "The Wind," "The Chariot," "I Died for Beauty," "Mysteries" from *The Poems* of Emily Dickinson, edited by Martha Dickinson Bianchi and Alfred Leete Hampson; "Emigravit," "A Dream," "Danger" by Helen Hunt Jackson.

Liveright Publishing Corporation for "They Went Forth to Battle, but They Always Fell" by Shaemas O'Sheel; "Voyages" II, VI, "Praise for an Urn," "The River," "The Dance," "Indiana," "Atlantis" from *The Bridge* by Hart Crane.

Macmillan Company for "The Darkling Thrush," "Afterwards," "Let Me Enjoy," "The Blinded Bird" from *Collected Poems* by Thomas Hardy; "To a Friend Whose Work Has Come to Nothing," "Against Unworthy Praise," "Sailing to Byzantium," "For His Own Epitaph" from *Collected Poems* by William Butler Yeats; "Eve," "The Bull" from *Poems* by Ralph Hodgson; "The Vindictive Staircase," "A Catch for Spring" from *Collected Poems* by Wilfrid Wilson Gibson; "The Plougher," "Shall I Go Bound and You Go Free," "No Child," "Monkeys" from *Poems* by Padraic Colum; "What Tomas an Buile Said in a Pub," "On a Lonely Spray," "The Pit of Bliss," "A Glass of Beer" from

Collected Poems by James Stephens; Selection from *Dauber,* "The Passing Strange" from *Poems* by John Masefield; "The Faun Tells of the Rout of the Amazons" from *Poems* by T. Sturge Moore; "Digdog" from *My Lady's Garland* and "O Come Out of the Lily" from *The Spirit Watches* by Ruth Pitter; "The Fish," "My Apish Cousins," "Poetry," "Roses Only" from *Selected Poetry* by Marianne Moore; "Abraham Lincoln Walks at Midnight," "The Eagle That Is Forgotten," "Aladdin and the Jinn" from *Collected Poems* by Vachel Lindsay; "Eros Turannos" from *Collected Poems* by Edwin Arlington Robinson; "Islands: A Song" from *The Garden Is Political* by John Malcolm Brinnin; "The Waggoner," "Thiepval Wood," "The Pike" from *Halfway House* by Edmund Blunden; "Bagley Wood" by Lionel Johnson; "To the Fallen," "A Glimpse of Time" by Laurence Binyon.

Virgil Markham for "The Man with the Hoe" by Edwin Markham.

Edgar Lee Masters for "Thomas Trevelyan," "Edmund Pollard," "Bert Kessler," "Petit the Poet" from *Spoon River Anthology* by Edgar Lee Masters.

Marianne Moore for "A Talisman" by Marianne Moore.

Thomas Nelson & Sons for "Drake's Drum" from *Collected Poems* by Sir Henry Newbolt.

New Directions for "Song," "Spring Song" by Theodore Spencer; "Sir Gawaine and the Green Knight" by Yvor Winters; "Train Ride," "Fish Food" by John Wheelwright; "Bearded Oaks," "Revelation" by Robert Penn Warren; "At the New Year" by Kenneth Patchen; " 'Mentrechè il Vento, Come Fa, Si Tace'," "Socrates' Ghost Must Haunt Me Now" by Delmore Schwartz.

Oxford University Press for "The Man Coming Toward You," "Leg in the Subway" by Oscar Williams; "The Groundhog" by Richard Eberhart; "My Delight and Thy Delight," "I Will Not Let Thee Go," "London Snow" from *The Shorter Poems of Robert Bridges;* "God's Grandeur," "Pied Beauty," "The Windhover," "Spring and Fall," "Carrion Comfort" by Gerard Manley Hopkins; "Leisure," "The Sleepers," "The Example," "A Great Time" from *Collected Poems of W. H. Davies.*

Ezra Pound for "Envoi (1919)," "The Tree," "The Tomb at Akr Çaar," "Portrait d'une Femme," "Apparuit," "A Virginal," "The Return," "The River-Merchant's Wife," "The Flame," "Dance Figure," "Lament of the Frontier Guard," "Taking Leave of a Friend."

Random House, Inc. for "The Glacier," "The Death Wish" by Louis MacNeice; " 'O what is that sound—'," "Song: To the Tune of 'Frankie & Johnny,' " Chorus: From *For the Time Being* by W. H. Auden; "The Express," "I Think Continually—," "Landscape near an Aerdrome" by Stephen Spender; "Tempt Me No More," "In Me Two Worlds" by C. Day Lewis; "Continent's End," "Apology for Bad Dreams," "Love the Wild Swan" by Robinson Jeffers.

Reynal and Hitchcock, Inc. "Poet," "The Twins," "Travelogue for

Exiles" "Nostalgia" from *V Letter and Other Poems* by Karl Shapiro, copyright, 1940.

Siegfried Sassoon "Everyone Sang," "Aftermath," "Grandeur of Ghosts" by Siegfried Sassoon.

Charles Scribner's Sons for "For a Dead Lady" from *The Town Down the River* by Edwin Arlington Robinson; "On the Death of a Metaphysician," "As in the Midst of Battle There Is Room," "Solipsism," "Odes" by George Santayana; "Hasbrouck and the Rose," "About Women" by H. Phelps Putnam; "Summer Wish" by Louise Bogan; "Ode to the Confederate Dead" by Allen Tate; "Earth" by John Hall Wheelock; "The Marshes of Glynn," "Opposition" by Sidney Lanier; "In Early Spring," "Chimes," "One Wept Whose Only Child Was Dead," "Renouncement" by Alice Meynell.

Martin Secker and Warburg Ltd. for "The Old Ships," "Gates of Damascus" from *Collected Poems* by James Elroy Flecker.

Thomas Seltzer, Inc. for "Haymaking" from *Collected Poems of Edward Thomas*.

Henry A. Stickney for "Be Still. The Hanging Gardens Were a Dream," "Live Blindly," "He Said: 'If in His Image I Was Made'," "On Some Shells Found Inland," "In Ampezzo," "Mt. Lykaion," "Near Helikon," "Fidelity," "Mnemosyne," "Now in the Palace Gardens" by Trumbell Stickney.

Leon Tebbetts Editions for "Confidence," "Warblers," "In Robin Hood's Cove" by Marsden Hartley.

Viking Press, Inc. for "The Image of Delight" from *A Son of Earth* by William Ellery Leonard, copyright, 1928, by The Viking Press, Inc.; "Be Beautiful, Noble, Like the Antique Ant," "God Said, 'I Made a Man'," "Now, If You Will Look in My Brain," "My Mouth Is Very Quiet," "The Way My Ideas Think Me," "Saw God Dead but Laughing" from *Have Come, Am Here* by José Garcia Villa, copyright, 1941, 1942, by The Viking Press, Inc.

A. P. Watt & Son for "Danny Deever," "The Ballad of East and West," "The Last Chantey" and "Jobson's Amen" by Rudyard Kipling.

Edmund Wilson for "Riverton," "A House of the Eighties" by Edmund Wilson.